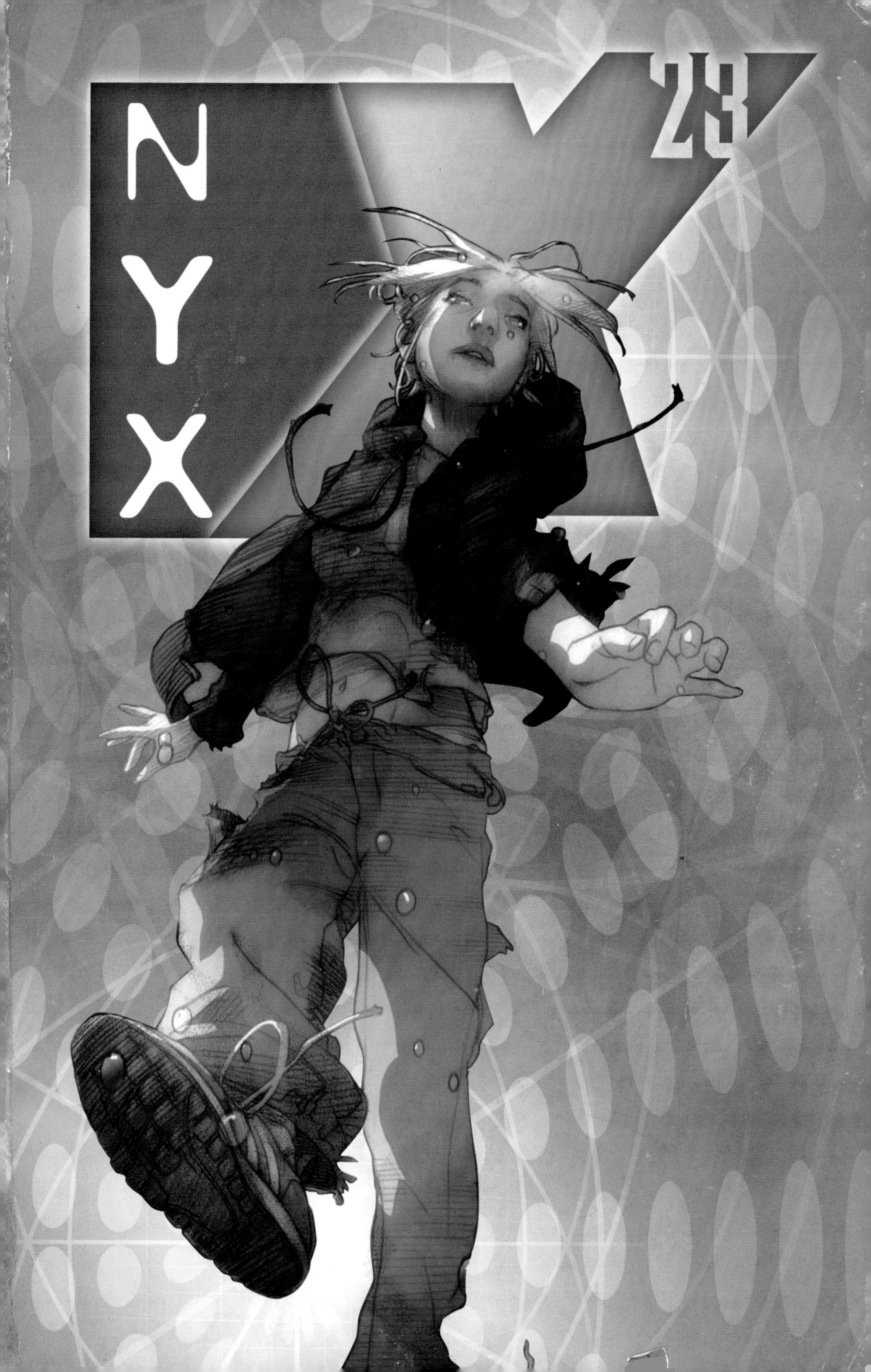
NYX
23

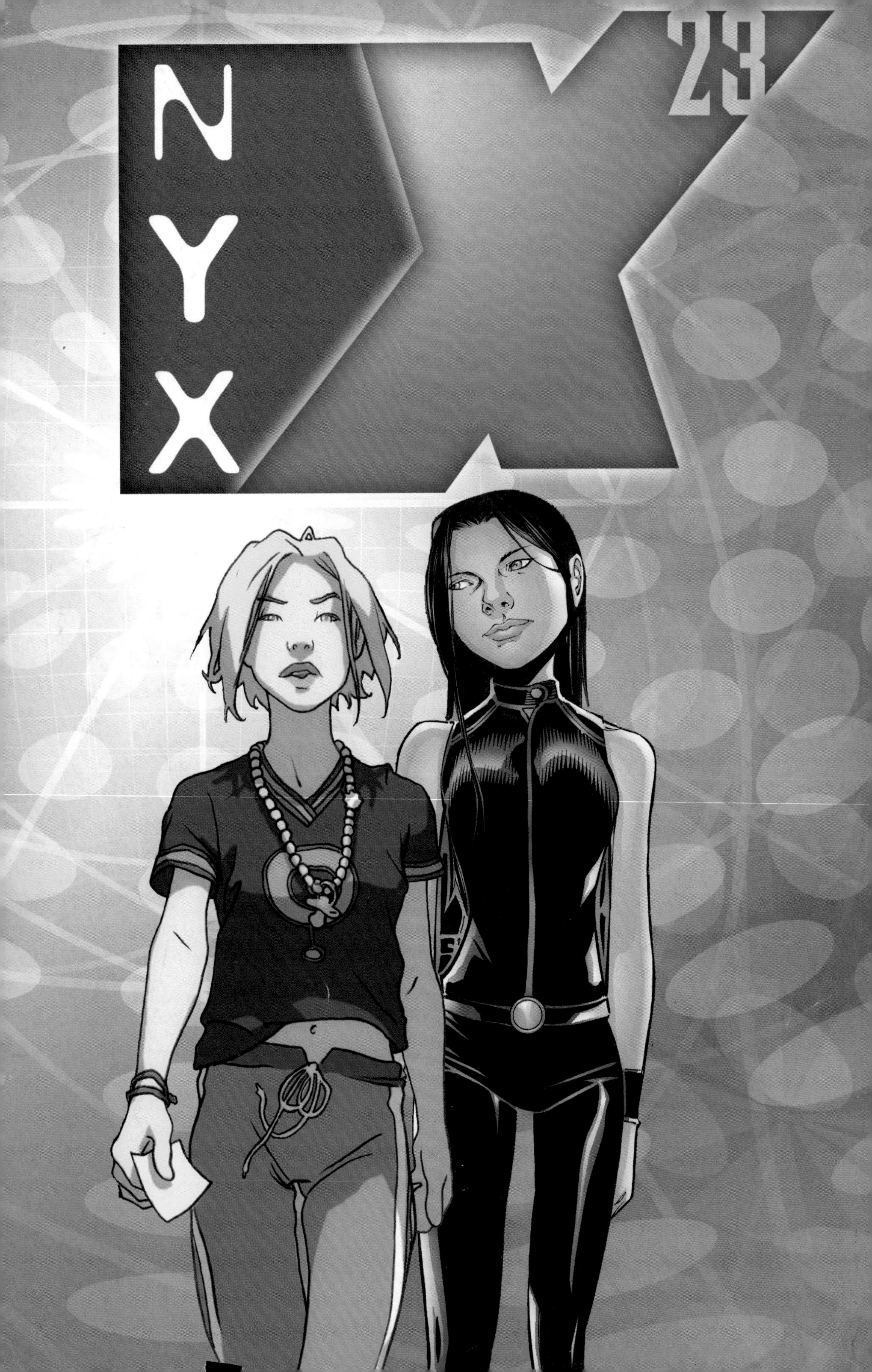
NYX
23

X-23

STORY BY CRAIG KYLE
writers CRAIG KYLE & CHRISTOPHER YOST
pencils BILLY TAN
inks JON SIBAL
colors BRIAN HABERLIN
letters CHRIS ELIOPOULOS
& VIRTUAL CALLIGRAPHY'S CORY PETIT
assistant editor CORY SEDLMEIER
editor AXEL ALONSO

X-23 CREATED BY CRAIG KYLE

NYX

writer JOE QUESADA
pencilers JOSHUA MIDDLETON & ROBERT TERANISHI
inkers NELSON & CHRIS SOTOMAYOR
colors JEAN-FRANCOIS BEAULIEU, JOSHUA MIDDLETON, &
SOTOCOLOR'S CHRIS SOTOMAYOR & FELIX SERRANO
letters CHRIS ELIOPOULOS
assistant editors MACKENZIE CADENHEAD,
C.B. CEBULSKI, & WARREN SIMONS

SPECIAL THANKS TO ZEB WELLS

NYX CREATED BY JOE QUESADA AND JOSH MIDDLETON

collection editor JENNIFER GRÜNWALD
senior editor, special projects JEFF YOUNGQUIST
assistant editor MICHAEL SHORT
director of sales DAVID GABRIEL
book designer MEGHAN KERNS
creative director TOM MARVELLI
editor in chief JOE QUESADA
publisher DAN BUCKLEY

INTRODUCTION

I can't believe you're really reading this... Well, I'd better be entertaining, as you've taken the time to read something involving comics that's missing all the beautiful pictures that make these words more interesting.

When Mike Marts asked me if I wanted to do the opening for this collected hardcover, I jumped at the chance. It's an honor for me to introduce a story that I have so much passion for, but keep in mind that this is my first time writing an introduction. Not wanting to screw it up, I asked Mike for a little reference on what other writers have done in the past. He was kind enough to send me a few samples... Samples written by Chris Claremont, J. Michael Straczynski and Brian K. Vaughan. Remind me NEVER to ask Mike for samples ever again. Had he included Brian Bendis, Grant Morrison and Mark Millar to the list I would still be staring at a blank computer screen while fighting bouts of panic and nausea. Fortunately, he didn't include those other writers so I'm just left with the panic and nausea.

So, X-23... Well, I created this character but it wasn't hard being that I stood on the shoulders of geniuses like Len Wein and Chris Claremont. Len Wein created Wolverine and by doing so made X-23 possible. But without Chris Claremont, there would be no X-23, as he is the writer that made me fall in love with comics. Uncanny X-Men issue #181 was my first comic book purchase. After reading that issue, I was hooked. I bought every issue from #181 back through Giant Size X-Men #1 and have collected comics for over 20 years. Jeez, I'm old.

I'm a fanboy and proudly so, but I'm not alone. Chris Yost is too. I hate to speak for Chris but since I'm writing this and he's not, what the hell. Chris is a comic book junkie. He knows more about the history and the characters of the Marvel Universe than anyone else I know. But besides being a comic freak he is also a great writer. He bangs out pages faster than I can form sentences and he makes writing look easy. For the record, it's not easy! In fact, some of us toil over this stuff for days, you hear that, mister show-off?! IT'S NOT EASY!!!

Sorry, I'm a Scorpio, we're emotional creatures...

Fortunately, Chris and I have worked on many Marvel projects together but until this series all of our work was in animation. We're extremely proud of our animation work but when the X-23 mini was offered to us, we were in shock. Writing a comic is like adding a verse to the comic bible. I mean, this is where all the best stories are told. No rules and no restrictions, just honest storytelling. In comics, if your story sucks you've got no one to blame for getting in your creative way, which is both awesome and scary... but mostly awesome... and a little scary... but awesome. Well, you know what I mean.

But that's enough about Chris and me. Let's talk about Billy Tan! What. A. Talent. Billy is more than just a gifted artist, he is also an excellent director. His work on the series exceeded my wildest expectations. No two shots were ever the same and he gave depth and complexity to every panel. Billy took a nearly mute child assassin and turned her into an emotional and intriguing character. I'm glad he was the one chosen to bring this story to life.

Creating a comic is a collective journey and each person involved in this series — especially Axel, Cory, Brian, John, Chris and Billy — put their best into every page. I also need to thank Avi, Alan, Dan and Joe for giving two unproven writers a chance to make this book. I'm glad we didn't let you down, or if we did, I'm glad you didn't tell us.

Now I'm sure you were hoping for a little more insight into X-23 but like I said I have no idea what I'm doing. BUT I was given an 800-word limit on this intro and we're only at 698. So here are some fun facts: X-23's mission watch is always set for 22 minutes because that is the length of a Saturday morning cartoon. X-23's bones are NOT laced with Adamantium. Greg Johnson before dying in our series was the Head Writer on X-Men: Evolution. X-23's real name Laura was inspired by Logan. All of the times shown on the two-page spread in issue 3 where X-23 kills around the globe are the birthdays of people I know. And I hate carrots!

Hope you enjoyed this intro but if you didn't you should read the ones written by Chris Claremont, J. Michael Straczynski and Brian K. Vaughan, they were excellent!

Mahalo, *1/2008 Aloha Friend 35*

Craig Kyle

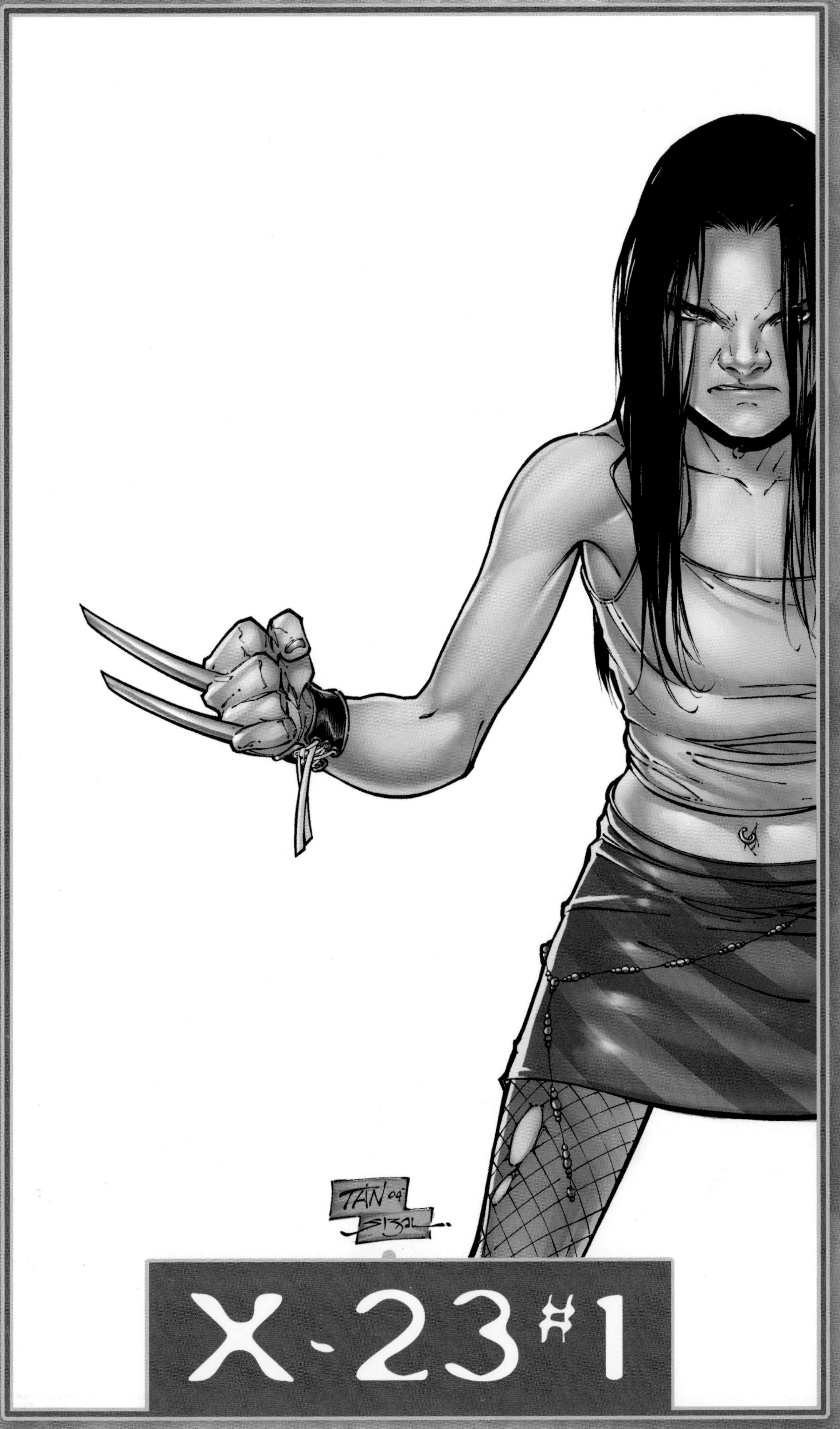
X-23 #1

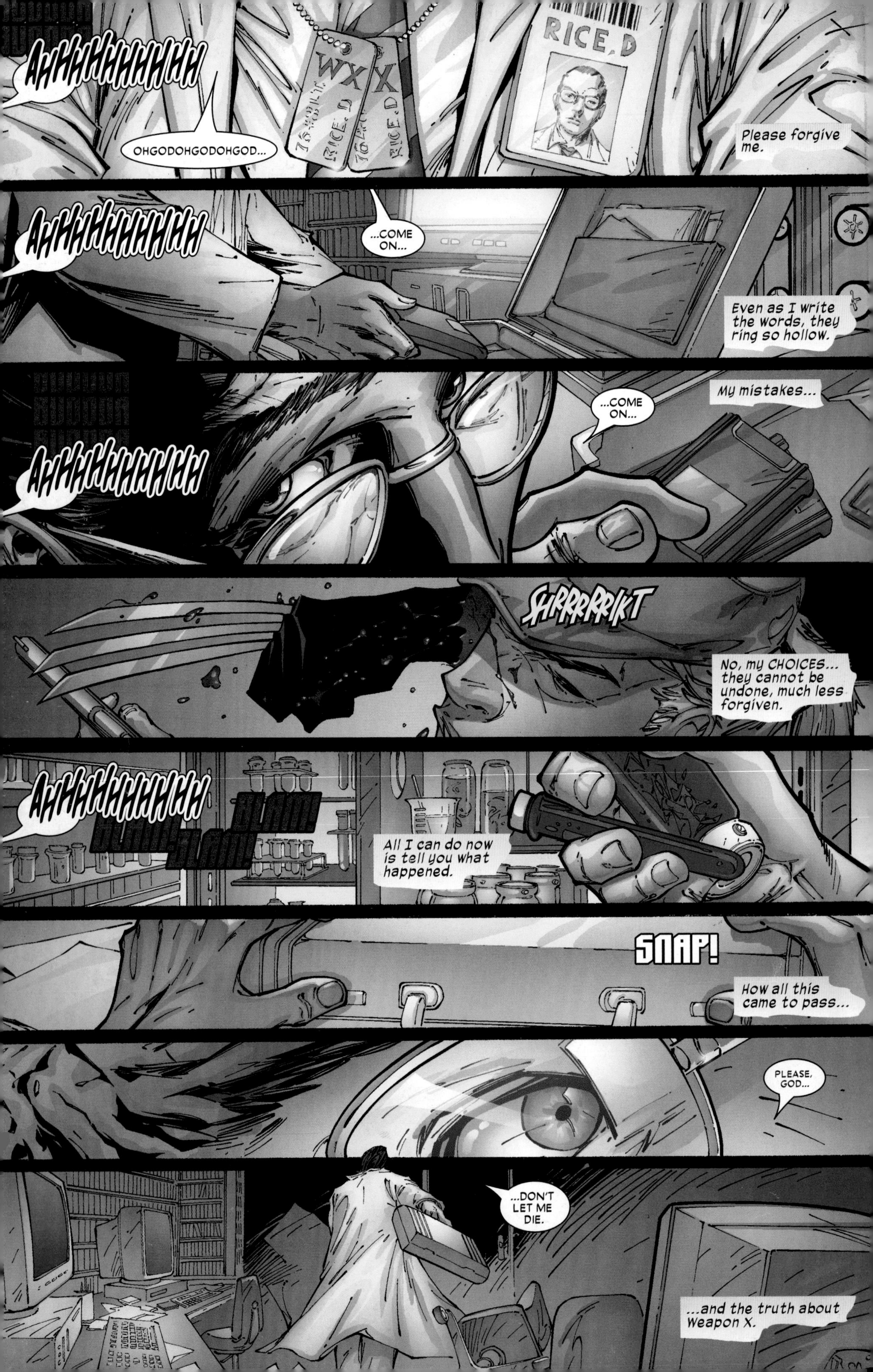
AHHHHHHHHHHH
OHGODOHGODOHGOD...
WXX
RICE, D
RICE, D
Please forgive me.
AHHHHHHHHHHH
...COME ON...
Even as I write the words, they ring so hollow.
My mistakes...
...COME ON...
AHHHHHHHHHHH
SHRRRRRIKT
No, my CHOICES... they cannot be undone, much less forgiven.
AHHHHHHHHHHH
BLAM!
BLAM!
BLAM!
All I can do now is tell you what happened.
SNAP!
How all this came to pass...
PLEASE, GOD...
...DON'T LET ME DIE.
...and the truth about Weapon X.

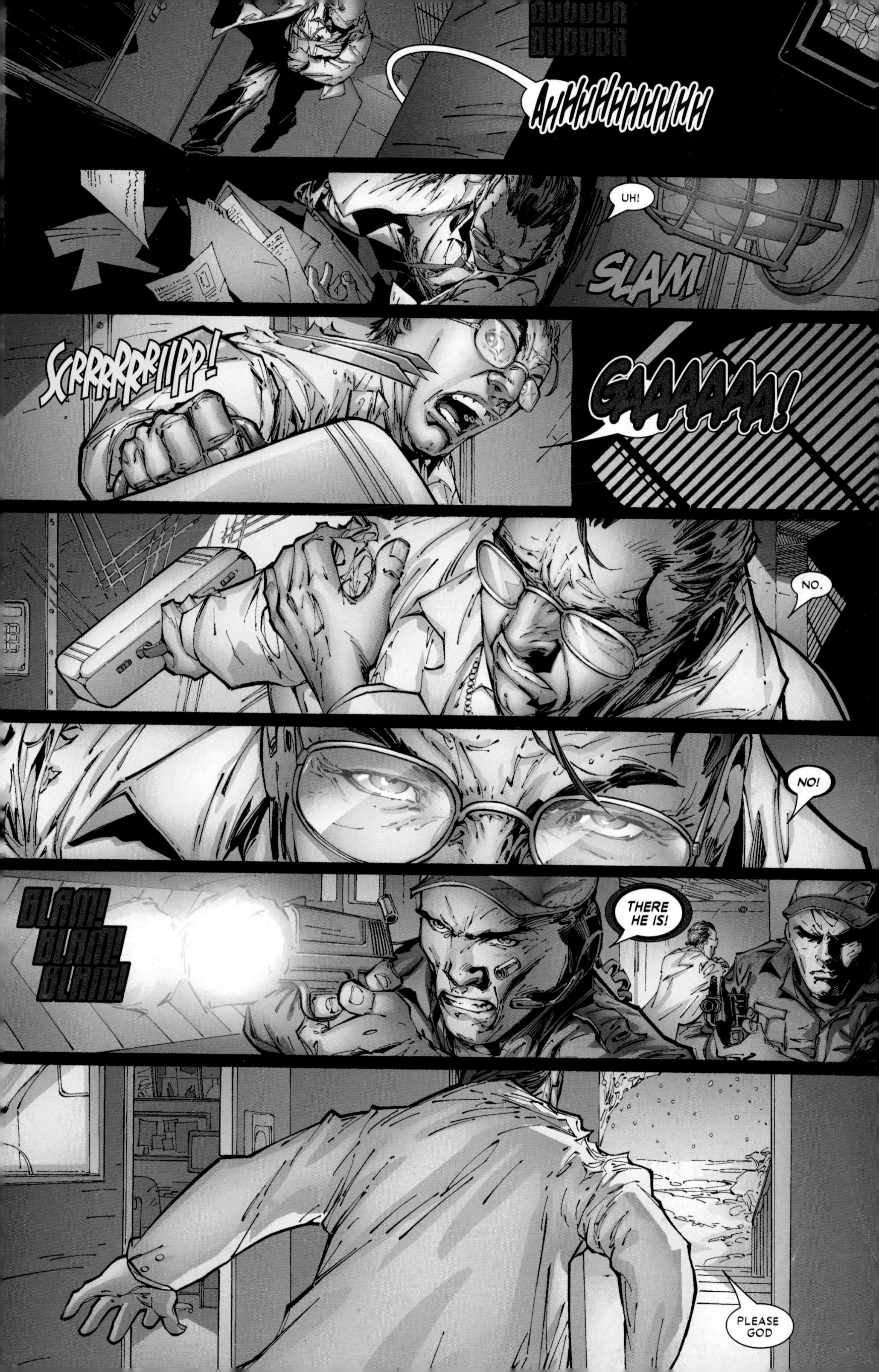

AHHHHHHHHHHH
UH!
SLAM
SCRRRRRRIIPP!
GAAAAAA!
NO.
NO!
BLAM! BLAM! BLAM!
THERE HE IS!
PLEASE GOD

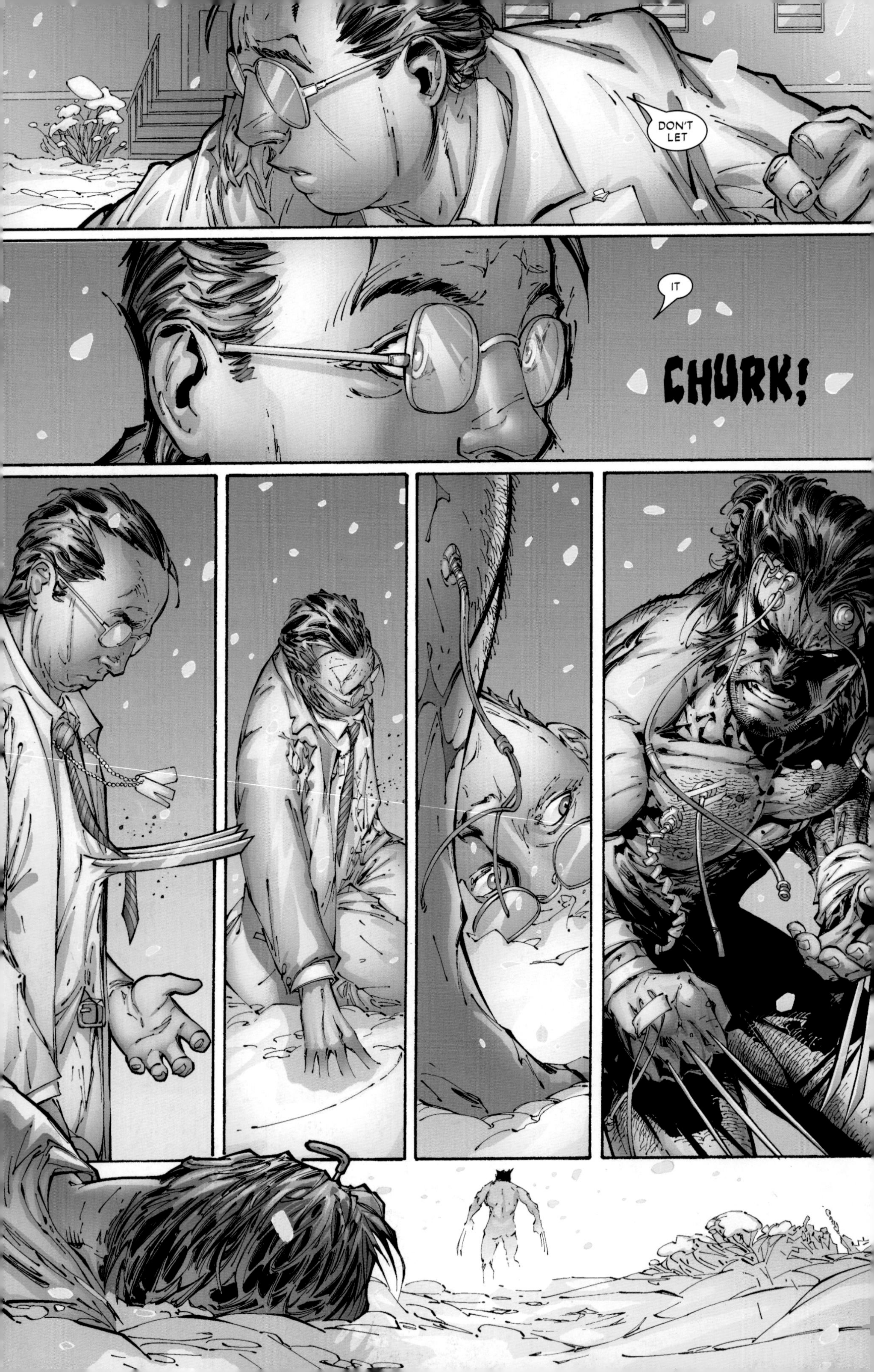
DON'T LET
IT
CHURK!

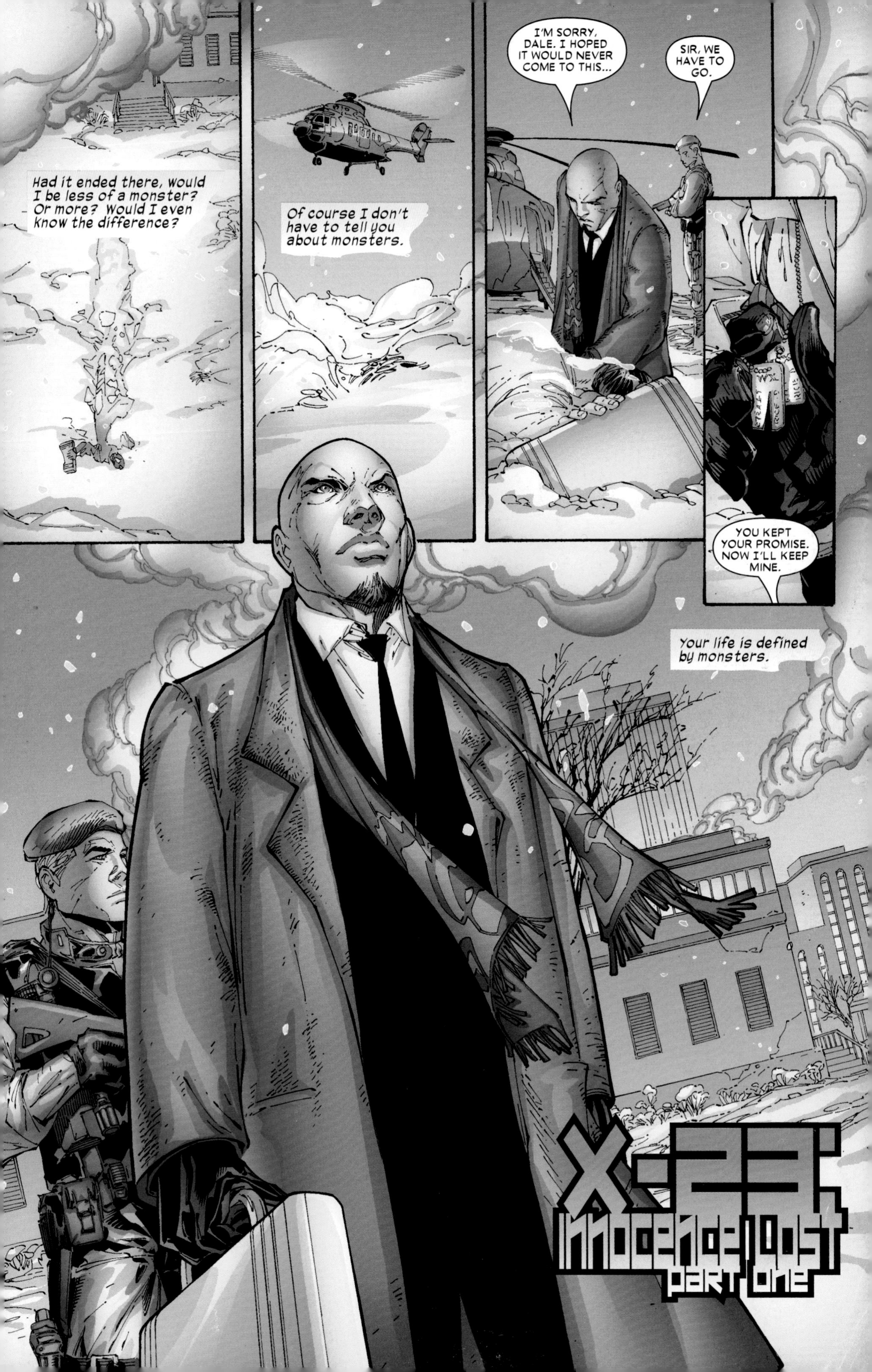

Had it ended there, would I be less of a monster? Or more? Would I even know the difference?
Of course I don't have to tell you about monsters.
I'M SORRY, DALE. I HOPED IT WOULD NEVER COME TO THIS...
SIR, WE HAVE TO GO.
YOU KEPT YOUR PROMISE. NOW I'LL KEEP MINE.
Your life is defined by monsters.
X-23
INNOCENCE LOST
PART ONE

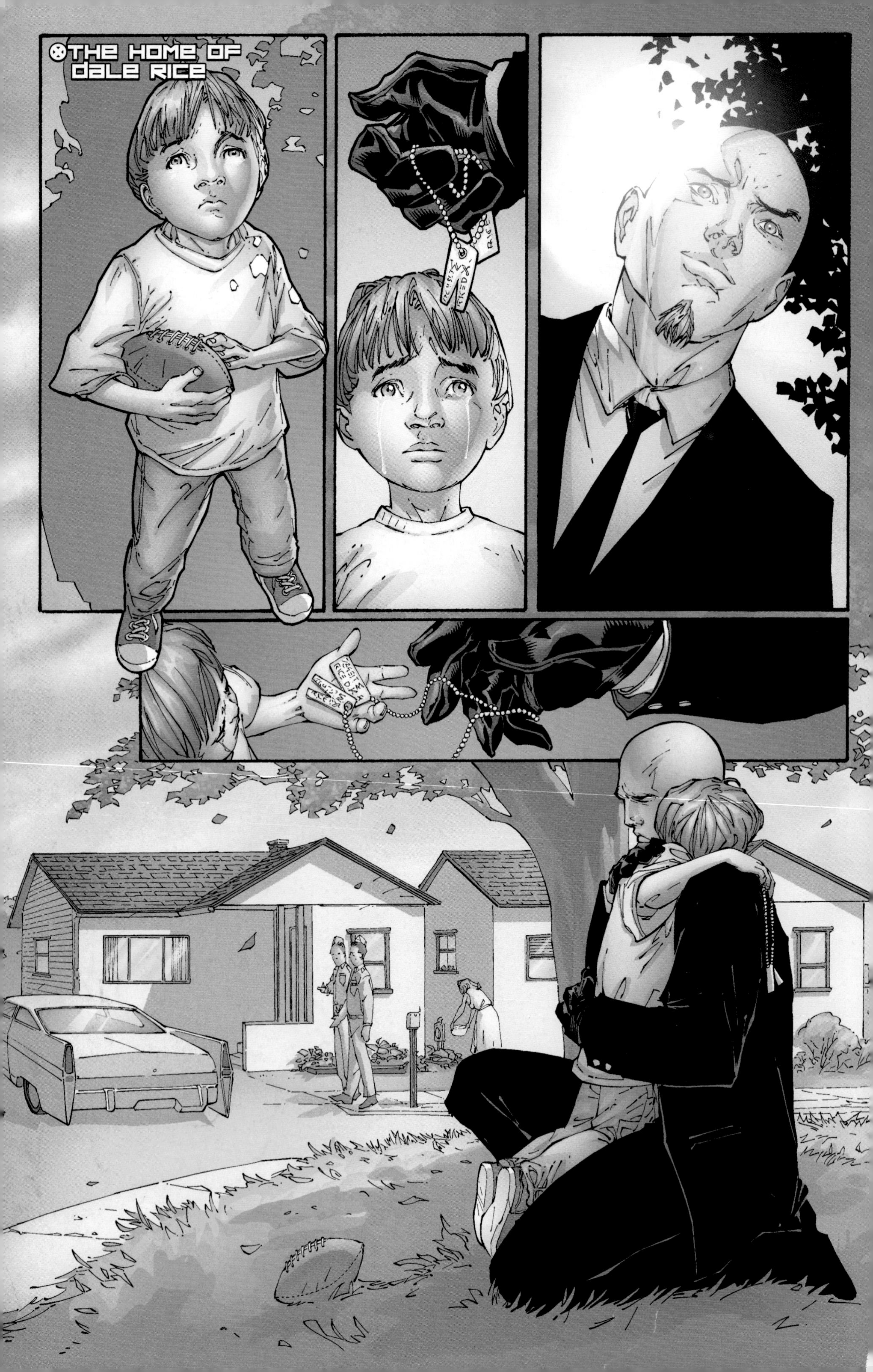
THE HOME OF DALE RICE

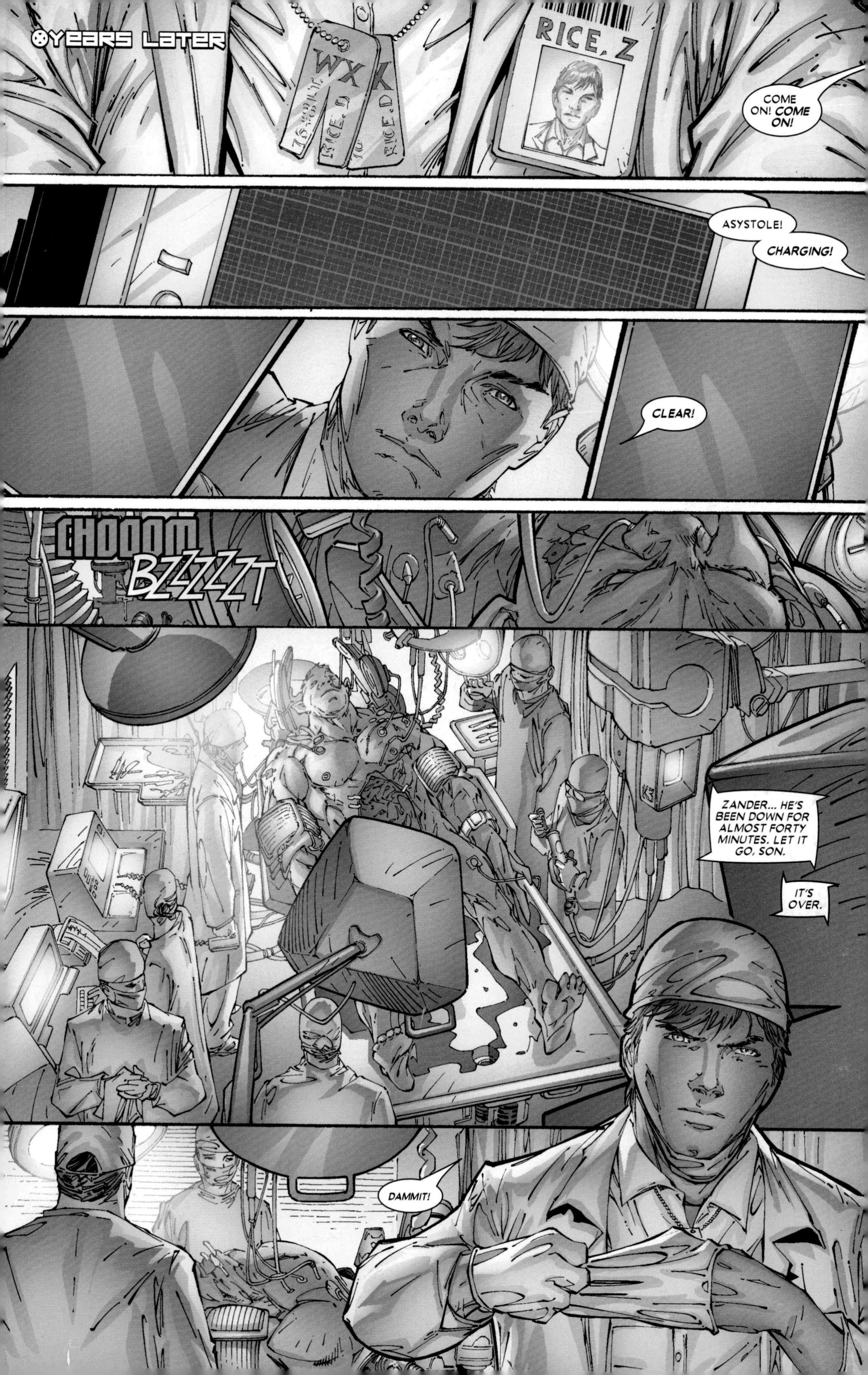
YEARS LATER
WXK
RICE, D
RICE, Z
COME ON! COME ON!
ASYSTOLE!
CHARGING!
CLEAR!
CHOOOM
BZZZZZT
ZANDER... HE'S BEEN DOWN FOR ALMOST FORTY MINUTES. LET IT GO, SON.
IT'S OVER.
DAMMIT!

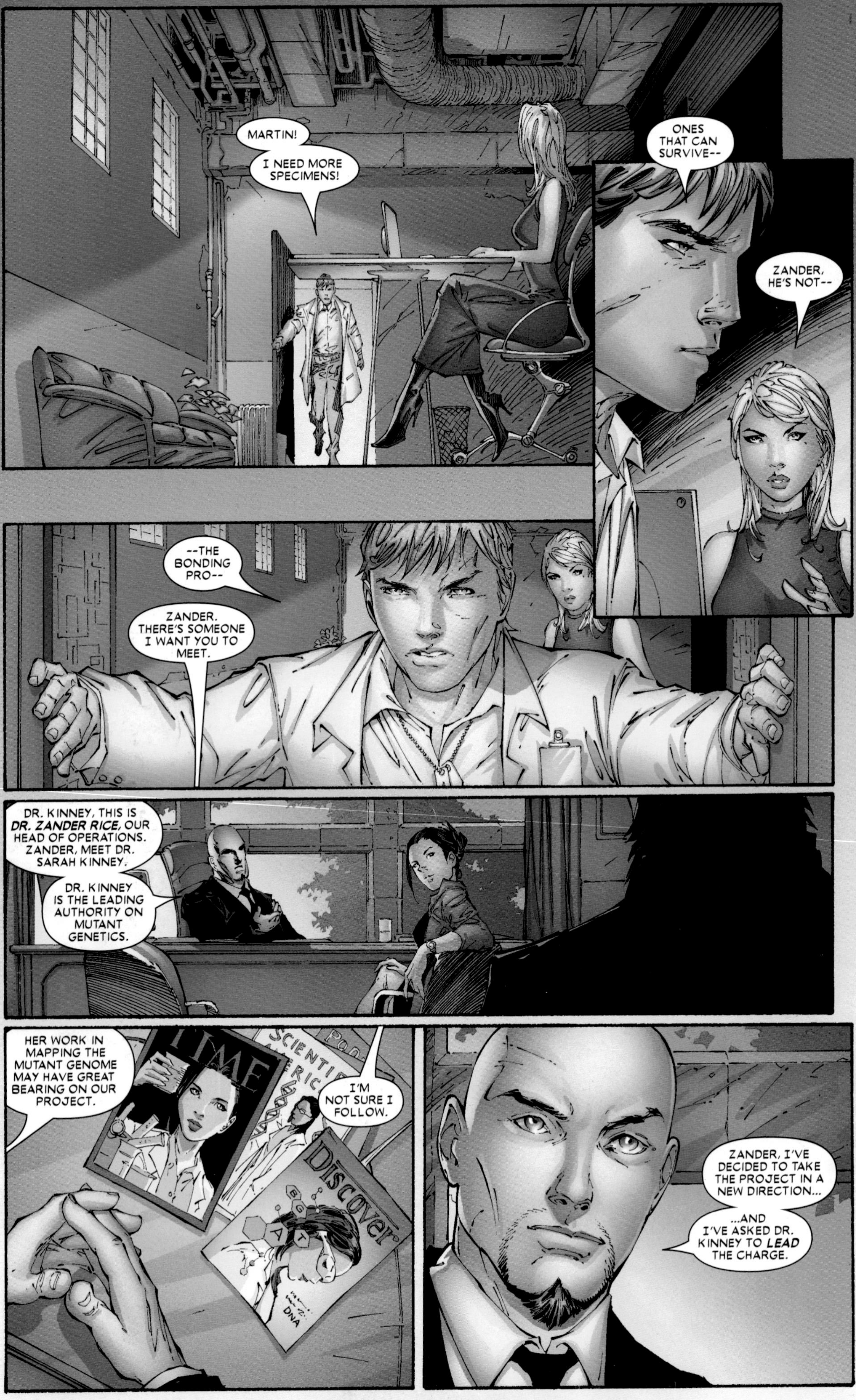
MARTIN!
I NEED MORE SPECIMENS!
ONES THAT CAN SURVIVE--
ZANDER, HE'S NOT--
--THE BONDING PRO--
ZANDER. THERE'S SOMEONE I WANT YOU TO MEET.
DR. KINNEY, THIS IS DR. ZANDER RICE, OUR HEAD OF OPERATIONS. ZANDER, MEET DR. SARAH KINNEY.
DR. KINNEY IS THE LEADING AUTHORITY ON MUTANT GENETICS.
HER WORK IN MAPPING THE MUTANT GENOME MAY HAVE GREAT BEARING ON OUR PROJECT.
TIME
SCIENTIFIC AMERICAN
Discover
DNA
I'M NOT SURE I FOLLOW.
ZANDER, I'VE DECIDED TO TAKE THE PROJECT IN A NEW DIRECTION...
...AND I'VE ASKED DR. KINNEY TO LEAD THE CHARGE.

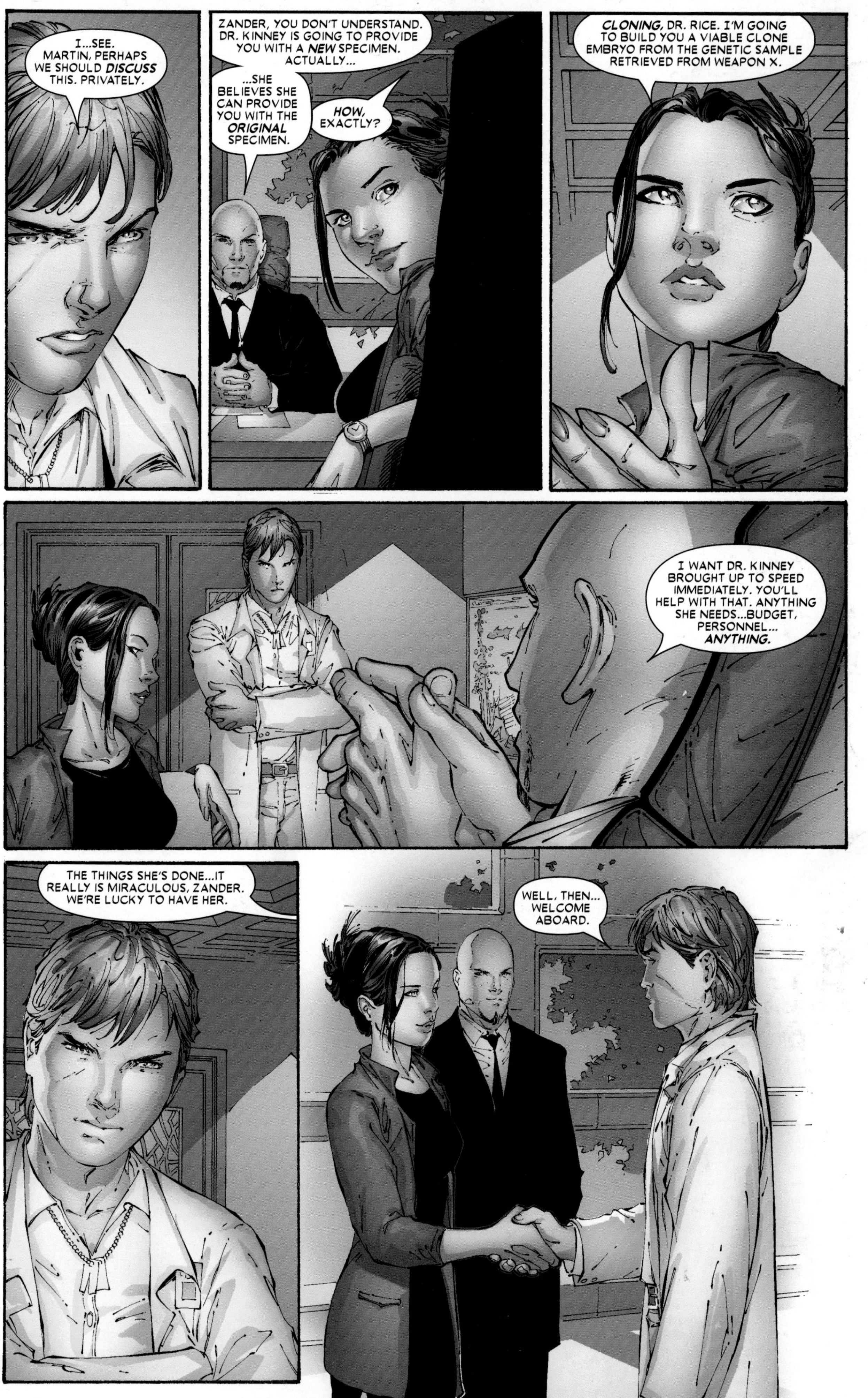
I...SEE. MARTIN, PERHAPS WE SHOULD DISCUSS THIS. PRIVATELY.
ZANDER, YOU DON'T UNDERSTAND. DR. KINNEY IS GOING TO PROVIDE YOU WITH A NEW SPECIMEN. ACTUALLY...
...SHE BELIEVES SHE CAN PROVIDE YOU WITH THE ORIGINAL SPECIMEN.
HOW, EXACTLY?
CLONING, DR. RICE. I'M GOING TO BUILD YOU A VIABLE CLONE EMBRYO FROM THE GENETIC SAMPLE RETRIEVED FROM WEAPON X.
I WANT DR. KINNEY BROUGHT UP TO SPEED IMMEDIATELY. YOU'LL HELP WITH THAT. ANYTHING SHE NEEDS...BUDGET, PERSONNEL... ANYTHING.
THE THINGS SHE'S DONE...IT REALLY IS MIRACULOUS, ZANDER. WE'RE LUCKY TO HAVE HER.
WELL, THEN... WELCOME ABOARD.

"UNLIMITED RESOURCES AND NO POLITICAL OR LEGAL RESTRAINTS ON YOUR WORK. *THAT'S* WHAT WE HAVE TO OFFER, DR. KINNEY..."

...HOWEVER, THERE ARE *SACRIFICES* INVOLVED. WE'VE ALL MADE THEM. PHYSICALLY, YOU'D BE TOTALLY CUT OFF FROM THE OUTSIDE WORLD, ALTHOUGH YOU CAN STILL RECEIVE MAIL AND PHONE CALLS THROUGH OUR ROUTING SYSTEM. AND OF COURSE YOU'D BE COMMITTED FOR THE LIFE OF THE PROJECT.

I ALSO NEED TO KNOW IF YOU CAN LIVE WITH THE MORAL IMPLICATIONS OF WHAT YOU'D BE DOING HERE.

NO GOVERNMENT INTERFERENCE. REMIND ME TO NEVER ASK HOW YOU MANAGE THAT.

"*MORAL IMPLICATIONS?* AND HERE I THOUGHT WE WERE TALKING ABOUT *SCIENCE.*"

POLICE REPORT.

OFFICERS WERE CALLED IN REPONSE TO AN ANONYMOUS TIP REGARDING SUSPECTED CHILD ABUSE. WHEN QUESTIONED, THE ALLEGED VICTIM SARAH KINNEY (AGE 8) WAS NON RESPONSIVE. NO APPARENT PHYSICAL SIGNS OF ABUSE PRESENT. SUBSEQUENT QUESTIONING OF ALLEGED VICTIM'S FATHER - RON KINNEY - AND MOTHER - LESLIE KINNEY - AS WELL AS FEMALE SIBLING DEBORAH KINNEY ALL DENIED ANY ALLEGATIONS OF ABUSE OCCURING IN HOME. AFTER SUSTAINED QUESTIONING, ALLEGED VICTIM WOULD NOT CONFIRM ANY ABUSE OCCURRED. PER PROCEDURE, WITHOUT SUBSTANTIVE EVIDENCE, REFERRED CASE TO DEPARTMENT OF CHILD AND FAMILY SERVICES...

"DR. SUTTER, I APPRECIATE YOUR CONCERN, BUT I'D WORRY MORE ABOUT YOUR MAN RICE CONSIDERING HIS WARM RECEPTION IN YOUR OFFICE."

"SHARING CONTROL WON'T BE EASY FOR HIM. HE'LL NEED TIME TO ADJUST. YOU HAVE TO UNDERSTAND...THE PROJECT WOULDN'T *EXIST* WITHOUT ZANDER'S FATHER."

"HE RETRIEVED THE SAMPLE YOU'LL BE WORKING WITH. AT THE COST OF HIS LIFE."

POLICE REPORT

CALLED IN REPONSE TO REGARDING SUSPECTED STIONED, THE ALLEGE 8) WAS NONRESPONS SIGNS OF ABUSE PR STIONING O

WE ALL MAKE SACRIFICES.

C3

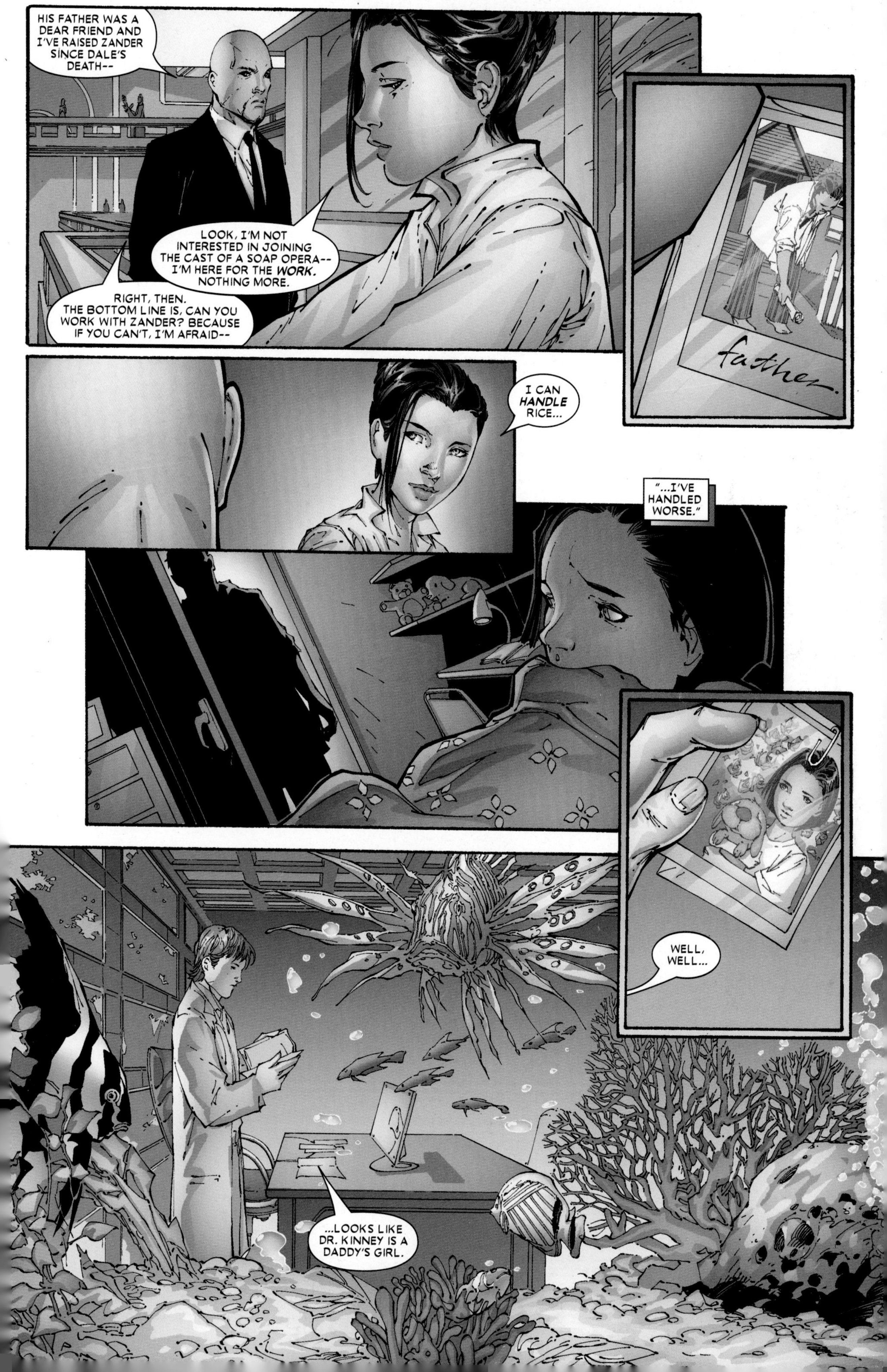
HIS FATHER WAS A DEAR FRIEND AND I'VE RAISED ZANDER SINCE DALE'S DEATH--
LOOK, I'M NOT INTERESTED IN JOINING THE CAST OF A SOAP OPERA-- I'M HERE FOR THE *WORK.* NOTHING MORE.
RIGHT, THEN. THE BOTTOM LINE IS, CAN YOU WORK WITH ZANDER? BECAUSE IF YOU CAN'T, I'M AFRAID--
father.
I CAN *HANDLE* RICE...
"...I'VE HANDLED WORSE."
WELL, WELL...
...LOOKS LIKE DR. KINNEY IS A DADDY'S GIRL.

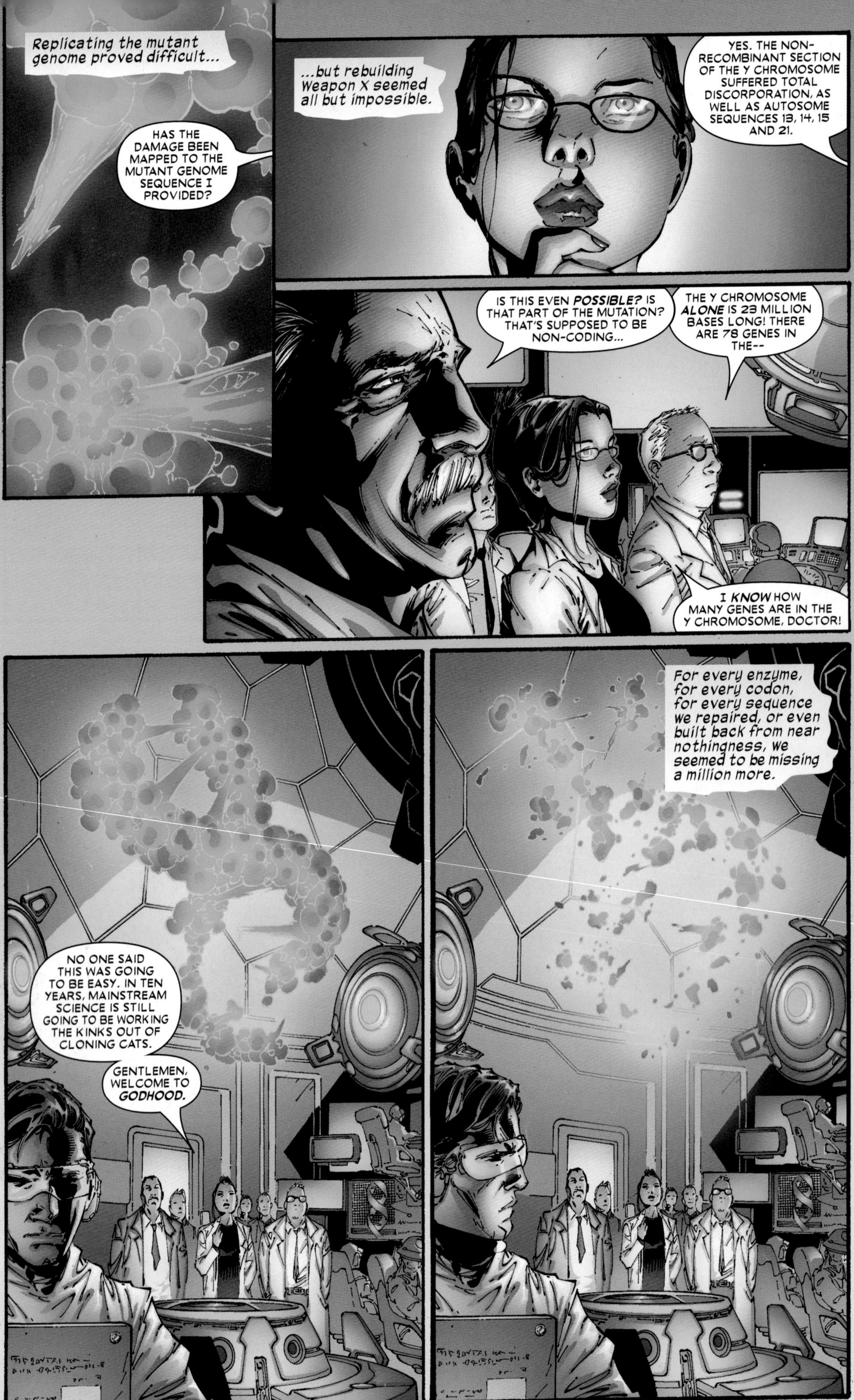

Replicating the mutant genome proved difficult...
HAS THE DAMAGE BEEN MAPPED TO THE MUTANT GENOME SEQUENCE I PROVIDED?
...but rebuilding Weapon X seemed all but impossible.
YES. THE NON-RECOMBINANT SECTION OF THE Y CHROMOSOME SUFFERED TOTAL DISCORPORATION, AS WELL AS AUTOSOME SEQUENCES 13, 14, 15 AND 21.
IS THIS EVEN POSSIBLE? IS THAT PART OF THE MUTATION? THAT'S SUPPOSED TO BE NON-CODING...
THE Y CHROMOSOME ALONE IS 23 MILLION BASES LONG! THERE ARE 78 GENES IN THE--
I KNOW HOW MANY GENES ARE IN THE Y CHROMOSOME, DOCTOR!
NO ONE SAID THIS WAS GOING TO BE EASY. IN TEN YEARS, MAINSTREAM SCIENCE IS STILL GOING TO BE WORKING THE KINKS OUT OF CLONING CATS.
GENTLEMEN, WELCOME TO GODHOOD.
For every enzyme, for every codon, for every sequence we repaired, or even built back from near nothingness, we seemed to be missing a million more.

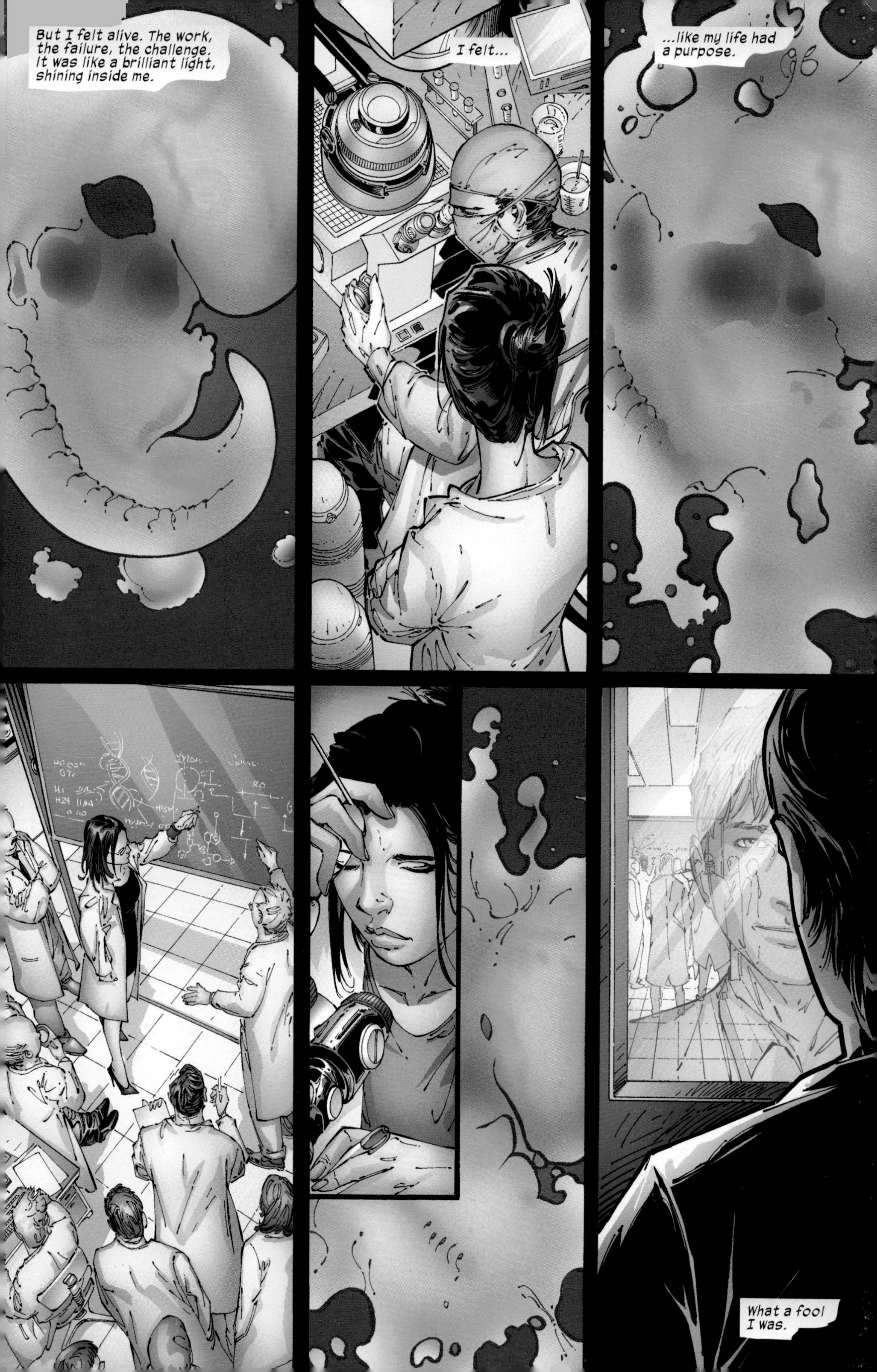
But I felt alive. The work, the failure, the challenge. It was like a brilliant light, shining inside me.
I felt...
...like my life had a purpose.
What a fool I was.

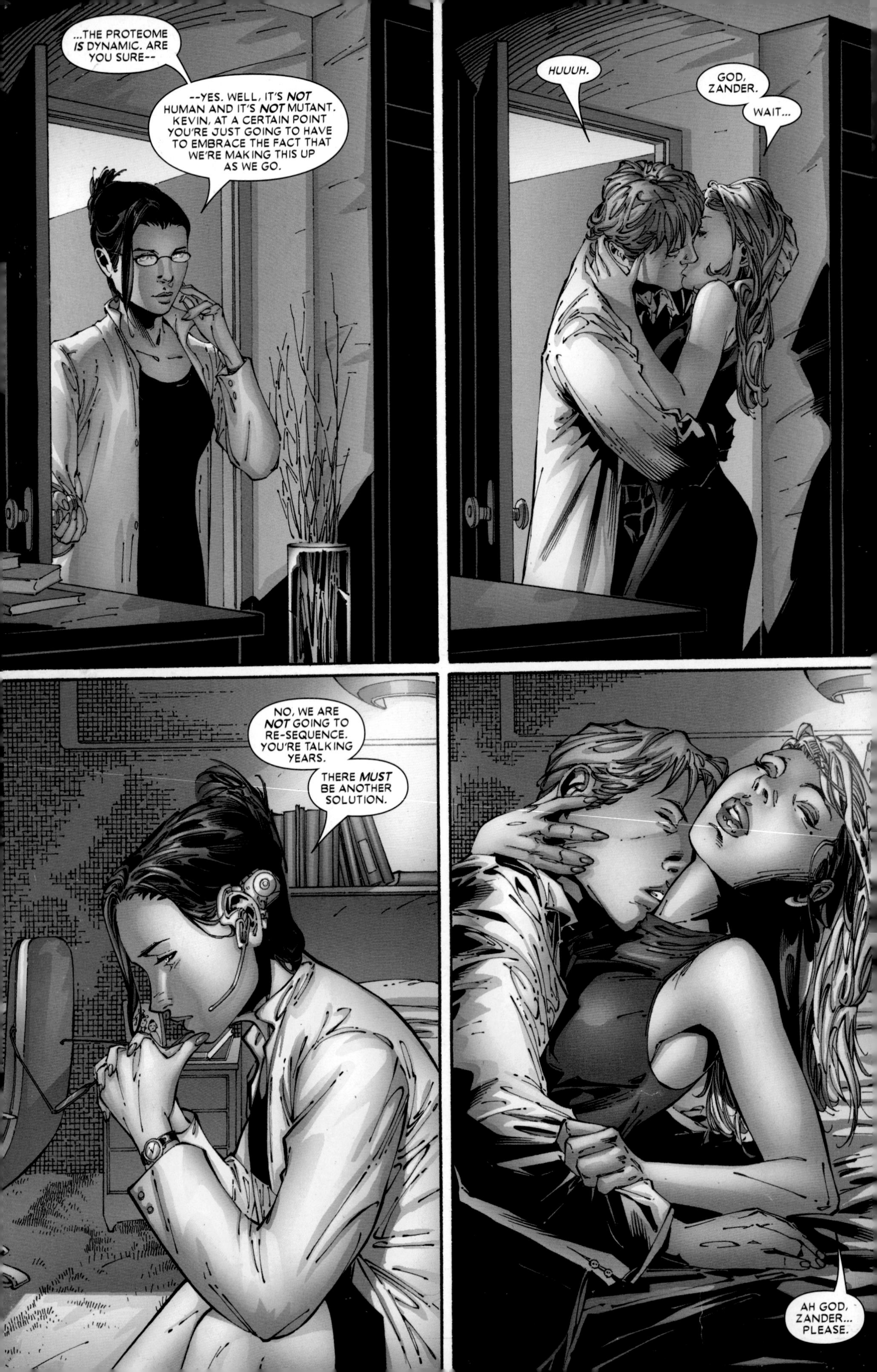
...THE PROTEOME IS DYNAMIC. ARE YOU SURE--
--YES. WELL, IT'S NOT HUMAN AND IT'S NOT MUTANT. KEVIN, AT A CERTAIN POINT YOU'RE JUST GOING TO HAVE TO EMBRACE THE FACT THAT WE'RE MAKING THIS UP AS WE GO.
HUUUH.
GOD, ZANDER.
WAIT...
NO, WE ARE NOT GOING TO RE-SEQUENCE. YOU'RE TALKING YEARS.
THERE MUST BE ANOTHER SOLUTION.
AH GOD, ZANDER... PLEASE.

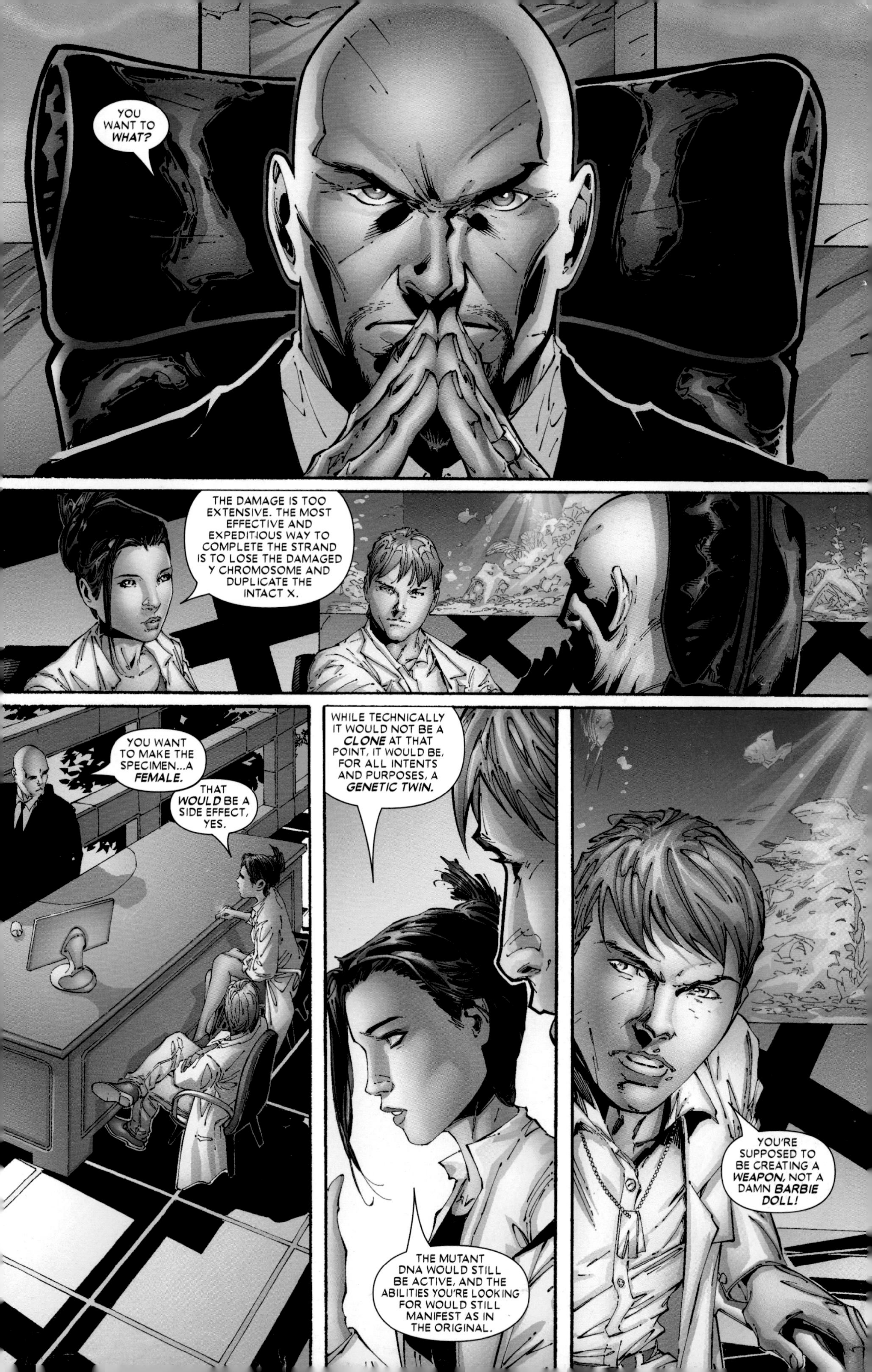
YOU WANT TO WHAT?
THE DAMAGE IS TOO EXTENSIVE. THE MOST EFFECTIVE AND EXPEDITIOUS WAY TO COMPLETE THE STRAND IS TO LOSE THE DAMAGED Y CHROMOSOME AND DUPLICATE THE INTACT X.
YOU WANT TO MAKE THE SPECIMEN...A FEMALE.
THAT WOULD BE A SIDE EFFECT, YES.
WHILE TECHNICALLY IT WOULD NOT BE A CLONE AT THAT POINT, IT WOULD BE, FOR ALL INTENTS AND PURPOSES, A GENETIC TWIN.
THE MUTANT DNA WOULD STILL BE ACTIVE, AND THE ABILITIES YOU'RE LOOKING FOR WOULD STILL MANIFEST AS IN THE ORIGINAL.
YOU'RE SUPPOSED TO BE CREATING A WEAPON, NOT A DAMN BARBIE DOLL!

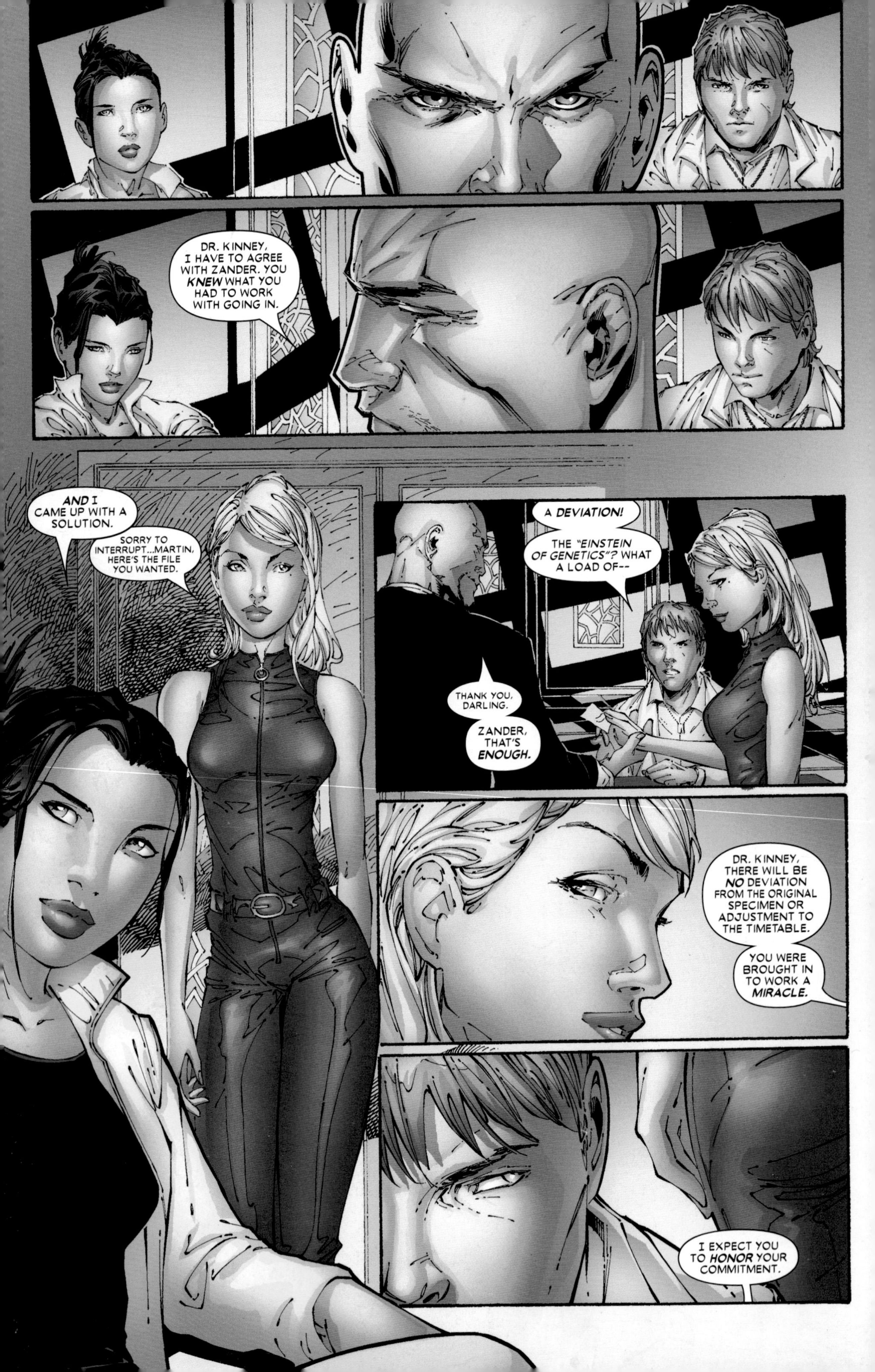
DR. KINNEY, I HAVE TO AGREE WITH ZANDER. YOU *KNEW* WHAT YOU HAD TO WORK WITH GOING IN.
AND I CAME UP WITH A SOLUTION.
SORRY TO INTERRUPT...MARTIN, HERE'S THE FILE YOU WANTED.
A *DEVIATION!*
THE *"EINSTEIN OF GENETICS"*? WHAT A LOAD OF--
THANK YOU, DARLING.
ZANDER, THAT'S *ENOUGH.*
DR. KINNEY, THERE WILL BE *NO* DEVIATION FROM THE ORIGINAL SPECIMEN OR ADJUSTMENT TO THE TIMETABLE.
YOU WERE BROUGHT IN TO WORK A *MIRACLE.*
I EXPECT YOU TO *HONOR* YOUR COMMITMENT.

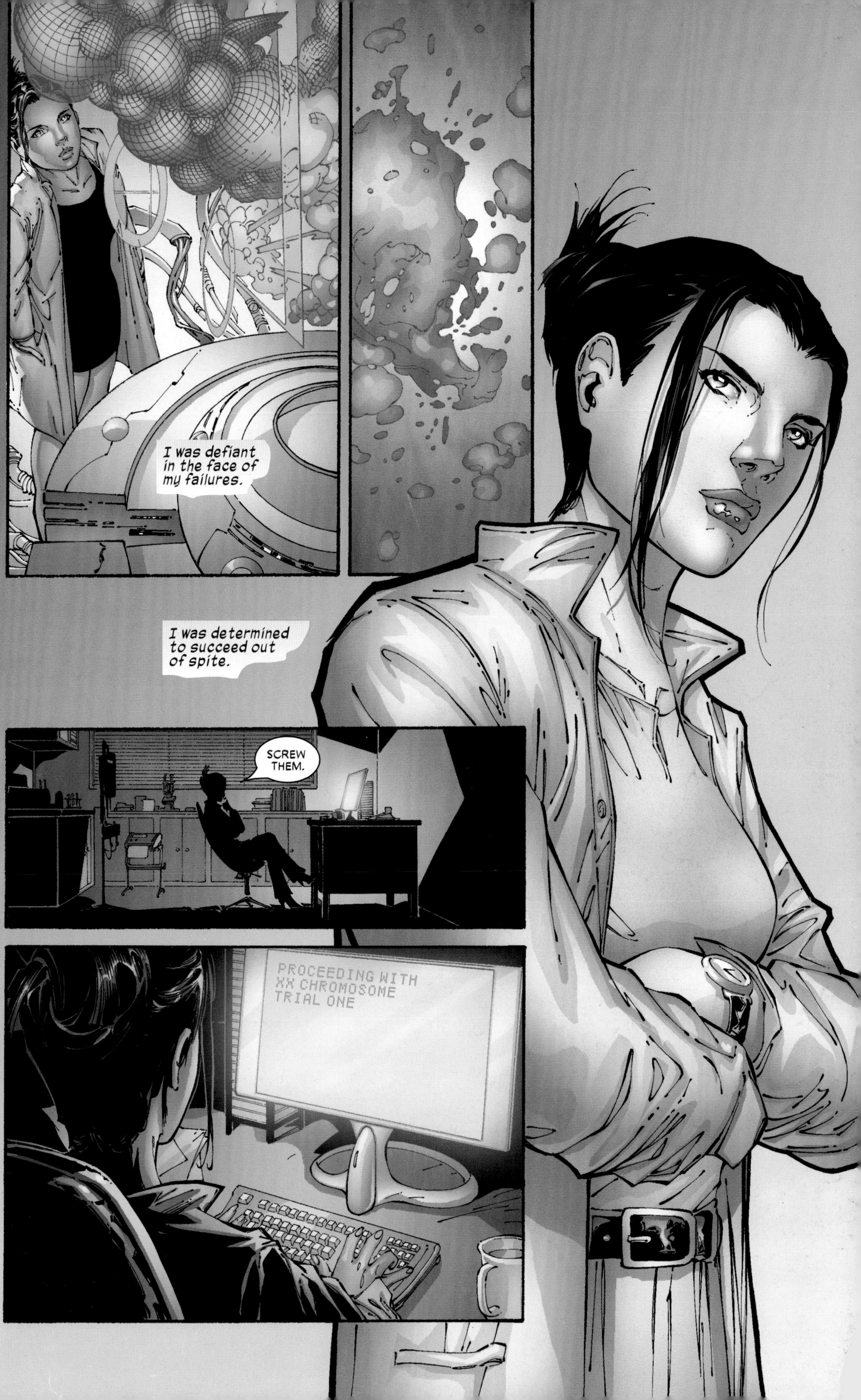
I was defiant in the face of my failures.
I was determined to succeed out of spite.
SCREW THEM.
PROCEEDING WITH XX CHROMOSOME TRIAL ONE

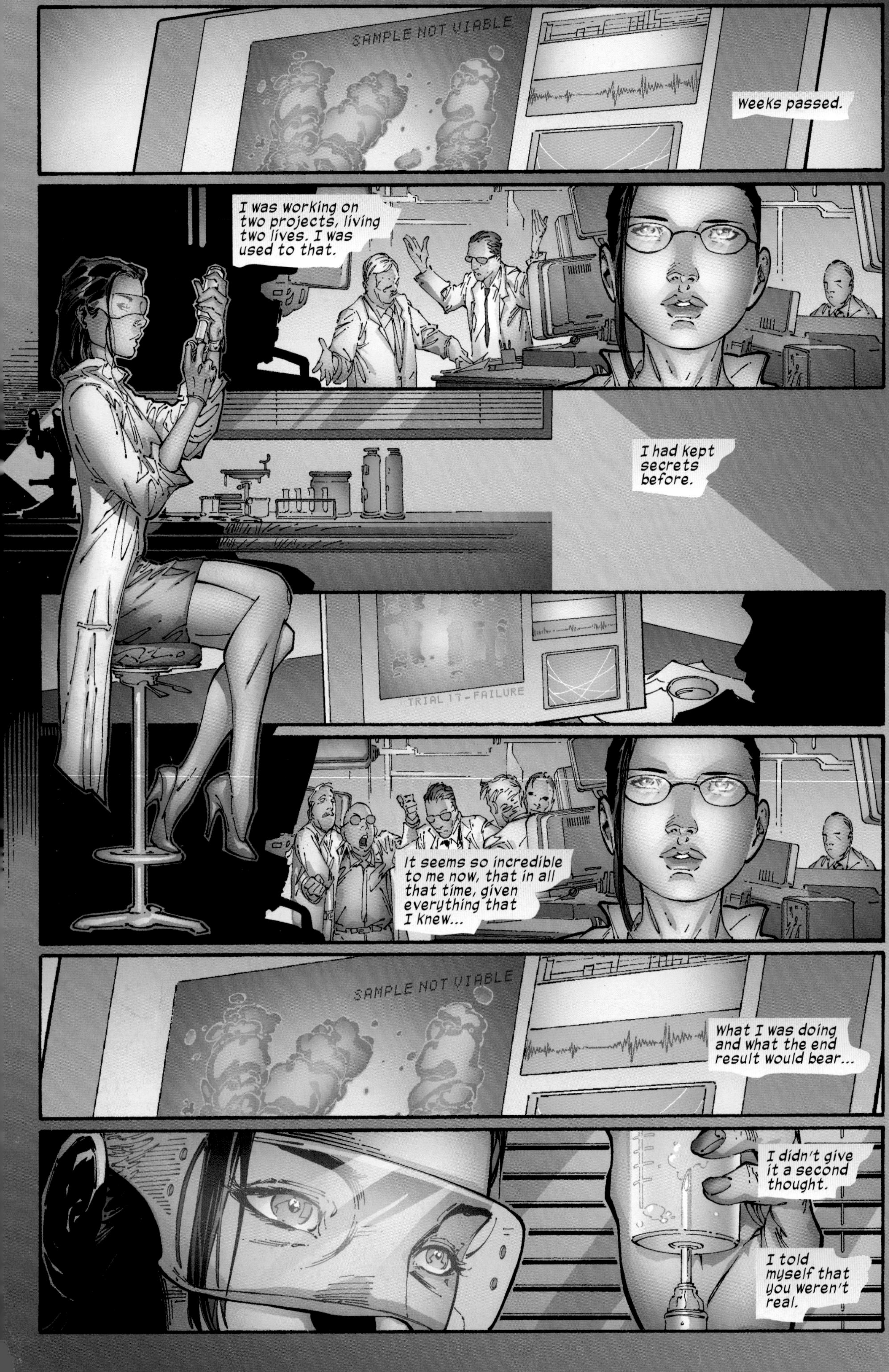
SAMPLE NOT VIABLE
Weeks passed.
I was working on two projects, living two lives. I was used to that.
I had kept secrets before.
TRIAL 17-FAILURE
It seems so incredible to me now, that in all that time, given everything that I knew...
SAMPLE NOT VIABLE
What I was doing and what the end result would bear...
I didn't give it a second thought.
I told myself that you weren't real.

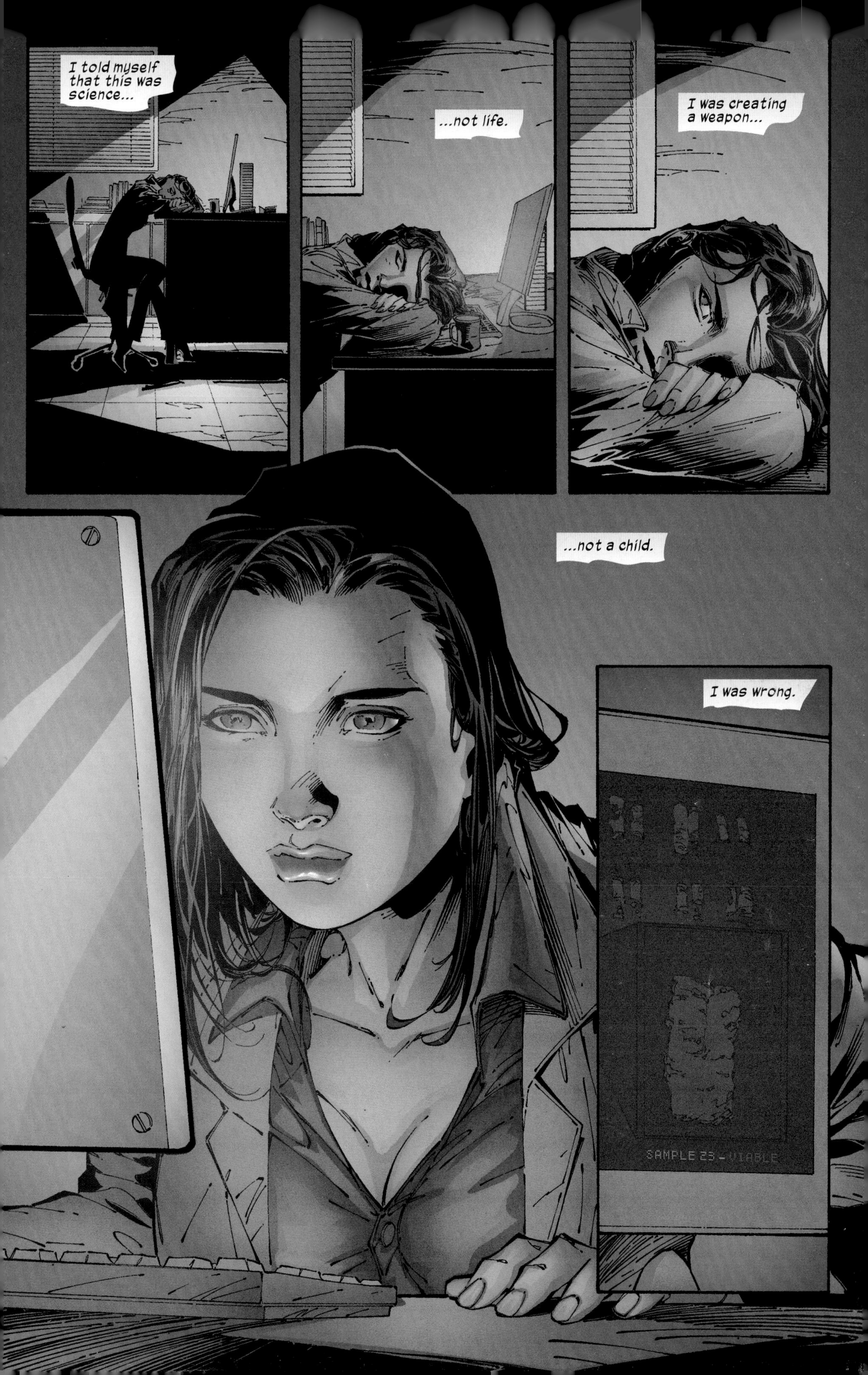
I told myself that this was science...
...not life.
I was creating a weapon...
...not a child.
I was wrong.
SAMPLE 23 - VIABLE

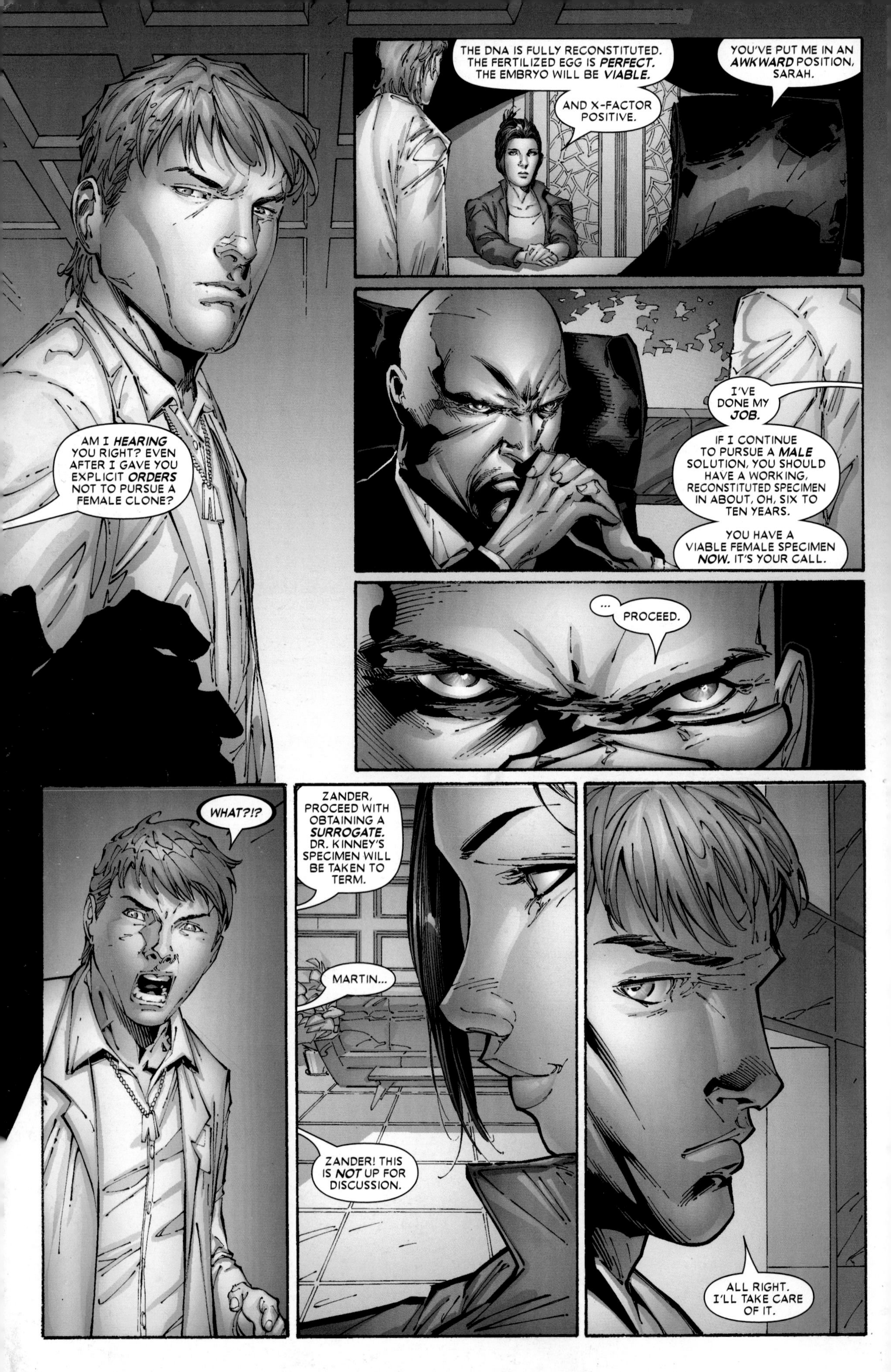
THE DNA IS FULLY RECONSTITUTED. THE FERTILIZED EGG IS PERFECT. THE EMBRYO WILL BE VIABLE.
AND X-FACTOR POSITIVE.
YOU'VE PUT ME IN AN AWKWARD POSITION, SARAH.
I'VE DONE MY JOB.
IF I CONTINUE TO PURSUE A MALE SOLUTION, YOU SHOULD HAVE A WORKING, RECONSTITUTED SPECIMEN IN ABOUT, OH, SIX TO TEN YEARS.
YOU HAVE A VIABLE FEMALE SPECIMEN NOW. IT'S YOUR CALL.
...
PROCEED.
AM I HEARING YOU RIGHT? EVEN AFTER I GAVE YOU EXPLICIT ORDERS NOT TO PURSUE A FEMALE CLONE?
WHAT?!?
ZANDER, PROCEED WITH OBTAINING A SURROGATE. DR. KINNEY'S SPECIMEN WILL BE TAKEN TO TERM.
MARTIN...
ZANDER! THIS IS NOT UP FOR DISCUSSION.
ALL RIGHT. I'LL TAKE CARE OF IT.

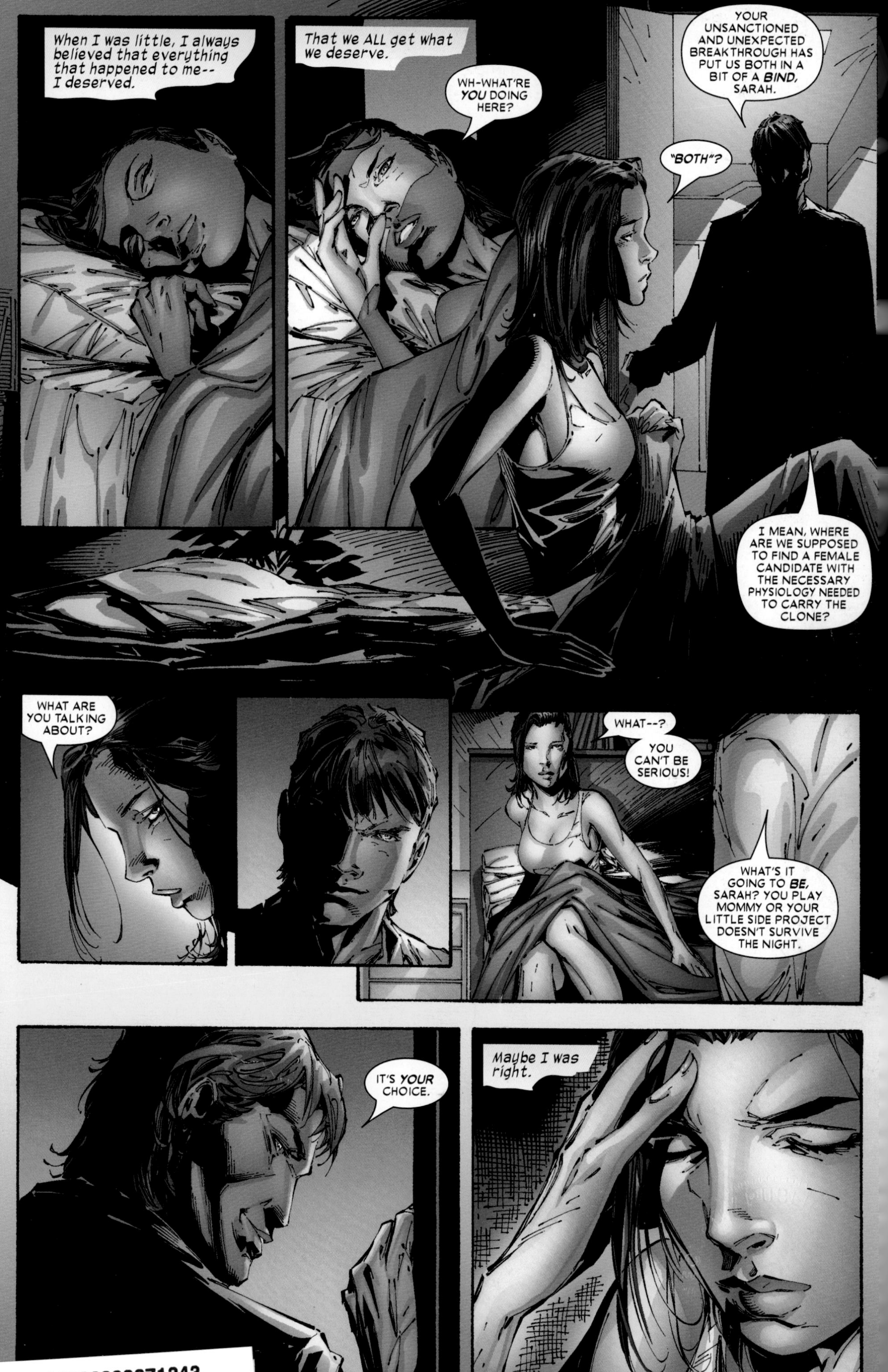
When I was little, I always believed that everything that happened to me-- I deserved.
That we ALL get what we deserve.
WH-WHAT'RE YOU DOING HERE?
YOUR UNSANCTIONED AND UNEXPECTED BREAKTHROUGH HAS PUT US BOTH IN A BIT OF A BIND, SARAH.
"BOTH"?
I MEAN, WHERE ARE WE SUPPOSED TO FIND A FEMALE CANDIDATE WITH THE NECESSARY PHYSIOLOGY NEEDED TO CARRY THE CLONE?
WHAT ARE YOU TALKING ABOUT?
WHAT--?
YOU CAN'T BE SERIOUS!
WHAT'S IT GOING TO BE, SARAH? YOU PLAY MOMMY OR YOUR LITTLE SIDE PROJECT DOESN'T SURVIVE THE NIGHT.
IT'S YOUR CHOICE.
Maybe I was right.

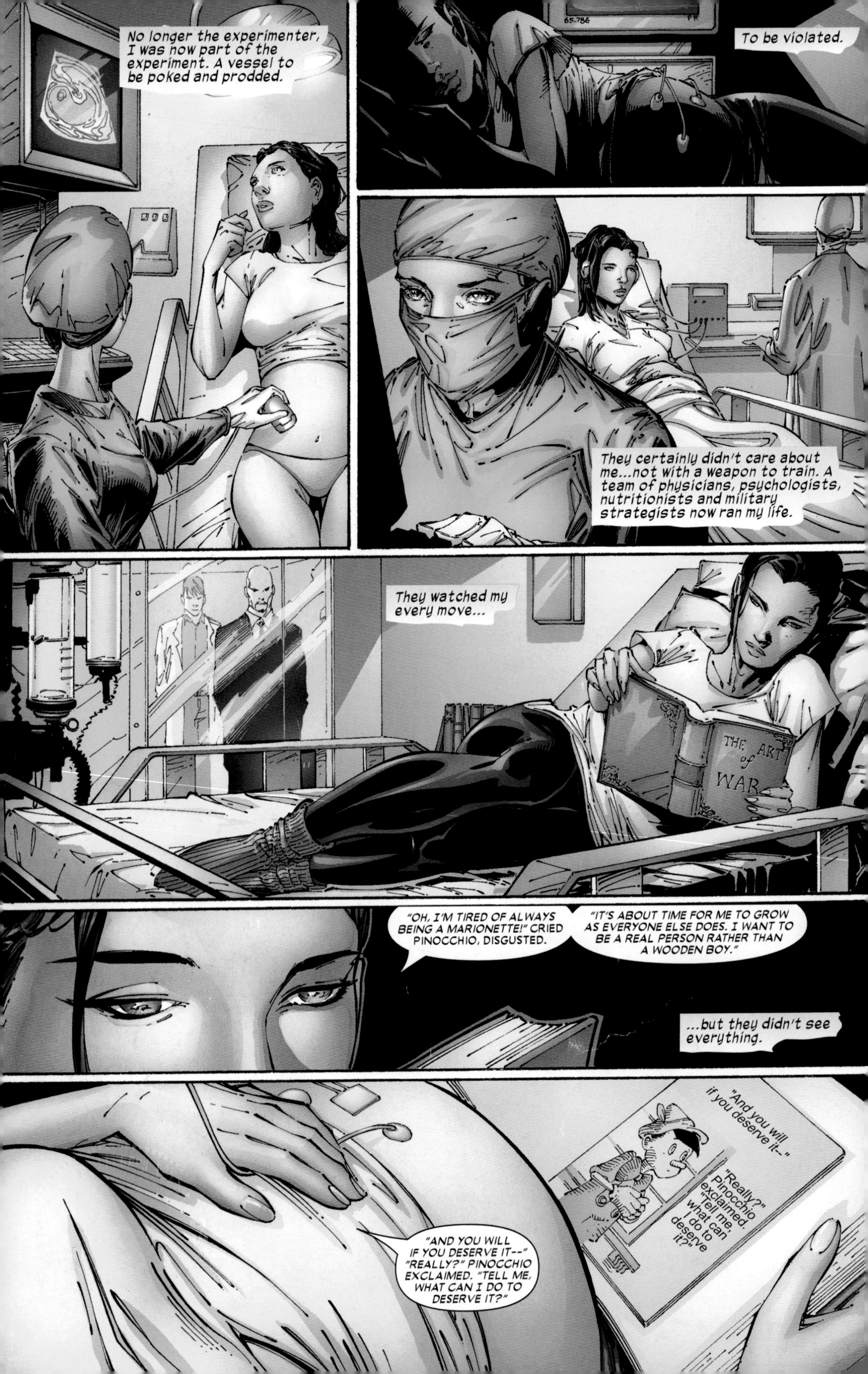
No longer the experimenter, I was now part of the experiment. A vessel to be poked and prodded.
To be violated.
They certainly didn't care about me...not with a weapon to train. A team of physicians, psychologists, nutritionists and military strategists now ran my life.
They watched my every move...
THE ART of WAR
"OH, I'M TIRED OF ALWAYS BEING A MARIONETTE!" CRIED PINOCCHIO, DISGUSTED.
"IT'S ABOUT TIME FOR ME TO GROW AS EVERYONE ELSE DOES. I WANT TO BE A REAL PERSON RATHER THAN A WOODEN BOY."
...but they didn't see everything.
"AND YOU WILL IF YOU DESERVE IT--" "REALLY?" PINOCCHIO EXCLAIMED. "TELL ME, WHAT CAN I DO TO DESERVE IT?"
"And you will if you deserve it--"
"Really?" Pinocchio exclaimed. "Tell me, what can I do to deserve it?"

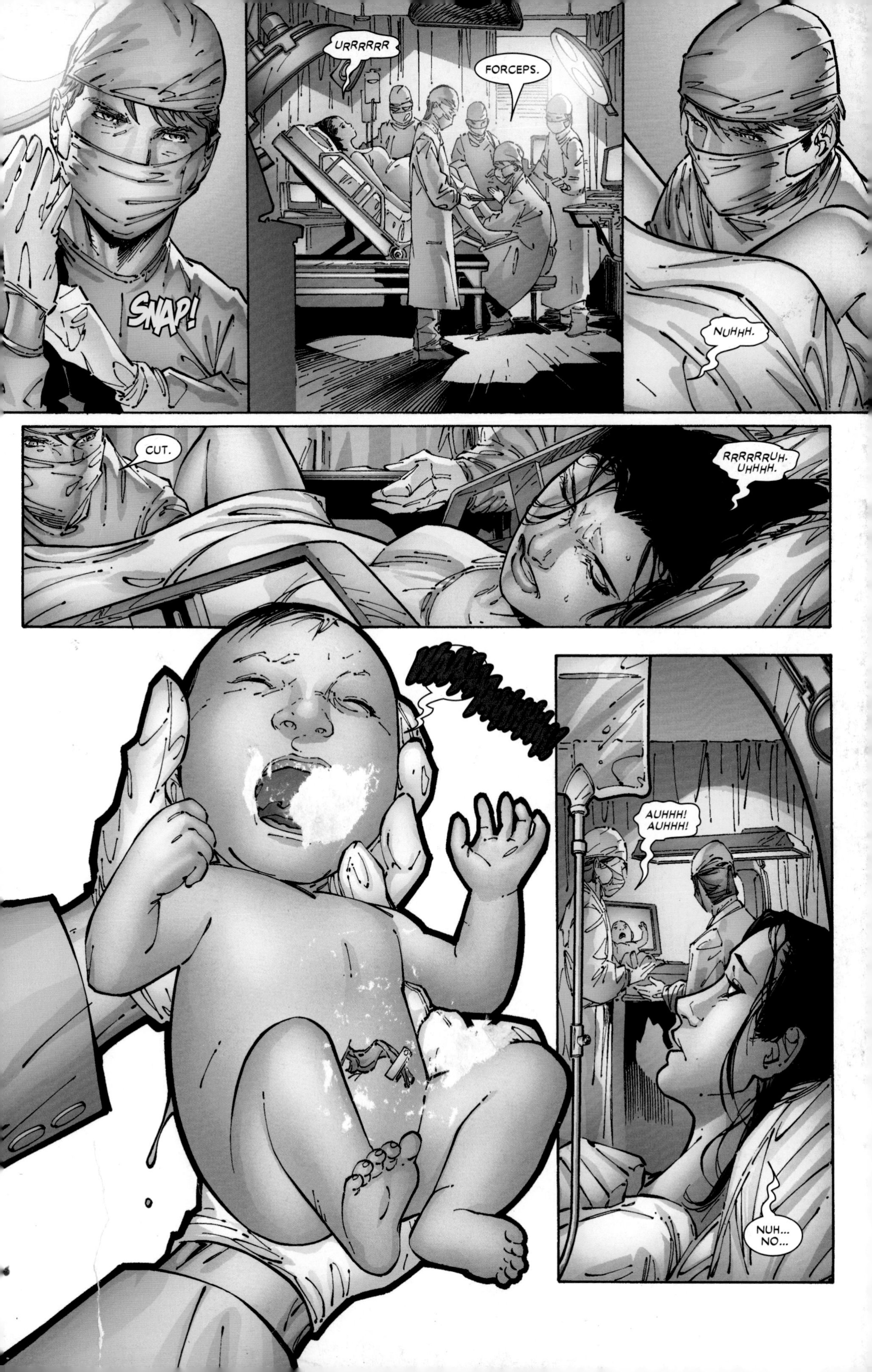
SNAP!
URRRRRR
FORCEPS.
NUHHH.
CUT.
RRRRRRUH. UHHHH.
AUHHH! AUHHH!
NUH... NO...

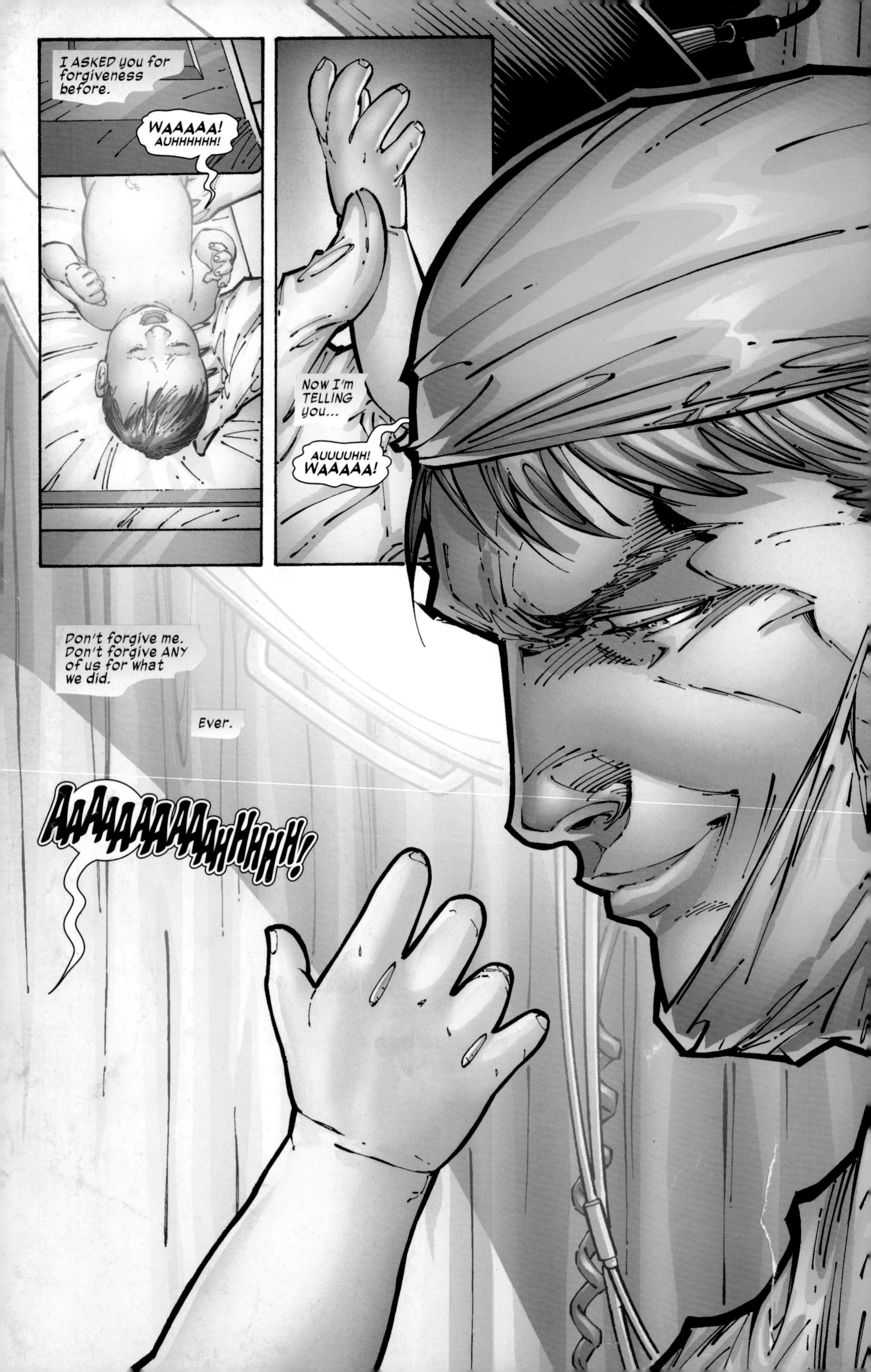
I ASKED you for forgiveness before.
WAAAAA! AUHHHHHH!
Now I'm TELLING you...
AUUUUHH! WAAAAA!
Don't forgive me. Don't forgive ANY of us for what we did.
Ever.
AAAAAAAAAAAAHHHHH!

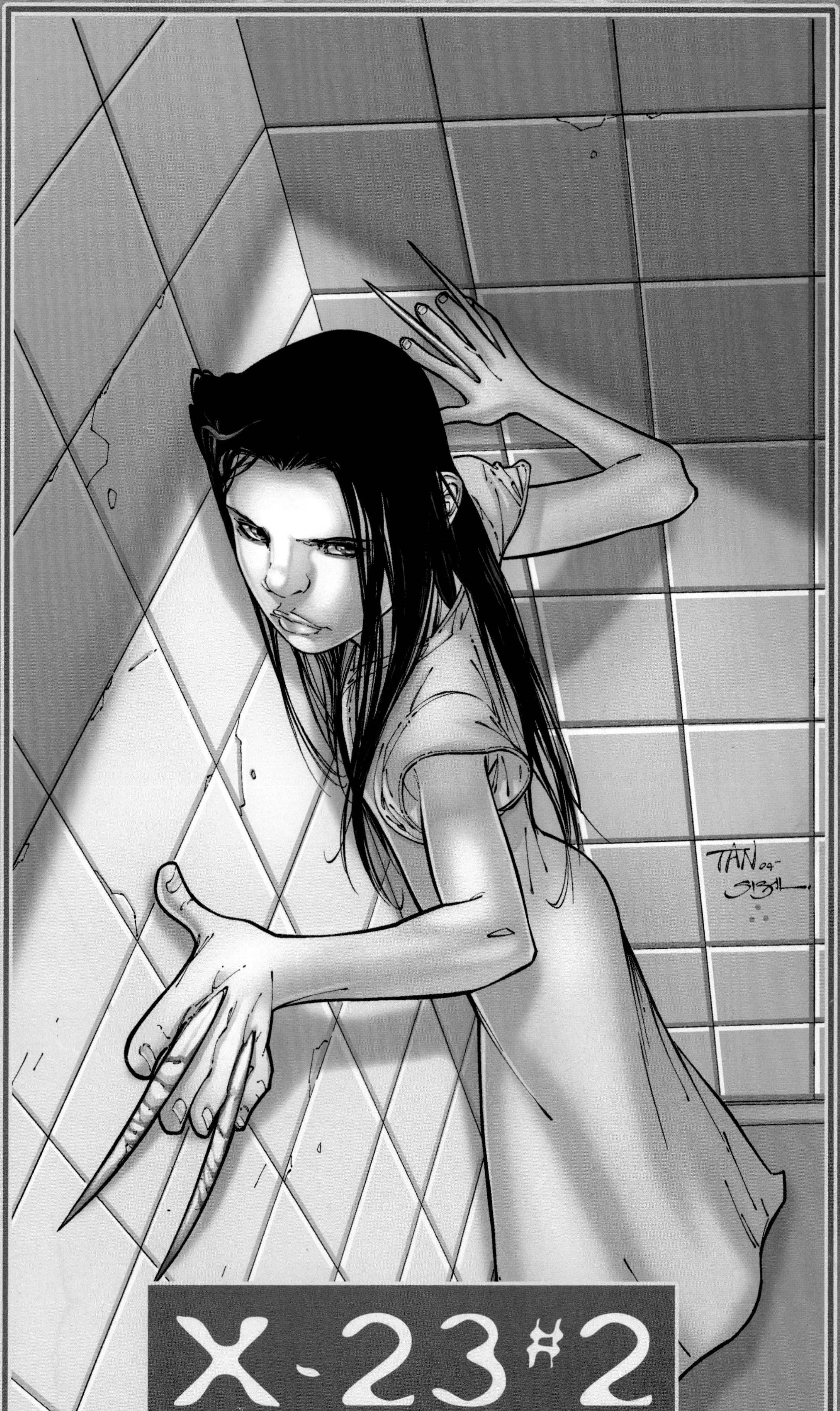
TAN 04
X-23 #2

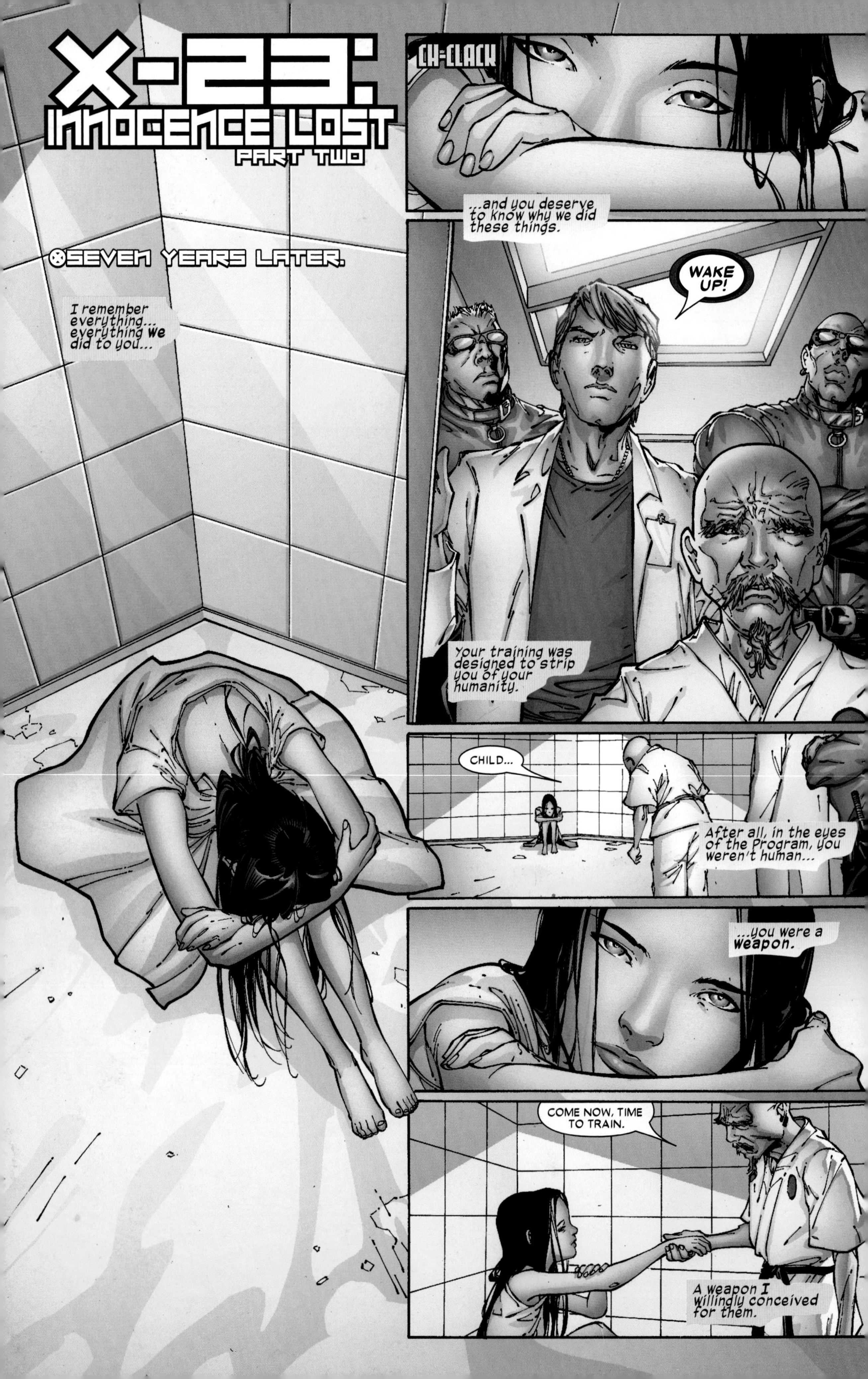
X-23: INNOCENCE LOST
PART TWO
SEVEN YEARS LATER.
I remember everything... everything we did to you...
CH-CLACK
...and you deserve to know why we did these things.
WAKE UP!
Your training was designed to strip you of your humanity.
CHILD...
After all, in the eyes of the Program, you weren't human...
...you were a weapon.
COME NOW, TIME TO TRAIN.
A weapon I willingly conceived for them.

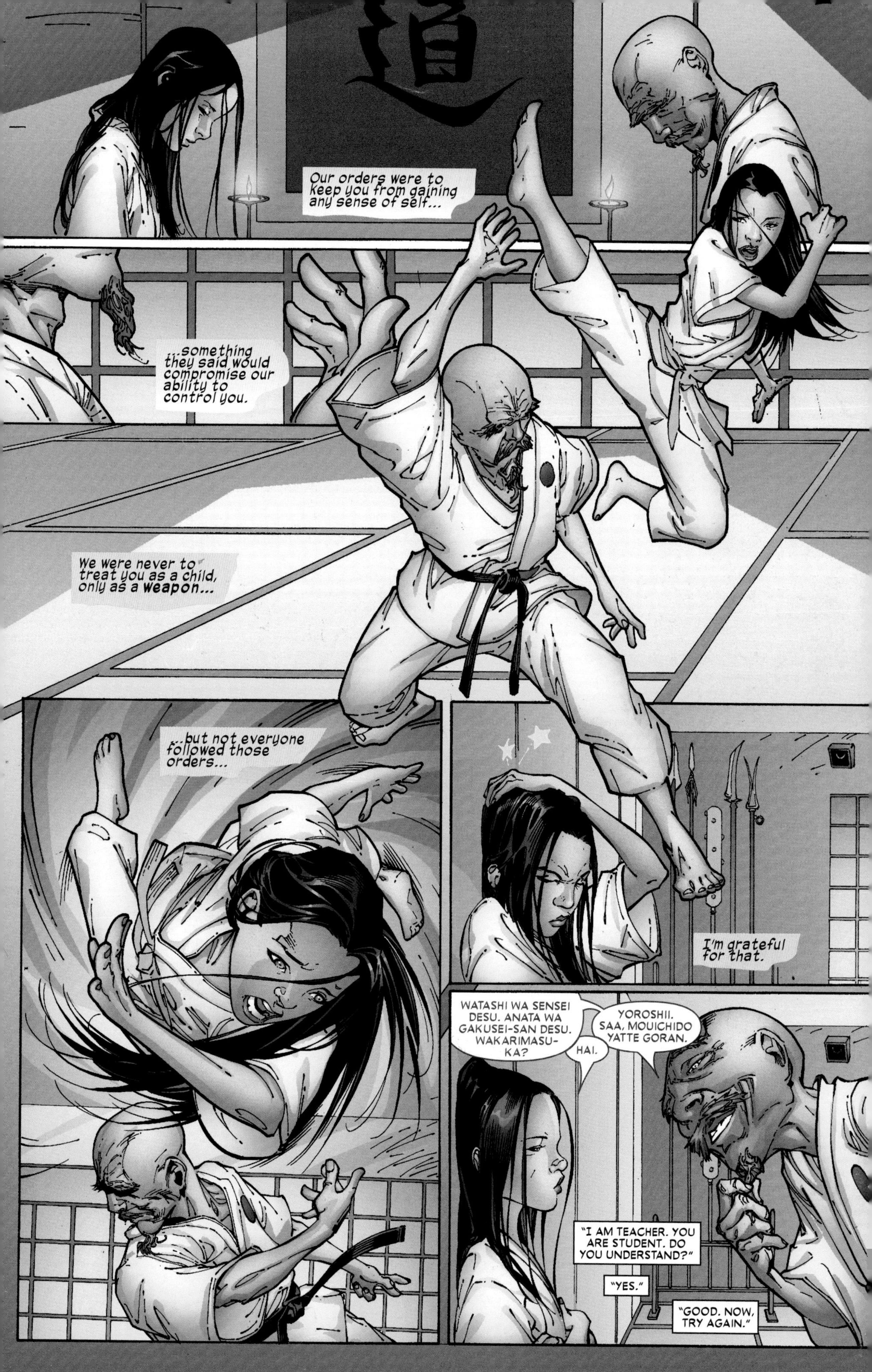
Our orders were to keep you from gaining any sense of self...
...something they said would compromise our ability to control you.
We were never to treat you as a child, only as a weapon...
...but not everyone followed those orders...
I'm grateful for that.
WATASHI WA SENSEI DESU. ANATA WA GAKUSEI-SAN DESU. WAKARIMASU-KA?
HAI.
YOROSHII. SAA, MOUICHIDO YATTE GORAN.
"I AM TEACHER. YOU ARE STUDENT. DO YOU UNDERSTAND?"
"YES."
"GOOD. NOW, TRY AGAIN."

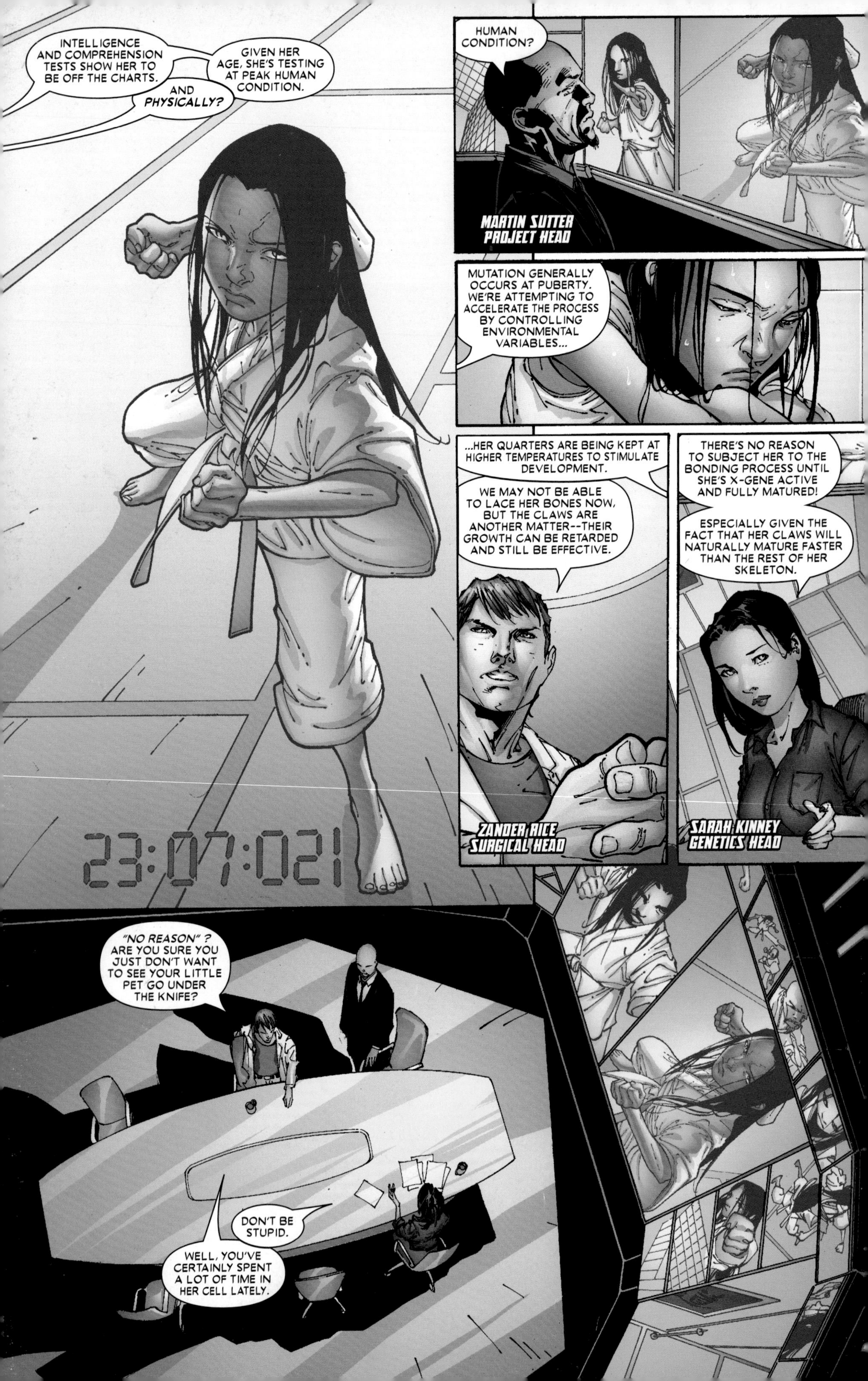
INTELLIGENCE AND COMPREHENSION TESTS SHOW HER TO BE OFF THE CHARTS.
AND *PHYSICALLY?*
GIVEN HER AGE, SHE'S TESTING AT PEAK HUMAN CONDITION.
23:07:021
HUMAN CONDITION?
MARTIN SUTTER
PROJECT HEAD
MUTATION GENERALLY OCCURS AT PUBERTY. WE'RE ATTEMPTING TO ACCELERATE THE PROCESS BY CONTROLLING ENVIRONMENTAL VARIABLES...
...HER QUARTERS ARE BEING KEPT AT HIGHER TEMPERATURES TO STIMULATE DEVELOPMENT.
WE MAY NOT BE ABLE TO LACE HER BONES NOW, BUT THE CLAWS ARE ANOTHER MATTER--THEIR GROWTH CAN BE RETARDED AND STILL BE EFFECTIVE.
ZANDER RICE
SURGICAL HEAD
THERE'S NO REASON TO SUBJECT HER TO THE BONDING PROCESS UNTIL SHE'S X-GENE ACTIVE AND FULLY MATURED!
ESPECIALLY GIVEN THE FACT THAT HER CLAWS WILL NATURALLY MATURE FASTER THAN THE REST OF HER SKELETON.
SARAH KINNEY
GENETICS HEAD
"NO REASON"? ARE YOU SURE YOU JUST DON'T WANT TO SEE YOUR LITTLE PET GO UNDER THE KNIFE?
DON'T BE STUPID.
WELL, YOU'VE CERTAINLY SPENT A LOT OF TIME IN HER CELL LATELY.

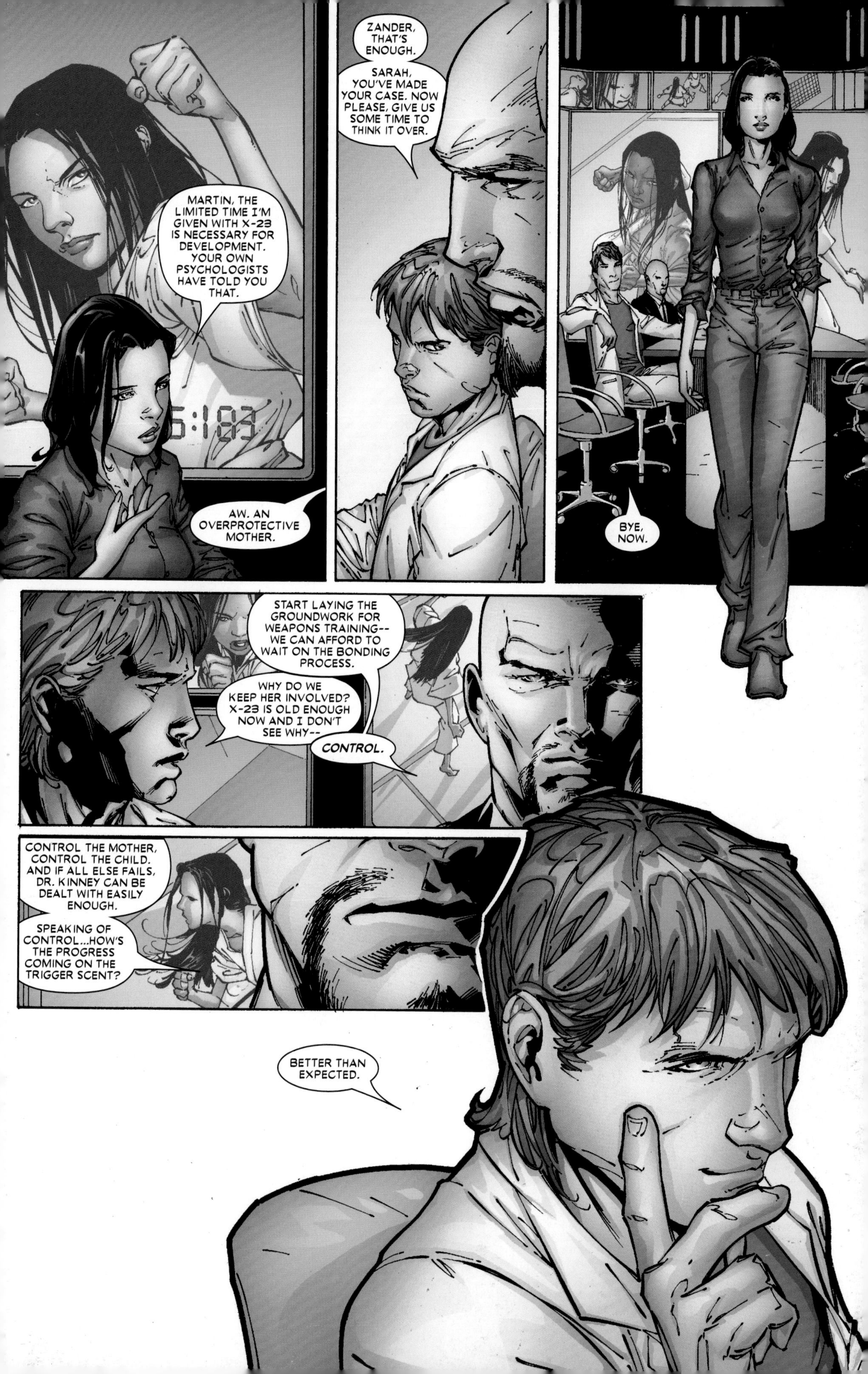
MARTIN, THE LIMITED TIME I'M GIVEN WITH X-23 IS NECESSARY FOR DEVELOPMENT. YOUR OWN PSYCHOLOGISTS HAVE TOLD YOU THAT.
AW. AN OVERPROTECTIVE MOTHER.
ZANDER, THAT'S ENOUGH.
SARAH, YOU'VE MADE YOUR CASE. NOW PLEASE, GIVE US SOME TIME TO THINK IT OVER.
BYE, NOW.
START LAYING THE GROUNDWORK FOR WEAPONS TRAINING-- WE CAN AFFORD TO WAIT ON THE BONDING PROCESS.
WHY DO WE KEEP HER INVOLVED? X-23 IS OLD ENOUGH NOW AND I DON'T SEE WHY--
CONTROL.
CONTROL THE MOTHER, CONTROL THE CHILD. AND IF ALL ELSE FAILS, DR. KINNEY CAN BE DEALT WITH EASILY ENOUGH.
SPEAKING OF CONTROL...HOW'S THE PROGRESS COMING ON THE TRIGGER SCENT?
BETTER THAN EXPECTED.

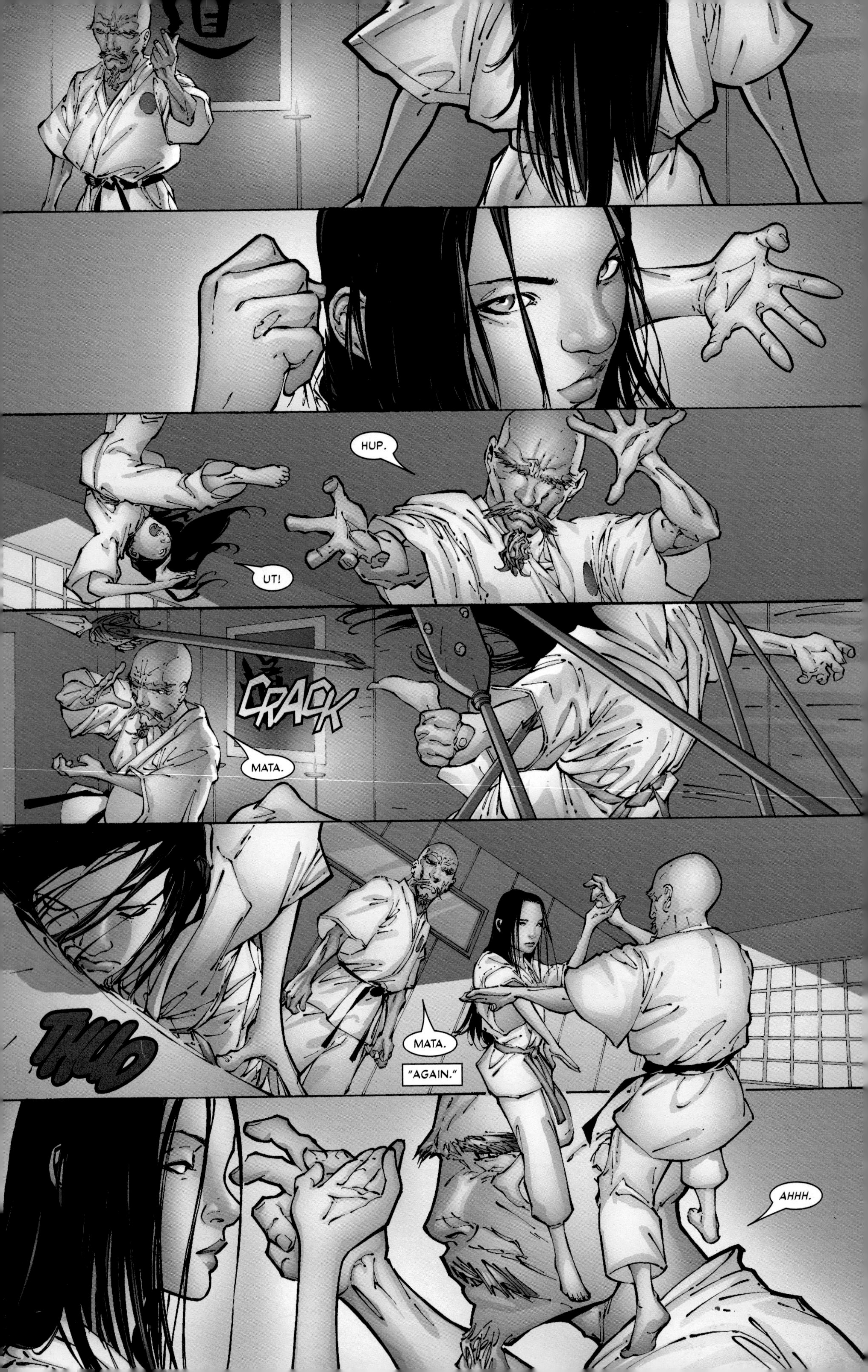
HUP.
UT!
CRACK
MATA.
THUD
MATA.
"AGAIN."
AHHH.

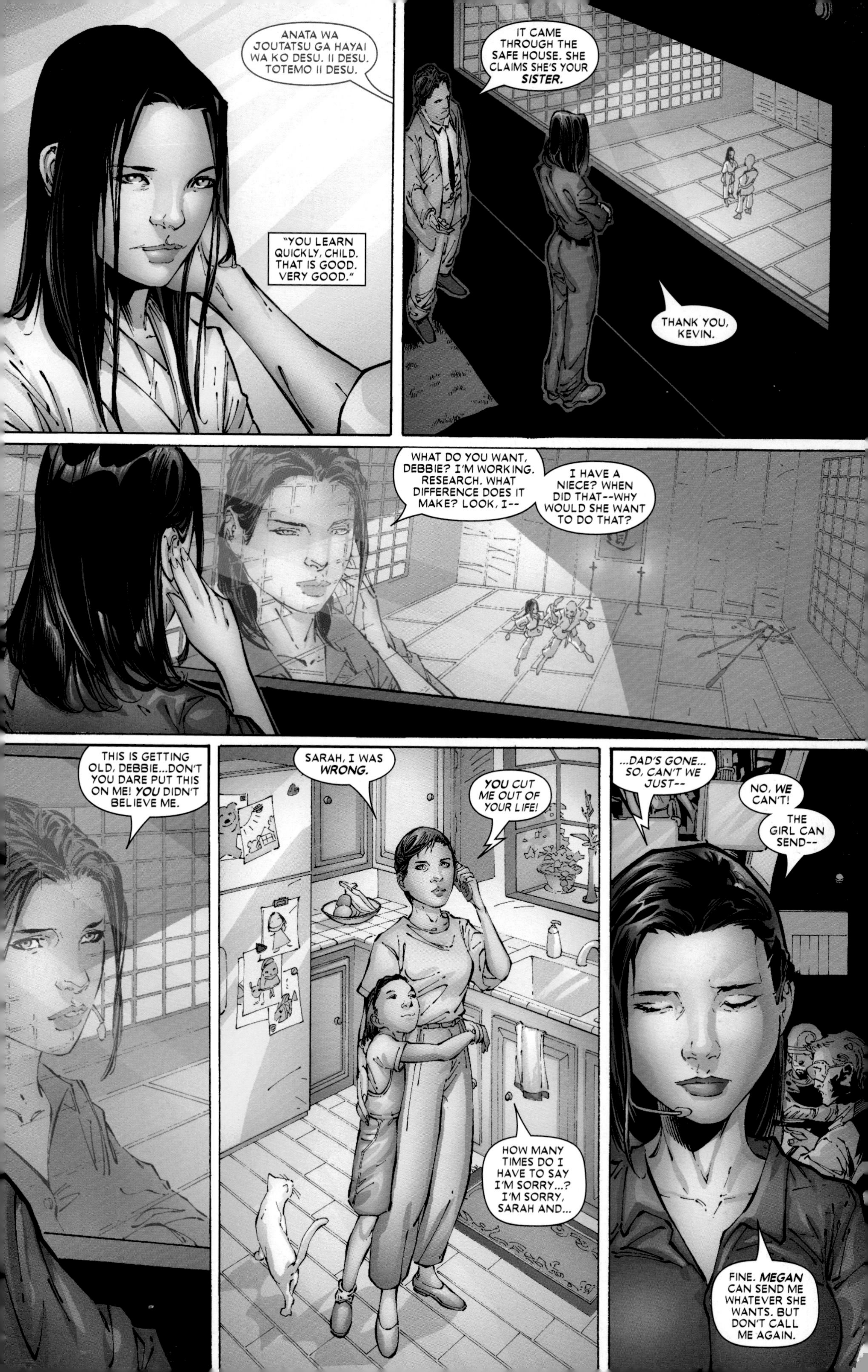
ANATA WA JOUTATSU GA HAYAI WA KO DESU. II DESU. TOTEMO II DESU.
"YOU LEARN QUICKLY, CHILD. THAT IS GOOD. VERY GOOD."
IT CAME THROUGH THE SAFE HOUSE. SHE CLAIMS SHE'S YOUR SISTER.
THANK YOU, KEVIN.
WHAT DO YOU WANT, DEBBIE? I'M WORKING. RESEARCH. WHAT DIFFERENCE DOES IT MAKE? LOOK, I--
I HAVE A NIECE? WHEN DID THAT--WHY WOULD SHE WANT TO DO THAT?
THIS IS GETTING OLD, DEBBIE...DON'T YOU DARE PUT THIS ON ME! YOU DIDN'T BELIEVE ME.
SARAH, I WAS WRONG.
YOU CUT ME OUT OF YOUR LIFE!
HOW MANY TIMES DO I HAVE TO SAY I'M SORRY...? I'M SORRY, SARAH AND...
...DAD'S GONE... SO, CAN'T WE JUST--
NO, WE CAN'T!
THE GIRL CAN SEND--
FINE. MEGAN CAN SEND ME WHATEVER SHE WANTS. BUT DON'T CALL ME AGAIN.

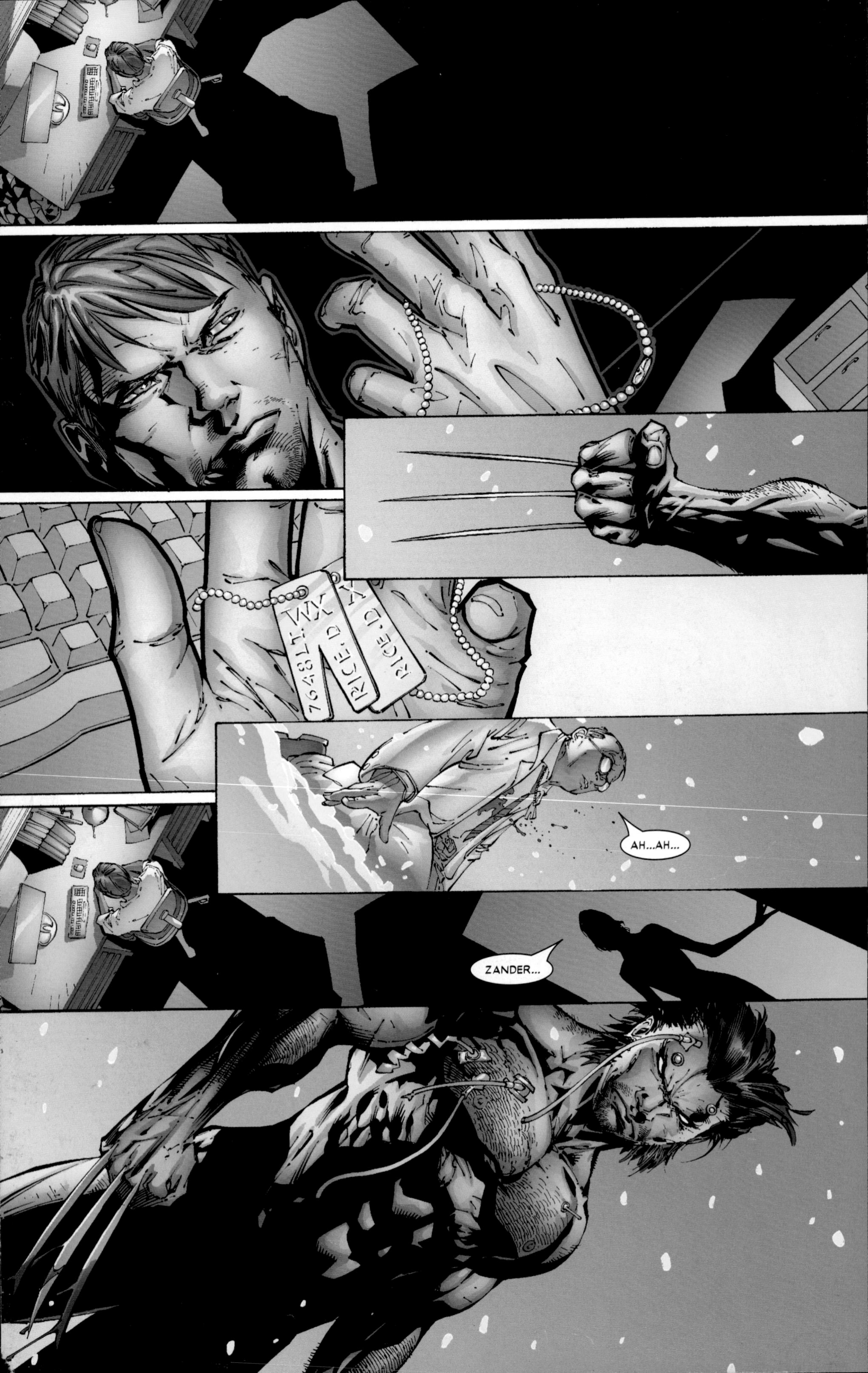
WX
7648LT
RICE.D
X
RICE.D
AH...AH...
ZANDER...

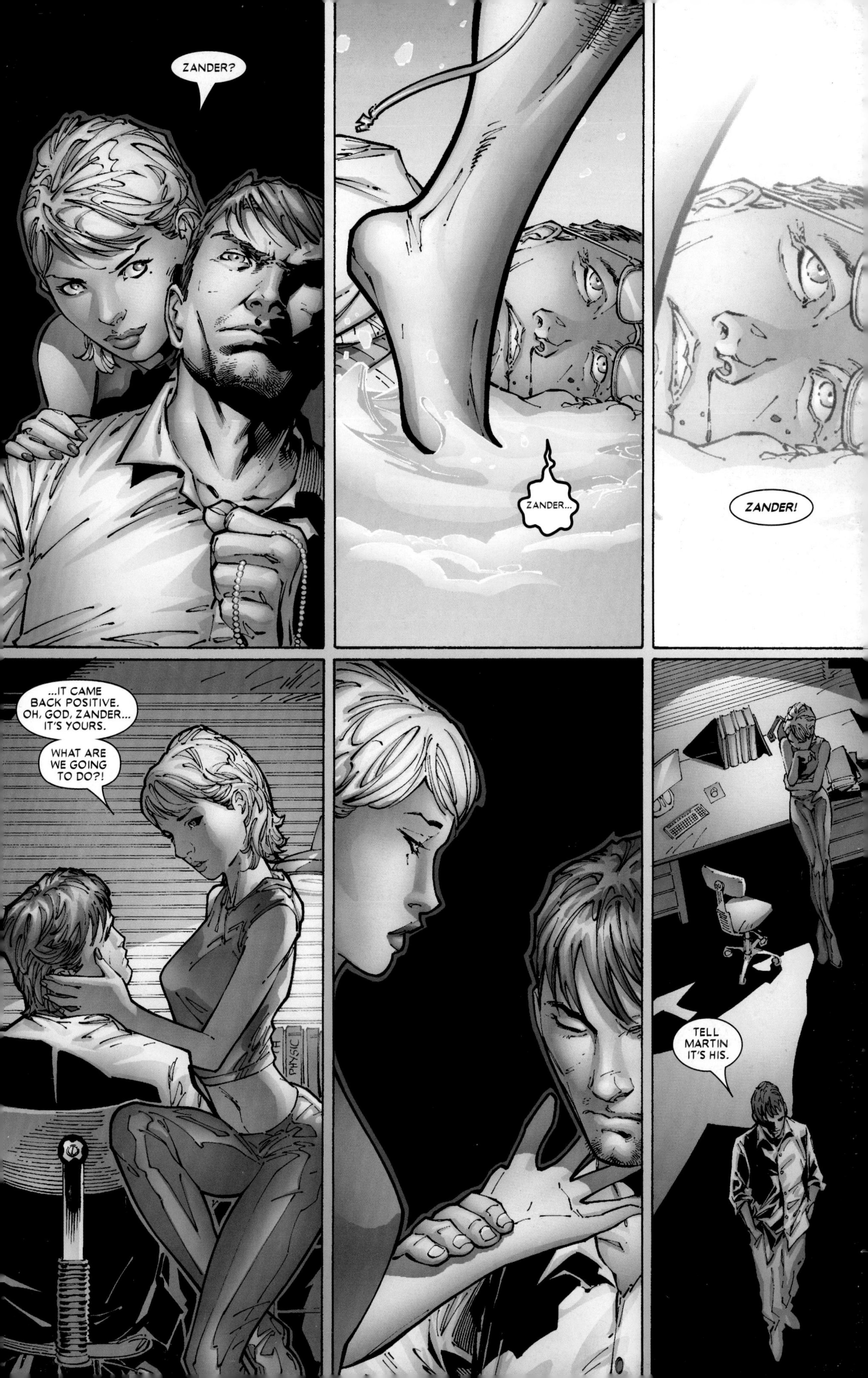

ZANDER?
ZANDER...
ZANDER!
...IT CAME BACK POSITIVE. OH, GOD, ZANDER... IT'S YOURS.
WHAT ARE WE GOING TO DO?!
PHYSIC
TELL MARTIN IT'S HIS.

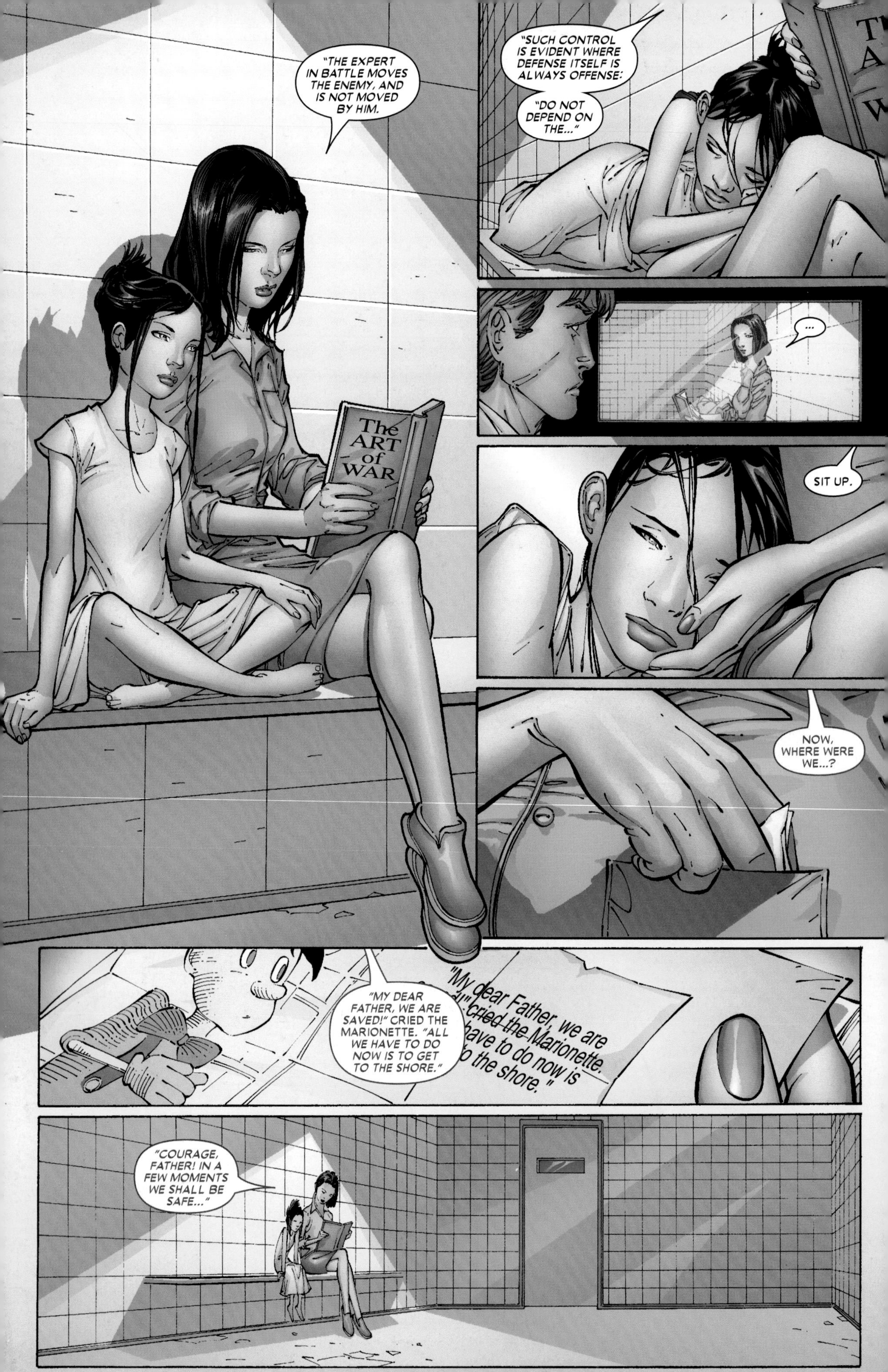
"THE EXPERT IN BATTLE MOVES THE ENEMY, AND IS NOT MOVED BY HIM.
The ART of WAR
"SUCH CONTROL IS EVIDENT WHERE DEFENSE ITSELF IS ALWAYS OFFENSE:
"DO NOT DEPEND ON THE..."
...
SIT UP.
NOW, WHERE WERE WE...?
"MY DEAR FATHER, WE ARE SAVED!" CRIED THE MARIONETTE. "ALL WE HAVE TO DO NOW IS TO GET TO THE SHORE."
"COURAGE, FATHER! IN A FEW MOMENTS WE SHALL BE SAFE..."

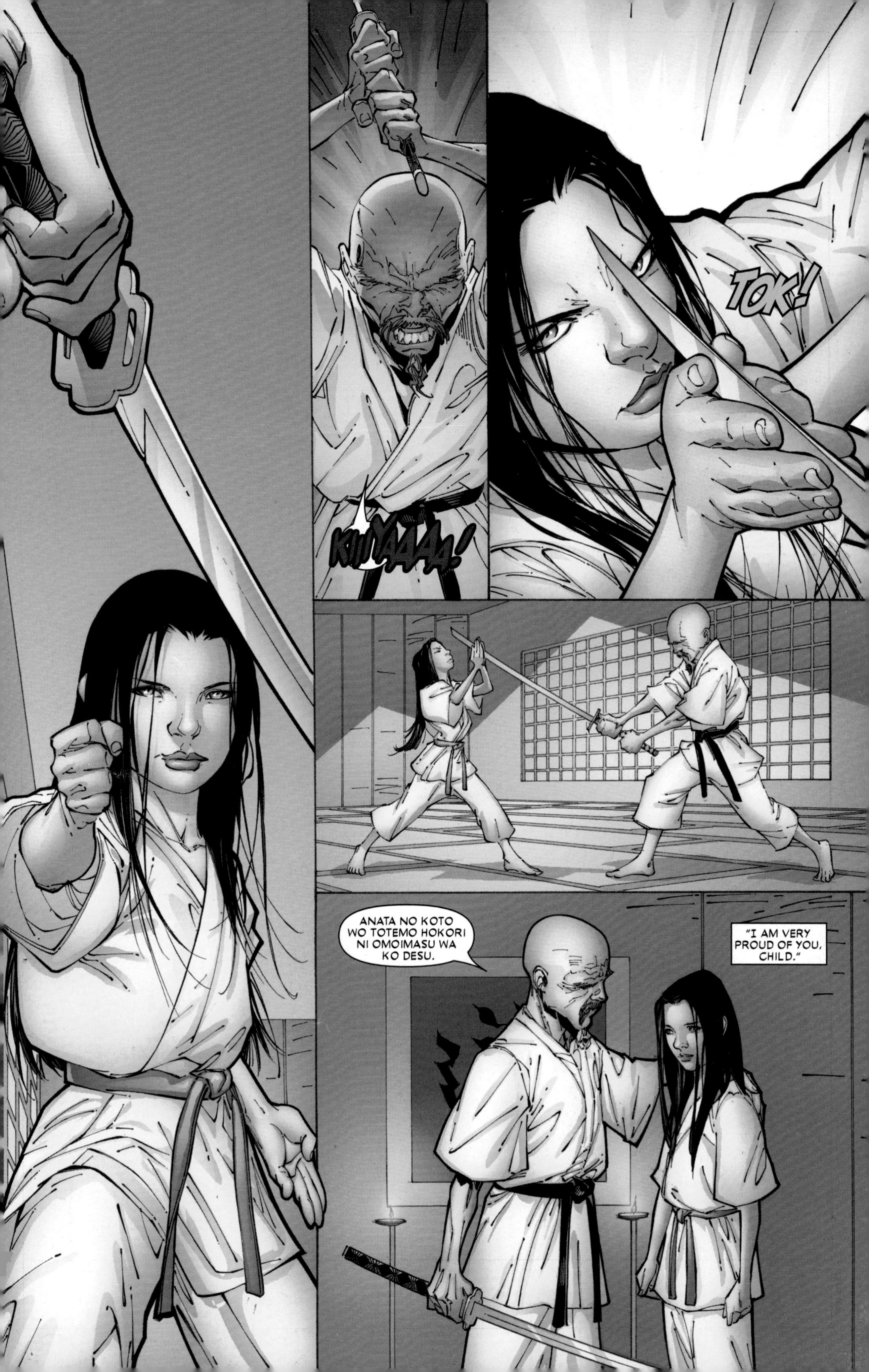
KIIIYAAAA!
TOK!
ANATA NO KOTO WO TOTEMO HOKORI NI OMOIMASU WA KO DESU.
"I AM VERY PROUD OF YOU, CHILD."

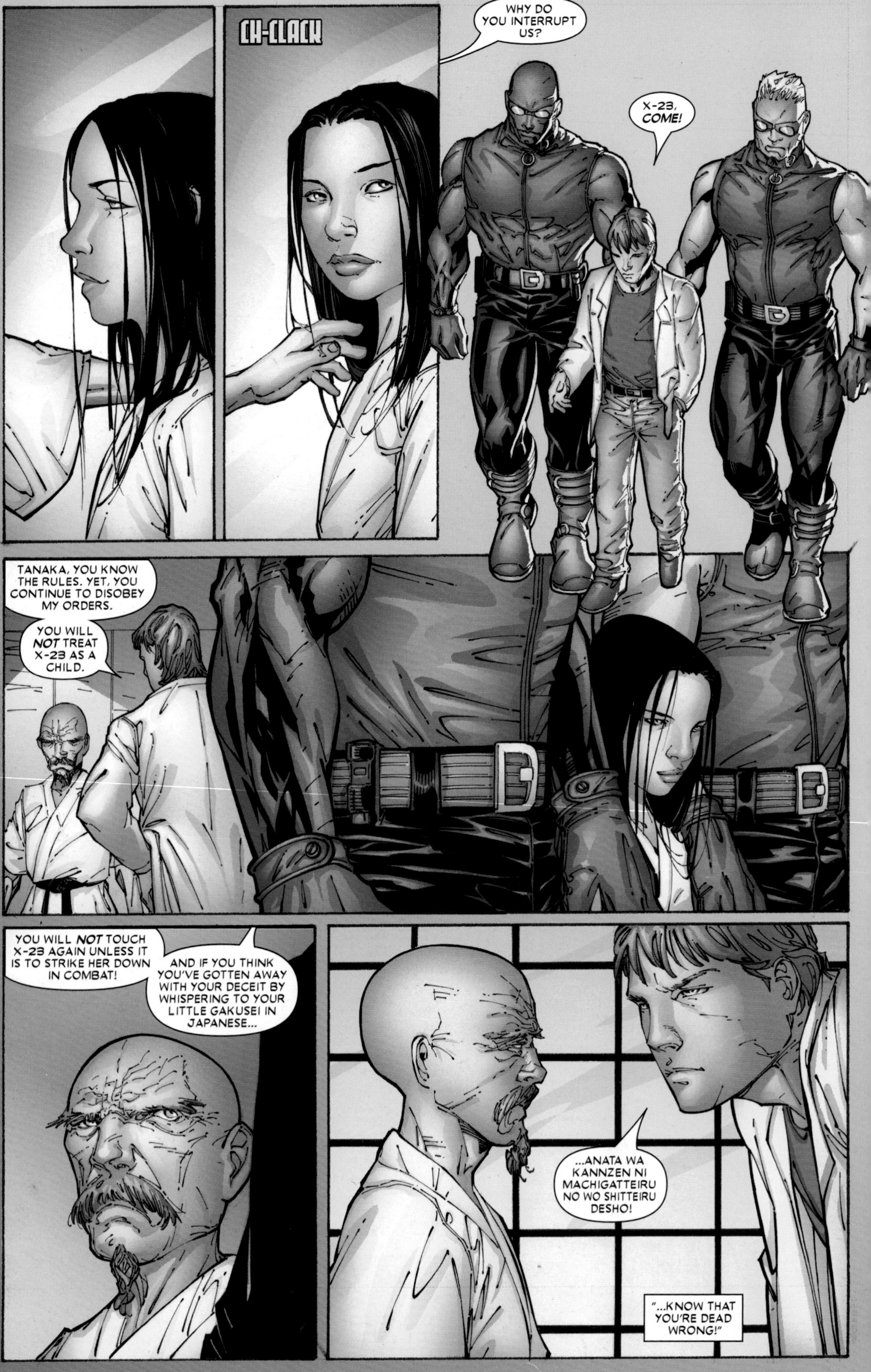
CH-CLACK
WHY DO YOU INTERRUPT US?
X-23, COME!
TANAKA, YOU KNOW THE RULES. YET, YOU CONTINUE TO DISOBEY MY ORDERS.
YOU WILL NOT TREAT X-23 AS A CHILD.
YOU WILL NOT TOUCH X-23 AGAIN UNLESS IT IS TO STRIKE HER DOWN IN COMBAT!
AND IF YOU THINK YOU'VE GOTTEN AWAY WITH YOUR DECEIT BY WHISPERING TO YOUR LITTLE GAKUSEI IN JAPANESE...
...ANATA WA KANNZEN NI MACHIGATTEIRU NO WO SHITTEIRU DESHO!
"...KNOW THAT YOU'RE DEAD WRONG!"

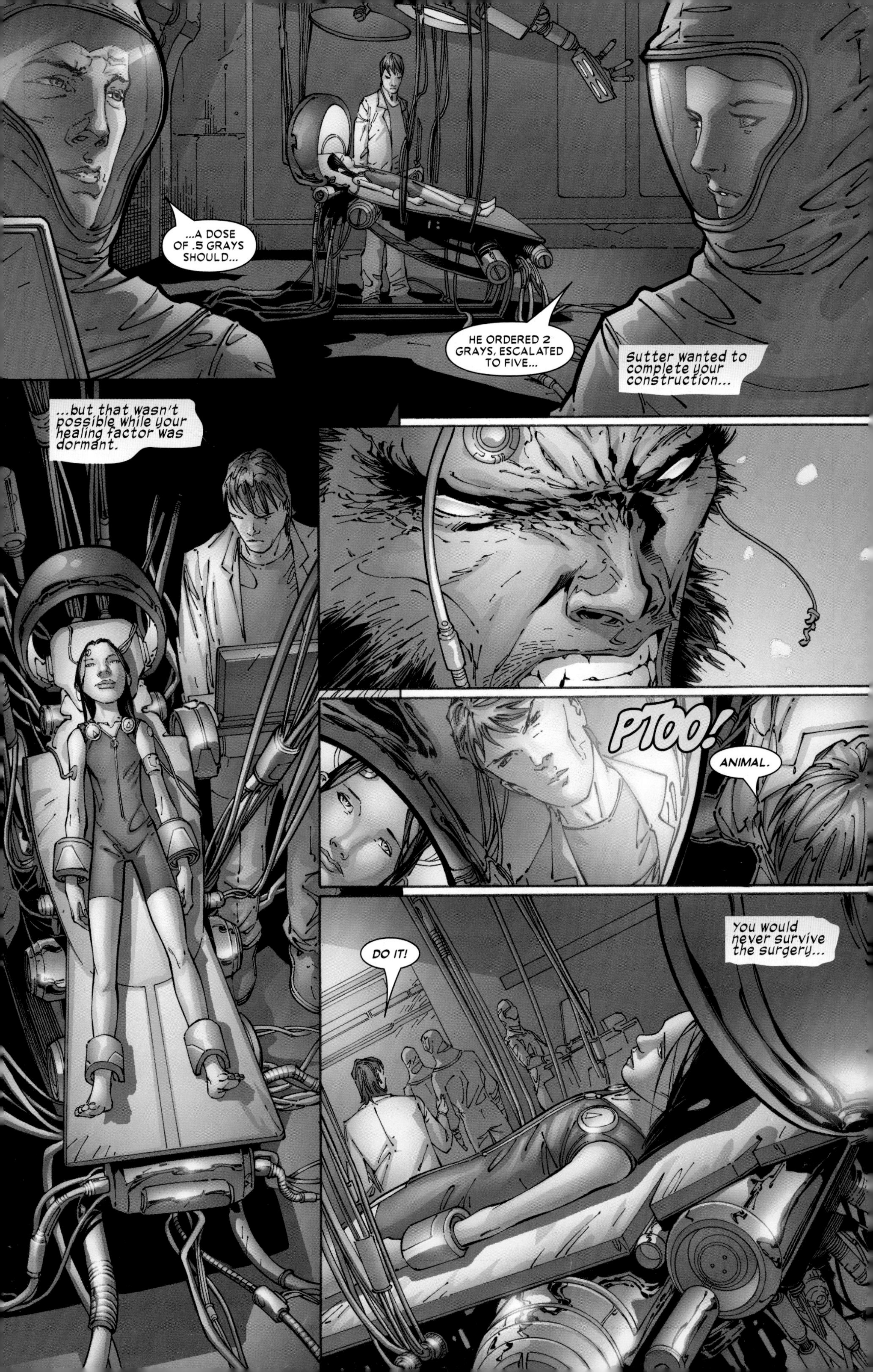
...A DOSE OF .5 GRAYS SHOULD...
HE ORDERED 2 GRAYS, ESCALATED TO FIVE...
Sutter wanted to complete your construction...
...but that wasn't possible while your healing factor was dormant.
PTOO!
ANIMAL.
DO IT!
You would never survive the surgery...

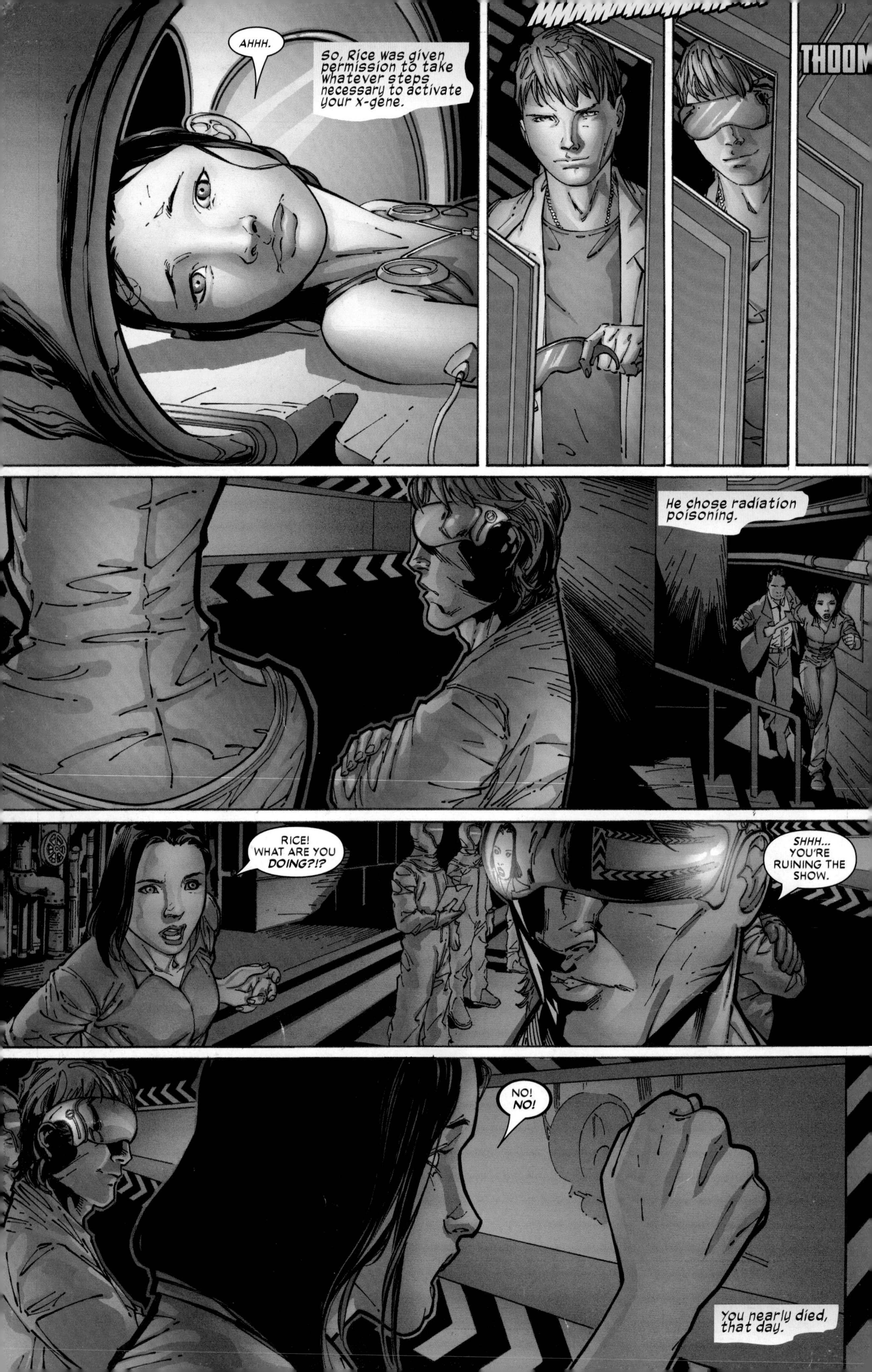
AHHH.
So, Rice was given permission to take whatever steps necessary to activate your x-gene.
THOOM
He chose radiation poisoning.
RICE! WHAT ARE YOU DOING?!?
SHHH... YOU'RE RUINING THE SHOW.
NO! NO!
You nearly died, that day.

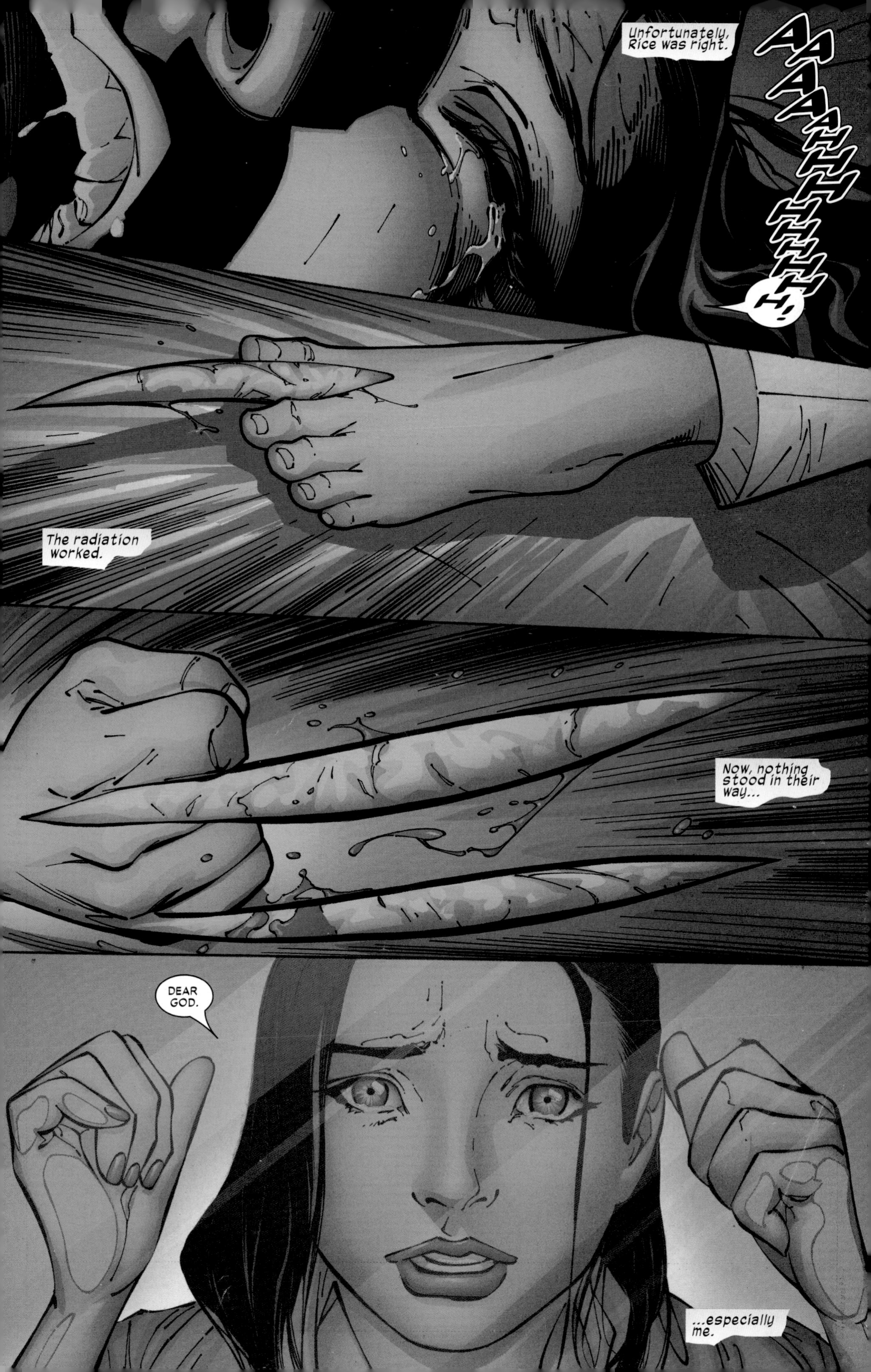
Unfortunately, Rice was right.
AAAAAHHHHHHHH!
The radiation worked.
Now, nothing stood in their way...
DEAR GOD.
...especially me.

ABSOLUTELY NOT! ZANDER HAS PREPARED FOR THIS HIS WHOLE LIFE. THERE'S NO REASON TO TAKE HIM OFF THE SURGERY.

MARTIN, YOU DON'T UNDERSTAND. HE'S BECOME TOO EMOTIONALLY MOTIVATED. HE'S LOST IT!

SARAH--

PLEASE...LET SOMEONE ELSE... LET ME HANDLE THE SURGERY! RICE CAN OVERSEE THE BONDING, BUT PLEASE...

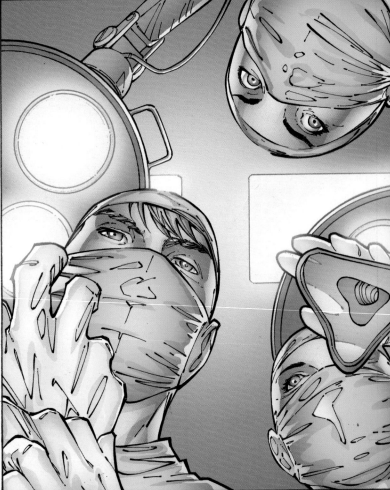

OUT OF THE QUESTION. NO ONE KNOWS ZANDER BETTER THAN ME. AND IF ANYONE HAS BECOME EMOTIONALLY INVESTED, SARAH...

...IT'S YOU.

STOP.

NO ANESTHESIA.

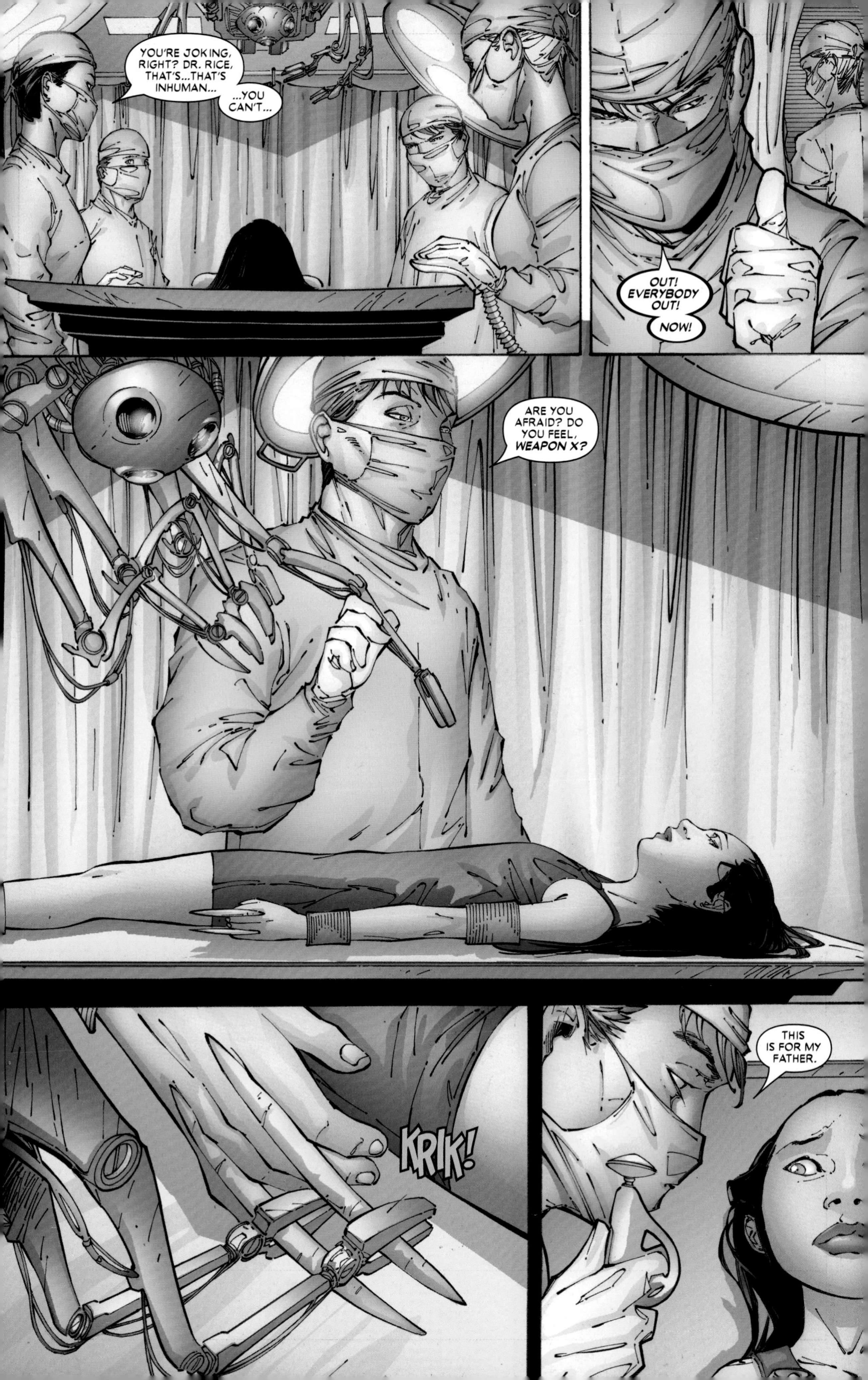
YOU'RE JOKING, RIGHT? DR. RICE, THAT'S...THAT'S INHUMAN...
...YOU CAN'T...
OUT! EVERYBODY OUT!
NOW!
ARE YOU AFRAID? DO YOU FEEL, WEAPON X?
KRIK!
THIS IS FOR MY FATHER.

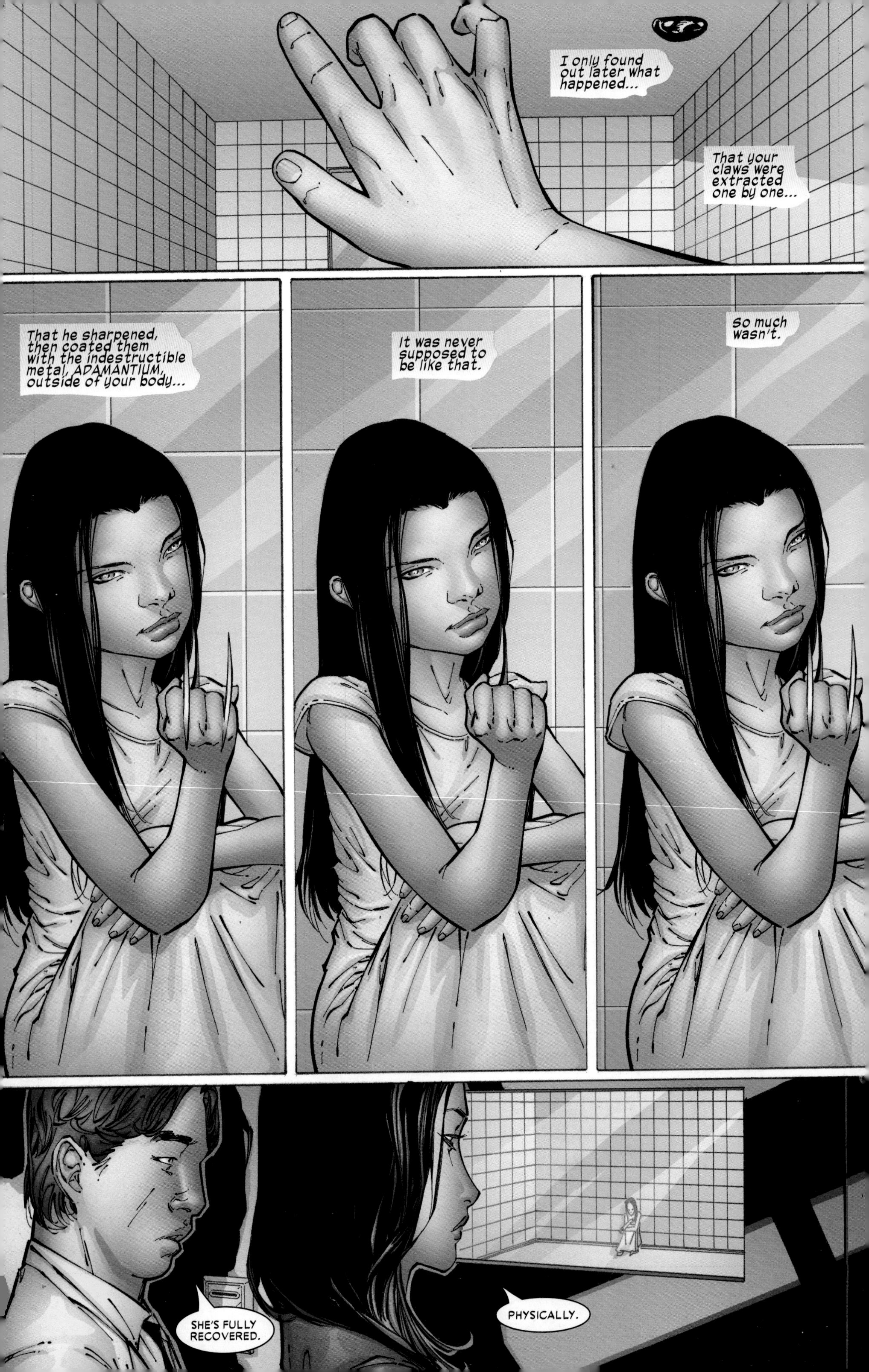
I only found out later what happened...
That your claws were extracted one by one...
That he sharpened, then coated them with the indestructible metal, ADAMANTIUM, outside of your body...
It was never supposed to be like that.
So much wasn't.
SHE'S FULLY RECOVERED.
PHYSICALLY.

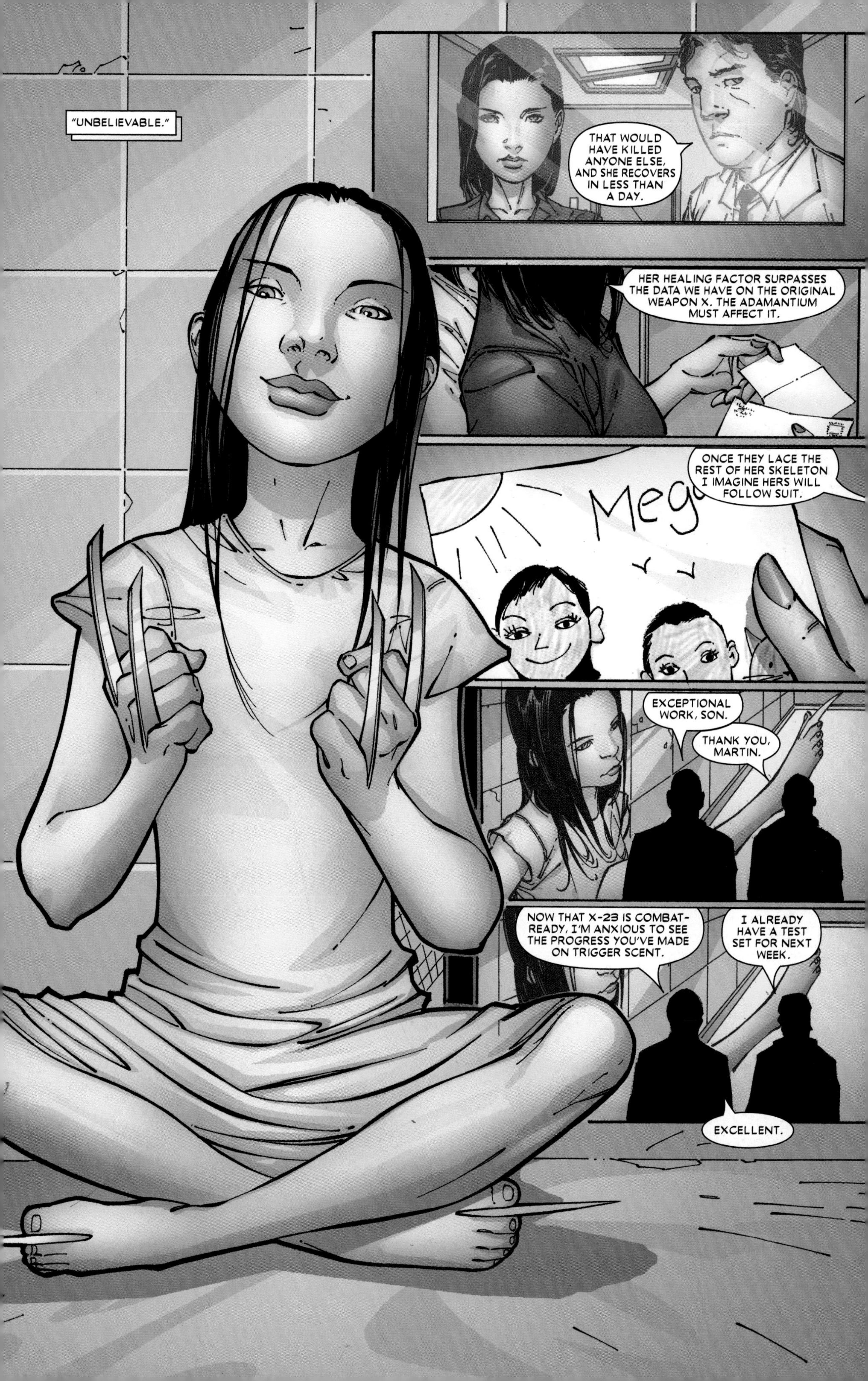
"UNBELIEVABLE."
THAT WOULD HAVE KILLED ANYONE ELSE, AND SHE RECOVERS IN LESS THAN A DAY.
HER HEALING FACTOR SURPASSES THE DATA WE HAVE ON THE ORIGINAL WEAPON X. THE ADAMANTIUM MUST AFFECT IT.
Meg
ONCE THEY LACE THE REST OF HER SKELETON I IMAGINE HERS WILL FOLLOW SUIT.
EXCEPTIONAL WORK, SON.
THANK YOU, MARTIN.
NOW THAT X-23 IS COMBAT-READY, I'M ANXIOUS TO SEE THE PROGRESS YOU'VE MADE ON TRIGGER SCENT.
I ALREADY HAVE A TEST SET FOR NEXT WEEK.
EXCELLENT.

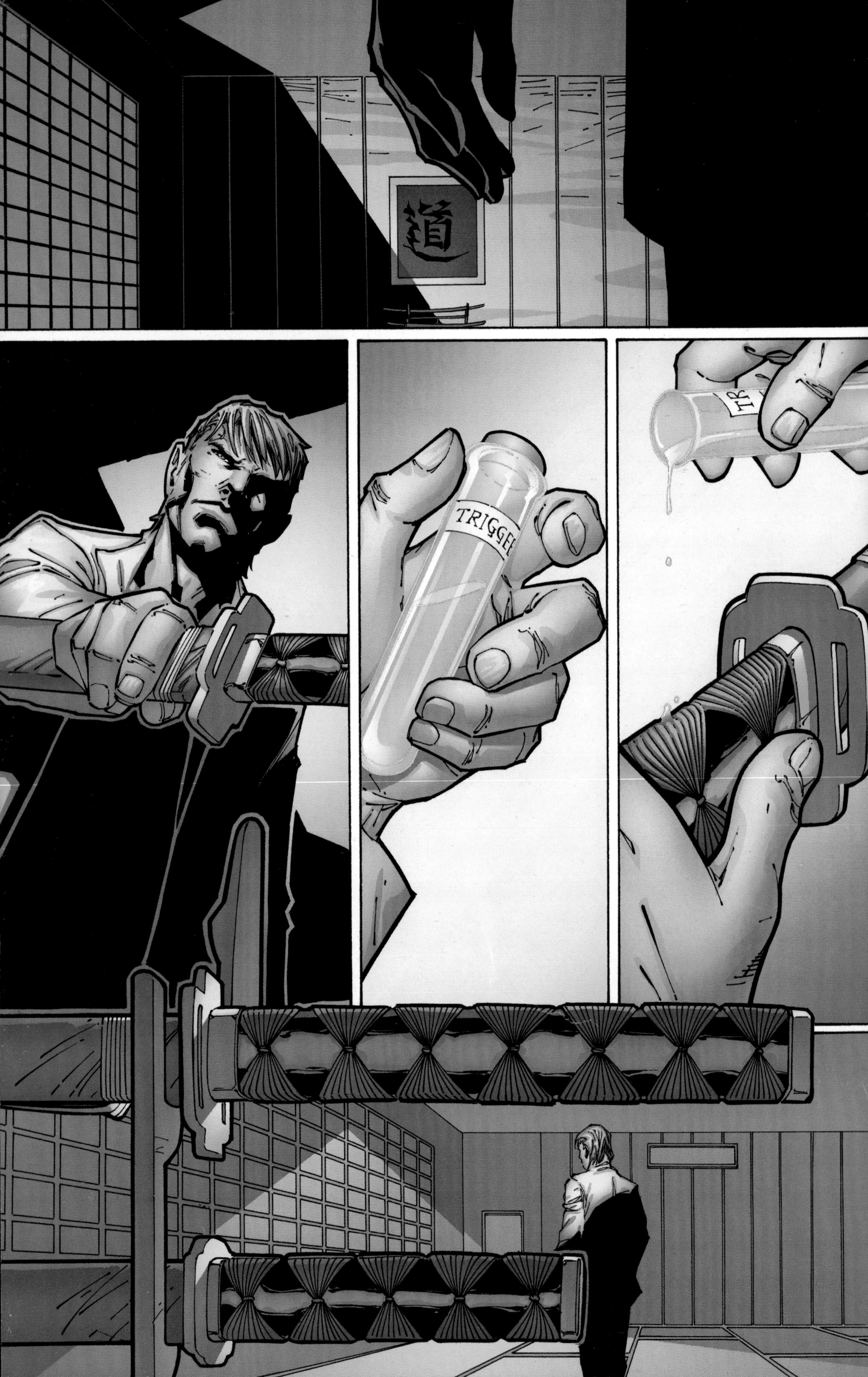
道
TRIGGE
TR

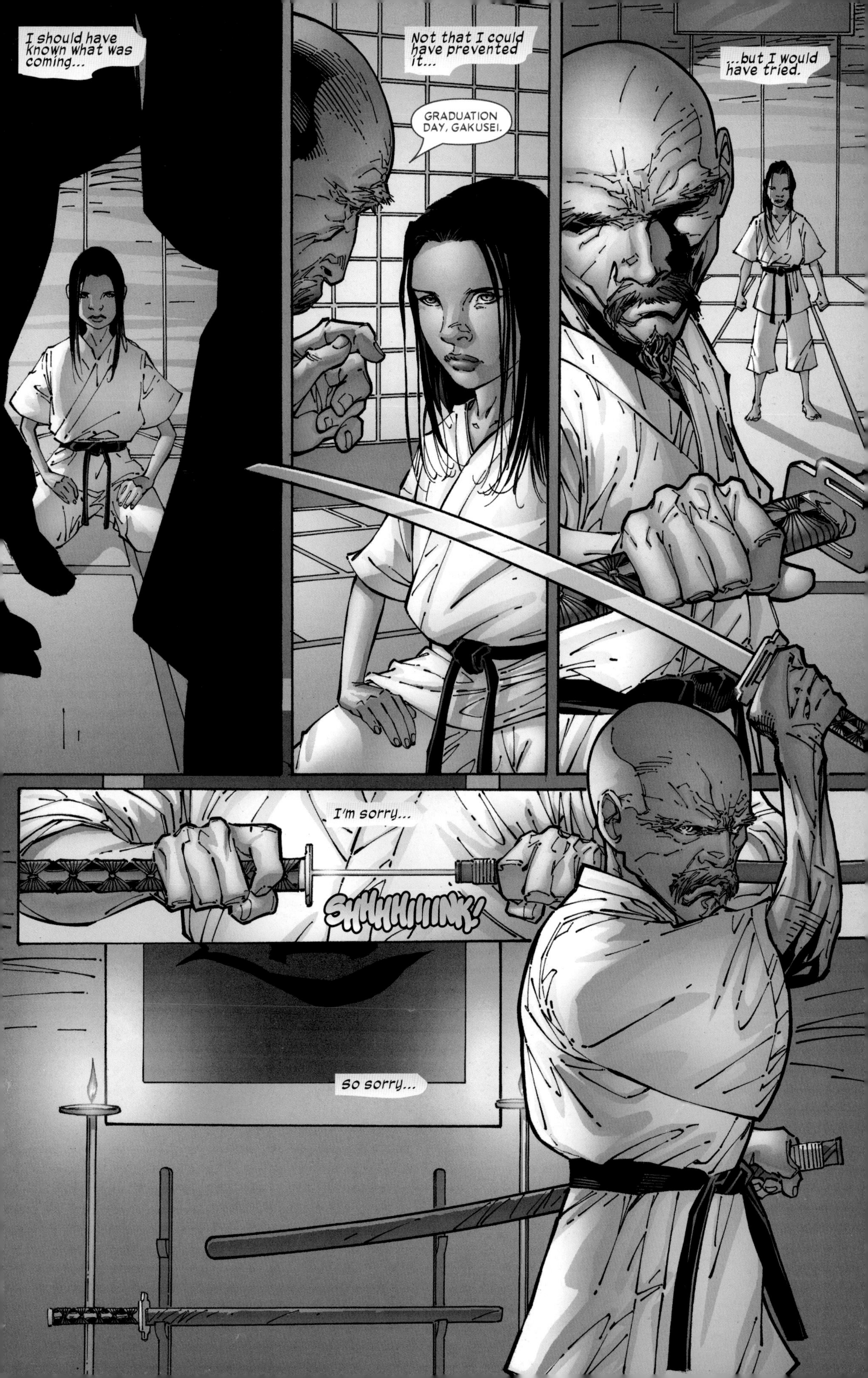
I should have known what was coming...
Not that I could have prevented it...
GRADUATION DAY, GAKUSEI.
...but I would have tried.
I'm sorry...
SHHHHIIIINK!
So sorry...

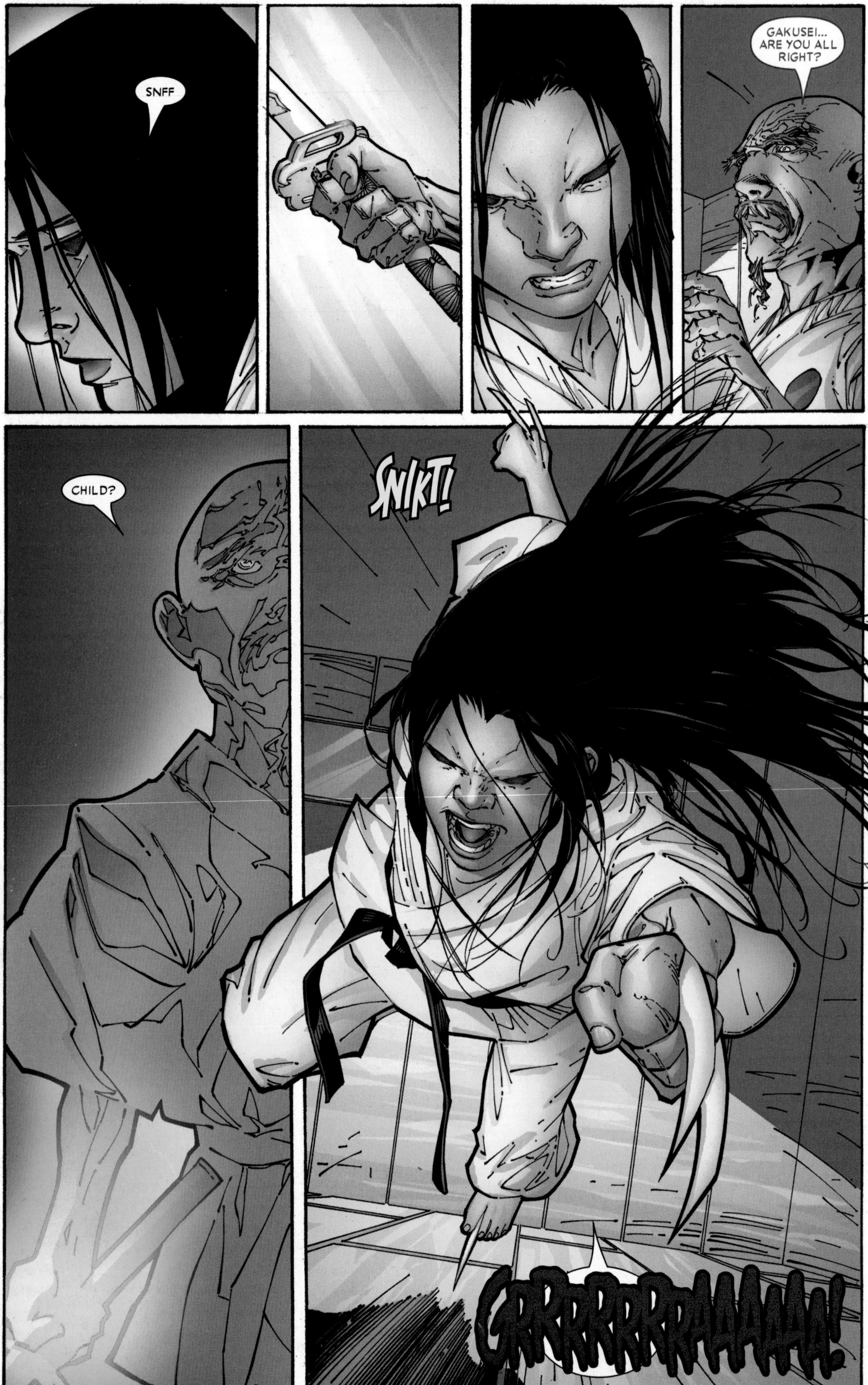
SNFF
GAKUSEI... ARE YOU ALL RIGHT?
CHILD?
SNIKT!
GRRRRRRRAAAAAA!

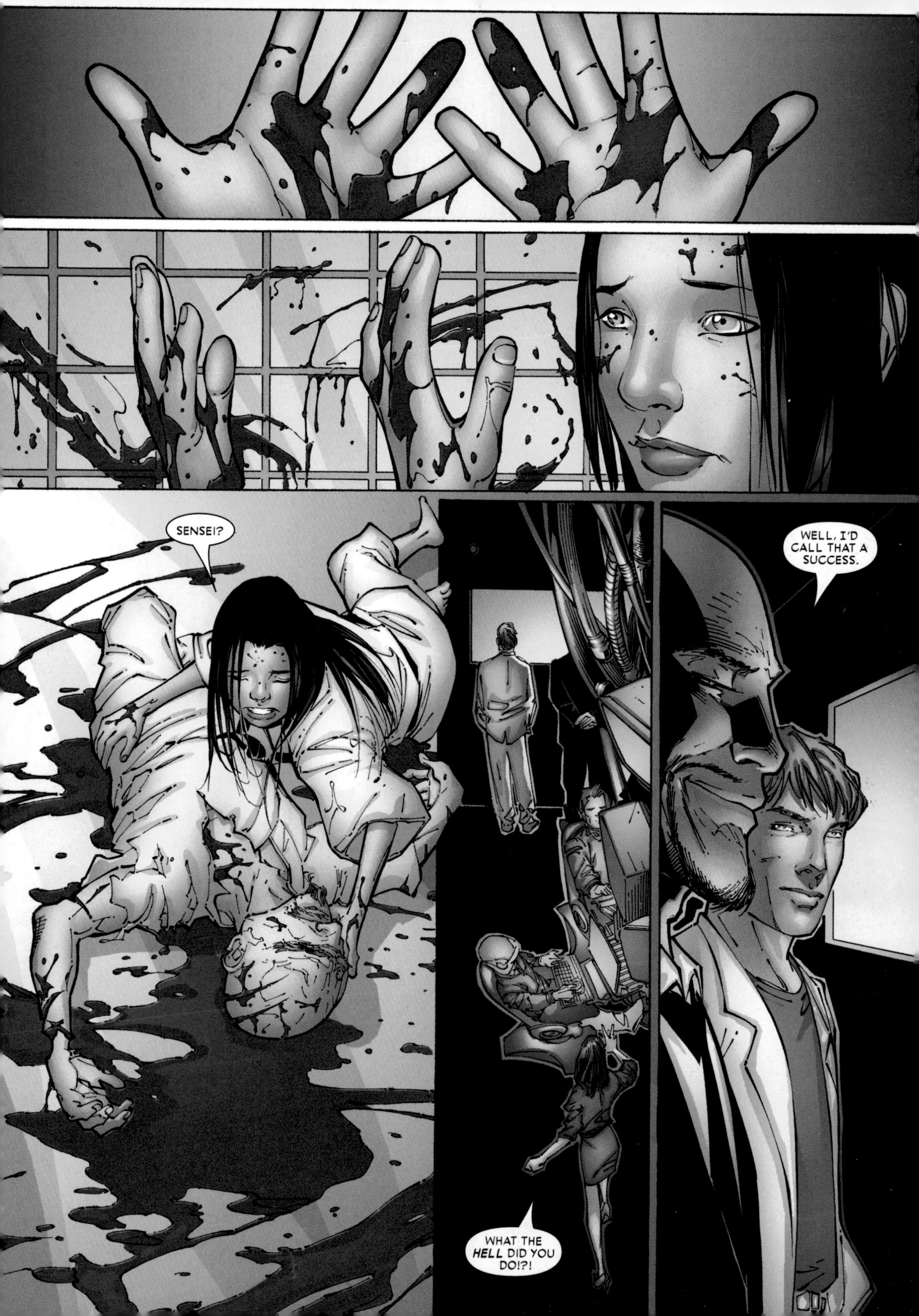
SENSEI?
WELL, I'D CALL THAT A SUCCESS.
WHAT THE **HELL** DID YOU DO!?!

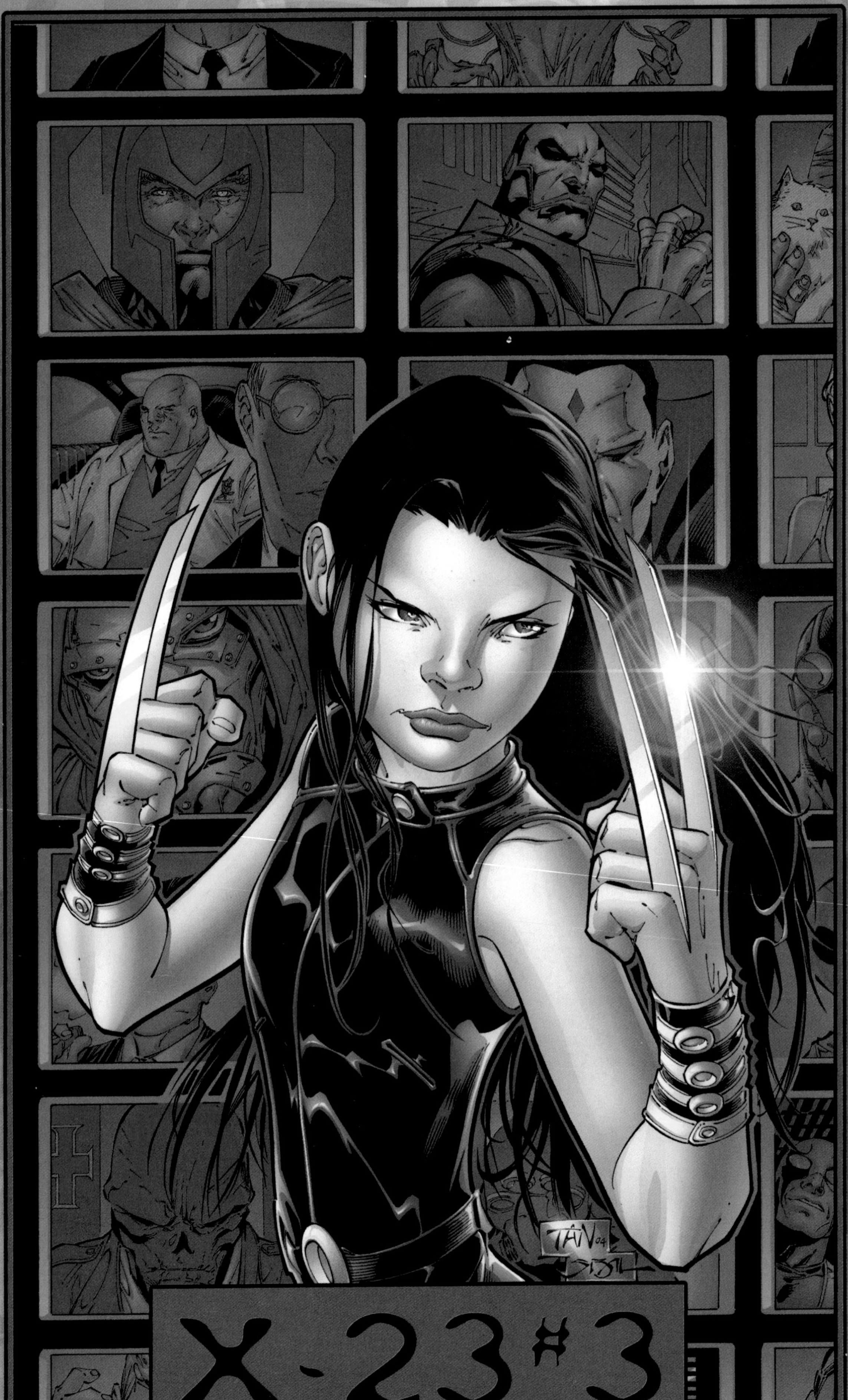
X-23 #3

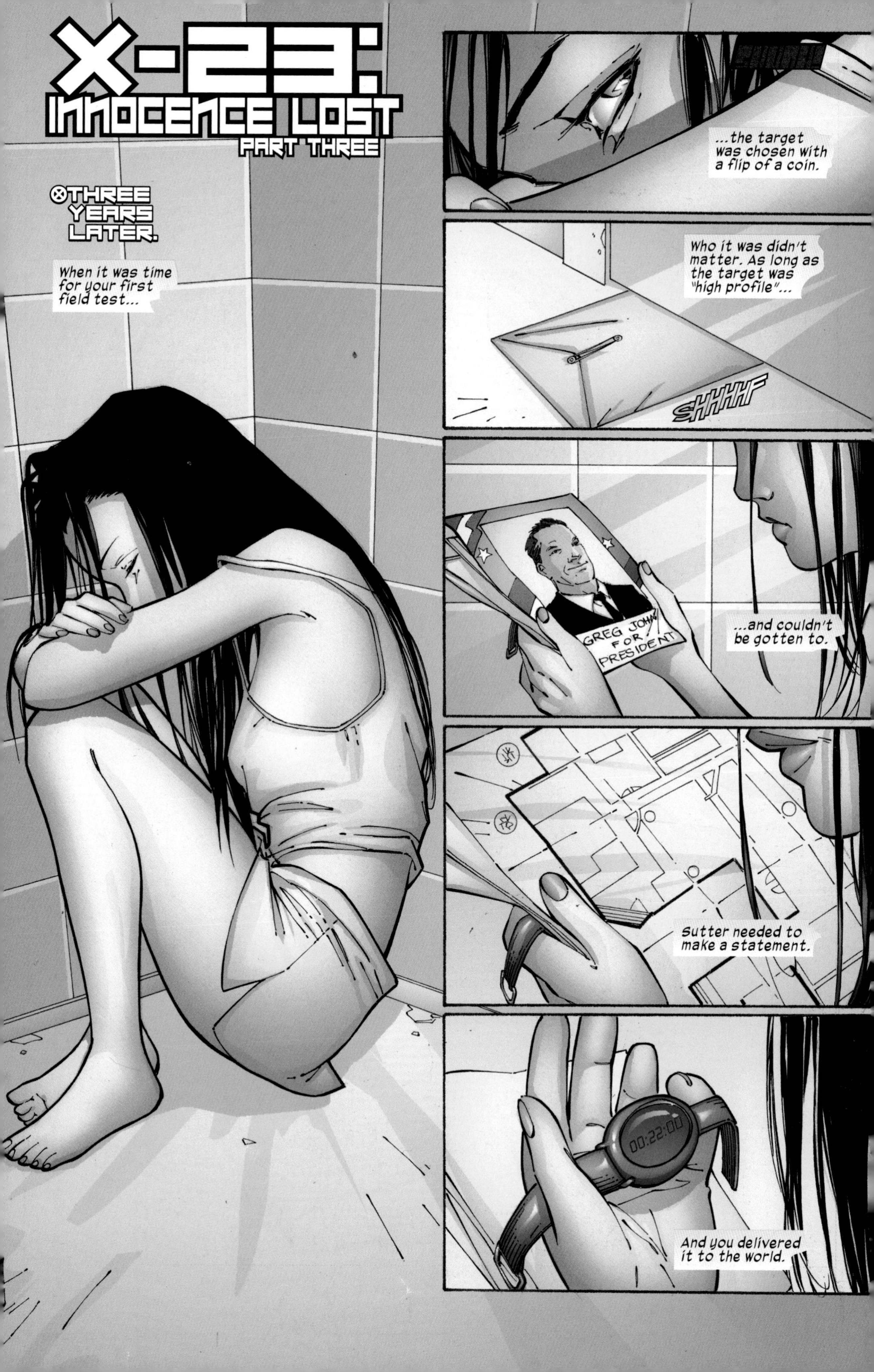

X-23: INNOCENCE LOST
PART THREE
THREE YEARS LATER.
When it was time for your first field test...
...the target was chosen with a flip of a coin.
Who it was didn't matter. As long as the target was "high profile"...
SHHHHF
GREG JOHN FOR PRESIDENT
...and couldn't be gotten to.
Sutter needed to make a statement.
00:22:00
And you delivered it to the world.

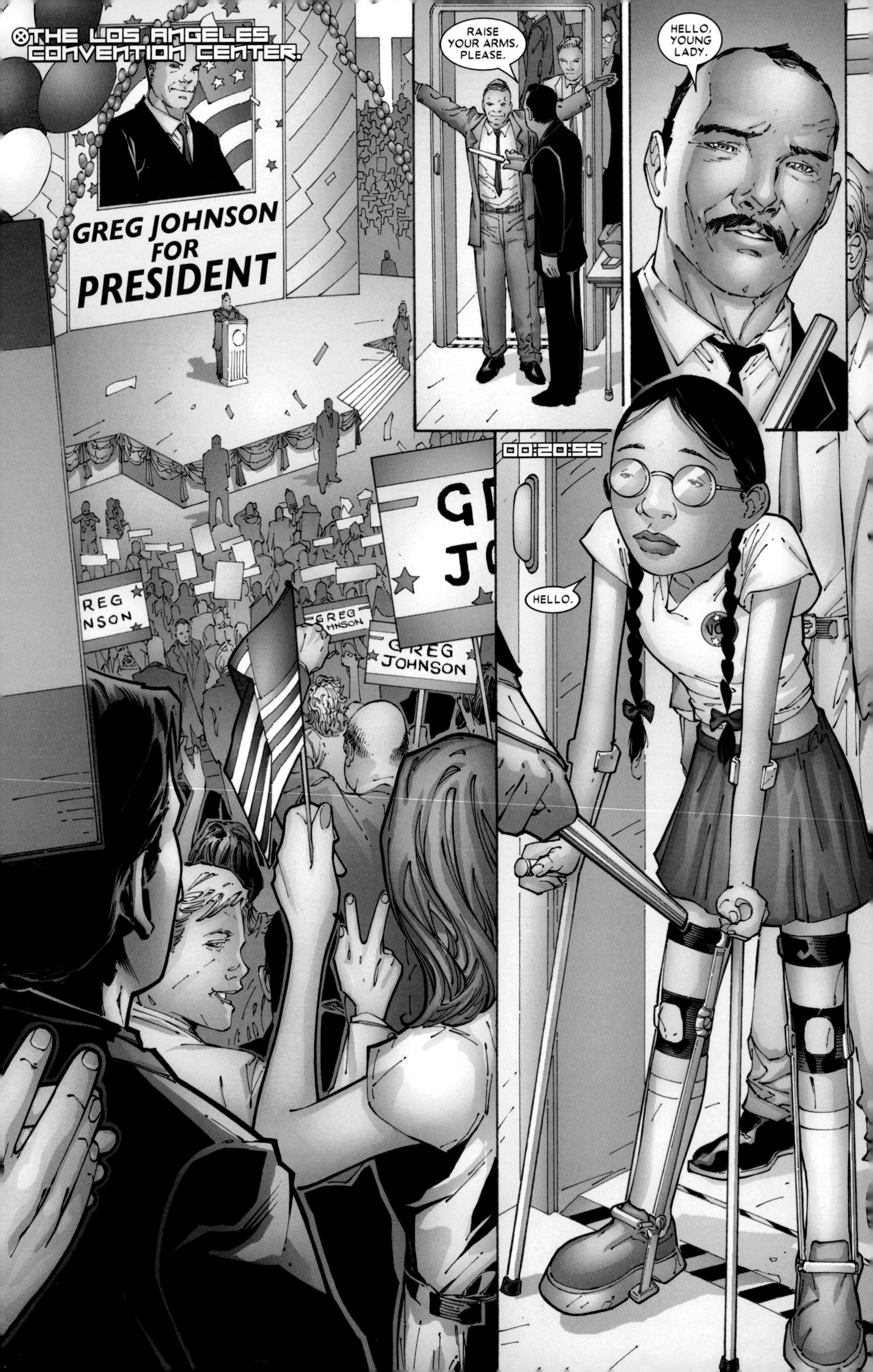
THE LOS ANGELES CONVENTION CENTER.
GREG JOHNSON FOR PRESIDENT
RAISE YOUR ARMS, PLEASE.
HELLO, YOUNG LADY.
00:20:55
HELLO.
GREG JOHNSON

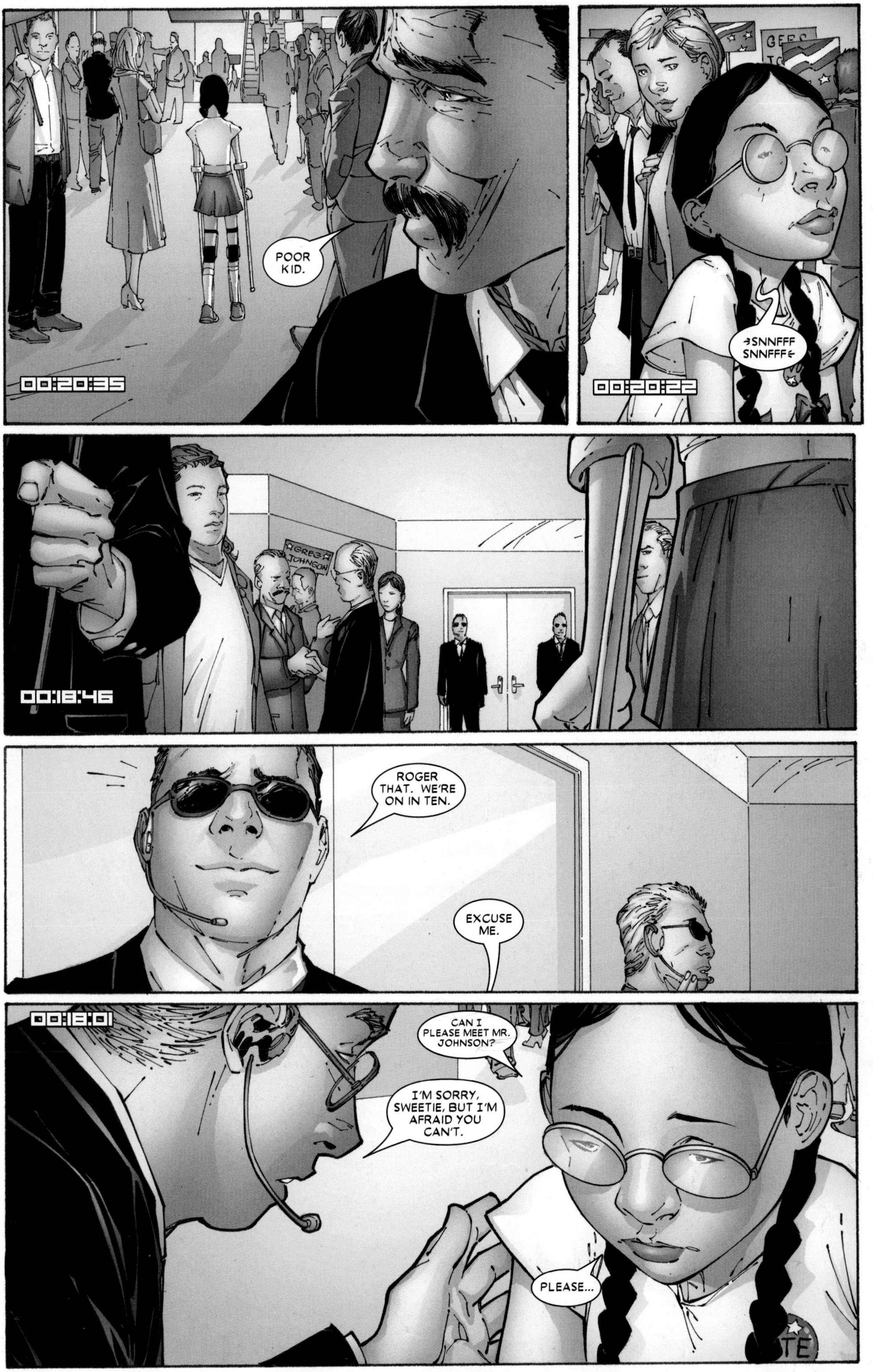
POOR KID.
00:20:35
SNNFFF SNNFFF
00:20:22
GREG JOHNSON
00:18:46
ROGER THAT. WE'RE ON IN TEN.
EXCUSE ME.
00:18:01
CAN I PLEASE MEET MR. JOHNSON?
I'M SORRY, SWEETIE, BUT I'M AFRAID YOU CAN'T.
PLEASE...

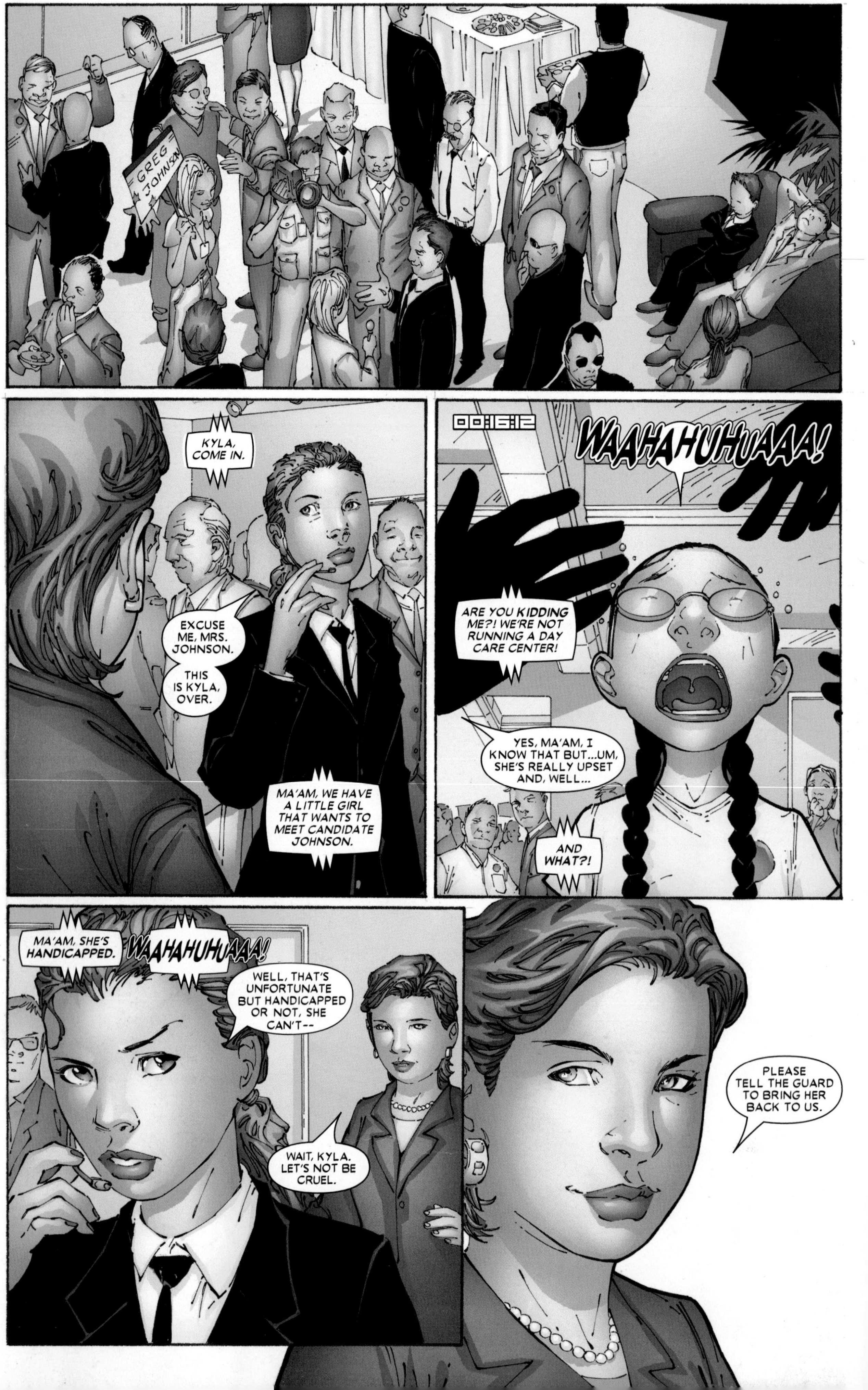
GREG JOHNSON
KYLA, COME IN.
EXCUSE ME, MRS. JOHNSON.
THIS IS KYLA, OVER.
MA'AM, WE HAVE A LITTLE GIRL THAT WANTS TO MEET CANDIDATE JOHNSON.
00:16:12
WAAHAHUHUAAA!
ARE YOU KIDDING ME?! WE'RE NOT RUNNING A DAY CARE CENTER!
YES, MA'AM, I KNOW THAT BUT...UM, SHE'S REALLY UPSET AND, WELL...
AND WHAT?!
MA'AM, SHE'S HANDICAPPED.
WAAHAHUHUAAA!
WELL, THAT'S UNFORTUNATE BUT HANDICAPPED OR NOT, SHE CAN'T--
WAIT, KYLA. LET'S NOT BE CRUEL.
PLEASE TELL THE GUARD TO BRING HER BACK TO US.

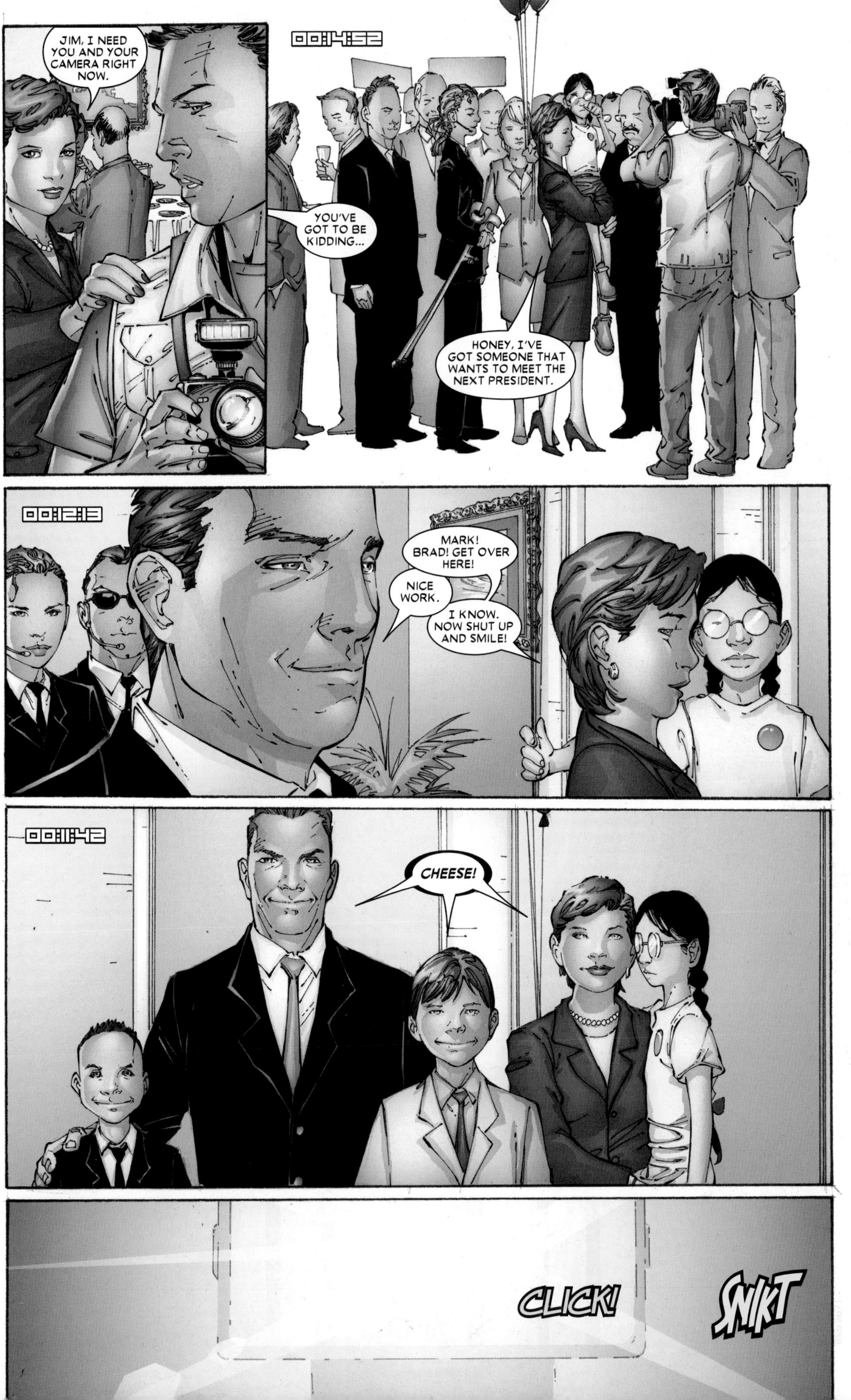
JIM, I NEED YOU AND YOUR CAMERA RIGHT NOW.
00:14:52
YOU'VE GOT TO BE KIDDING...
HONEY, I'VE GOT SOMEONE THAT WANTS TO MEET THE NEXT PRESIDENT.
00:12:13
MARK! BRAD! GET OVER HERE!
NICE WORK.
I KNOW. NOW SHUT UP AND SMILE!
00:11:42
CHEESE!
CLICK!
SNIKT

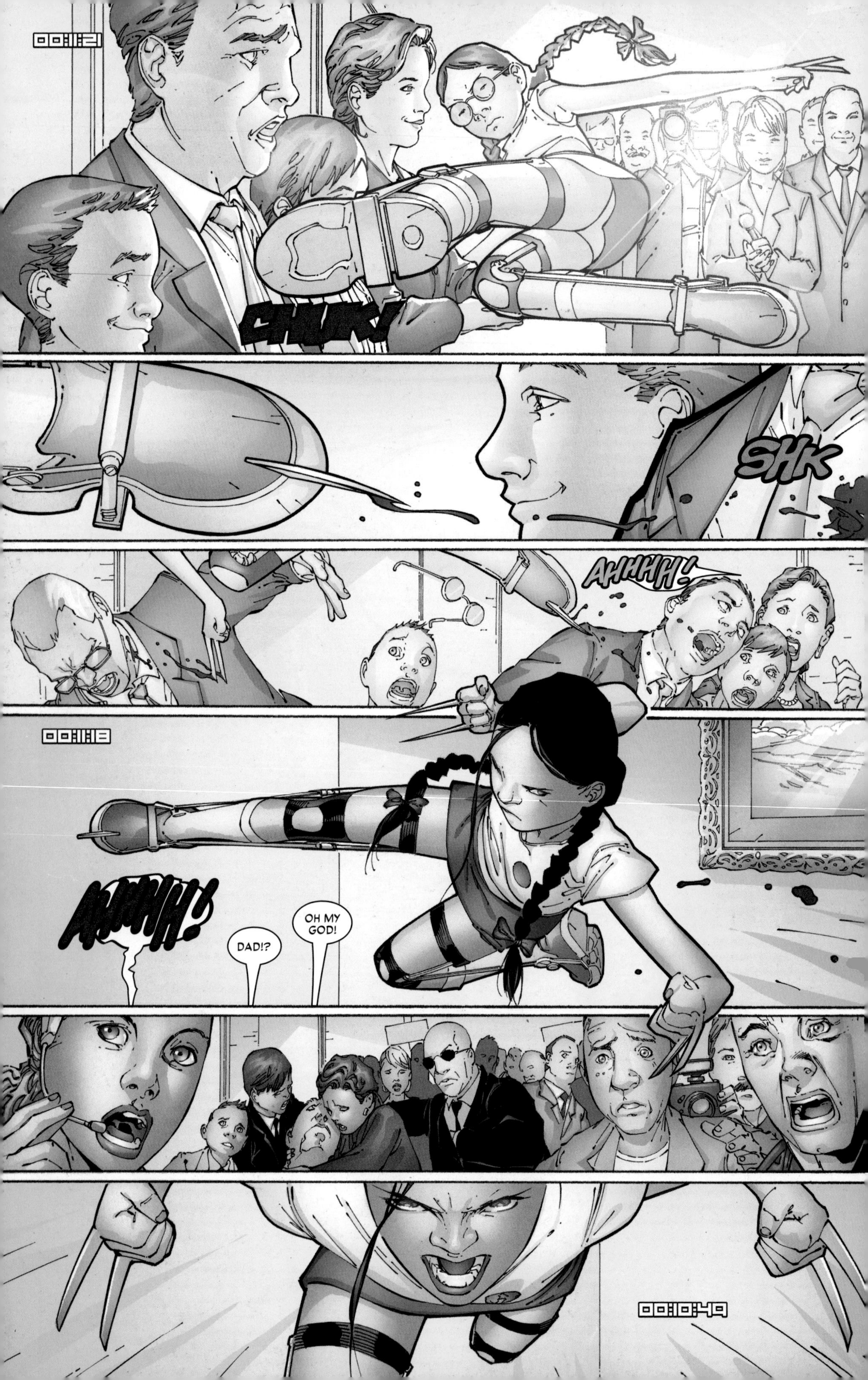

00:11:21
CHUK!
SHK
AHHHH!
00:11:18
AHHHH!
DAD!?
OH MY GOD!
00:10:49

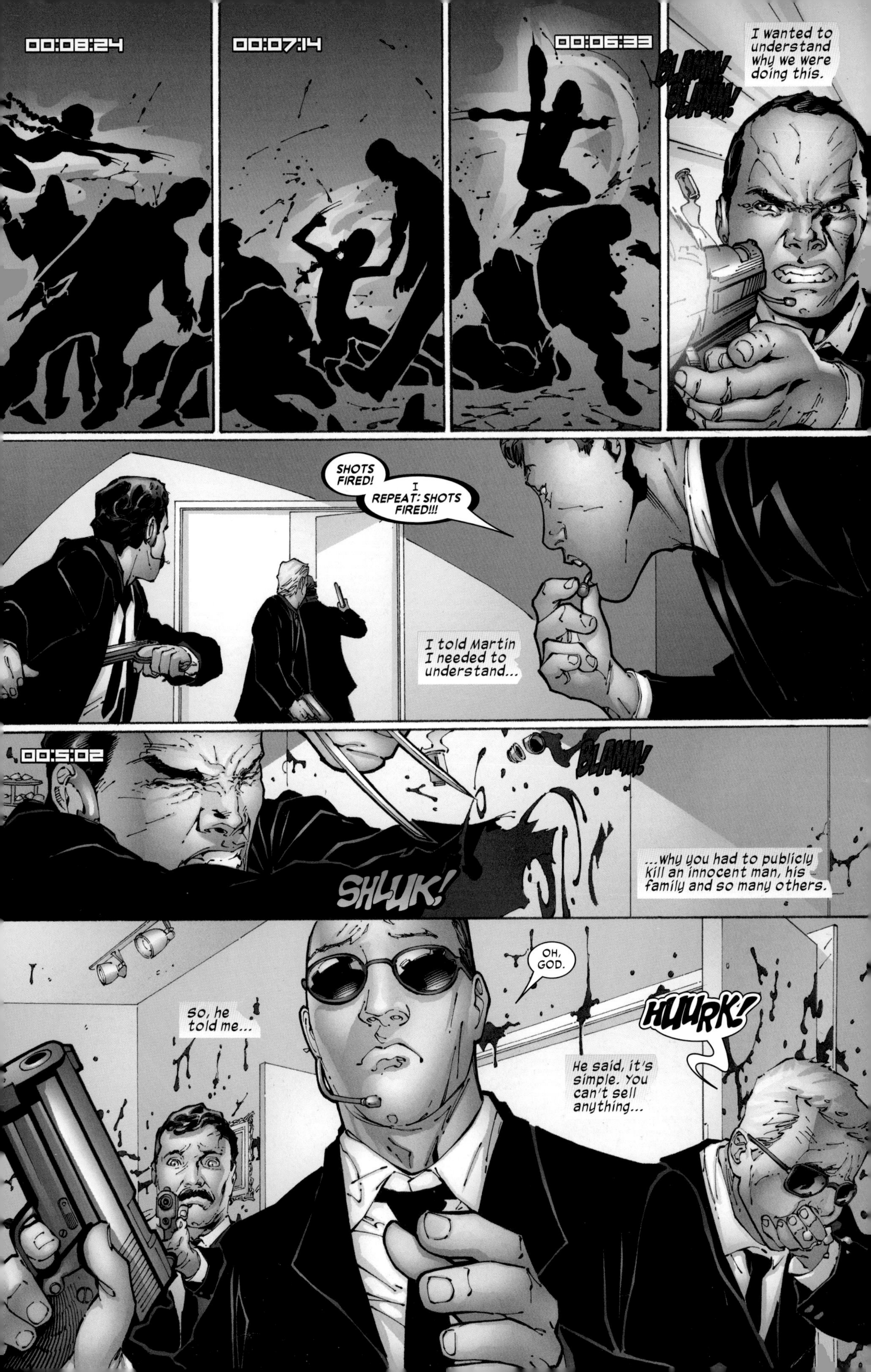

00:08:24
00:07:14
00:06:33
BLAMM! BLAMM!
I wanted to understand why we were doing this.
SHOTS FIRED!
I REPEAT: SHOTS FIRED!!!
I told Martin I needed to understand...
00:5:02
BLAMM!
SHLUK!
...why you had to publicly kill an innocent man, his family and so many others.
OH, GOD.
So, he told me...
HUURK!
He said, it's simple. You can't sell anything...

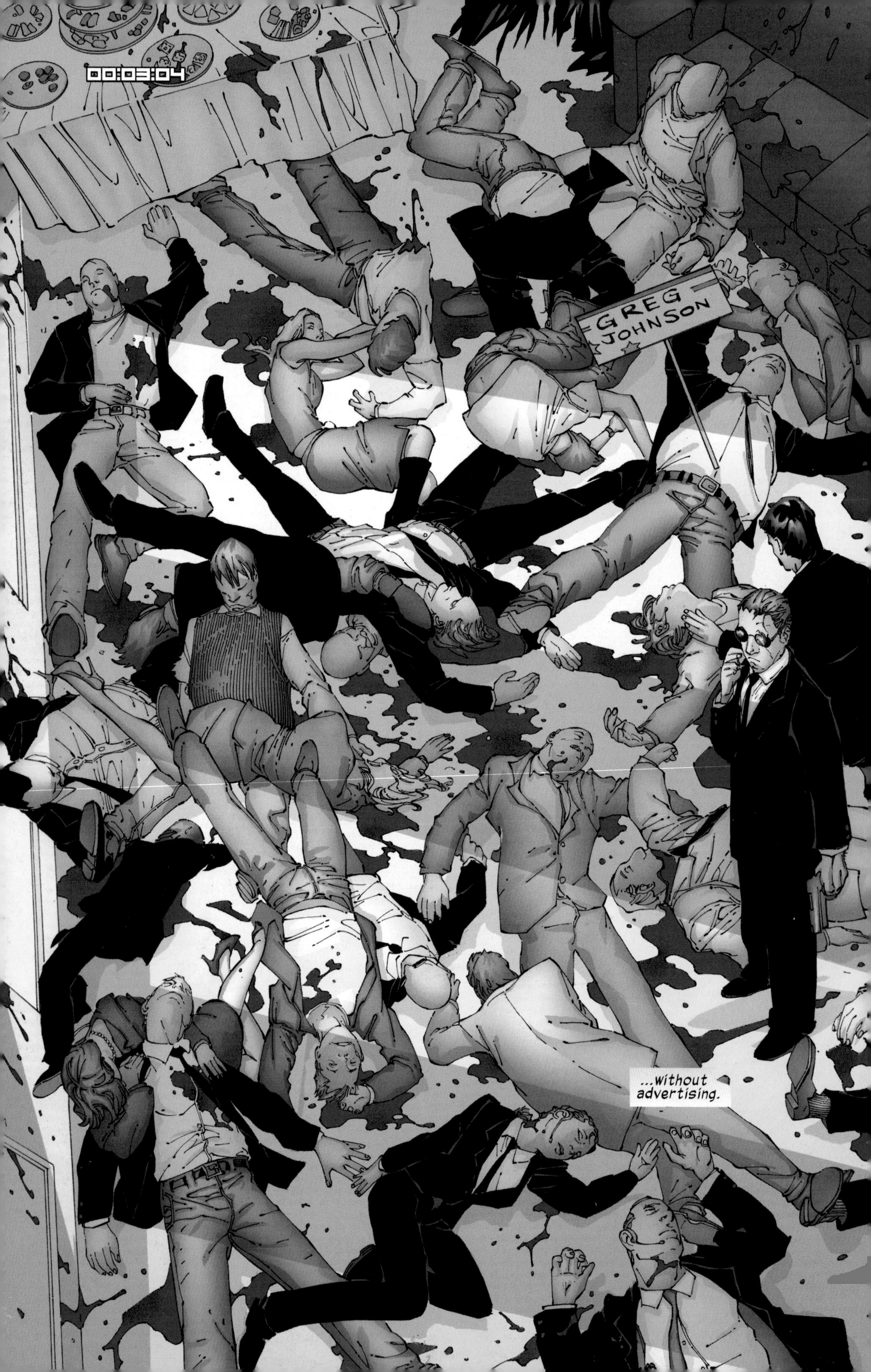
00:03:04
GREG JOHNSON
...without advertising.

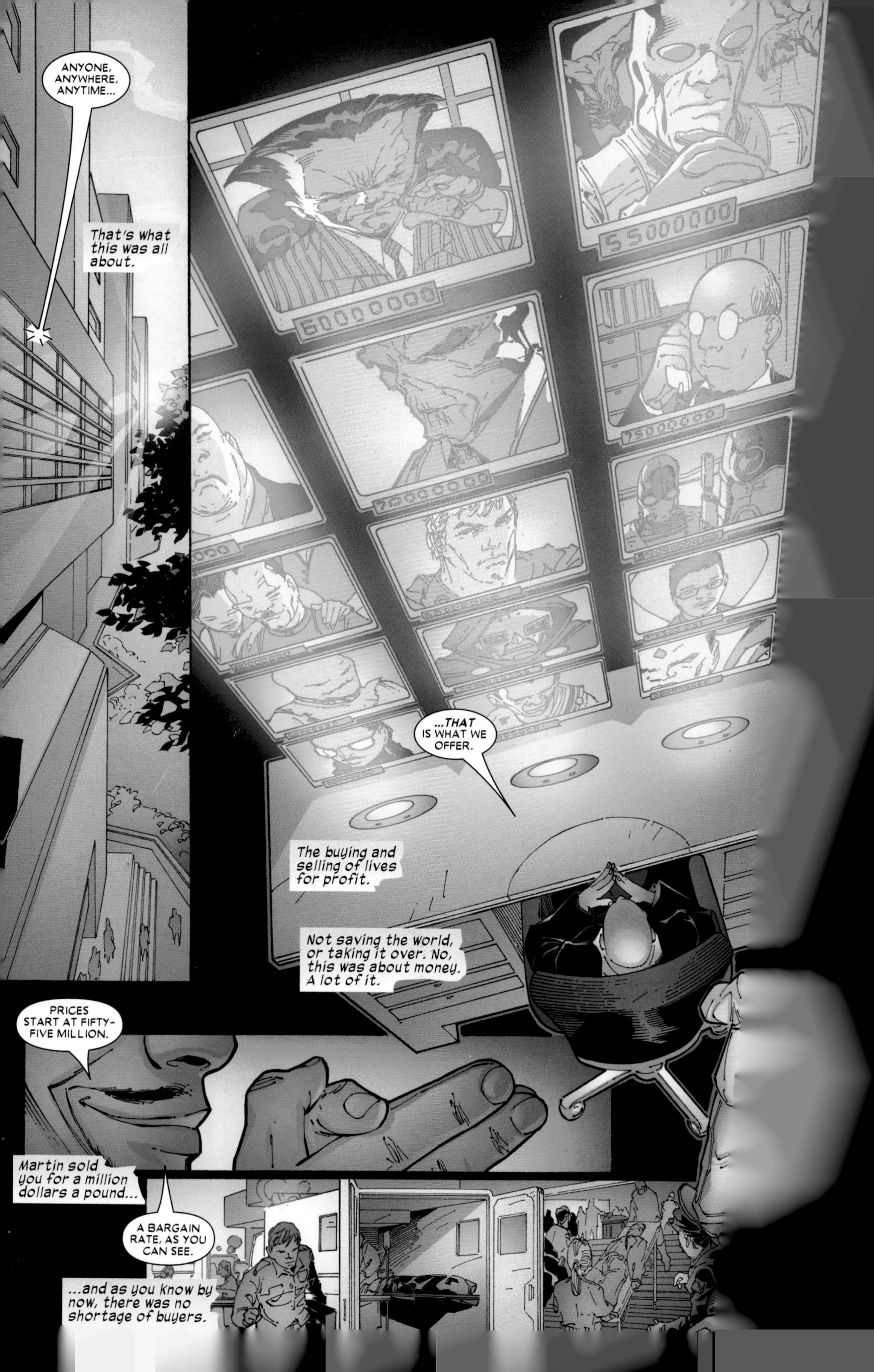
ANYONE, ANYWHERE, ANYTIME...
That's what this was all about.
...THAT IS WHAT WE OFFER.
The buying and selling of lives for profit.
Not saving the world, or taking it over. No, this was about money. A lot of it.
PRICES START AT FIFTY-FIVE MILLION.
Martin sold you for a million dollars a pound...
A BARGAIN RATE, AS YOU CAN SEE.
...and as you know by now, there was no shortage of buyers.

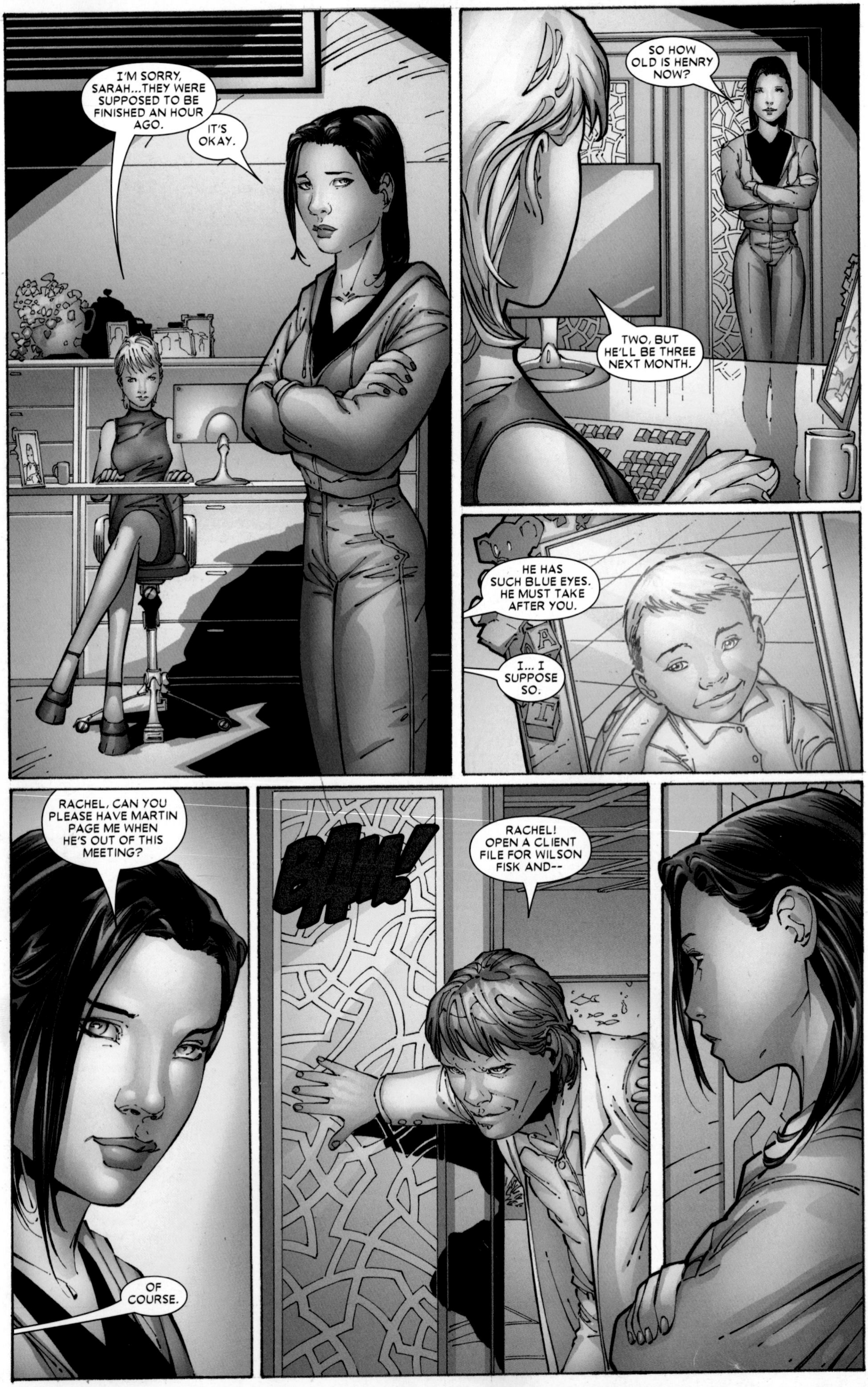
I'M SORRY, SARAH...THEY WERE SUPPOSED TO BE FINISHED AN HOUR AGO.
IT'S OKAY.
SO HOW OLD IS HENRY NOW?
TWO, BUT HE'LL BE THREE NEXT MONTH.
HE HAS SUCH BLUE EYES. HE MUST TAKE AFTER YOU.
I... I SUPPOSE SO.
RACHEL, CAN YOU PLEASE HAVE MARTIN PAGE ME WHEN HE'S OUT OF THIS MEETING?
OF COURSE.
BAM!
RACHEL! OPEN A CLIENT FILE FOR WILSON FISK AND--

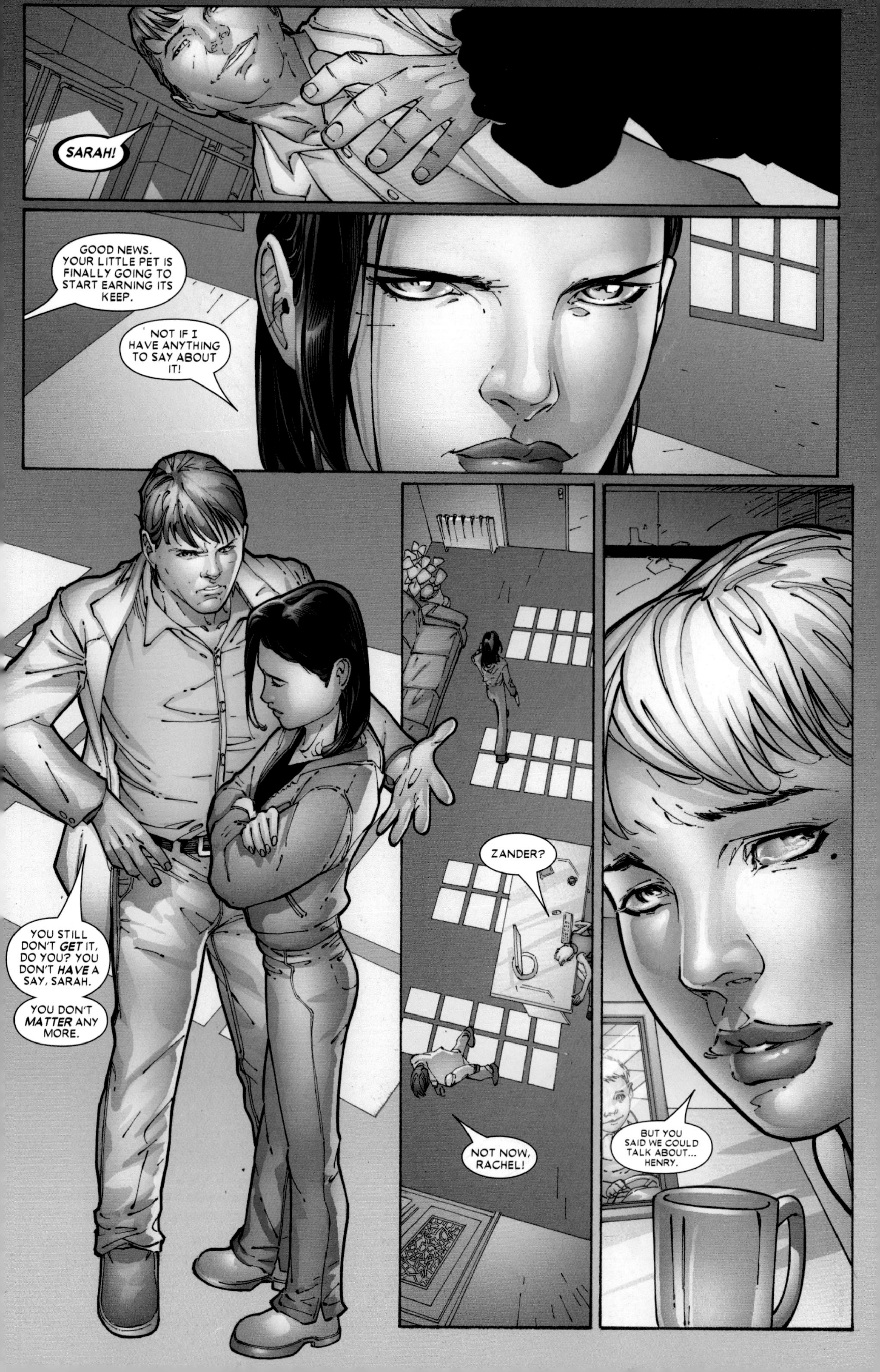
SARAH!
GOOD NEWS. YOUR LITTLE PET IS FINALLY GOING TO START EARNING ITS KEEP.
NOT IF I HAVE ANYTHING TO SAY ABOUT IT!
YOU STILL DON'T GET IT, DO YOU? YOU DON'T HAVE A SAY, SARAH.
YOU DON'T MATTER ANY MORE.
ZANDER?
NOT NOW, RACHEL!
BUT YOU SAID WE COULD TALK ABOUT... HENRY.

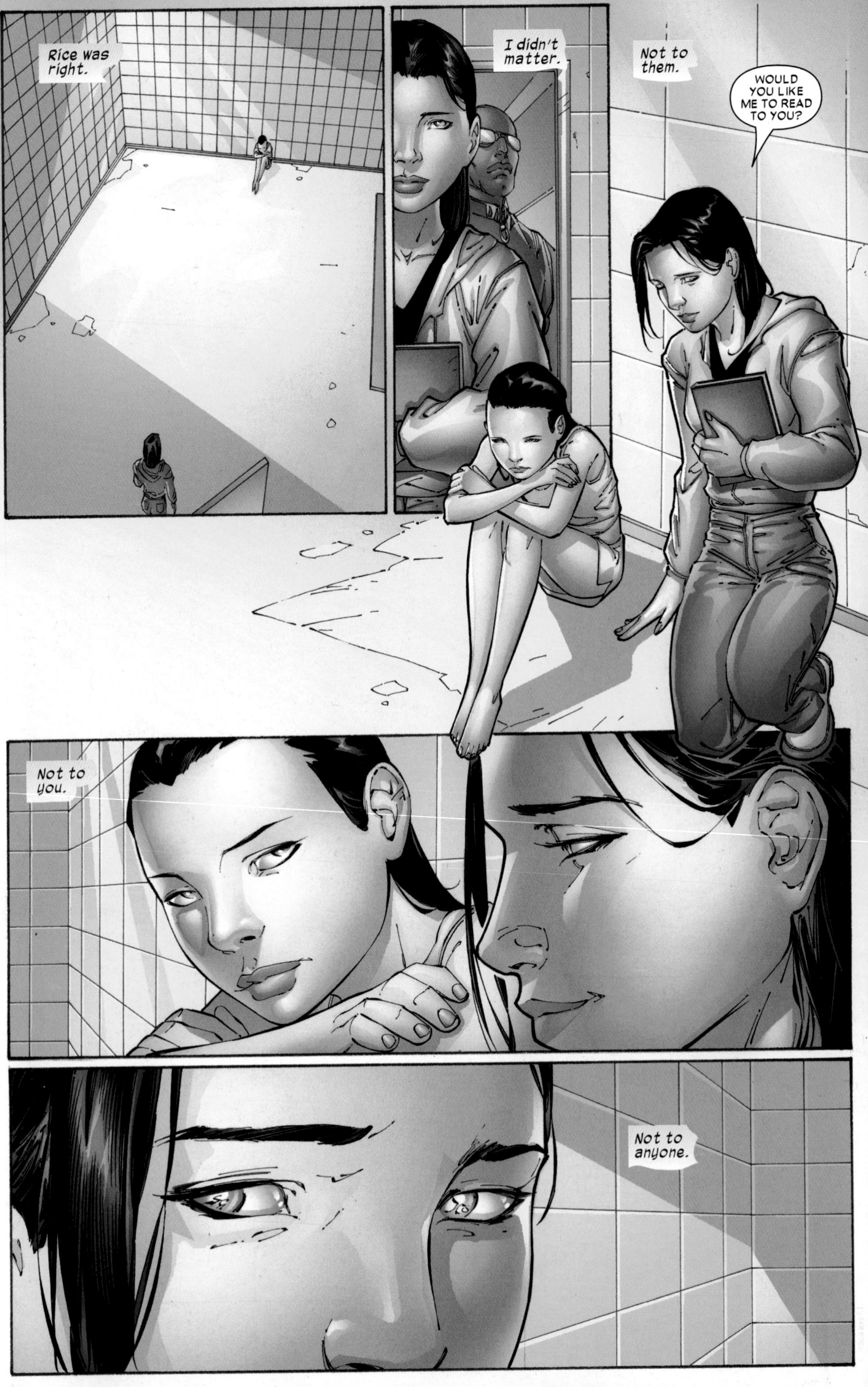
Rice was right.
I didn't matter.
Not to them.
WOULD YOU LIKE ME TO READ TO YOU?
Not to you.
Not to anyone.

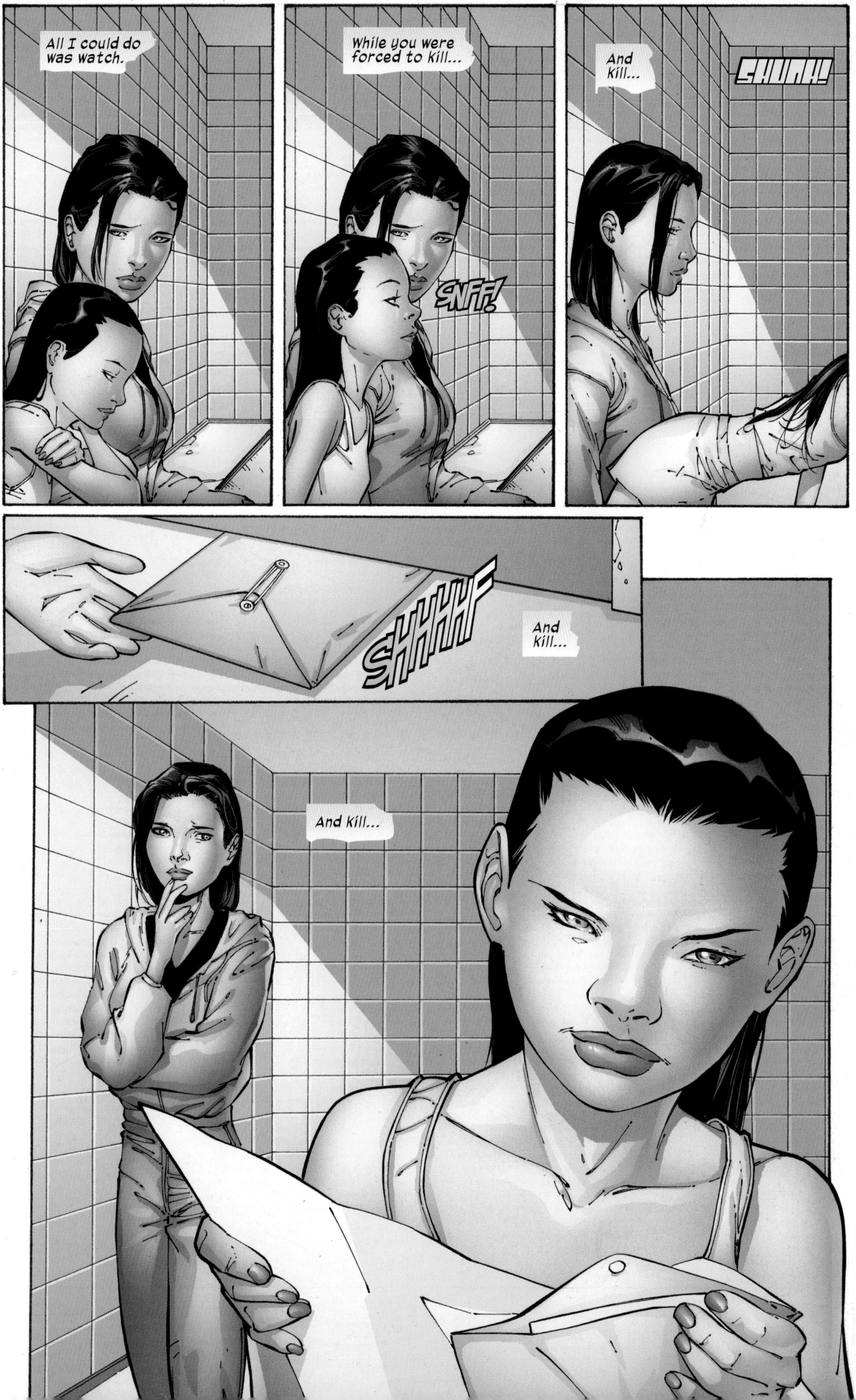
All I could do was watch.
While you were forced to kill...
SNFF!
And kill...
SHUNK!
SHHHF
And kill...
And kill...

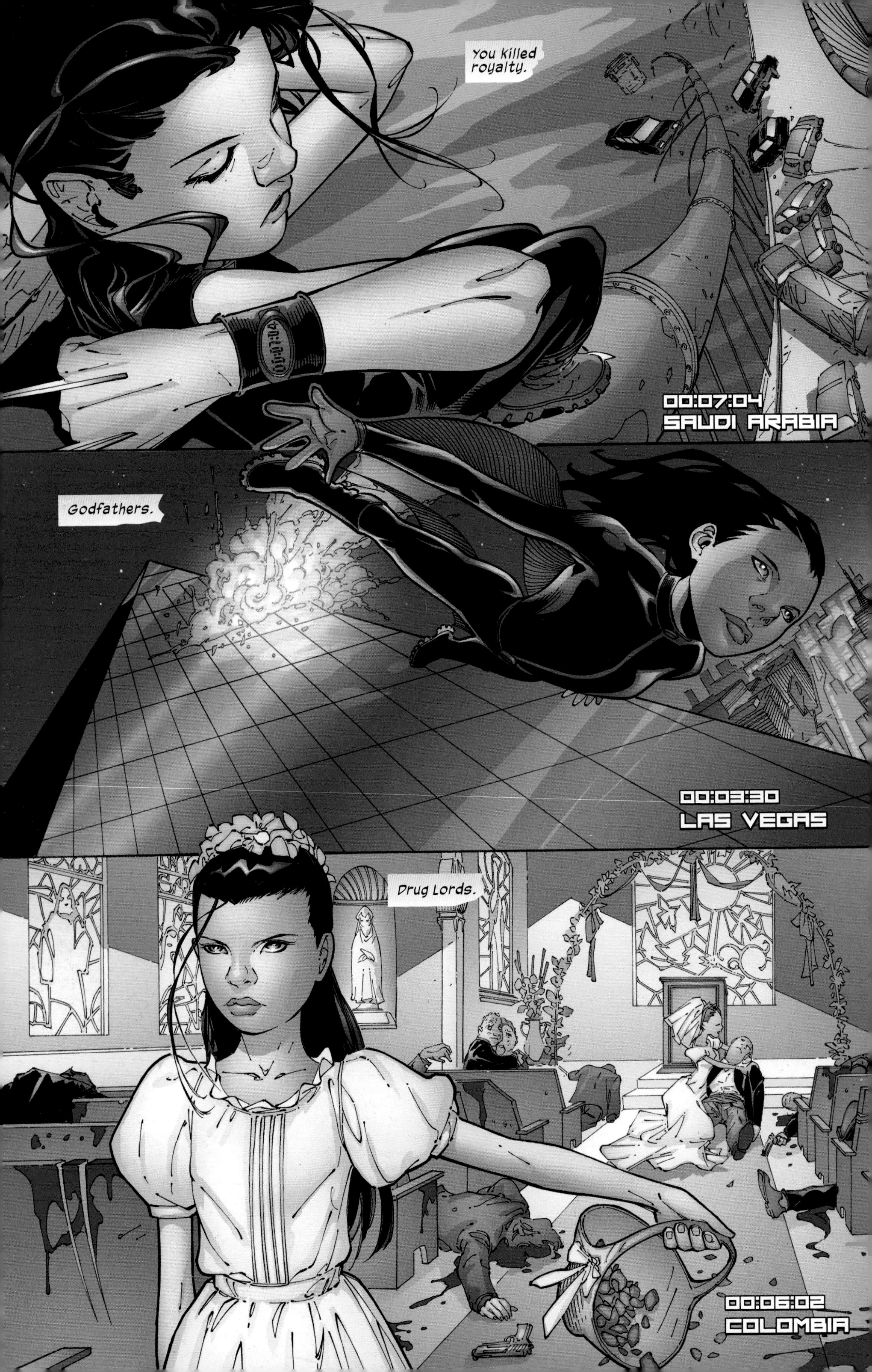
You killed royalty.
00:07:04
SAUDI ARABIA
Godfathers.
00:03:30
LAS VEGAS
Drug Lords.
00:06:02
COLOMBIA

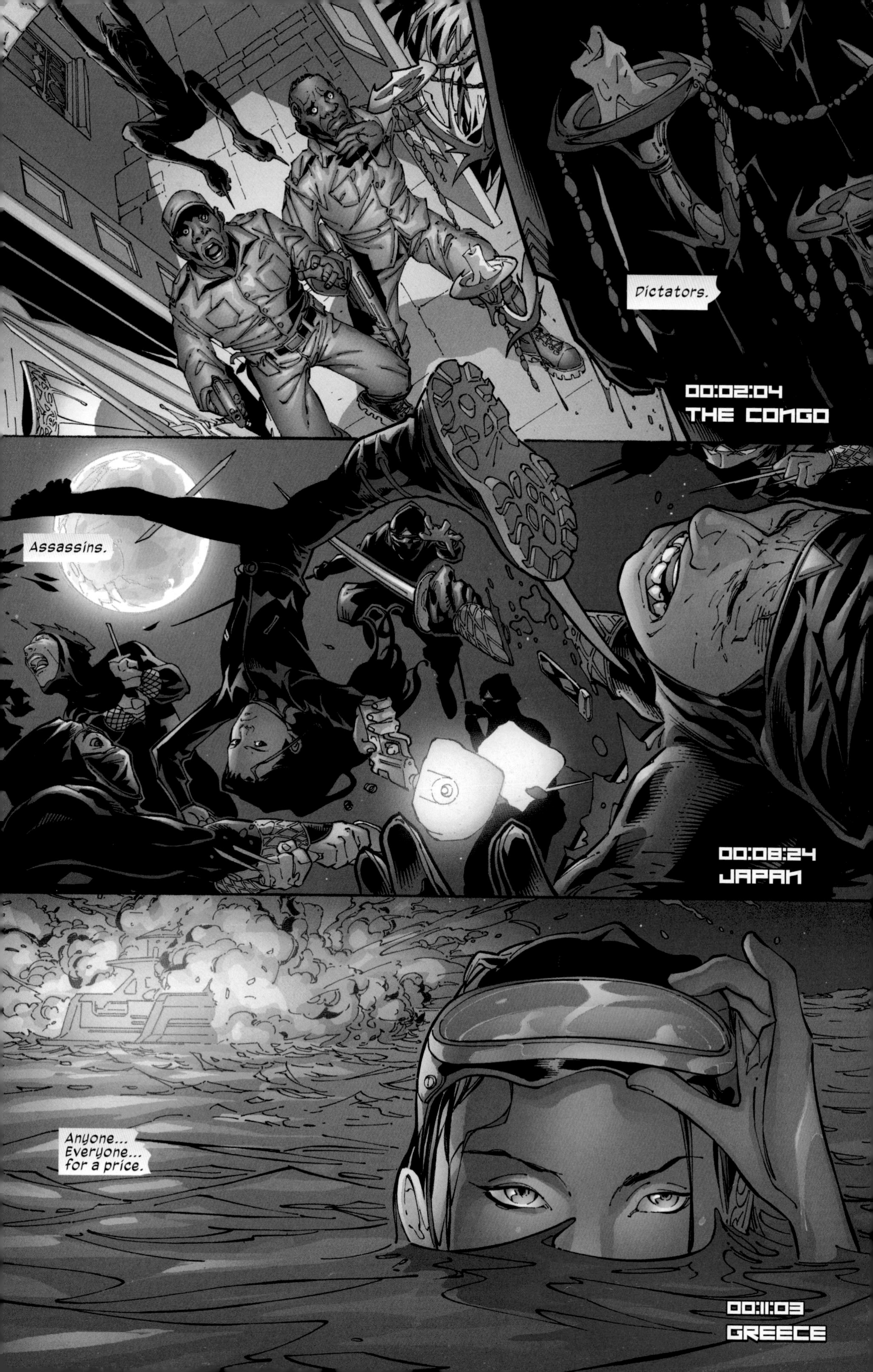
Dictators.
00:02:04
THE CONGO
Assassins.
00:08:24
JAPAN
Anyone...
Everyone...
for a price.
00:11:03
GREECE

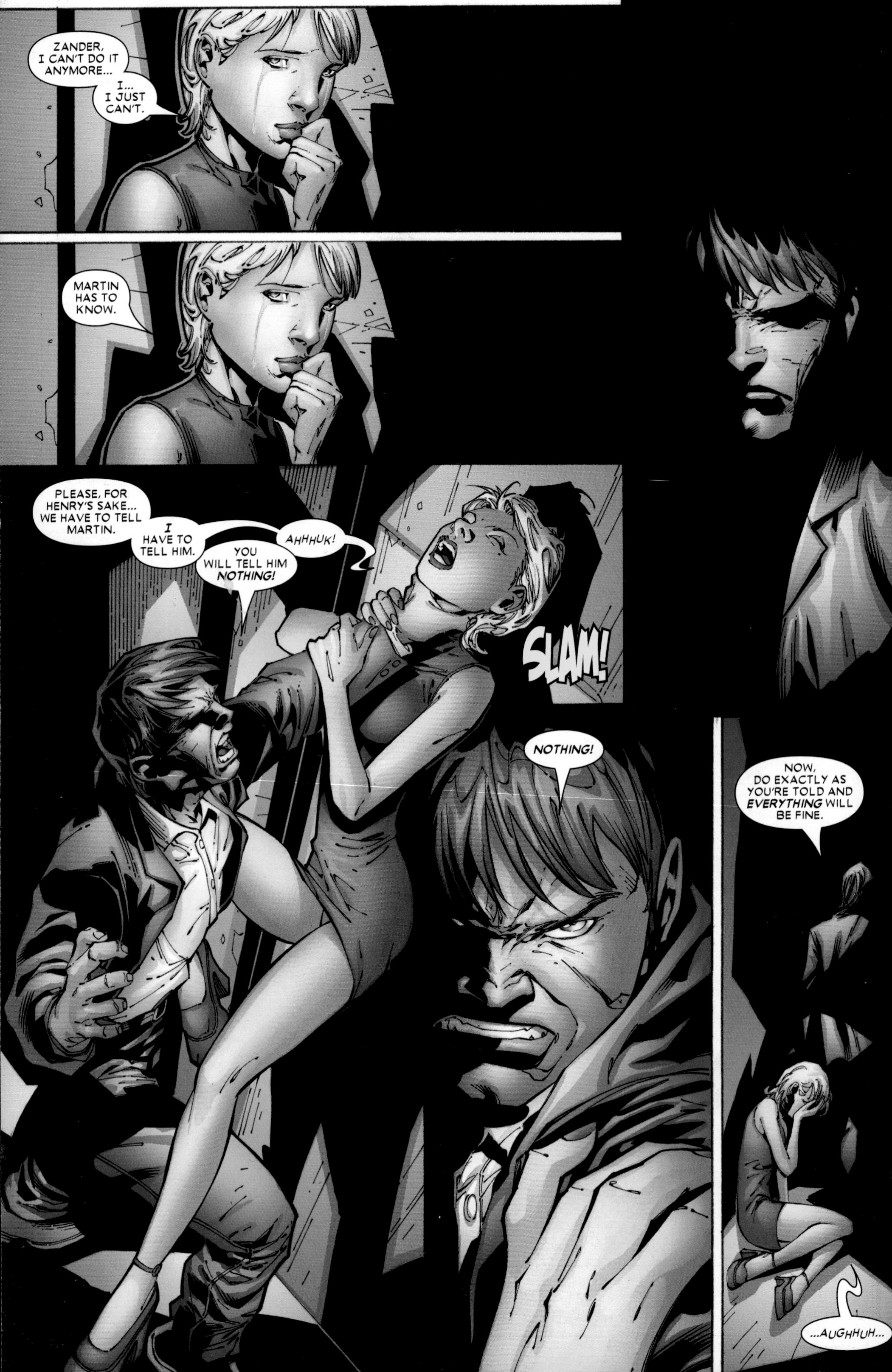
ZANDER, I CAN'T DO IT ANYMORE...
I... I JUST CAN'T.
MARTIN HAS TO KNOW.
PLEASE, FOR HENRY'S SAKE... WE HAVE TO TELL MARTIN.
I HAVE TO TELL HIM.
AHHHUK!
YOU WILL TELL HIM NOTHING!
SLAM!
NOTHING!
NOW, DO EXACTLY AS YOU'RE TOLD AND EVERYTHING WILL BE FINE.
...AUGHHUH...

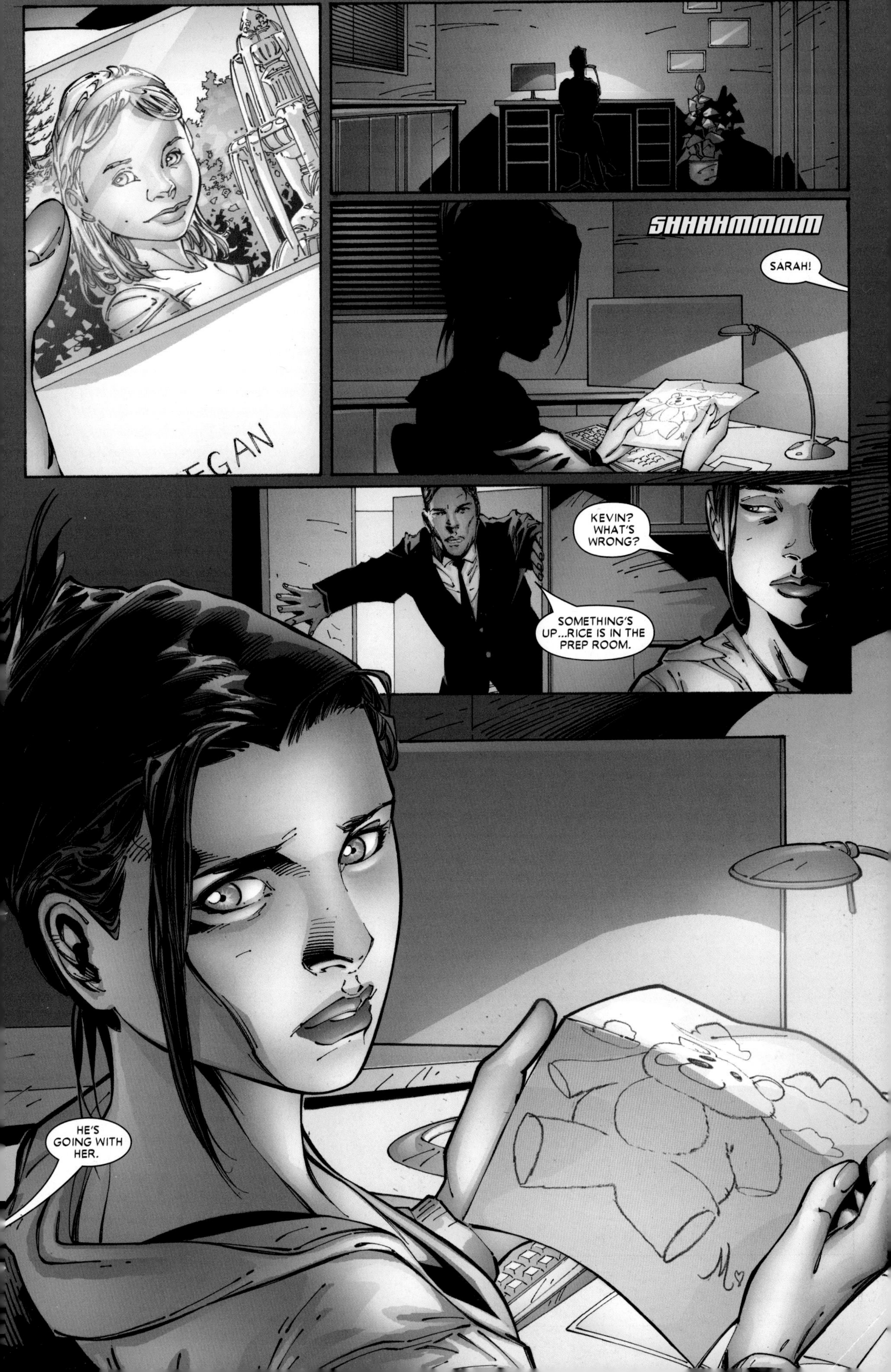
EGAN
SHHHHMMMM
SARAH!
KEVIN? WHAT'S WRONG?
SOMETHING'S UP...RICE IS IN THE PREP ROOM.
HE'S GOING WITH HER.

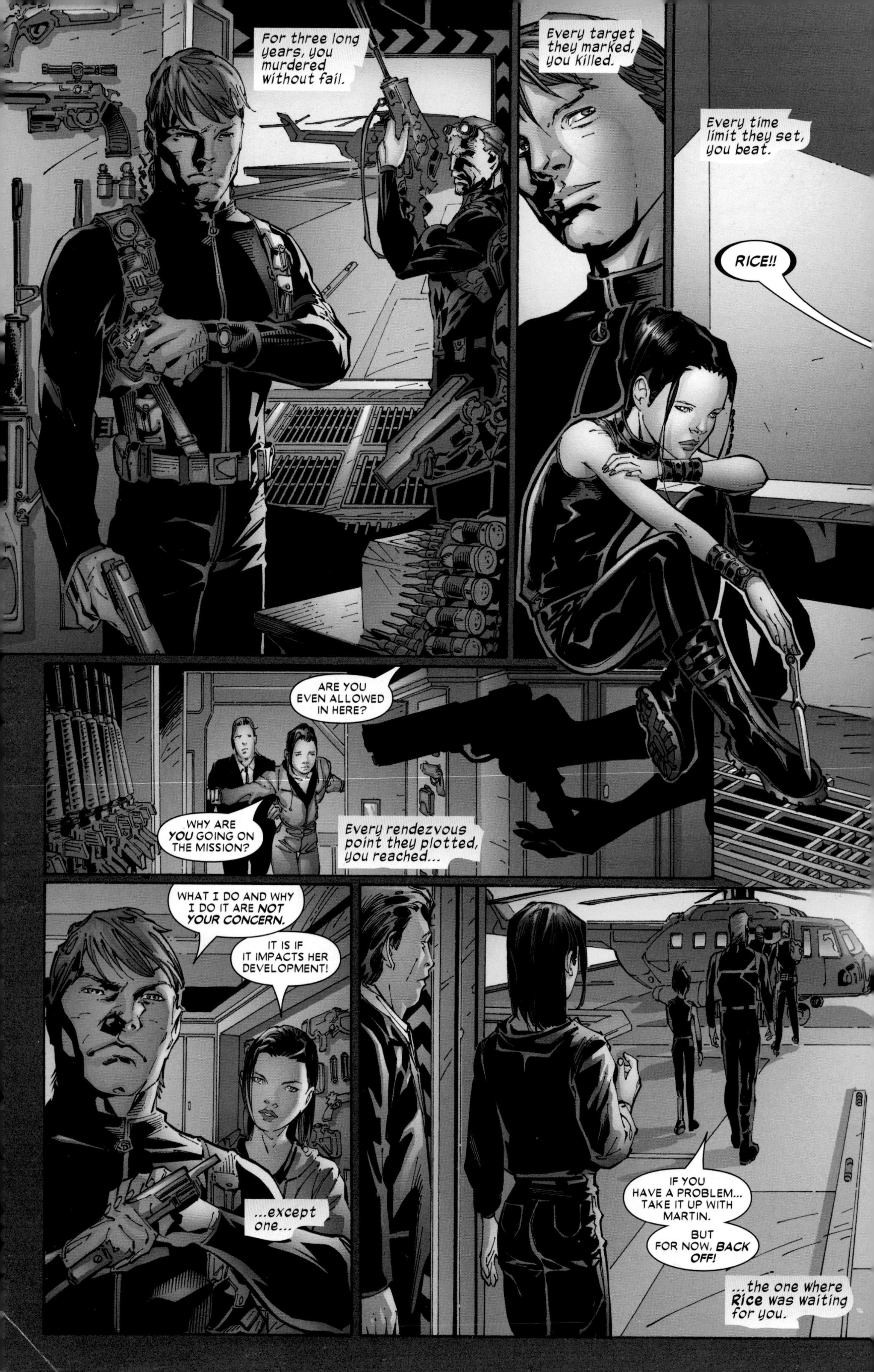

For three long years, you murdered without fail.
Every target they marked, you killed.
Every time limit they set, you beat.
RICE!!
ARE YOU EVEN ALLOWED IN HERE?
WHY ARE YOU GOING ON THE MISSION?
Every rendezvous point they plotted, you reached...
WHAT I DO AND WHY I DO IT ARE NOT YOUR CONCERN.
IT IS IF IT IMPACTS HER DEVELOPMENT!
...except one...
IF YOU HAVE A PROBLEM... TAKE IT UP WITH MARTIN.
BUT FOR NOW, BACK OFF!
...the one where Rice was waiting for you.

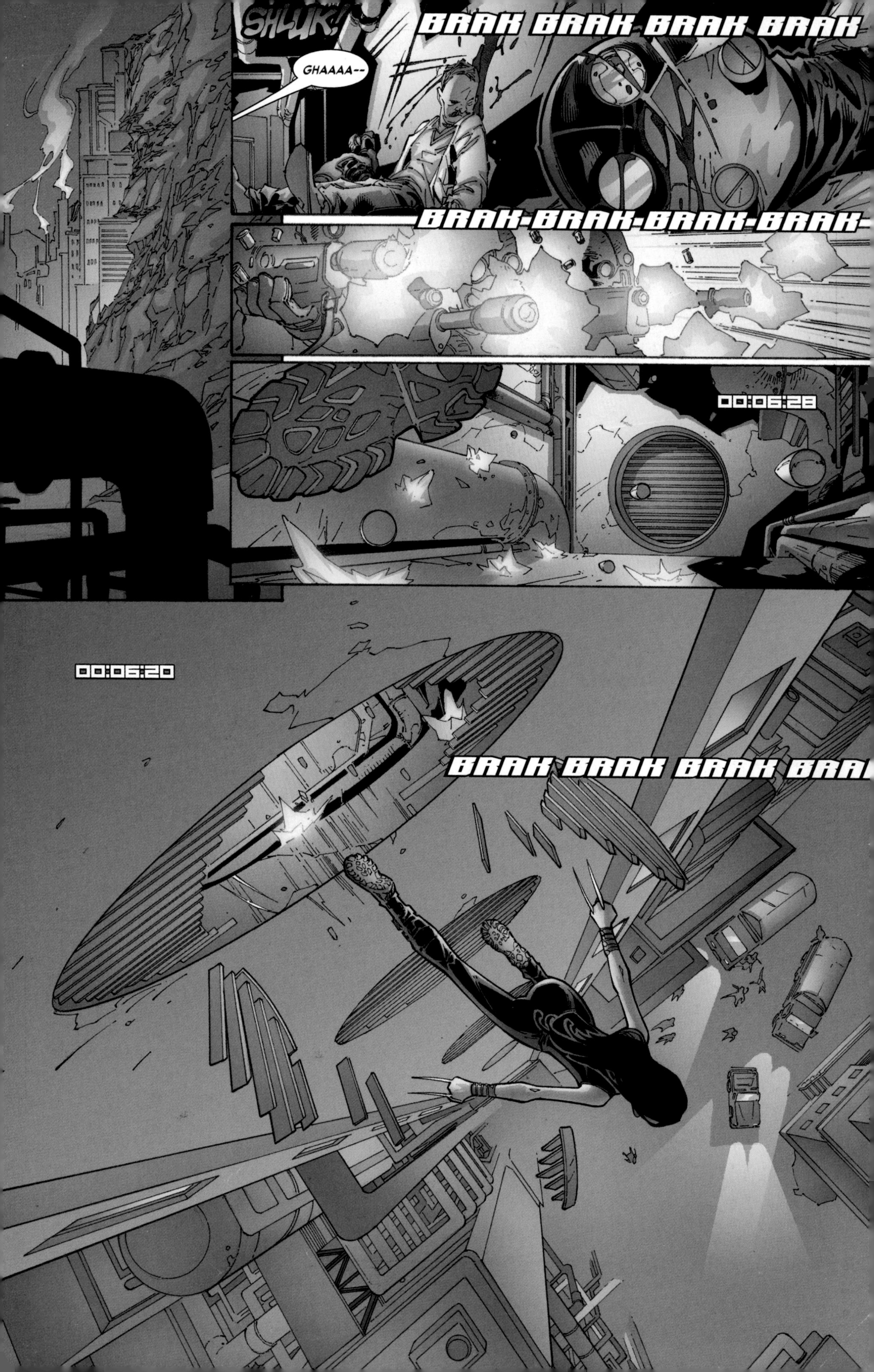
SHLUK!
BRAK BRAK BRAK BRAK
GHAAAA--
BRAK-BRAK-BRAK-BRAK-
00:06:28
00:06:20
BRAK BRAK BRAK BRA

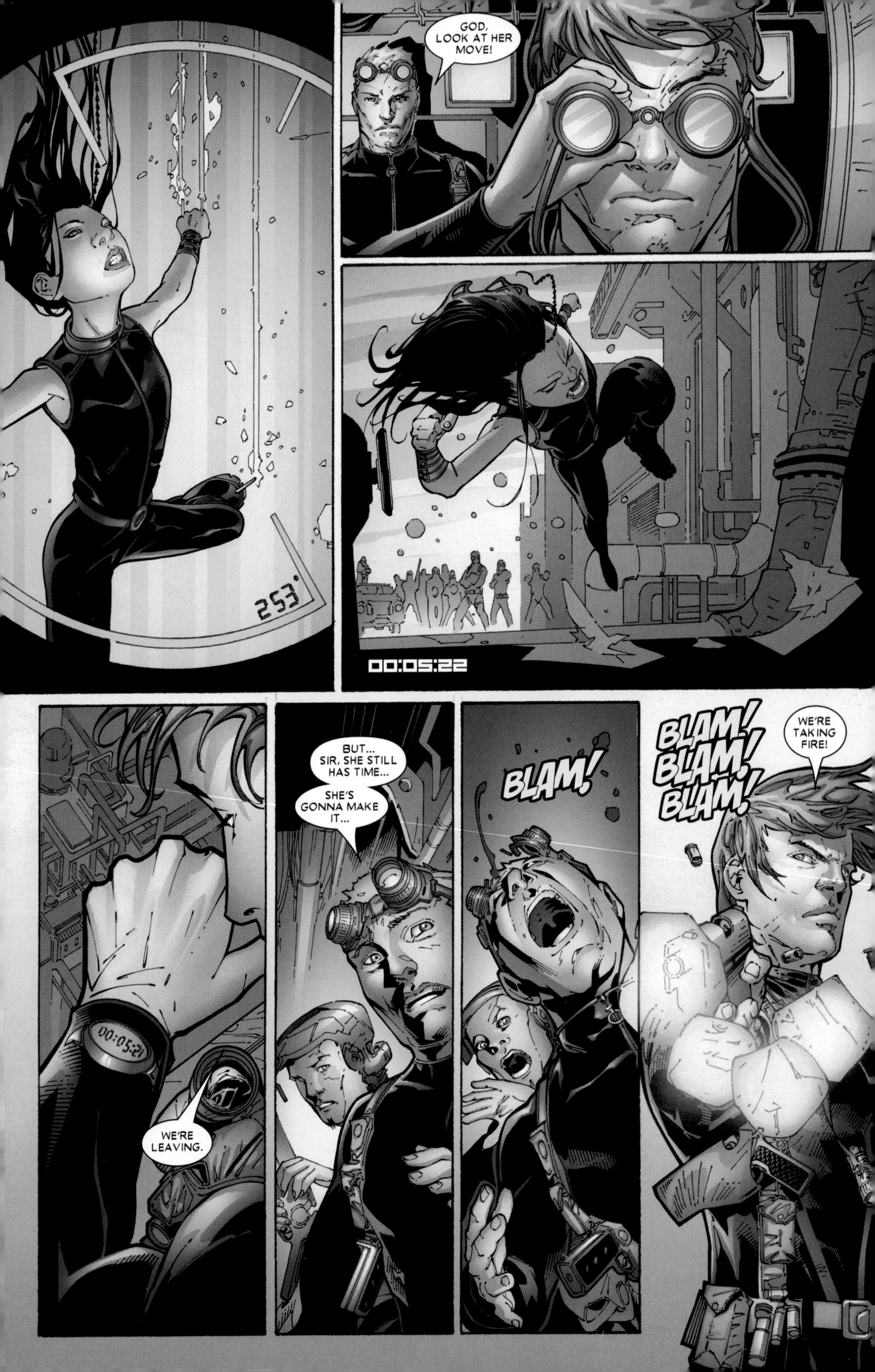

253°
GOD, LOOK AT HER MOVE!
00:05:22
00:05:21
WE'RE LEAVING.
BUT... SIR, SHE STILL HAS TIME...
SHE'S GONNA MAKE IT...
BLAM!
BLAM! BLAM! BLAM!
WE'RE TAKING FIRE!

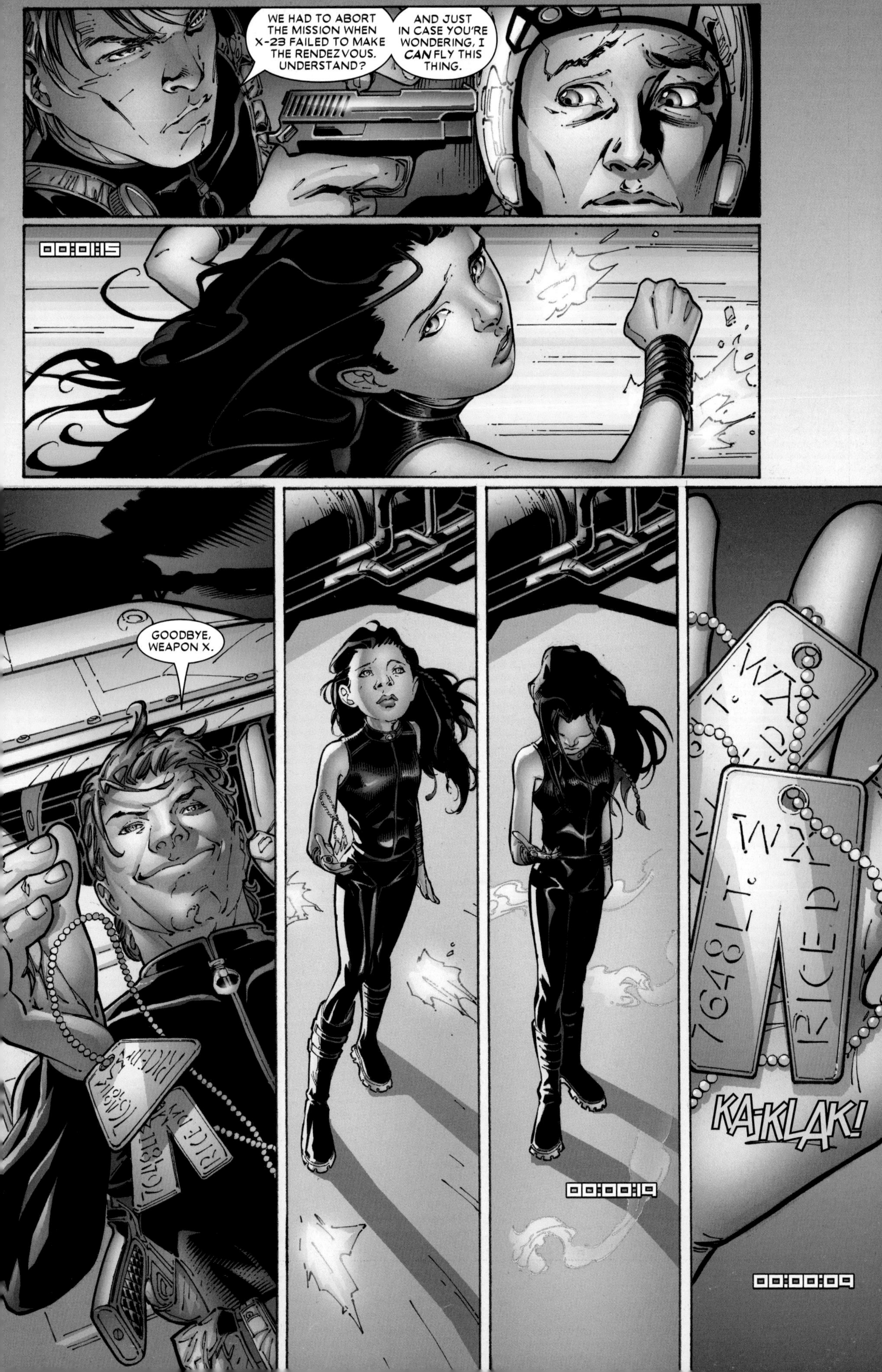
WE HAD TO ABORT THE MISSION WHEN X-23 FAILED TO MAKE THE RENDEZVOUS. UNDERSTAND?
AND JUST IN CASE YOU'RE WONDERING, I CAN FLY THIS THING.
00:01:15
GOODBYE, WEAPON X.
00:00:19
KA-KLAK!
00:00:09

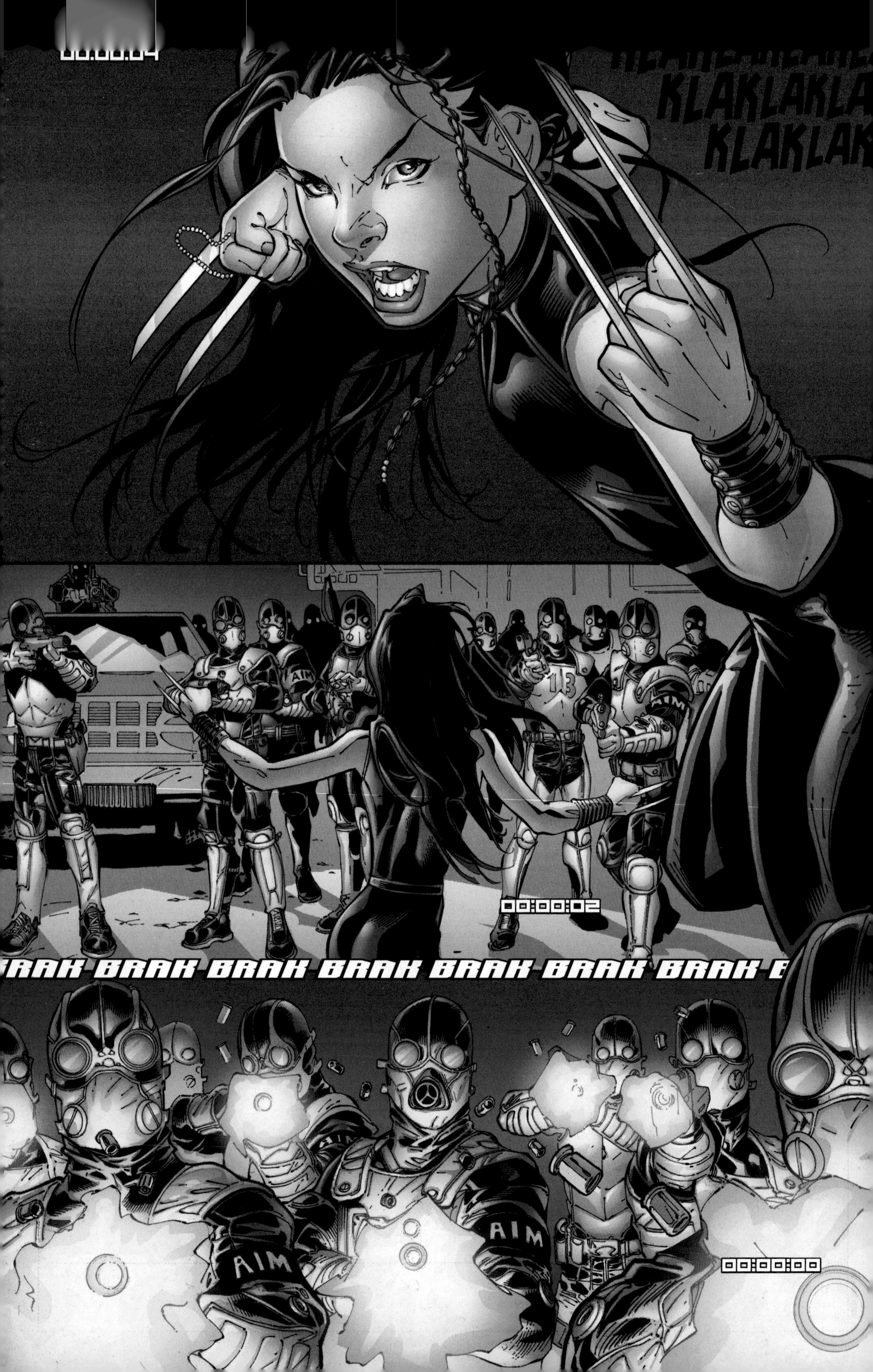

00:00:04
KLAKLAKLA
KLAKLAK
00:00:02
BRAK BRAK BRAK BRAK BRAK BRAK
00:00:00

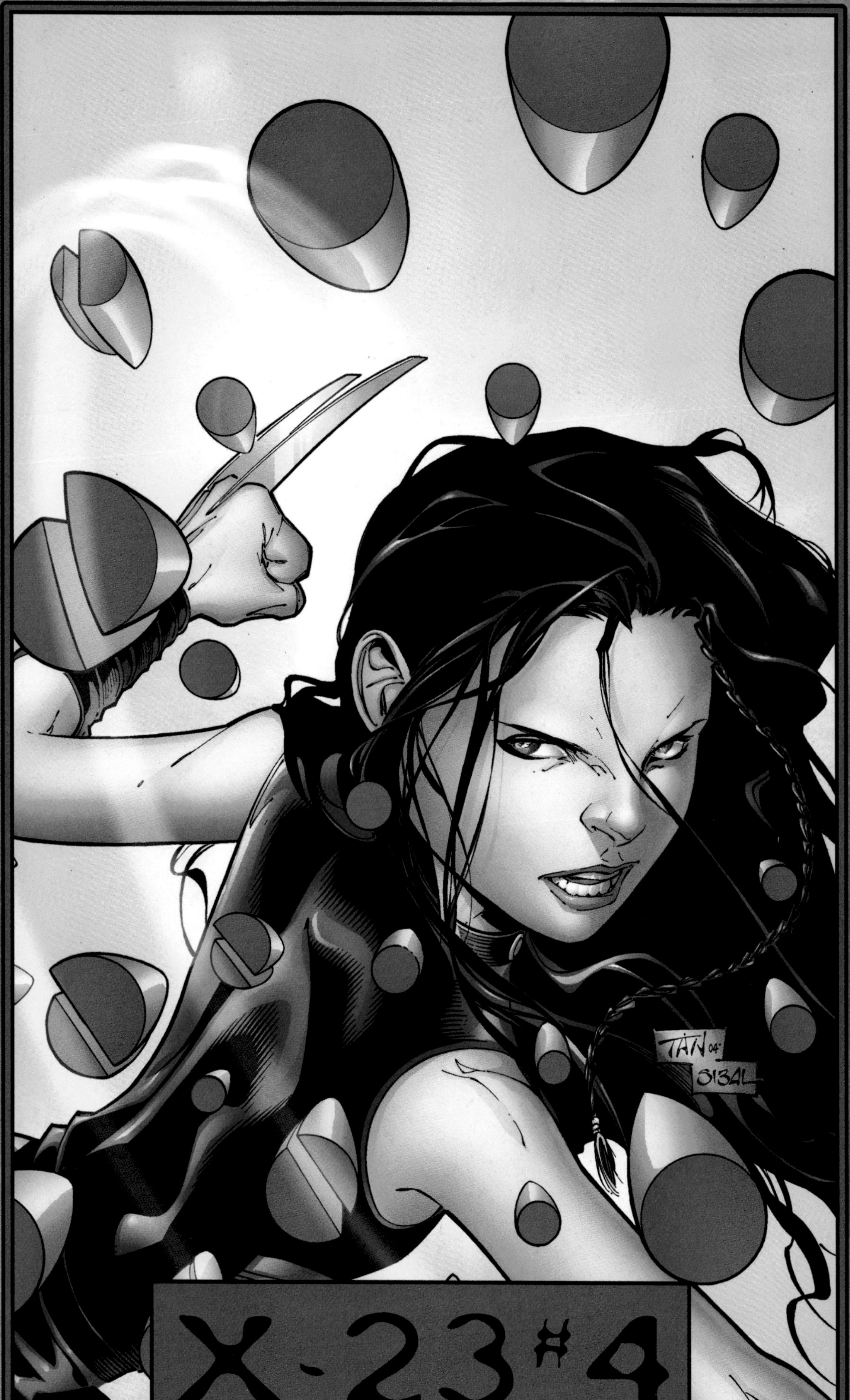
TAN 04
SIBAL
X-23 #4

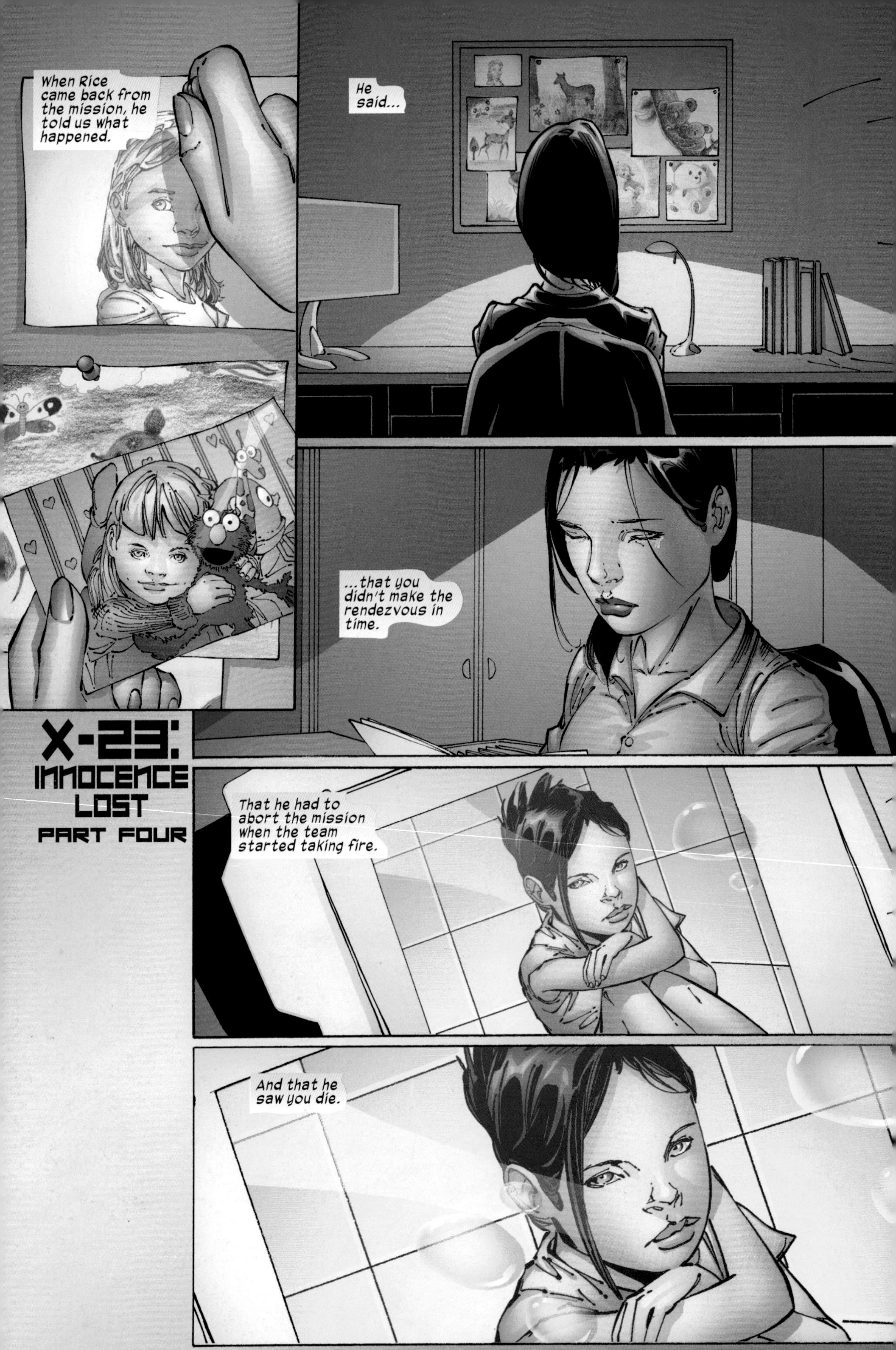
When Rice came back from the mission, he told us what happened.
He said...
...that you didn't make the rendezvous in time.
X-23: INNOCENCE LOST PART FOUR
That he had to abort the mission when the team started taking fire.
And that he saw you die.

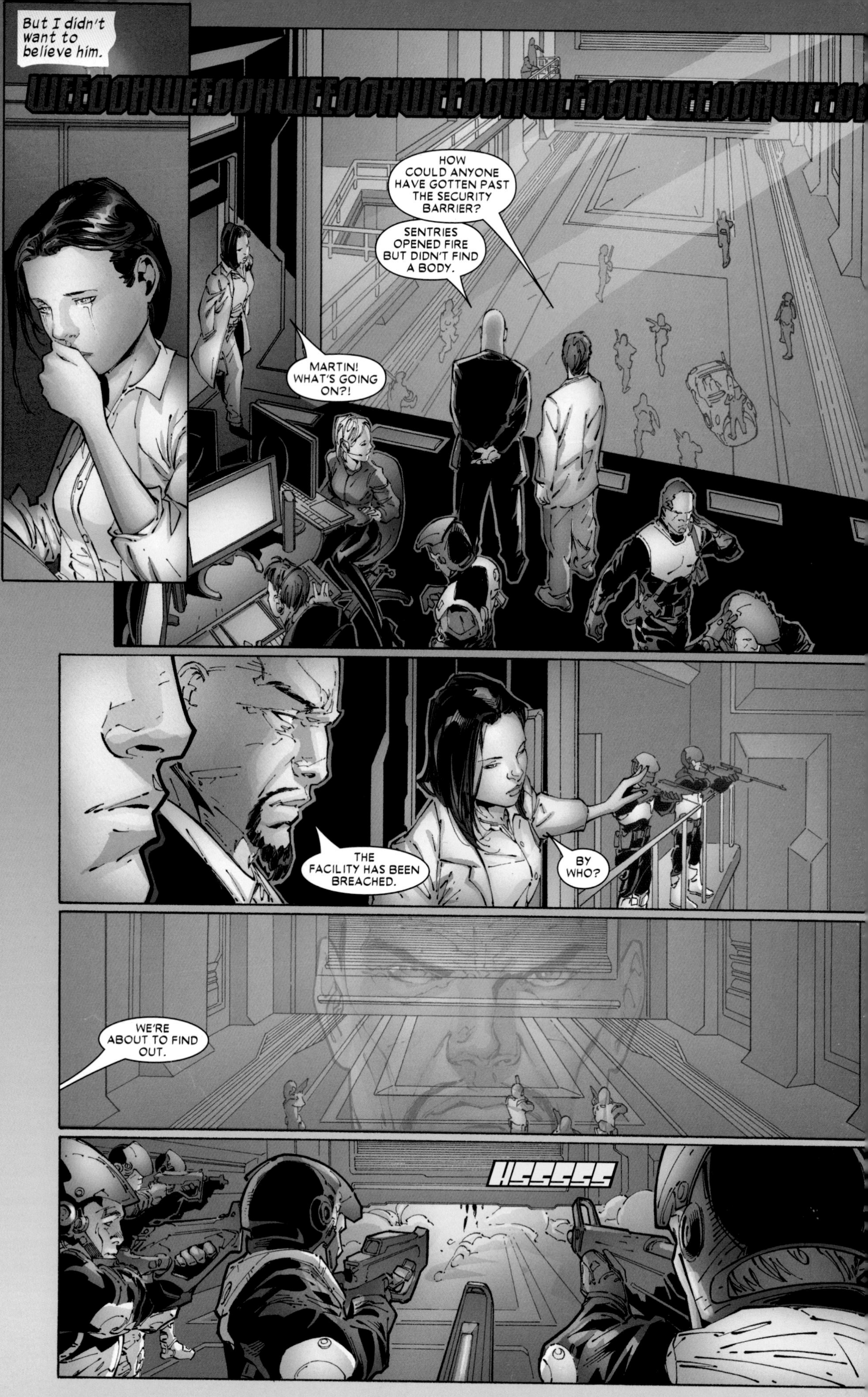
But I didn't want to believe him.
WEEOOHWEEOOHWEEOOHWEEOOHWEEOOHWEEOOHWEEO
HOW COULD ANYONE HAVE GOTTEN PAST THE SECURITY BARRIER?
SENTRIES OPENED FIRE BUT DIDN'T FIND A BODY.
MARTIN! WHAT'S GOING ON?!
THE FACILITY HAS BEEN BREACHED.
BY WHO?
WE'RE ABOUT TO FIND OUT.
HSSSSS

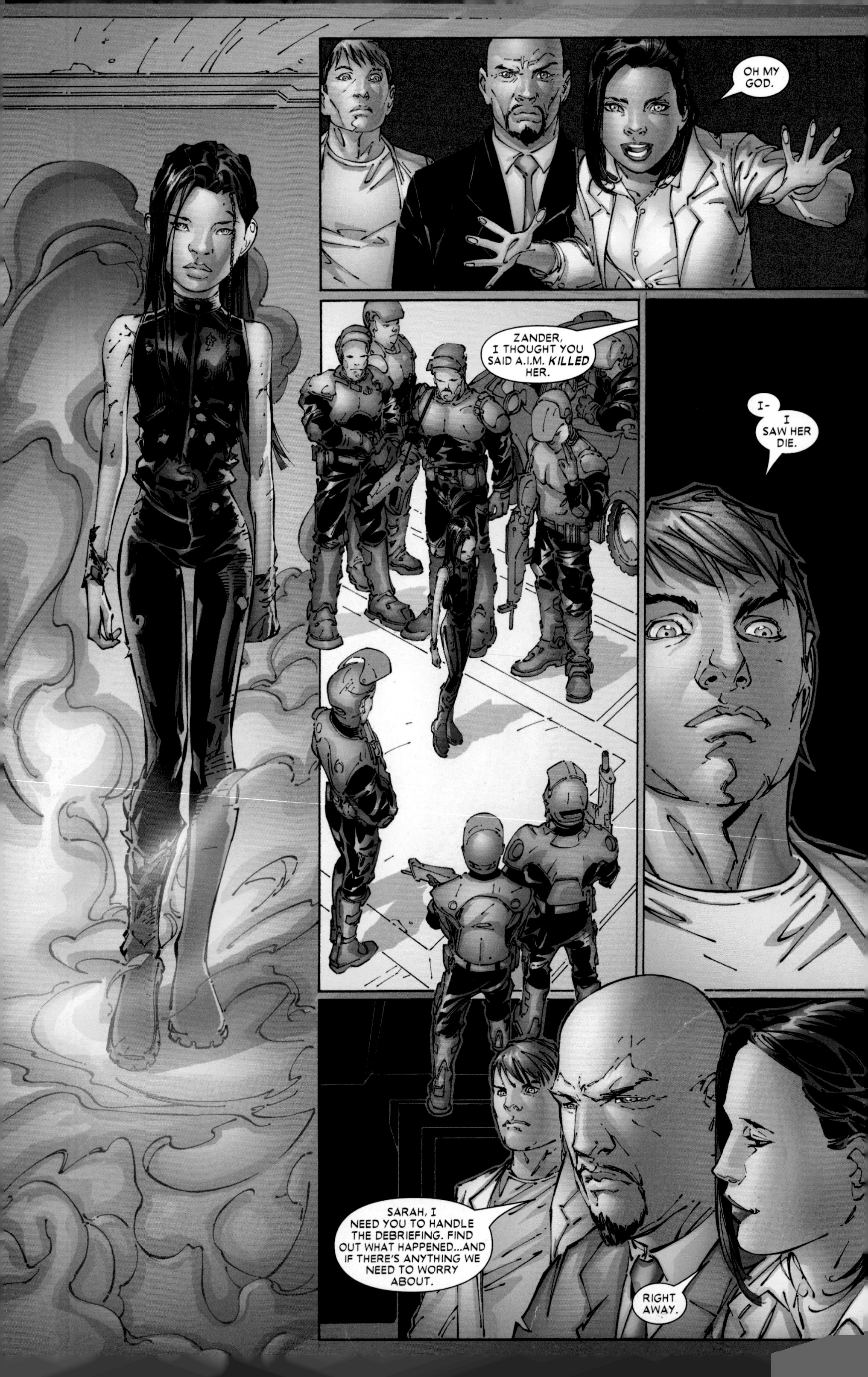
OH MY GOD.
ZANDER, I THOUGHT YOU SAID A.I.M. *KILLED* HER.
I-
I SAW HER DIE.
SARAH, I NEED YOU TO HANDLE THE DEBRIEFING. FIND OUT WHAT HAPPENED...AND IF THERE'S ANYTHING WE NEED TO WORRY ABOUT.
RIGHT AWAY.

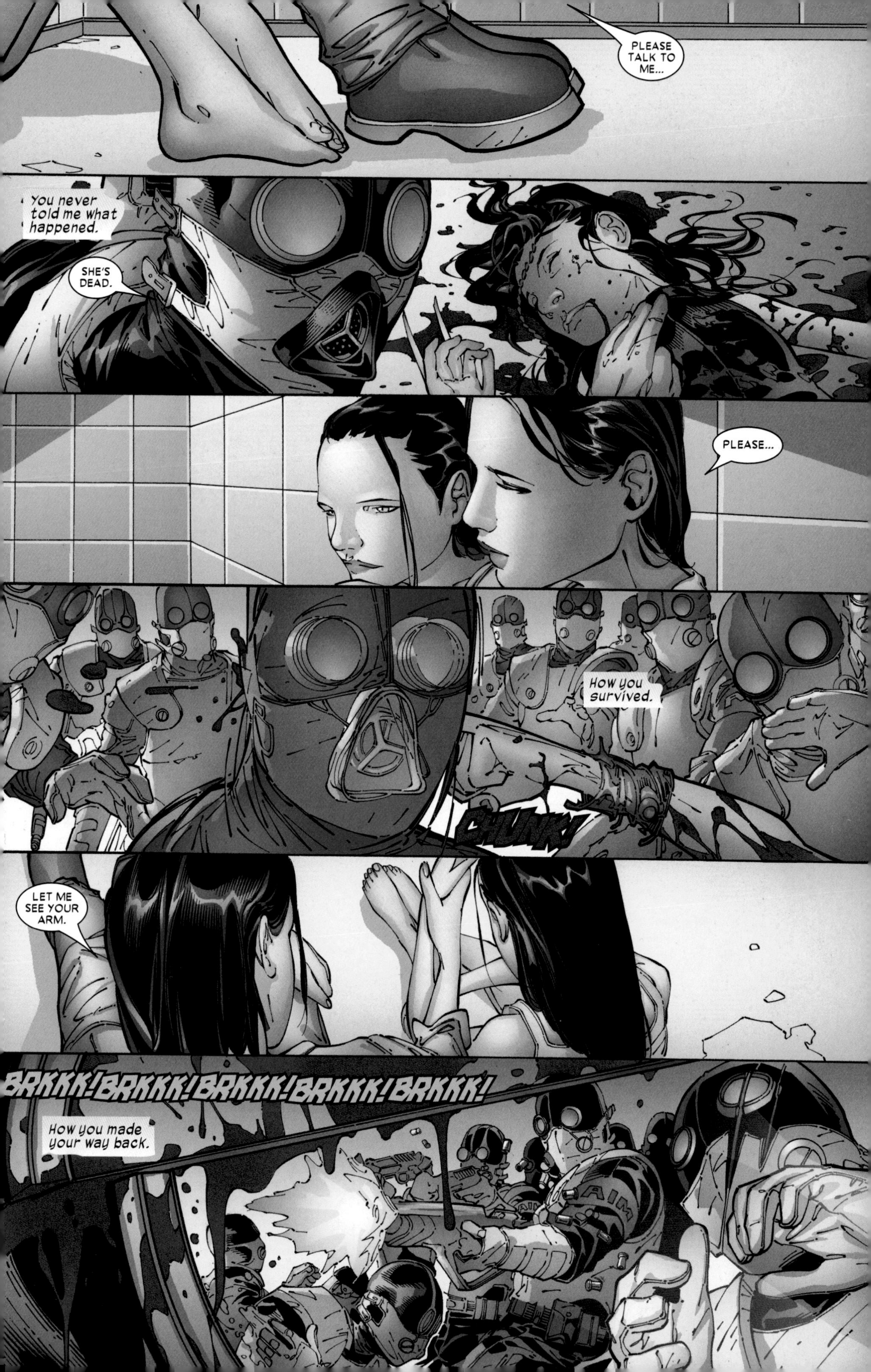
PLEASE TALK TO ME...
You never told me what happened.
SHE'S DEAD.
PLEASE...
How you survived.
CHUNK!
LET ME SEE YOUR ARM.
BRKKK! BRKKK! BRKKK! BRKKK! BRKKK!
How you made your way back.
AIM

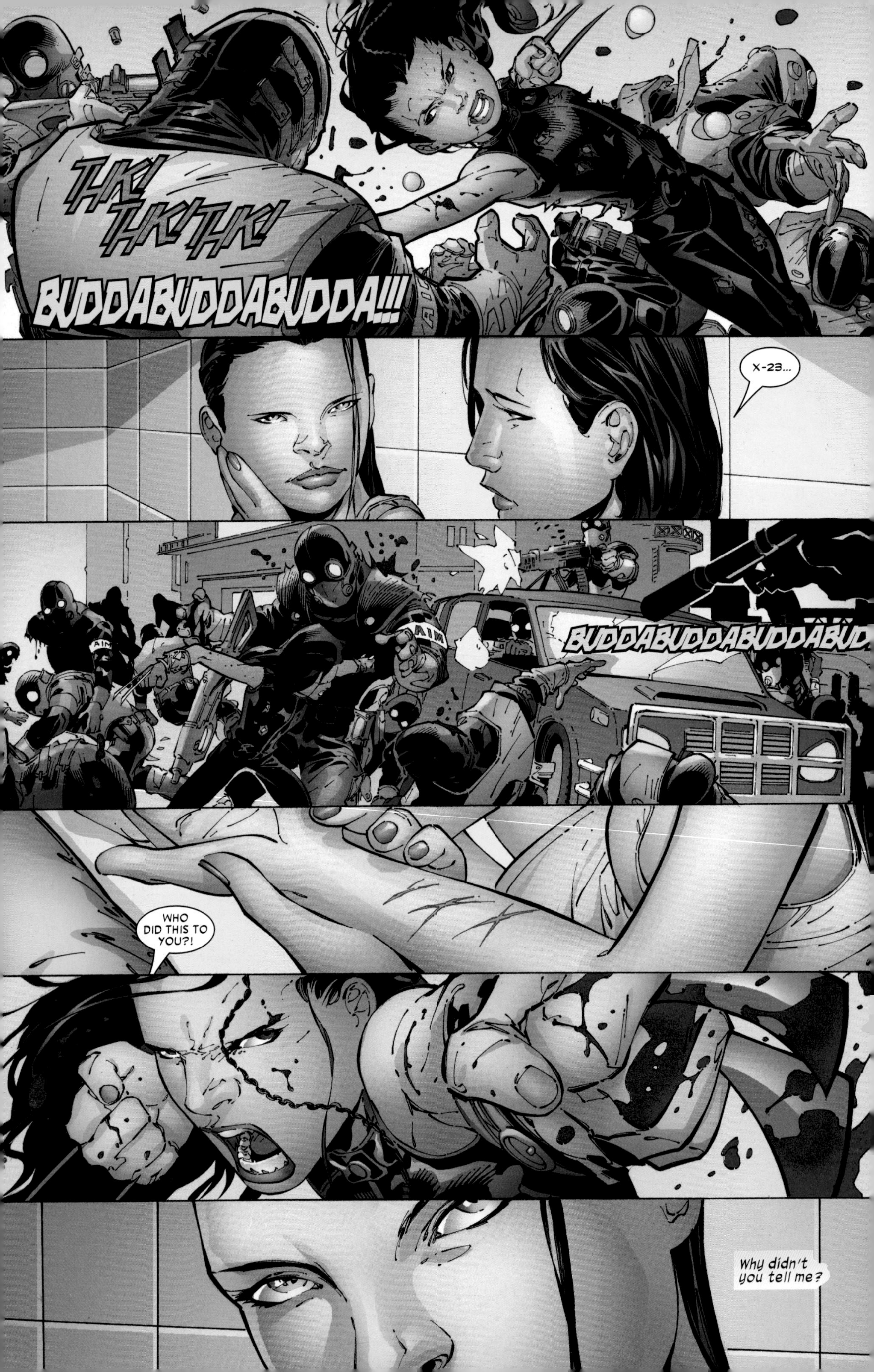
THK! THK! THK!
BUDDABUDDABUDDA!!!
X-23...
BUDDABUDDABUDDABUD
WHO DID THIS TO YOU?!
Why didn't you tell me?

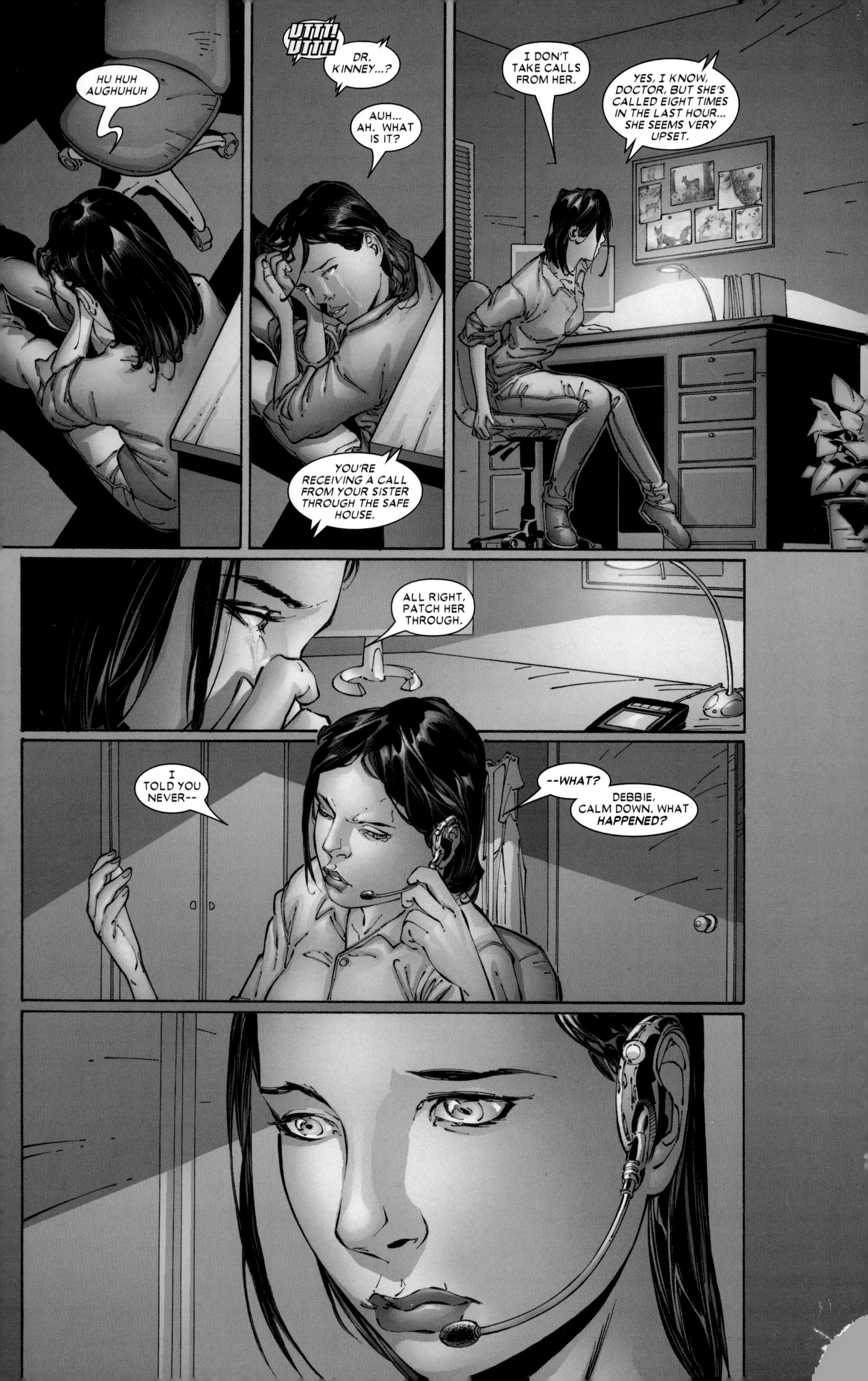
HU HUH AUGHUHUH
UTTT! UTTT!
DR. KINNEY...?
AUH... AH. WHAT IS IT?
YOU'RE RECEIVING A CALL FROM YOUR SISTER THROUGH THE SAFE HOUSE.
I DON'T TAKE CALLS FROM HER.
YES, I KNOW, DOCTOR, BUT SHE'S CALLED EIGHT TIMES IN THE LAST HOUR... SHE SEEMS VERY UPSET.
ALL RIGHT, PATCH HER THROUGH.
I TOLD YOU NEVER--
--WHAT?
DEBBIE, CALM DOWN. WHAT HAPPENED?

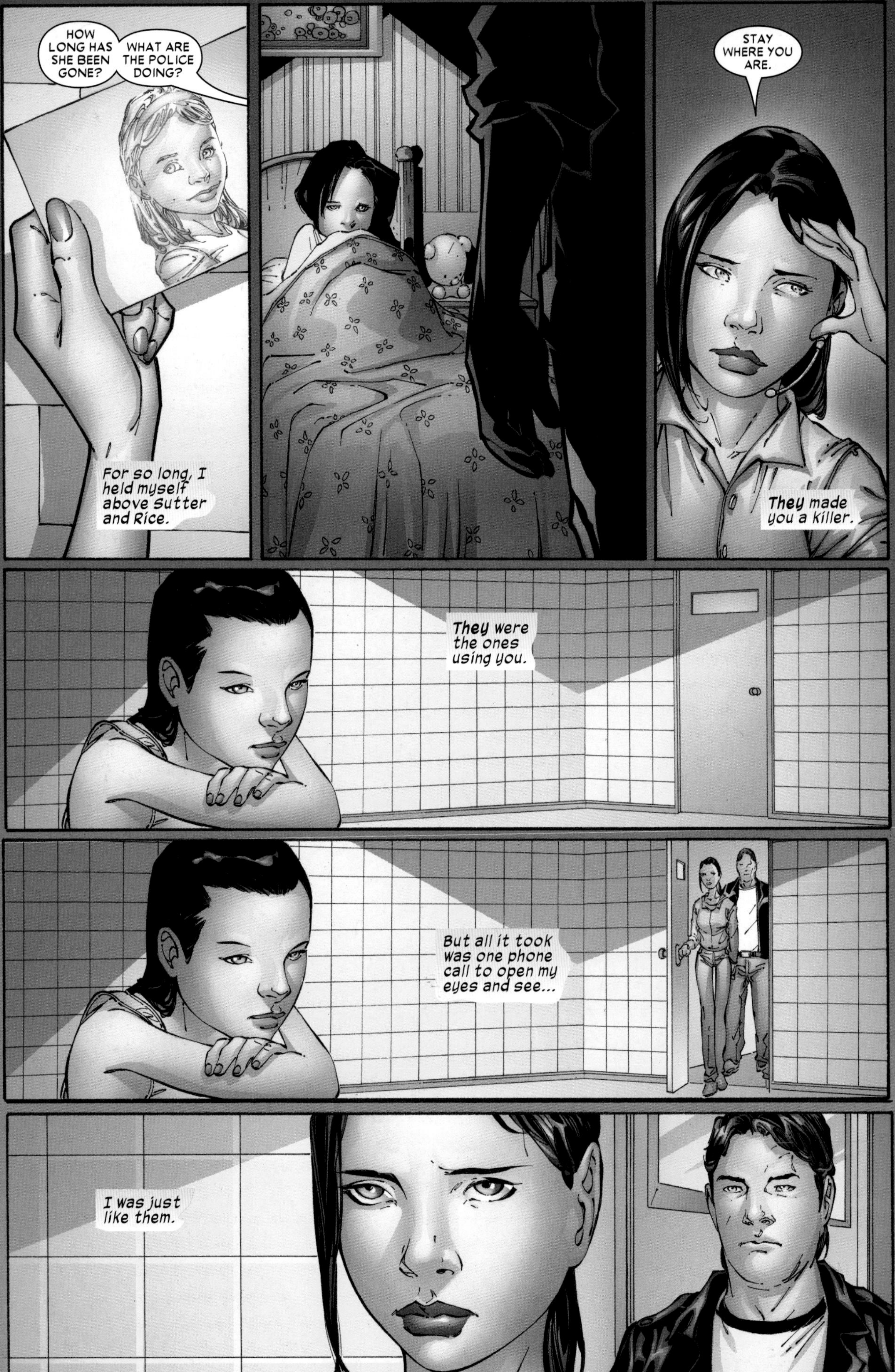
HOW LONG HAS SHE BEEN GONE?
WHAT ARE THE POLICE DOING?
For so long, I held myself above Sutter and Rice.
STAY WHERE YOU ARE.
They made you a killer.
They were the ones using you.
But all it took was one phone call to open my eyes and see...
I was just like them.

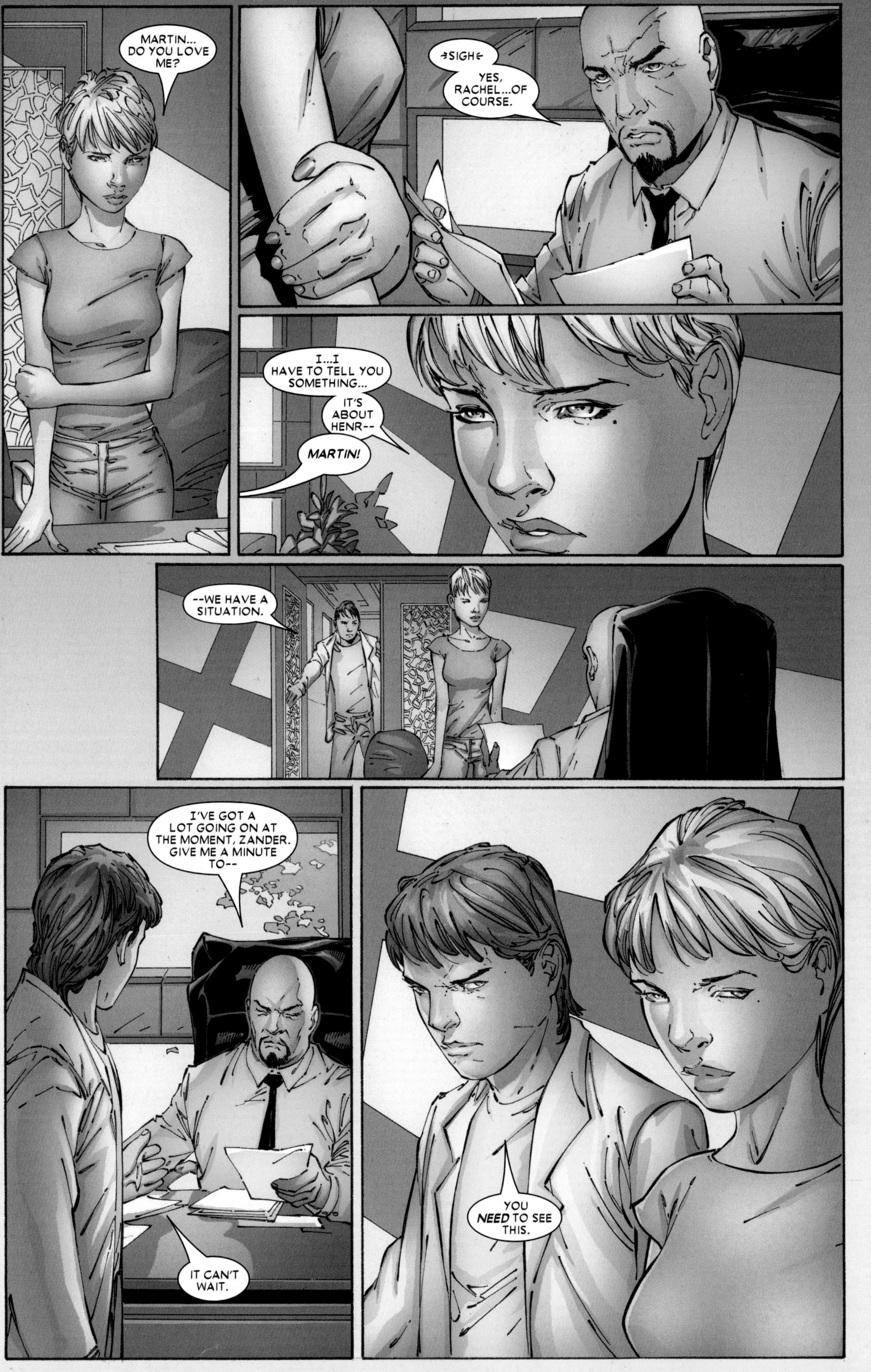
MARTIN... DO YOU LOVE ME?
SIGH
YES, RACHEL...OF COURSE.
I...I HAVE TO TELL YOU SOMETHING...
IT'S ABOUT HENR--
MARTIN!
--WE HAVE A SITUATION.
I'VE GOT A LOT GOING ON AT THE MOMENT, ZANDER. GIVE ME A MINUTE TO--
IT CAN'T WAIT.
YOU NEED TO SEE THIS.

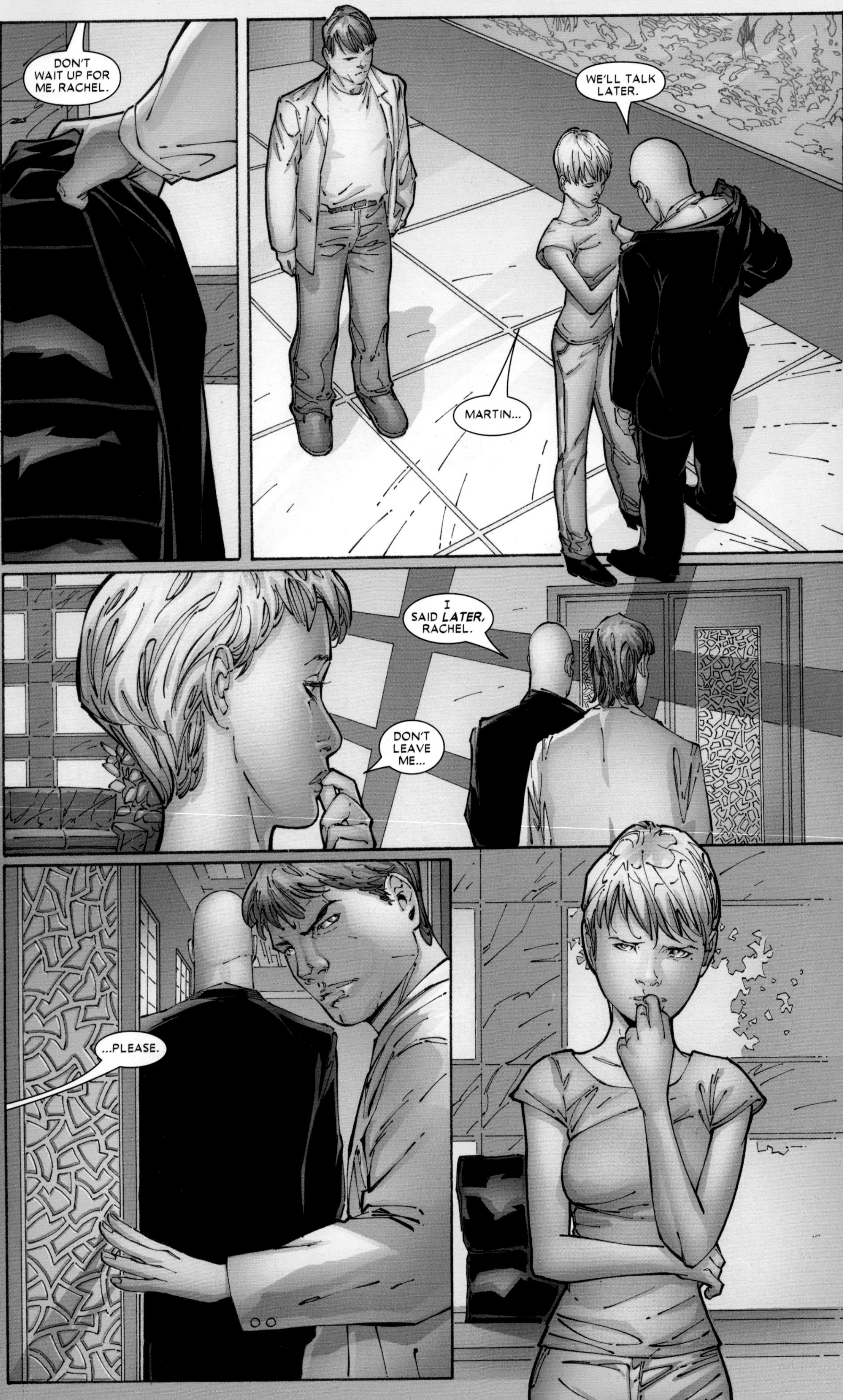
DON'T WAIT UP FOR ME, RACHEL.
WE'LL TALK LATER.
MARTIN...
I SAID LATER, RACHEL.
DON'T LEAVE ME...
...PLEASE.

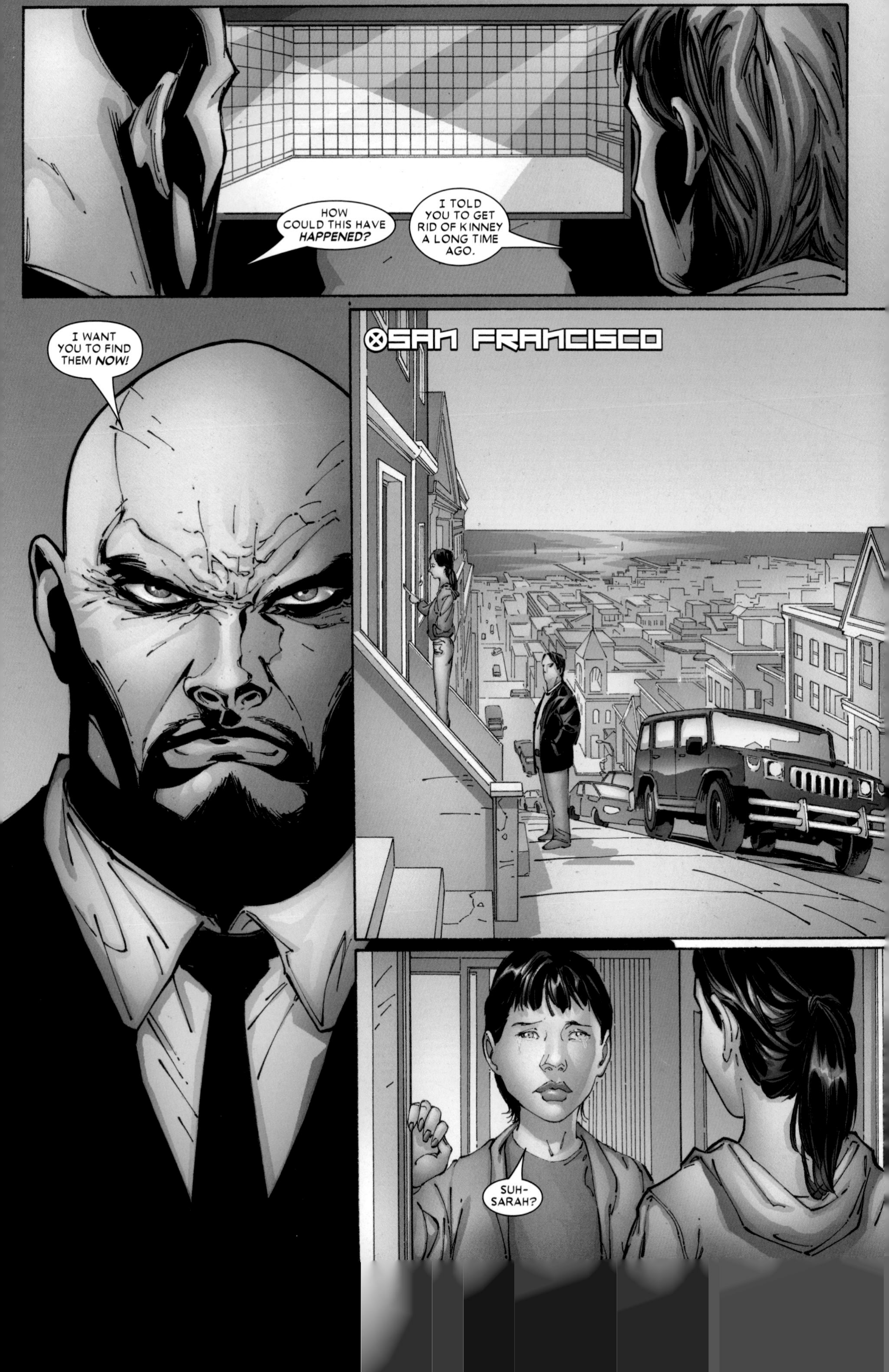

HOW COULD THIS HAVE HAPPENED?
I TOLD YOU TO GET RID OF KINNEY A LONG TIME AGO.
I WANT YOU TO FIND THEM NOW!
SAN FRANCISCO
SUH-SARAH?

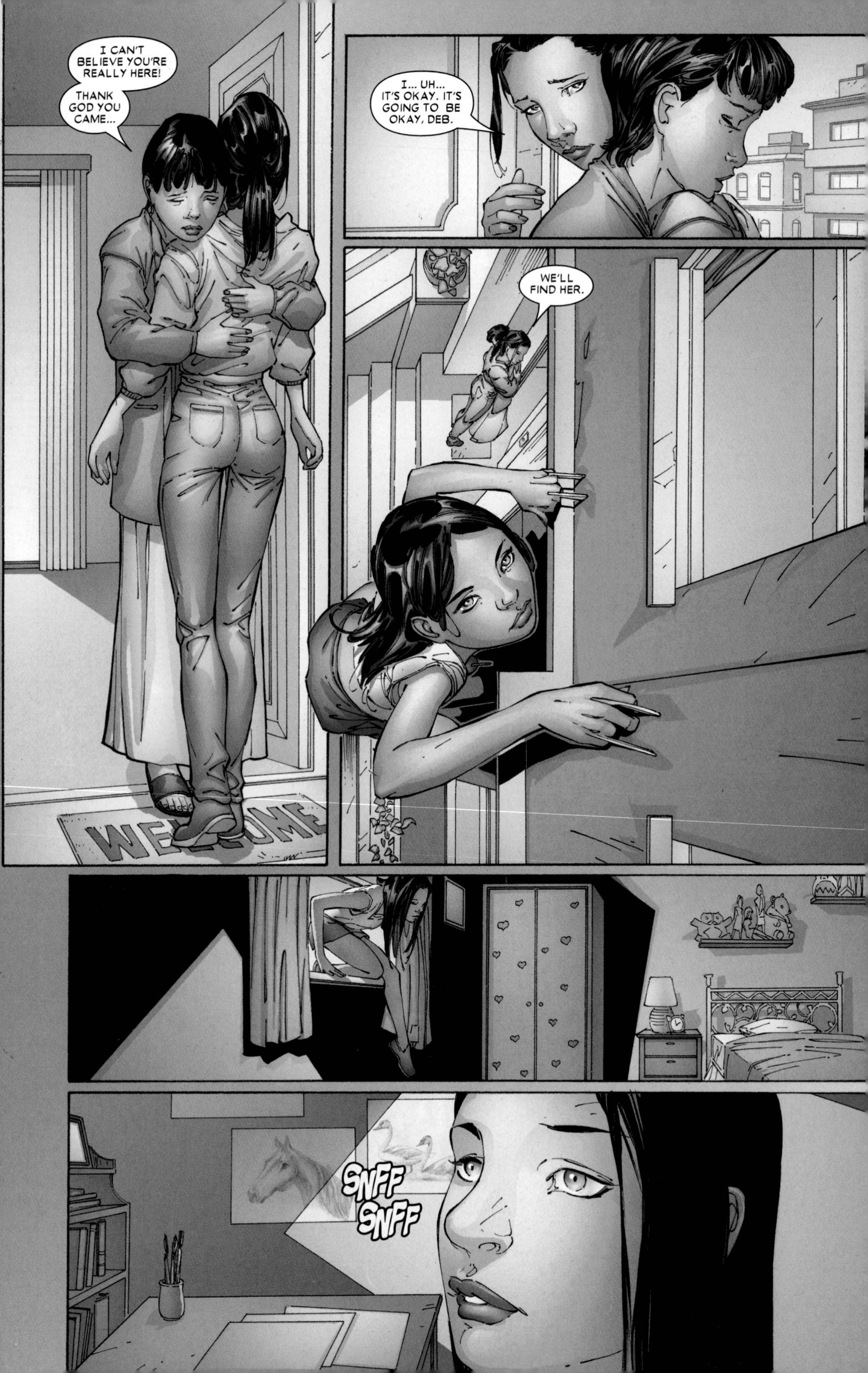
I CAN'T BELIEVE YOU'RE REALLY HERE!
THANK GOD YOU CAME...
I... UH... IT'S OKAY. IT'S GOING TO BE OKAY, DEB.
WE'LL FIND HER.
SNFF SNFF

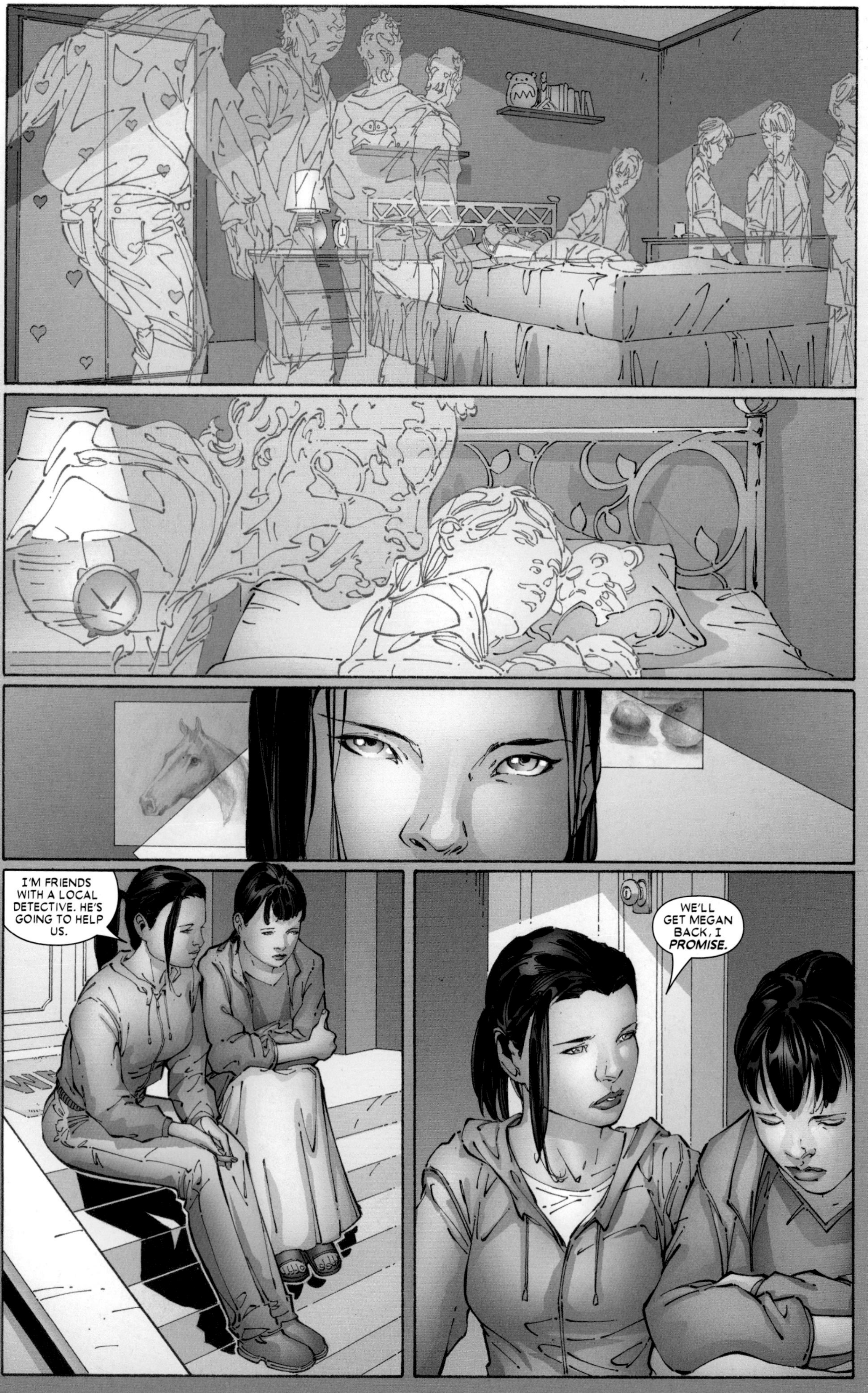
I'M FRIENDS WITH A LOCAL DETECTIVE. HE'S GOING TO HELP US.
WE'LL GET MEGAN BACK, I *PROMISE.*

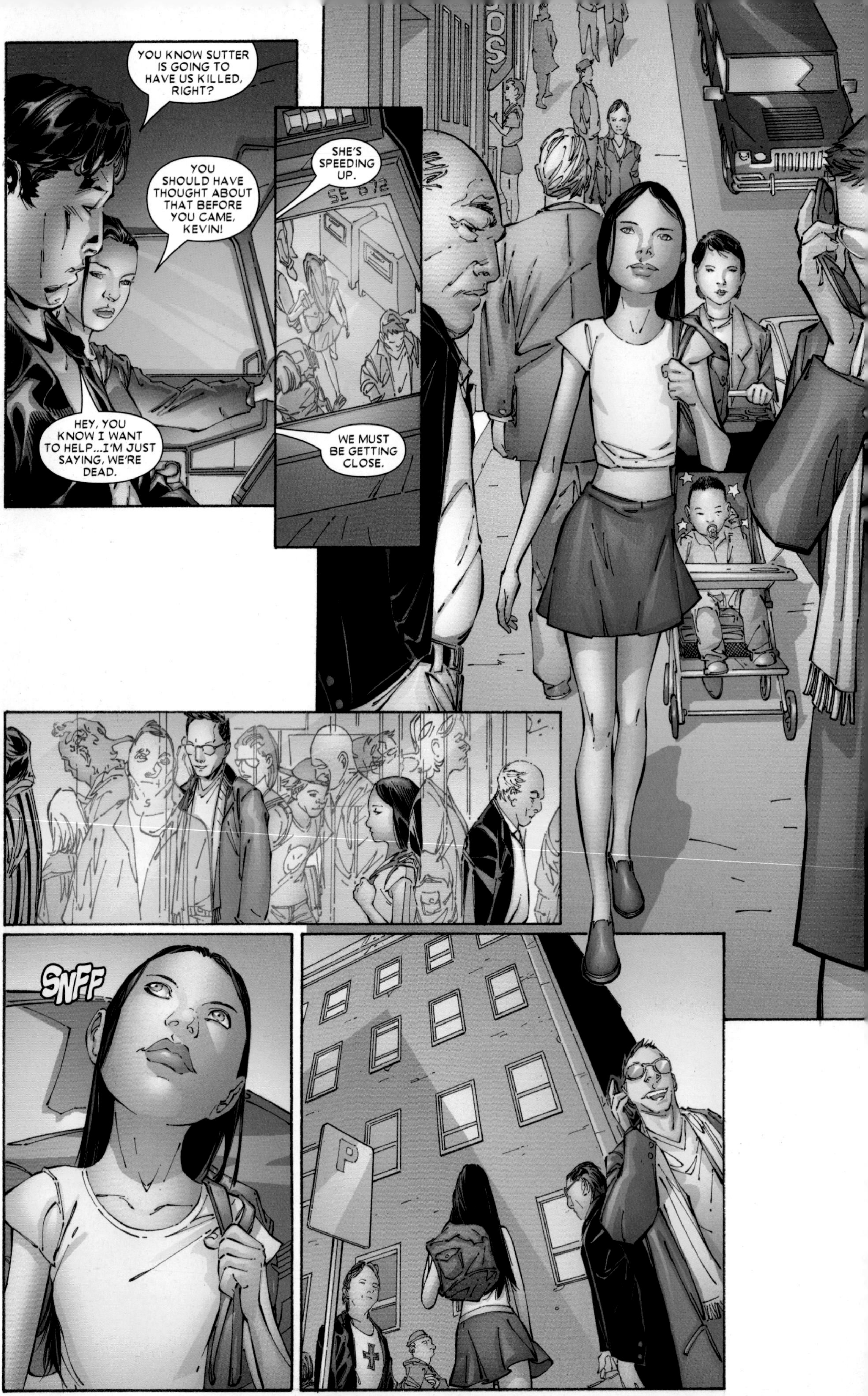
YOU KNOW SUTTER IS GOING TO HAVE US KILLED, RIGHT?
YOU SHOULD HAVE THOUGHT ABOUT THAT BEFORE YOU CAME, KEVIN!
HEY, YOU KNOW I WANT TO HELP...I'M JUST SAYING, WE'RE DEAD.
SHE'S SPEEDING UP.
WE MUST BE GETTING CLOSE.
SNFF

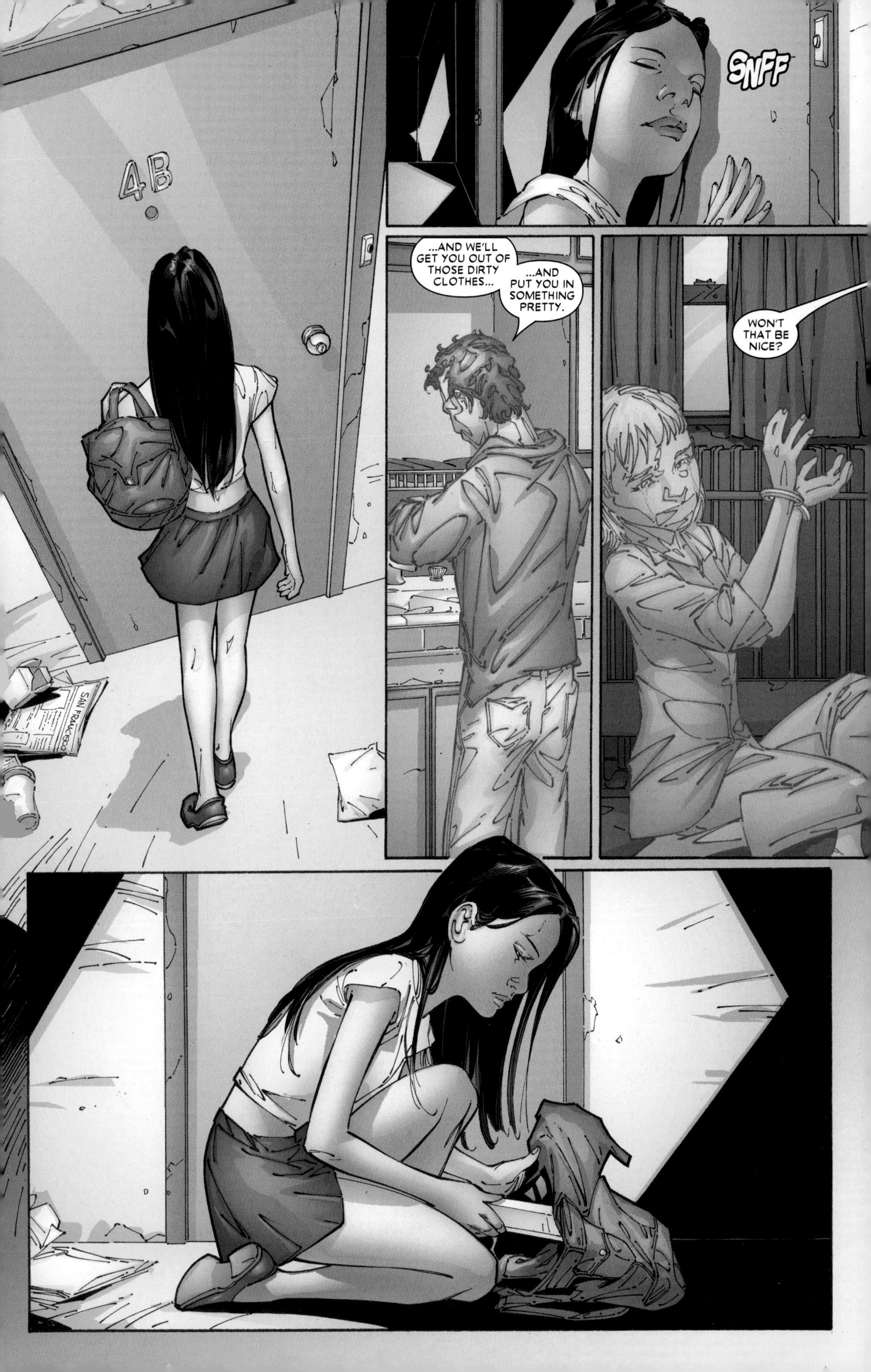

SNFF
...AND WE'LL GET YOU OUT OF THOSE DIRTY CLOTHES...
...AND PUT YOU IN SOMETHING PRETTY.
WON'T THAT BE NICE?
4B
SAN FRANCISCO

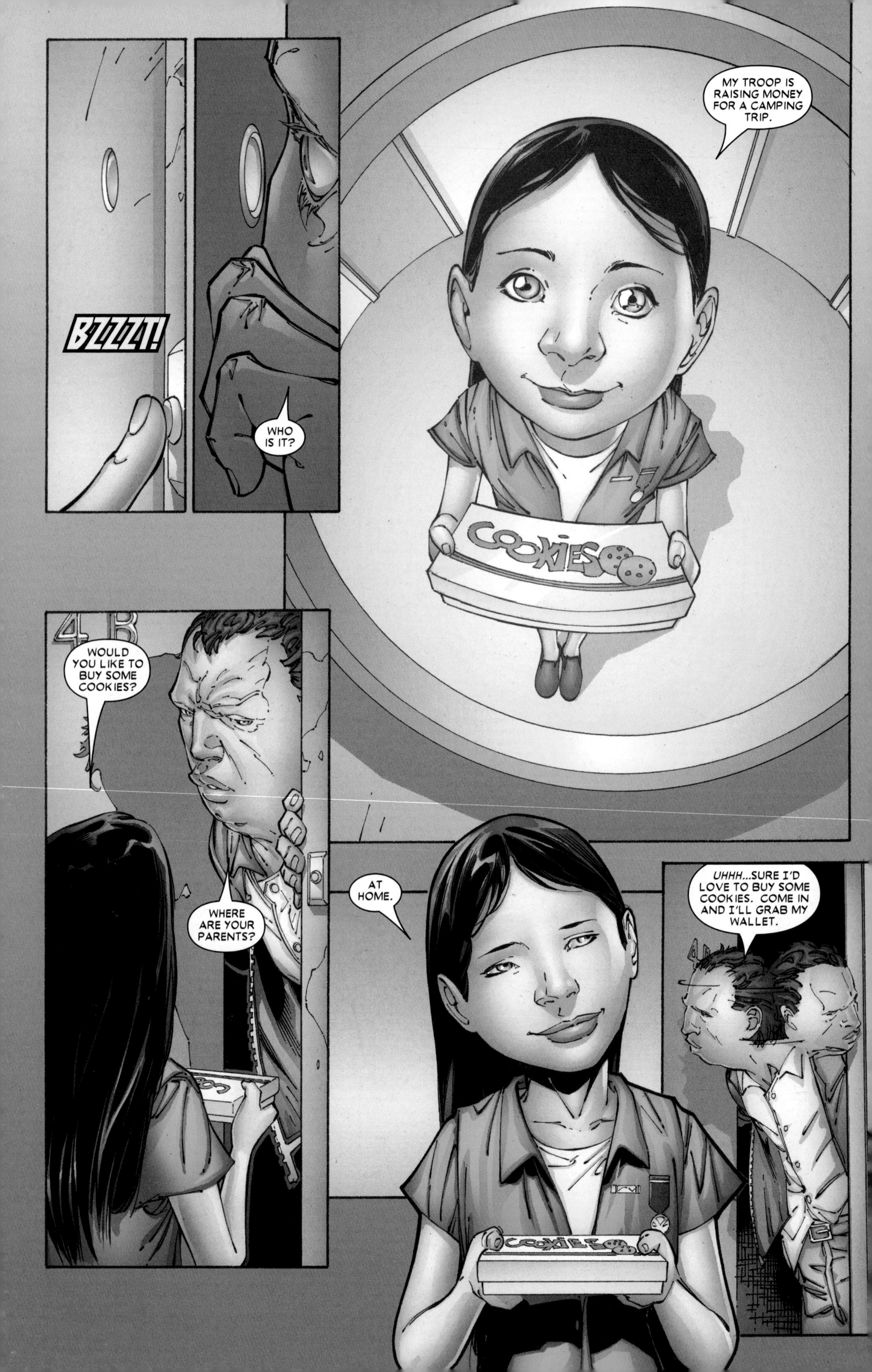
BZZZT!
WHO IS IT?
MY TROOP IS RAISING MONEY FOR A CAMPING TRIP.
COOKIES
WOULD YOU LIKE TO BUY SOME COOKIES?
WHERE ARE YOUR PARENTS?
AT HOME.
UHHH...SURE I'D LOVE TO BUY SOME COOKIES. COME IN AND I'LL GRAB MY WALLET.
COOKIES

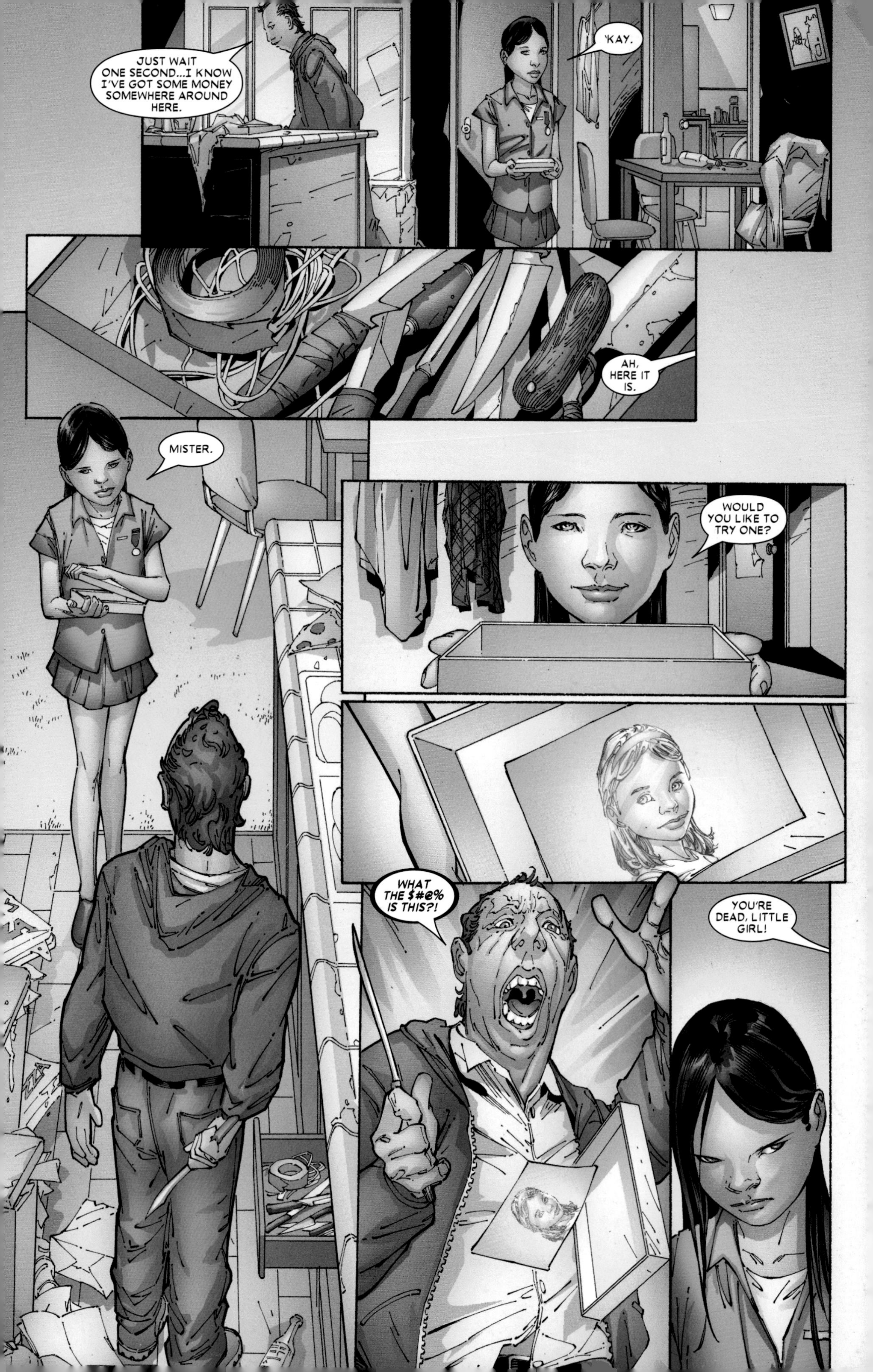
JUST WAIT ONE SECOND...I KNOW I'VE GOT SOME MONEY SOMEWHERE AROUND HERE.
'KAY.
AH, HERE IT IS.
MISTER.
WOULD YOU LIKE TO TRY ONE?
WHAT THE $#@% IS THIS?!
YOU'RE DEAD, LITTLE GIRL!

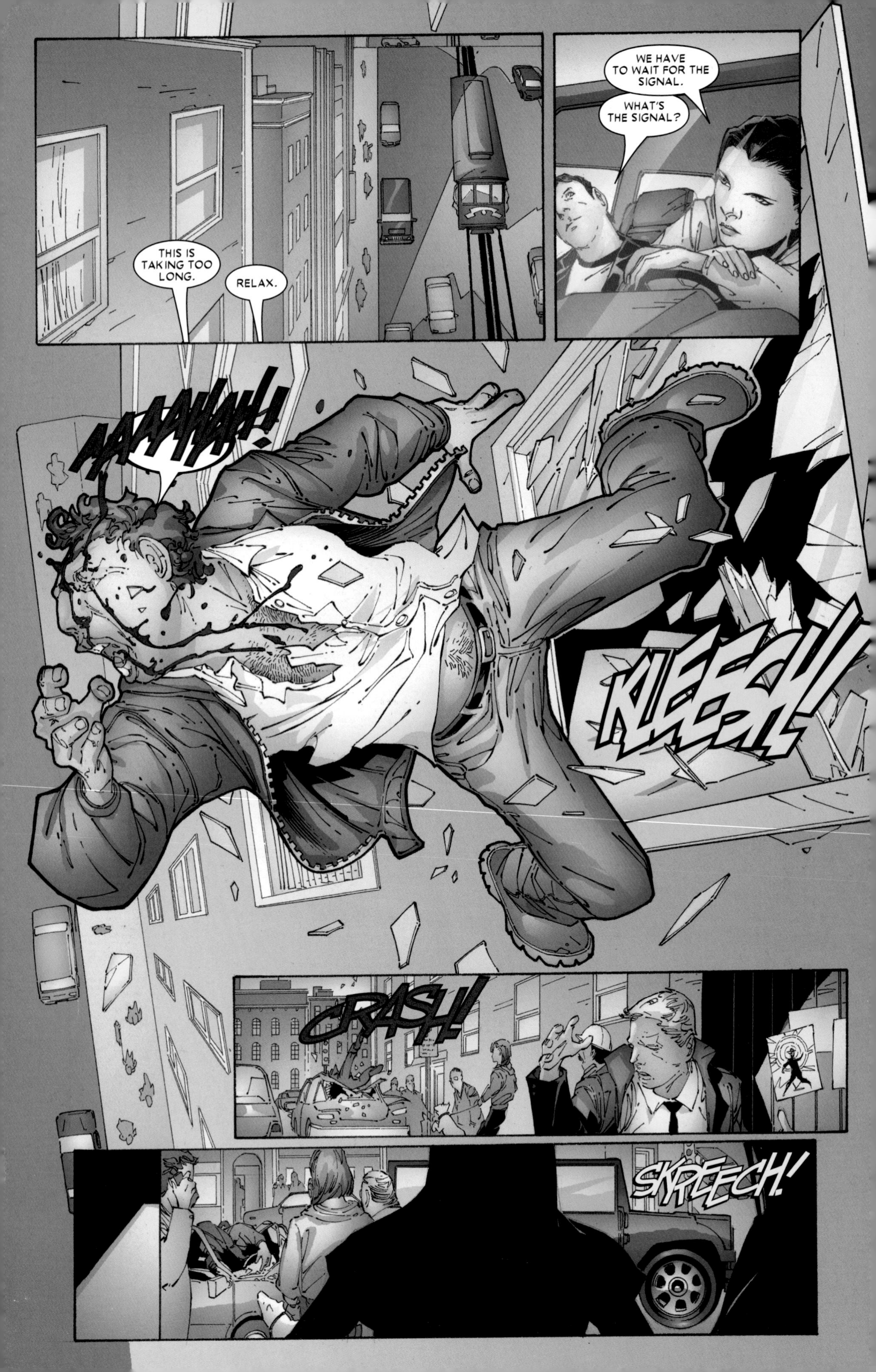

THIS IS TAKING TOO LONG.
RELAX.
WE HAVE TO WAIT FOR THE SIGNAL.
WHAT'S THE SIGNAL?
AAAAAAH!
KLEEESH!
CRASH!
SKREEECH!

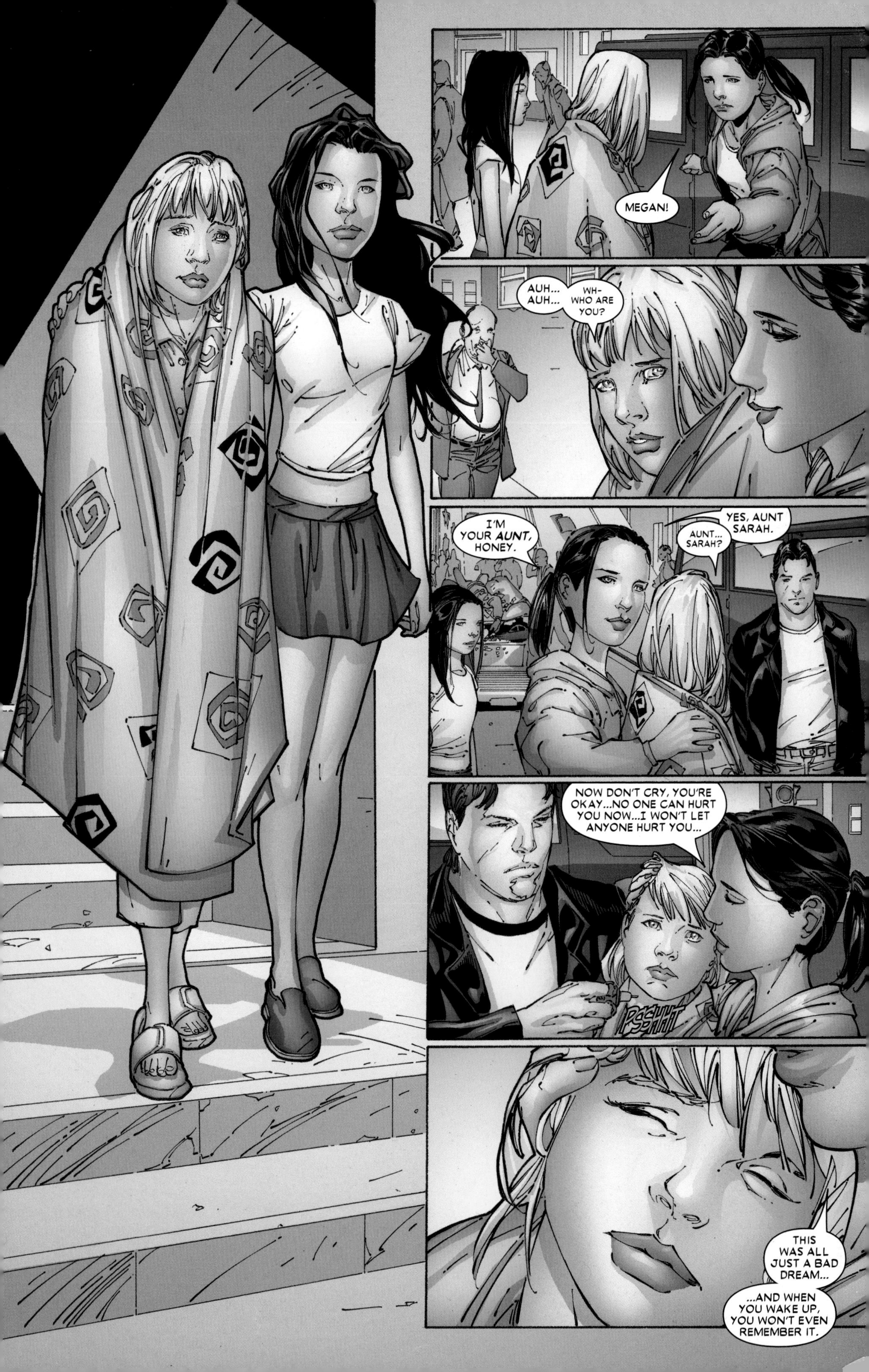
MEGAN!
AUH... AUH...
WH- WHO ARE YOU?
I'M YOUR *AUNT*, HONEY.
AUNT... SARAH?
YES, AUNT SARAH.
NOW DON'T CRY, YOU'RE OKAY...NO ONE CAN HURT YOU NOW...I WON'T LET ANYONE HURT YOU...
PSSHHT
THIS WAS ALL JUST A BAD DREAM...
...AND WHEN YOU WAKE UP, YOU WON'T EVEN REMEMBER IT.

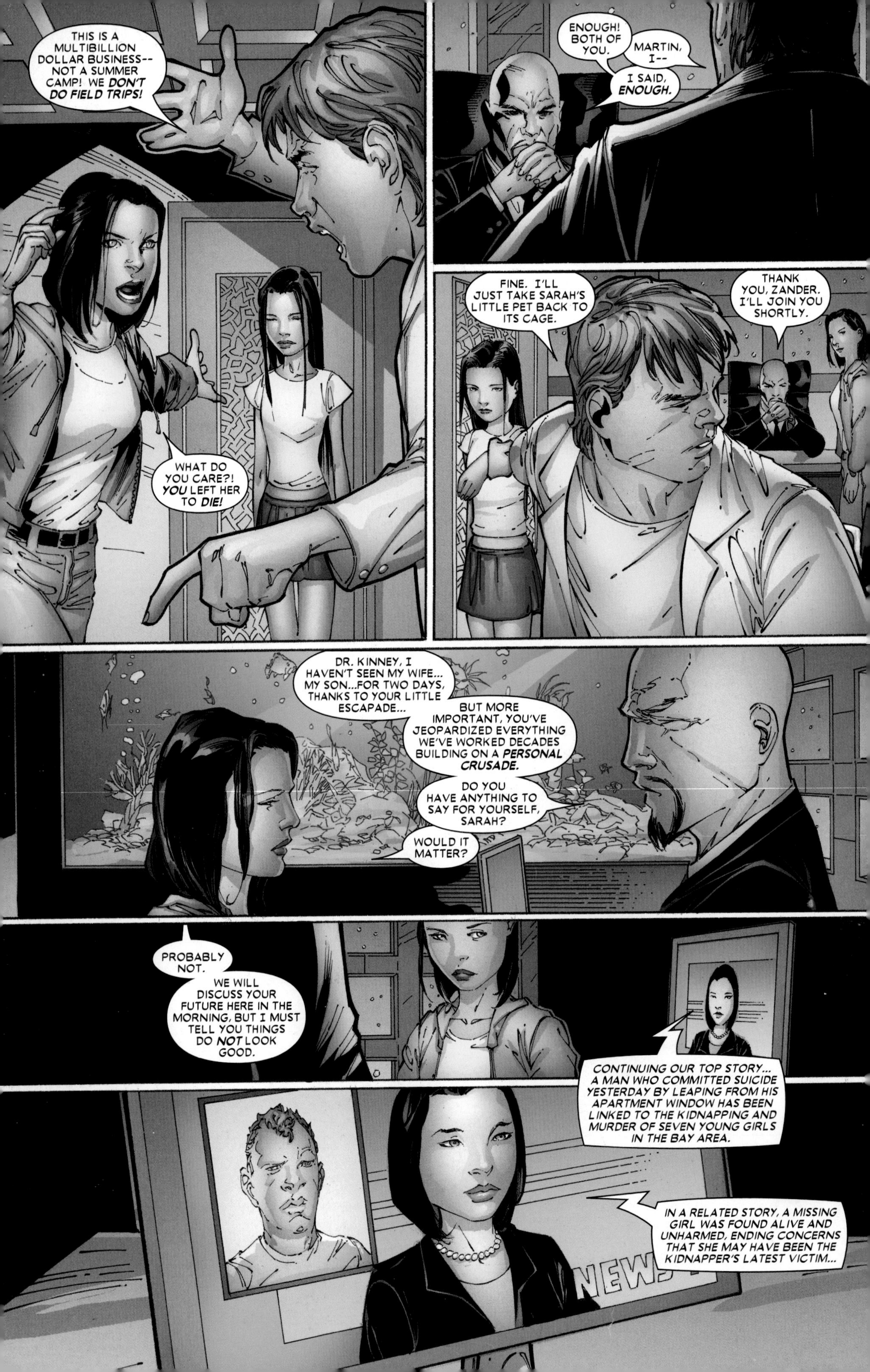
THIS IS A MULTIBILLION DOLLAR BUSINESS-- NOT A SUMMER CAMP! WE DON'T DO FIELD TRIPS!
WHAT DO YOU CARE?! YOU LEFT HER TO DIE!
ENOUGH! BOTH OF YOU.
MARTIN, I--
I SAID, ENOUGH.
FINE. I'LL JUST TAKE SARAH'S LITTLE PET BACK TO ITS CAGE.
THANK YOU, ZANDER. I'LL JOIN YOU SHORTLY.
DR. KINNEY, I HAVEN'T SEEN MY WIFE... MY SON...FOR TWO DAYS, THANKS TO YOUR LITTLE ESCAPADE...
BUT MORE IMPORTANT, YOU'VE JEOPARDIZED EVERYTHING WE'VE WORKED DECADES BUILDING ON A PERSONAL CRUSADE.
DO YOU HAVE ANYTHING TO SAY FOR YOURSELF, SARAH?
WOULD IT MATTER?
PROBABLY NOT.
WE WILL DISCUSS YOUR FUTURE HERE IN THE MORNING, BUT I MUST TELL YOU THINGS DO NOT LOOK GOOD.
CONTINUING OUR TOP STORY... A MAN WHO COMMITTED SUICIDE YESTERDAY BY LEAPING FROM HIS APARTMENT WINDOW HAS BEEN LINKED TO THE KIDNAPPING AND MURDER OF SEVEN YOUNG GIRLS IN THE BAY AREA.
NEWS
IN A RELATED STORY, A MISSING GIRL WAS FOUND ALIVE AND UNHARMED, ENDING CONCERNS THAT SHE MAY HAVE BEEN THE KIDNAPPER'S LATEST VICTIM...

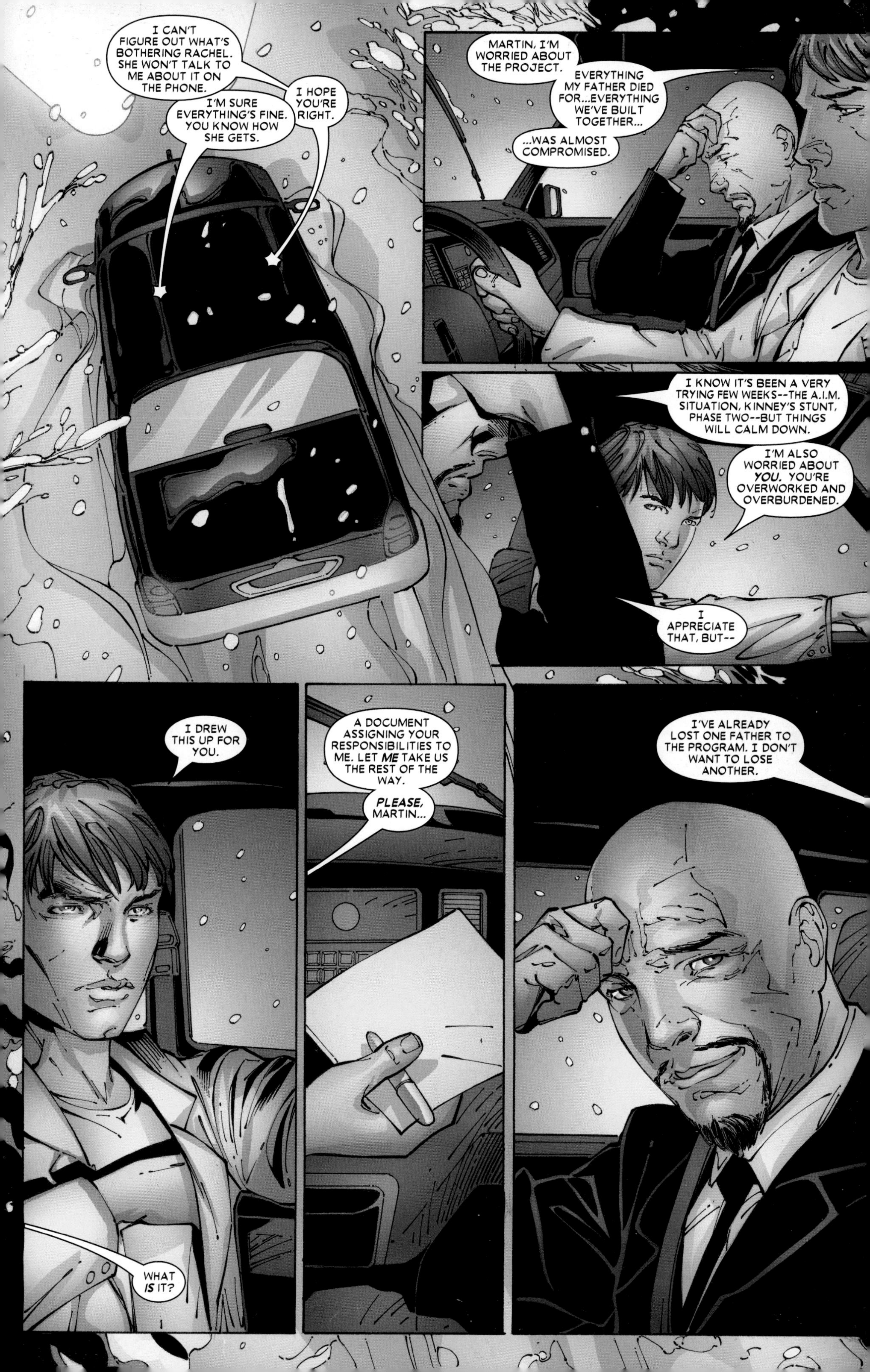
I CAN'T FIGURE OUT WHAT'S BOTHERING RACHEL. SHE WON'T TALK TO ME ABOUT IT ON THE PHONE.
I'M SURE EVERYTHING'S FINE. YOU KNOW HOW SHE GETS.
I HOPE YOU'RE RIGHT.
MARTIN, I'M WORRIED ABOUT THE PROJECT.
EVERYTHING MY FATHER DIED FOR...EVERYTHING WE'VE BUILT TOGETHER...
...WAS ALMOST COMPROMISED.
I KNOW IT'S BEEN A VERY TRYING FEW WEEKS--THE A.I.M. SITUATION, KINNEY'S STUNT, PHASE TWO--BUT THINGS WILL CALM DOWN.
I'M ALSO WORRIED ABOUT YOU. YOU'RE OVERWORKED AND OVERBURDENED.
I APPRECIATE THAT, BUT--
I DREW THIS UP FOR YOU.
WHAT IS IT?
A DOCUMENT ASSIGNING YOUR RESPONSIBILITIES TO ME. LET ME TAKE US THE REST OF THE WAY.
PLEASE, MARTIN...
I'VE ALREADY LOST ONE FATHER TO THE PROGRAM. I DON'T WANT TO LOSE ANOTHER.

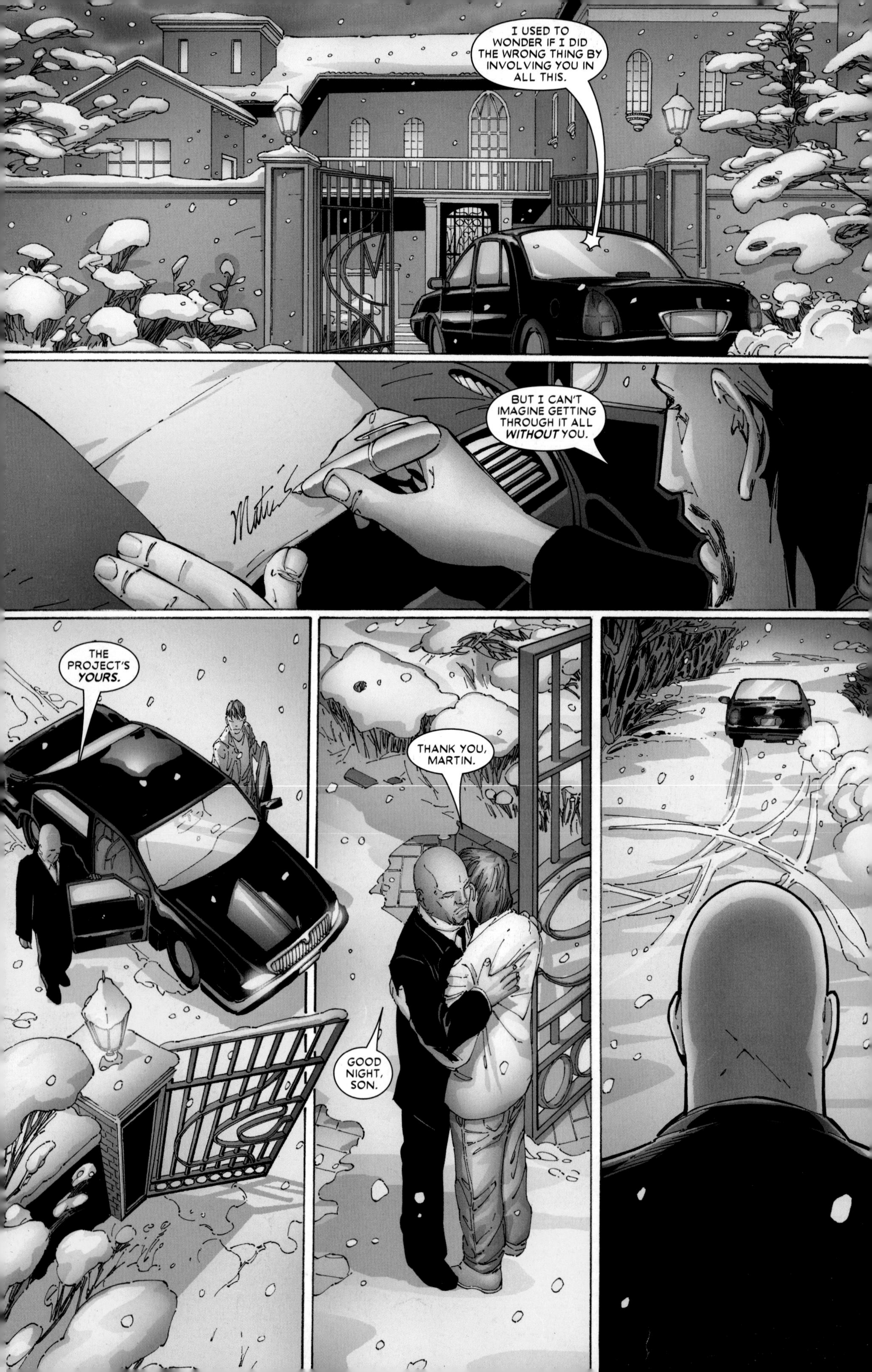
I USED TO WONDER IF I DID THE WRONG THING BY INVOLVING YOU IN ALL THIS.
BUT I CAN'T IMAGINE GETTING THROUGH IT ALL *WITHOUT* YOU.
THE PROJECT'S *YOURS.*
THANK YOU, MARTIN.
GOOD NIGHT, SON.

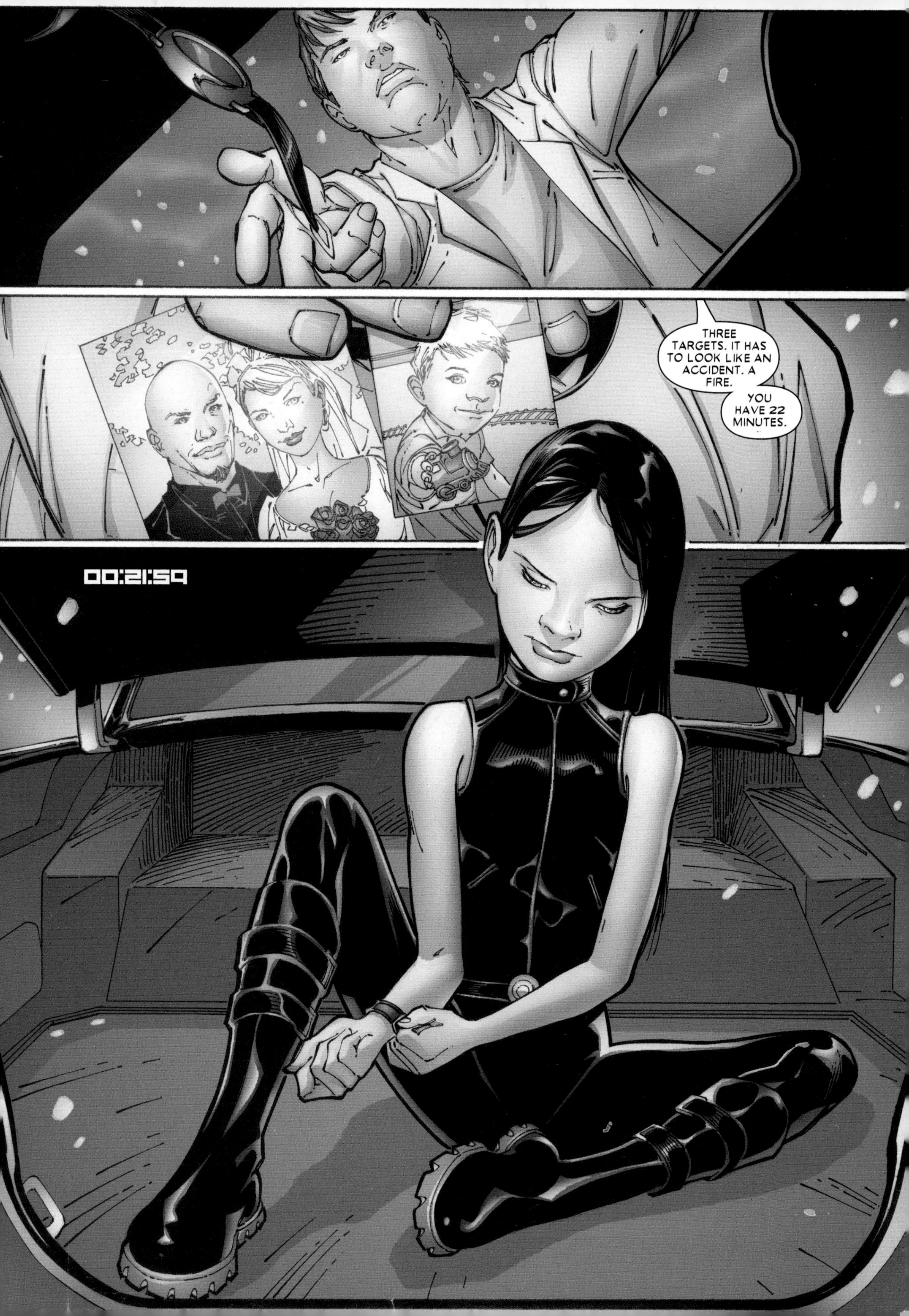
THREE TARGETS. IT HAS TO LOOK LIKE AN ACCIDENT. A FIRE.
YOU HAVE 22 MINUTES.
00:21:59

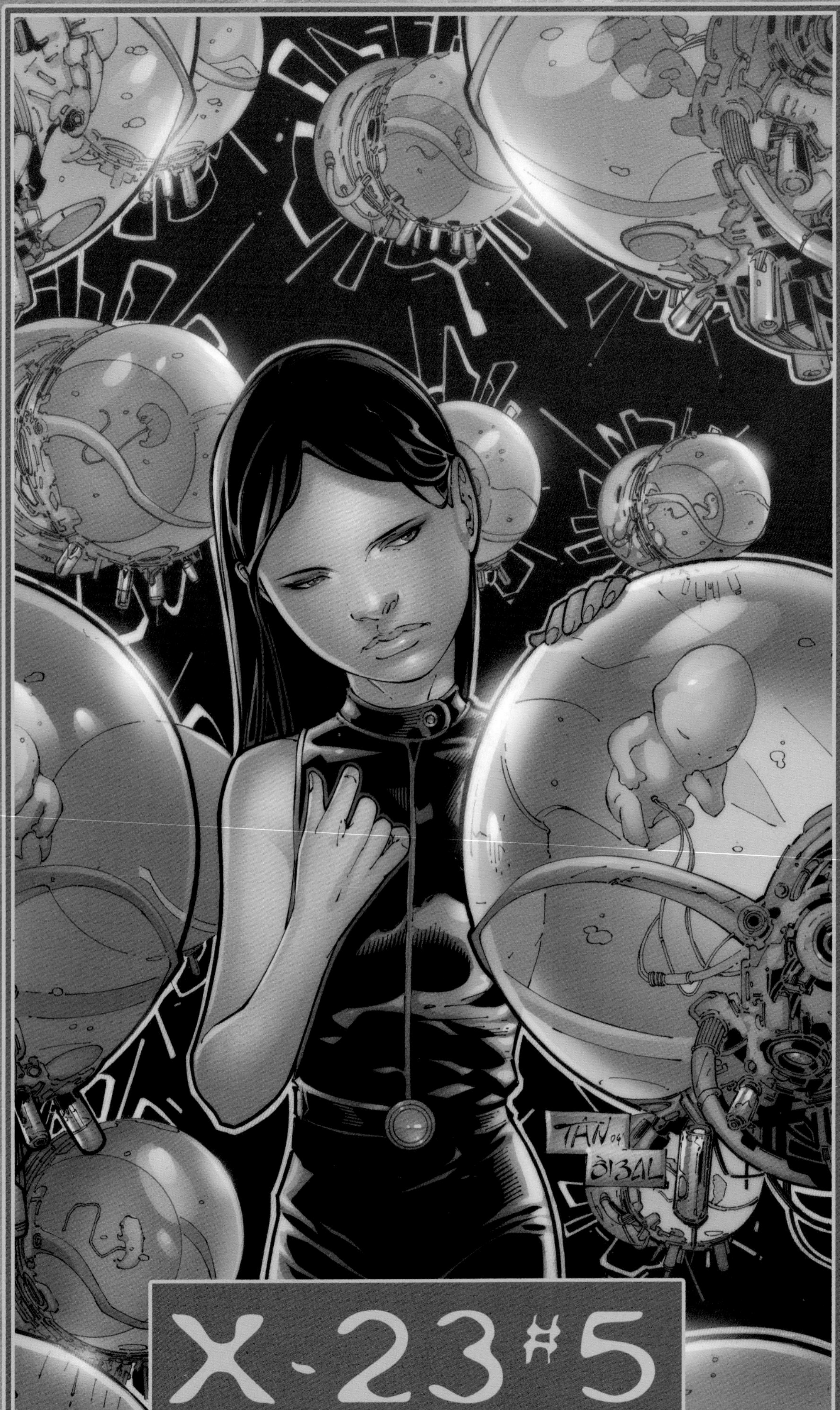
TAN 04
SIBAL
X-23 #5

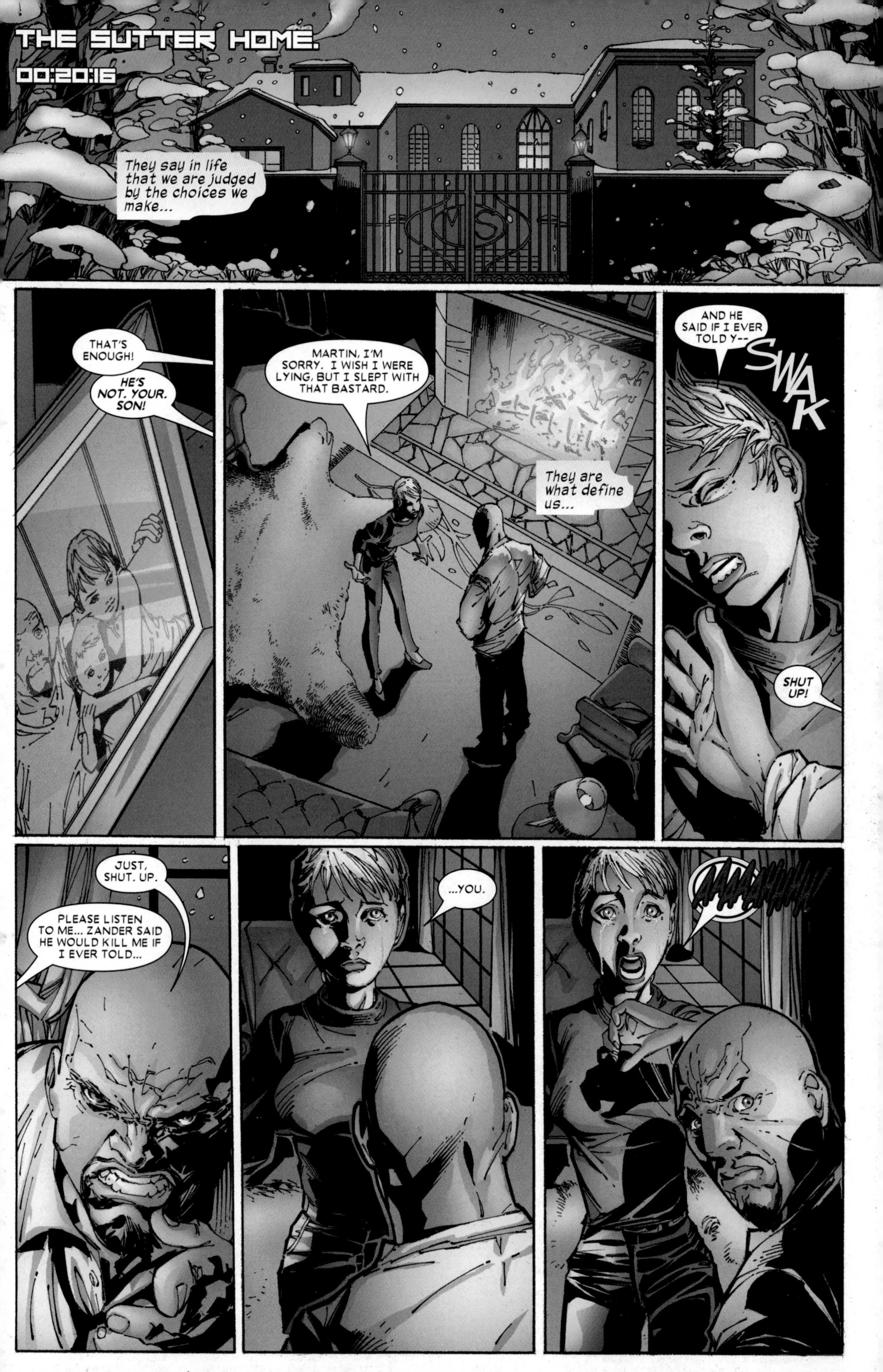
THE SUTTER HOME.
00:20:16
They say in life that we are judged by the choices we make...
THAT'S ENOUGH!
HE'S NOT. YOUR. SON!
MARTIN, I'M SORRY. I WISH I WERE LYING, BUT I SLEPT WITH THAT BASTARD.
They are what define us...
AND HE SAID IF I EVER TOLD Y--
SWAK
SHUT UP!
JUST, SHUT. UP.
PLEASE LISTEN TO ME... ZANDER SAID HE WOULD KILL ME IF I EVER TOLD...
...YOU.
AAAAHHHH!

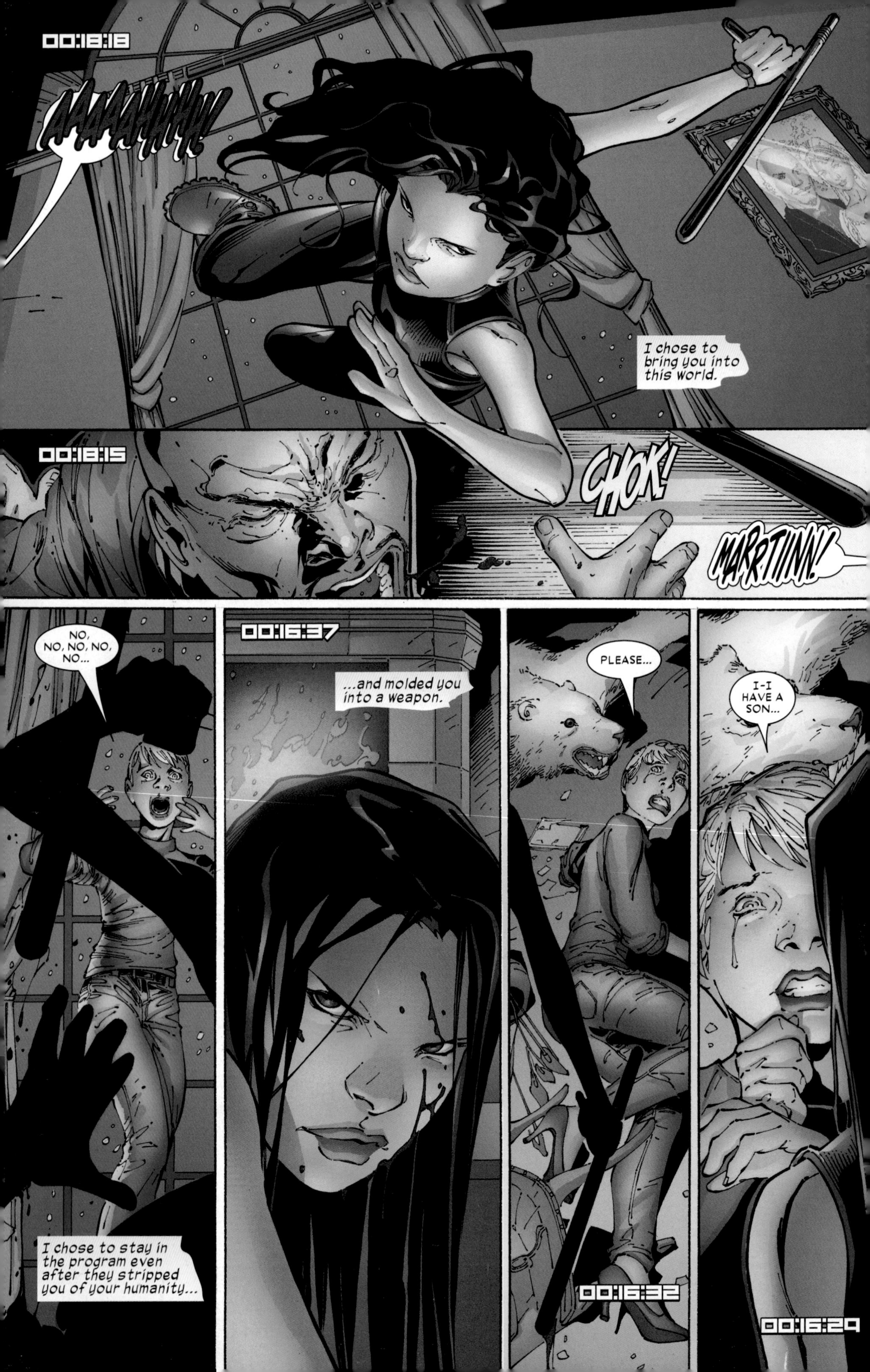

00:18:18
AAAAAHHHH!
I chose to bring you into this world.
00:18:15
CHOK!
MARRTINN!
NO, NO, NO, NO, NO...
I chose to stay in the program even after they stripped you of your humanity...
00:16:37
...and molded you into a weapon.
PLEASE...
00:16:32
I-I HAVE A SON...
00:16:29

00:11:58

-GASP!-

For all
the pain...

I'm responsible
for everything that
has happened...

00:12:21

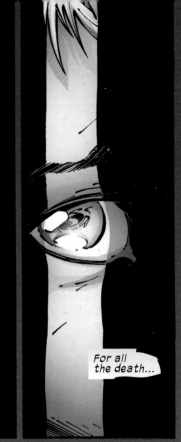

For all
the death...

For everything
you've suffered...

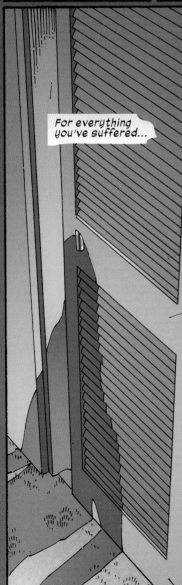

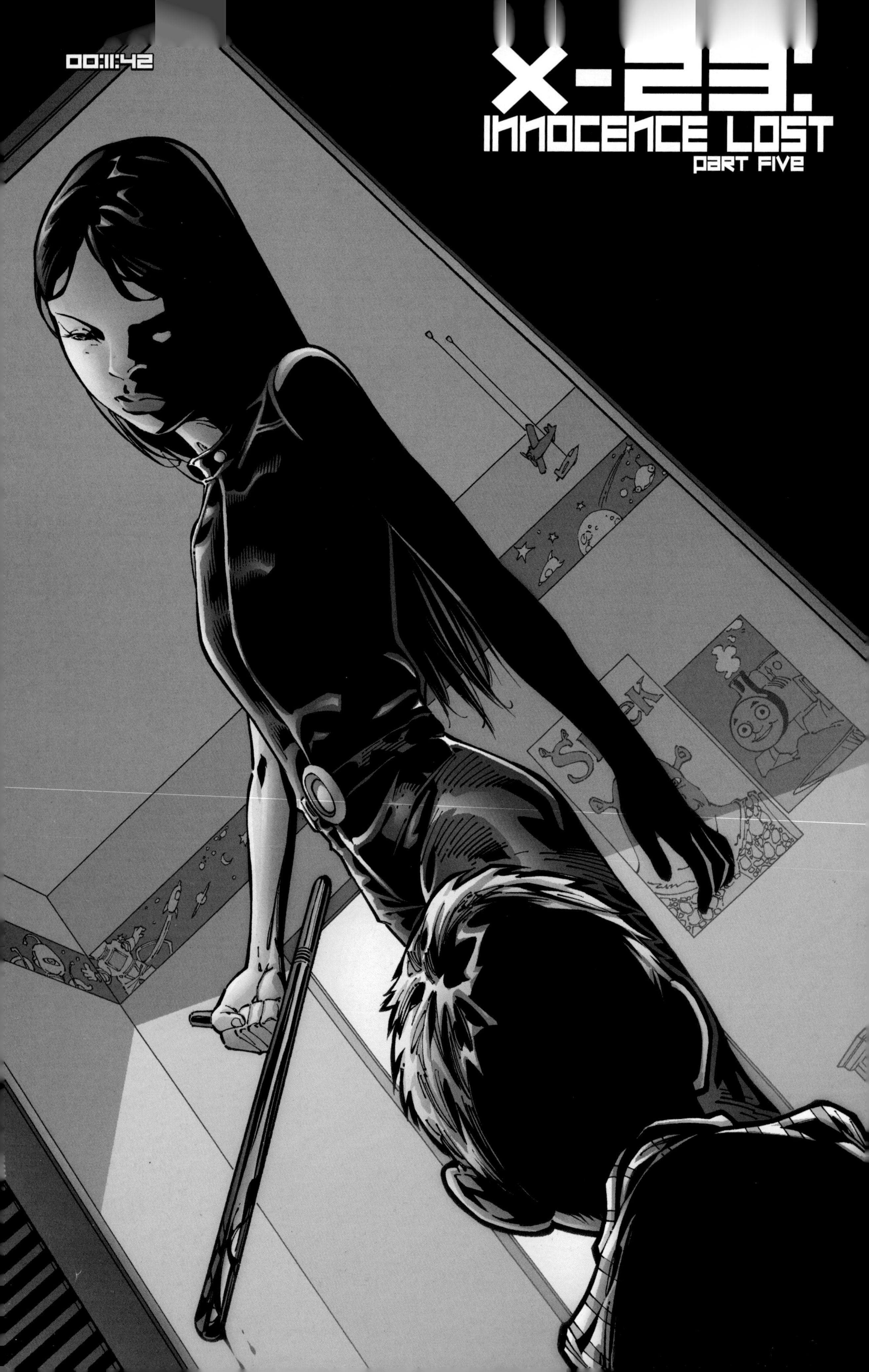

00:11:42
X-23:
INNOCENCE LOST
PART FIVE

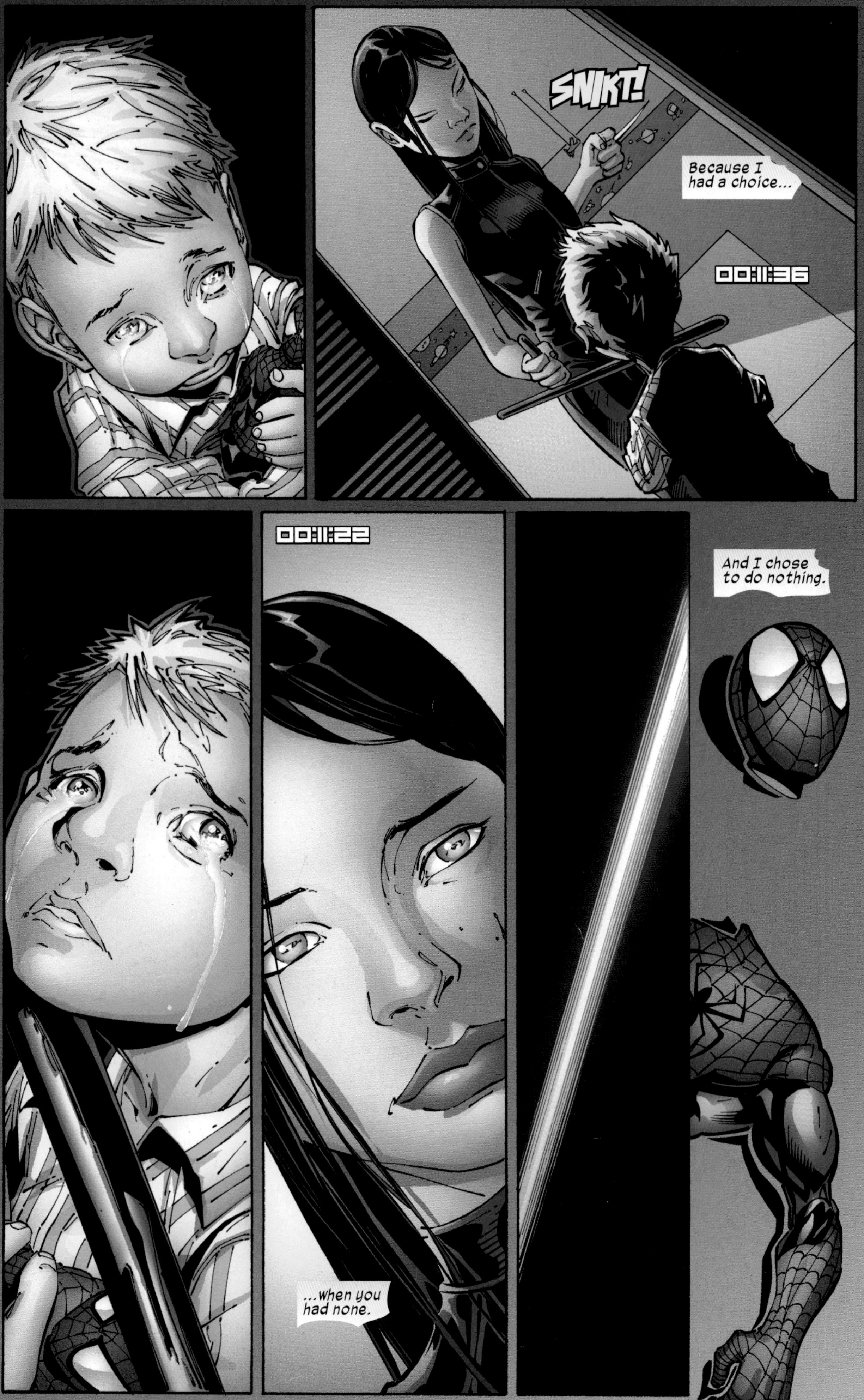
SNIKT!
Because I had a choice...
00:11:36
00:11:22
...when you had none.
And I chose to do nothing.

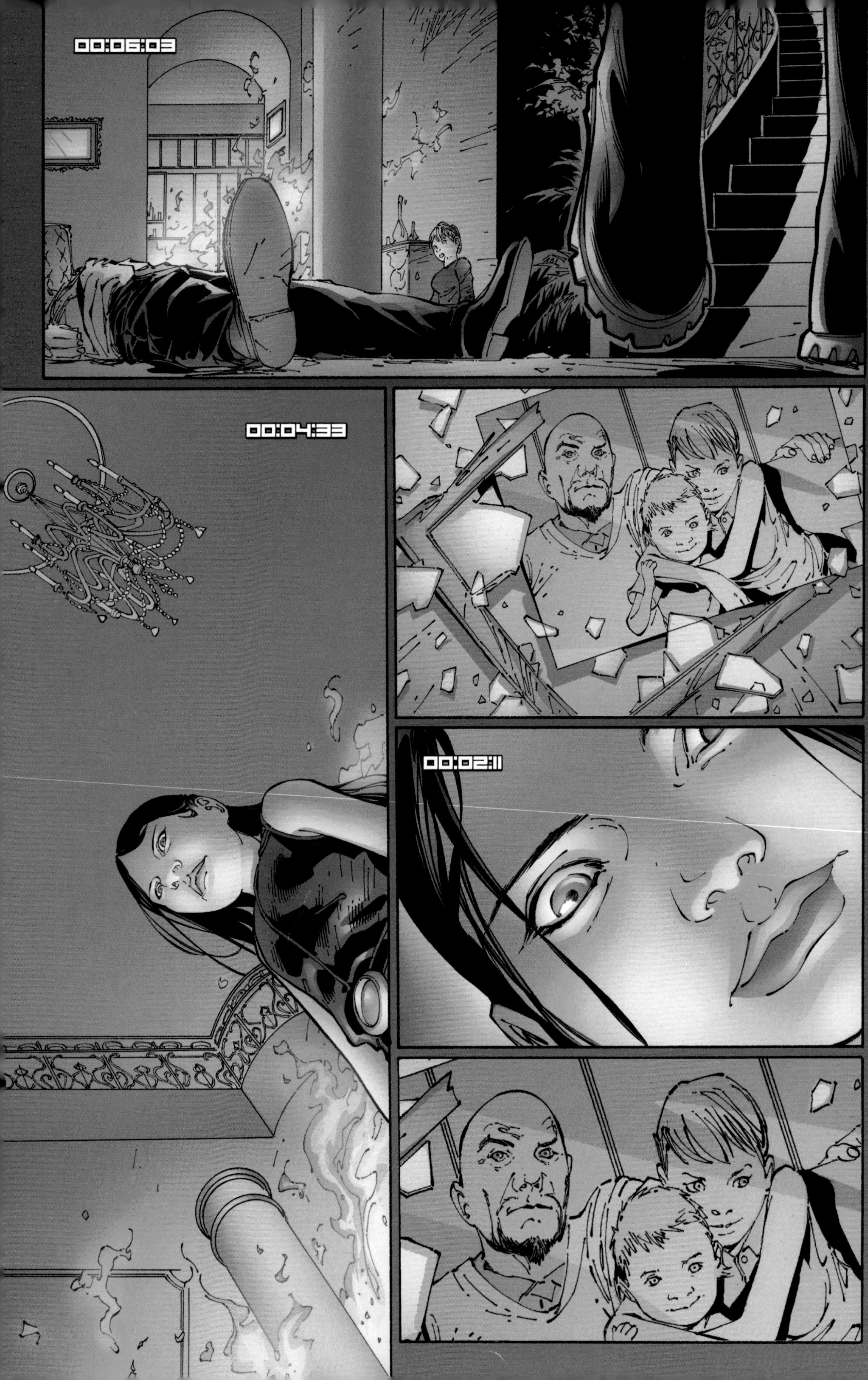
00:06:03
00:04:33
00:02:11

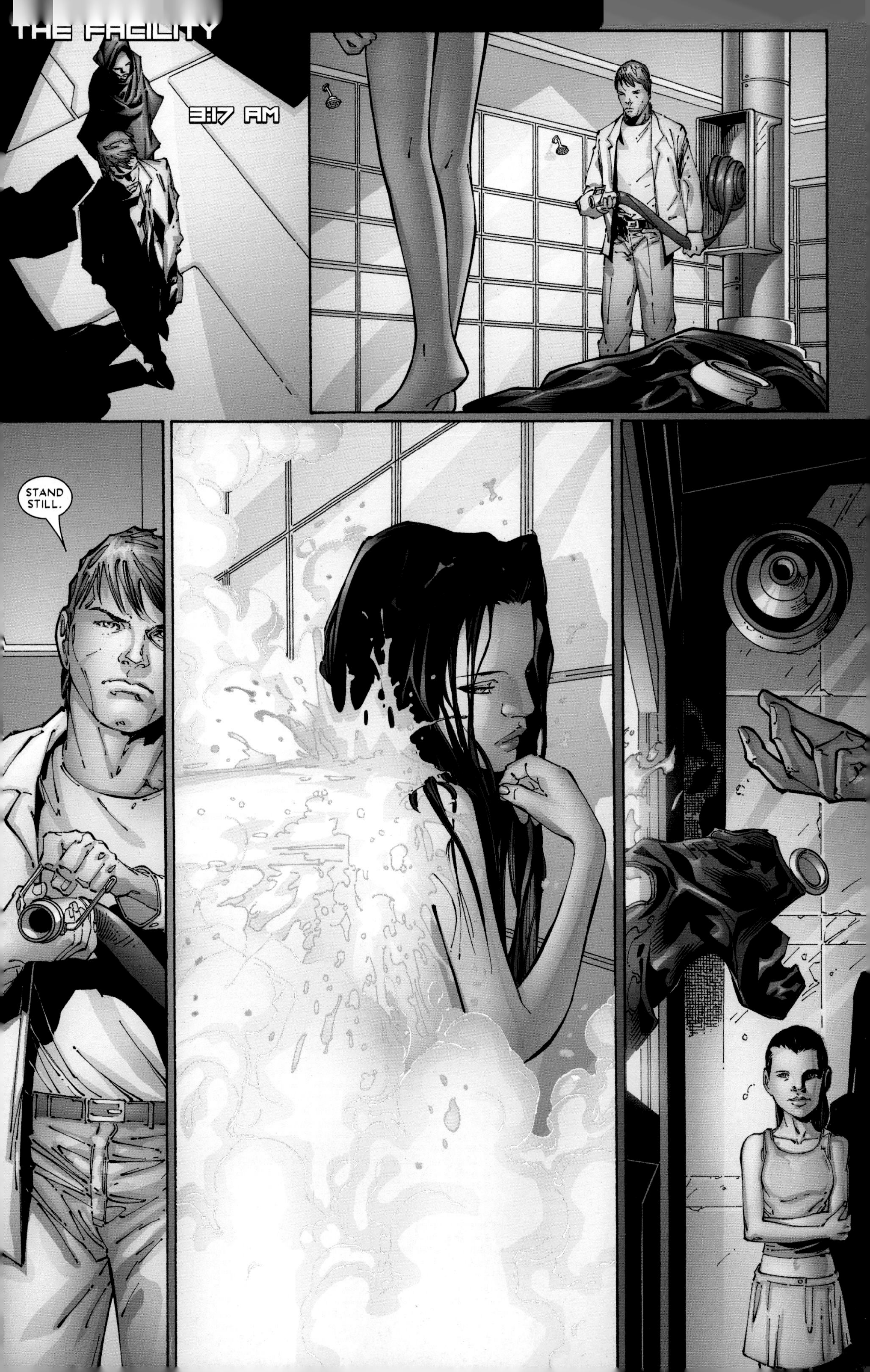
THE FACILITY
3:17 AM
STAND STILL.

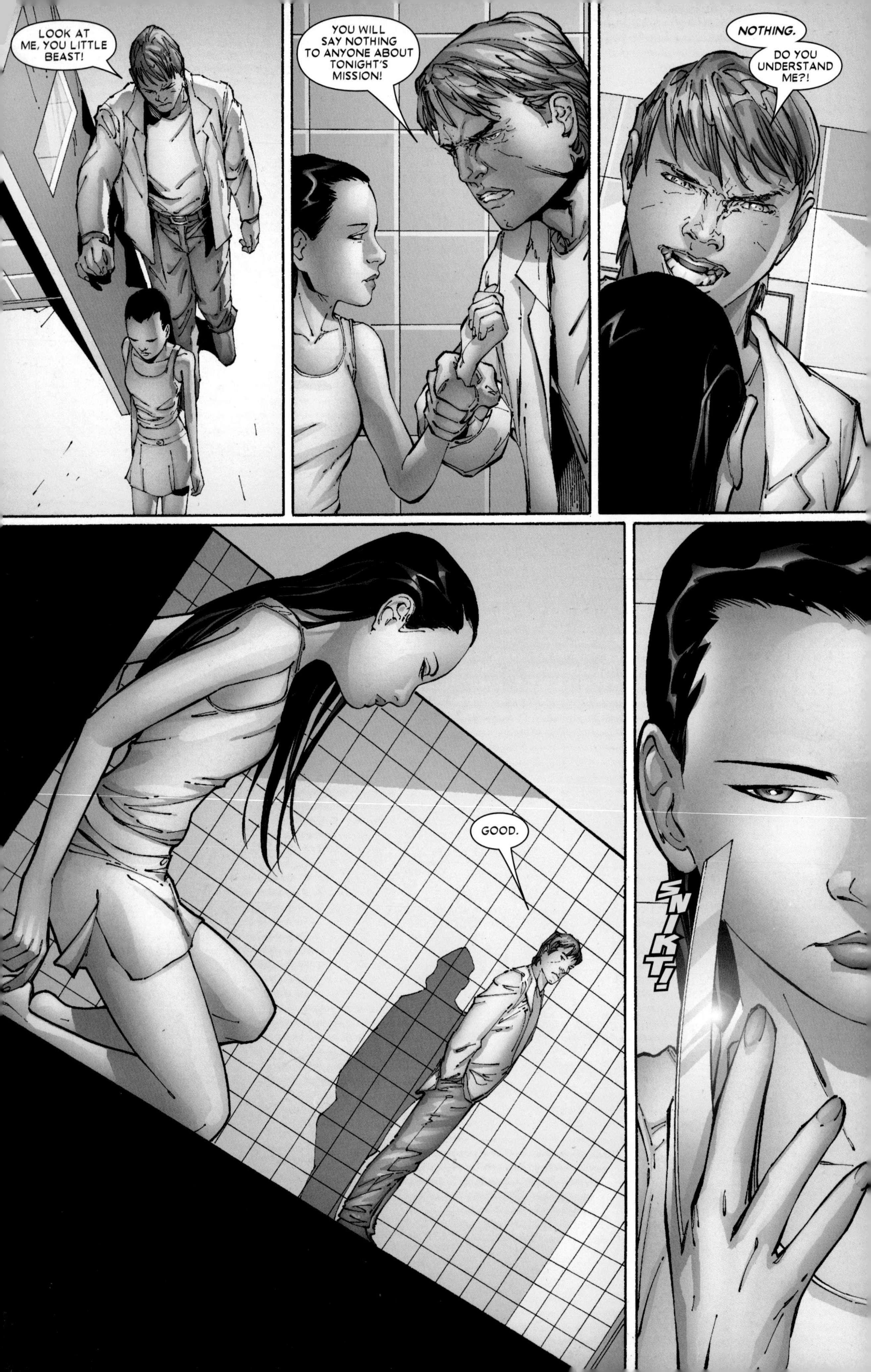
LOOK AT ME, YOU LITTLE BEAST!
YOU WILL SAY NOTHING TO ANYONE ABOUT TONIGHT'S MISSION!
NOTHING.
DO YOU UNDERSTAND ME?!
GOOD.
SNIKT!

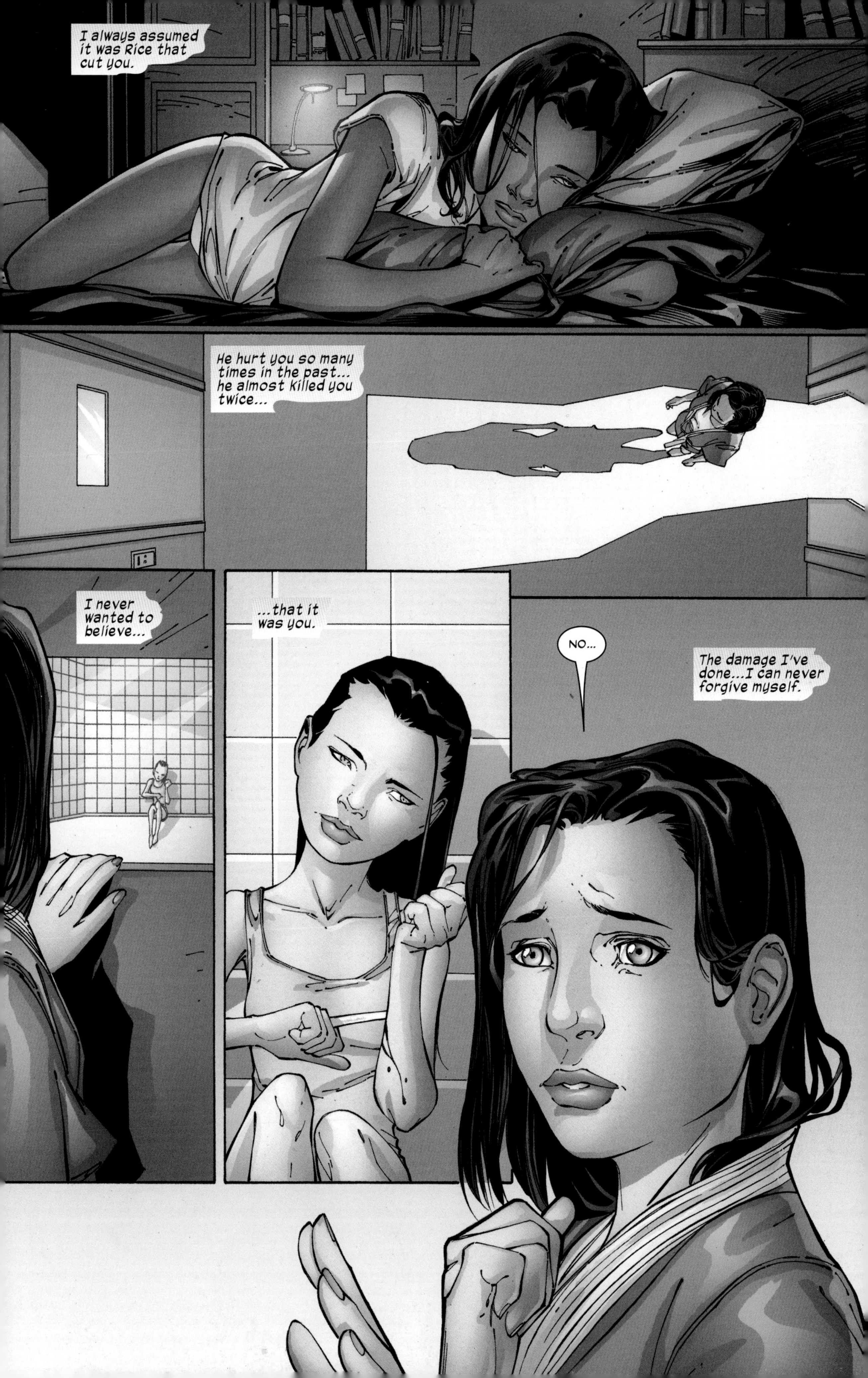
I always assumed it was Rice that cut you.
He hurt you so many times in the past... he almost killed you twice...
I never wanted to believe...
...that it was you.
NO...
The damage I've done...I can never forgive myself.

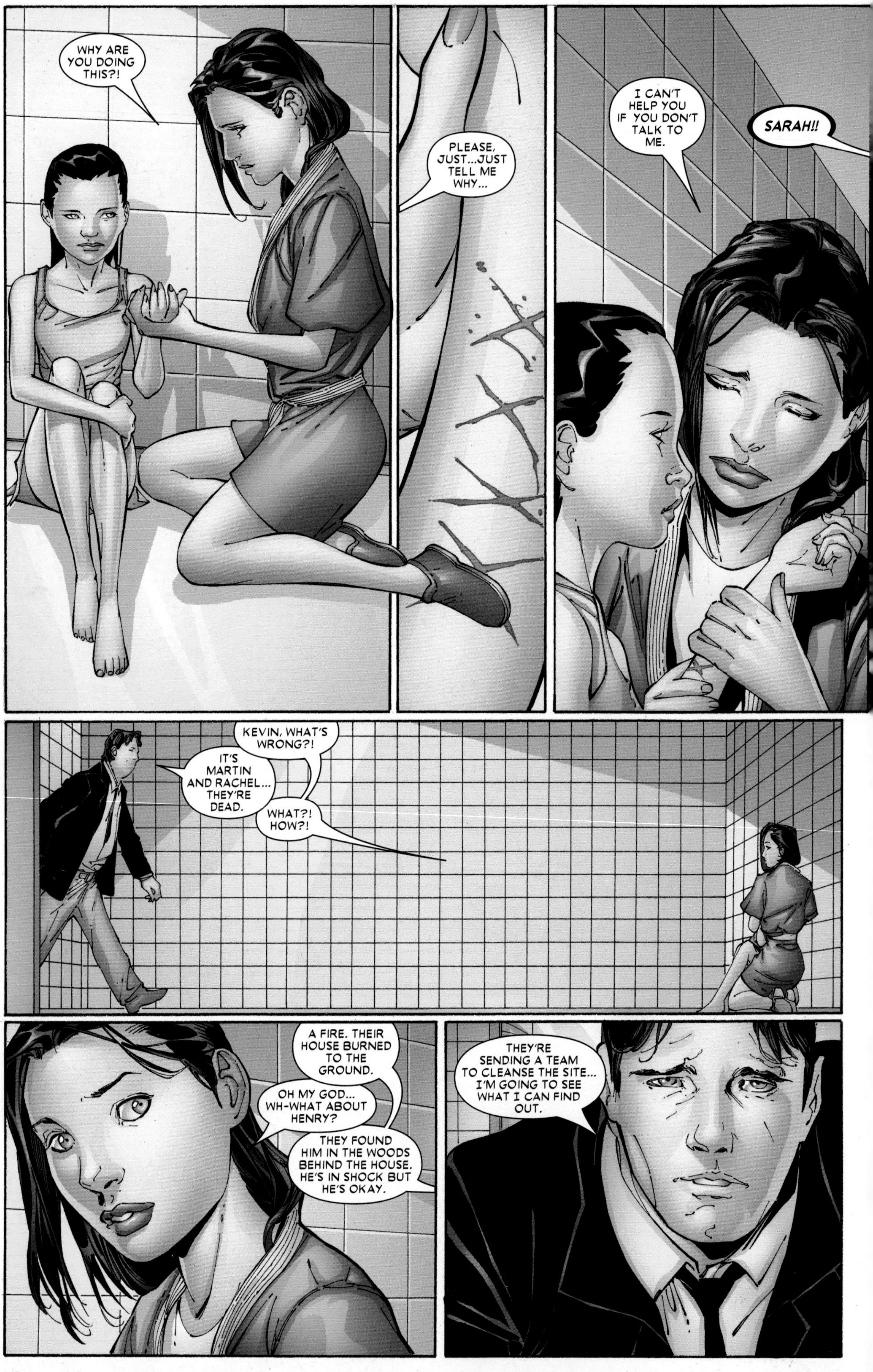

WHY ARE YOU DOING THIS?!
PLEASE, JUST...JUST TELL ME WHY...
I CAN'T HELP YOU IF YOU DON'T TALK TO ME.
SARAH!!
KEVIN, WHAT'S WRONG?!
IT'S MARTIN AND RACHEL... THEY'RE DEAD.
WHAT?! HOW?!
A FIRE. THEIR HOUSE BURNED TO THE GROUND.
OH MY GOD... WH-WHAT ABOUT HENRY?
THEY FOUND HIM IN THE WOODS BEHIND THE HOUSE. HE'S IN SHOCK BUT HE'S OKAY.
THEY'RE SENDING A TEAM TO CLEANSE THE SITE... I'M GOING TO SEE WHAT I CAN FIND OUT.

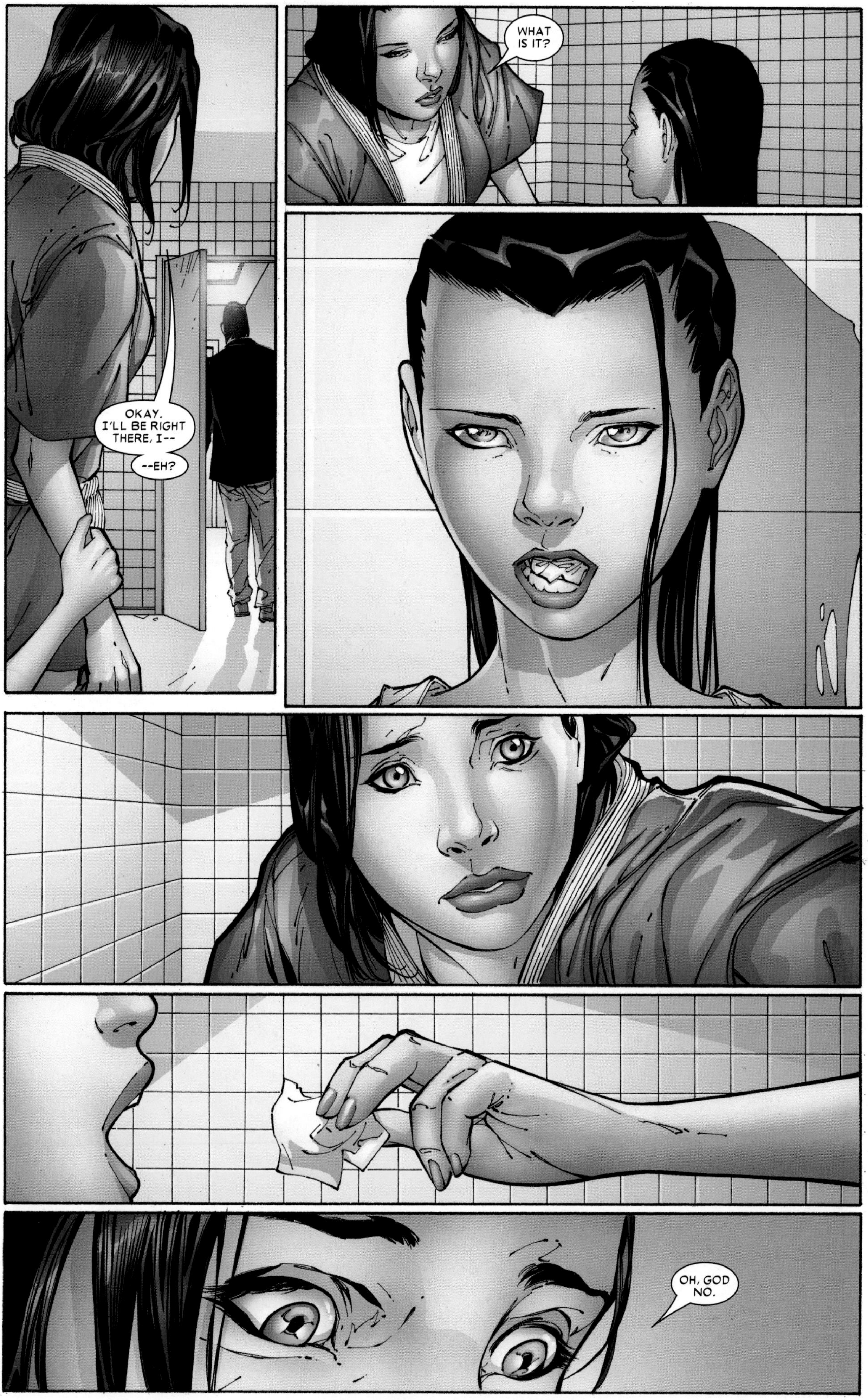
OKAY. I'LL BE RIGHT THERE, I--
--EH?
WHAT IS IT?
OH, GOD NO.

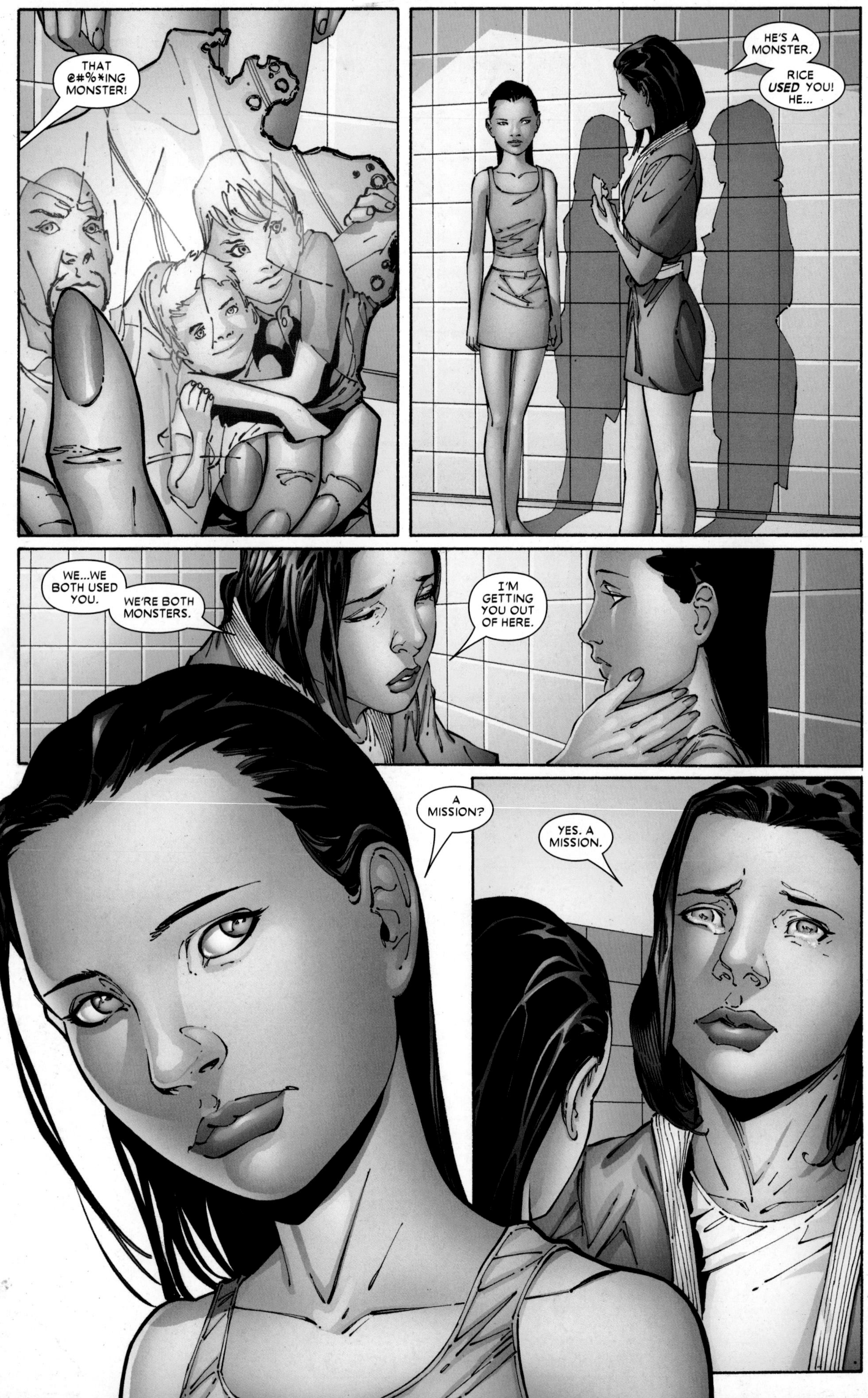
THAT @#%*ING MONSTER!
HE'S A MONSTER.
RICE USED YOU! HE...
WE...WE BOTH USED YOU.
WE'RE BOTH MONSTERS.
I'M GETTING YOU OUT OF HERE.
A MISSION?
YES. A MISSION.

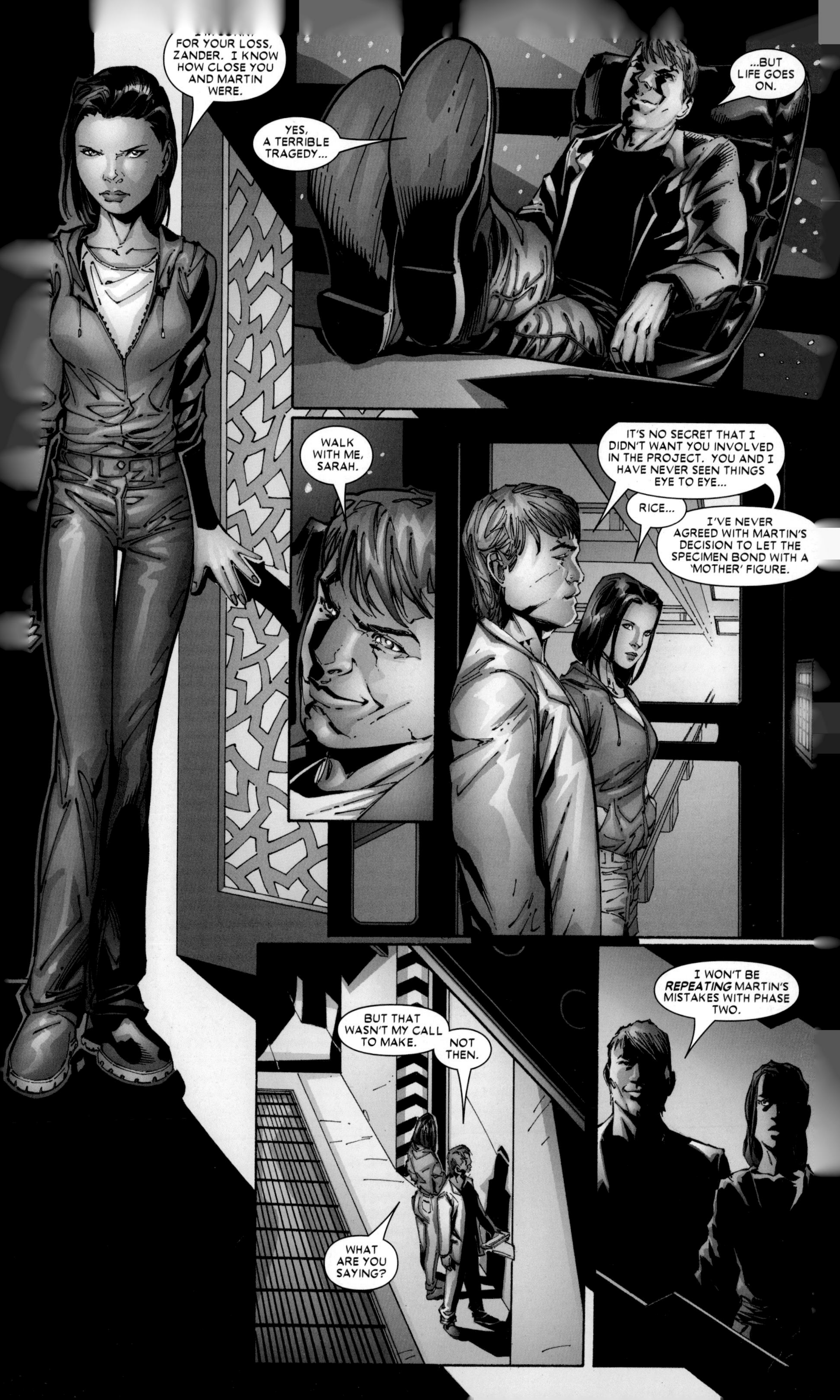
FOR YOUR LOSS, ZANDER. I KNOW HOW CLOSE YOU AND MARTIN WERE.
YES, A TERRIBLE TRAGEDY...
...BUT LIFE GOES ON.
WALK WITH ME, SARAH.
IT'S NO SECRET THAT I DIDN'T WANT YOU INVOLVED IN THE PROJECT. YOU AND I HAVE NEVER SEEN THINGS EYE TO EYE...
RICE...
I'VE NEVER AGREED WITH MARTIN'S DECISION TO LET THE SPECIMEN BOND WITH A 'MOTHER' FIGURE.
BUT THAT WASN'T MY CALL TO MAKE.
NOT THEN.
WHAT ARE YOU SAYING?
I WON'T BE *REPEATING* MARTIN'S MISTAKES WITH PHASE TWO.

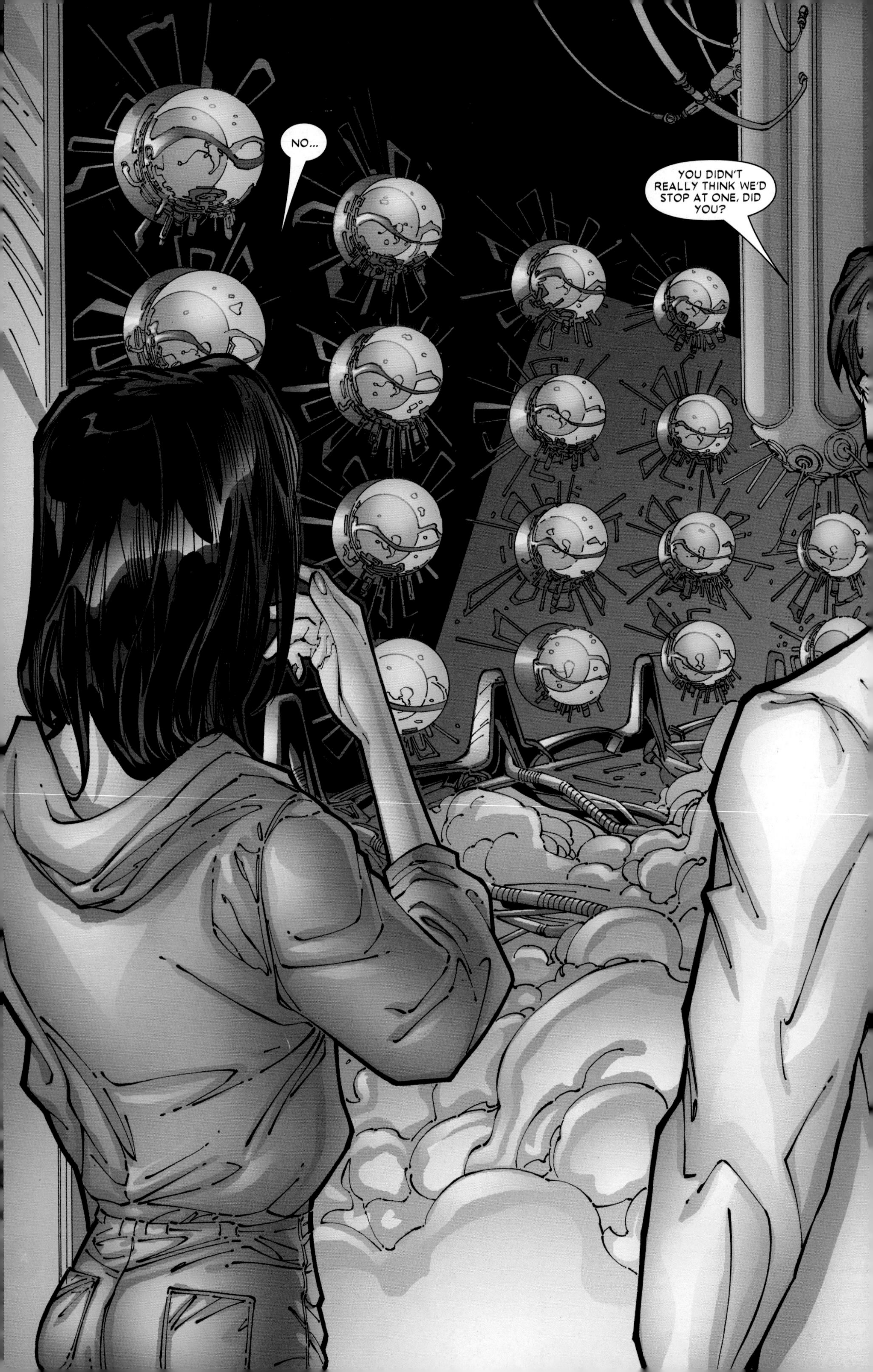
NO...
YOU DIDN'T REALLY THINK WE'D STOP AT ONE, DID YOU?

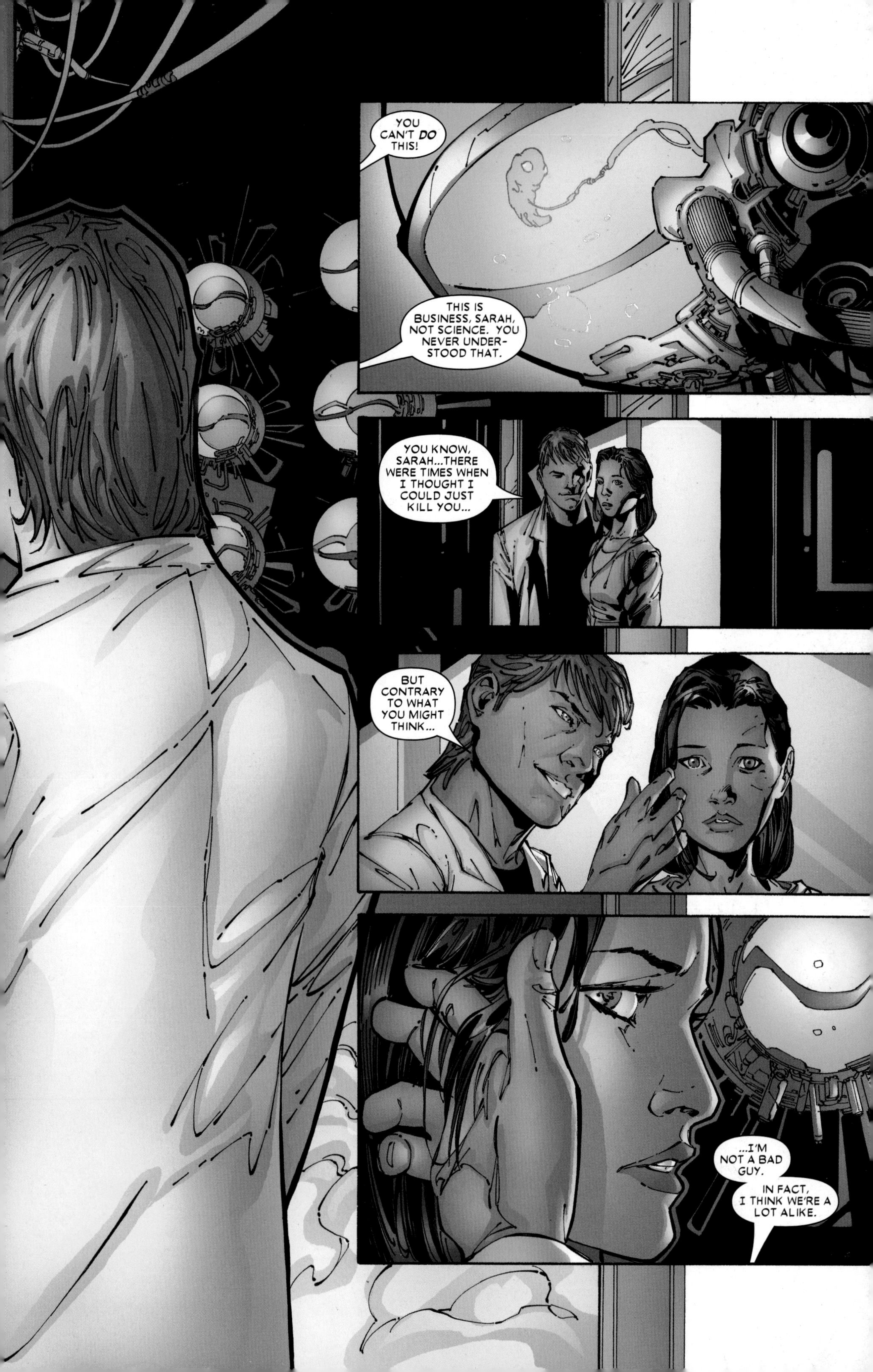
YOU CAN'T DO THIS!
THIS IS BUSINESS, SARAH, NOT SCIENCE. YOU NEVER UNDER-STOOD THAT.
YOU KNOW, SARAH...THERE WERE TIMES WHEN I THOUGHT I COULD JUST KILL YOU...
BUT CONTRARY TO WHAT YOU MIGHT THINK...
...I'M NOT A BAD GUY.
IN FACT, I THINK WE'RE A LOT ALIKE.

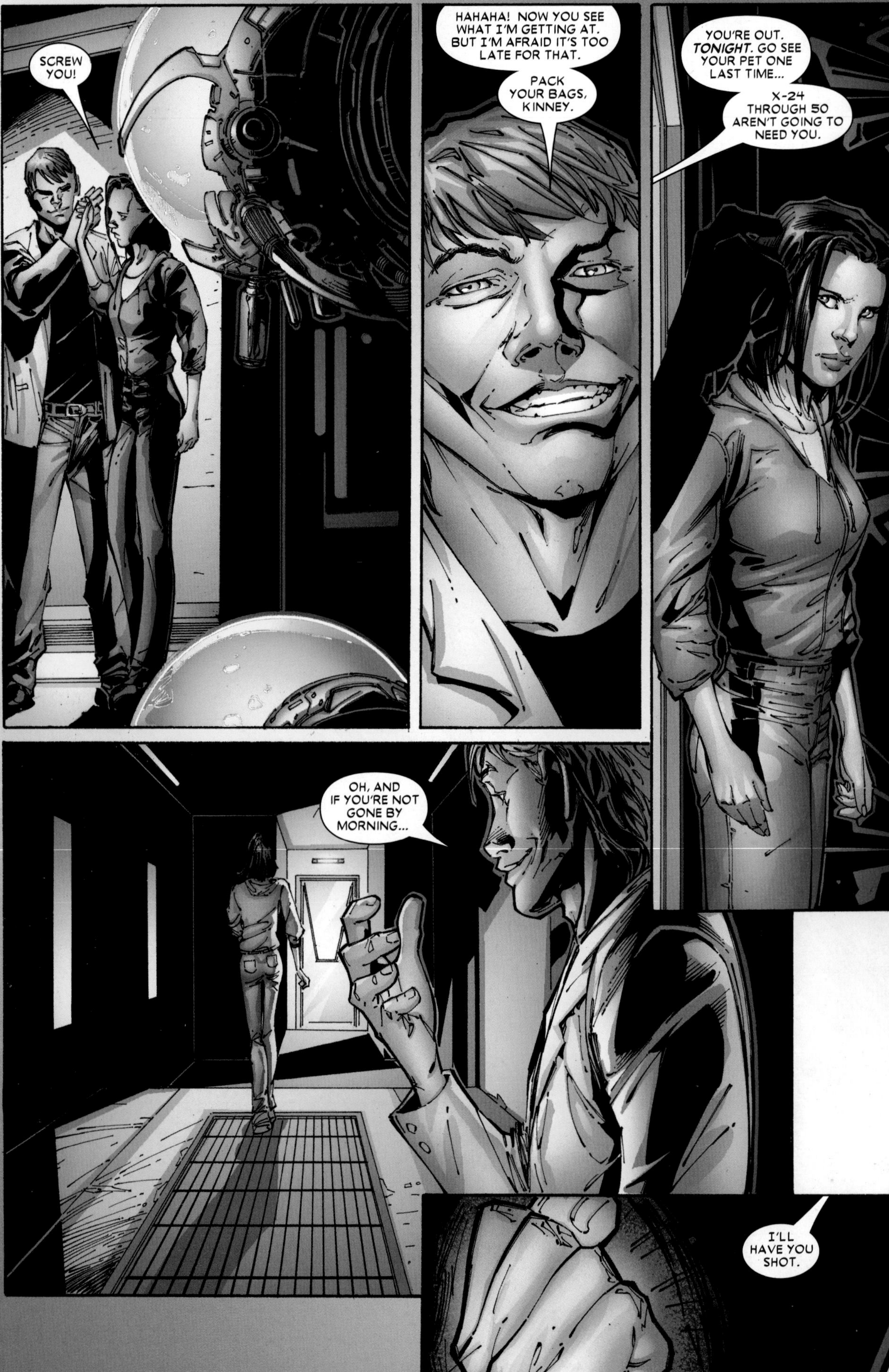
SCREW YOU!
HAHAHA! NOW YOU SEE WHAT I'M GETTING AT. BUT I'M AFRAID IT'S TOO LATE FOR THAT.
PACK YOUR BAGS, KINNEY.
YOU'RE OUT. *TONIGHT.* GO SEE YOUR PET ONE LAST TIME...
X-24 THROUGH 50 AREN'T GOING TO NEED YOU.
OH, AND IF YOU'RE NOT GONE BY MORNING...
I'LL HAVE YOU SHOT.

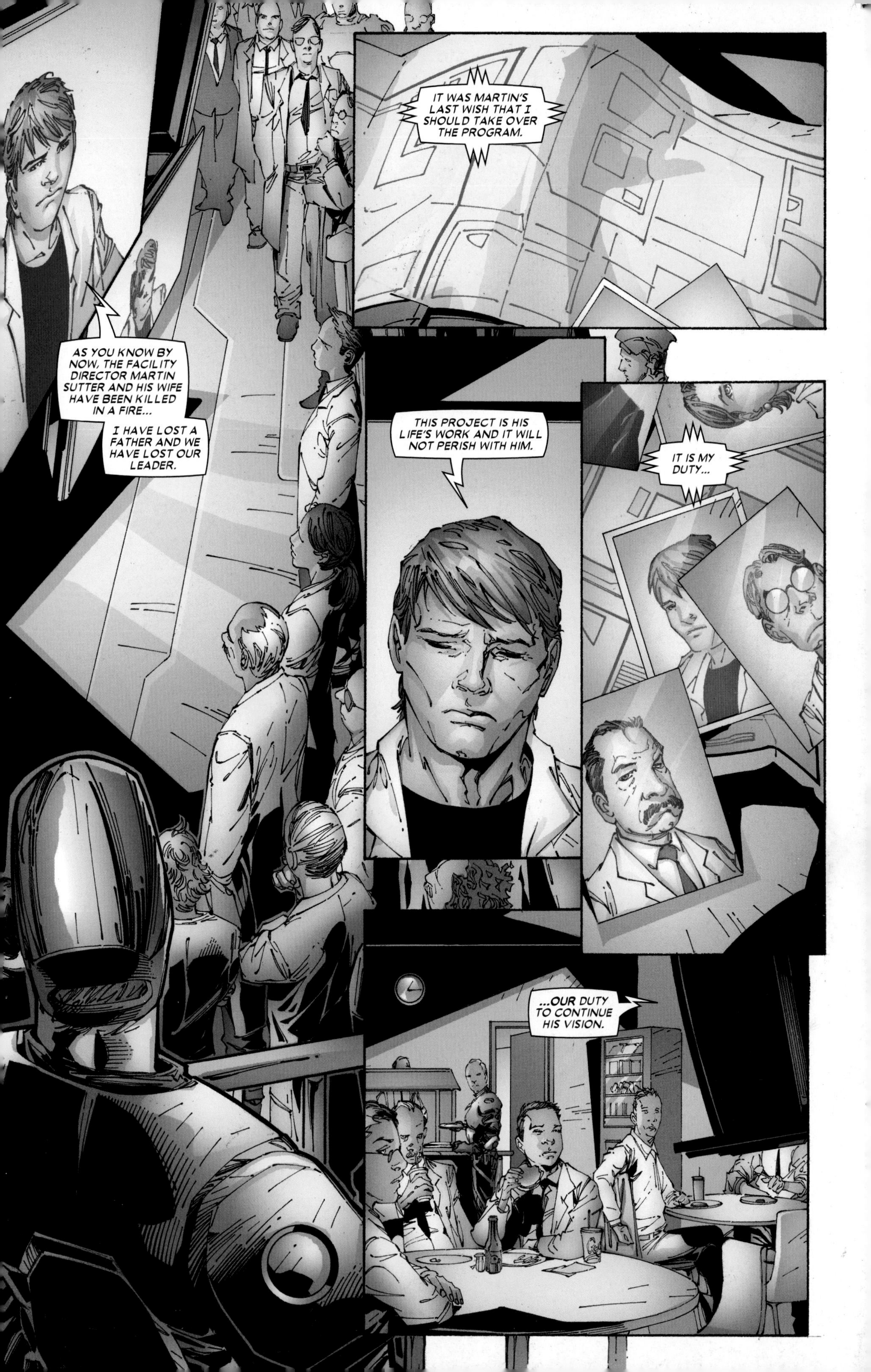
AS YOU KNOW BY NOW, THE FACILITY DIRECTOR MARTIN SUTTER AND HIS WIFE HAVE BEEN KILLED IN A FIRE...
I HAVE LOST A FATHER AND WE HAVE LOST OUR LEADER.
IT WAS MARTIN'S LAST WISH THAT I SHOULD TAKE OVER THE PROGRAM.
THIS PROJECT IS HIS LIFE'S WORK AND IT WILL NOT PERISH WITH HIM.
IT IS MY DUTY...
...OUR DUTY TO CONTINUE HIS VISION.

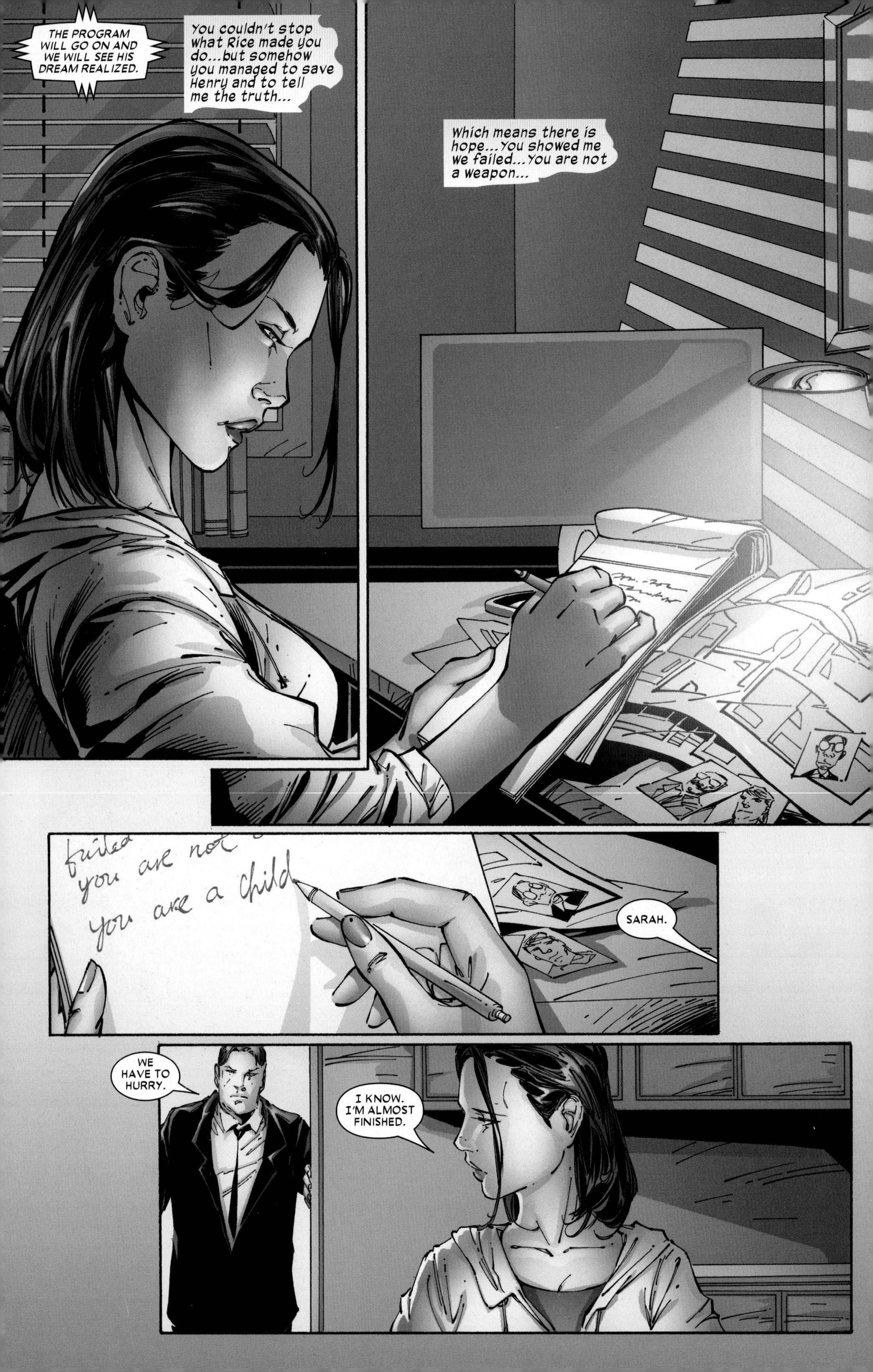
THE PROGRAM WILL GO ON AND WE WILL SEE HIS DREAM REALIZED.
You couldn't stop what Rice made you do...but somehow you managed to save Henry and to tell me the truth...
Which means there is hope...You showed me we failed...You are not a weapon...
failed
you are not
you are a child
SARAH.
WE HAVE TO HURRY.
I KNOW. I'M ALMOST FINISHED.

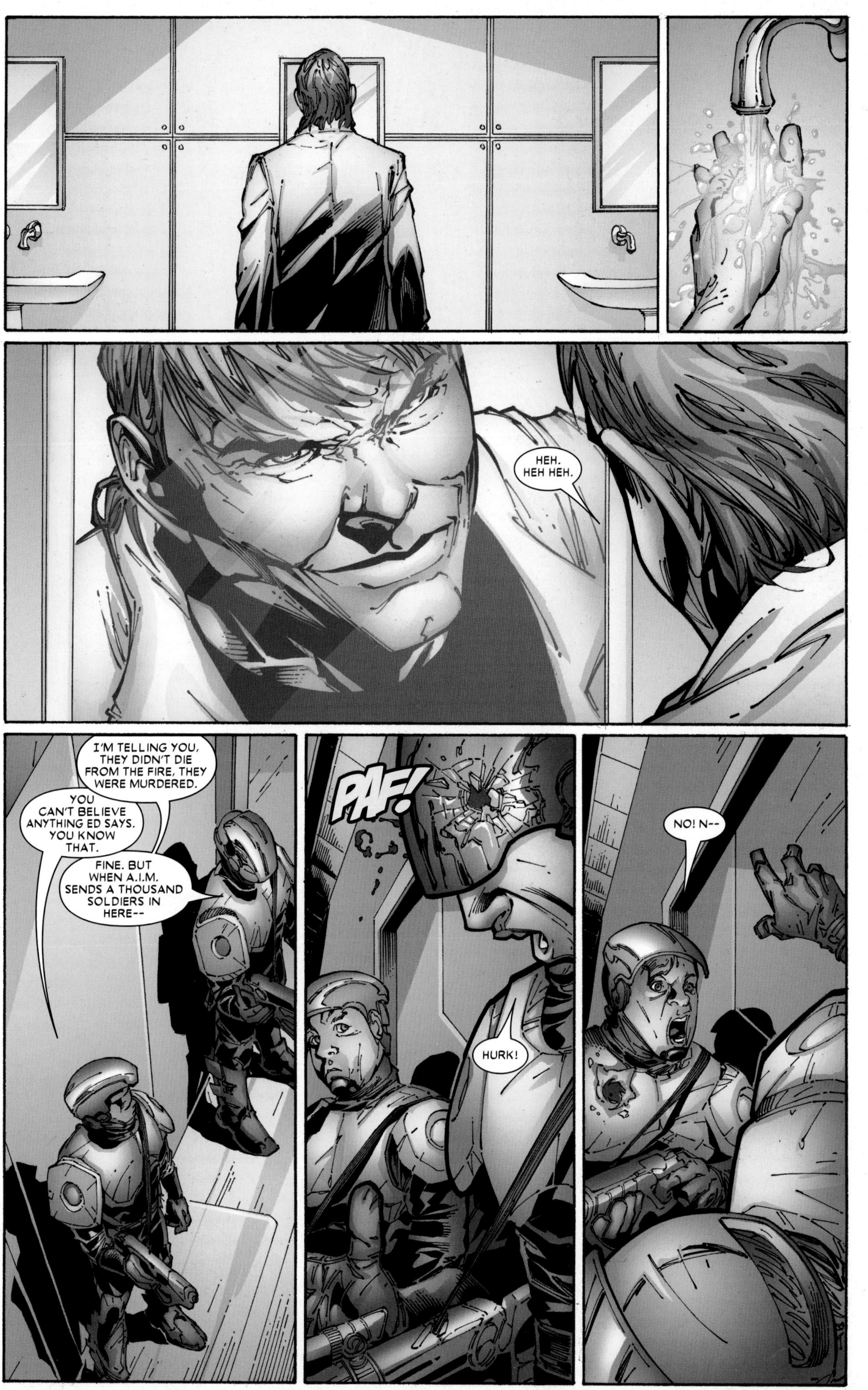

HEH.
HEH HEH.
I'M TELLING YOU, THEY DIDN'T DIE FROM THE FIRE, THEY WERE MURDERED.
YOU CAN'T BELIEVE ANYTHING ED SAYS. YOU KNOW THAT.
FINE. BUT WHEN A.I.M. SENDS A THOUSAND SOLDIERS IN HERE--
PAF!
HURK!
NO! N--

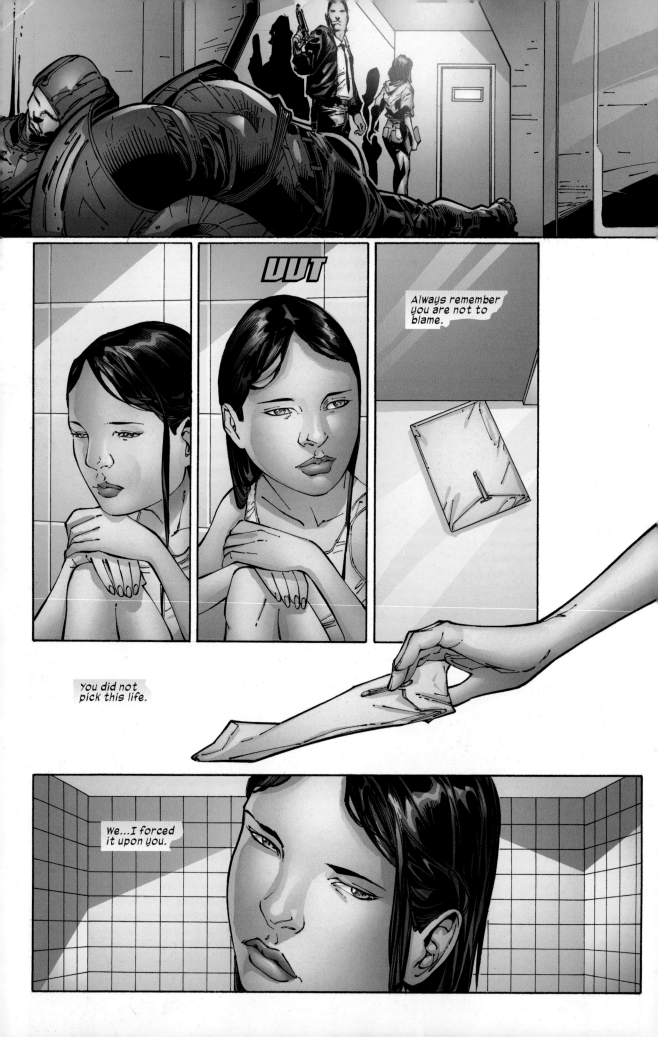

UVT

Always remember you are not to blame.

You did not pick this life.

We...I forced it upon you.

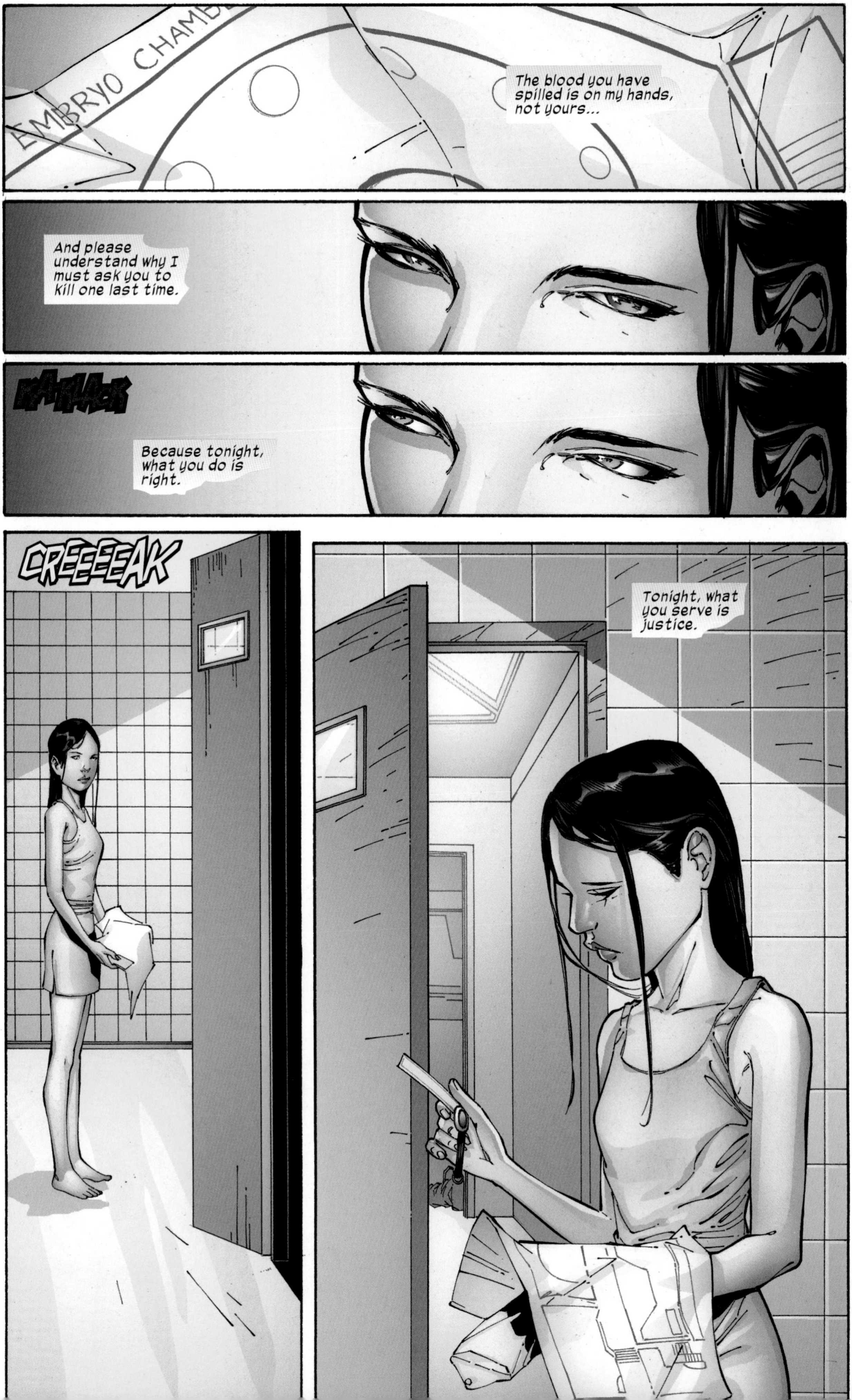
EMBRYO CHAMB
The blood you have spilled is on my hands, not yours...
And please understand why I must ask you to kill one last time.
Because tonight, what you do is right.
CREEEEAK
Tonight, what you serve is justice.

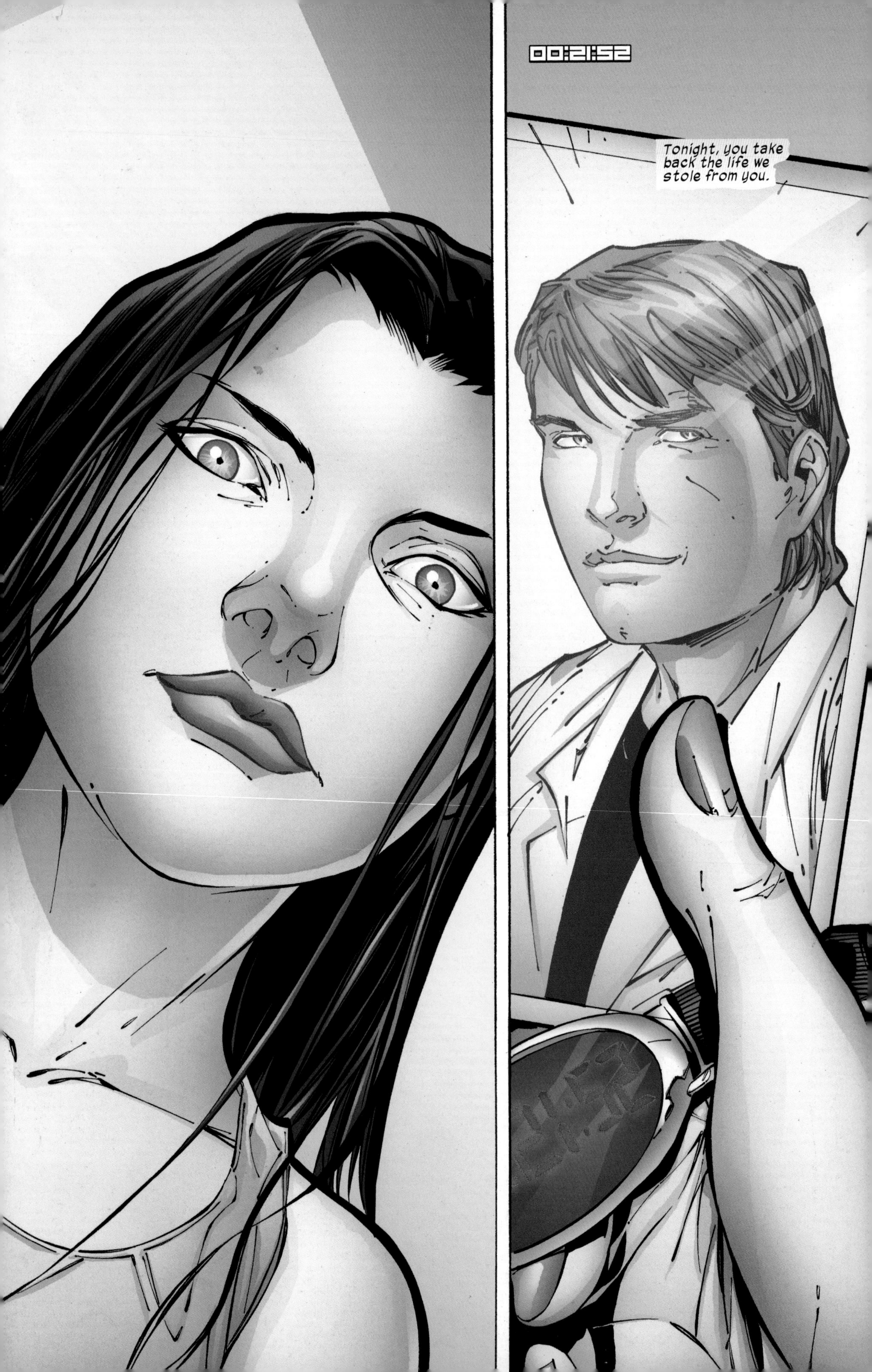
00:21:52
Tonight, you take back the life we stole from you.

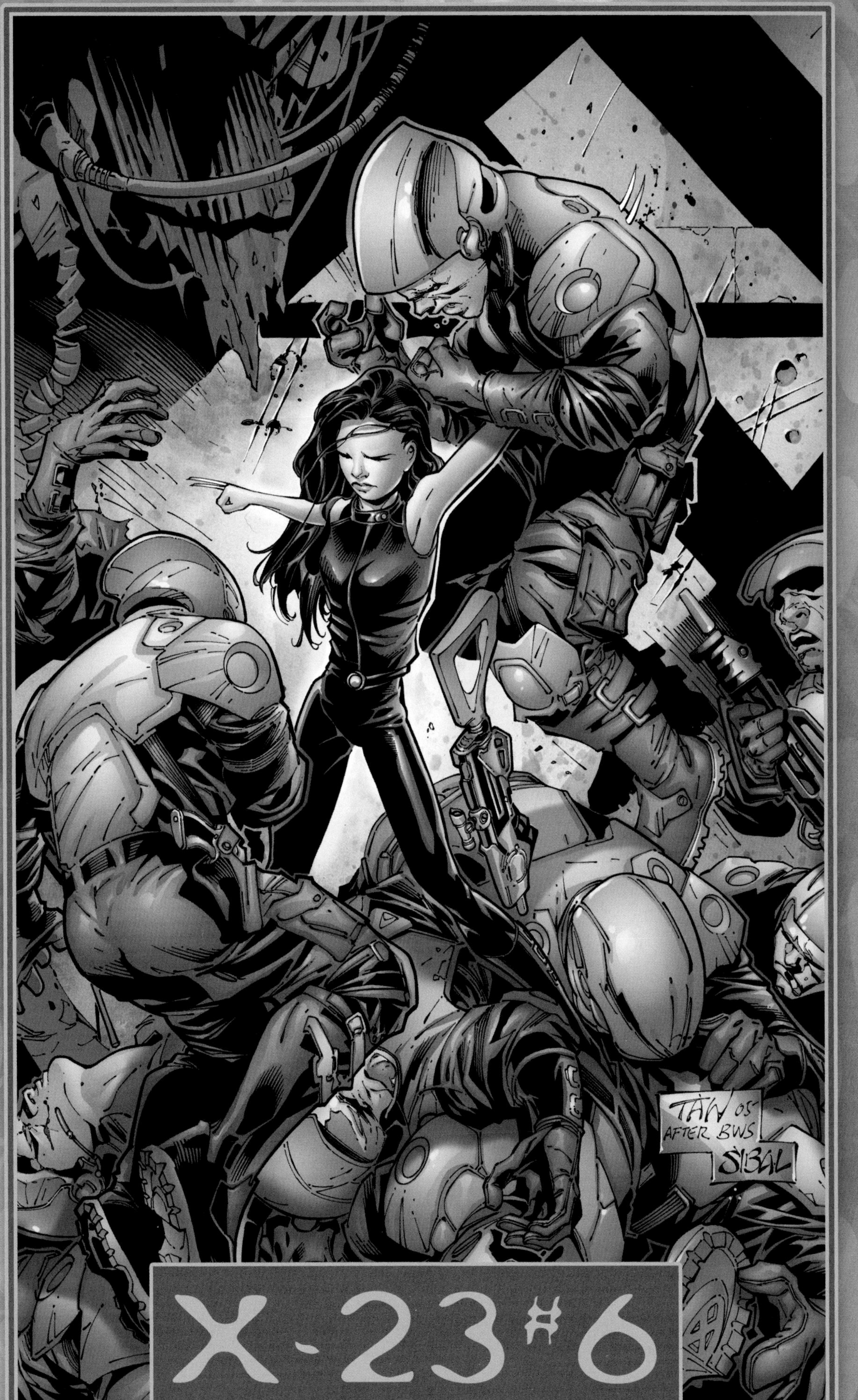
TAN 05
AFTER BWS
SIBAL
X-23 #6

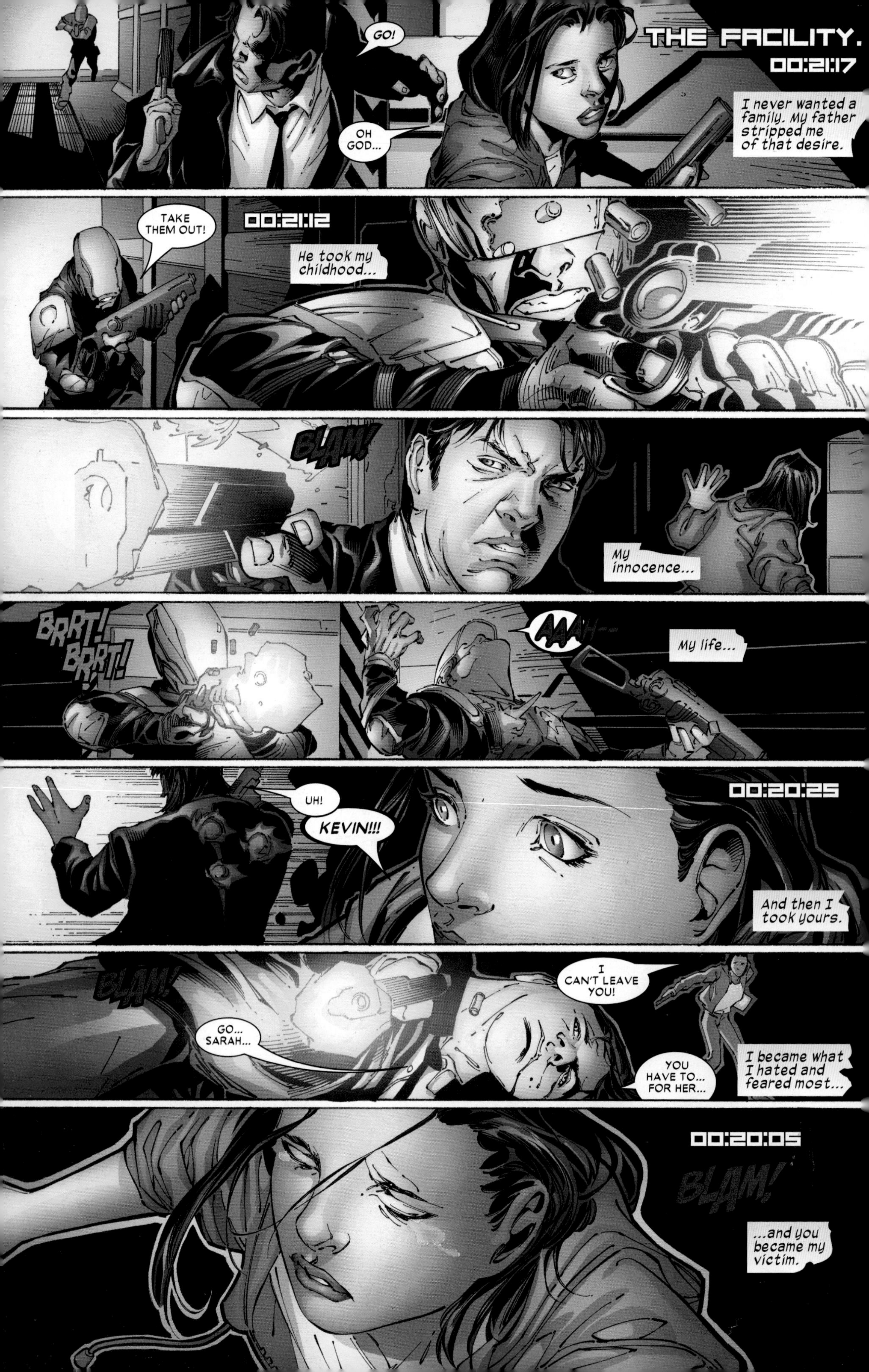
THE FACILITY.
00:21:17
GO!
OH GOD...
I never wanted a family. My father stripped me of that desire.
TAKE THEM OUT!
00:21:12
He took my childhood...
BLAM!
My innocence...
BRRT! BRRT!
AAAH
My life...
UH!
KEVIN!!!
00:20:25
And then I took yours.
BLAM!
I CAN'T LEAVE YOU!
GO... SARAH...
YOU HAVE TO... FOR HER...
I became what I hated and feared most...
00:20:05
BLAM!
...and you became my victim.

SECTOR ELEVEN, REPORT. I REPEAT...

VMMM

WHA--

But then you showed me hope.

I'M SORRY.

BLAM!

Not when you saved Megan, but when you saved Henry.

`00:19:17`

You showed me that we can choose to be something other than what we have been forced to be...

`00:19:15`

PLEASE, GOD...

That we can be something better than what we believe we are.

`00:19:01`

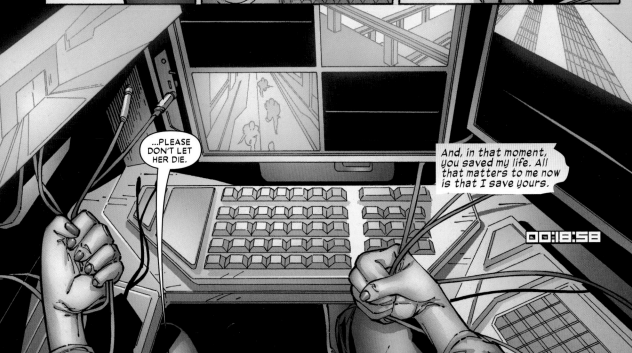

...PLEASE DON'T LET HER DIE.

And, in that moment, you saved my life. All that matters to me now is that I save yours.

`00:18:58`

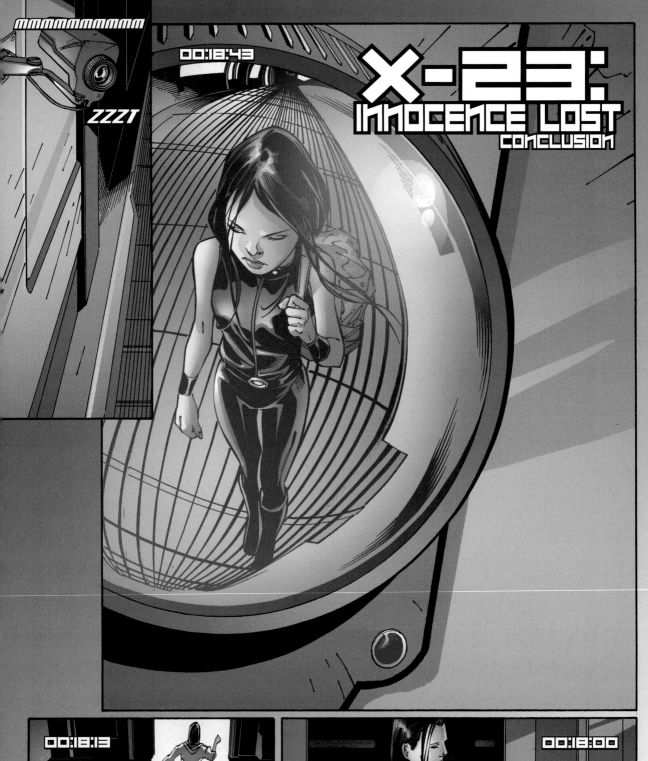

X-23:
INNOCENCE LOST
CONCLUSION

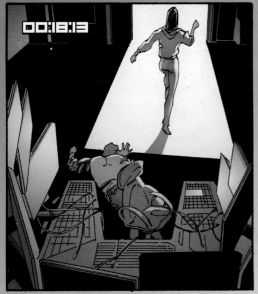

00:18:13

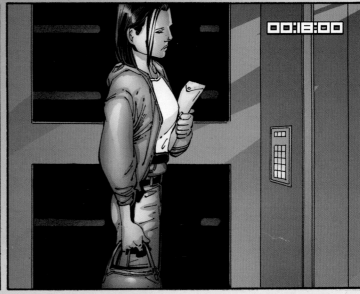

00:18:00

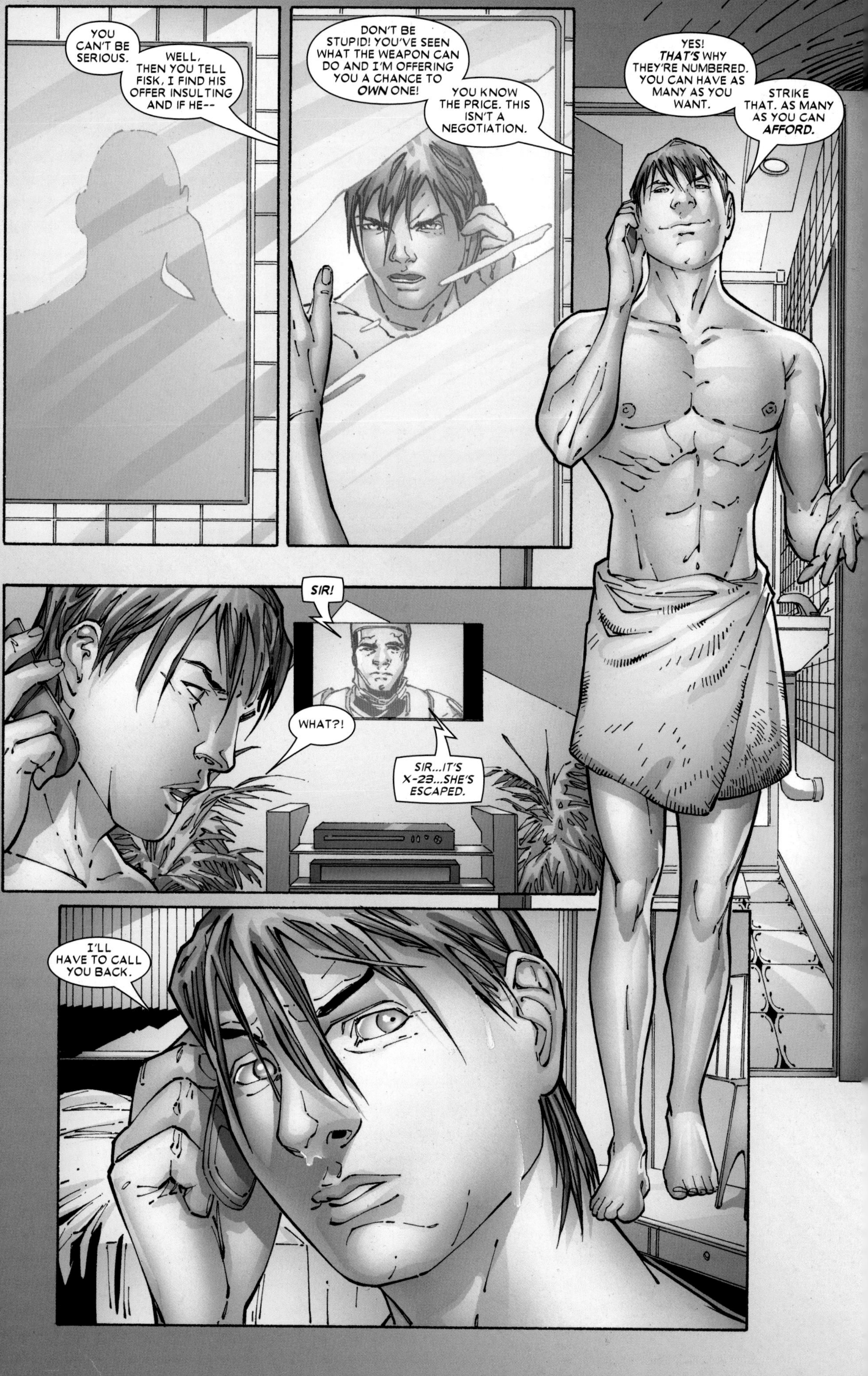
YOU CAN'T BE SERIOUS.
WELL, THEN YOU TELL FISK, I FIND HIS OFFER INSULTING AND IF HE--
DON'T BE STUPID! YOU'VE SEEN WHAT THE WEAPON CAN DO AND I'M OFFERING YOU A CHANCE TO OWN ONE!
YOU KNOW THE PRICE. THIS ISN'T A NEGOTIATION.
YES! THAT'S WHY THEY'RE NUMBERED. YOU CAN HAVE AS MANY AS YOU WANT.
STRIKE THAT. AS MANY AS YOU CAN AFFORD.
SIR!
WHAT?!
SIR...IT'S X-23...SHE'S ESCAPED.
I'LL HAVE TO CALL YOU BACK.

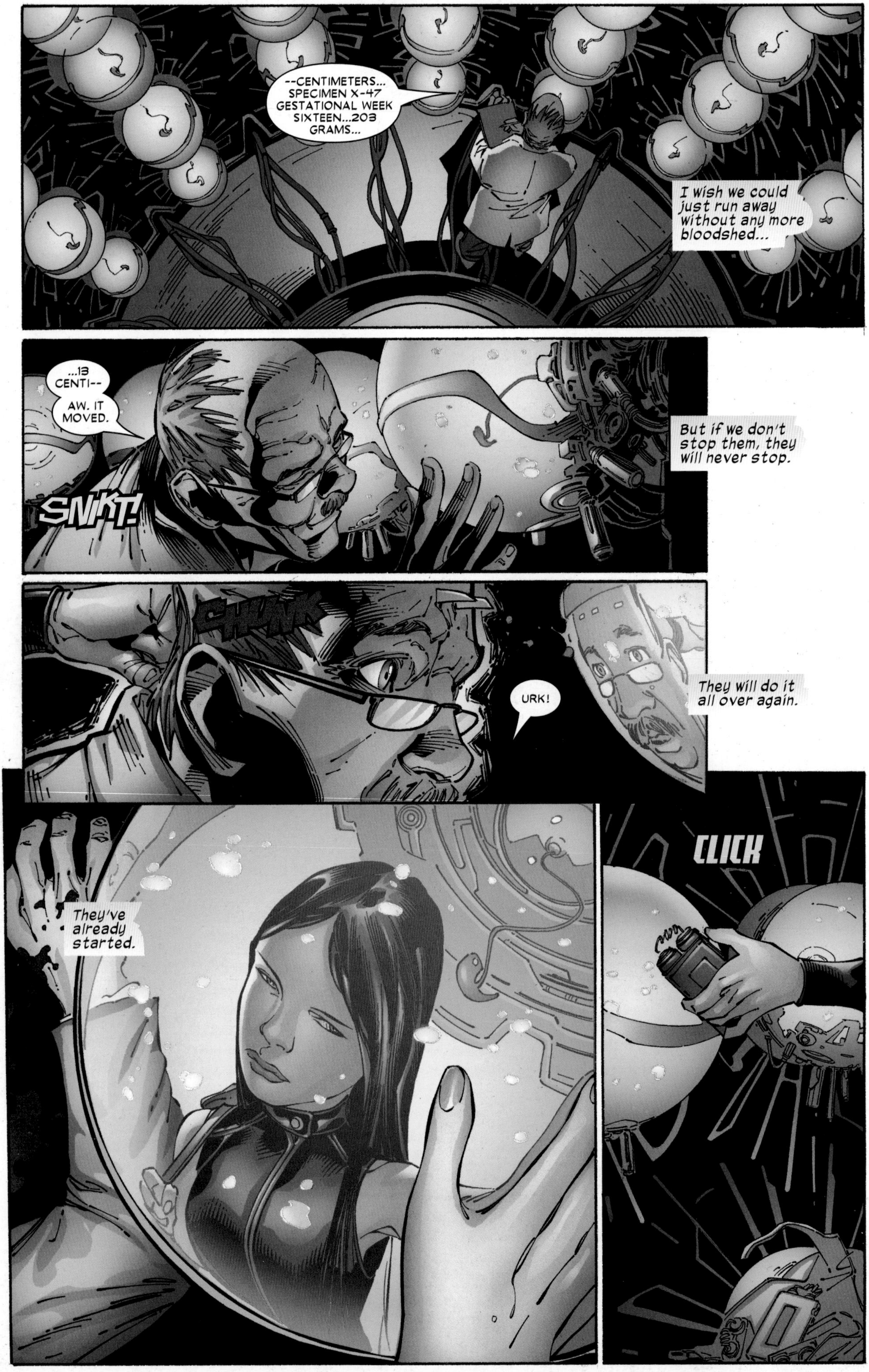
--CENTIMETERS... SPECIMEN X-47 GESTATIONAL WEEK SIXTEEN...203 GRAMS...
I wish we could just run away without any more bloodshed...
...13 CENTI--
AW. IT MOVED.
SNIKT!
But if we don't stop them, they will never stop.
CHUNK
URK!
They will do it all over again.
They've already started.
CLICK

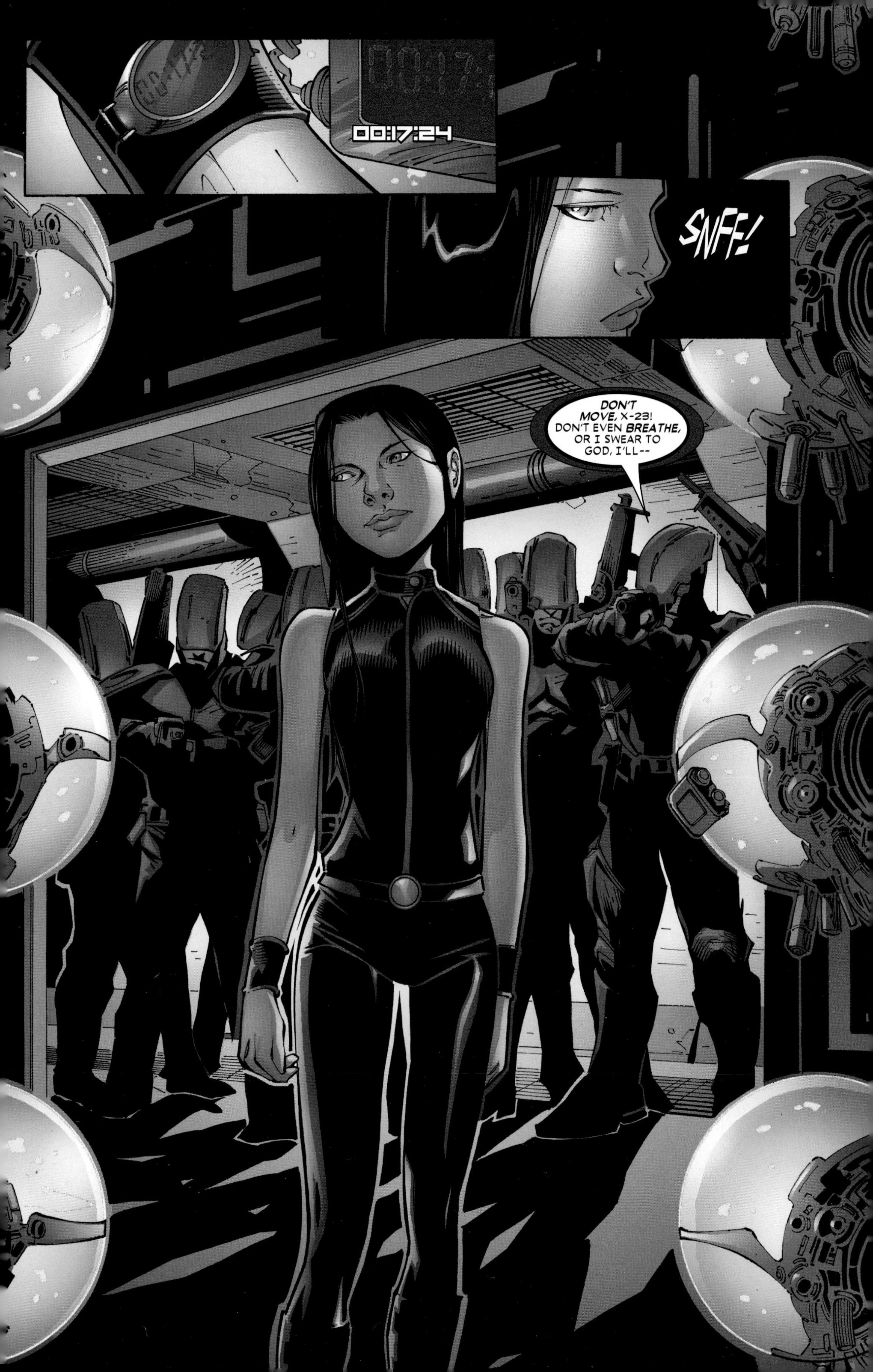
00:17:24
SNFF!
DON'T MOVE, X-23! DON'T EVEN BREATHE, OR I SWEAR TO GOD, I'LL--

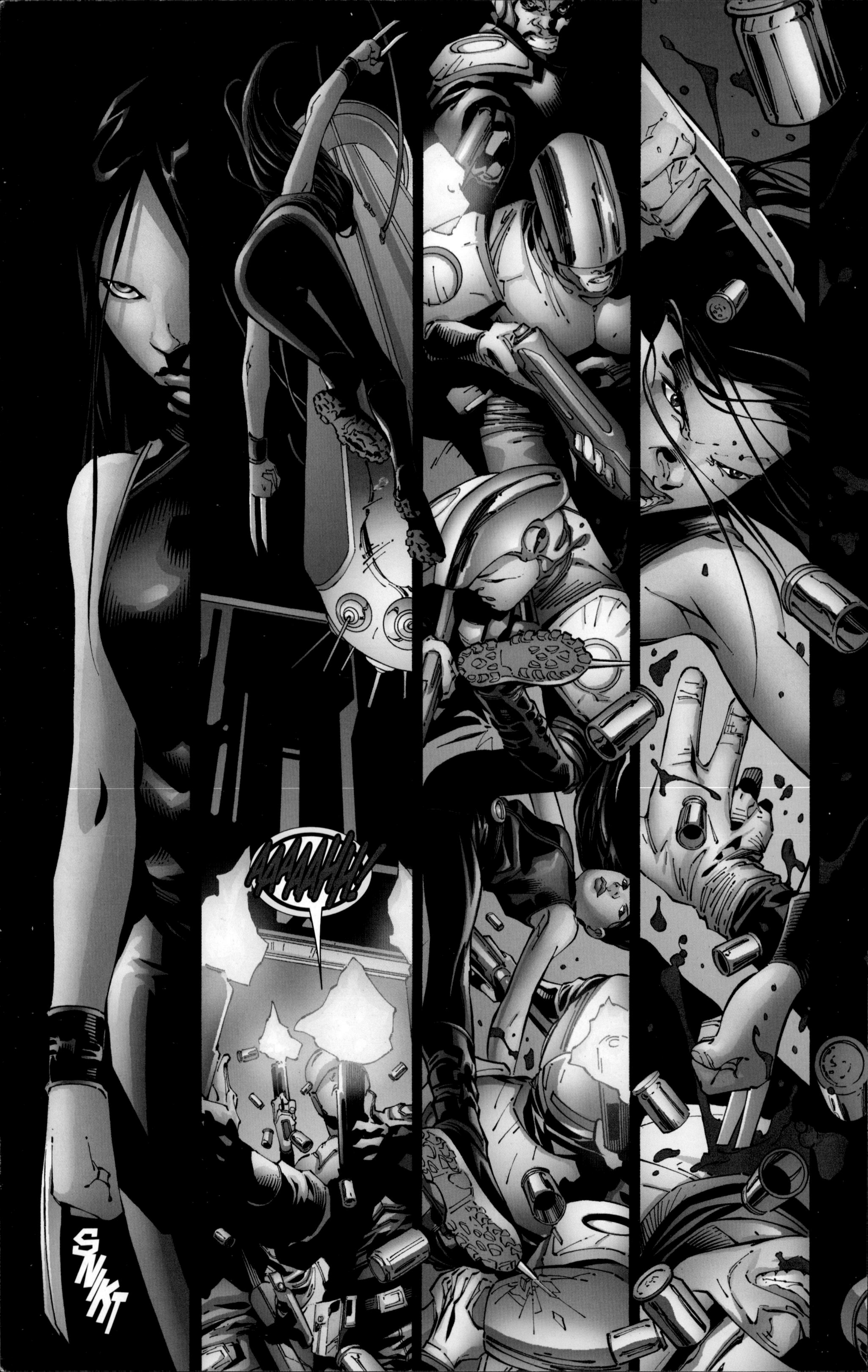
AAAAAHH!
SNIKT

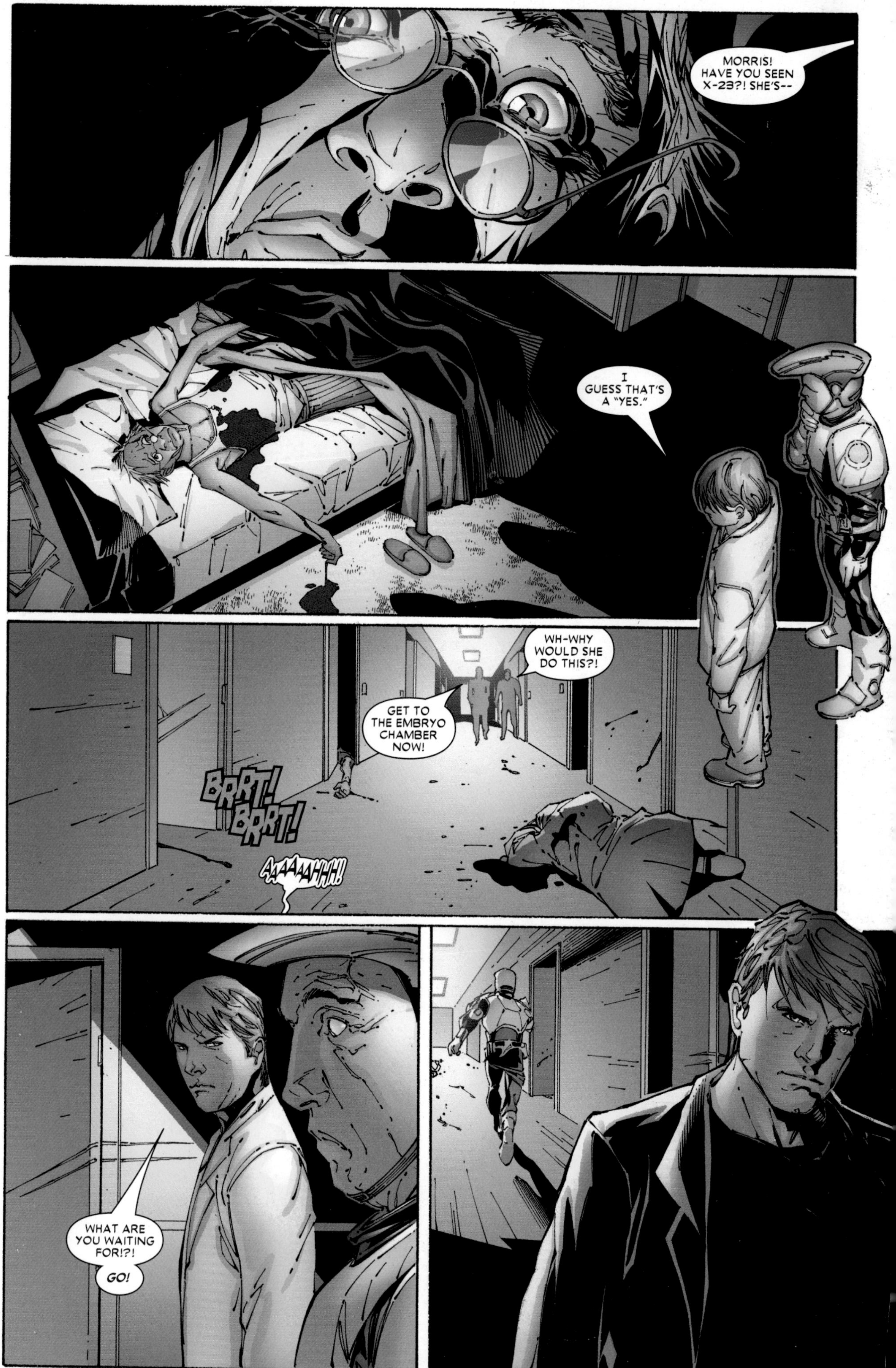
MORRIS! HAVE YOU SEEN X-23?! SHE'S--
I GUESS THAT'S A "YES."
WH-WHY WOULD SHE DO THIS?!
GET TO THE EMBRYO CHAMBER NOW!
BRRT! BRRT!
AAAAAHHH!
WHAT ARE YOU WAITING FOR!?!
GO!

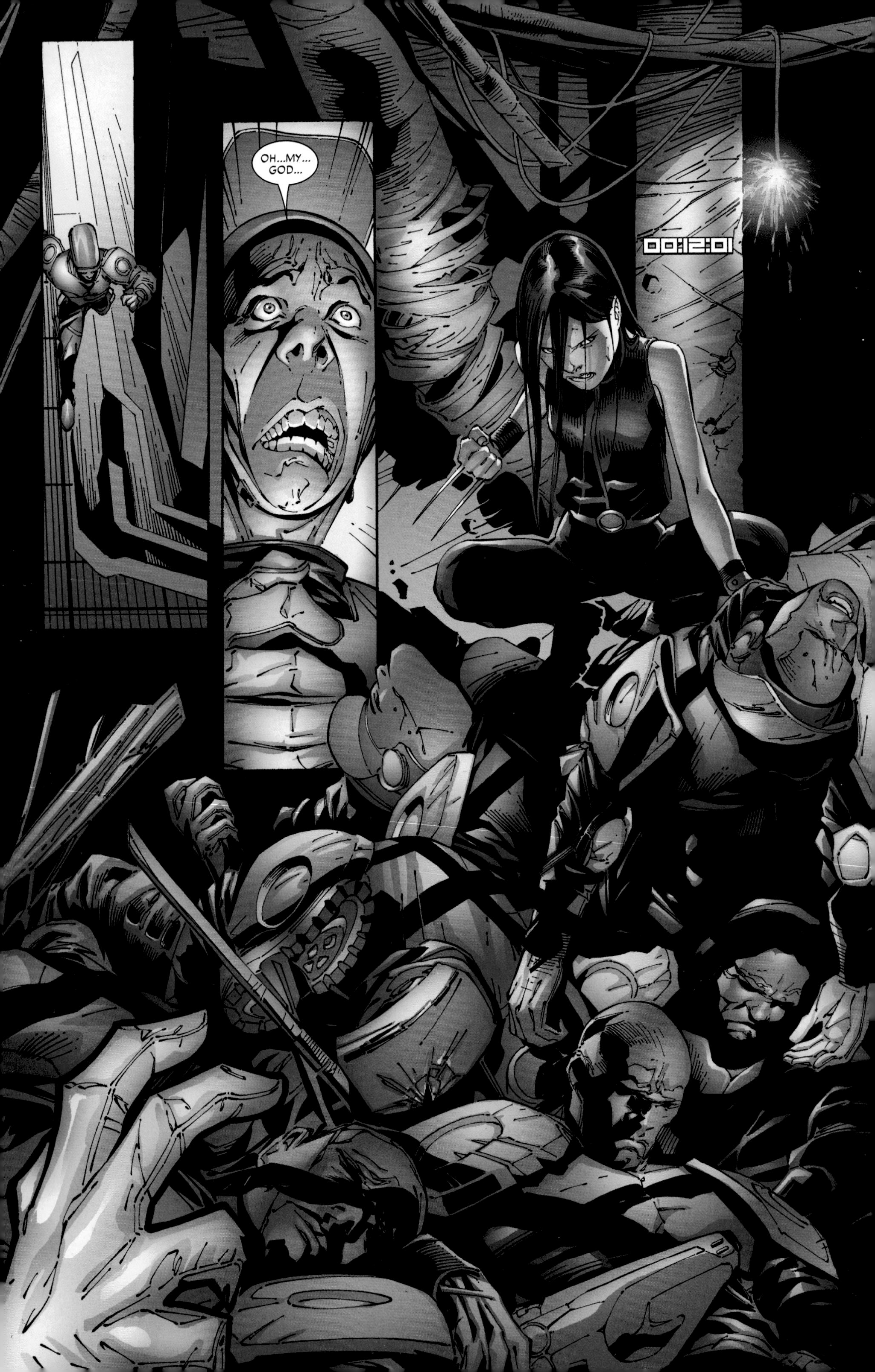
OH...MY... GOD...
00:12:01

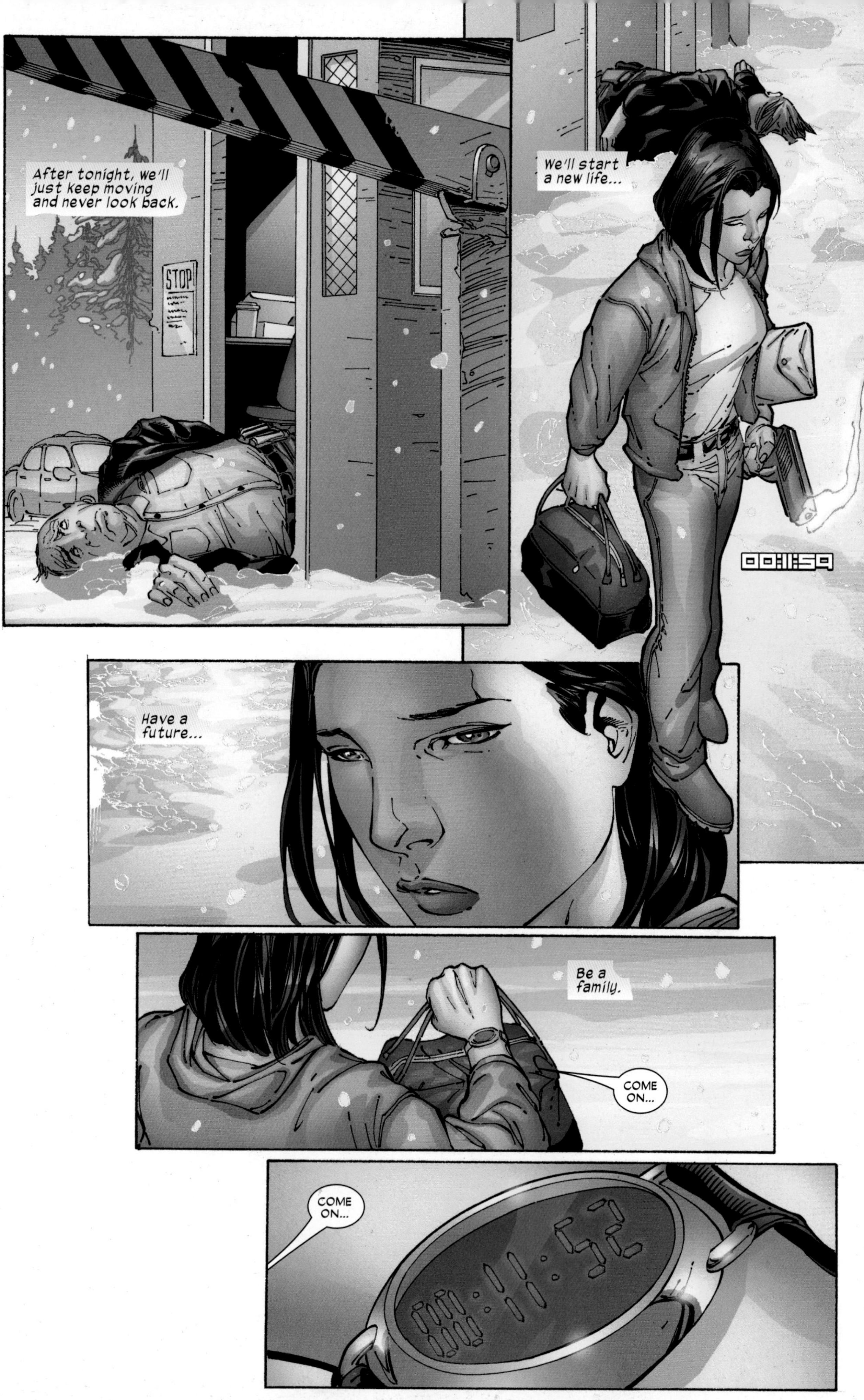
After tonight, we'll just keep moving and never look back.
STOP
We'll start a new life...
00:11:59
Have a future...
Be a family.
COME ON...
COME ON...

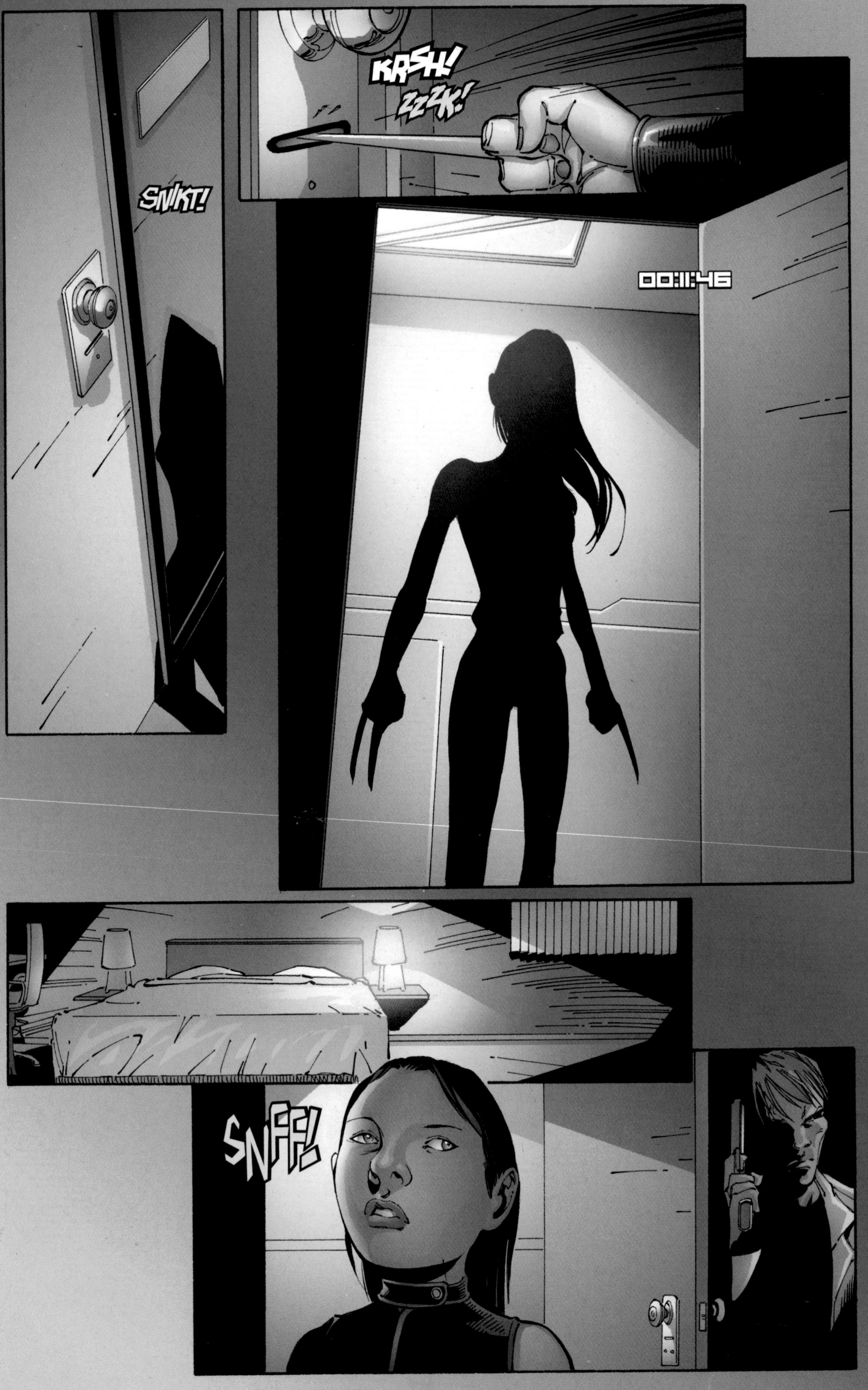
SNIKT!
KRSH!
ZZZK!
00:11:46
SNFF!

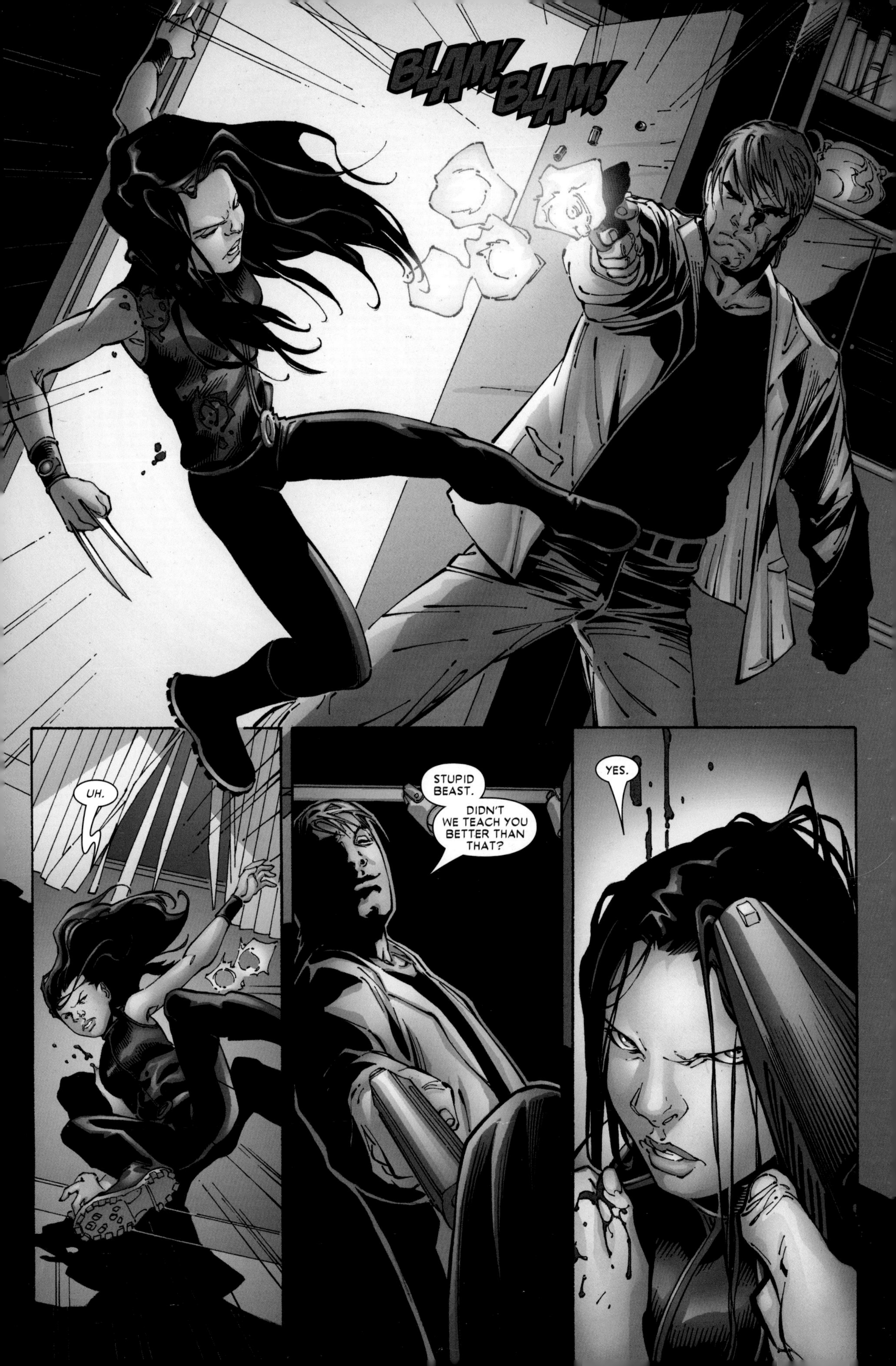
BLAM! BLAM!
UH.
STUPID BEAST.
DIDN'T WE TEACH YOU BETTER THAN THAT?
YES.

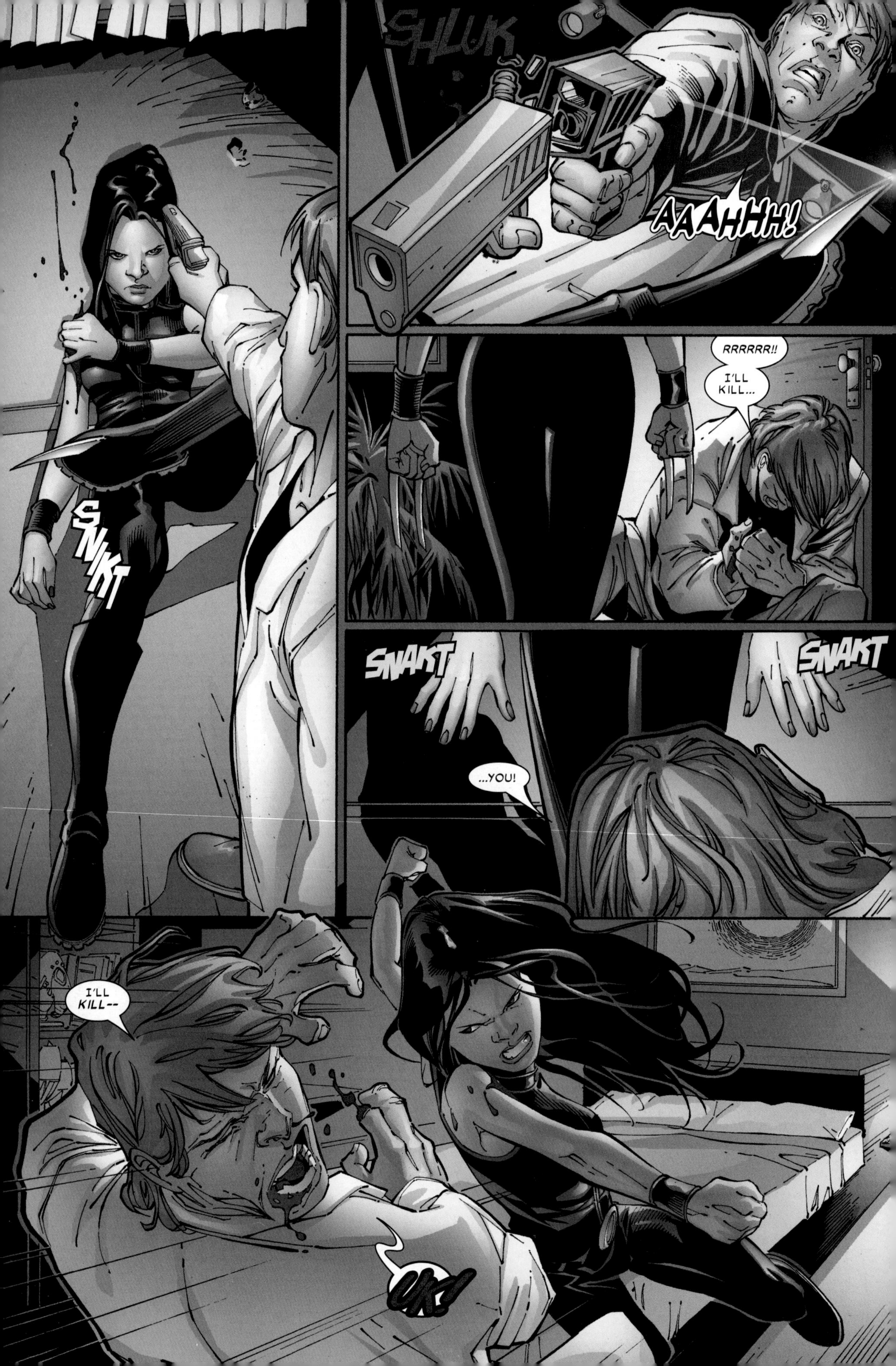
SNIKT
SHLUK
AAAHHH!
RRRRRR!!
I'LL KILL...
SNAKT
SNAKT
...YOU!
I'LL KILL--
UK!

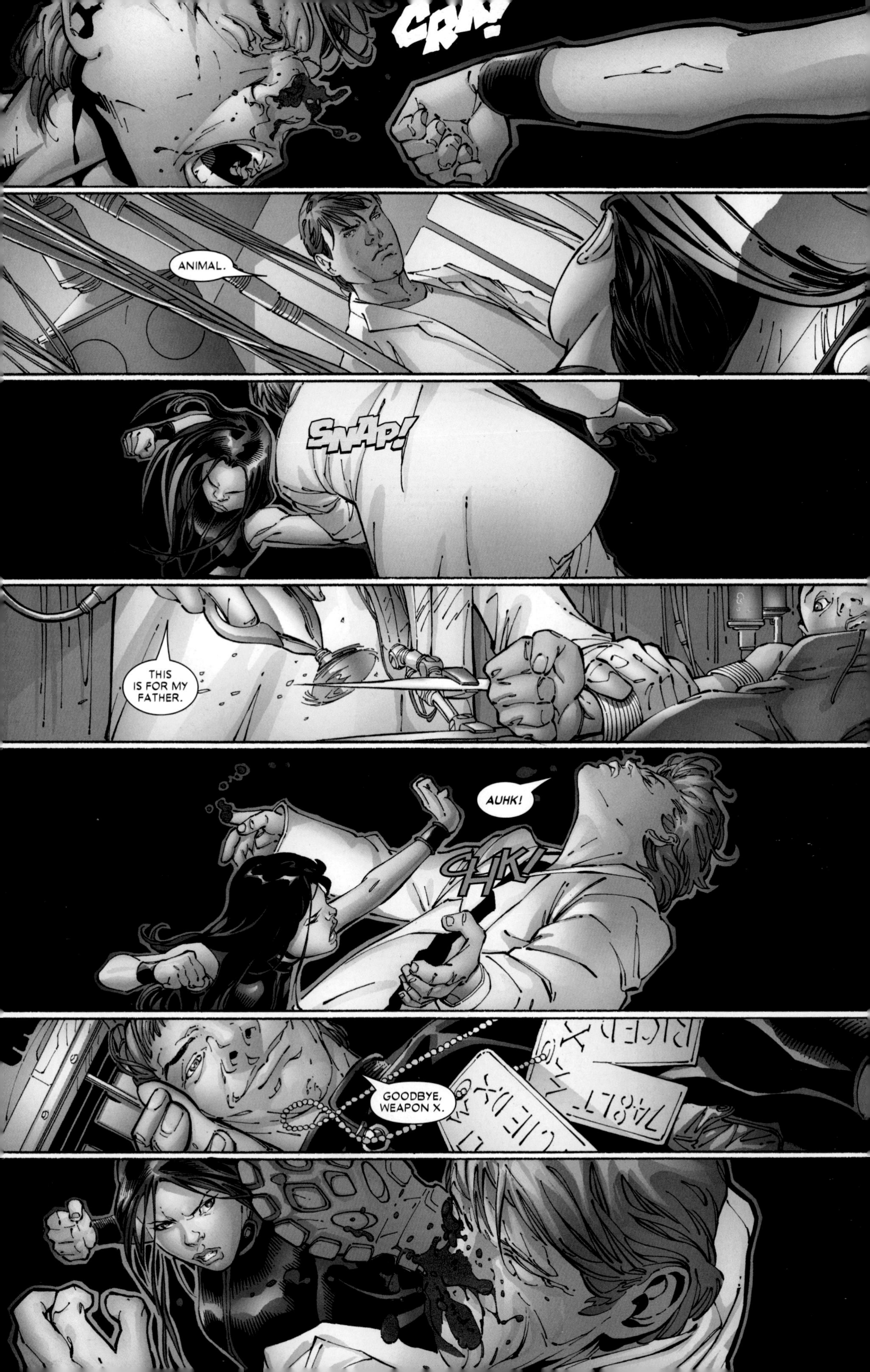
CRK!
ANIMAL.
SNAP!
THIS IS FOR MY FATHER.
AUHK!
CHK!
GOODBYE, WEAPON X.

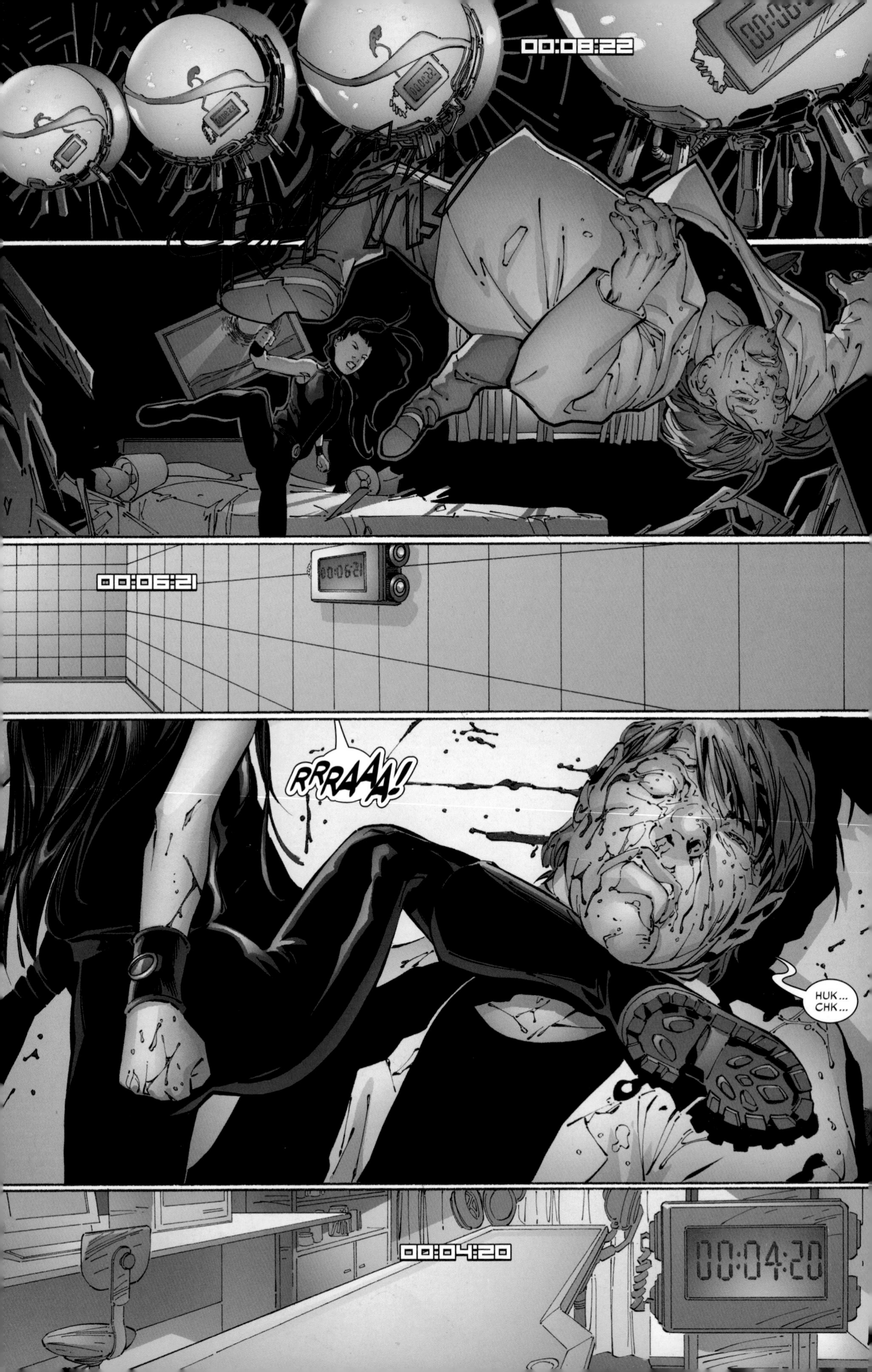
00:08:22
00:06:21
RRRAAA!
HUK...
CHK...
00:04:20
00:04:20

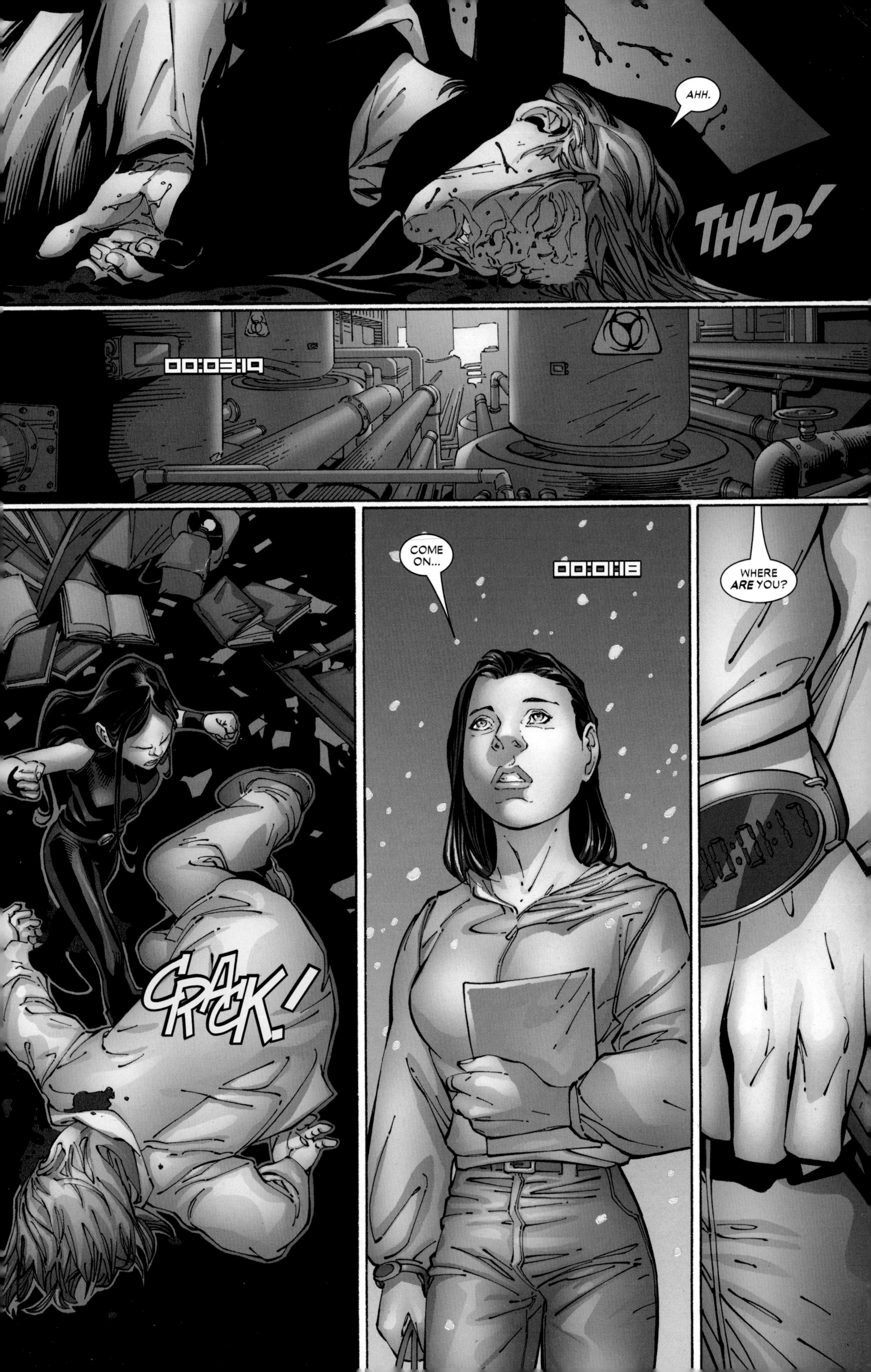
AHH.
THUD!
00:03:19
CRACK!
COME ON...
00:01:18
WHERE ARE YOU?

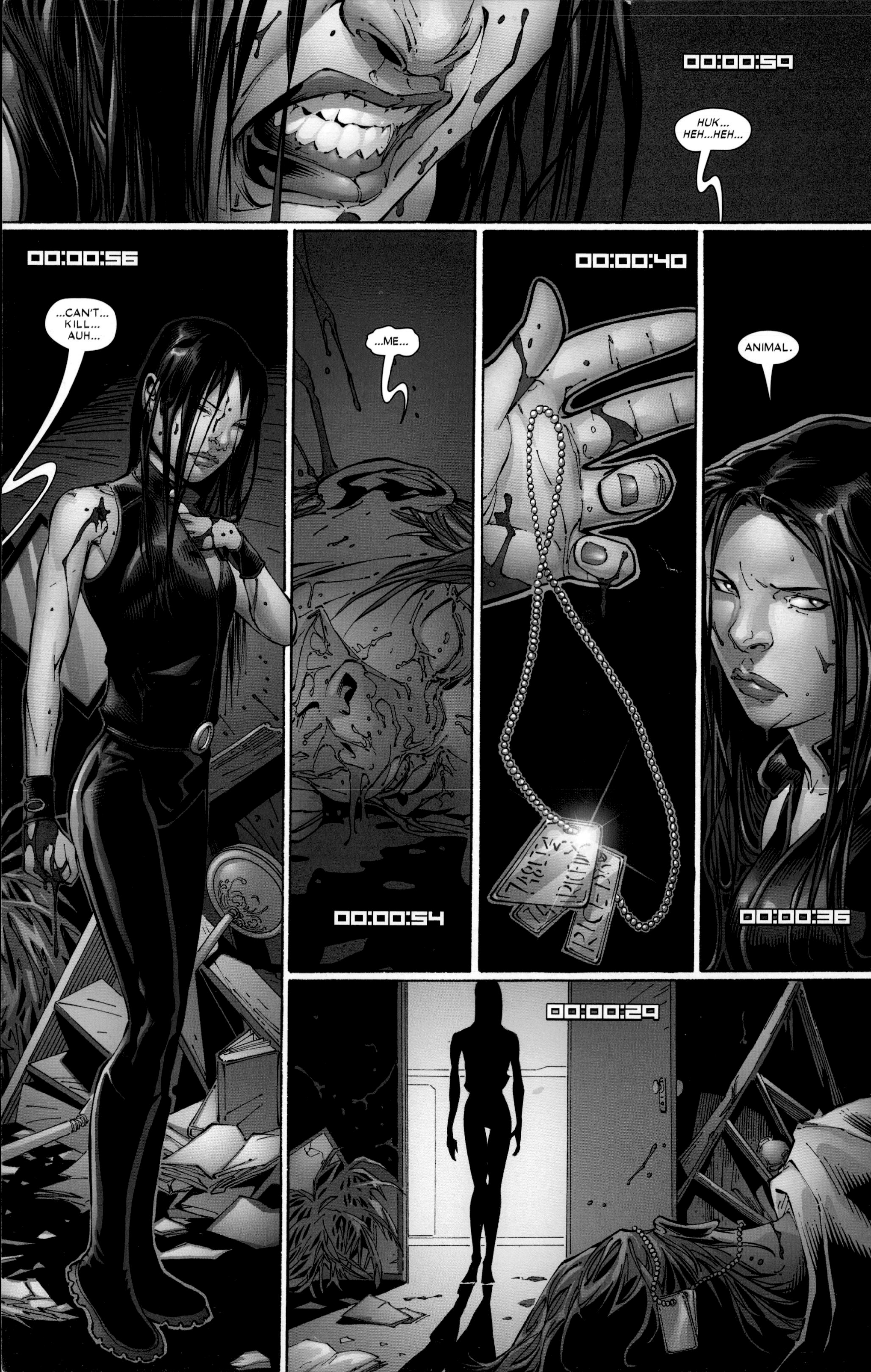
00:00:59
HUK... HEH...HEH...
00:00:56
...CAN'T... KILL... AUH...
...ME...
00:00:54
00:00:40
00:00:36
ANIMAL.
00:00:29

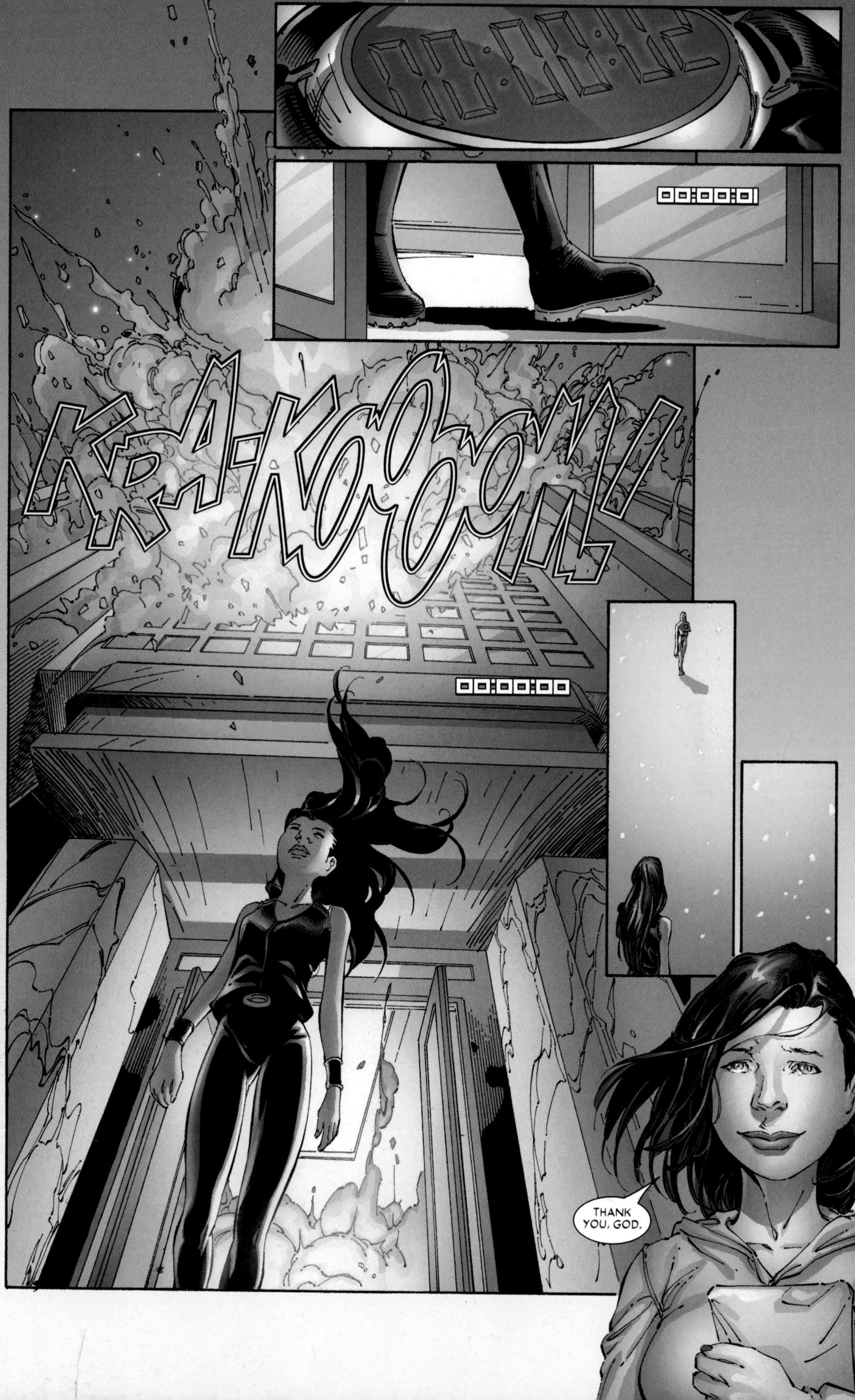
00:00:01
KRA-KOOOOM!!
00:00:00
THANK YOU, GOD.

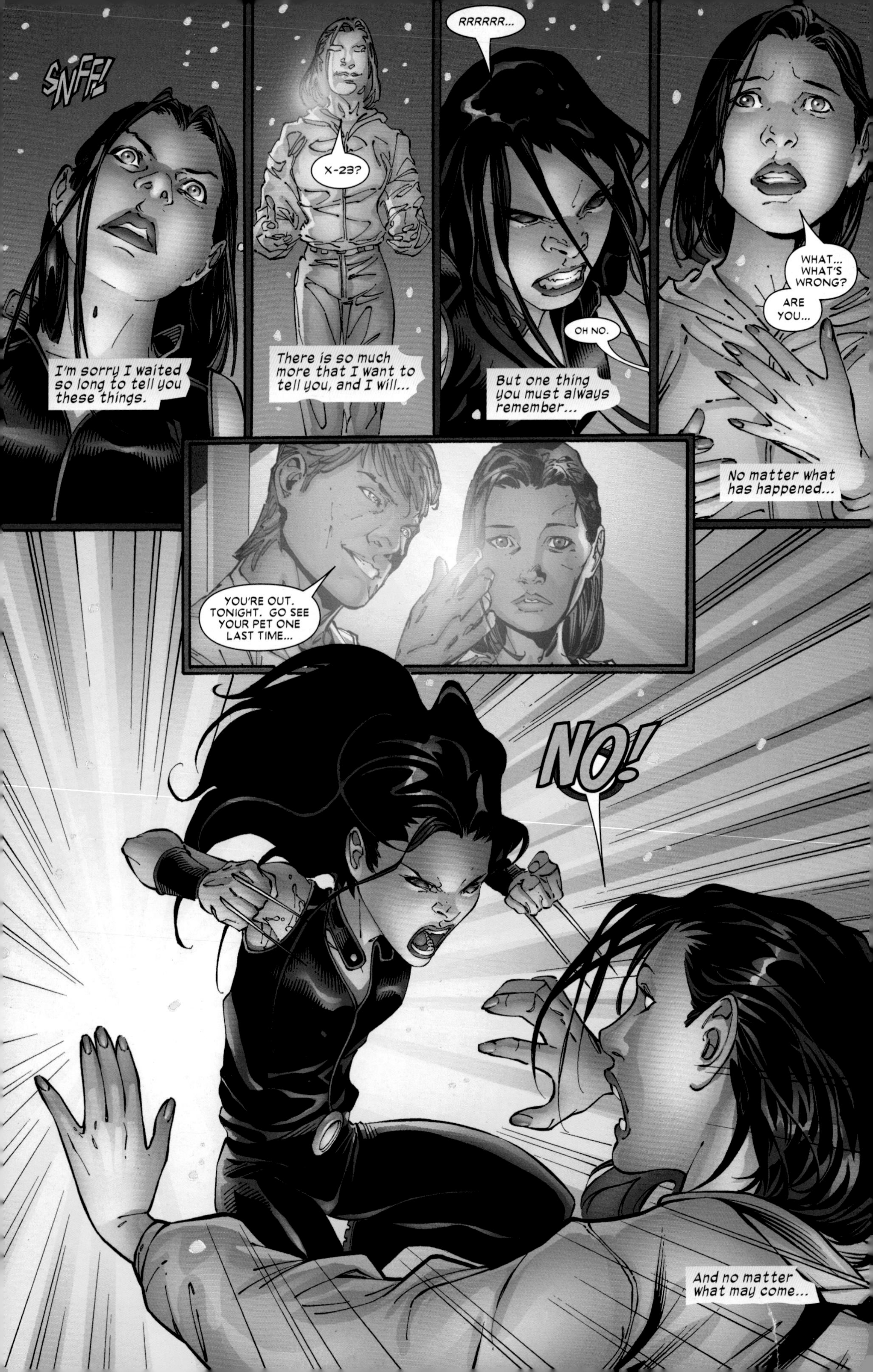
SNFF!
I'm sorry I waited so long to tell you these things.
X-23?
There is so much more that I want to tell you, and I will...
RRRRRR...
OH NO.
But one thing you must always remember...
WHAT... WHAT'S WRONG?
ARE YOU...
No matter what has happened...
YOU'RE OUT. TONIGHT. GO SEE YOUR PET ONE LAST TIME...
NO!
And no matter what may come...

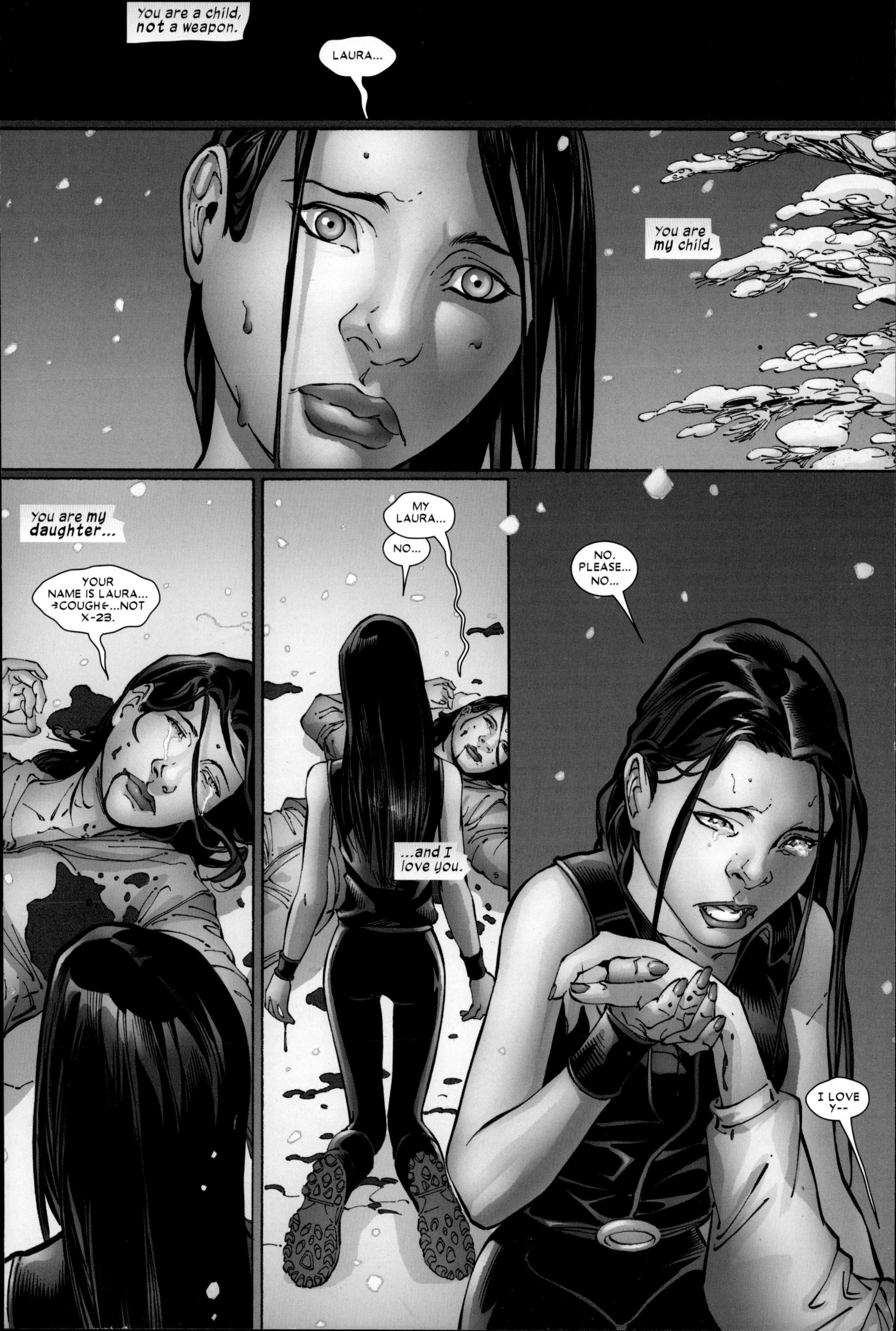
You are a child, not a weapon.
LAURA...
You are my child.
You are my daughter...
YOUR NAME IS LAURA... →COUGH←...NOT X-23.
MY LAURA...
NO...
...and I love you.
NO. PLEASE... NO...
I LOVE Y--

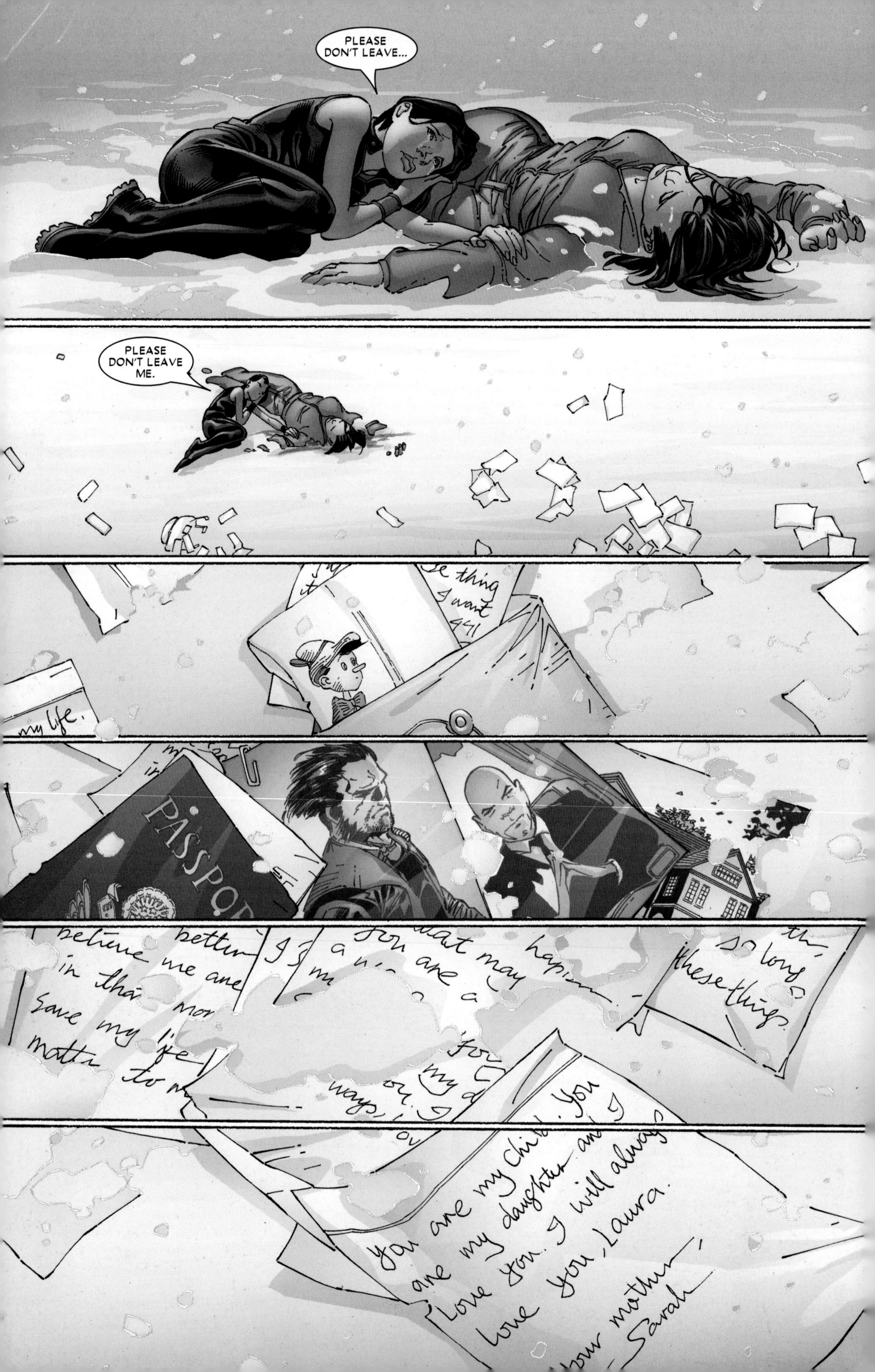
PLEASE DON'T LEAVE...
PLEASE DON'T LEAVE ME.
my life.
these things.
You are my chil
are my daughter and I
Love you. I will always
Love you, Laura.
our mother
Sarah

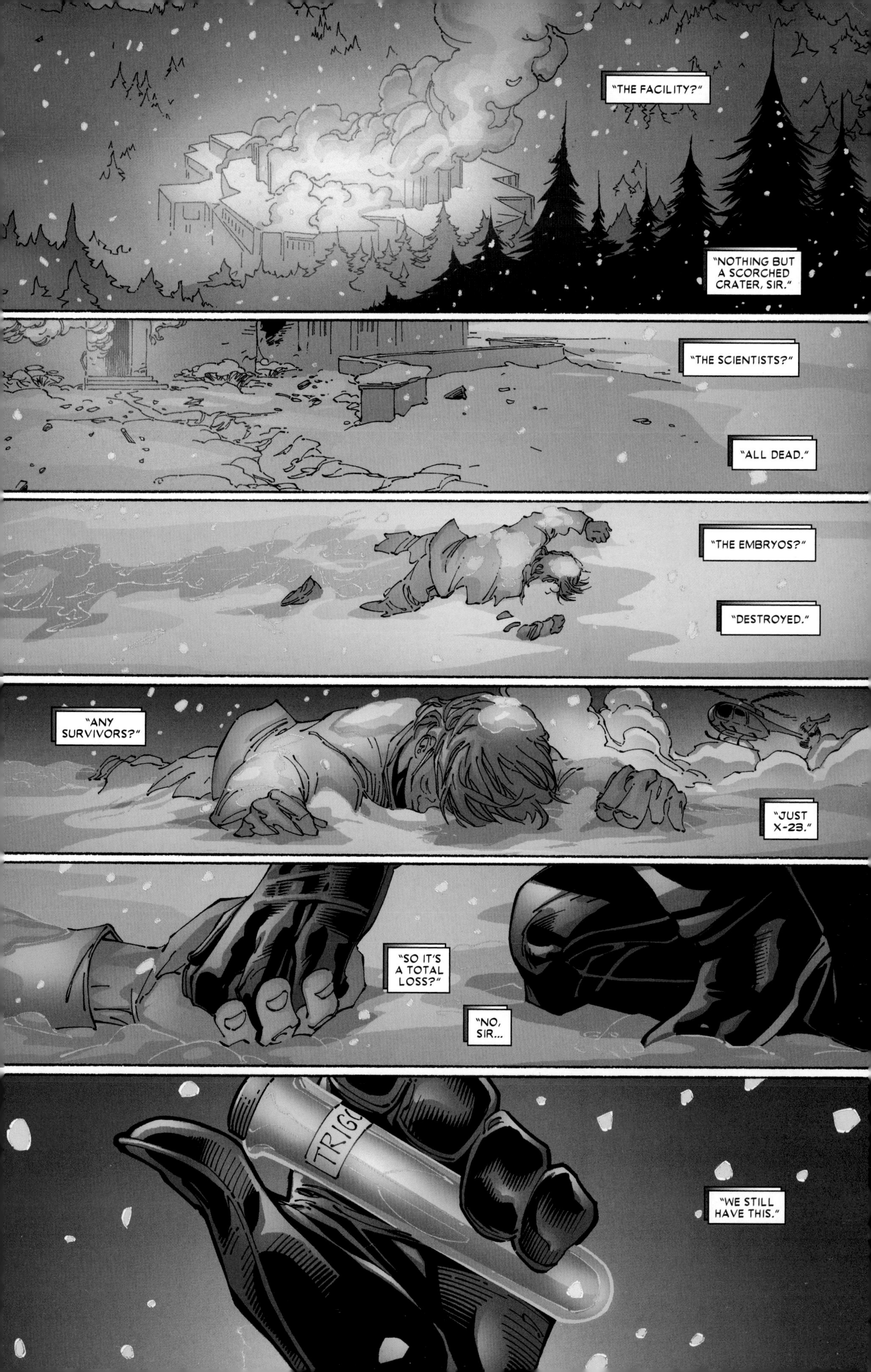
"THE FACILITY?"
"NOTHING BUT A SCORCHED CRATER, SIR."
"THE SCIENTISTS?"
"ALL DEAD."
"THE EMBRYOS?"
"DESTROYED."
"ANY SURVIVORS?"
"JUST X-23."
"SO IT'S A TOTAL LOSS?"
"NO, SIR...
"WE STILL HAVE THIS."

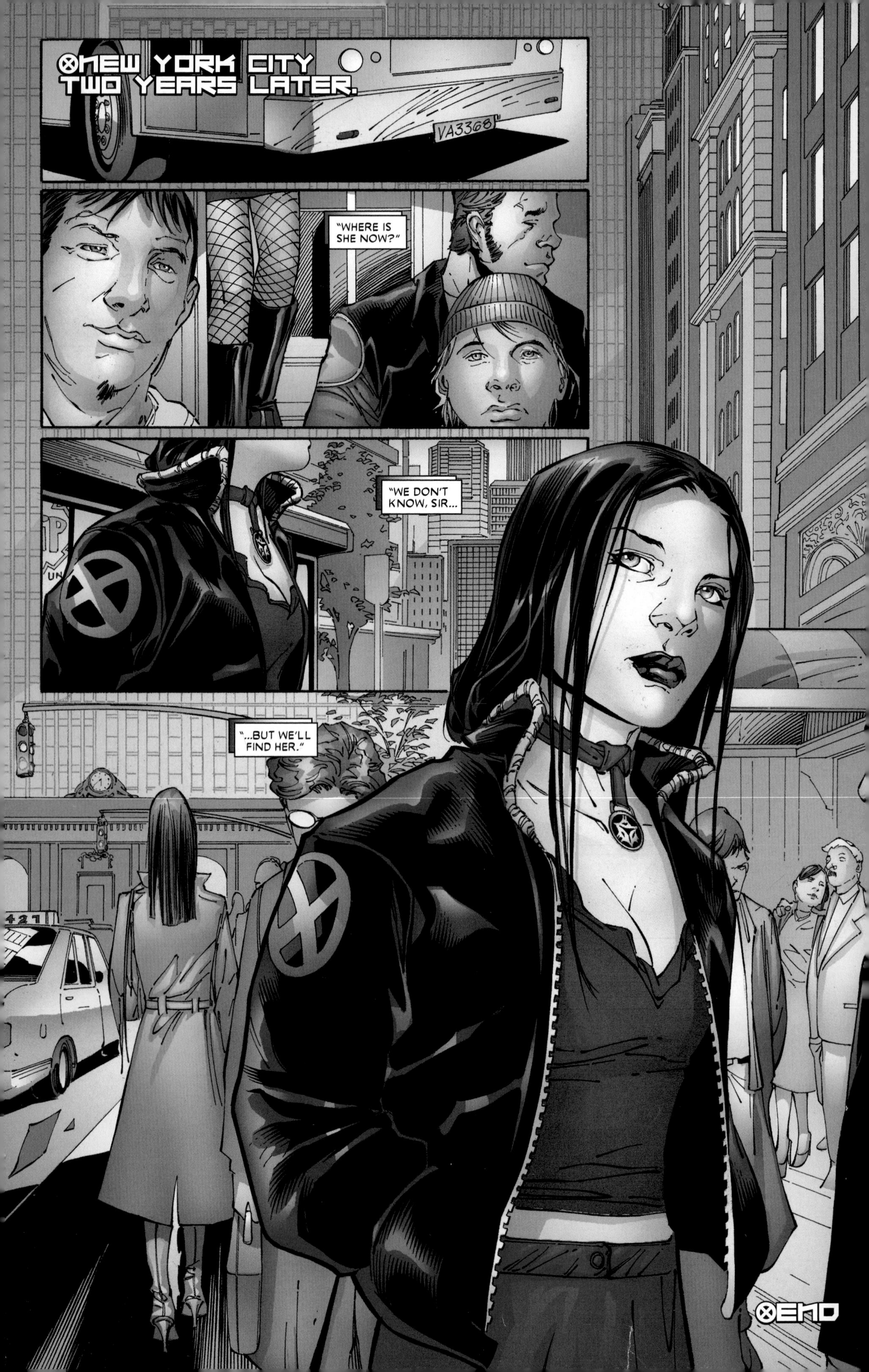
NEW YORK CITY
TWO YEARS LATER.
VA3368
"WHERE IS SHE NOW?"
"WE DON'T KNOW, SIR...
"...BUT WE'LL FIND HER."
427
END

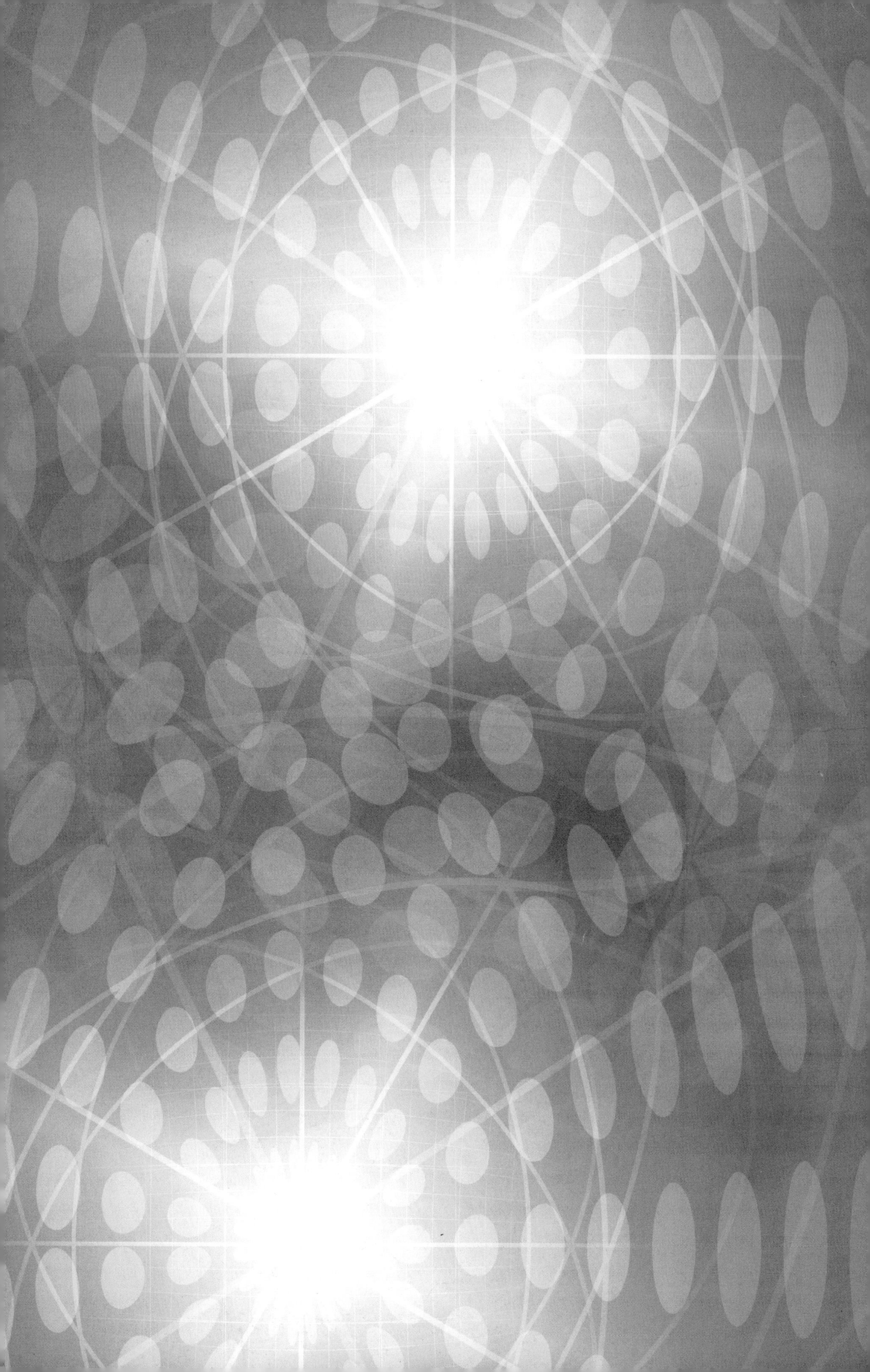

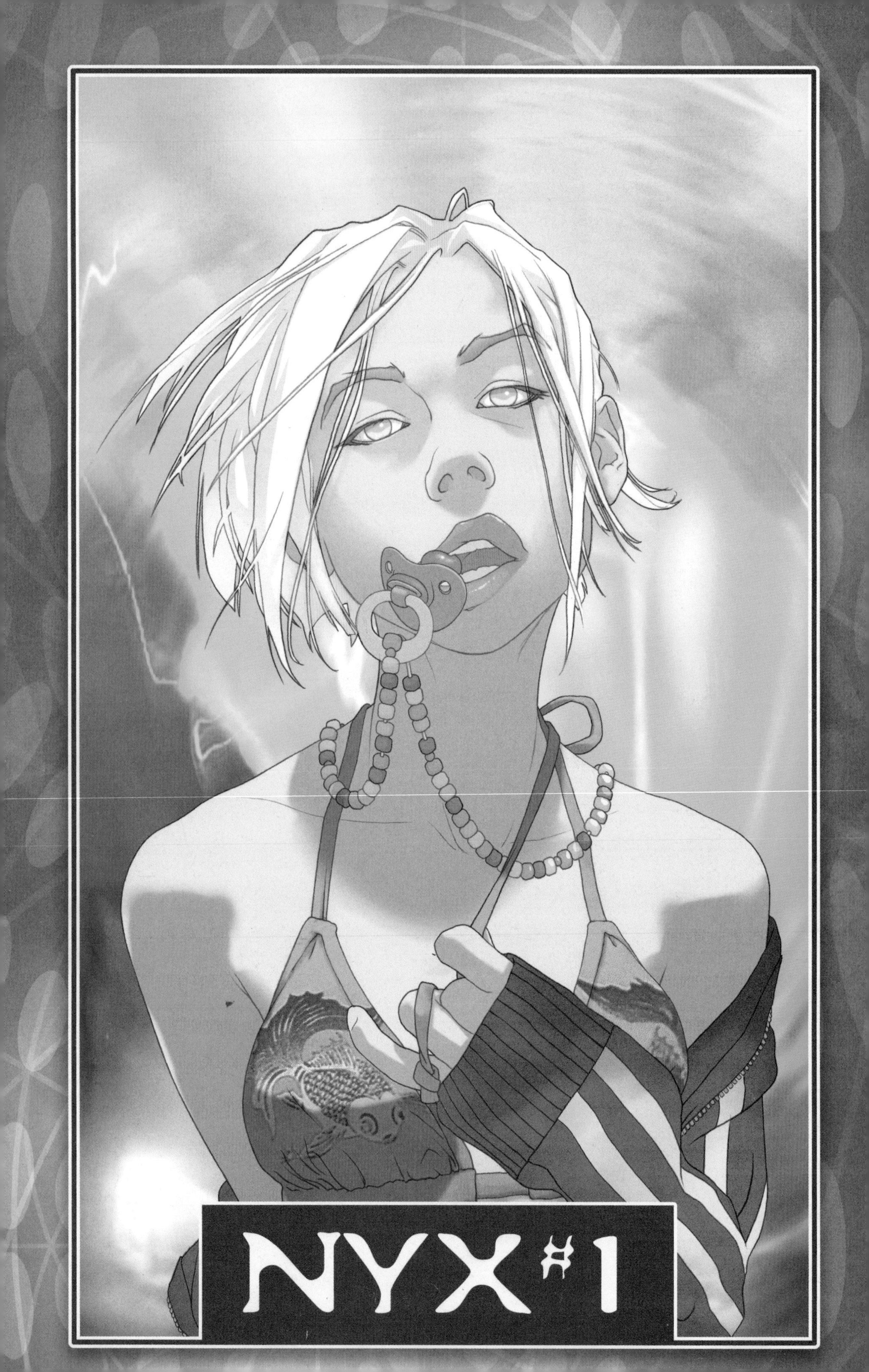
NYX #1

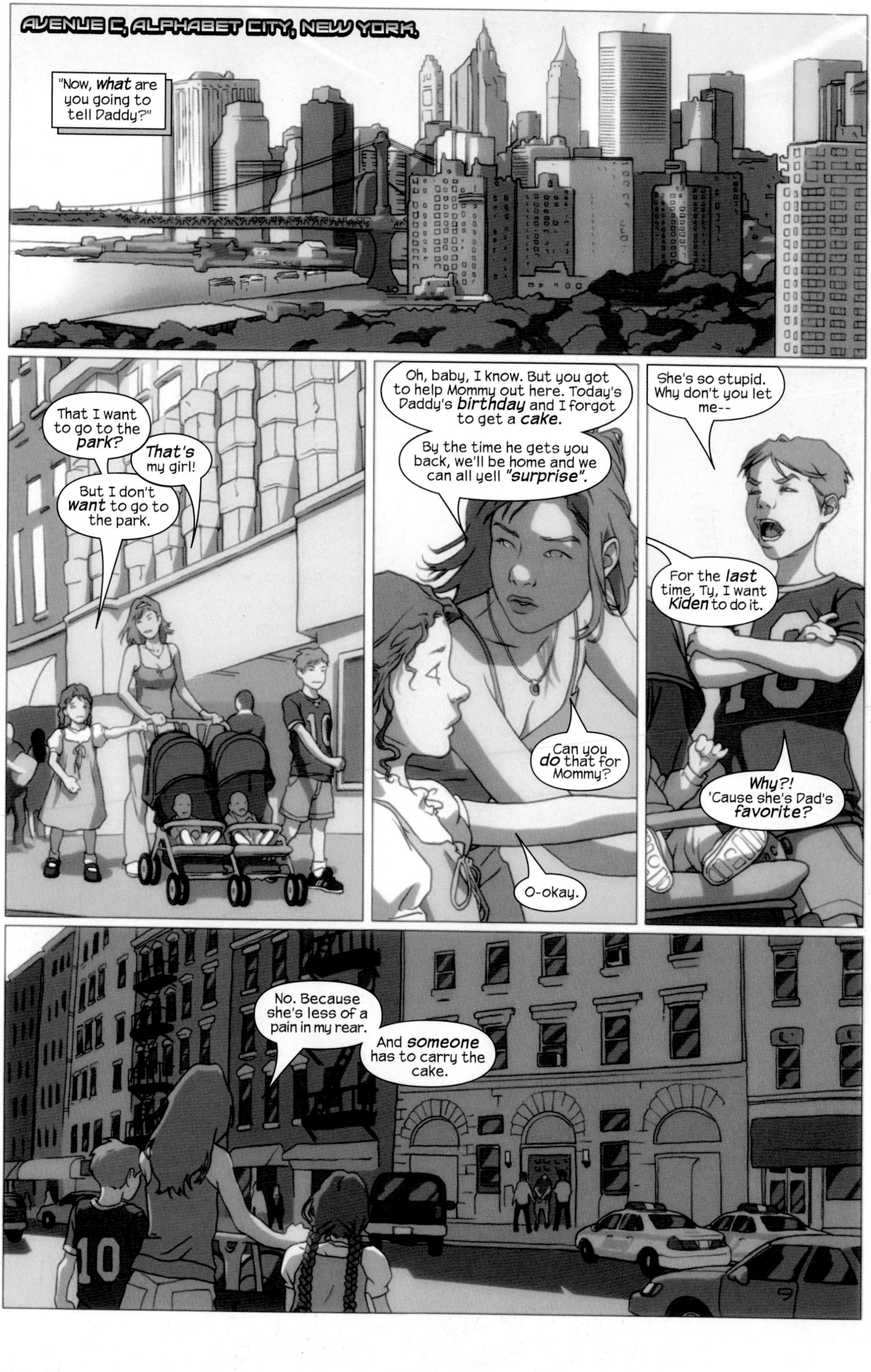
AVENUE C, ALPHABET CITY, NEW YORK.
"Now, what are you going to tell Daddy?"
That I want to go to the park?
That's my girl!
But I don't want to go to the park.
Oh, baby, I know. But you got to help Mommy out here. Today's Daddy's birthday and I forgot to get a cake.
By the time he gets you back, we'll be home and we can all yell "surprise".
Can you do that for Mommy?
O-okay.
She's so stupid. Why don't you let me--
For the last time, Ty, I want Kiden to do it.
Why?! 'Cause she's Dad's favorite?
No. Because she's less of a pain in my rear.
And someone has to carry the cake.

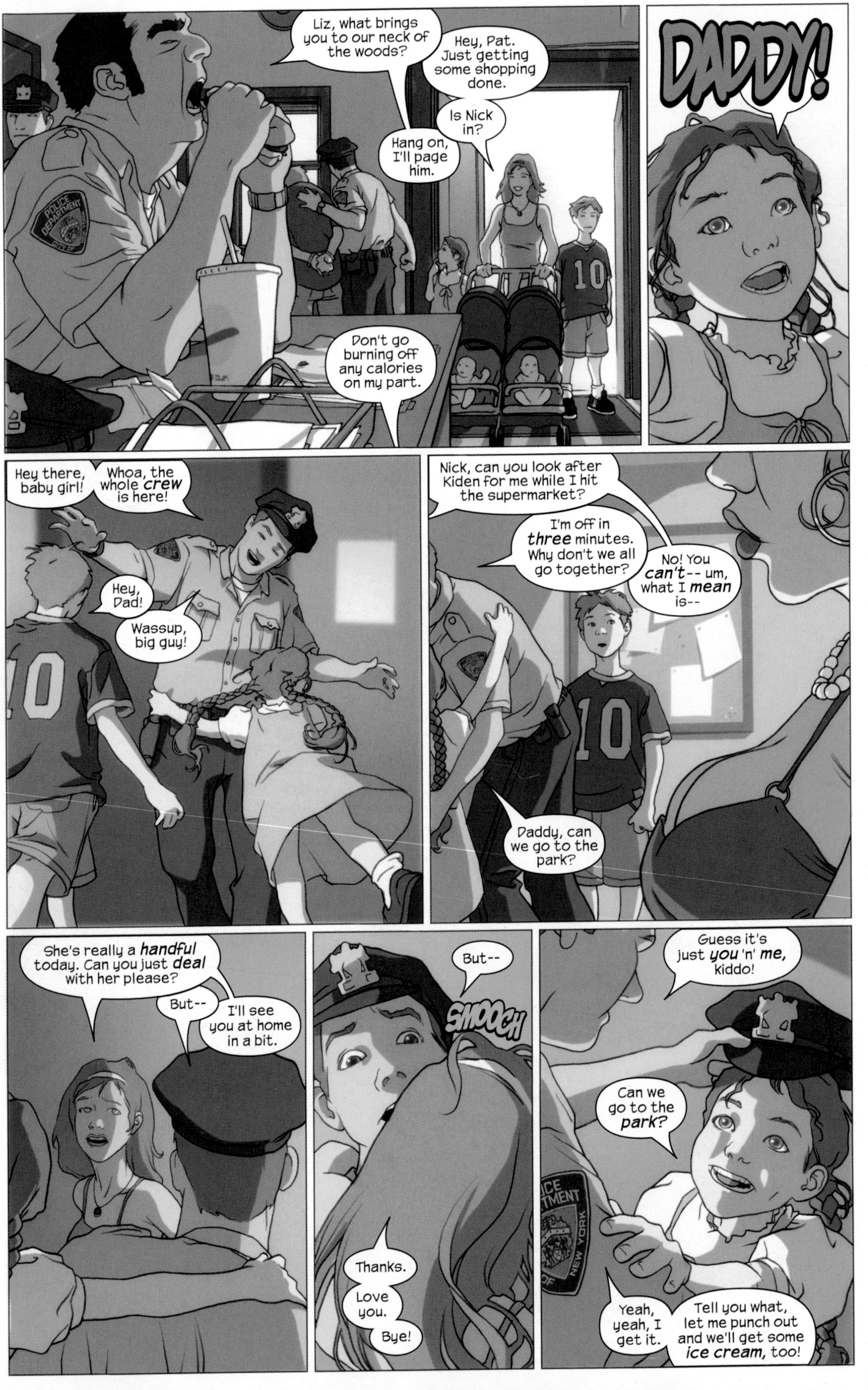

Liz, what brings you to our neck of the woods?
Hey, Pat. Just getting some shopping done.
Is Nick in?
Hang on, I'll page him.
Don't go burning off any calories on my part.
DADDY!
Hey there, baby girl!
Whoa, the whole crew is here!
Hey, Dad!
Wassup, big guy!
Nick, can you look after Kiden for me while I hit the supermarket?
I'm off in three minutes. Why don't we all go together?
No! You can't-- um, what I mean is--
Daddy, can we go to the park?
She's really a handful today. Can you just deal with her please?
But--
I'll see you at home in a bit.
But--
SMOOCH
Thanks.
Love you.
Bye!
Guess it's just you 'n' me, kiddo!
Can we go to the park?
Yeah, yeah, I get it.
Tell you what, let me punch out and we'll get some ice cream, too!

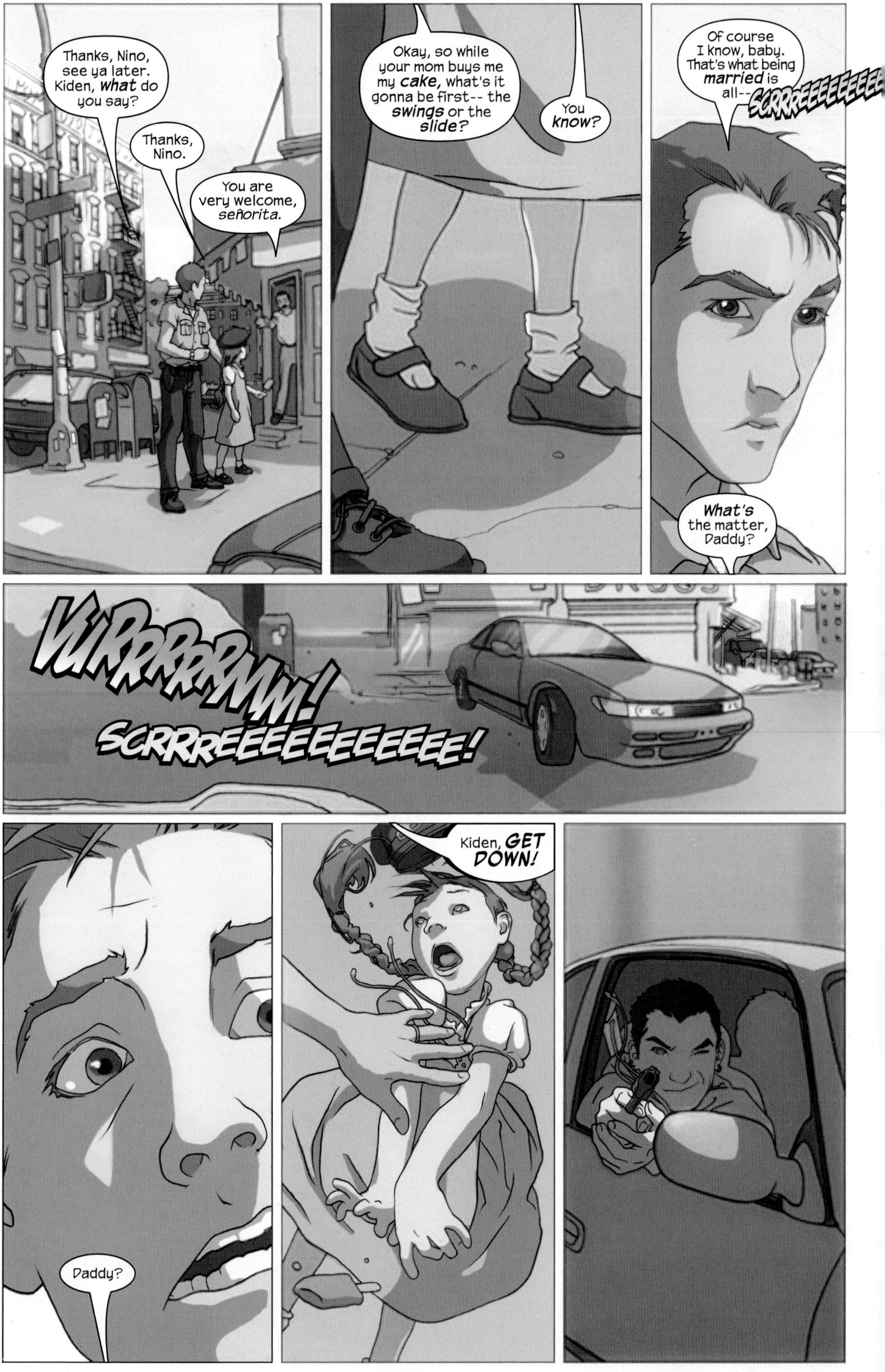
Thanks, Nino, see ya later. Kiden, *what* do you say?
Thanks, Nino.
You are very welcome, *señorita.*
Okay, so while your mom buys me my *cake,* what's it gonna be first-- the *swings* or the *slide?*
You *know?*
Of course I know, baby. That's what being *married* is all--
SCRRREEEEEEEEE
What's the matter, Daddy?
VURRRRRNNM!
SCRRREEEEEEEEEEEEE!
Daddy?
Kiden, **GET DOWN!**

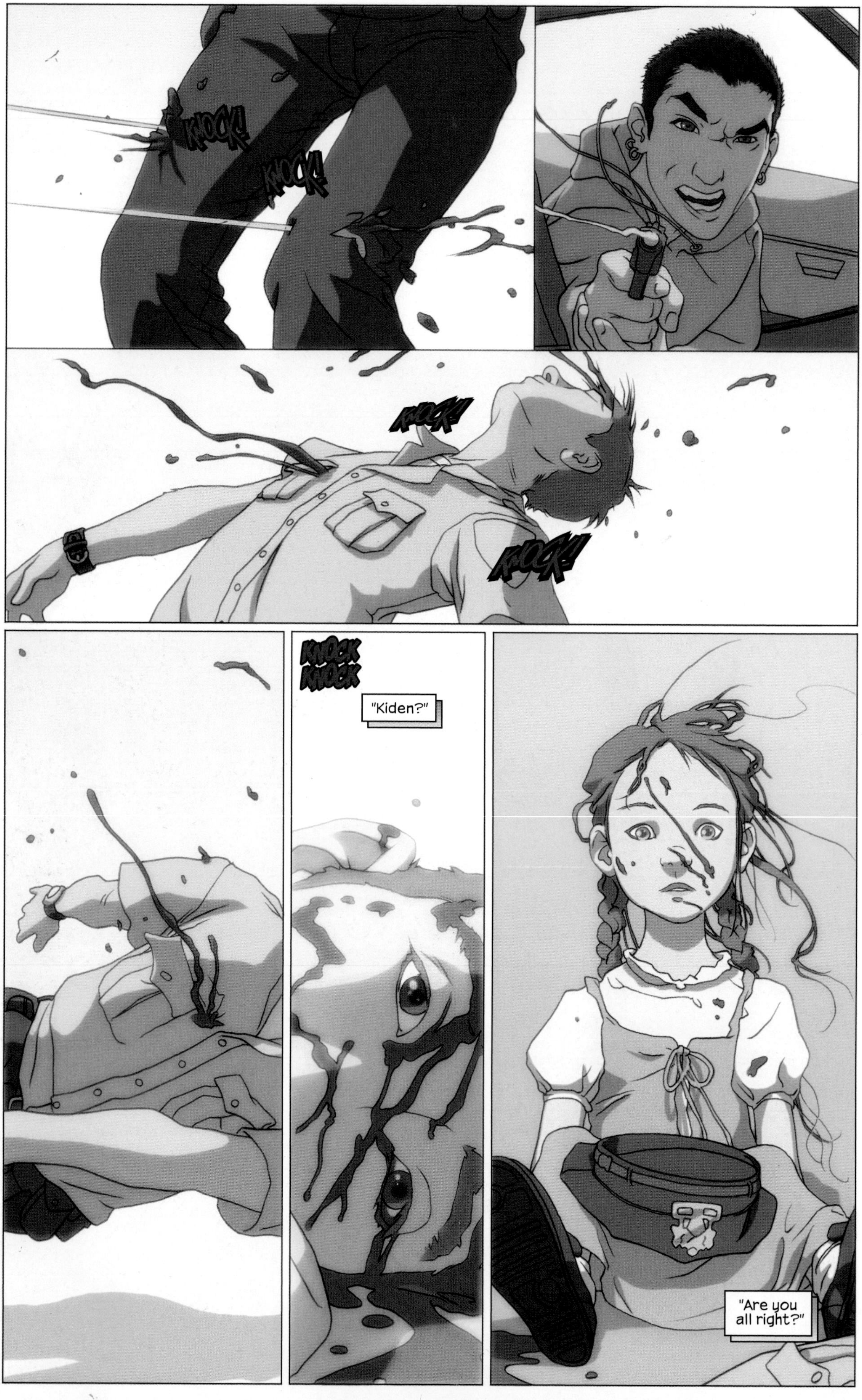
KNOCK!
KNOCK!
KNOCK!
KNOCK!
KNOCK
KNOCK
"Kiden?"
"Are you all right?"

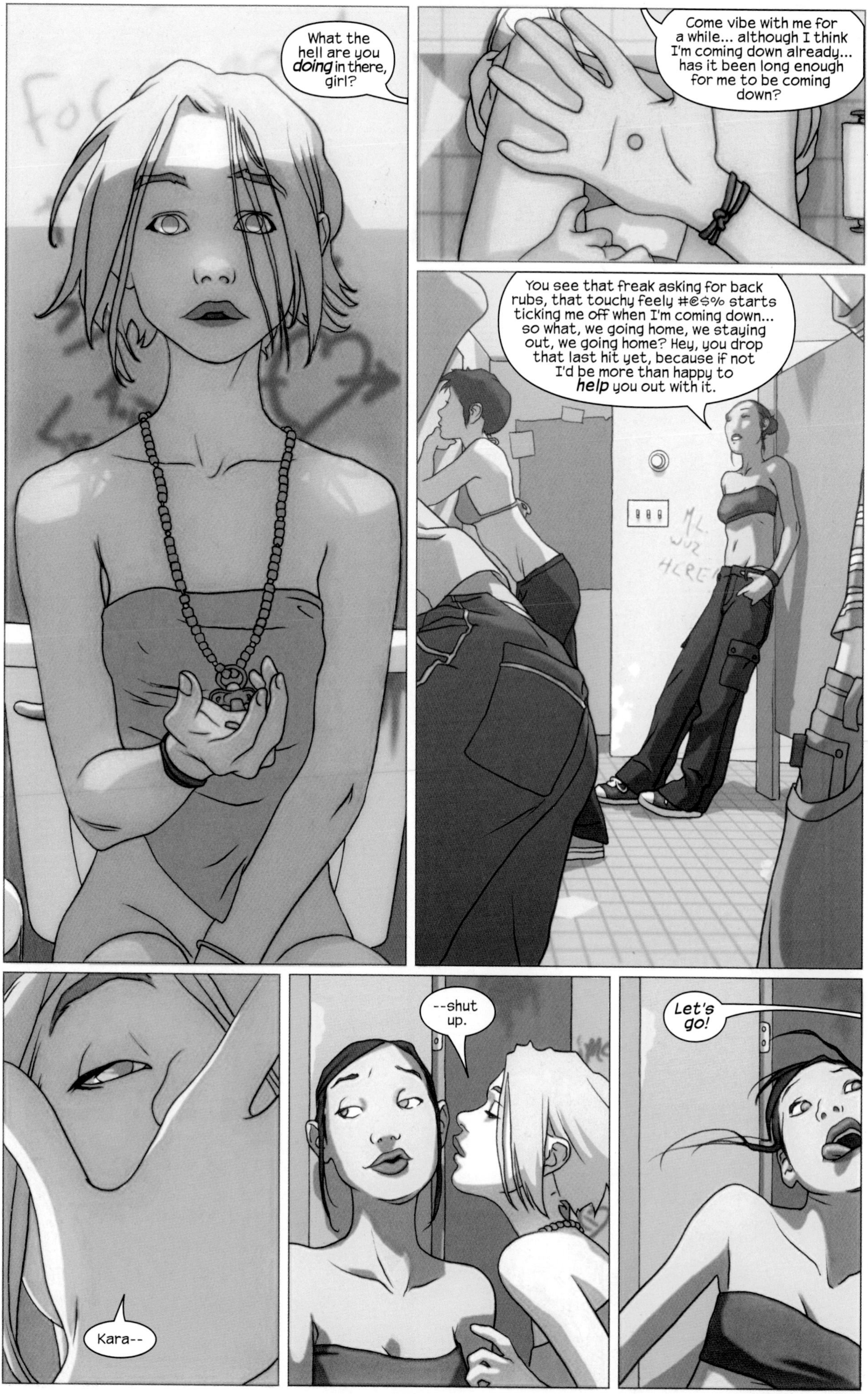
What the hell are you doing in there, girl?
Come vibe with me for a while... although I think I'm coming down already... has it been long enough for me to be coming down?
You see that freak asking for back rubs, that touchy feely #@$% starts ticking me off when I'm coming down... so what, we going home, we staying out, we going home? Hey, you drop that last hit yet, because if not I'd be more than happy to help you out with it.
M.L. WUZ HERE
Kara--
--shut up.
Let's go!

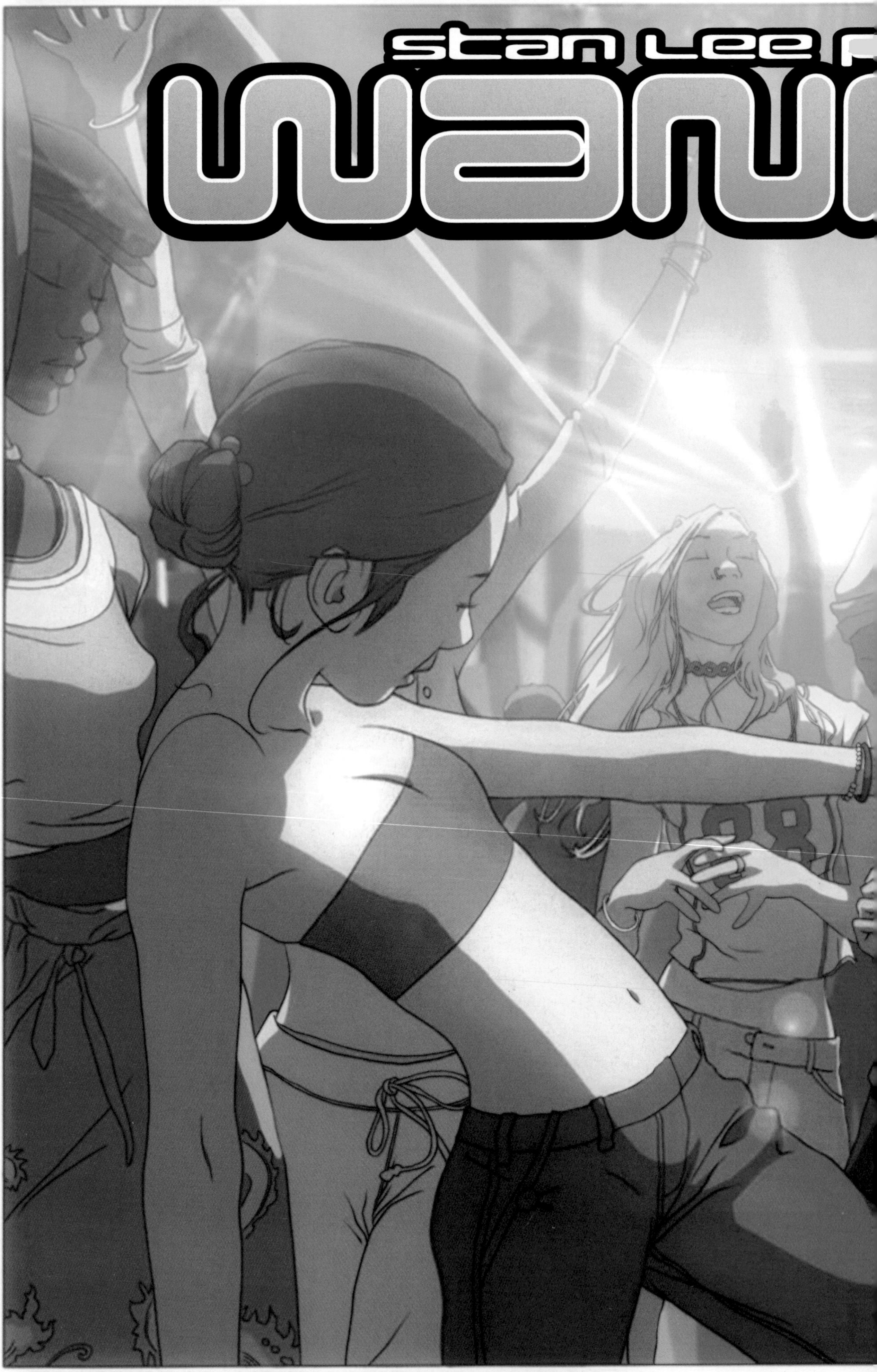
stan Lee

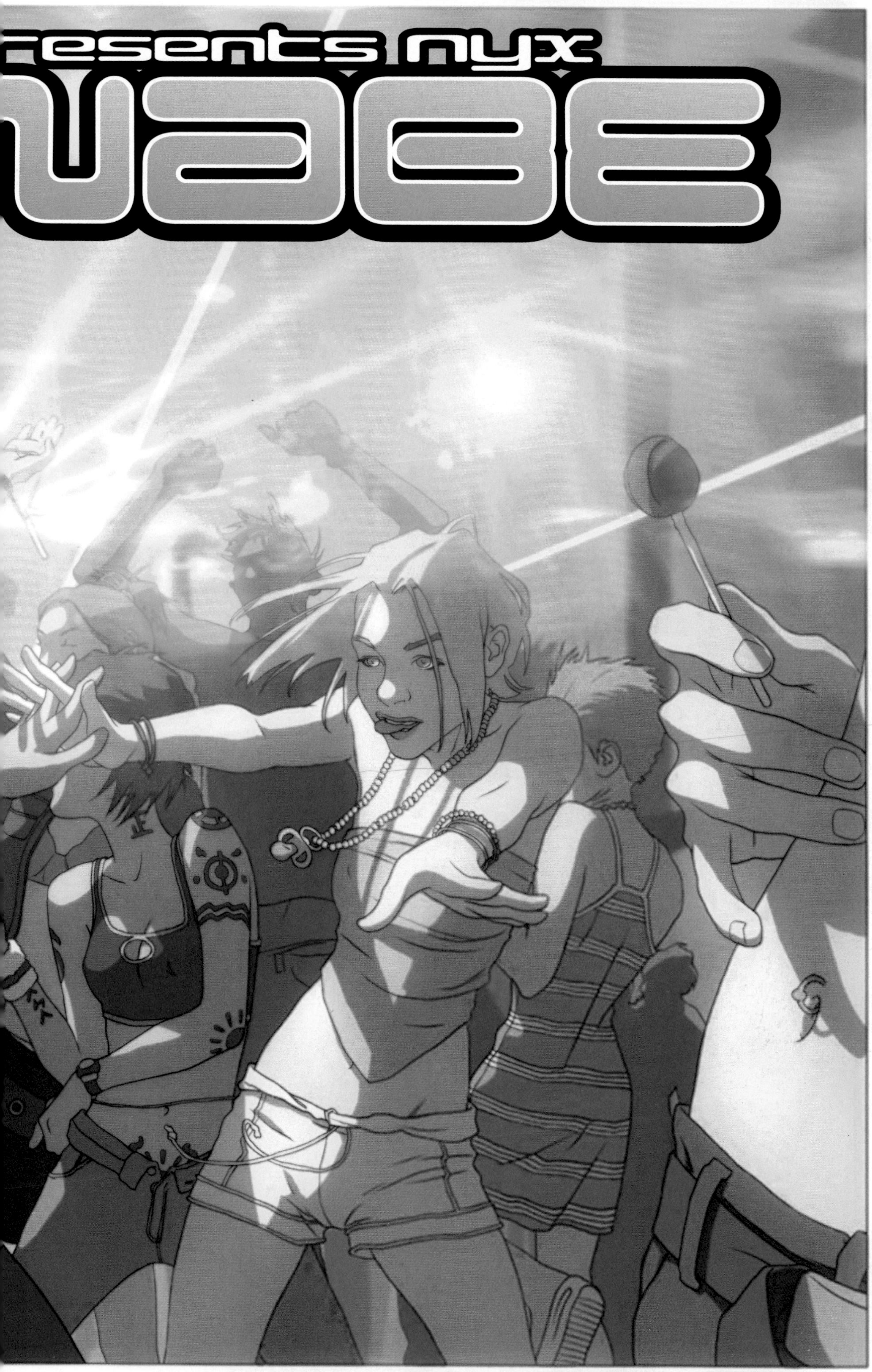

resents nyx

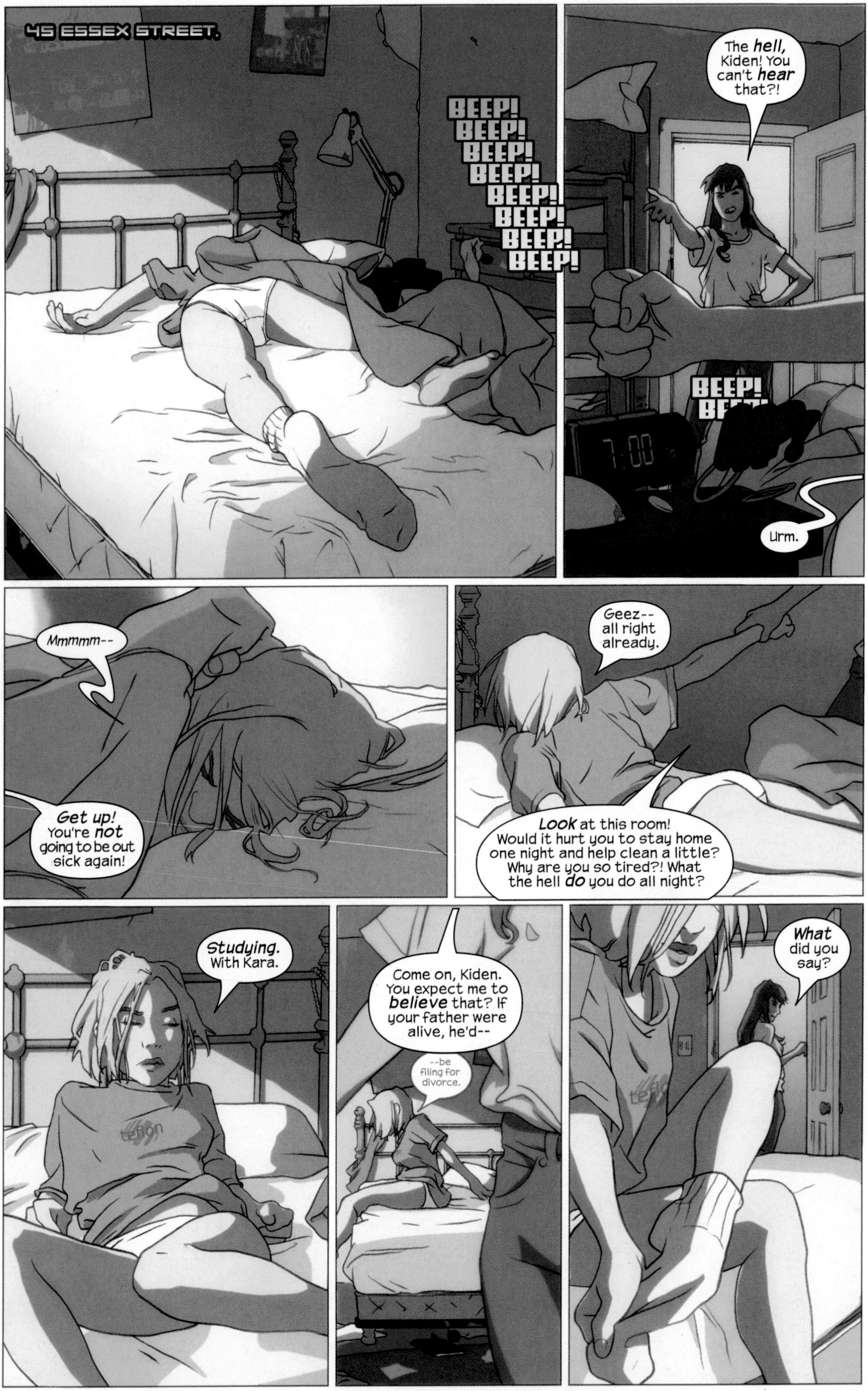
45 ESSEX STREET.
BEEP! BEEP! BEEP! BEEP! BEEP! BEEP! BEEP! BEEP!
The hell, Kiden! You can't hear that?!
BEEP!
Urm.
Mmmmm--
Get up! You're not going to be out sick again!
Geez-- all right already.
Look at this room! Would it hurt you to stay home one night and help clean a little? Why are you so tired?! What the hell do you do all night?
Studying. With Kara.
Come on, Kiden. You expect me to believe that? If your father were alive, he'd--
--be filing for divorce.
What did you say?

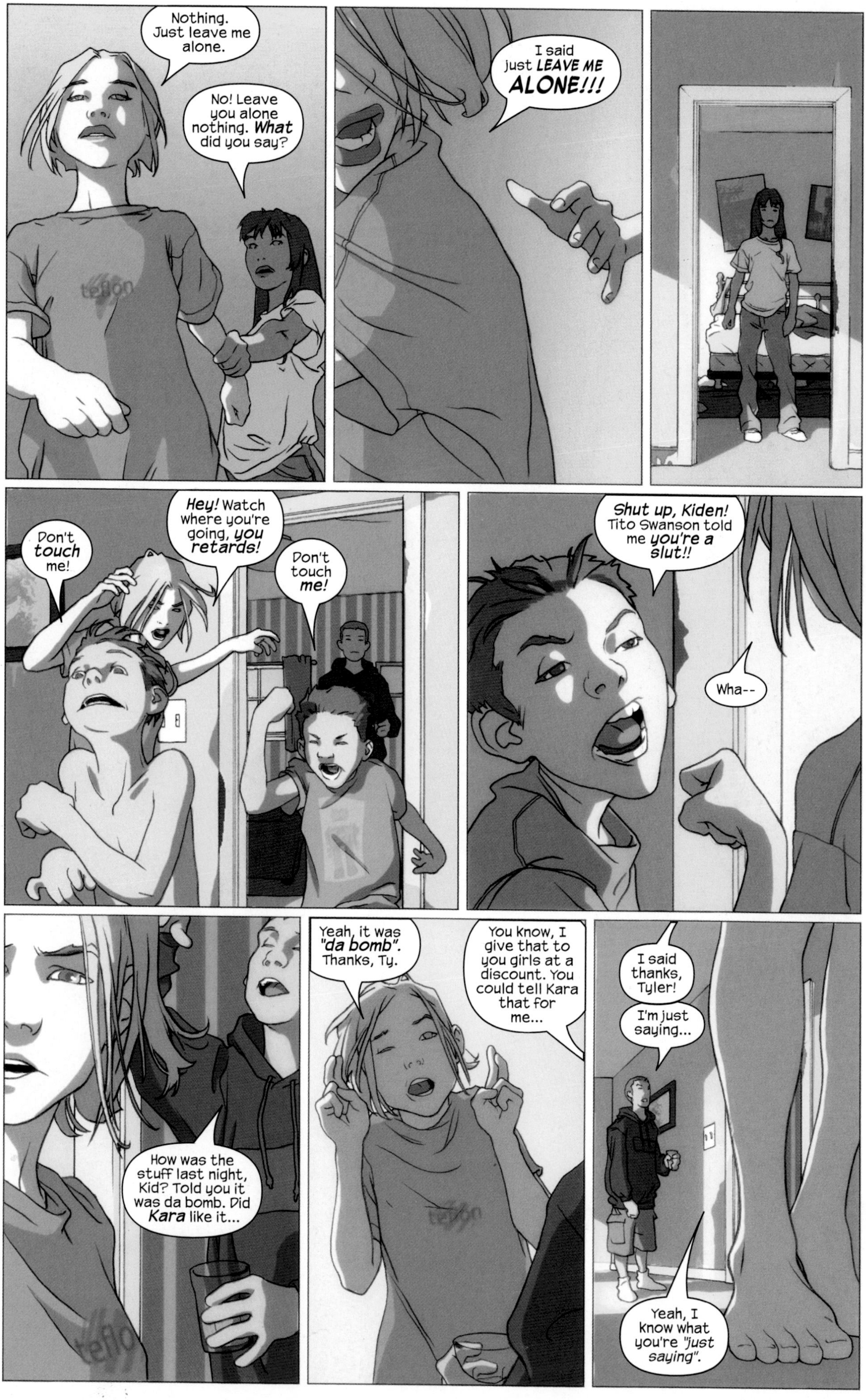
Nothing. Just leave me alone.
No! Leave you alone nothing. *What* did you say?
I said just ***LEAVE ME ALONE!!!***
Don't ***touch*** *me!*
Hey! Watch where you're going, ***you retards!***
Don't touch ***me!***
Shut up, Kiden! Tito Swanson told me ***you're a slut!!***
Wha--
How was the stuff last night, Kid? Told you it was da bomb. Did ***Kara*** like it...
Yeah, it was ***"da bomb"***. Thanks, Ty.
You know, I give that to you girls at a discount. You could tell Kara that for me...
I said thanks, Tyler!
I'm just saying...
Yeah, I know what you're *"just saying"*.

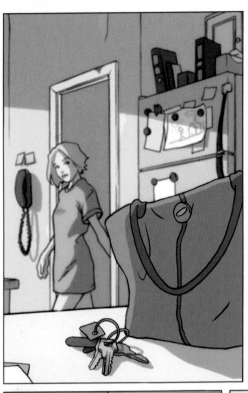

Kiden?

I'm sorry. I didn't mean to--

No, Mom-- it's okay. It was my fault. I shouldn't have said what I said.

Stop. Don't apologize, Kid. Look I know what-- I mean you're sixteen, it's--

Look, can we just sit and talk... just once like we're not enemies?

Yeah, Mom, sure. I'd like that.

Maybe when I get back from school.

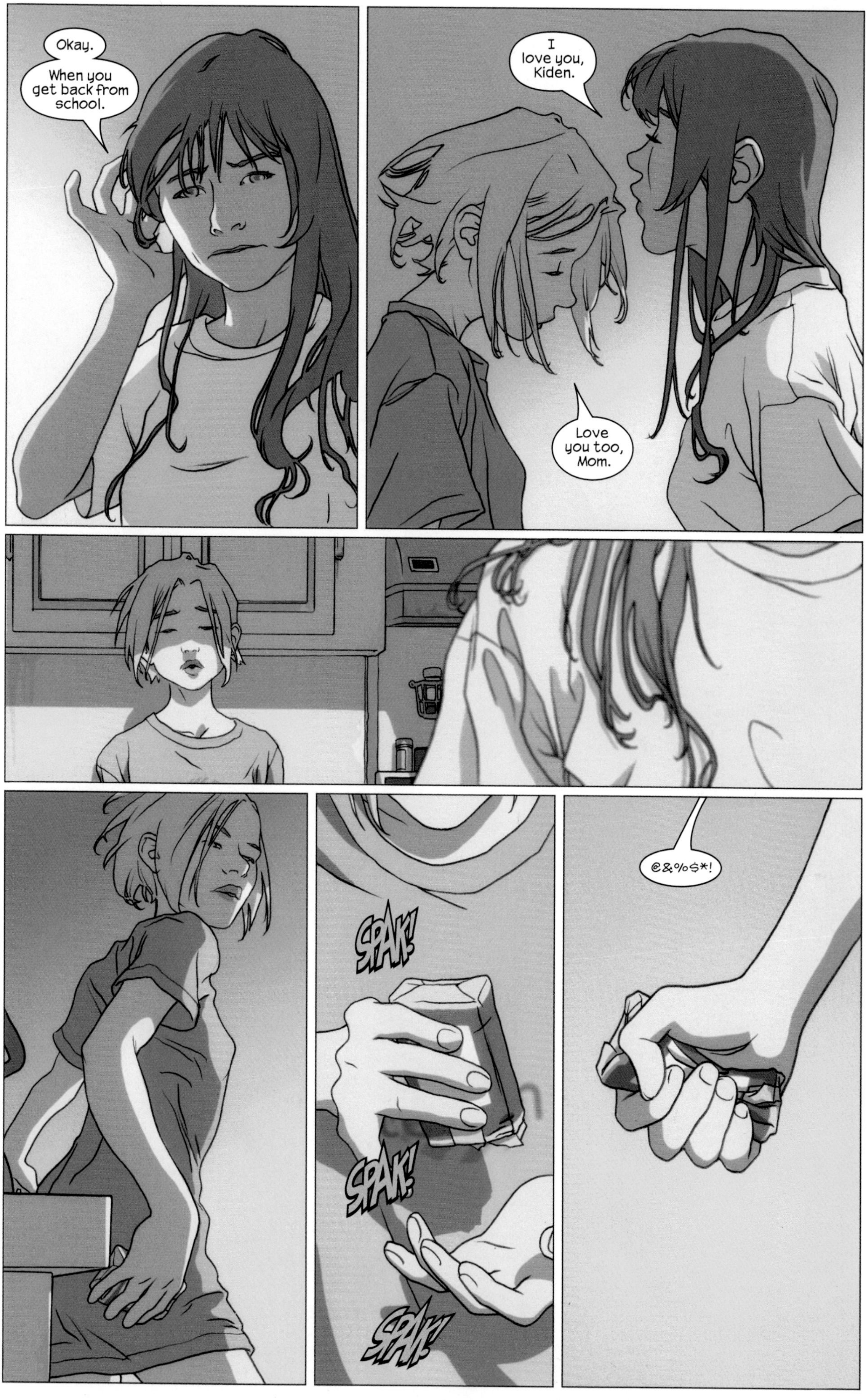
Okay.
When you get back from school.
I love you, Kiden.
Love you too, Mom.
SPAK!
SPAK!
SPAK!
@&%$*!

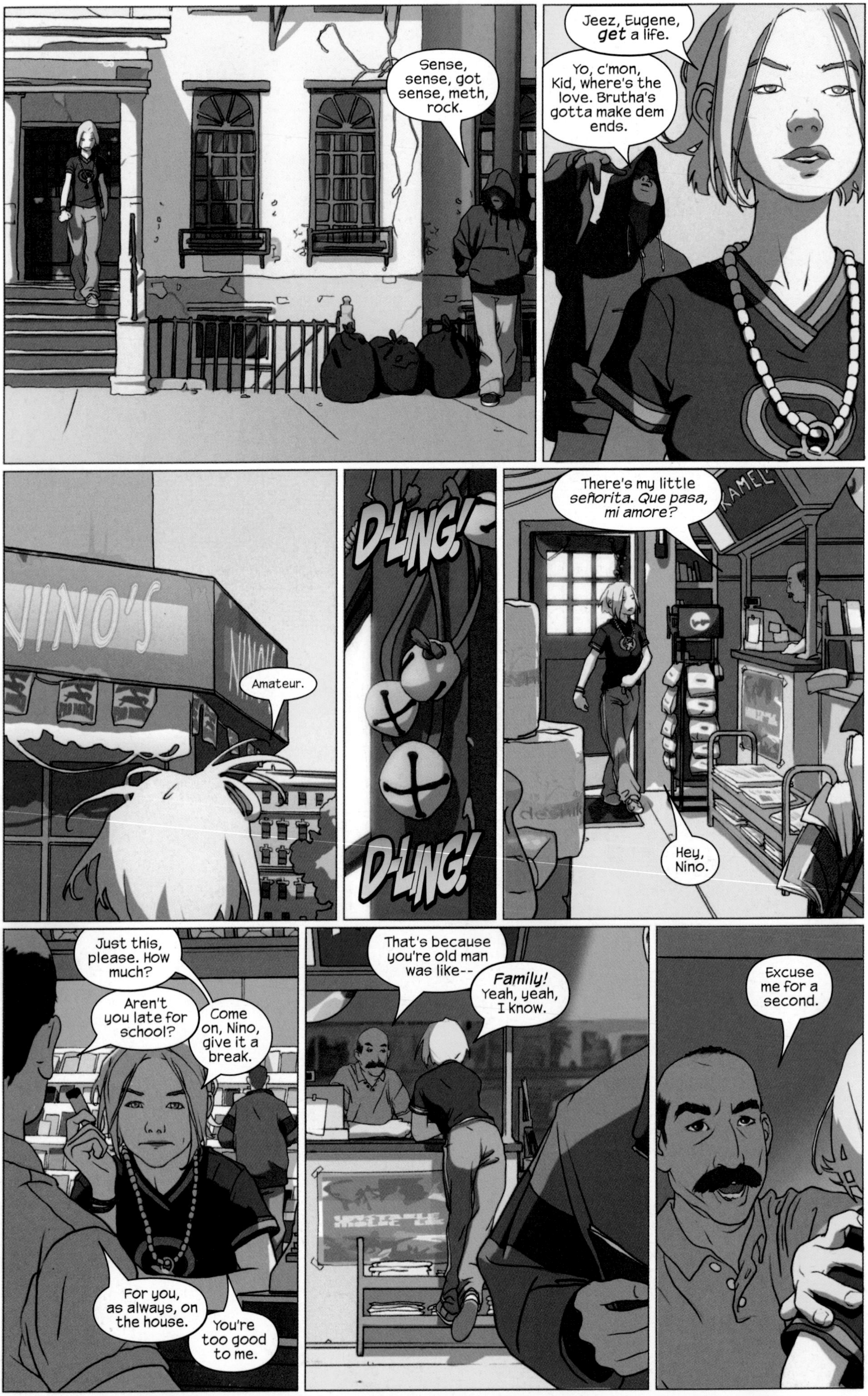

Sense, sense, got sense, meth, rock.
Jeez, Eugene, *get* a life.
Yo, c'mon, Kid, where's the love. Brutha's gotta make dem ends.
NINO'S
Amateur.
D-LING!
D-LING!
There's my little señorita. Que pasa, mi amore?
Hey, Nino.
Just this, please. How much?
Aren't you late for school?
Come on, Nino, give it a break.
For you, as always, on the house.
You're too good to me.
That's because you're old man was like--
Family! Yeah, yeah, I know.
Excuse me for a second.

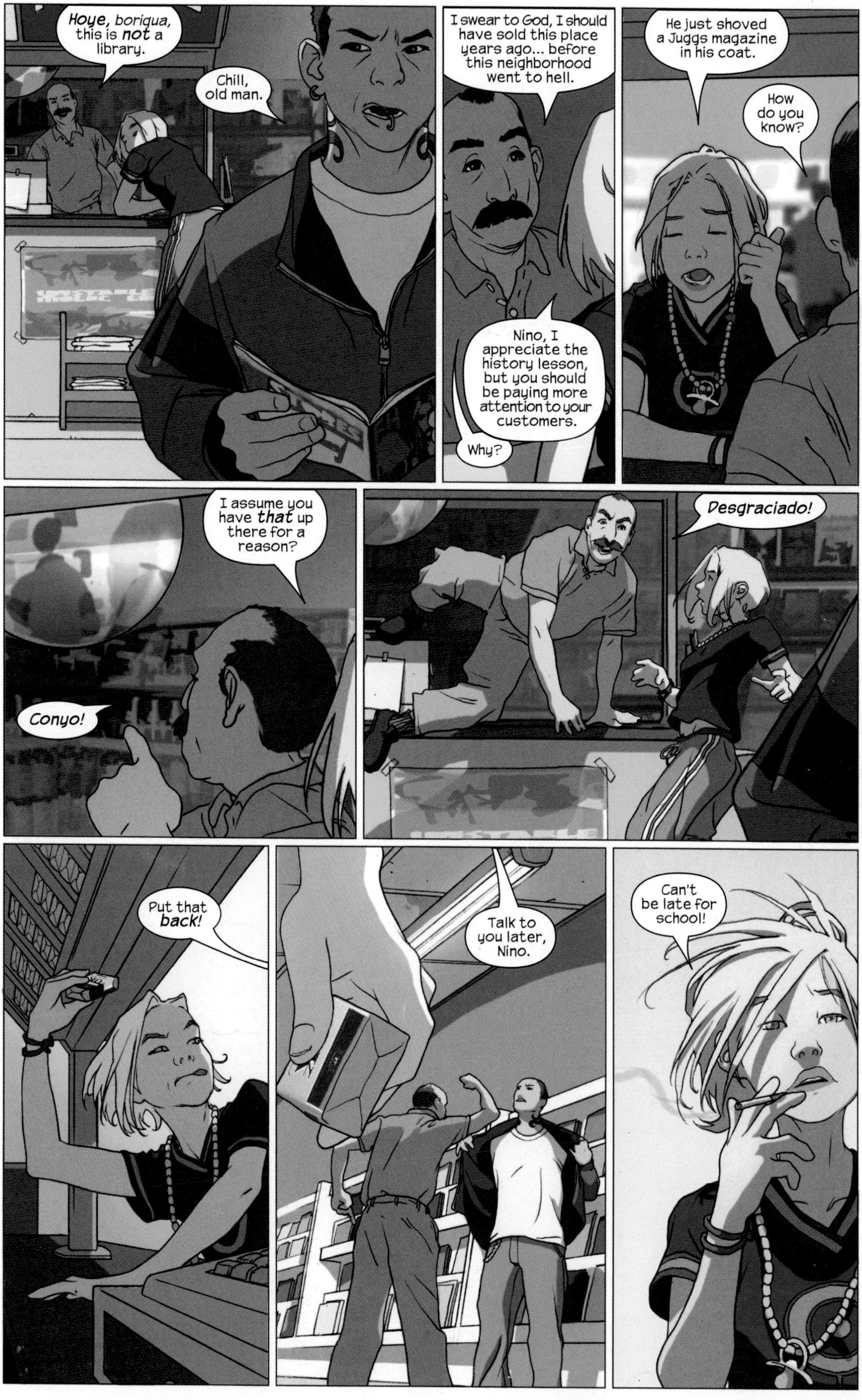
Hoye, boriqua, this is not a library.
Chill, old man.
I swear to God, I should have sold this place years ago... before this neighborhood went to hell.
Nino, I appreciate the history lesson, but you should be paying more attention to your customers.
Why?
He just shoved a Juggs magazine in his coat.
How do you know?
I assume you have that up there for a reason?
Conyo!
Desgraciado!
Put that back!
Talk to you later, Nino.
Can't be late for school!

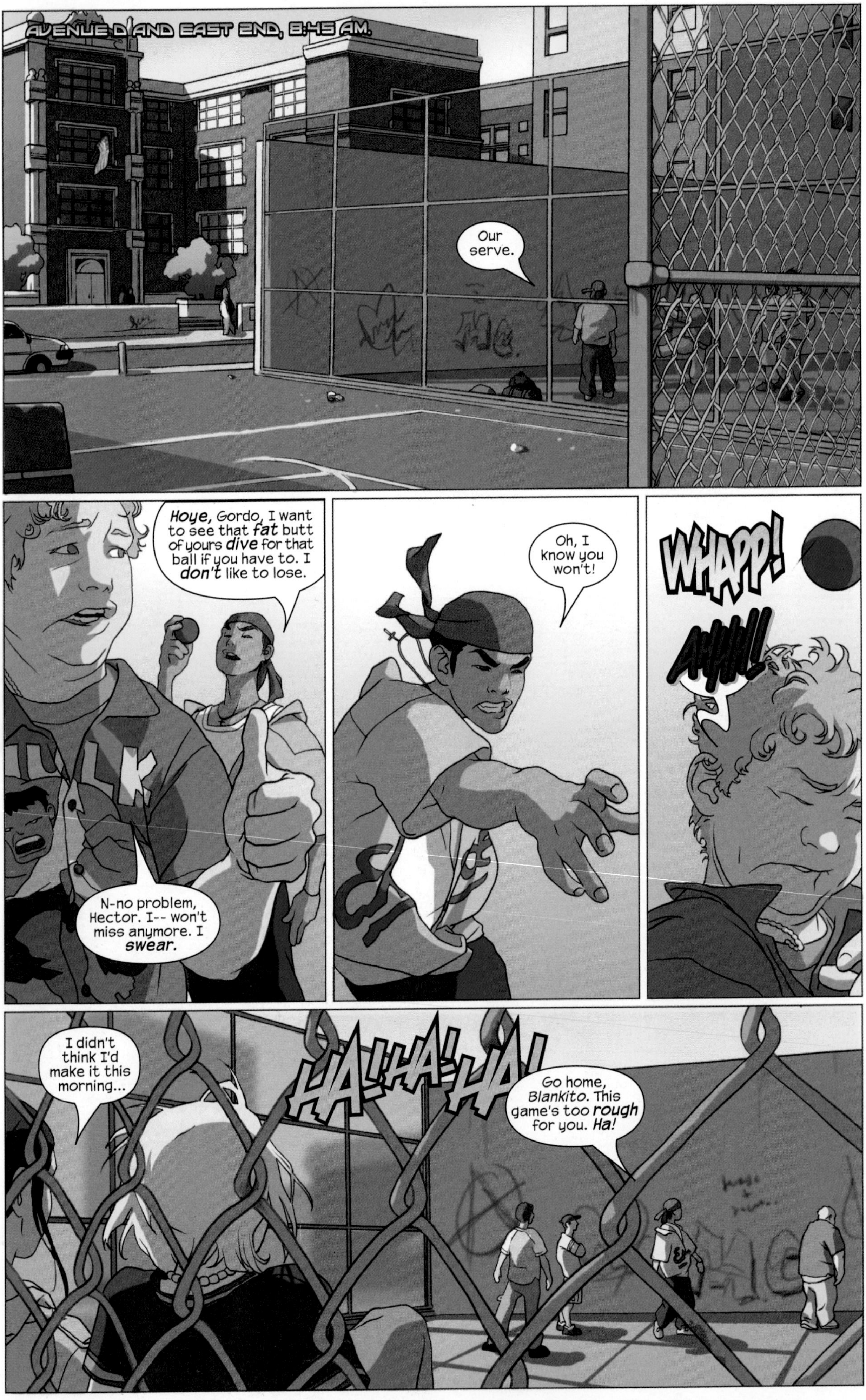
AVENUE D AND EAST 2ND, 8:45 AM.
Our serve.
Hoye, Gordo, I want to see that fat butt of yours dive for that ball if you have to. I don't like to lose.
N-no problem, Hector. I-- won't miss anymore. I swear.
Oh, I know you won't!
WHAPP!
AHHH!!
I didn't think I'd make it this morning...
HA! HA! HA!
Go home, Blankito. This game's too rough for you. Ha!

...my mom was completely passed out, and I came down so hard I started to cry watching a rerun of "Full House".

Heh. That's a sure sign of brain damage.

I wish my mom could just pass out for a bit.

It's like she wants to be Super Mom, but then have us pay for it with her misery. Tonight she wants to do the *talk*.

Uh-oh. Beware the dreaded "talk".

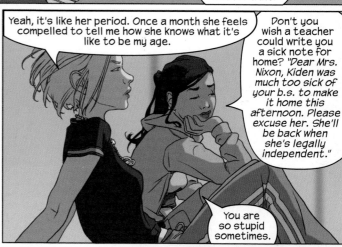

Yeah, it's like her period. Once a month she feels compelled to tell me how she knows what it's like to be my age.

Don't you wish a teacher could write you a sick note for home? "Dear Mrs. Nixon, Kiden was much too sick of your b.s. to make it home this afternoon. Please excuse her. She'll be back when she's legally independent."

You are so stupid sometimes.

Stupid is as stupid does.

Your mom tell you that, or one of her hippie boyfriends...

Oh, please, you wish you were me.

You're right. Why can't my mom find a boyfriend and make someone else miserable for a change?

Share the wealth, ya know!

It's worked for me.

BAP!

HEY!

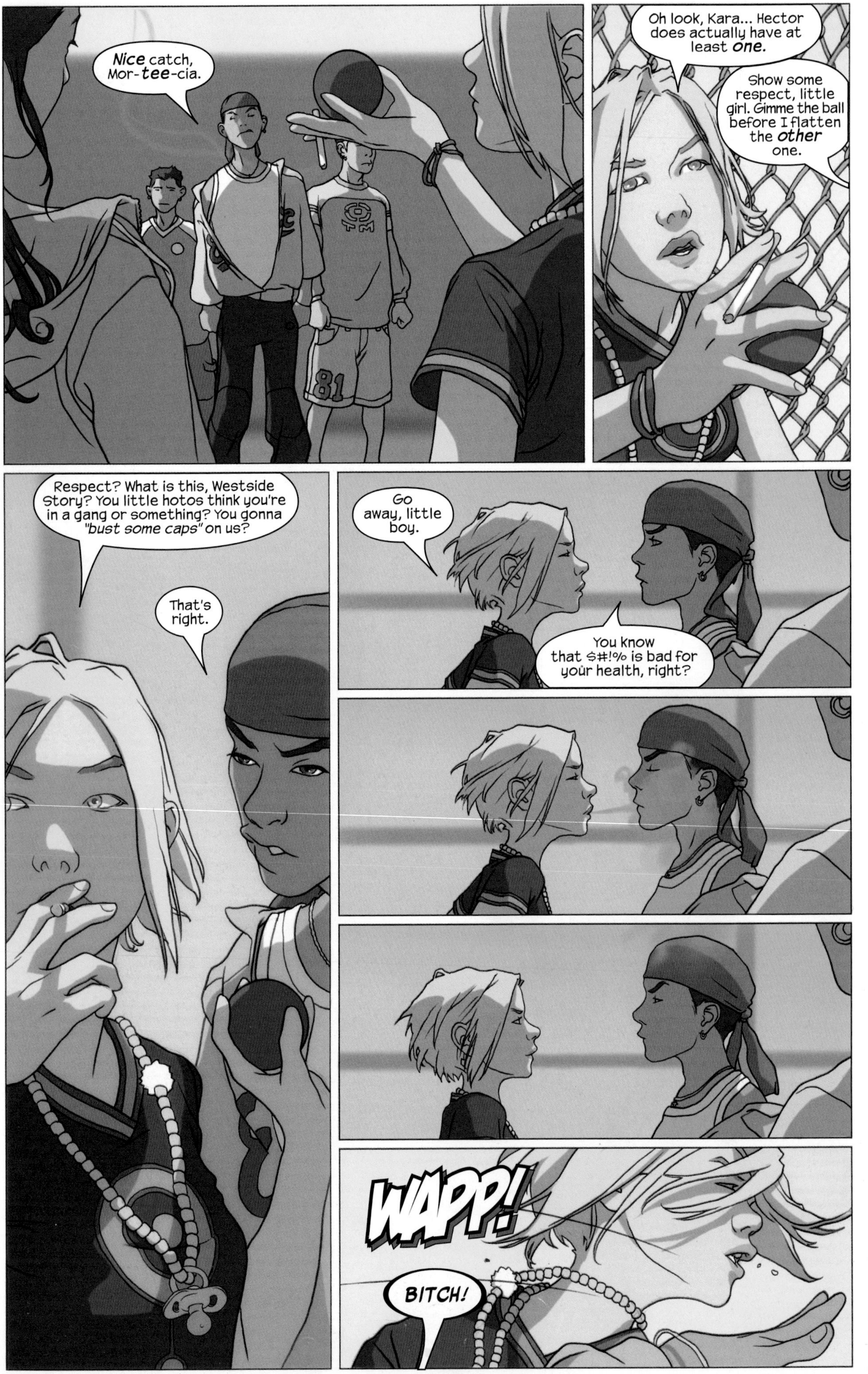

Nice catch, Mor-tee-cia.
Oh look, Kara... Hector does actually have at least one.
Show some respect, little girl. Gimme the ball before I flatten the other one.
Respect? What is this, Westside Story? You little hotos think you're in a gang or something? You gonna "bust some caps" on us?
That's right.
Go away, little boy.
You know that $#!% is bad for your health, right?
WAPP!
BITCH!

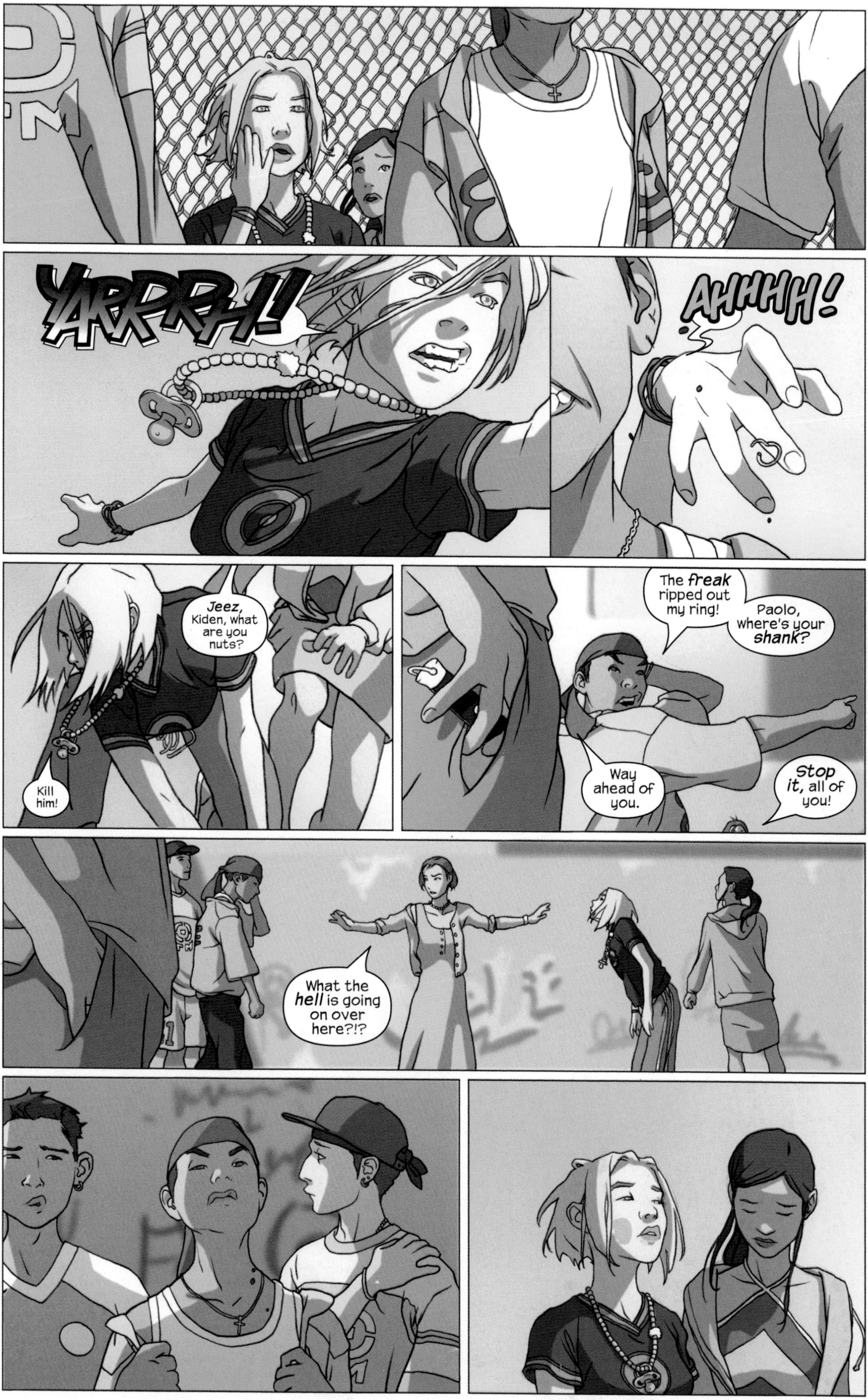
YARRRGH!
AHHHH!
Jeez, Kiden, what are you nuts?
Kill him!
The freak ripped out my ring!
Paolo, where's your shank?
Way ahead of you.
Stop it, all of you!
What the hell is going on over here?!?

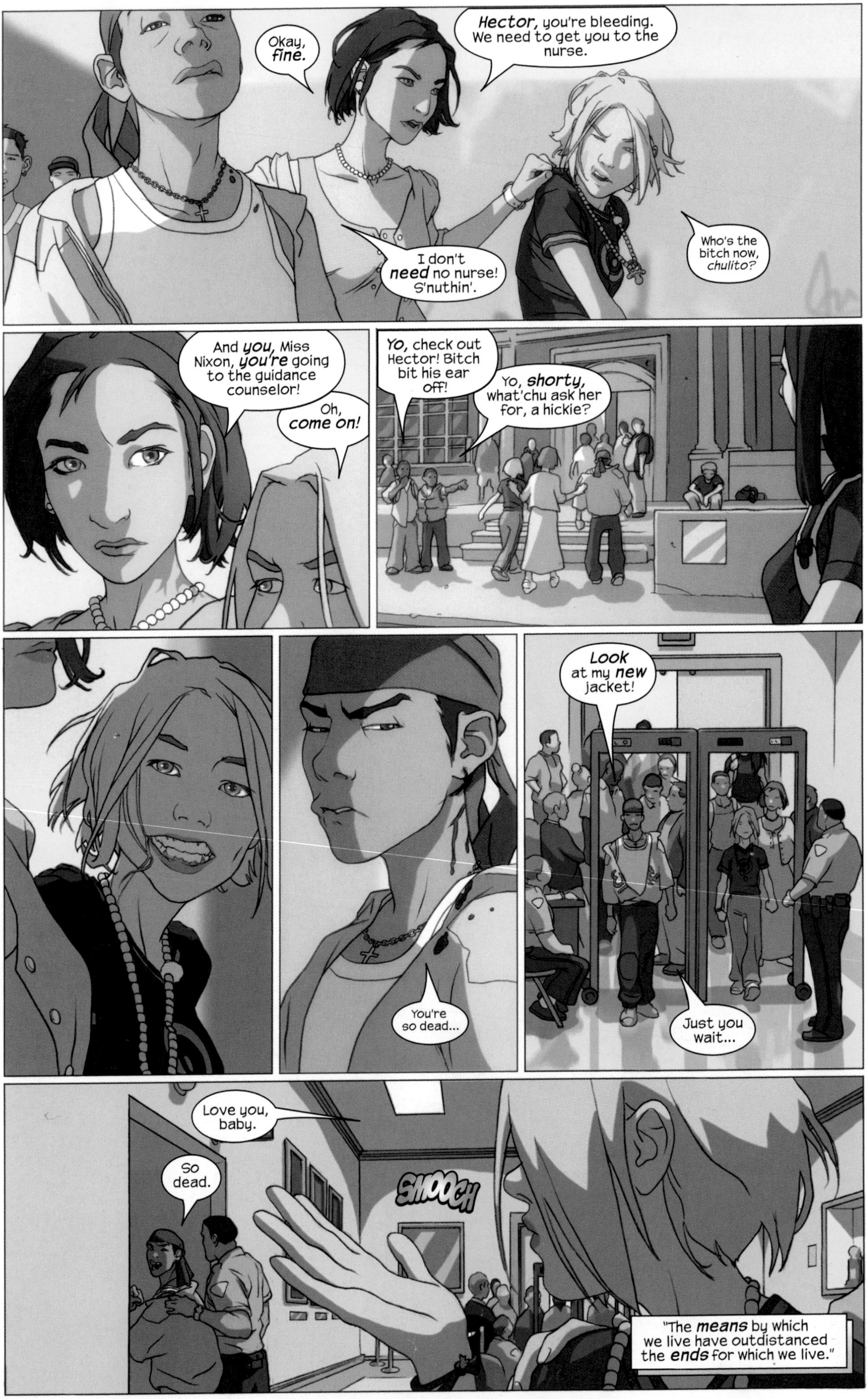
Okay, fine.
Hector, you're bleeding. We need to get you to the nurse.
I don't need no nurse! S'nuthin'.
Who's the bitch now, chulito?
And you, Miss Nixon, you're going to the guidance counselor!
Oh, come on!
Yo, check out Hector! Bitch bit his ear off!
Yo, shorty, what'chu ask her for, a hickie?
You're so dead...
Look at my new jacket!
Just you wait...
Love you, baby.
So dead.
SMOOCH
"The means by which we live have outdistanced the ends for which we live."

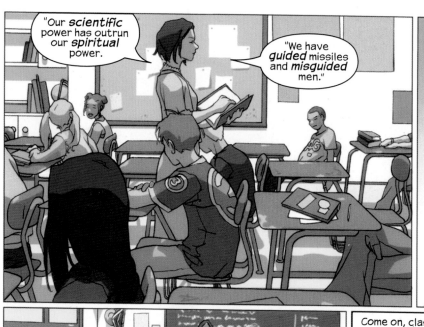

"Our *scientific* power has outrun our *spiritual* power.

"We have *guided* missiles and *misguided* men."

What did Doctor King mean by this?

Come on, class, we have *three* minutes before the bell rings.

Anybody?

It means we're all doomed.

...I assume you have a note from the guidance counselor for me?

Yeah, thanks a hell of a whole lot.

Very good. Take your seat.

Miss Nixon...

Now, the truth of the matter is that Miss Nixon isn't entirely wrong.

Hey, Ms. Palmer, that would be the *first* time this semester!

BWAHA-HA-HA-HA-HA!

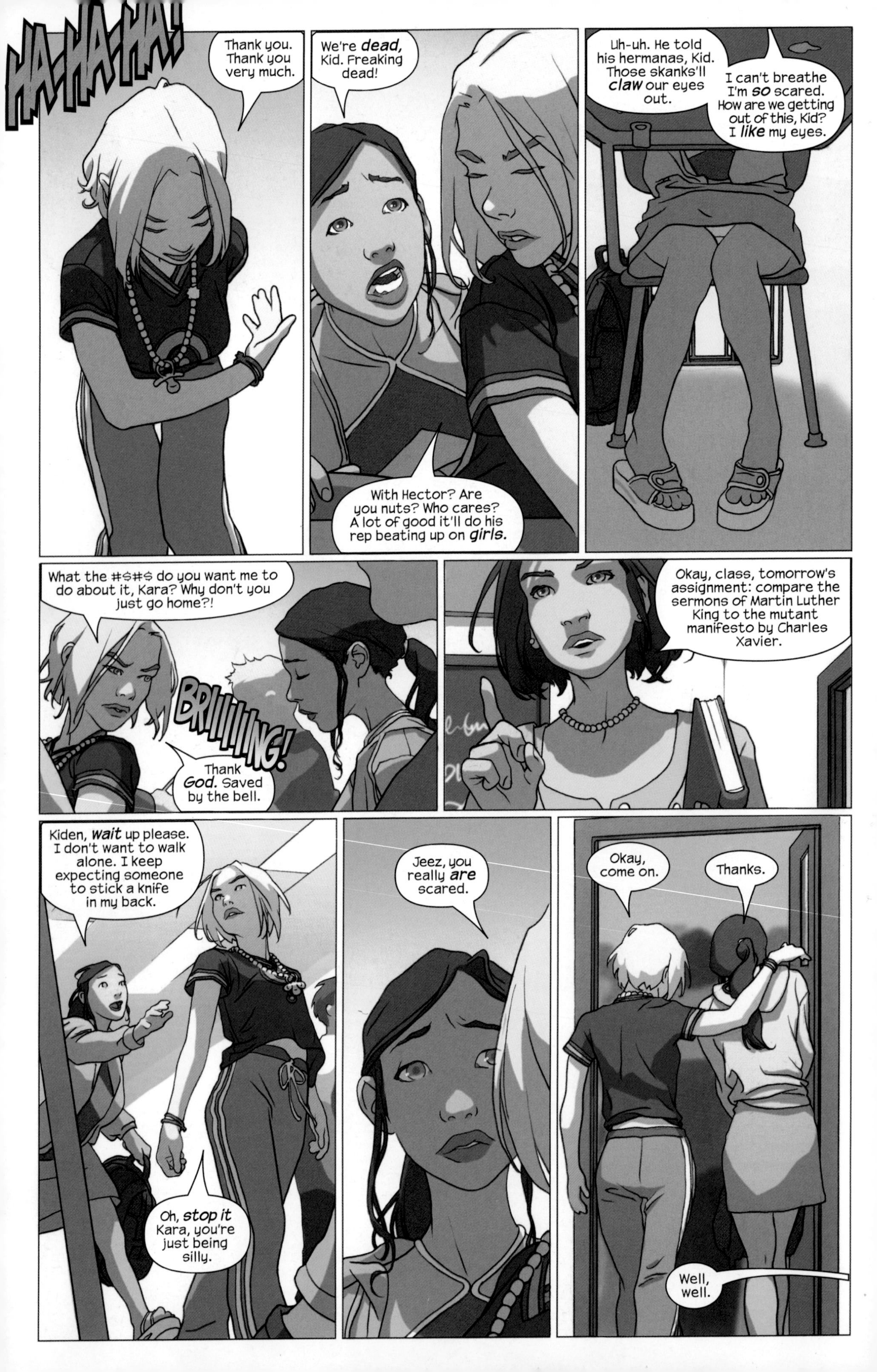
HA-HA-HA!
Thank you. Thank you very much.
We're *dead,* Kid. Freaking dead!
With Hector? Are you nuts? Who cares? A lot of good it'll do his rep beating up on *girls.*
Uh-uh. He told his hermanas, Kid. Those skanks'll *claw* our eyes out.
I can't breathe I'm *so* scared. How are we getting out of this, Kid? I *like* my eyes.
What the #$#$ do you want me to do about it, Kara? Why don't you just go home?!
BRIIIIIING!
Thank *God.* Saved by the bell.
Okay, class, tomorrow's assignment: compare the sermons of Martin Luther King to the mutant manifesto by Charles Xavier.
Kiden, *wait* up please. I don't want to walk alone. I keep expecting someone to stick a knife in my back.
Oh, *stop it* Kara, you're just being silly.
Jeez, you really *are* scared.
Okay, come on.
Thanks.
Well, well.

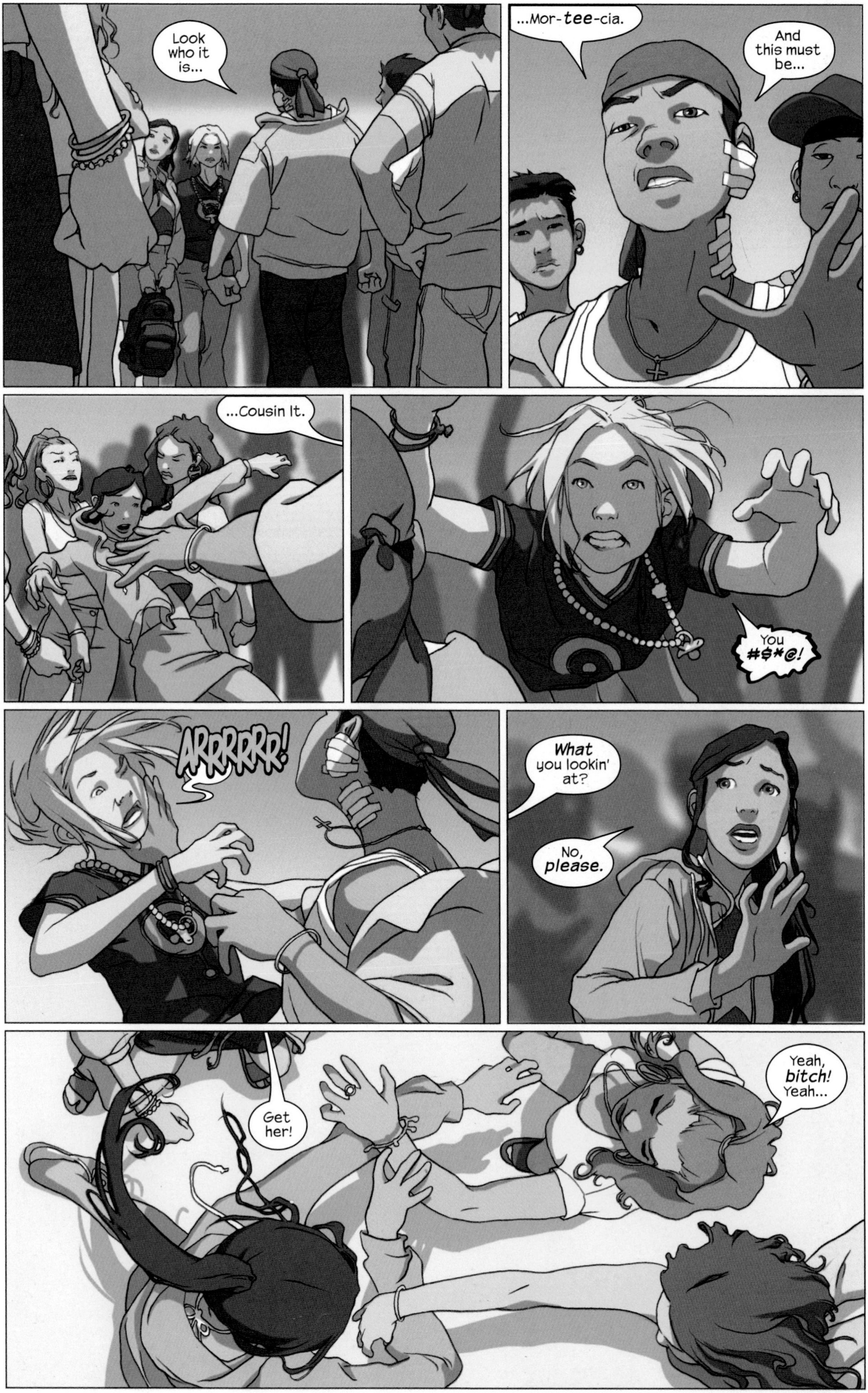

Look who it is...
...Mor-tee-cia.
And this must be...
...Cousin It.
You #$*@!
ARRRRRR!
What you lookin' at?
No, please.
Get her!
Yeah, bitch! Yeah...

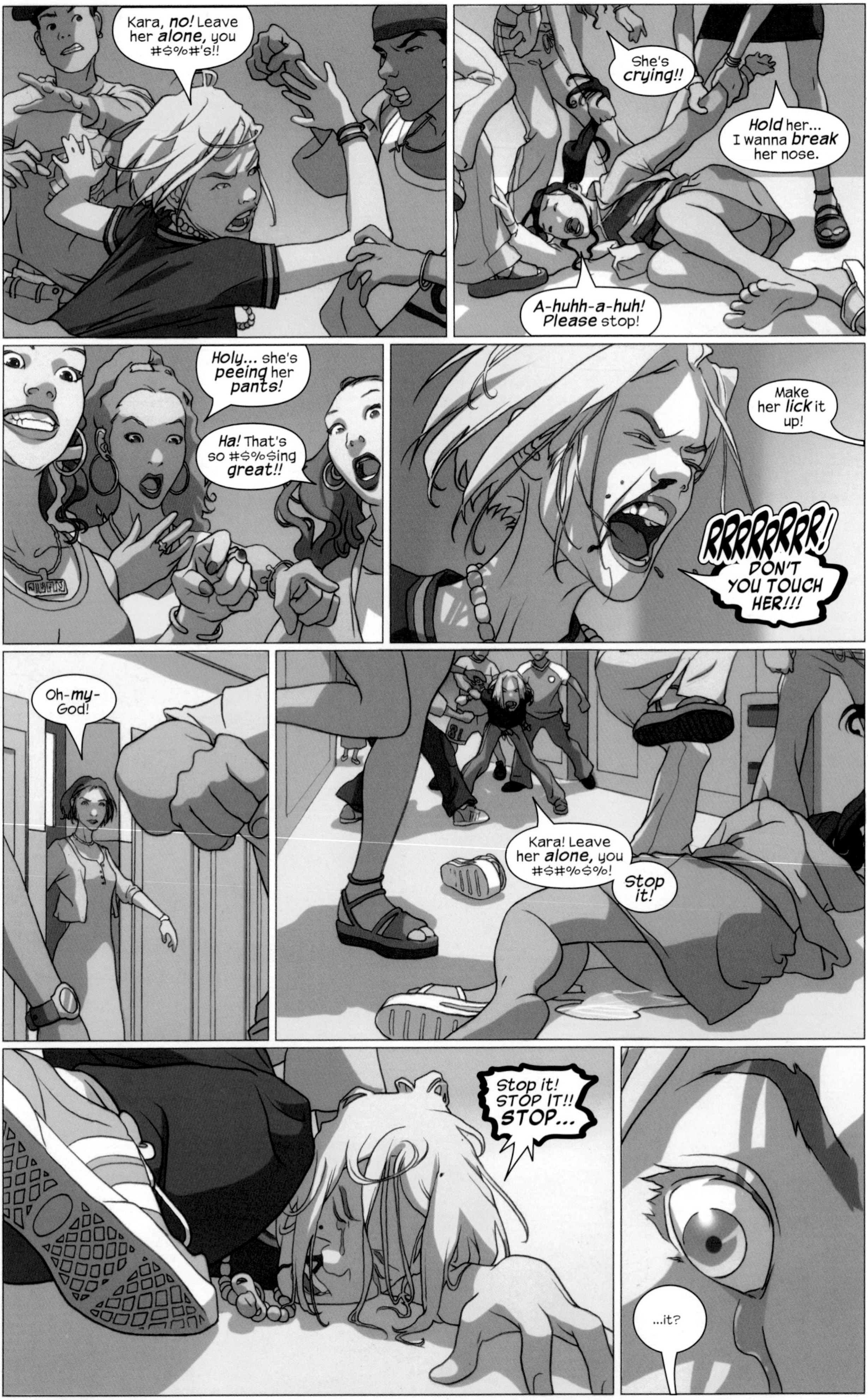
Kara, no! Leave her alone, you #$%#'s!!
She's crying!!
Hold her... I wanna break her nose.
A-huhh-a-huh! Please stop!
Holy... she's peeing her pants!
Ha! That's so #$%$ing great!!
Make her lick it up!
RRRRRRRR! DON'T YOU TOUCH HER!!!
Oh-my-God!
Kara! Leave her alone, you #$#%$%!
Stop it!
Stop it! STOP IT!! STOP...
...it?

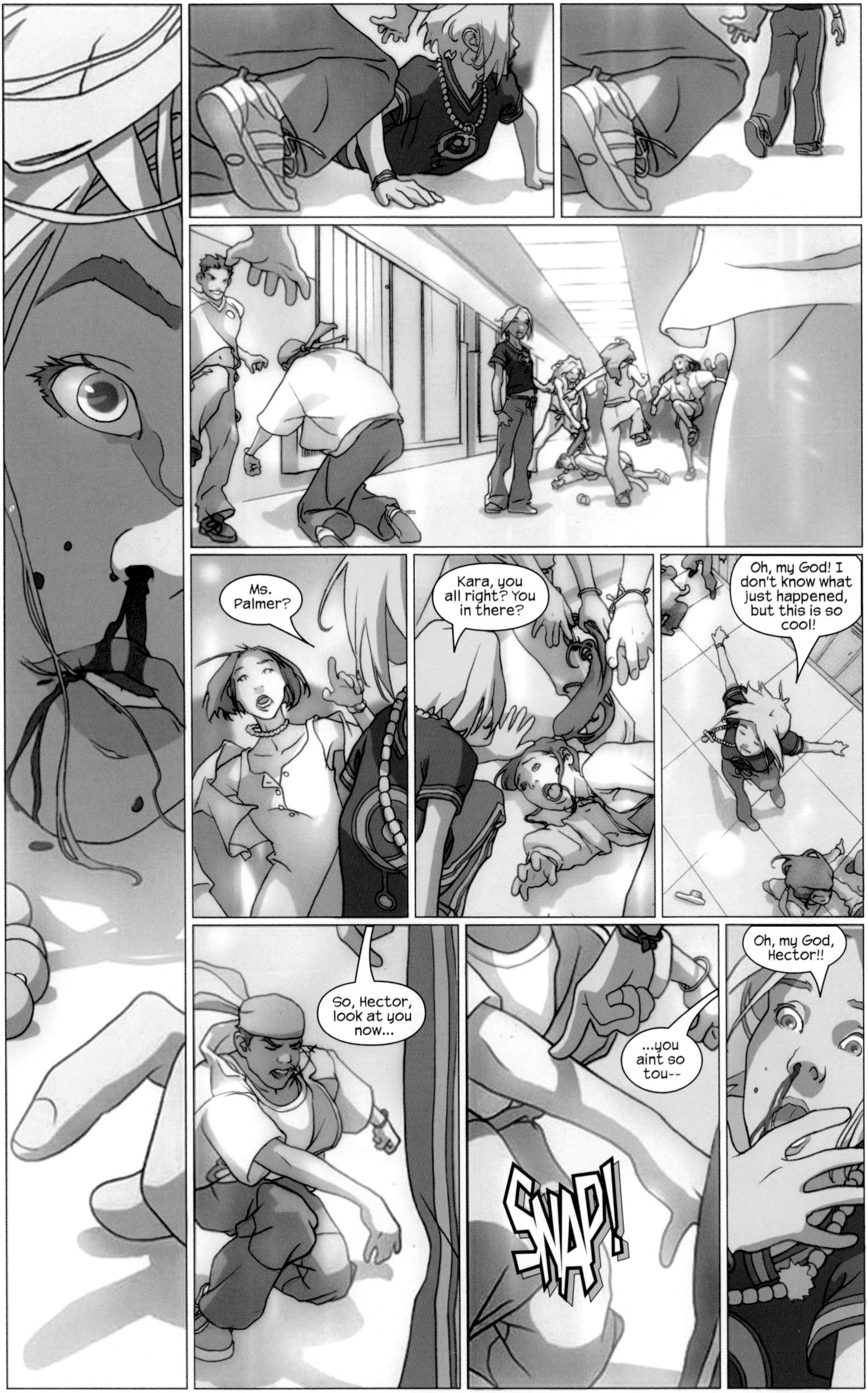

Ms. Palmer?
Kara, you all right? You in there?
Oh, my God! I don't know what just happened, but this is so cool!
So, Hector, look at you now...
...you aint so tou--
SNAP!
Oh, my God, Hector!!

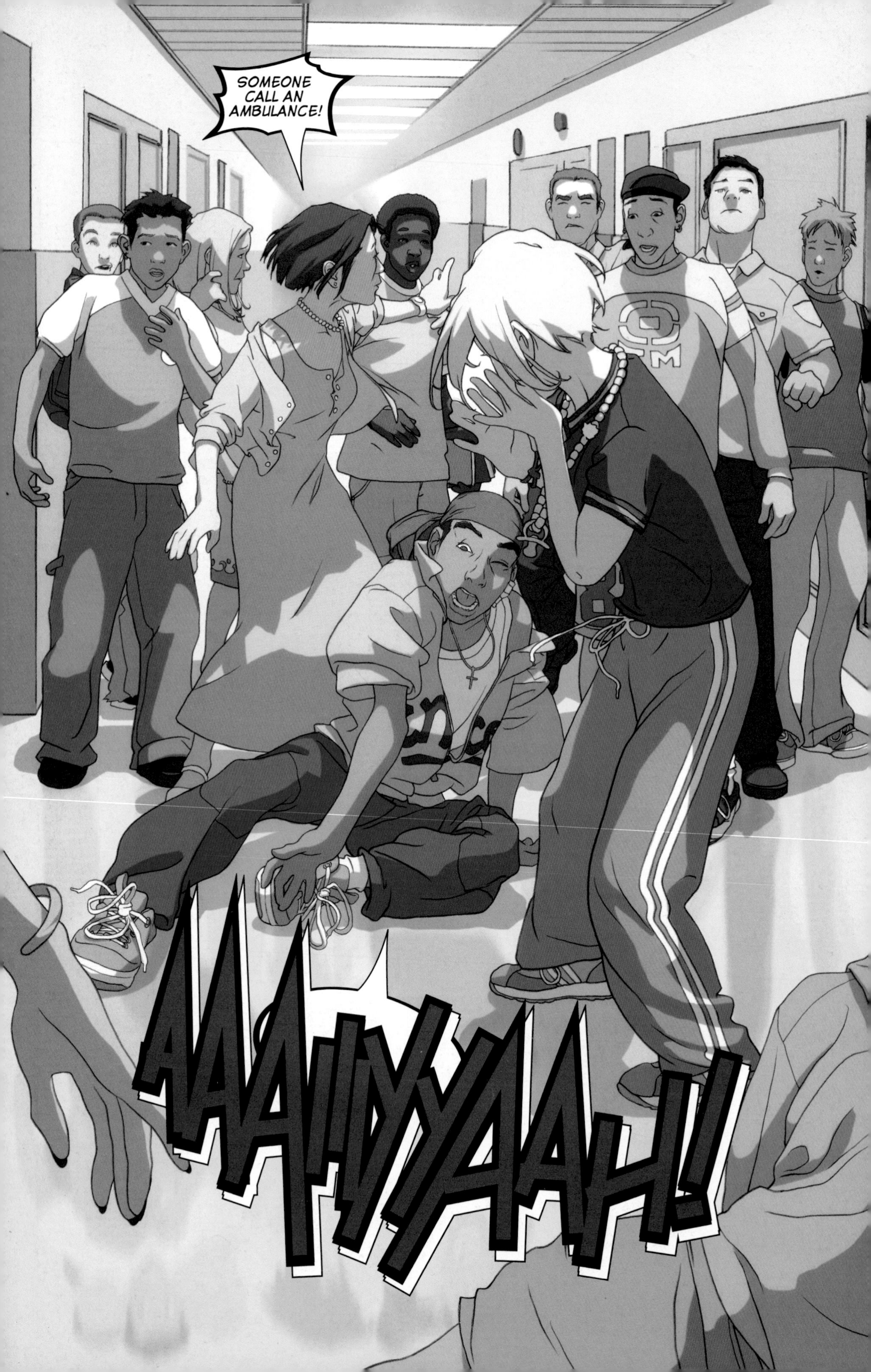
SOMEONE CALL AN AMBULANCE!
AAAHHYAAH!!

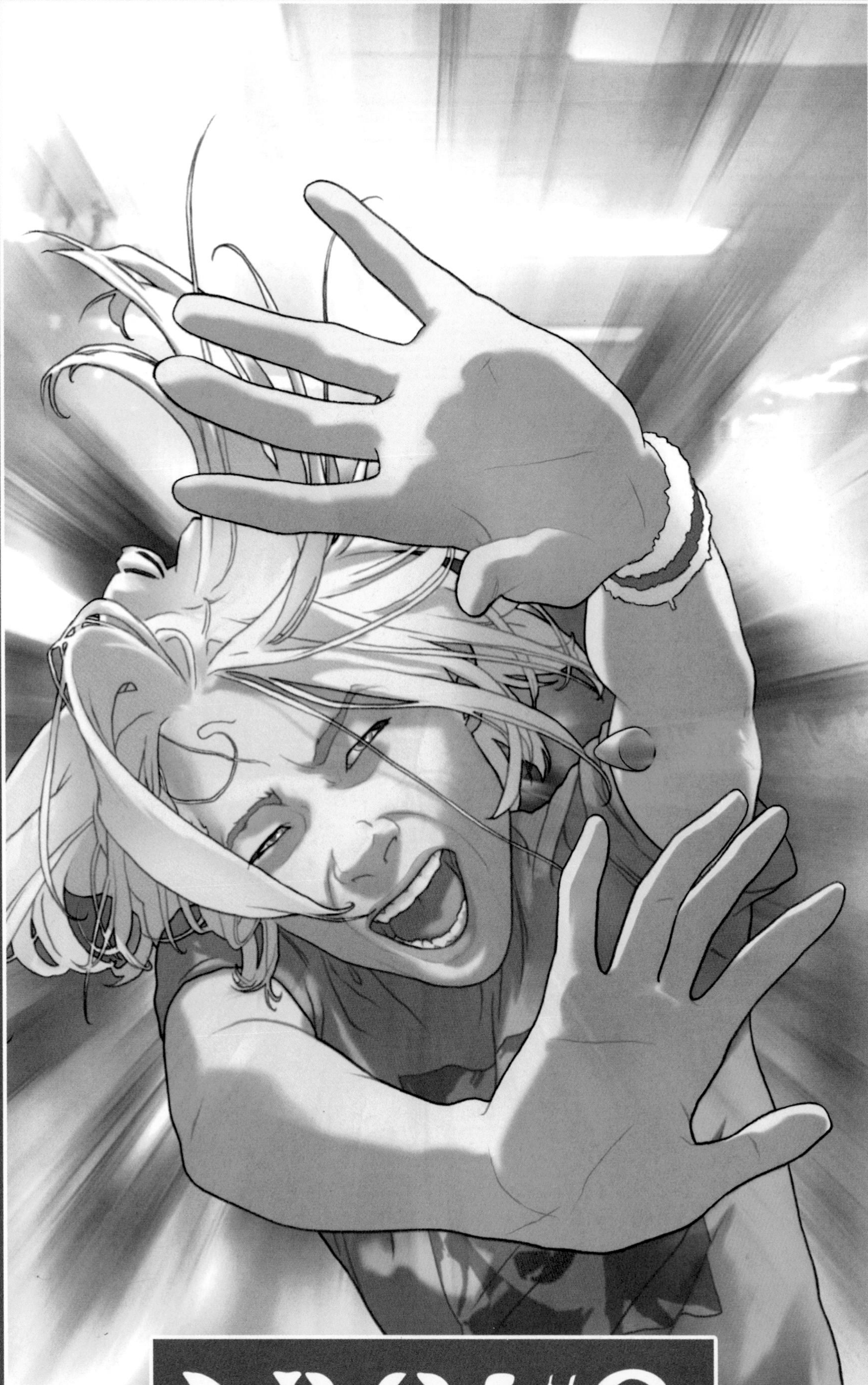

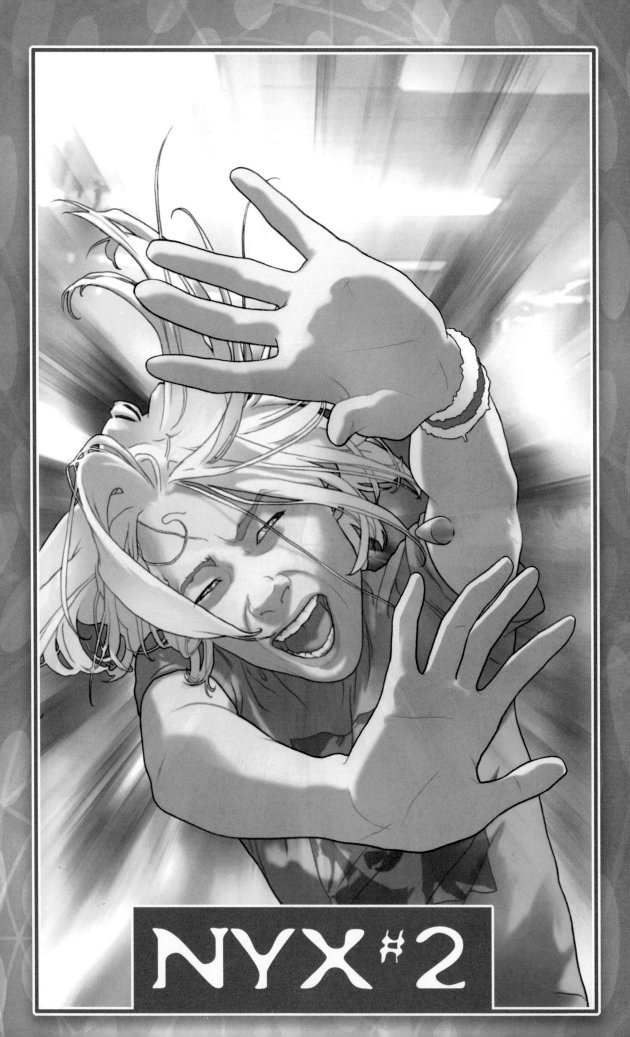

NYX #2

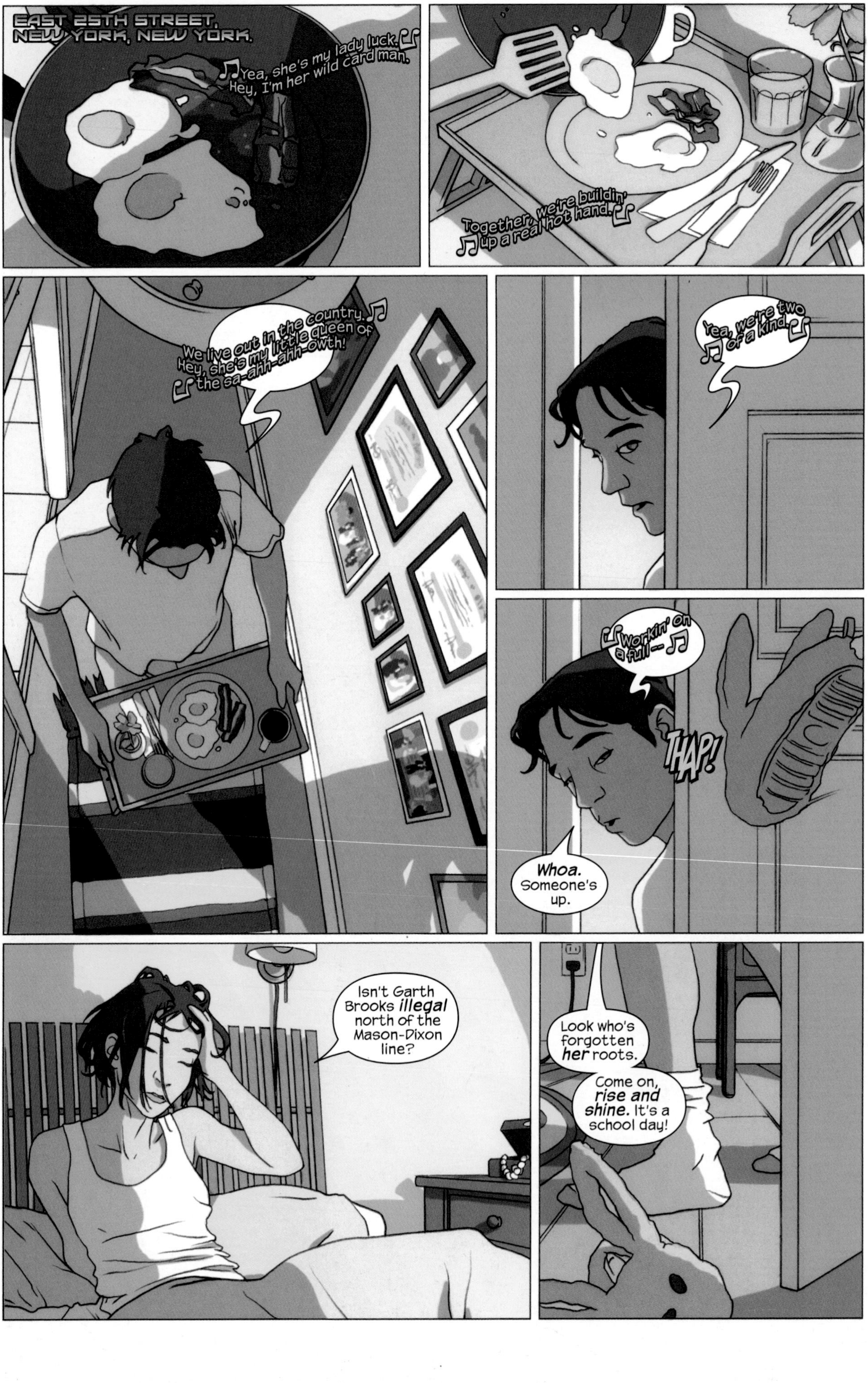

EAST 25TH STREET, NEW YORK, NEW YORK.
Yea, she's my lady luck. Hey, I'm her wild card man.
Together, we're buildin' up a real hot hand.
We live out in the country. Hey, she's my little queen of the sa-ahh-ahh-owth!
Yea, we're two of a kind.
Workin' on a full--
THAP!
Whoa. Someone's up.
Isn't Garth Brooks illegal north of the Mason-Dixon line?
Look who's forgotten her roots.
Come on, rise and shine. It's a school day!

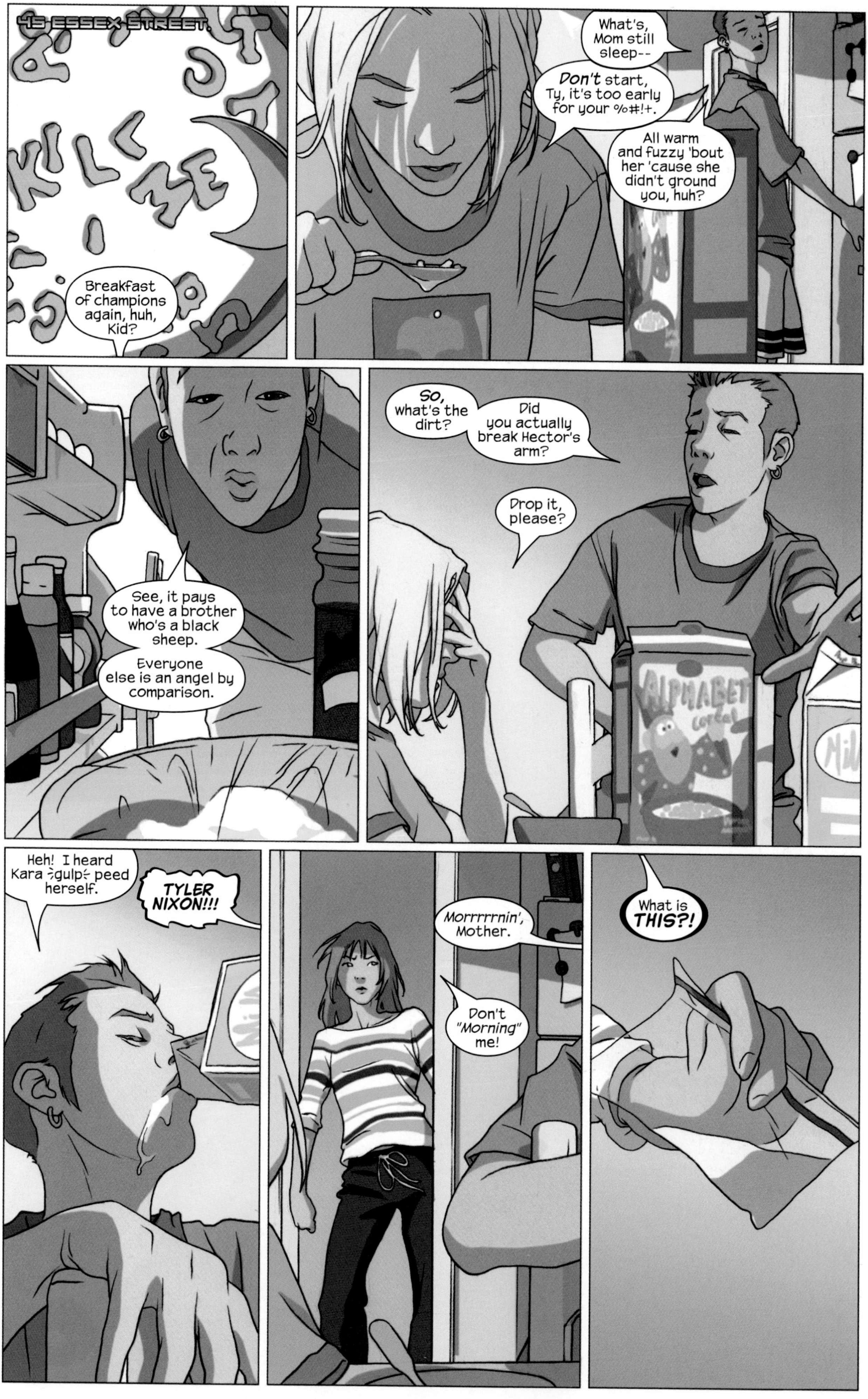
43 ESSEX STREET.
KILL ME
Breakfast of champions again, huh, Kid?
What's, Mom still sleep--
Don't start, Ty, it's too early for your %#!+.
All warm and fuzzy 'bout her 'cause she didn't ground you, huh?
See, it pays to have a brother who's a black sheep.
Everyone else is an angel by comparison.
So, what's the dirt?
Did you actually break Hector's arm?
Drop it, please?
ALPHABET cereal
Heh! I heard Kara <gulp> peed herself.
TYLER NIXON!!!
Morrrrrnin', Mother.
Don't "Morning" me!
What is THIS?!

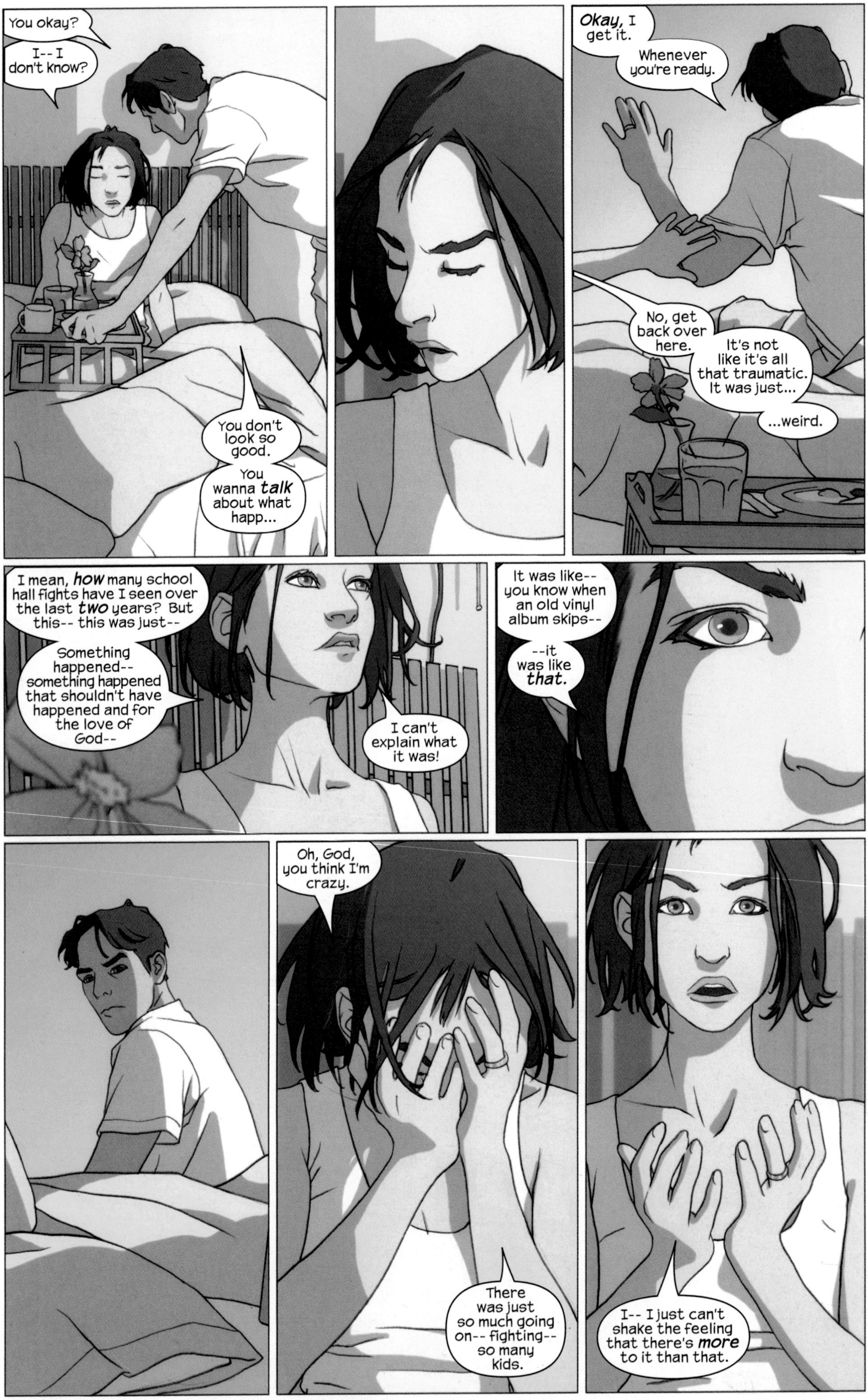
You okay?
I-- I don't know?
You don't look so good.
You wanna *talk* about what happ...
Okay, I get it.
Whenever you're ready.
No, get back over here.
It's not like it's all that traumatic. It was just...
...weird.
I mean, *how* many school hall fights have I seen over the last *two* years? But this-- this was just--
Something happened-- something happened that shouldn't have happened and for the love of God--
I can't explain what it was!
It was like-- you know when an old vinyl album skips--
--it was like *that.*
Oh, God, you think I'm crazy.
There was just so much going on-- fighting-- so many kids.
I-- I just can't shake the feeling that there's *more* to it than that.

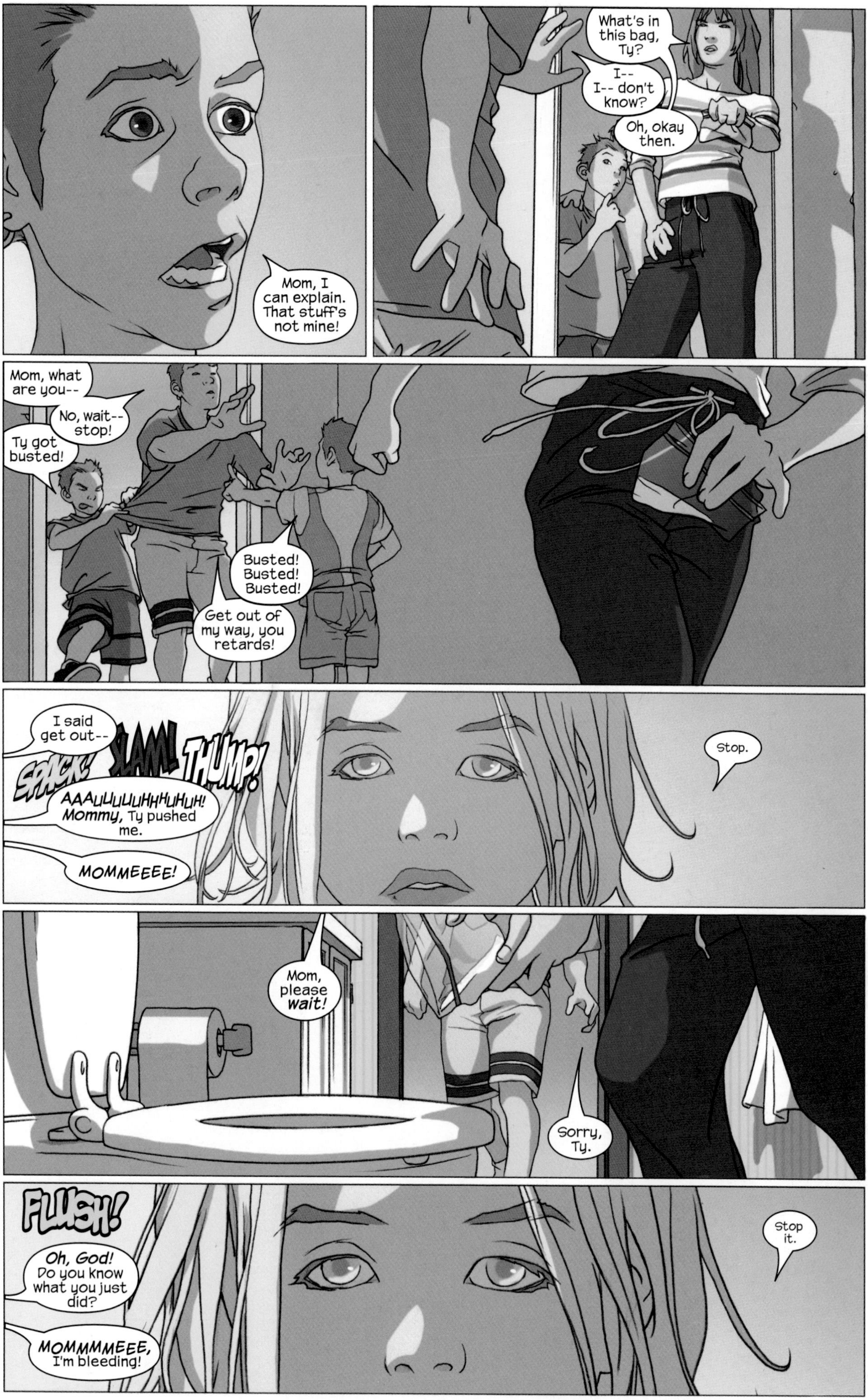
Mom, I can explain. That stuff's not mine!
What's in this bag, Ty?
I-- I-- don't know?
Oh, okay then.
Mom, what are you--
No, wait-- stop!
Ty got busted!
Busted! Busted! Busted!
Get out of my way, you retards!
I said get out--
SPACK!
SLAM!
THUMP!
AAAUUUUUHHHUHUH! Mommy, Ty pushed me.
MOMMEEEE!
Stop.
Mom, please wait!
Sorry, Ty.
FLUSH!
Oh, God! Do you know what you just did?
MOMMMMEEE, I'm bleeding!
Stop it.

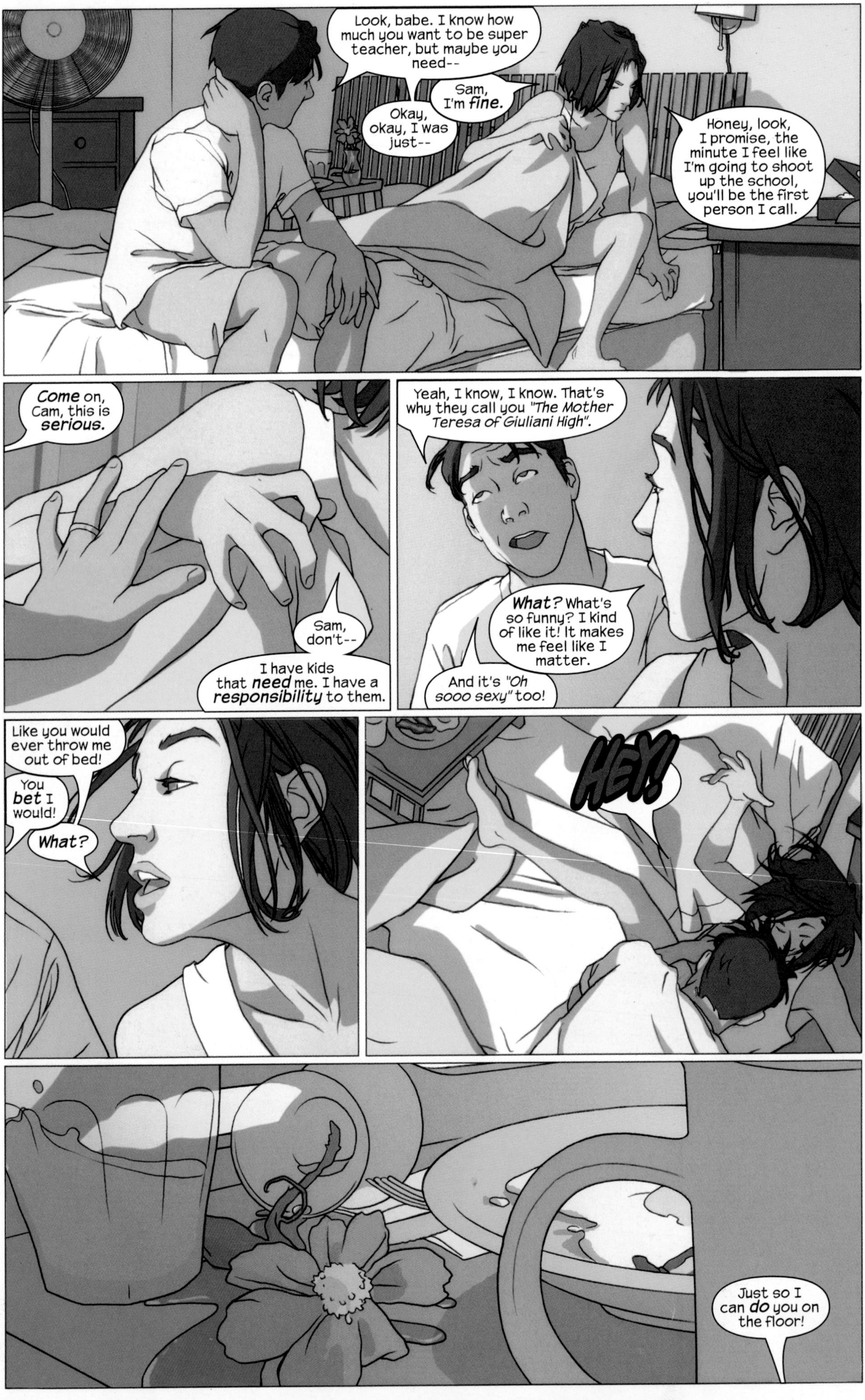
Look, babe. I know how much you want to be super teacher, but maybe you need--
Sam, I'm *fine.*
Okay, okay, I was just--
Honey, look, I promise, the minute I feel like I'm going to shoot up the school, you'll be the first person I call.
Come on, Cam, this is *serious.*
Sam, don't--
I have kids that *need* me. I have a *responsibility* to them.
Yeah, I know, I know. That's why they call you *"The Mother Teresa of Giuliani High".*
What? What's so funny? I kind of like it! It makes me feel like I matter.
And it's *"Oh sooo sexy"* too!
Like you would ever throw me out of bed!
You *bet* I would!
What?
HEY!
Just so I can *do* you on the floor!

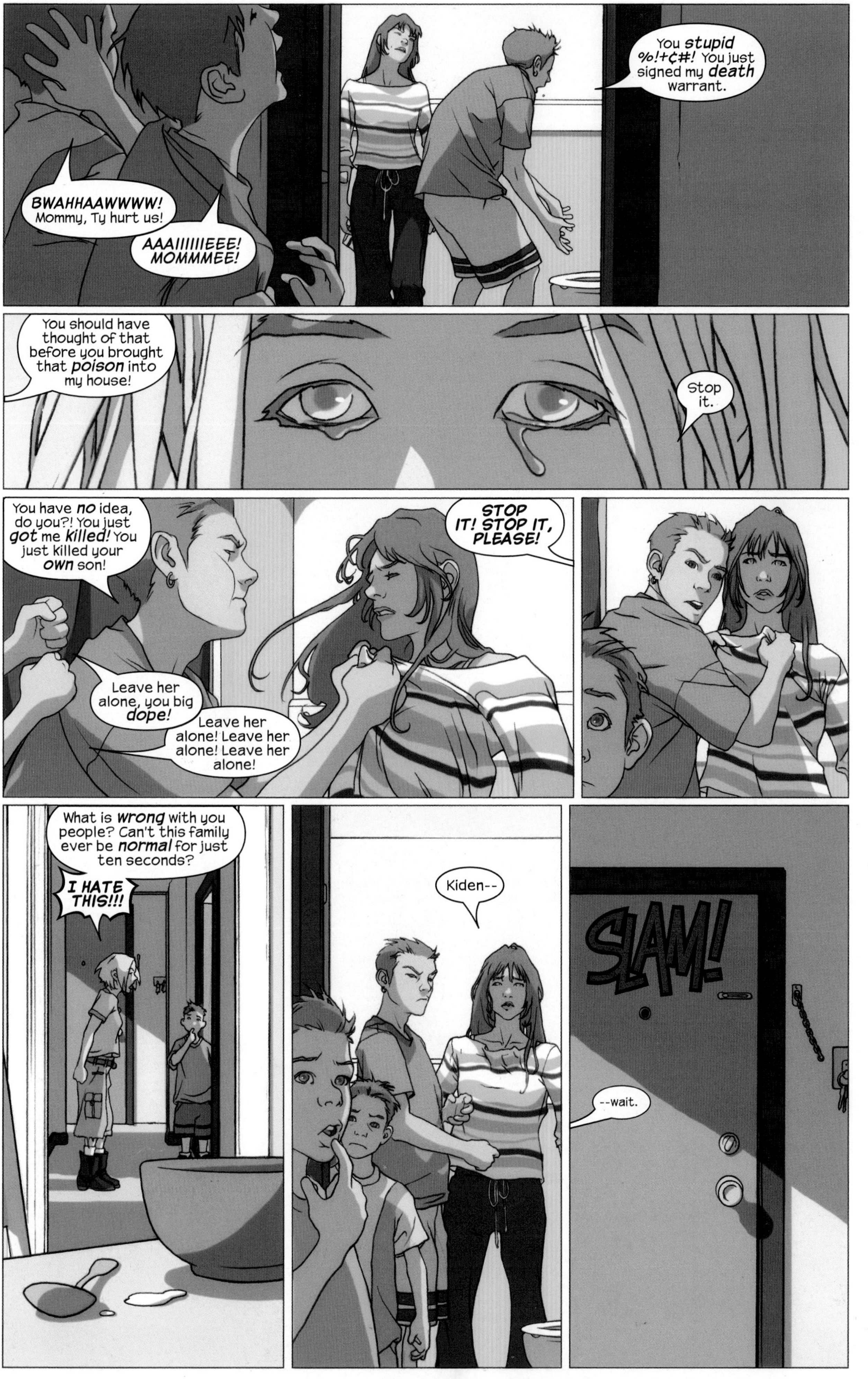
You stupid %!+¢#! You just signed my death warrant.
BWAHHAAWWWW! Mommy, Ty hurt us!
AAAIIIIIIEEE! MOMMMEE!
You should have thought of that before you brought that poison into my house!
Stop it.
You have no idea, do you?! You just got me killed! You just killed your own son!
STOP IT! STOP IT, PLEASE!
Leave her alone, you big dope!
Leave her alone! Leave her alone! Leave her alone!
What is wrong with you people? Can't this family ever be normal for just ten seconds?
I HATE THIS!!!
Kiden--
SLAM!
--wait.

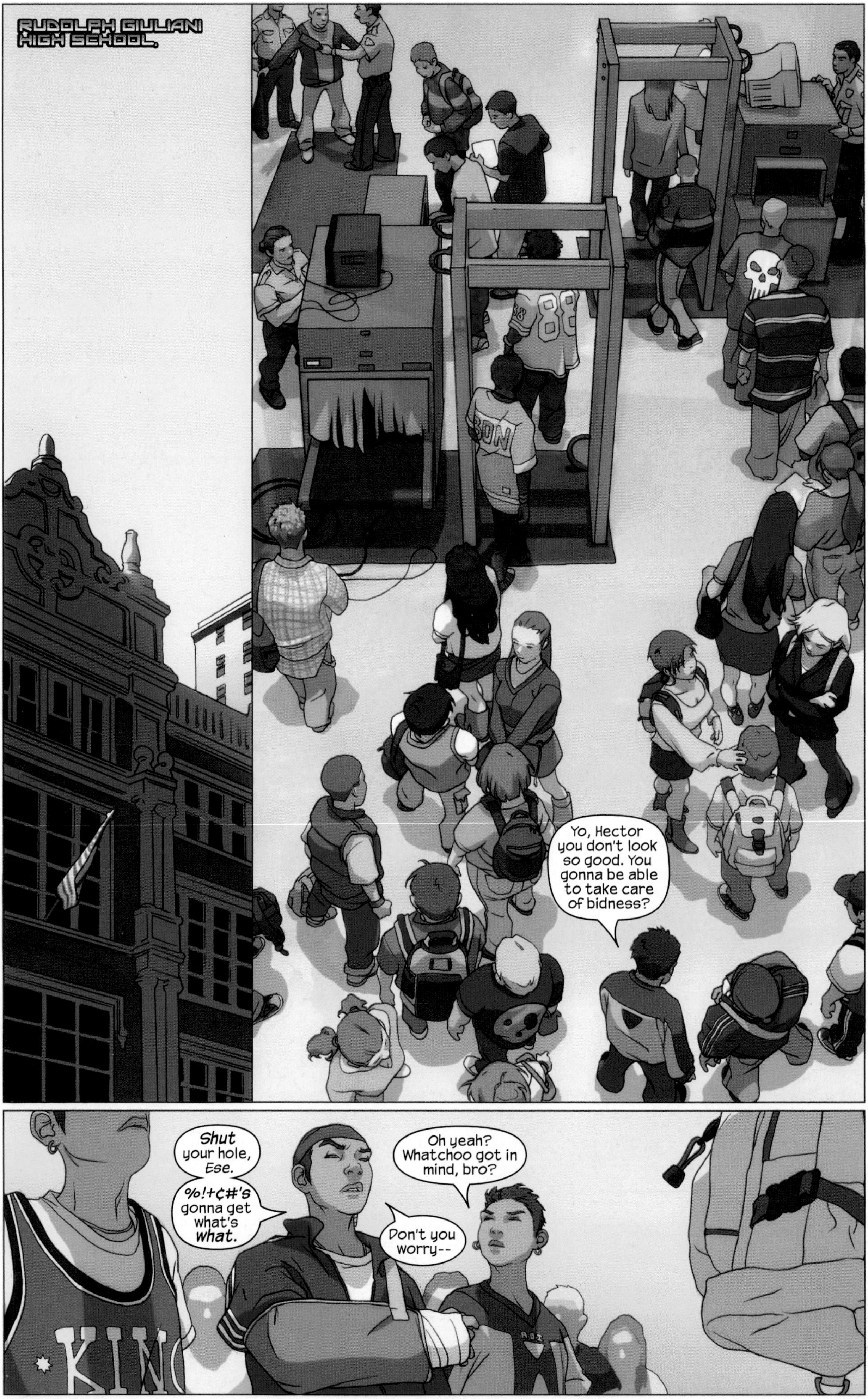
RUDOLPH GIULIANI HIGH SCHOOL.
Yo, Hector you don't look so good. You gonna be able to take care of bidness?
Shut your hole, Ese.
%!+¢#'s gonna get what's what.
Oh yeah? Whatchoo got in mind, bro?
Don't you worry--

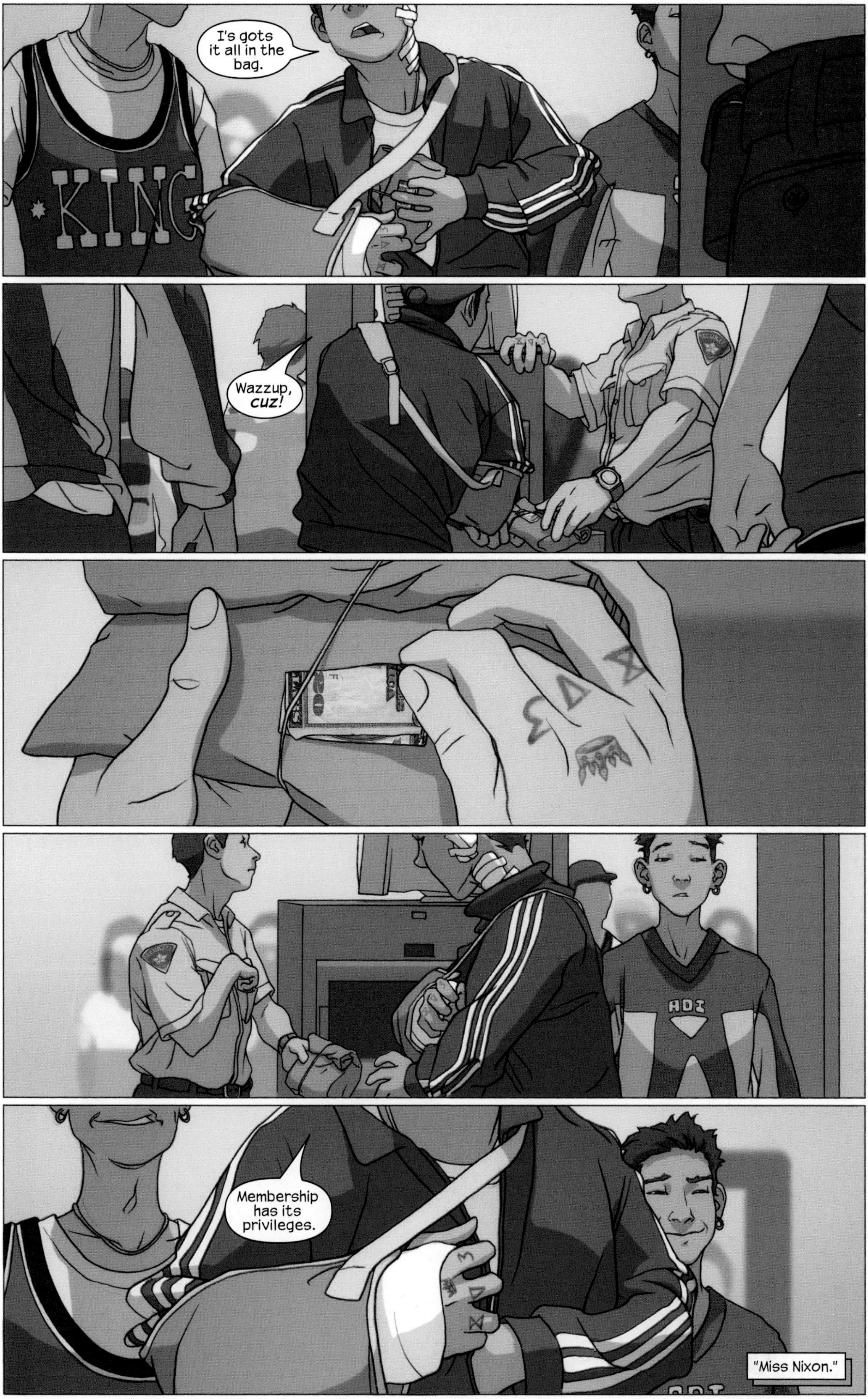

I's gots it all in the bag.
Wazzup, *cuz!*
Membership has its privileges.
"Miss Nixon."

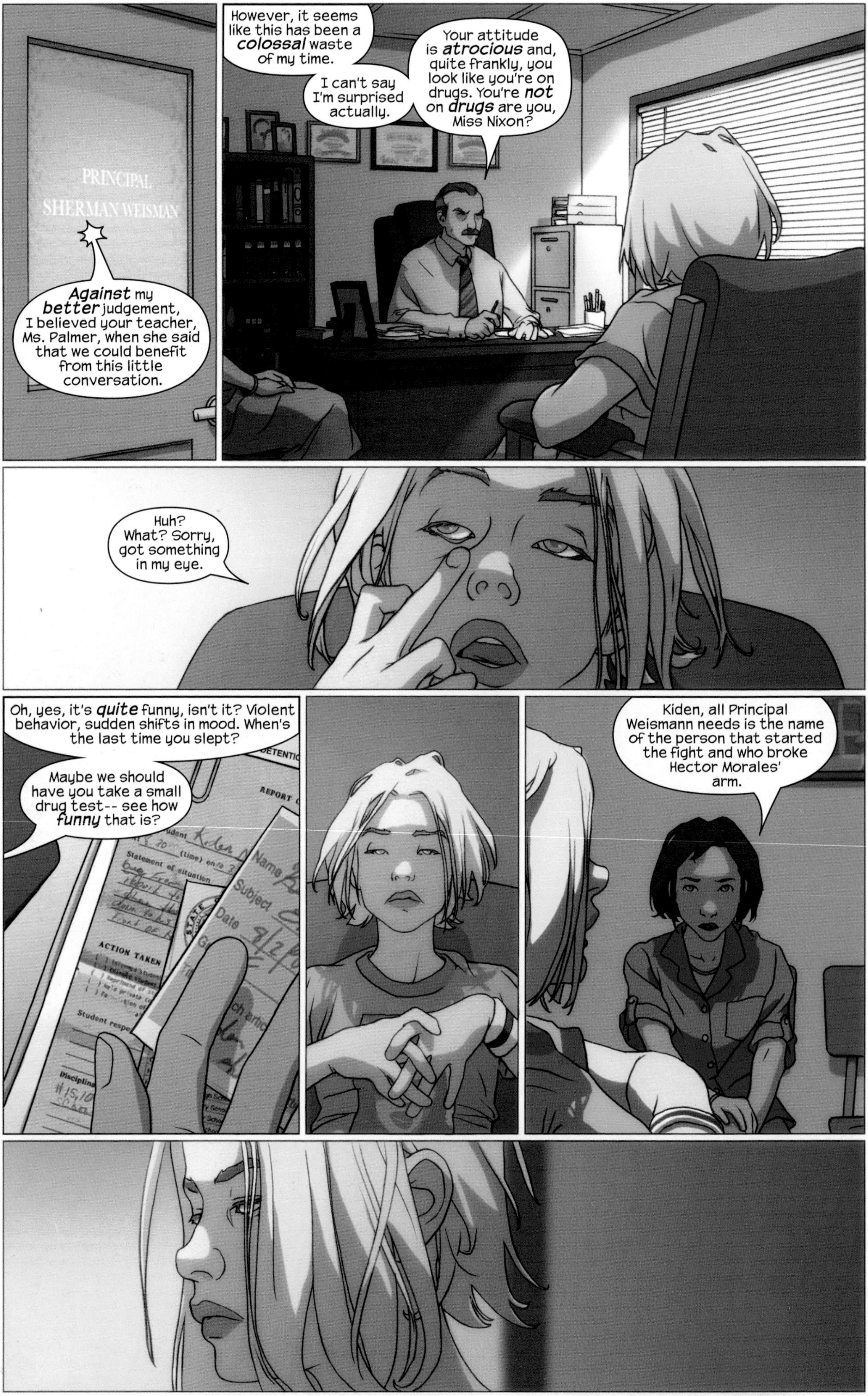
PRINCIPAL
SHERMAN WEISMAN
Against my better judgement, I believed your teacher, Ms. Palmer, when she said that we could benefit from this little conversation.
However, it seems like this has been a colossal waste of my time.
I can't say I'm surprised actually.
Your attitude is atrocious and, quite frankly, you look like you're on drugs. You're not on drugs are you, Miss Nixon?
Huh? What? Sorry, got something in my eye.
Oh, yes, it's quite funny, isn't it? Violent behavior, sudden shifts in mood. When's the last time you slept?
Maybe we should have you take a small drug test-- see how funny that is?
Kiden, all Principal Weismann needs is the name of the person that started the fight and who broke Hector Morales' arm.

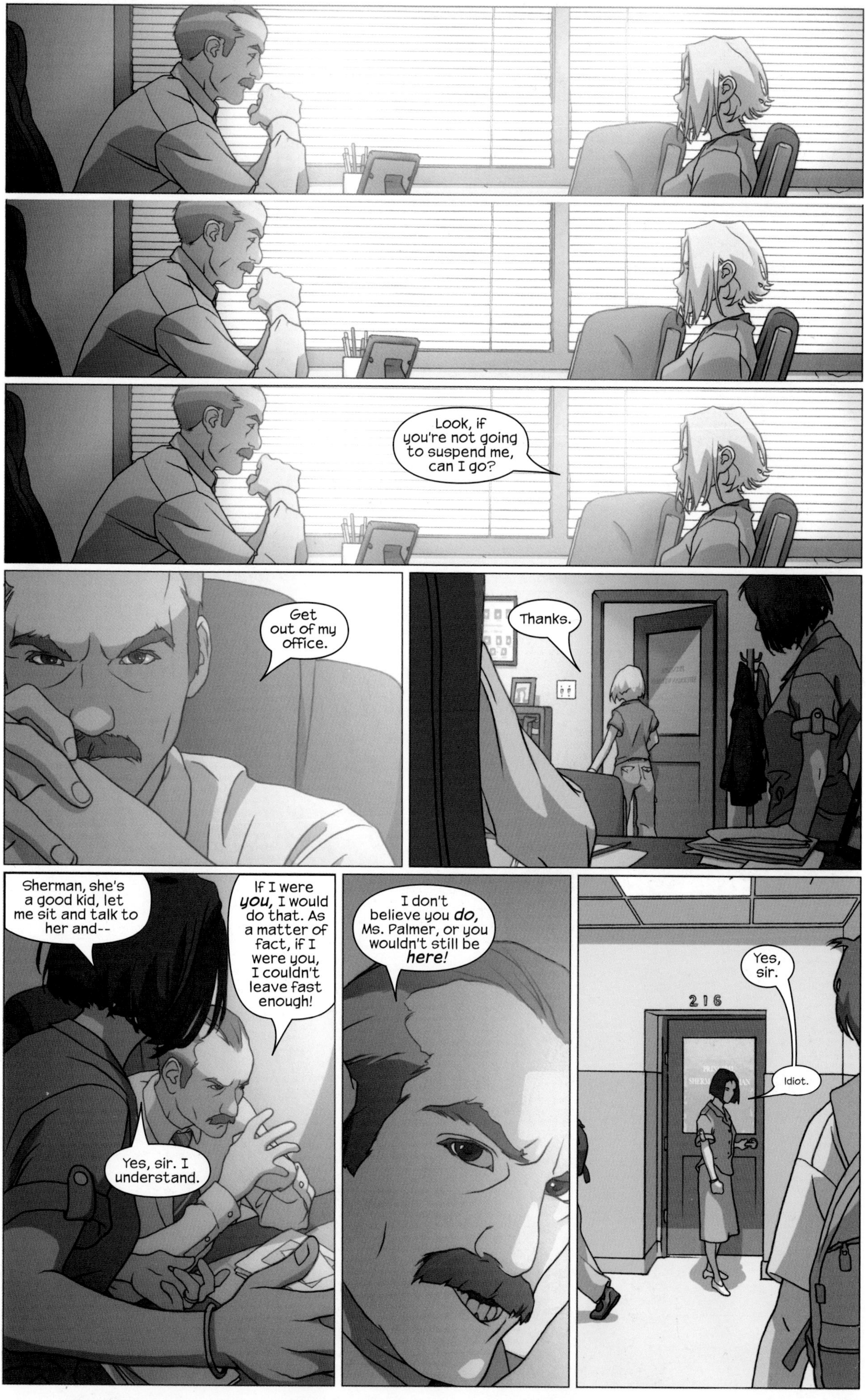

Look, if you're not going to suspend me, can I go?
Get out of my office.
Thanks.
Sherman, she's a good kid, let me sit and talk to her and--
If I were *you,* I would do that. As a matter of fact, if I were you, I couldn't leave fast enough!
Yes, sir. I understand.
I don't believe you *do,* Ms. Palmer, or you wouldn't still be *here!*
Yes, sir.
216
Idiot.

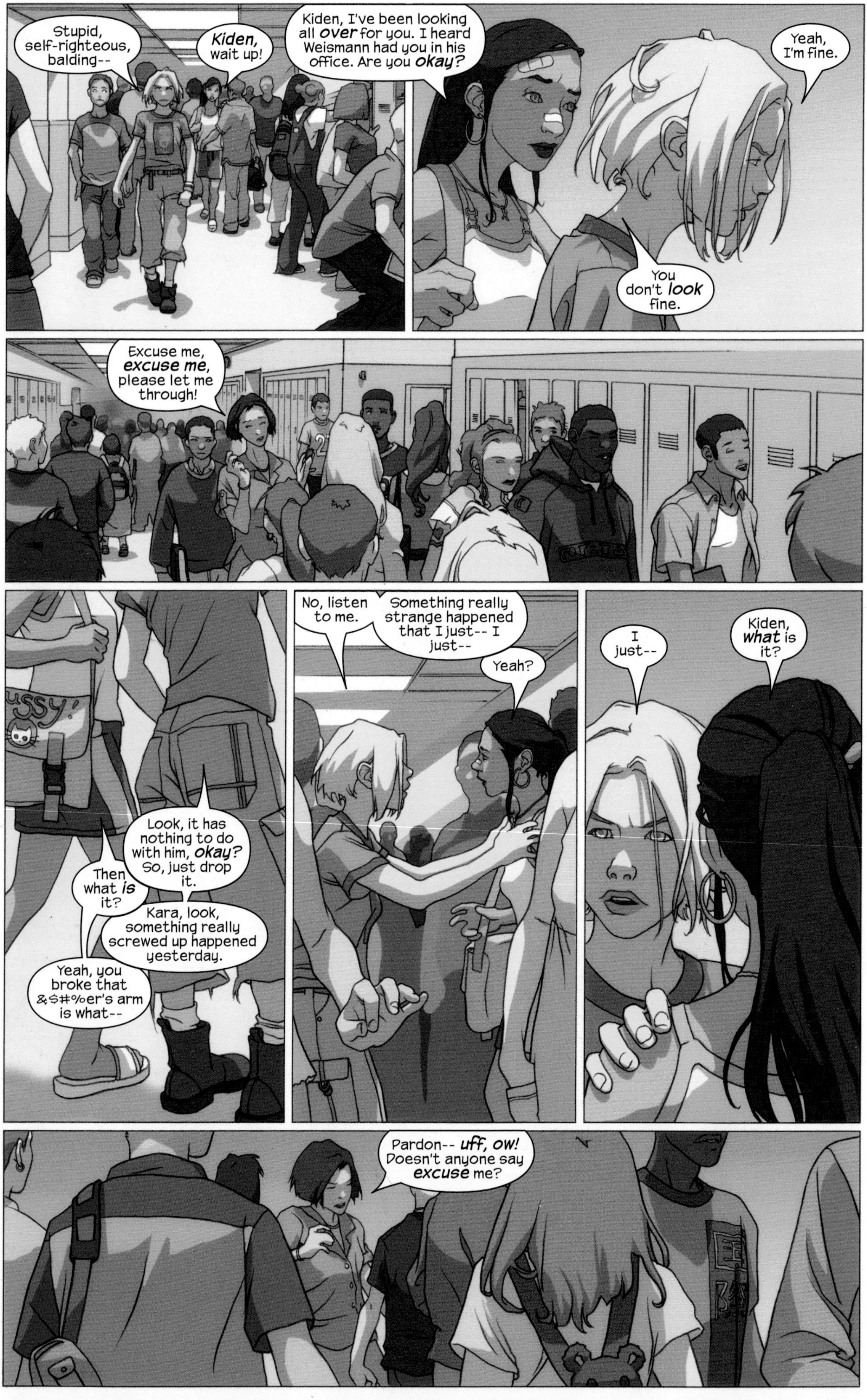
Stupid, self-righteous, balding--
Kiden, wait up!
Kiden, I've been looking all over for you. I heard Weismann had you in his office. Are you okay?
Yeah, I'm fine.
You don't look fine.
Excuse me, excuse me, please let me through!
Look, it has nothing to do with him, okay? So, just drop it.
Then what is it?
Kara, look, something really screwed up happened yesterday.
Yeah, you broke that &$#%er's arm is what--
No, listen to me.
Something really strange happened that I just-- I just--
Yeah?
I just--
Kiden, what is it?
Pardon-- uff, ow! Doesn't anyone say excuse me?

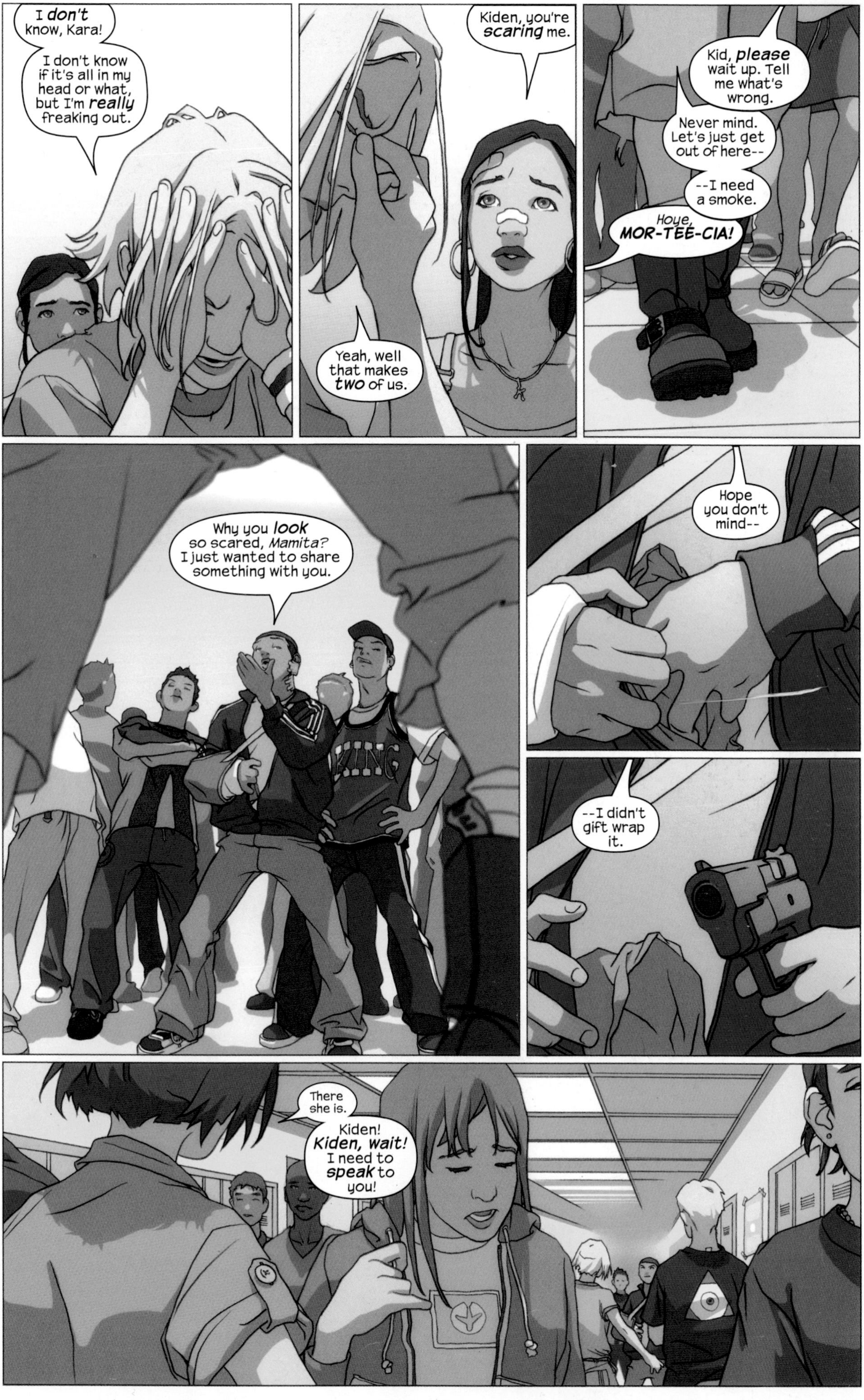
I don't know, Kara!
I don't know if it's all in my head or what, but I'm really freaking out.
Kiden, you're scaring me.
Yeah, well that makes two of us.
Kid, please wait up. Tell me what's wrong.
Never mind. Let's just get out of here--
--I need a smoke.
Hoye, MOR-TEE-CIA!
Why you look so scared, Mamita? I just wanted to share something with you.
Hope you don't mind--
--I didn't gift wrap it.
There she is.
Kiden! Kiden, wait! I need to speak to you!

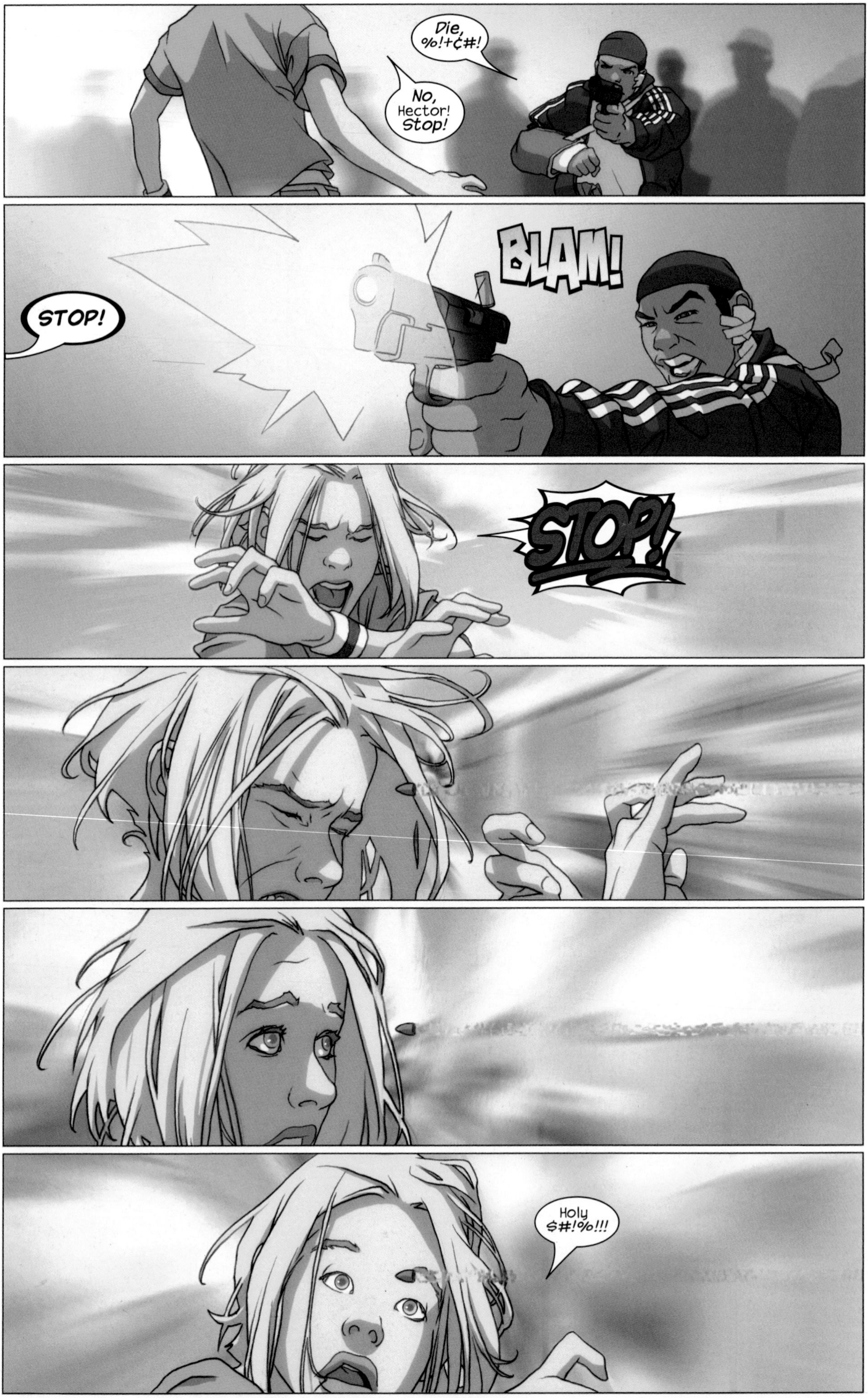
Die, %!+¢#!
No, Hector! Stop!
BLAM!
STOP!
STOP!
Holy $#!%!!!

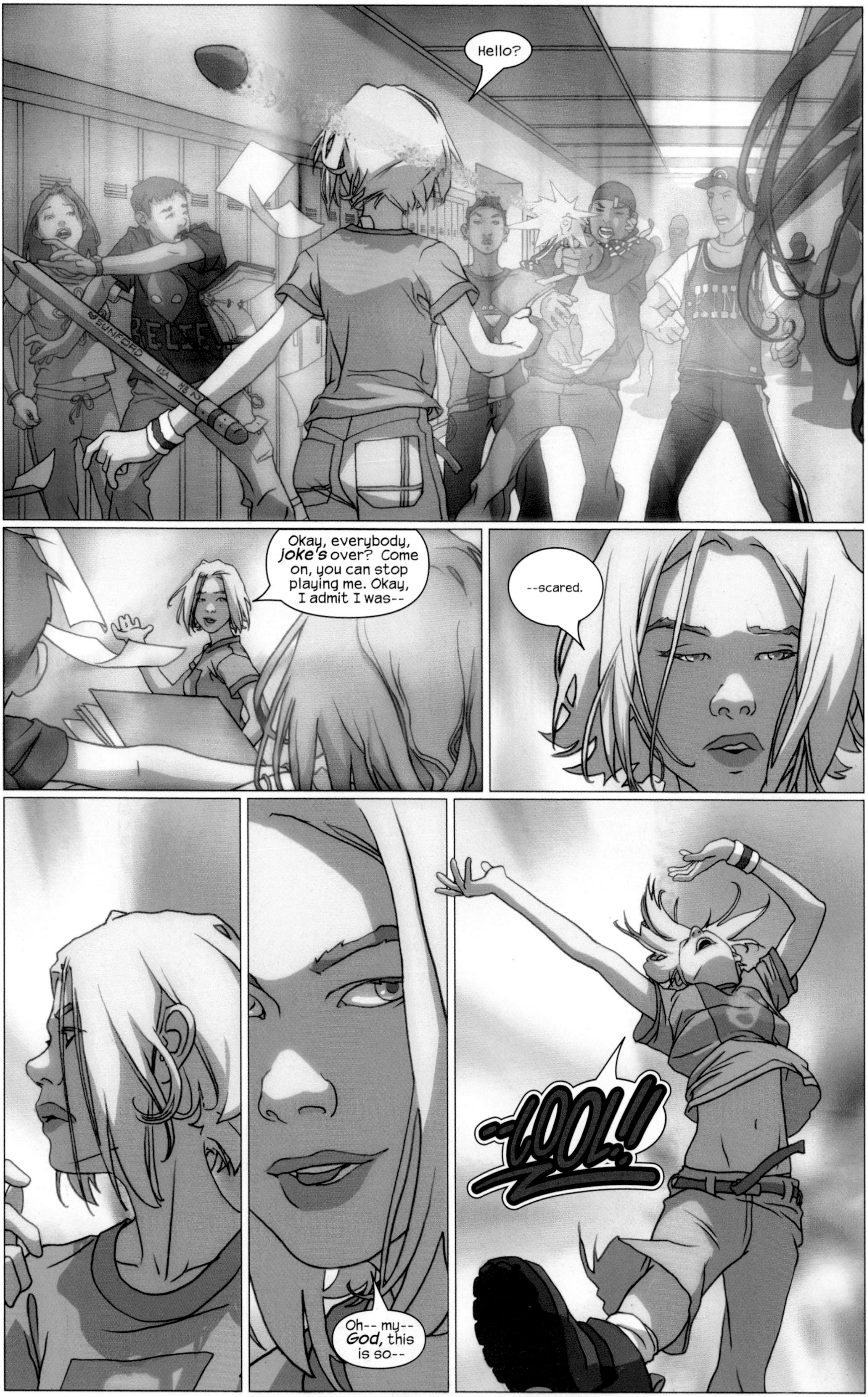
Hello?
Okay, everybody, joke's over? Come on, you can stop playing me. Okay, I admit I was--
--scared.
Oh-- my-- God, this is so--
--COOL!!

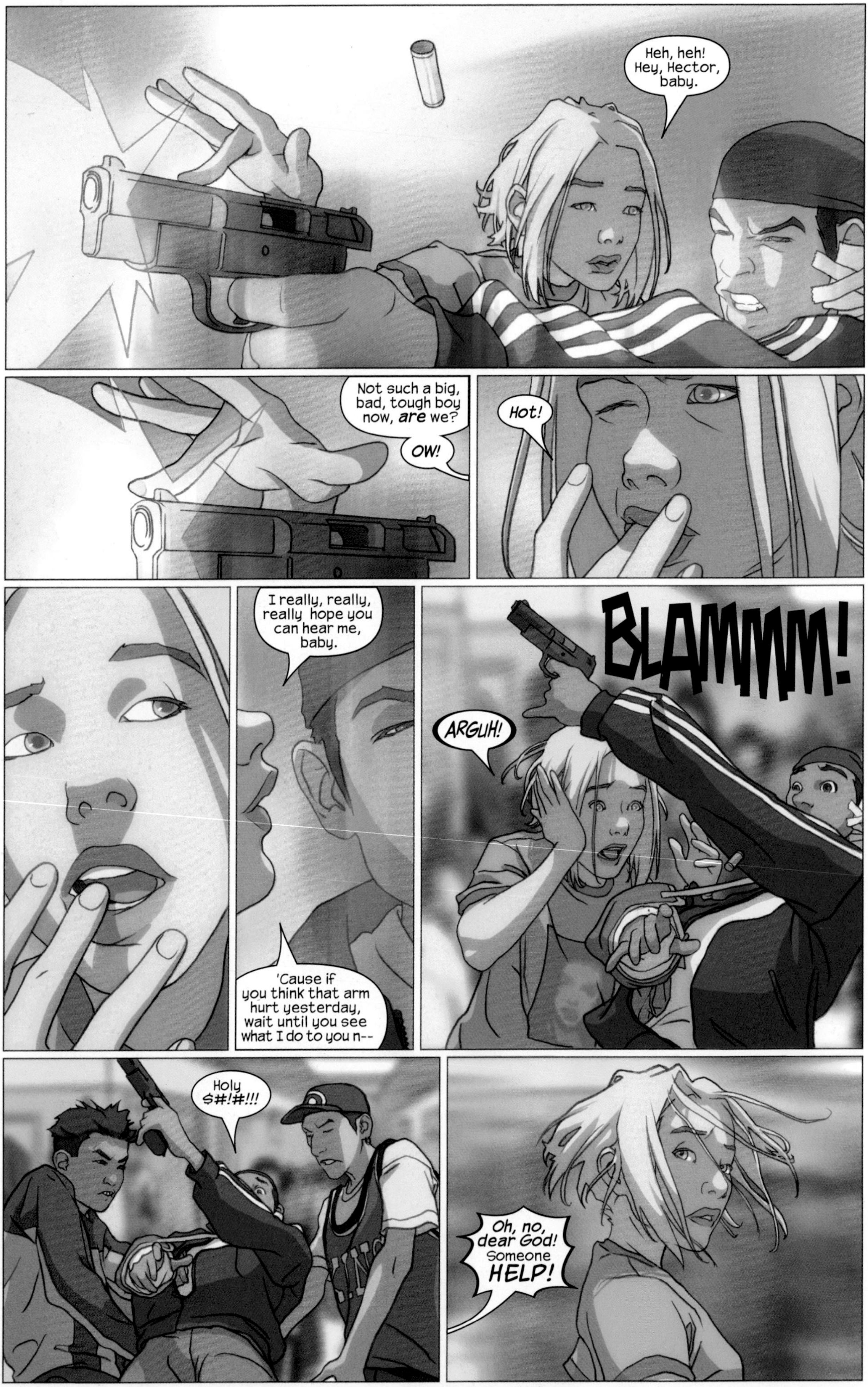
Heh, heh! Hey, Hector, baby.
Not such a big, bad, tough boy now, are we?
OW!
Hot!
I really, really, really hope you can hear me, baby.
'Cause if you think that arm hurt yesterday, wait until you see what I do to you n--
BLAMMM!
ARGUH!
Holy $#!#!!!
Oh, no, dear God! Someone HELP!

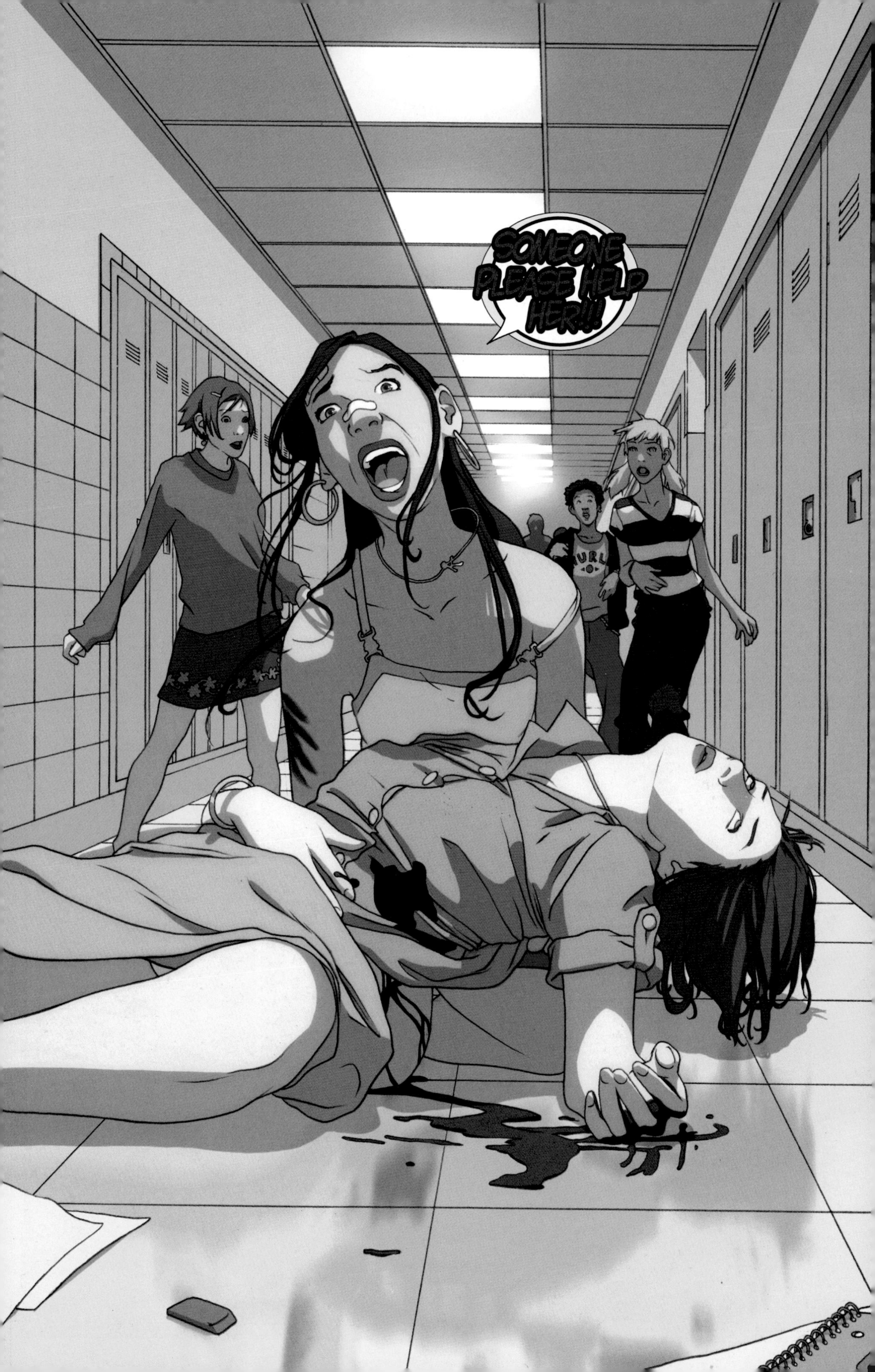
SOMEONE PLEASE HELP HER!!!

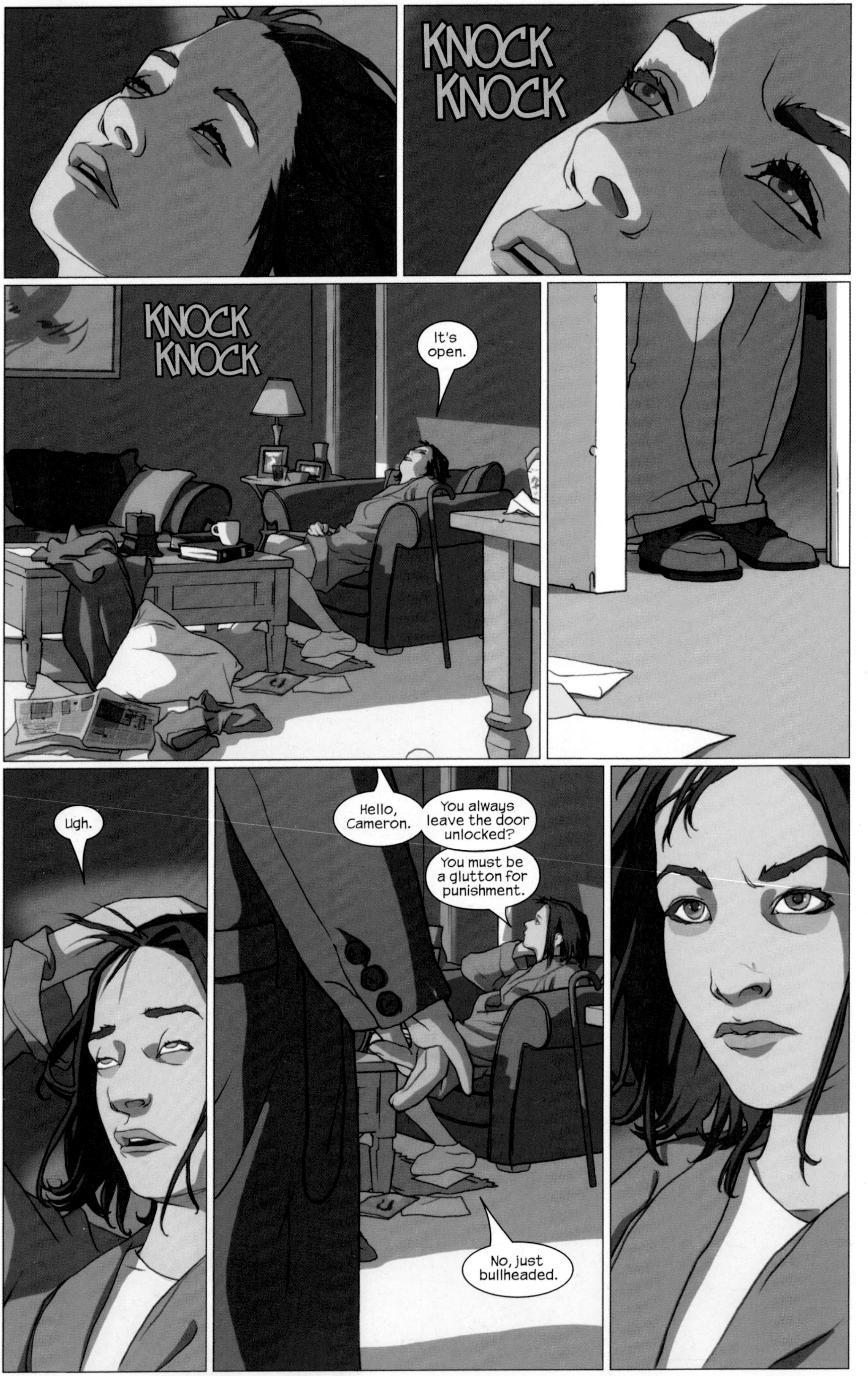
KNOCK KNOCK
KNOCK KNOCK
It's open.
Ugh.
Hello, Cameron.
You always leave the door unlocked?
You must be a glutton for punishment.
No, just bullheaded.

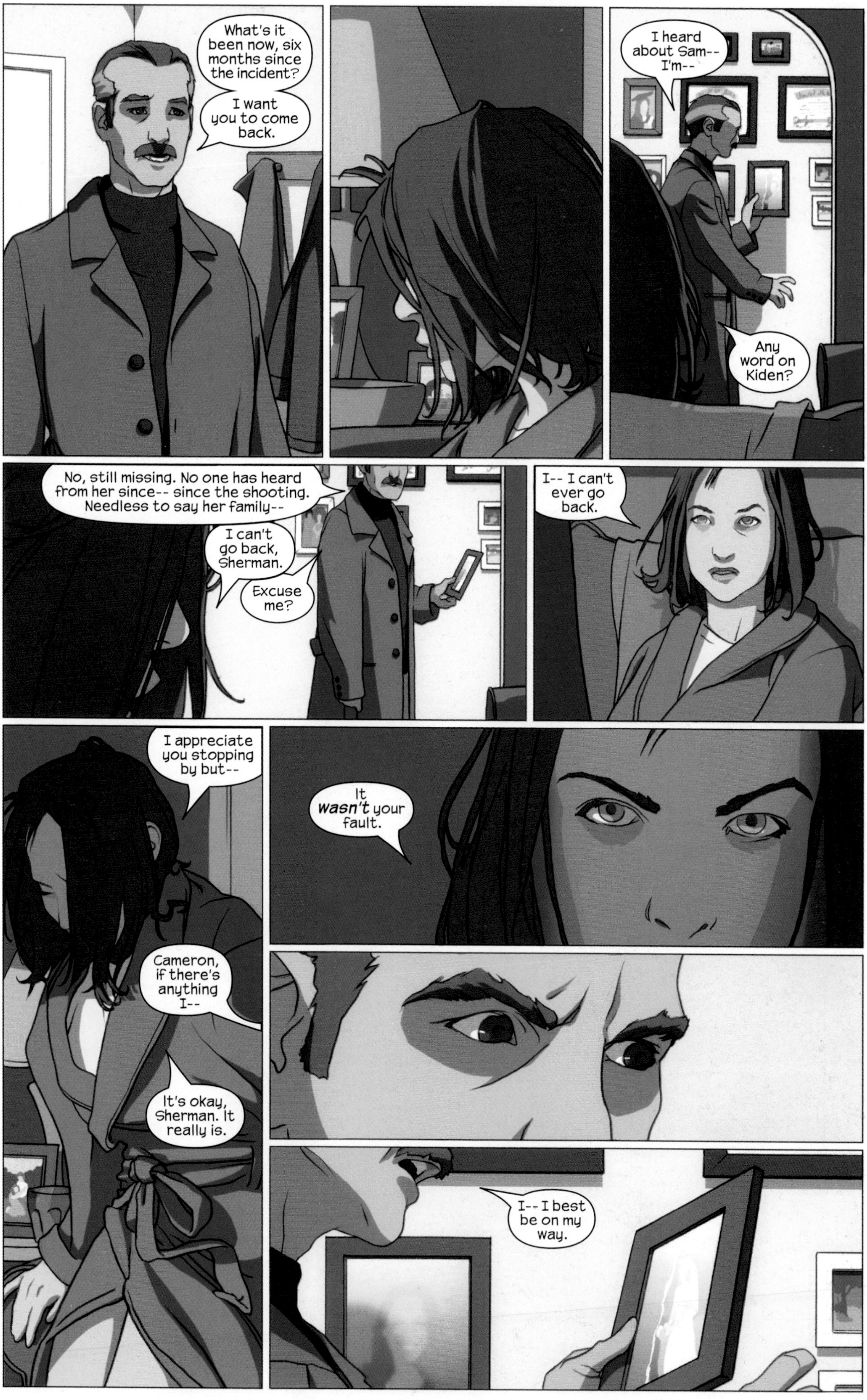
What's it been now, six months since the incident?
I want you to come back.
I heard about Sam-- I'm--
Any word on Kiden?
No, still missing. No one has heard from her since-- since the shooting. Needless to say her family--
I can't go back, Sherman.
Excuse me?
I-- I can't ever go back.
I appreciate you stopping by but--
It *wasn't* your fault.
Cameron, if there's anything I--
It's okay, Sherman. It really is.
I-- I best be on my way.

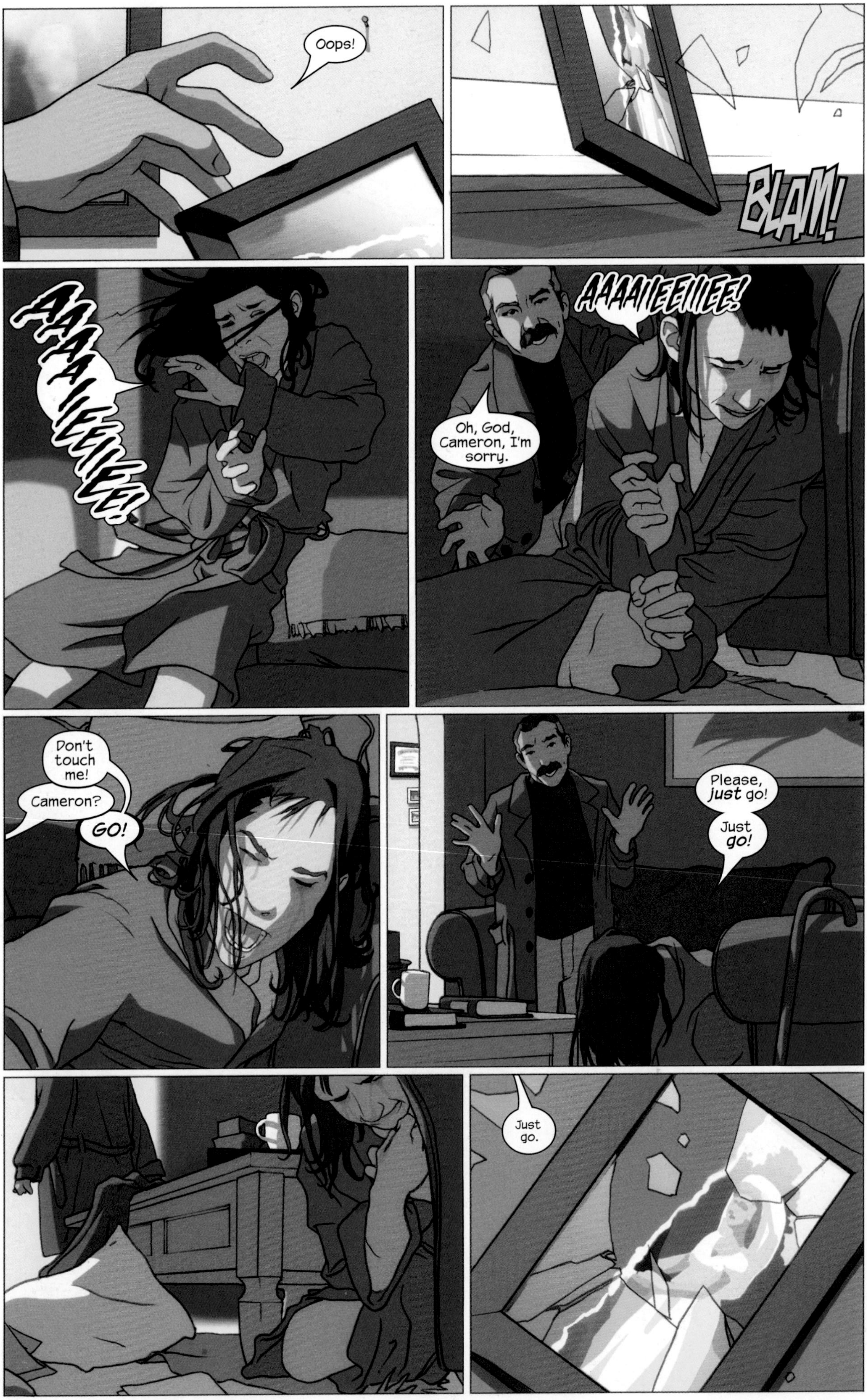
Oops!
BLAM!
AAAAAIIEEIIEE!
AAAAIIEEIIIEE!
Oh, God, Cameron, I'm sorry.
Don't touch me!
Cameron?
GO!
Please, *just* go!
Just *go!*
Just go.

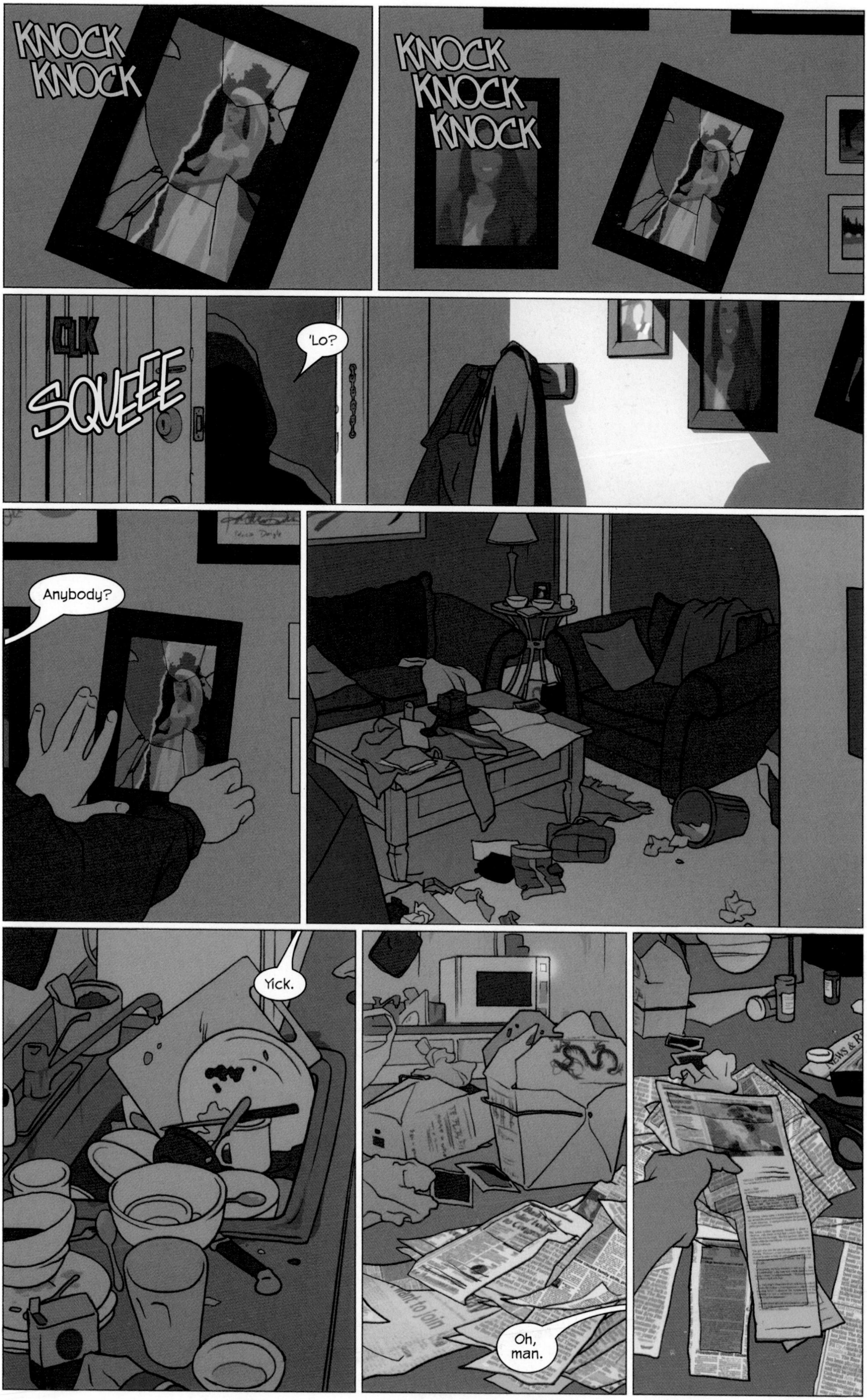
KNOCK KNOCK
KNOCK KNOCK KNOCK
CLK
SQUEEE
'Lo?
Anybody?
Yick.
Oh, man.

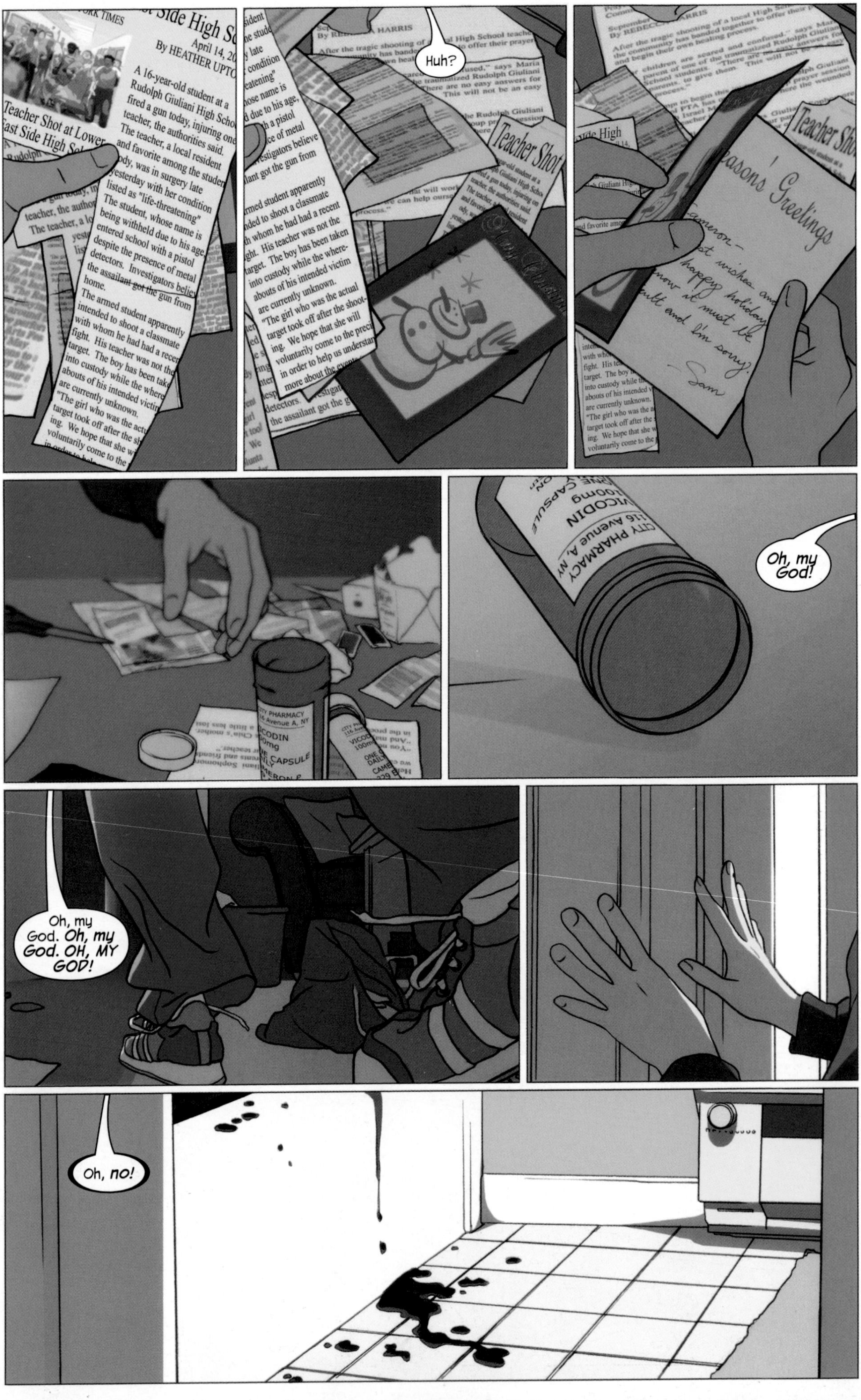
Huh?
Oh, my God!
Oh, my God. Oh, my God. OH, MY GOD!
Oh, no!

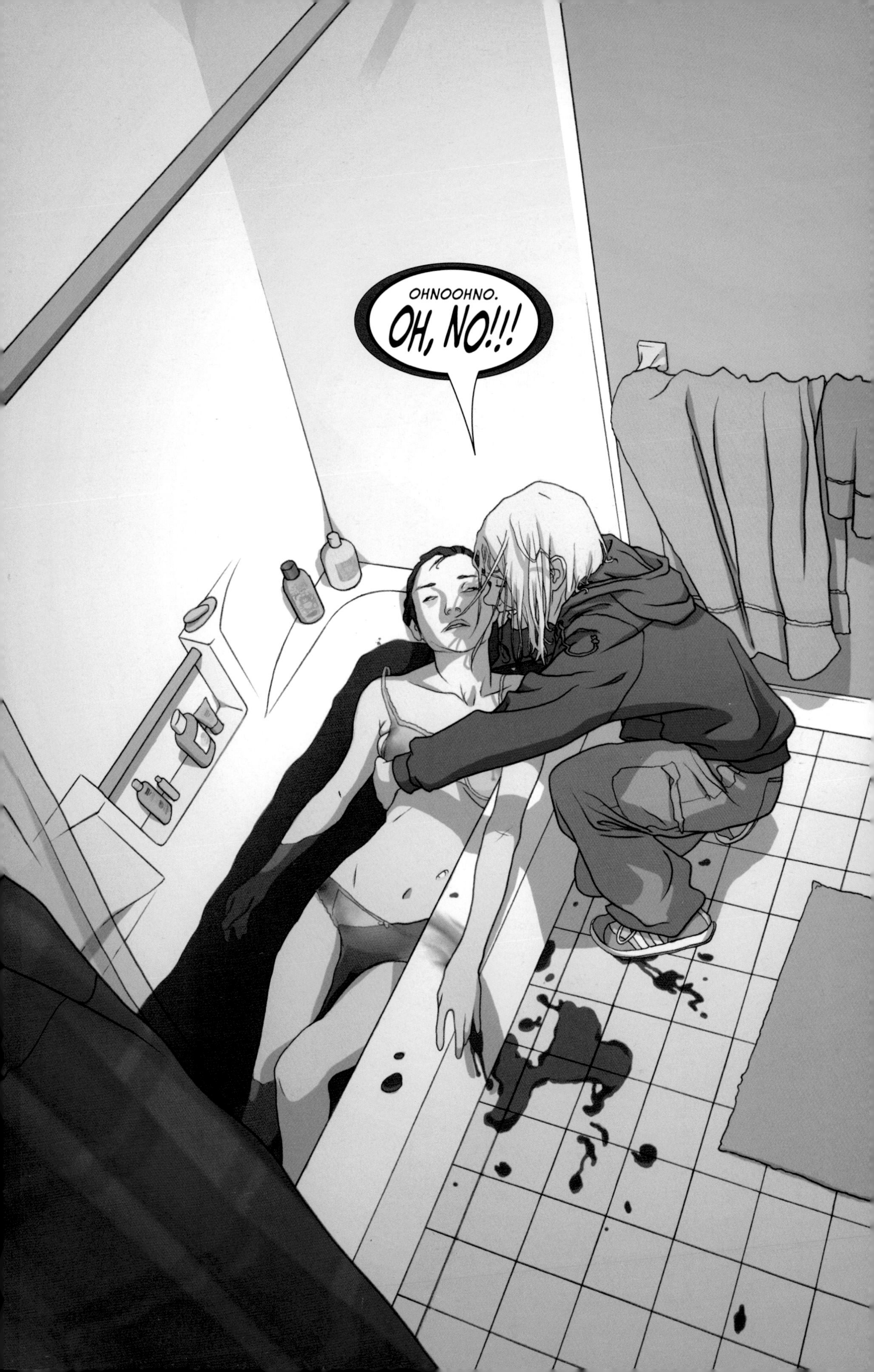
OHNOOHNO.
OH, NO!!!

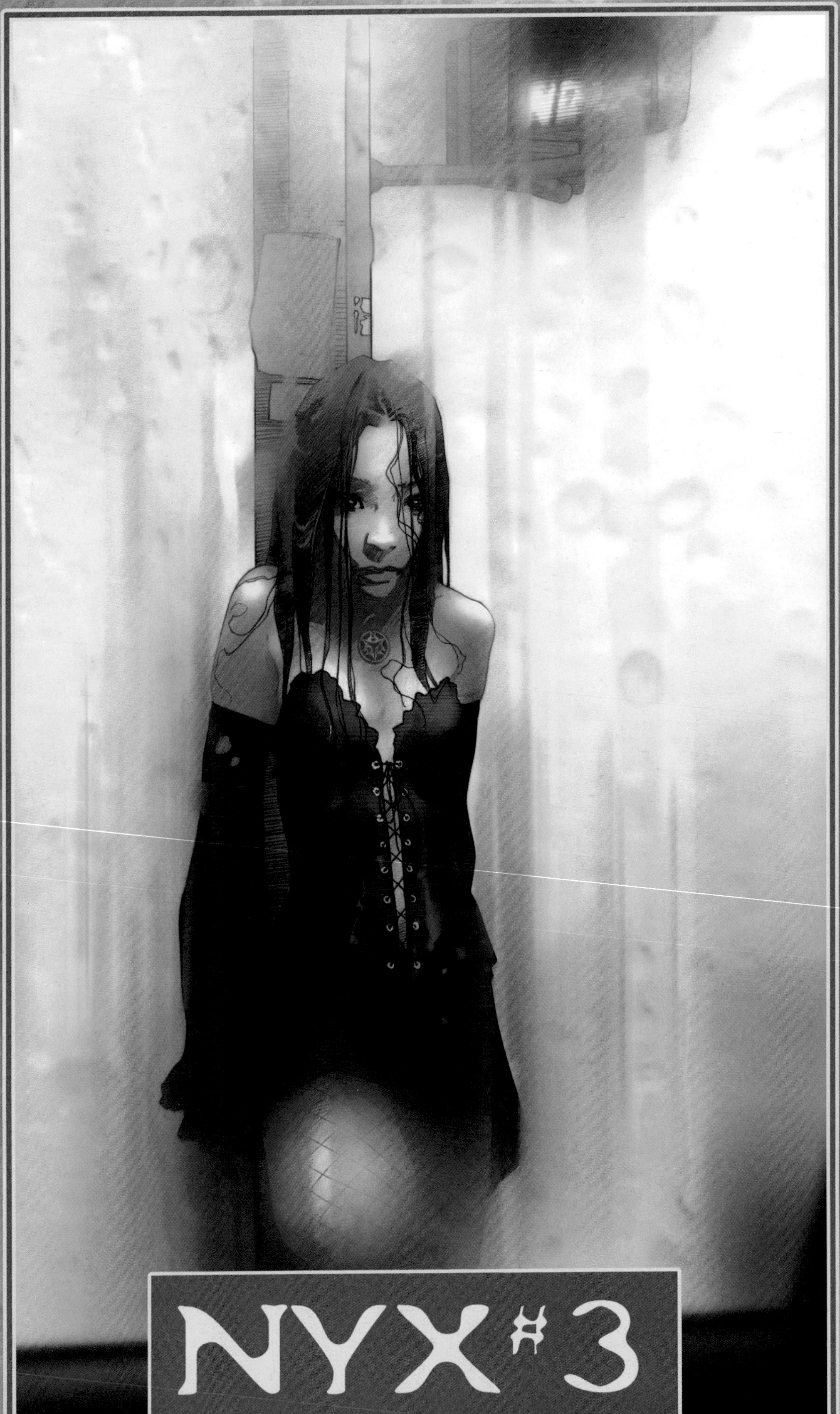
NYX #3

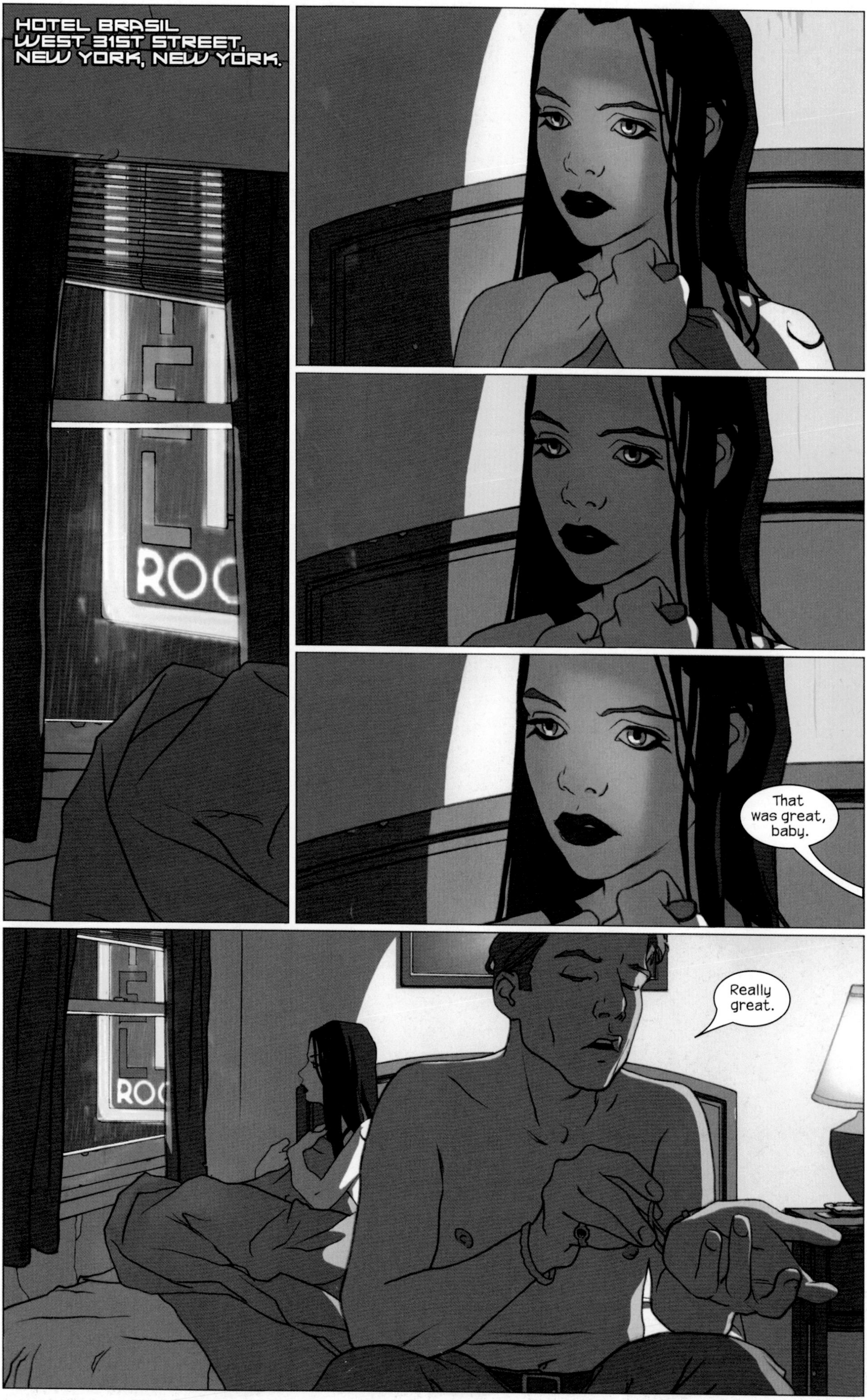
HOTEL BRASIL
WEST 31ST STREET,
NEW YORK, NEW YORK.
ROO
That was great, baby.
ROO
Really great.

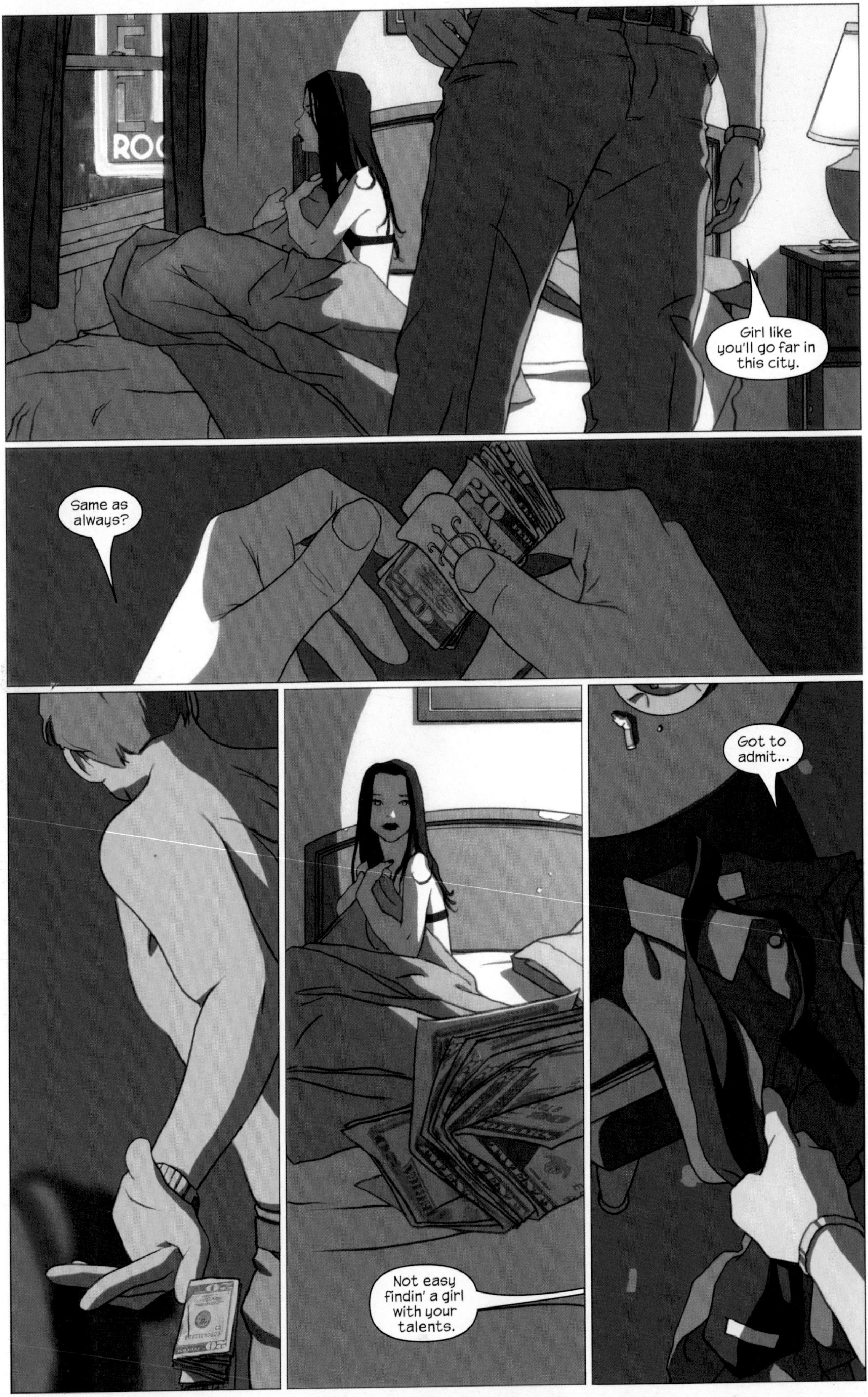
Girl like you'll go far in this city.
Same as always?
Got to admit...
Not easy findin' a girl with your talents.

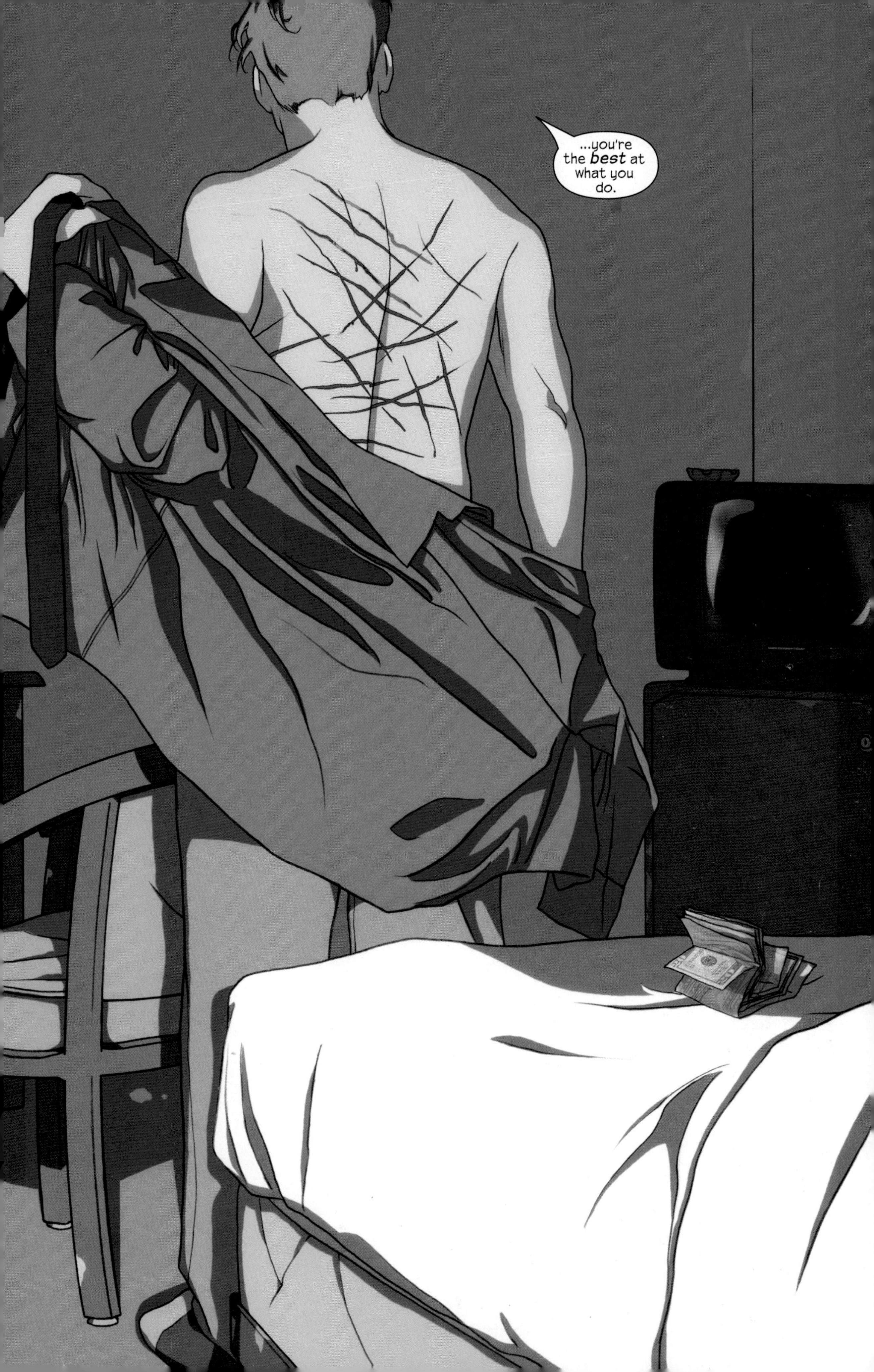
...you're the *best* at what you do.

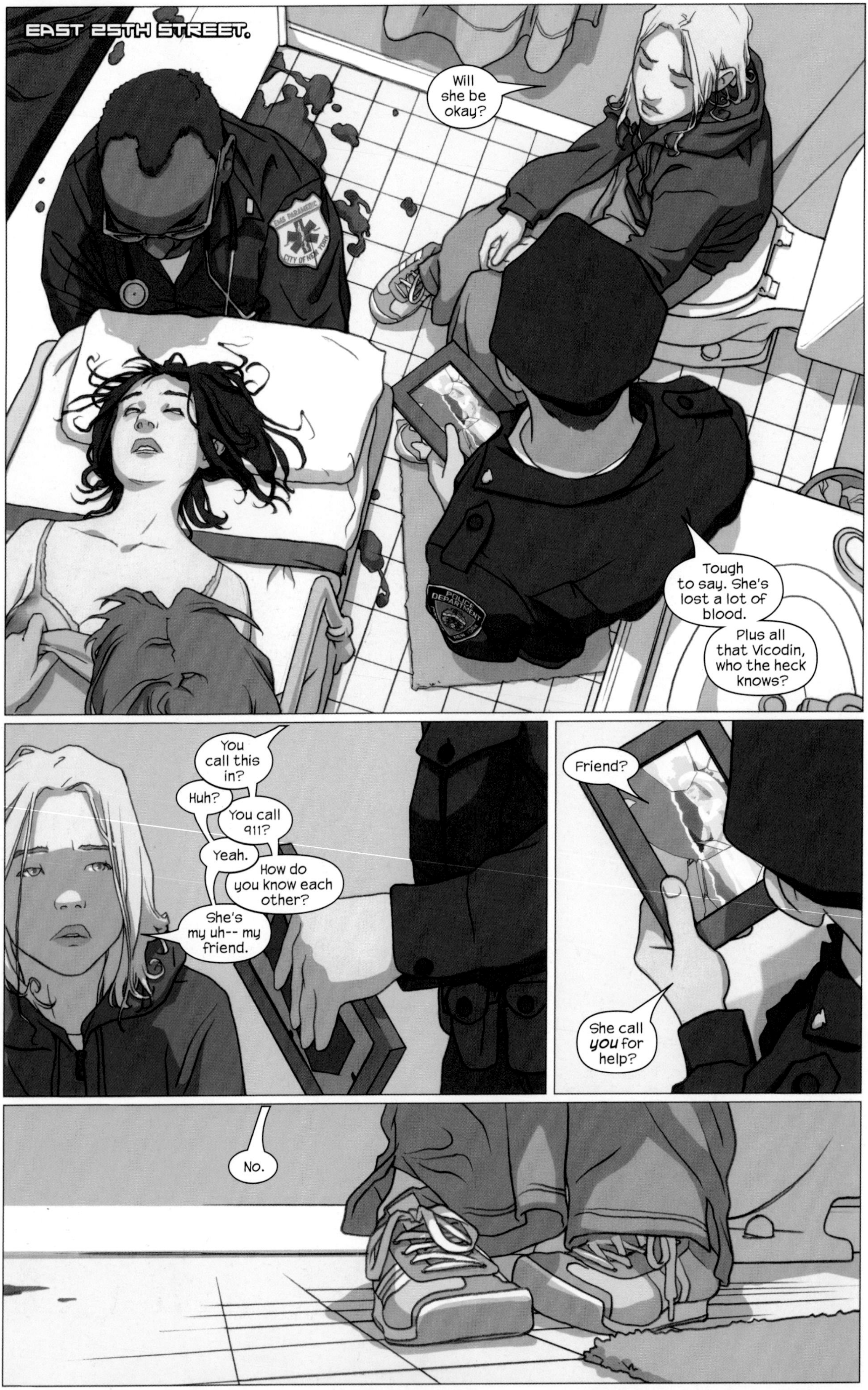
EAST 25TH STREET.
Will she be okay?
EMS PARAMEDIC CITY OF NEW YORK
Tough to say. She's lost a lot of blood.
Plus all that Vicodin, who the heck knows?
POLICE DEPARTMENT
You call this in?
Huh?
You call 911?
Yeah.
How do you know each other?
She's my uh-- my friend.
Friend?
She call *you* for help?
No.

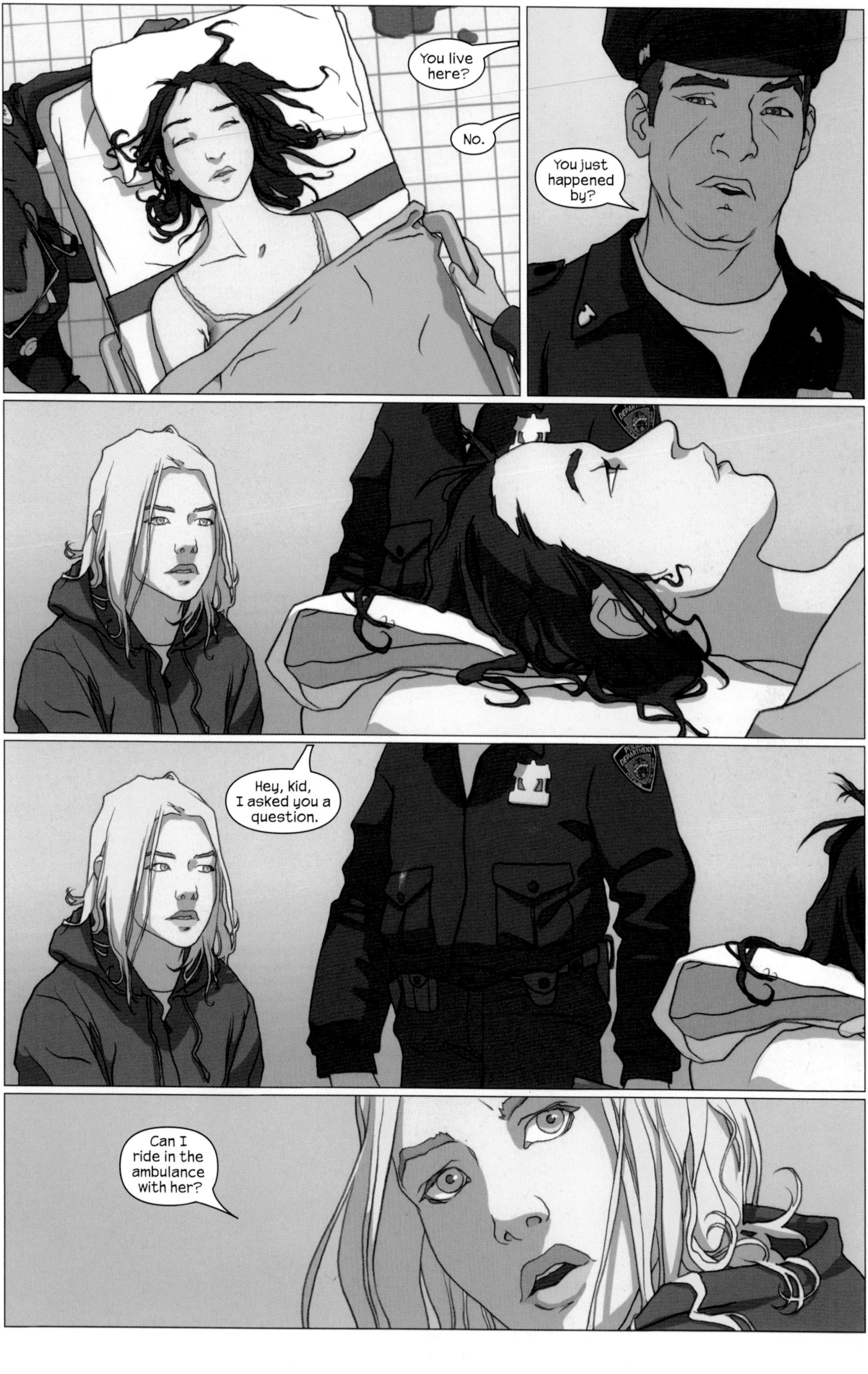
You live here?
No.
You just happened by?
Hey, kid, I asked you a question.
Can I ride in the ambulance with her?

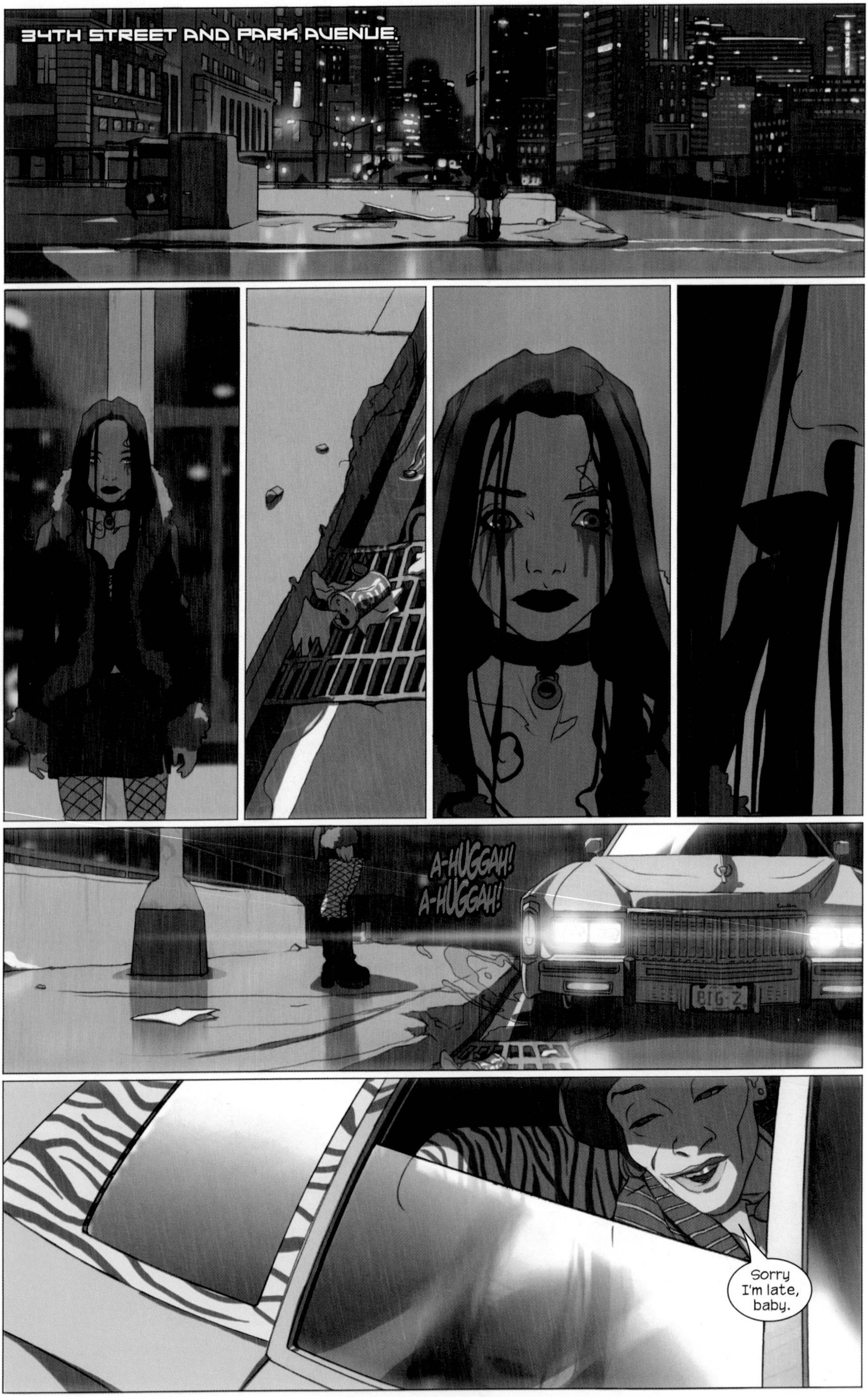
34TH STREET AND PARK AVENUE.
A-HUGGAH!
A-HUGGAH!
BIG-Z
Sorry I'm late, baby.

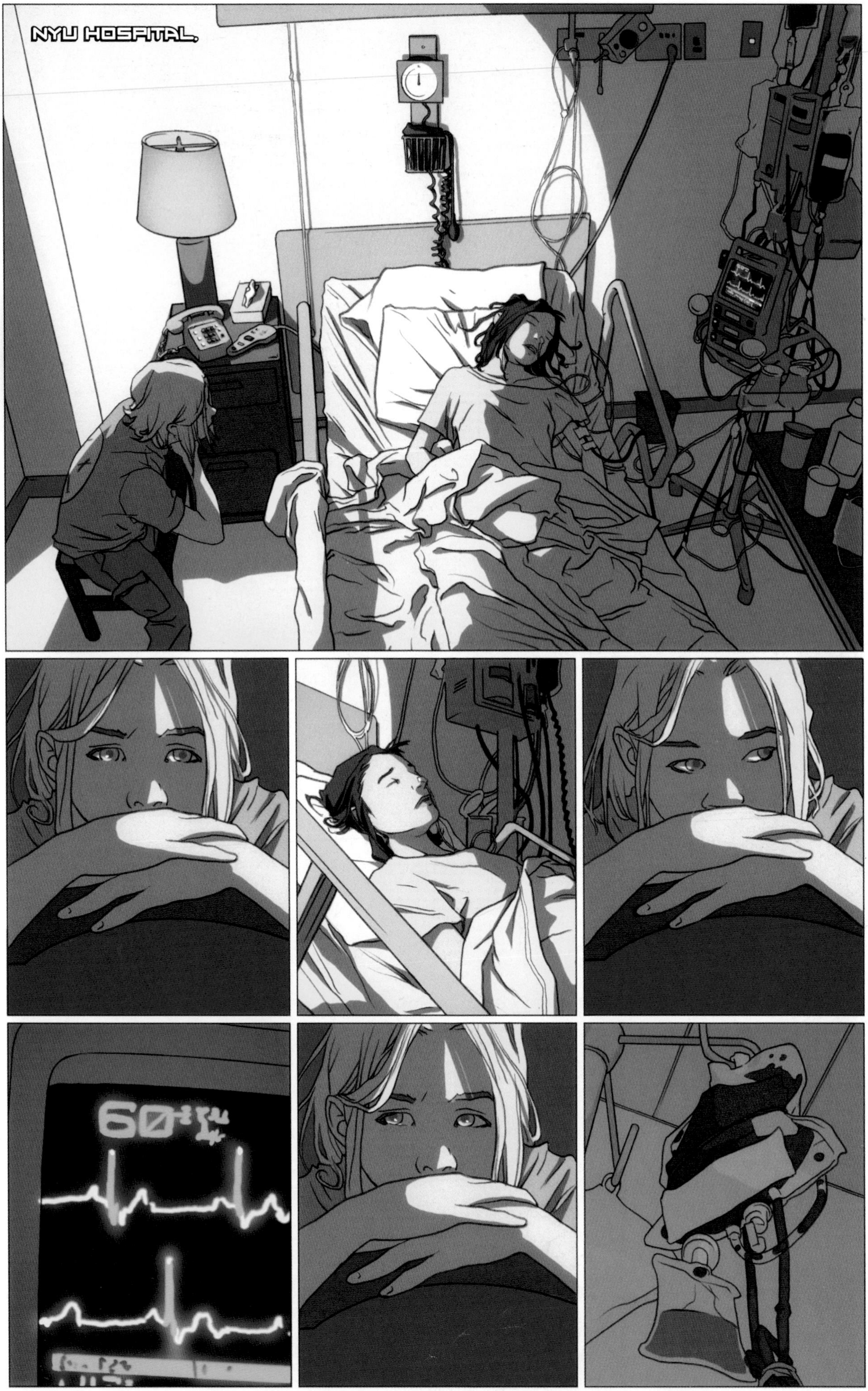
NYU HOSPITAL.
60

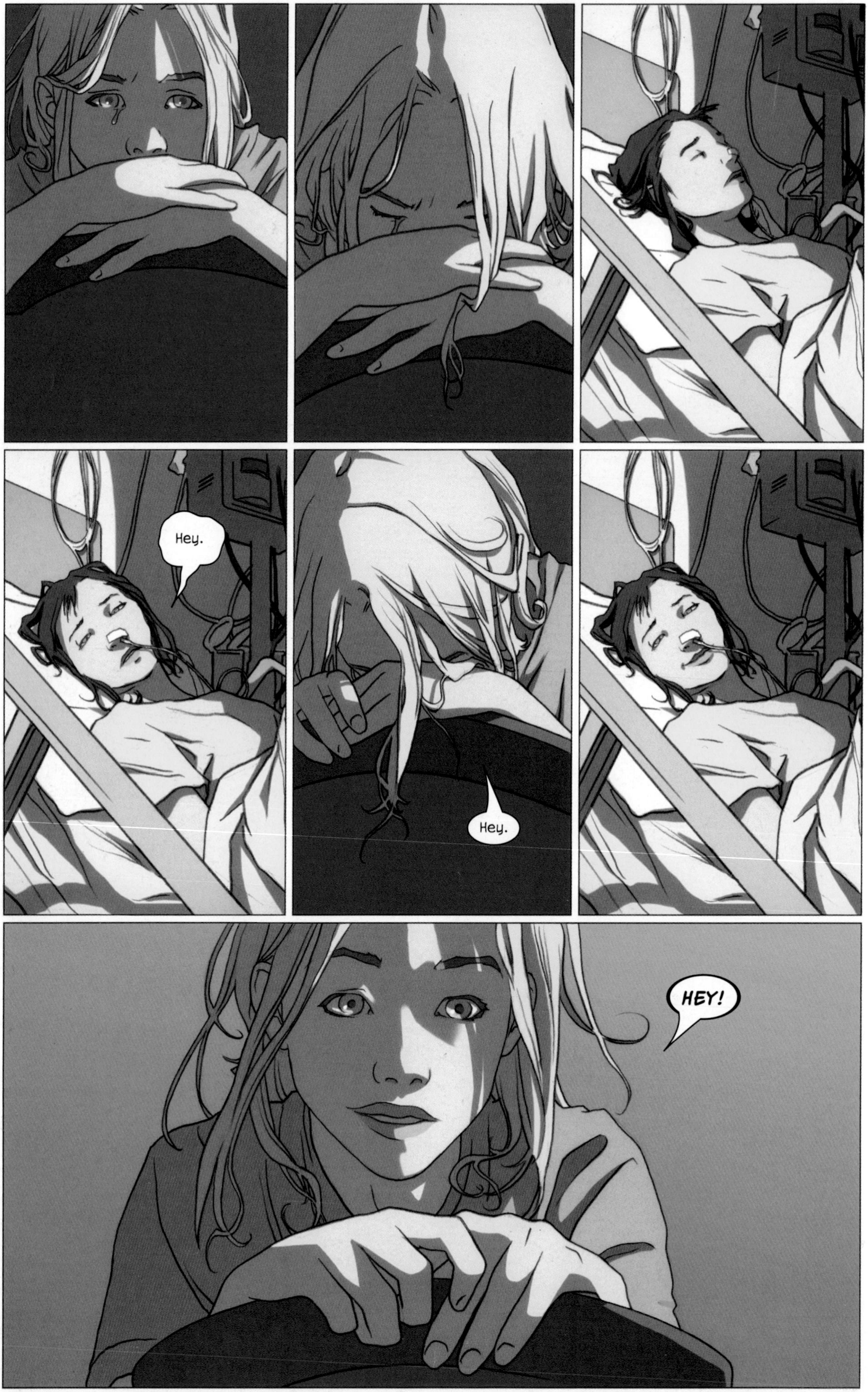
Hey.
Hey.
HEY!

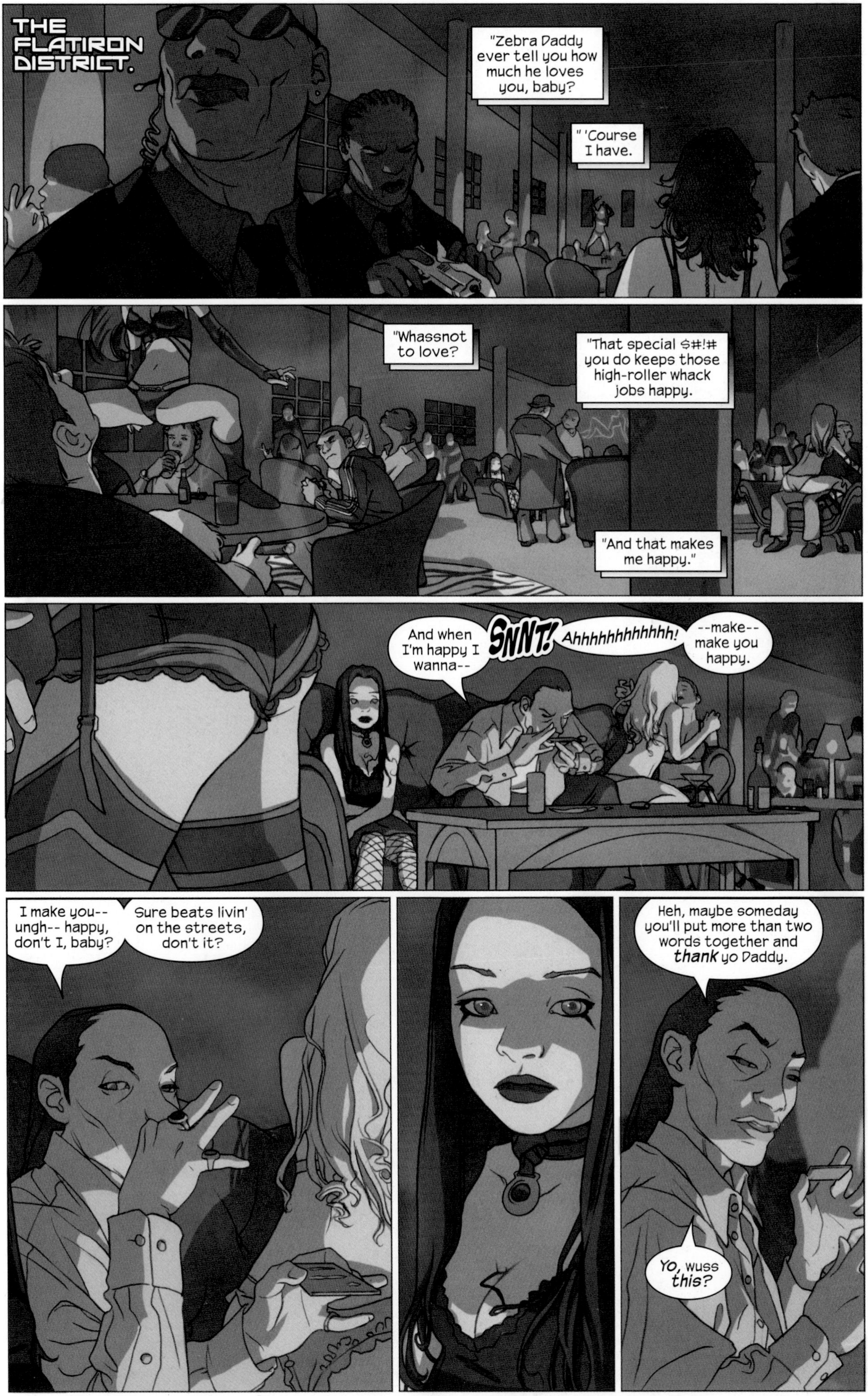
THE FLATIRON DISTRICT.
"Zebra Daddy ever tell you how much he loves you, baby?
" 'Course I have.
"Whassnot to love?
"That special $#!# you do keeps those high-roller whack jobs happy.
"And that makes me happy."
And when I'm happy I wanna--
SNNT!
Ahhhhhhhhhhhh!
--make-- make you happy.
I make you-- ungh-- happy, don't I, baby?
Sure beats livin' on the streets, don't it?
Heh, maybe someday you'll put more than two words together and *thank* yo Daddy.
YO, wuss *this?*

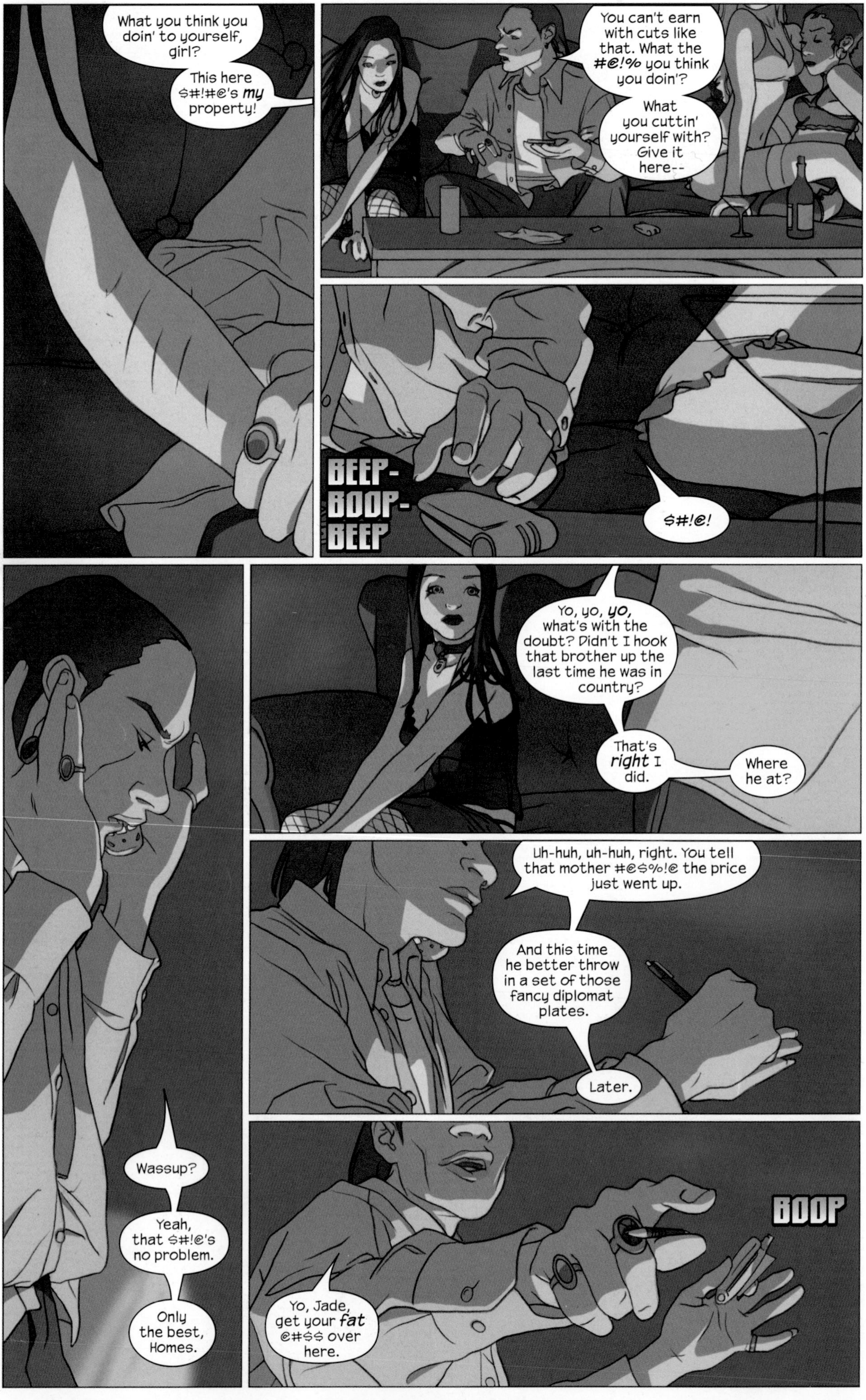
What you think you doin' to yourself, girl?
This here $#!#@'s my property!
You can't earn with cuts like that. What the #@!% you think you doin'?
What you cuttin' yourself with? Give it here--
BEEP-BOOP-BEEP
$#!@!
Yo, yo, yo, what's with the doubt? Didn't I hook that brother up the last time he was in country?
That's right I did.
Where he at?
Uh-huh, uh-huh, right. You tell that mother #@$%!@ the price just went up.
And this time he better throw in a set of those fancy diplomat plates.
Later.
Wassup?
Yeah, that $#!@'s no problem.
Only the best, Homes.
BOOP
Yo, Jade, get your fat @#$$ over here.

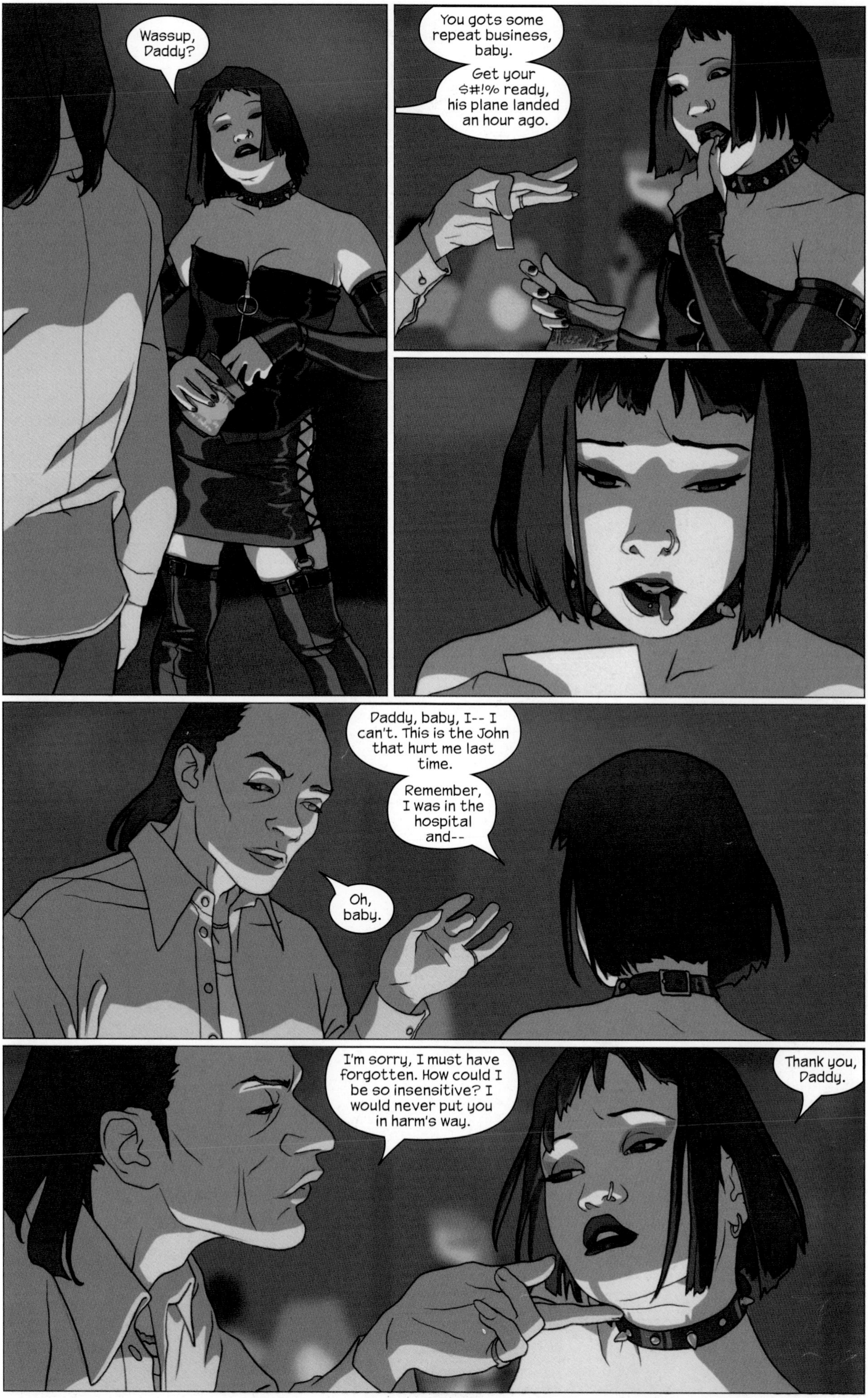
Wassup, Daddy?
You gots some repeat business, baby.
Get your $#!% ready, his plane landed an hour ago.
Daddy, baby, I-- I can't. This is the John that hurt me last time.
Remember, I was in the hospital and--
Oh, baby.
I'm sorry, I must have forgotten. How could I be so insensitive? I would never put you in harm's way.
Thank you, Daddy.

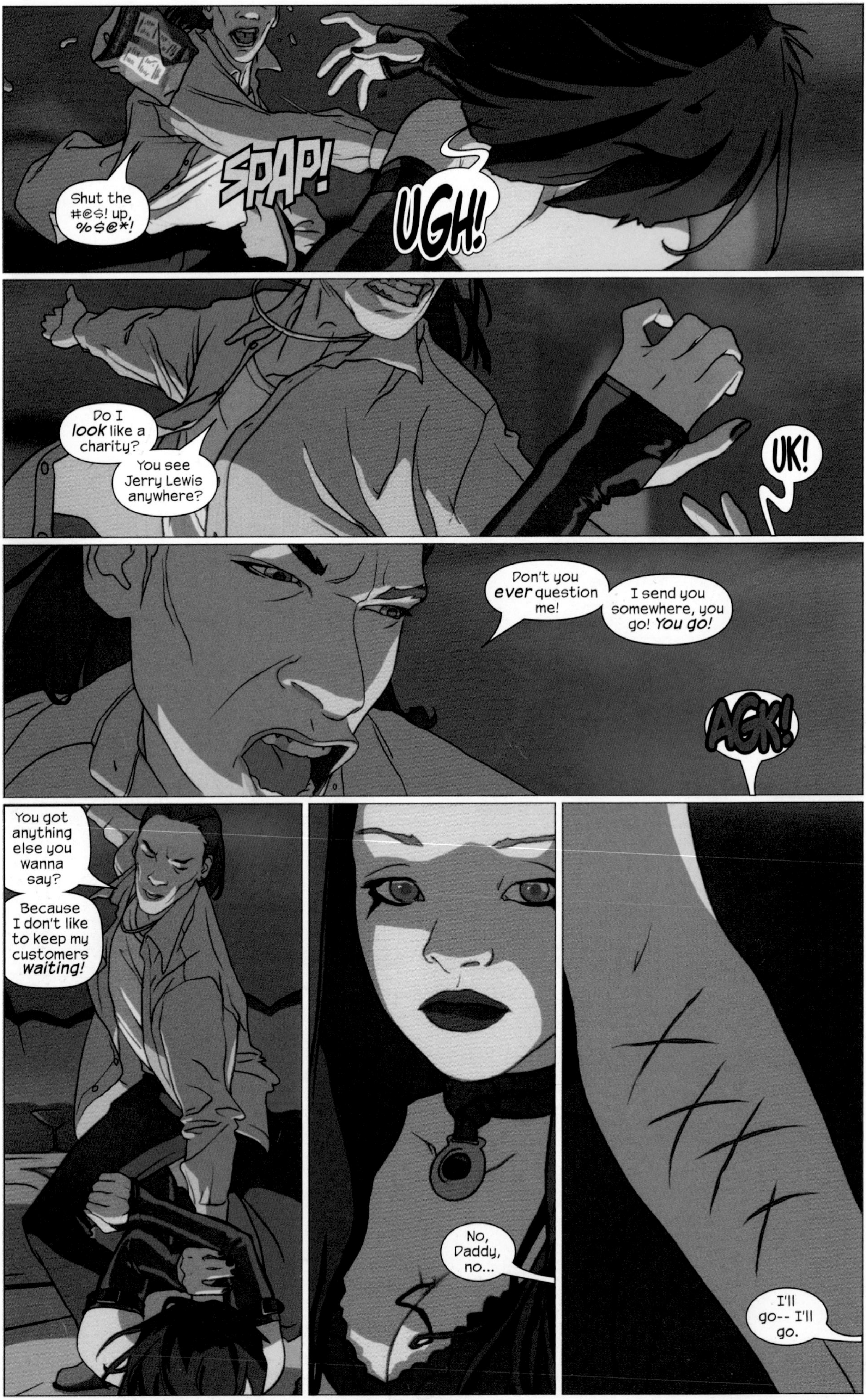

SPAP!
Shut the #@$! up, %$@*!
UGH!
Do I *look* like a charity?
You see Jerry Lewis anywhere?
UK!
Don't you *ever* question me!
I send you somewhere, you go! *You go!*
AGK!
You got anything else you wanna say?
Because I don't like to keep my customers *waiting!*
No, Daddy, no...
I'll go-- I'll go.

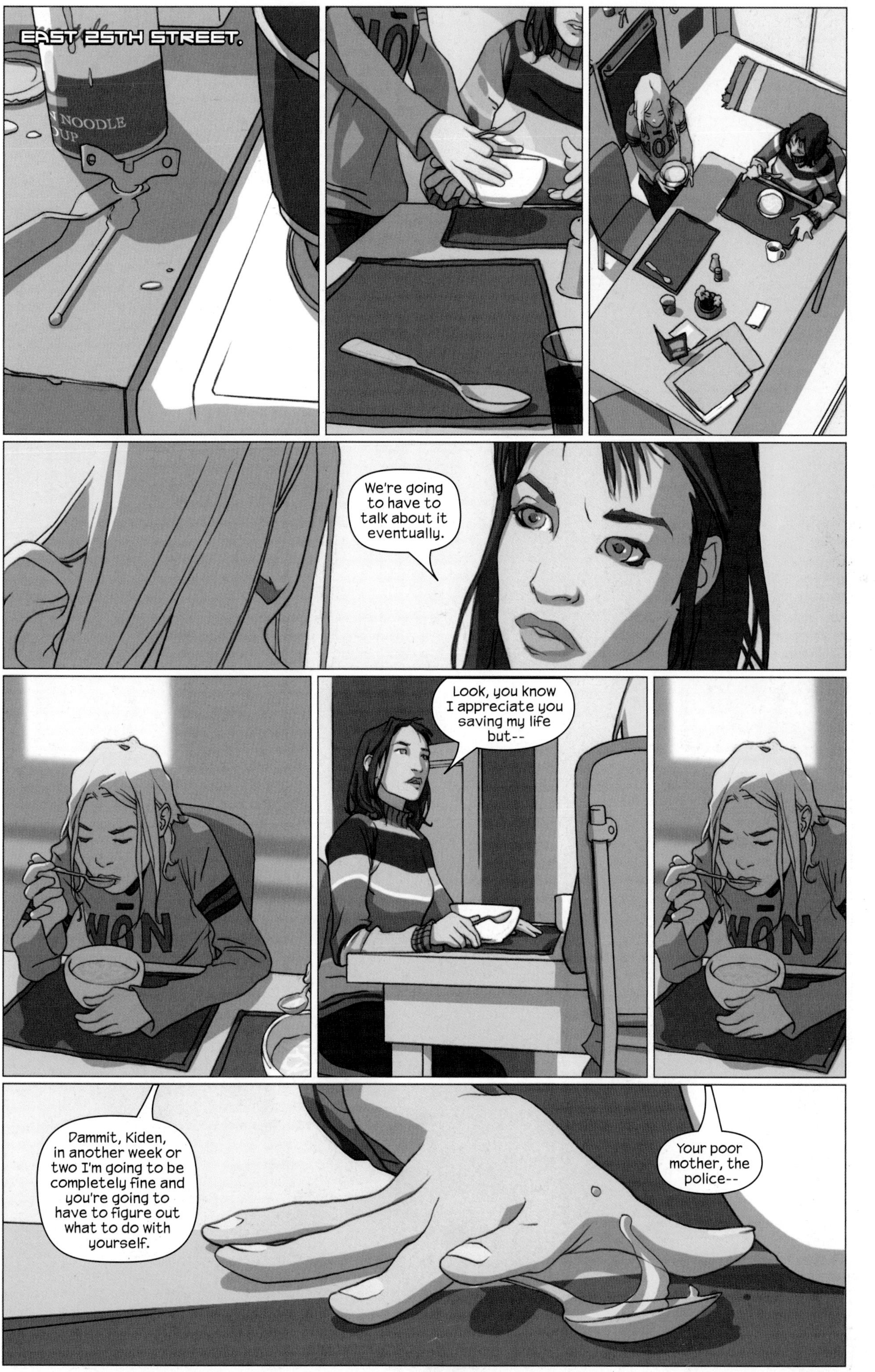

EAST 25TH STREET.
N NOODLE
OUP
We're going to have to talk about it eventually.
Look, you know I appreciate you saving my life but--
Dammit, Kiden, in another week or two I'm going to be completely fine and you're going to have to figure out what to do with yourself.
Your poor mother, the police--

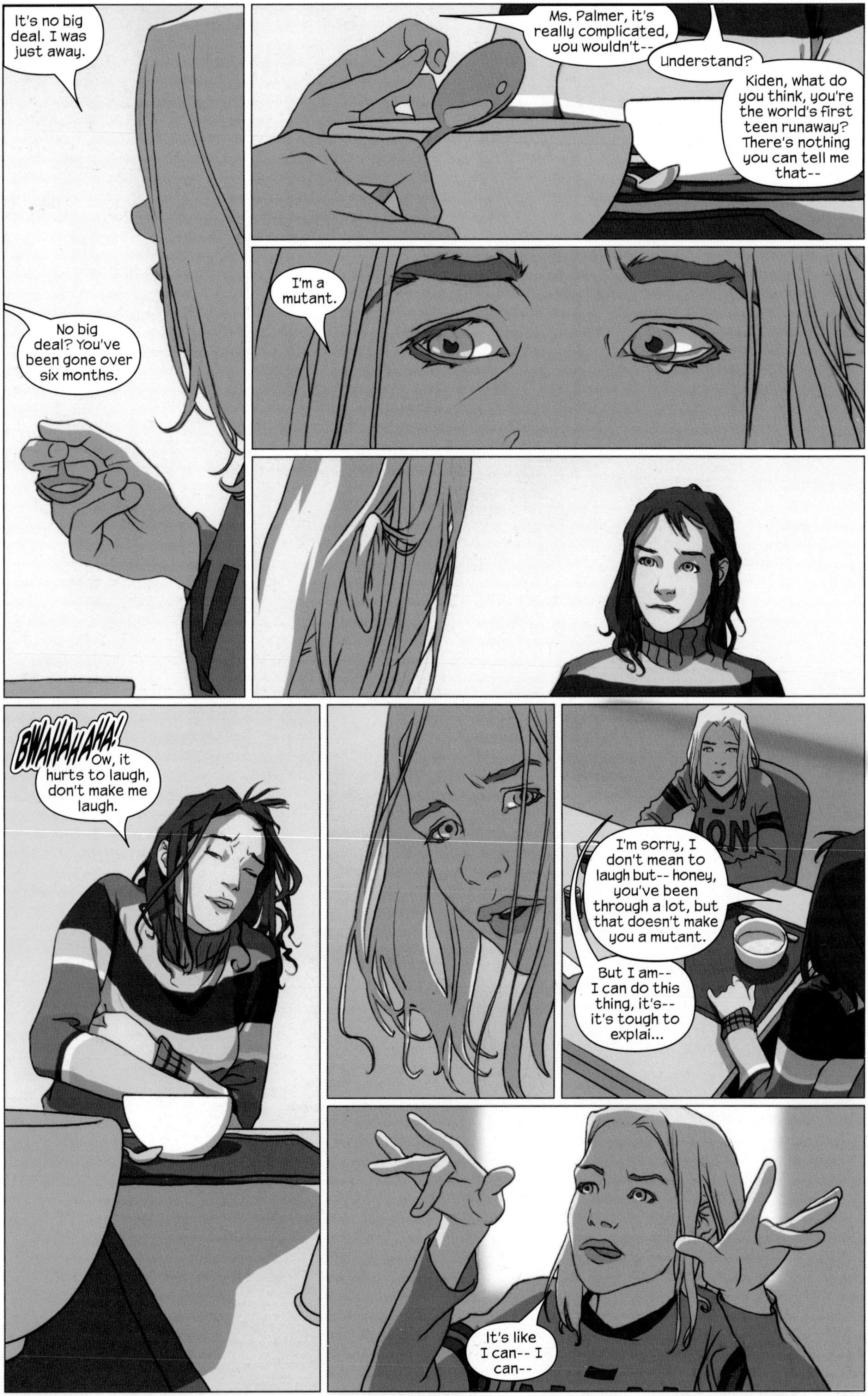
It's no big deal. I was just away.
Ms. Palmer, it's really complicated, you wouldn't--
Understand?
Kiden, what do you think, you're the world's first teen runaway? There's nothing you can tell me that--
No big deal? You've been gone over six months.
I'm a mutant.
BWAHAHAHA!
Ow, it hurts to laugh, don't make me laugh.
I'm sorry, I don't mean to laugh but-- honey, you've been through a lot, but that doesn't make you a mutant.
But I am-- I can do this thing, it's-- it's tough to explai...
It's like I can-- I can--

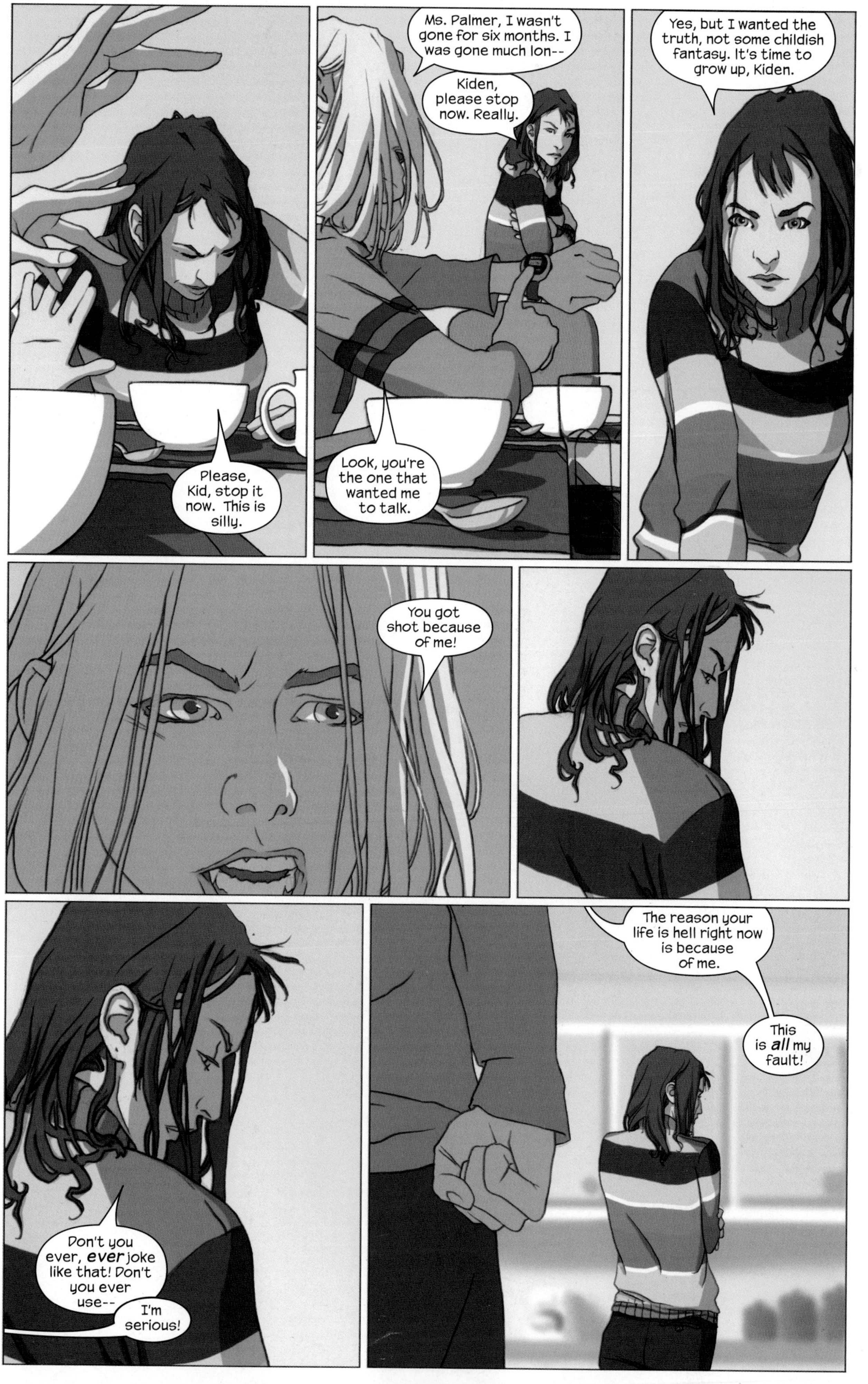
Please, Kid, stop it now. This is silly.
Ms. Palmer, I wasn't gone for six months. I was gone much lon--
Kiden, please stop now. Really.
Look, you're the one that wanted me to talk.
Yes, but I wanted the truth, not some childish fantasy. It's time to grow up, Kiden.
You got shot because of me!
Don't you ever, **ever** joke like that! Don't you ever use--
I'm serious!
The reason your life is hell right now is because of me.
This is ***all*** my fault!

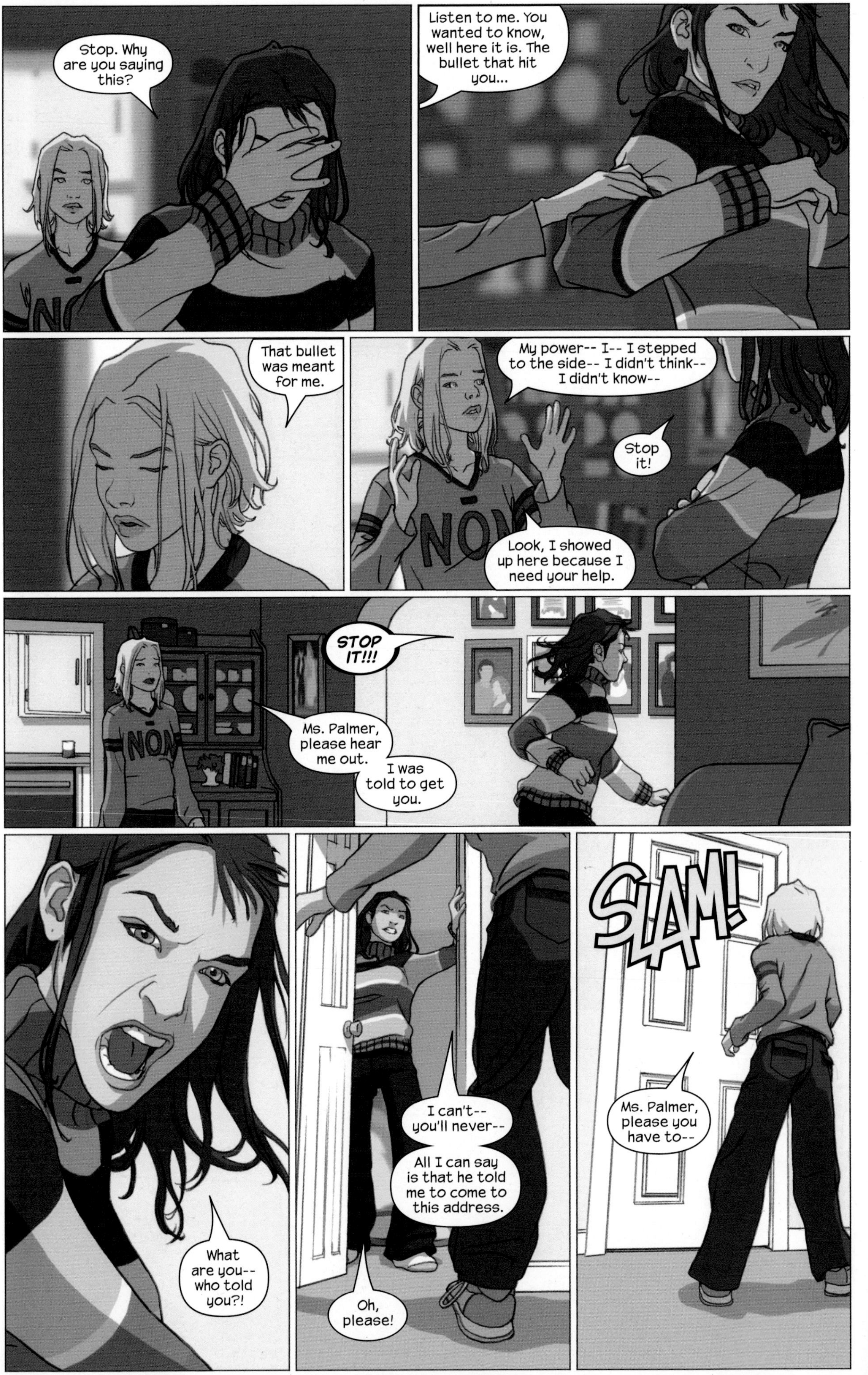
Stop. Why are you saying this?
Listen to me. You wanted to know, well here it is. The bullet that hit you...
That bullet was meant for me.
My power-- I-- I stepped to the side-- I didn't think-- I didn't know--
Stop it!
Look, I showed up here because I need your help.
STOP IT!!!
Ms. Palmer, please hear me out.
I was told to get you.
What are you-- who told you?!
I can't-- you'll never--
All I can say is that he told me to come to this address.
Oh, please!
SLAM!
Ms. Palmer, please you have to--

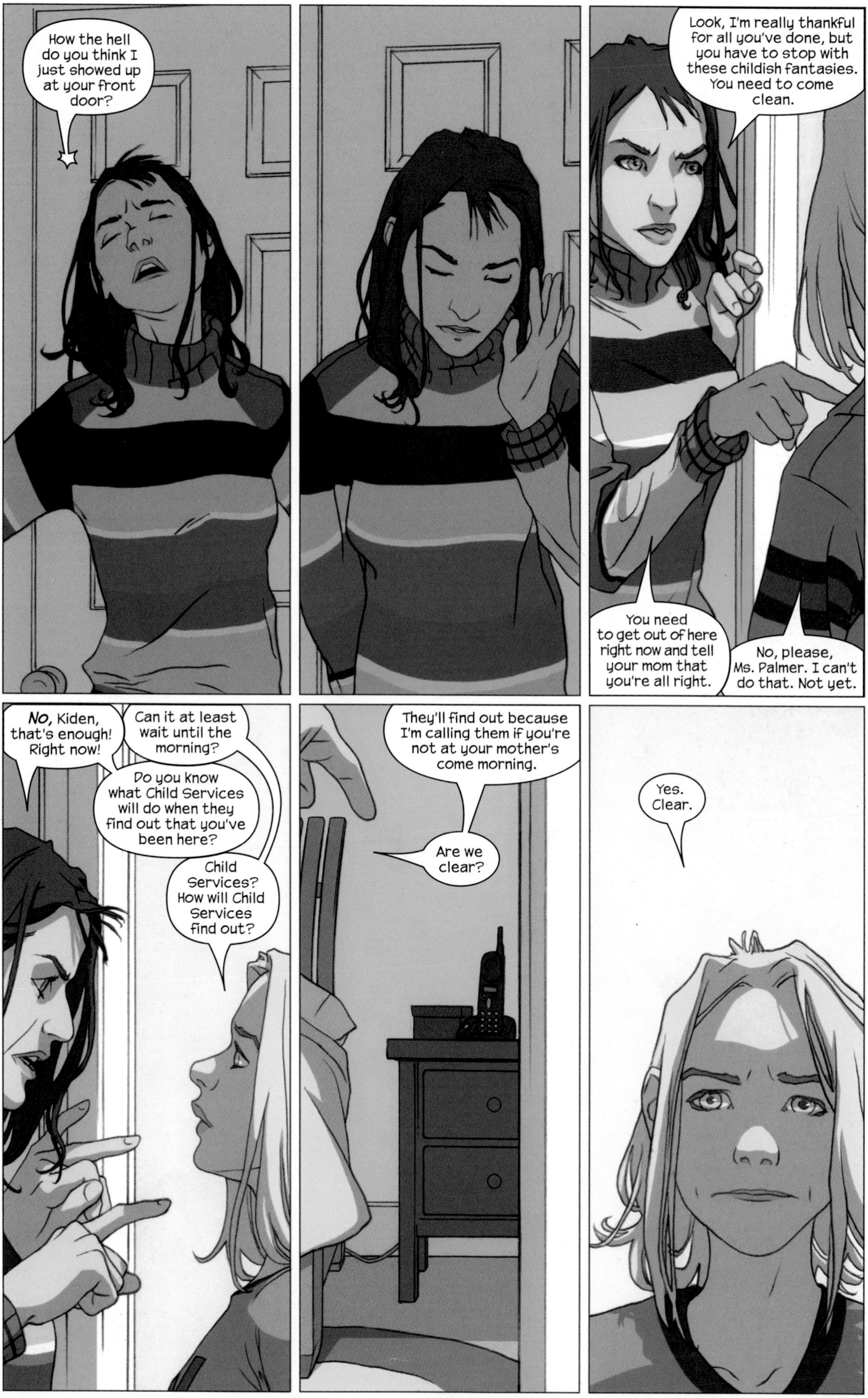
How the hell do you think I just showed up at your front door?
Look, I'm really thankful for all you've done, but you have to stop with these childish fantasies. You need to come clean.
You need to get out of here right now and tell your mom that you're all right.
No, please, Ms. Palmer. I can't do that. Not yet.
No, Kiden, that's enough! Right now!
Can it at least wait until the morning?
Do you know what Child Services will do when they find out that you've been here?
Child Services? How will Child Services find out?
They'll find out because I'm calling them if you're not at your mother's come morning.
Are we clear?
Yes. Clear.

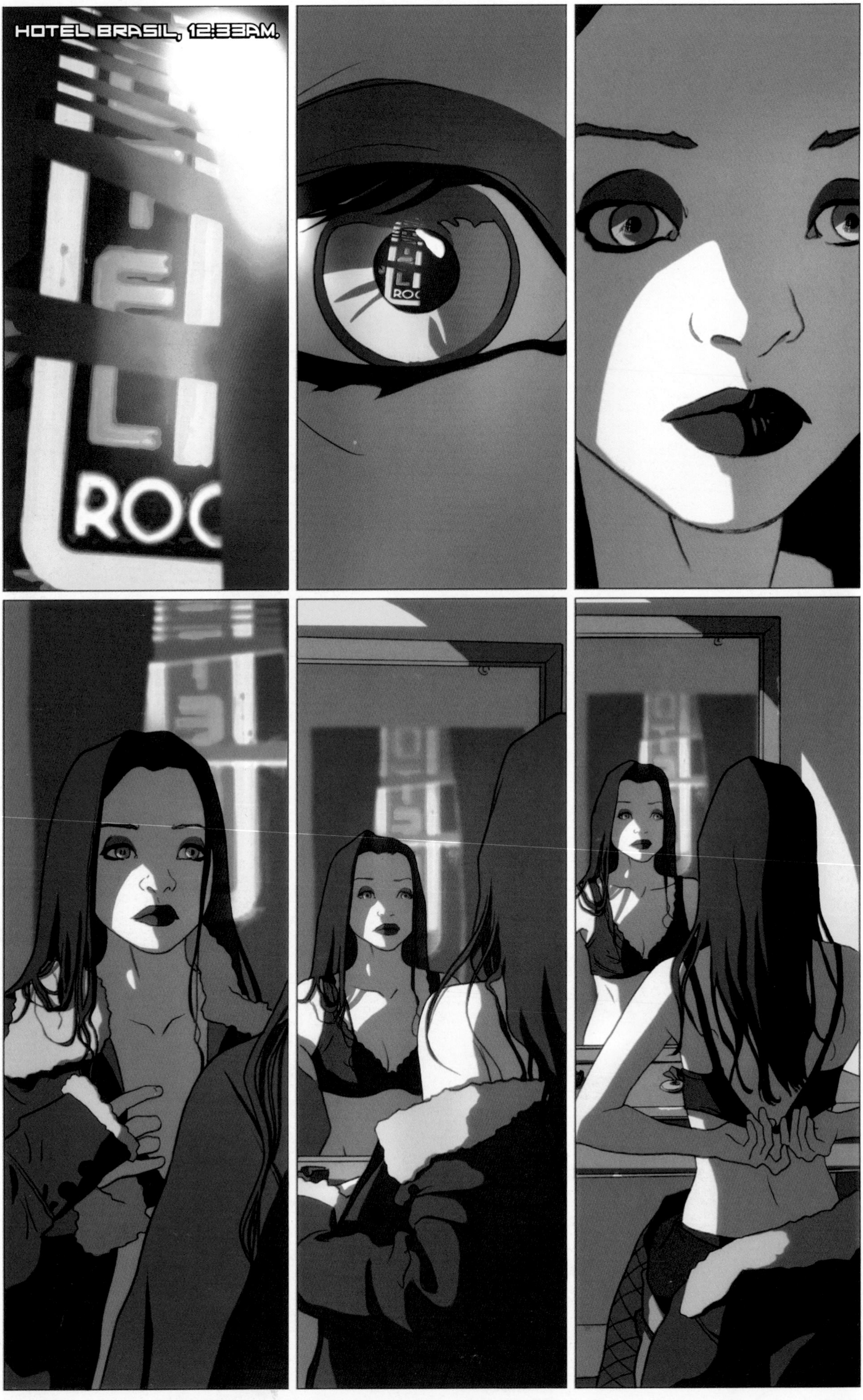

HOTEL BRASIL, 12:33AM.

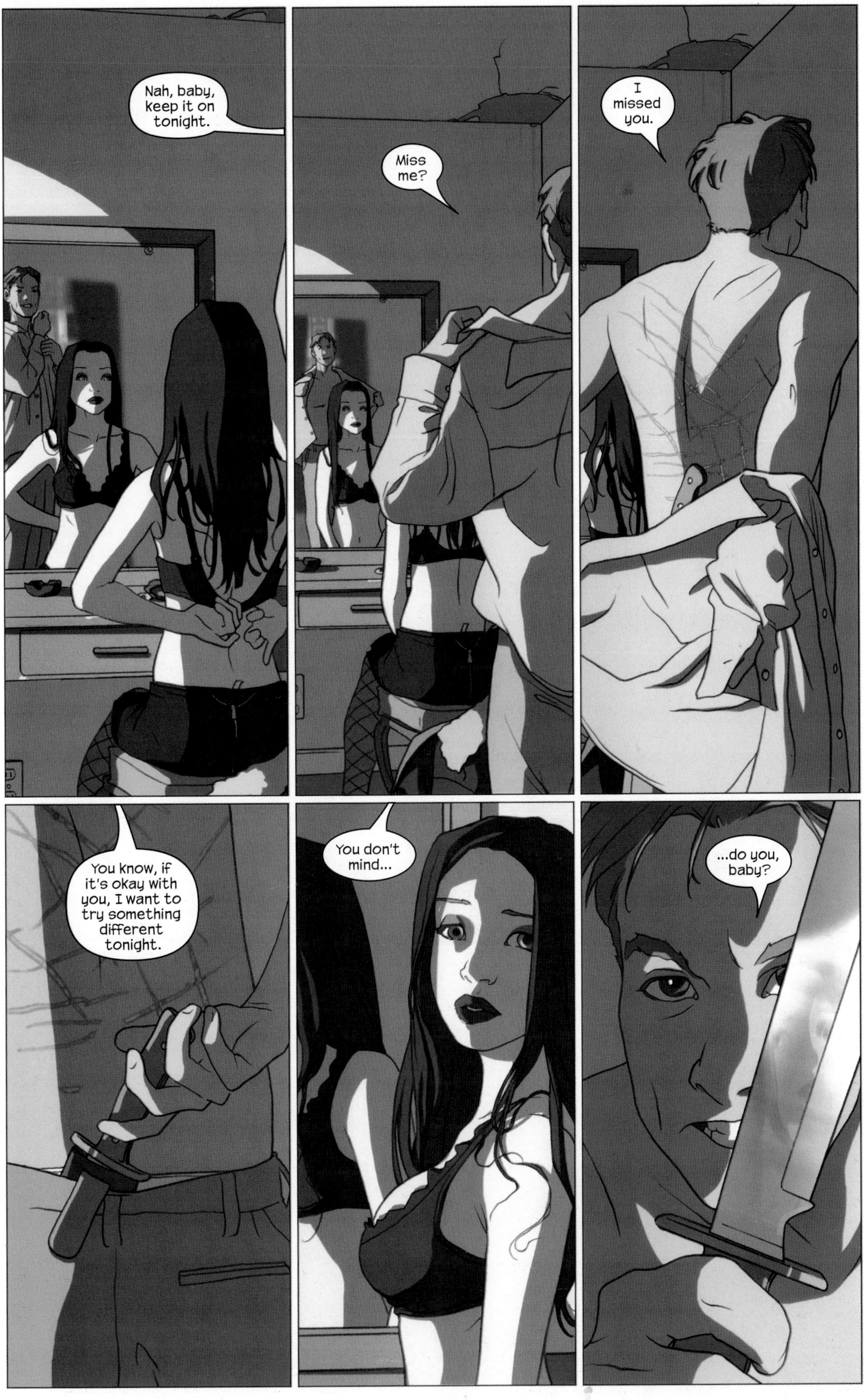
Nah, baby, keep it on tonight.
Miss me?
I missed you.
You know, if it's okay with you, I want to try something different tonight.
You don't mind...
...do you, baby?

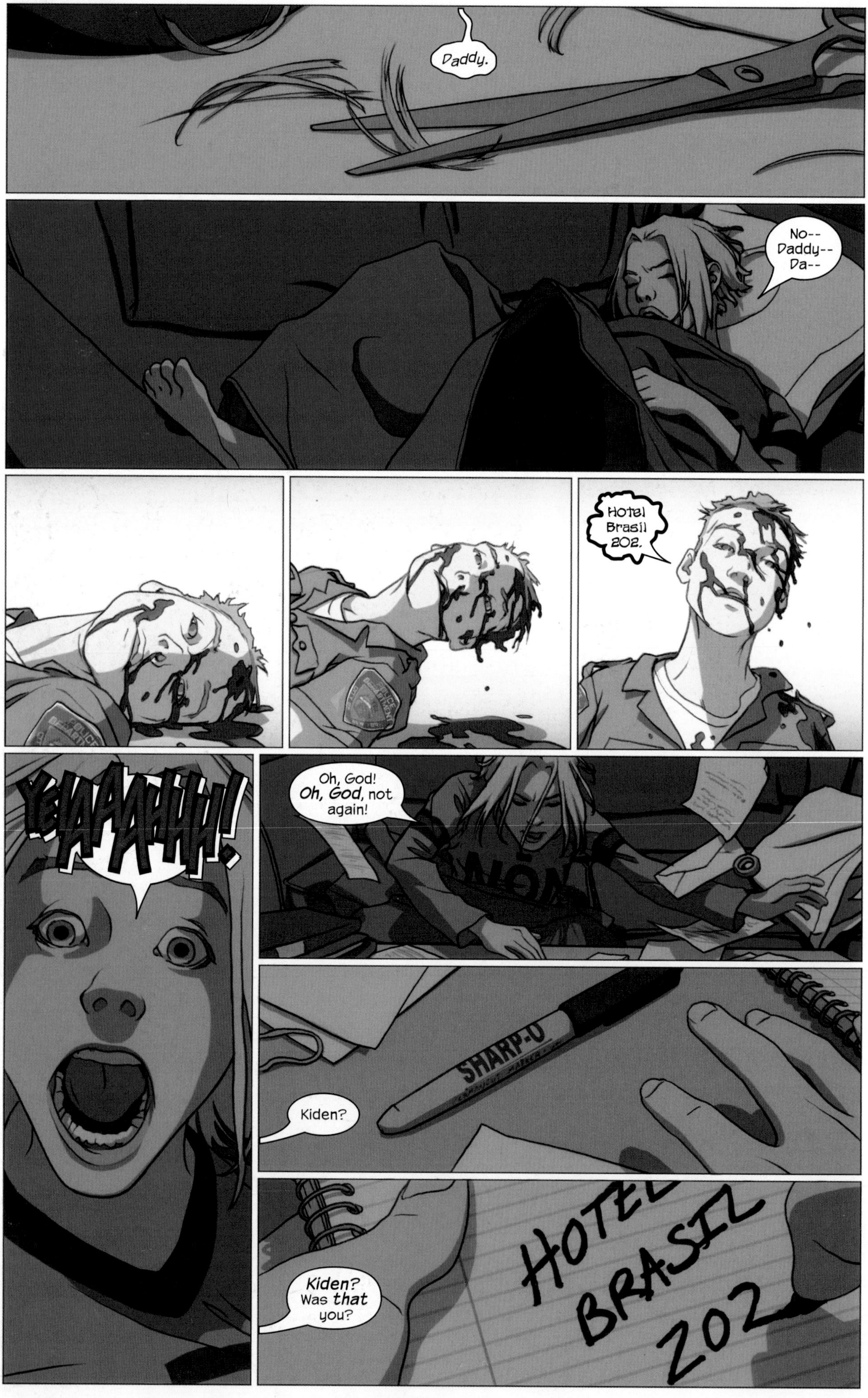
Daddy.
No-- Daddy-- Da--
Hotel Brasil 202.
YEAAAHHH!
Oh, God! Oh, God, not again!
SHARP-O
Kiden?
Kiden? Was that you?
HOTEL BRASIL 202

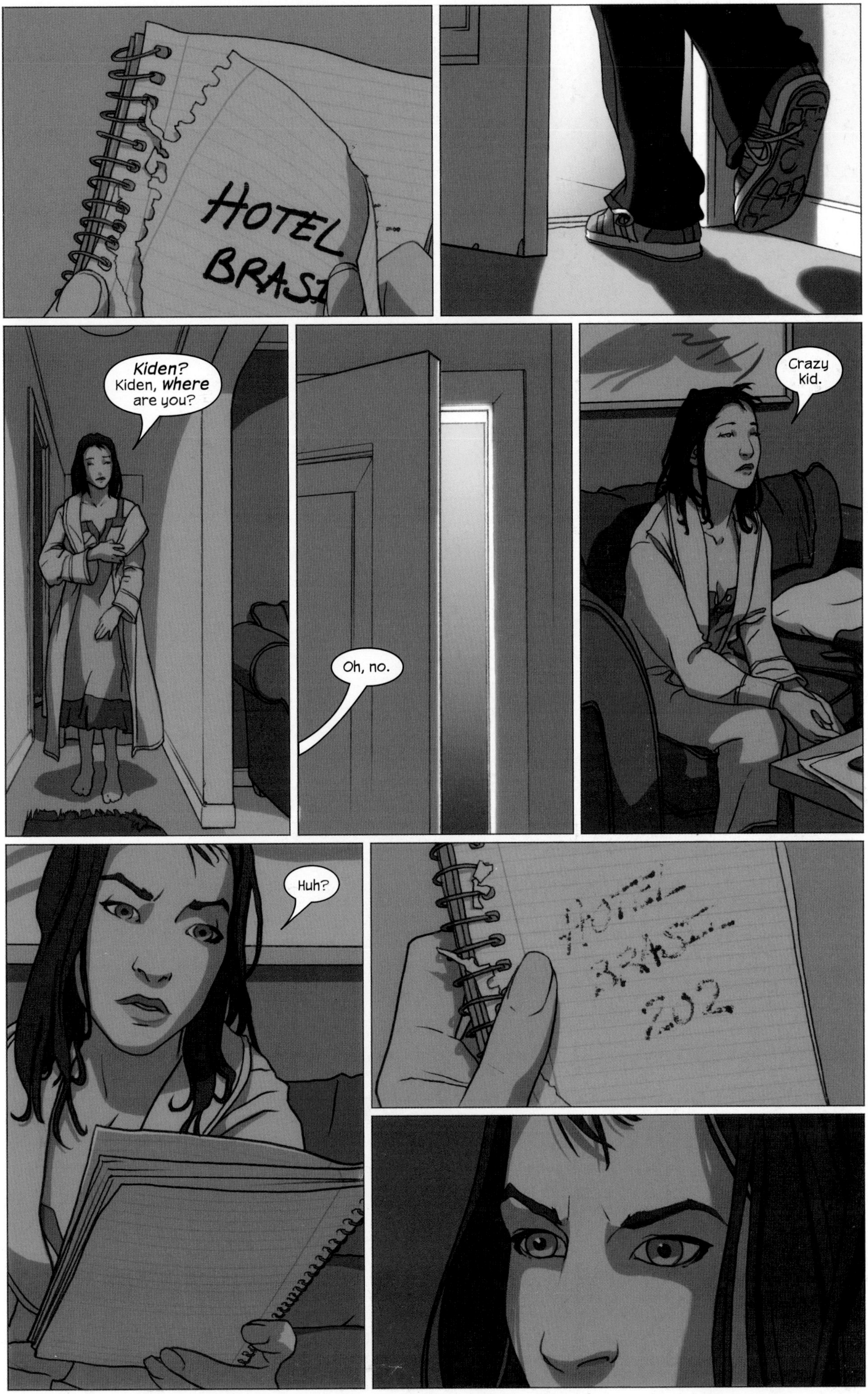
HOTEL BRASI
Kiden? Kiden, where are you?
Oh, no.
Crazy kid.
Huh?
HOTEL BRASI-- 202

Watch where you're going, #$¢%!¢!

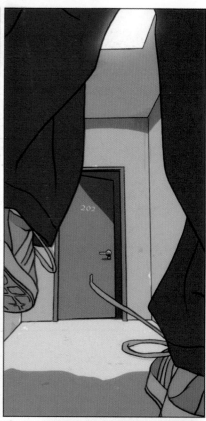

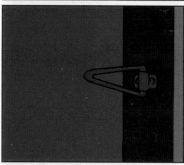

Keep the change.

What the #$¢% is this, *amateur* night?

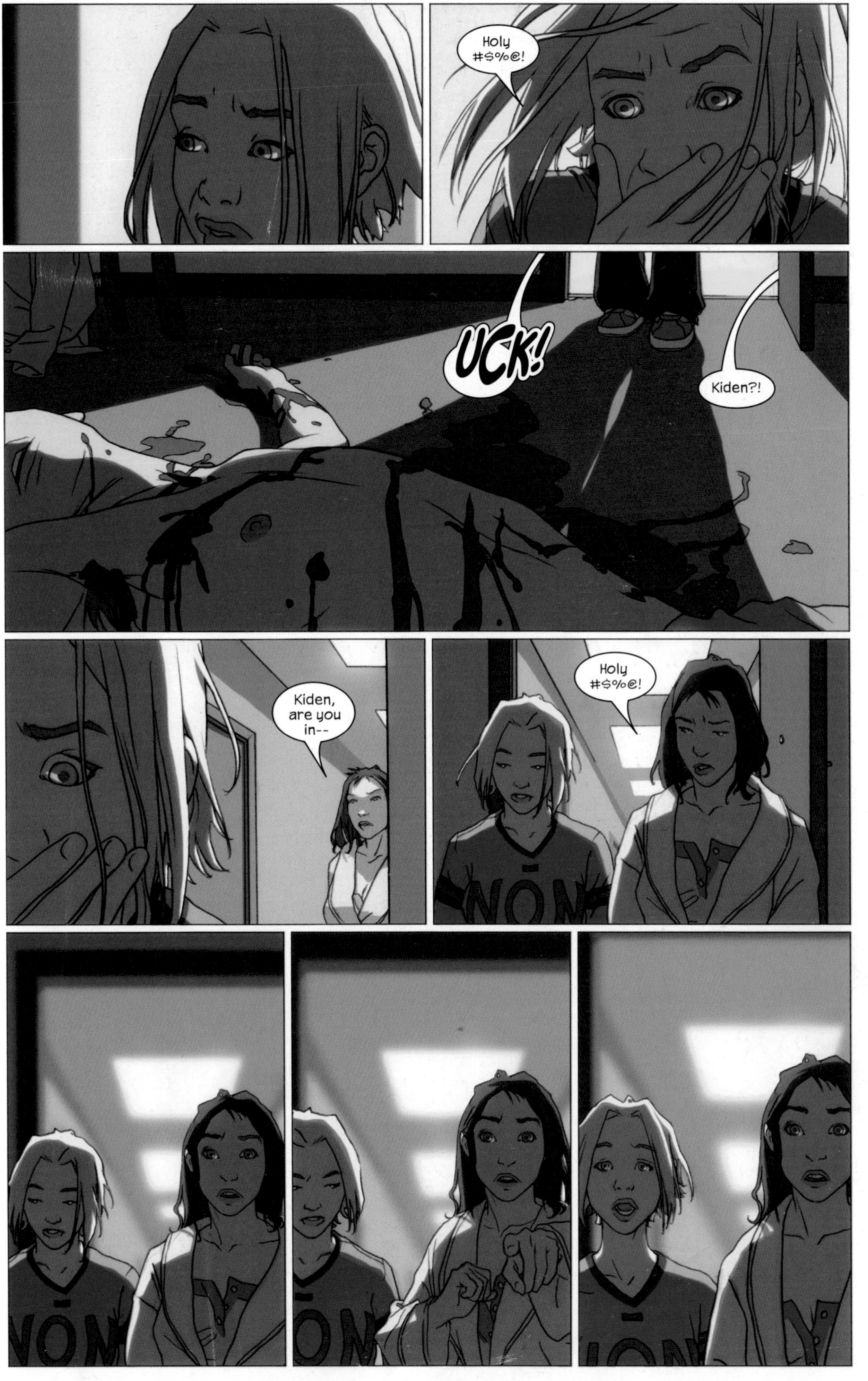

Holy #$%@!
UCK!
Kiden?!
Kiden, are you in--
Holy #$%@!
NON

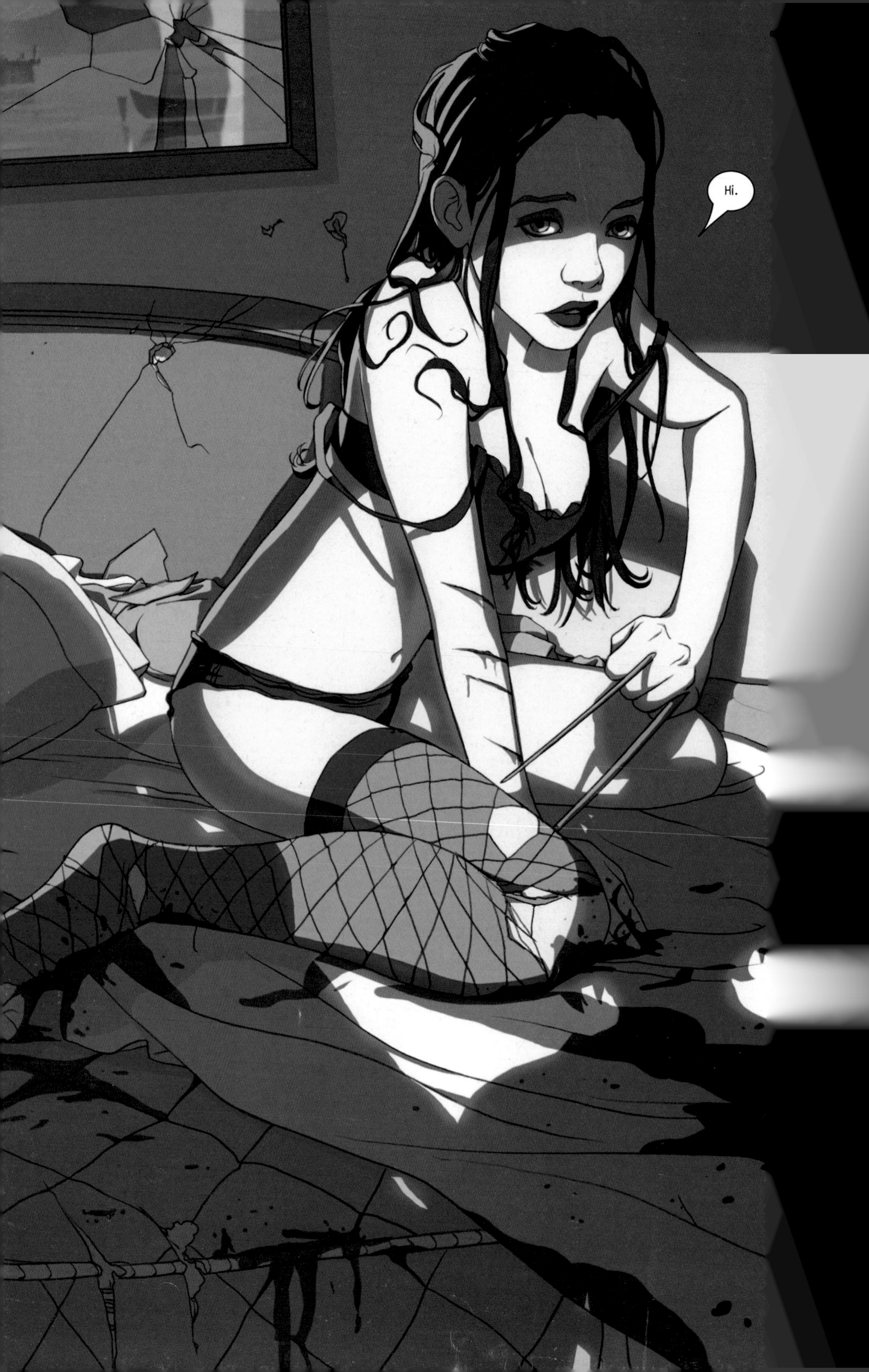
Hi.

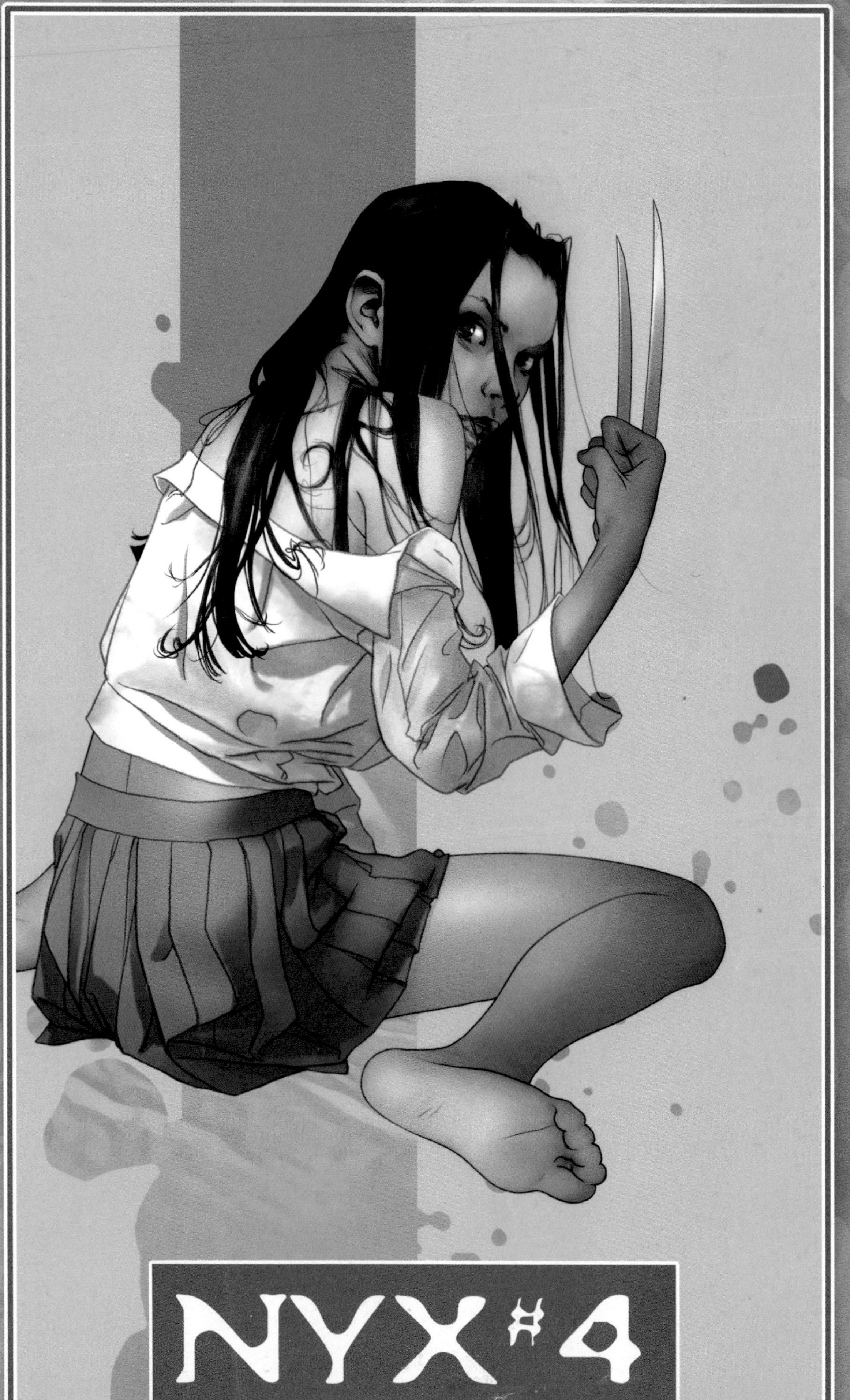
NYX #4

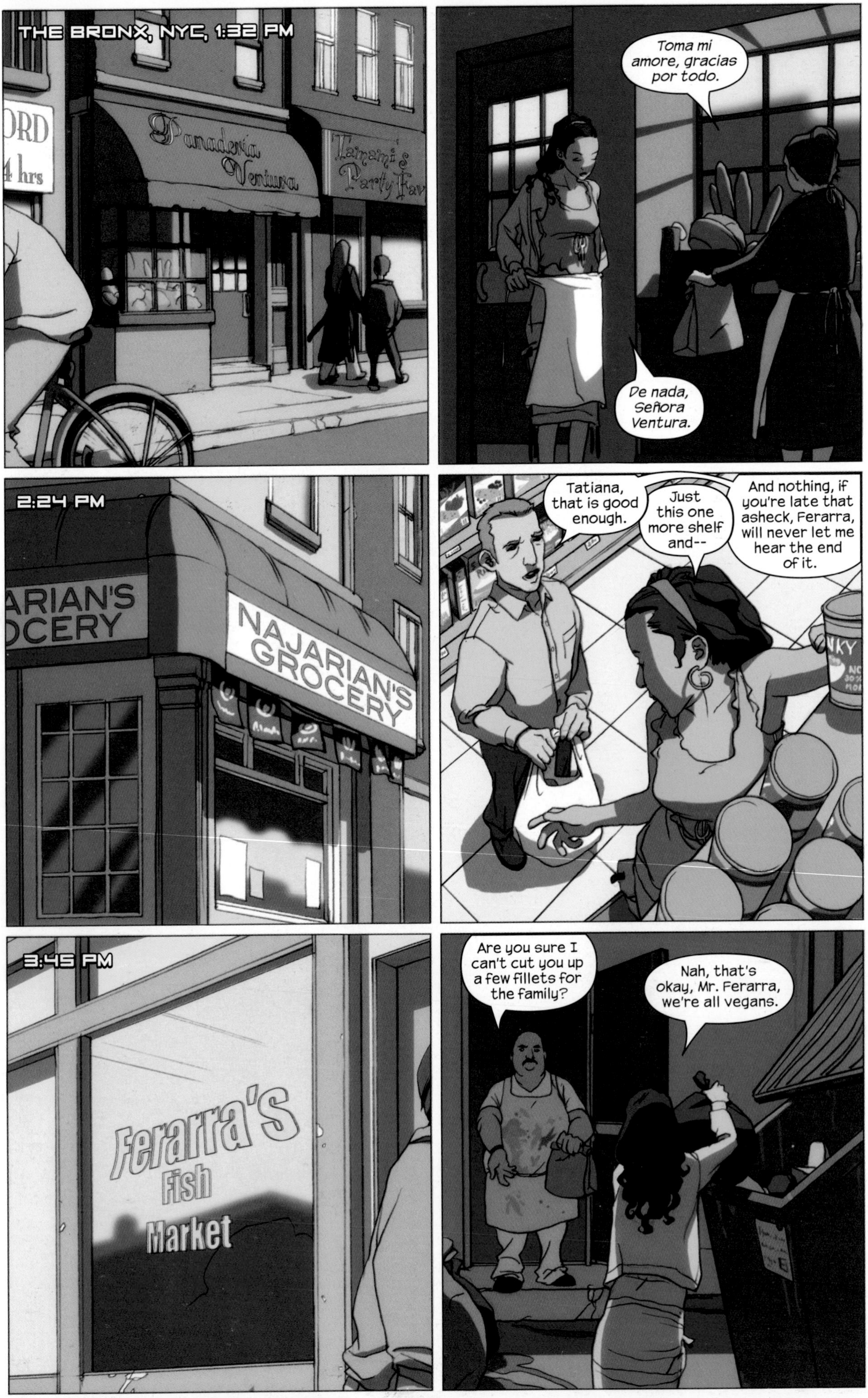
THE BRONX, NYC, 1:32 PM
Panadería Ventura
Toma mi amore, gracias por todo.
De nada, Señora Ventura.
2:24 PM
NAJARIAN'S GROCERY
Tatiana, that is good enough.
Just this one more shelf and--
And nothing, if you're late that asheck, Ferarra, will never let me hear the end of it.
3:45 PM
Ferarra's Fish Market
Are you sure I can't cut you up a few fillets for the family?
Nah, that's okay, Mr. Ferarra, we're all vegans.

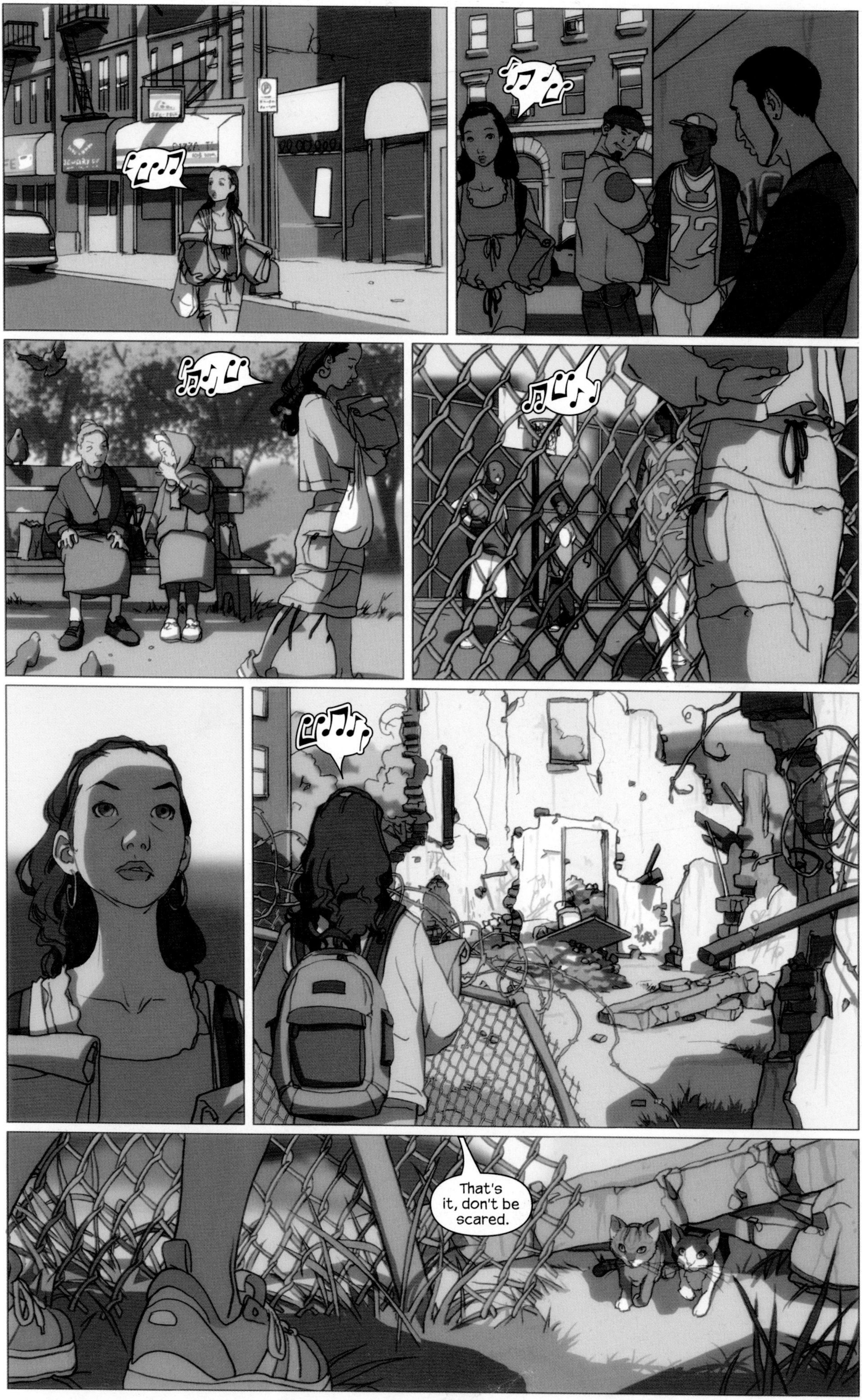
That's it, don't be scared.

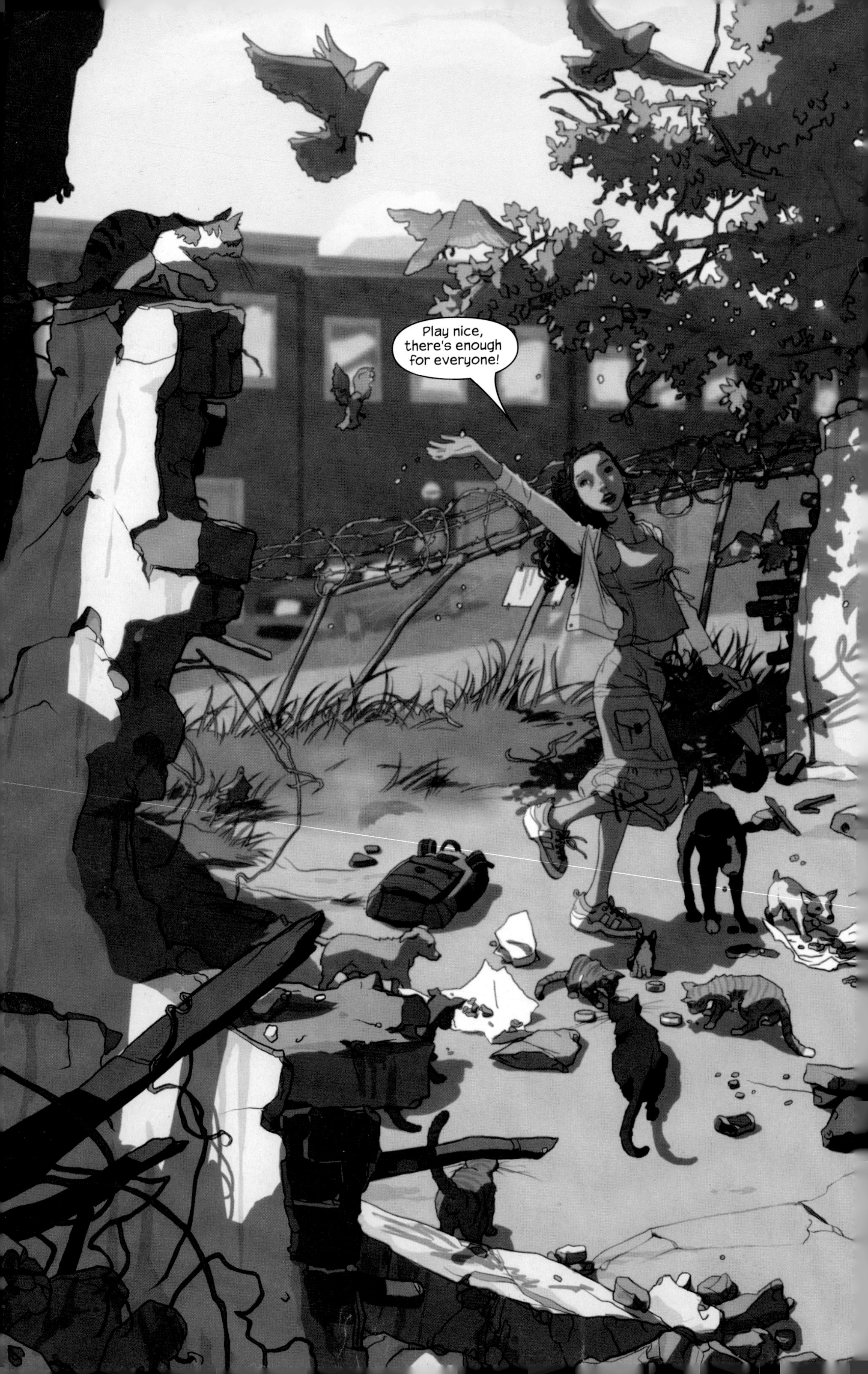
Play nice, there's enough for everyone!

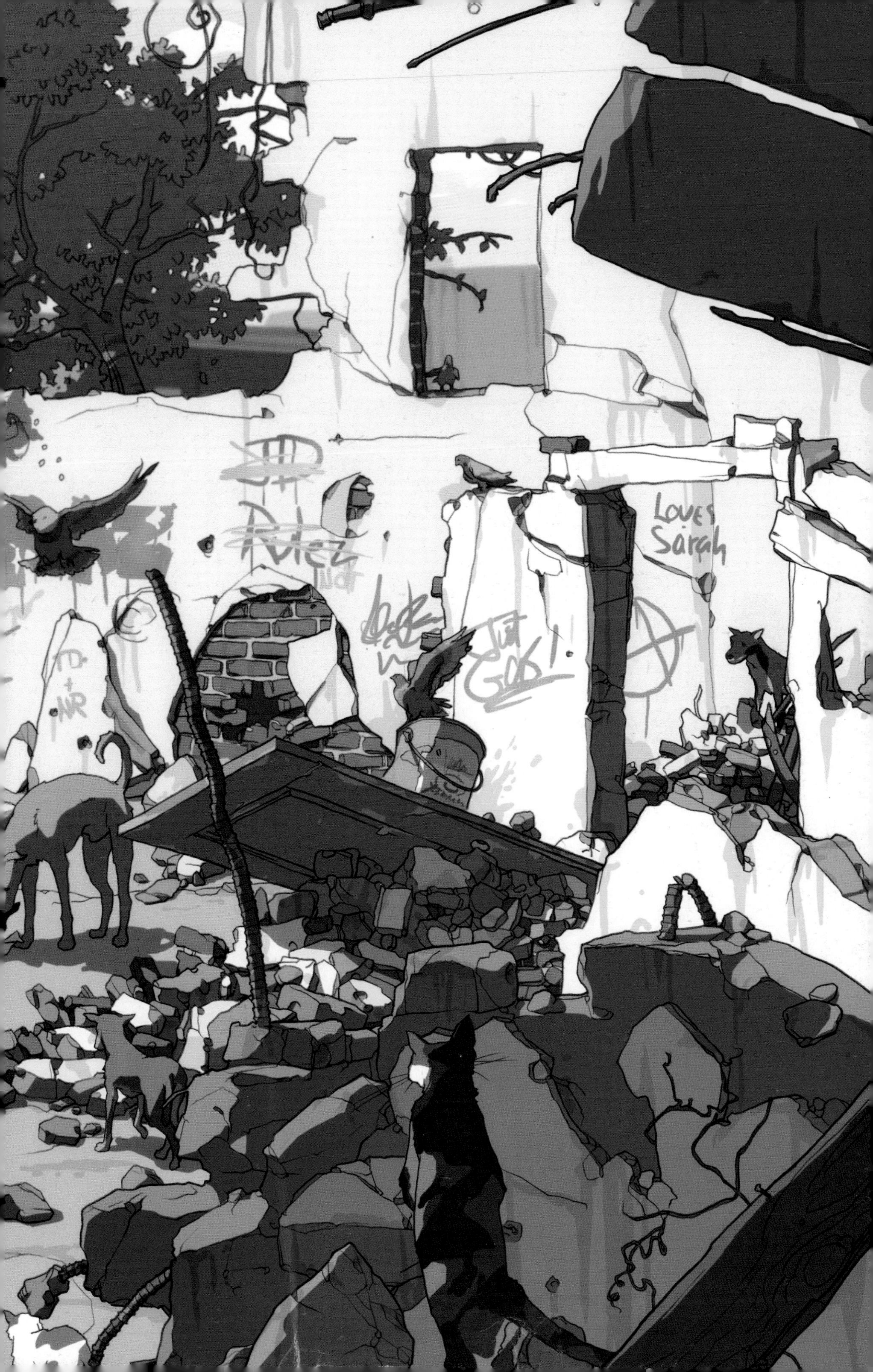
Loves Sarah
Rulez
Just GO!

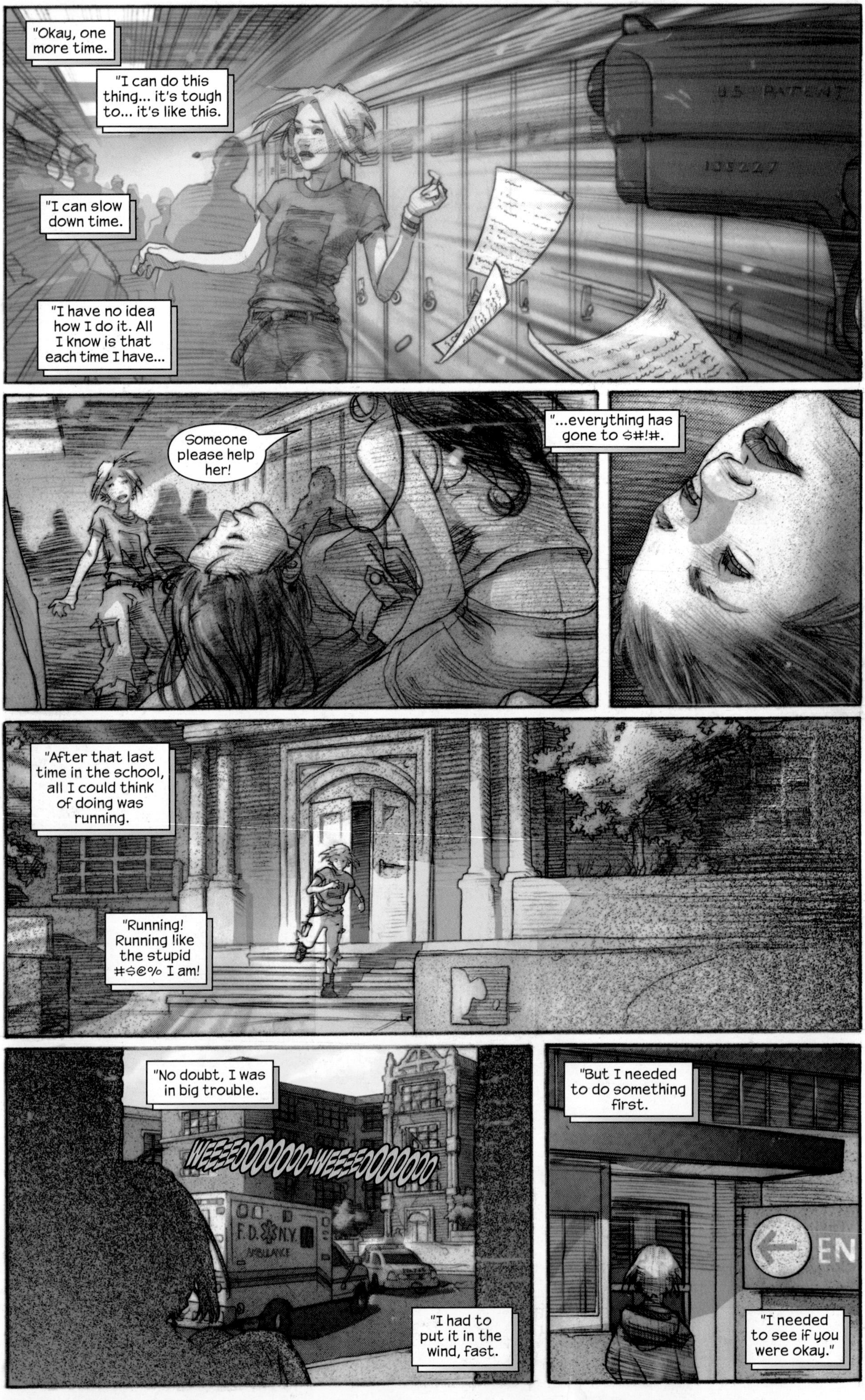
"Okay, one more time.
"I can do this thing... it's tough to... it's like this.
"I can slow down time.
"I have no idea how I do it. All I know is that each time I have...
Someone please help her!
"...everything has gone to $#!#.
"After that last time in the school, all I could think of doing was running.
"Running! Running like the stupid #$@% I am!
"No doubt, I was in big trouble.
WEEEEOOOOOOO-WEEEEOOOOOOO
F.D.N.Y.
"I had to put it in the wind, fast.
"But I needed to do something first.
"I needed to see if you were okay."

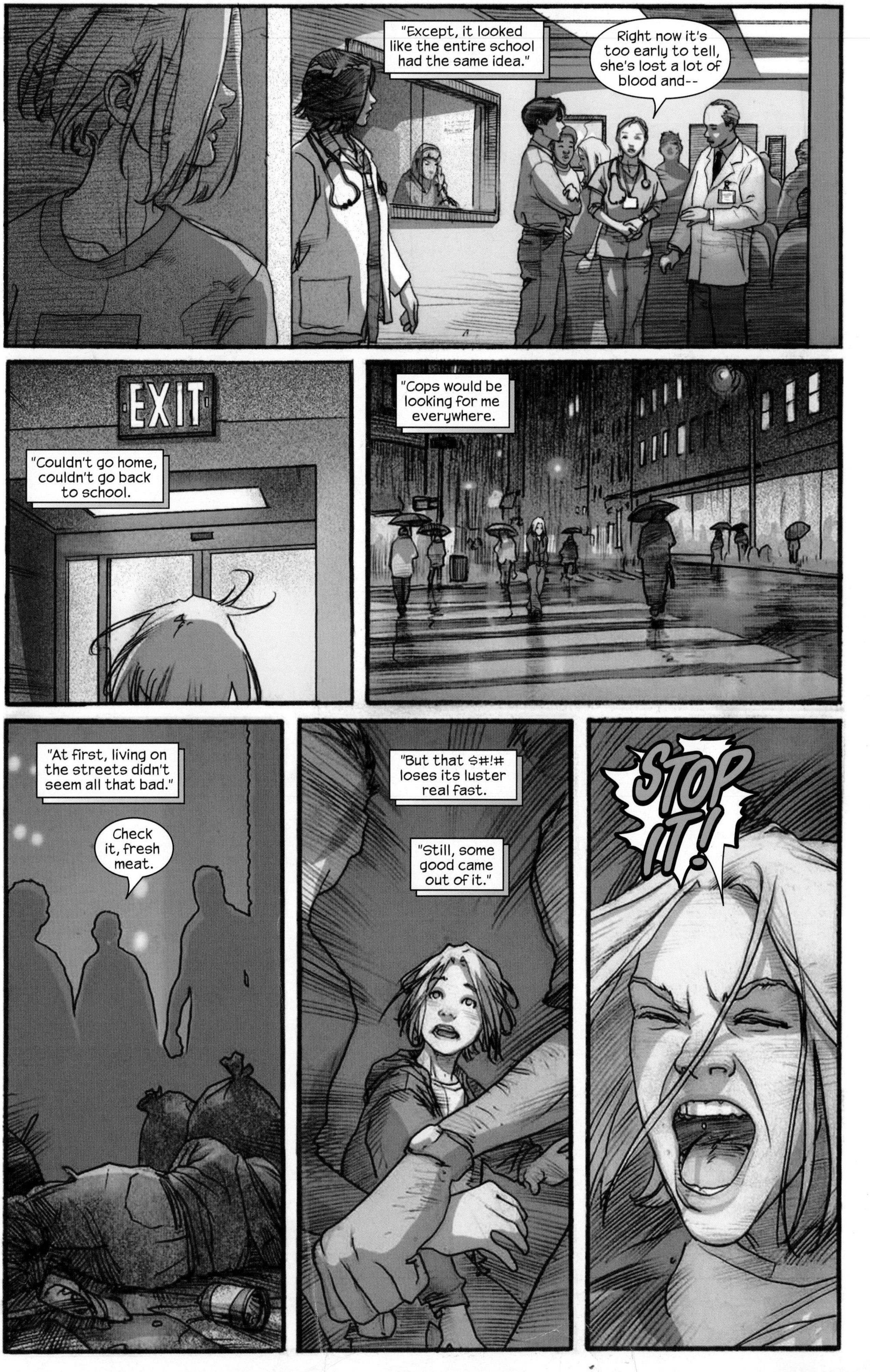
"Except, it looked like the entire school had the same idea."
Right now it's too early to tell, she's lost a lot of blood and--
EXIT
"Couldn't go home, couldn't go back to school.
"Cops would be looking for me everywhere.
"At first, living on the streets didn't seem all that bad."
Check it, fresh meat.
"But that $#!# loses its luster real fast.
"Still, some good came out of it."
STOP IT!

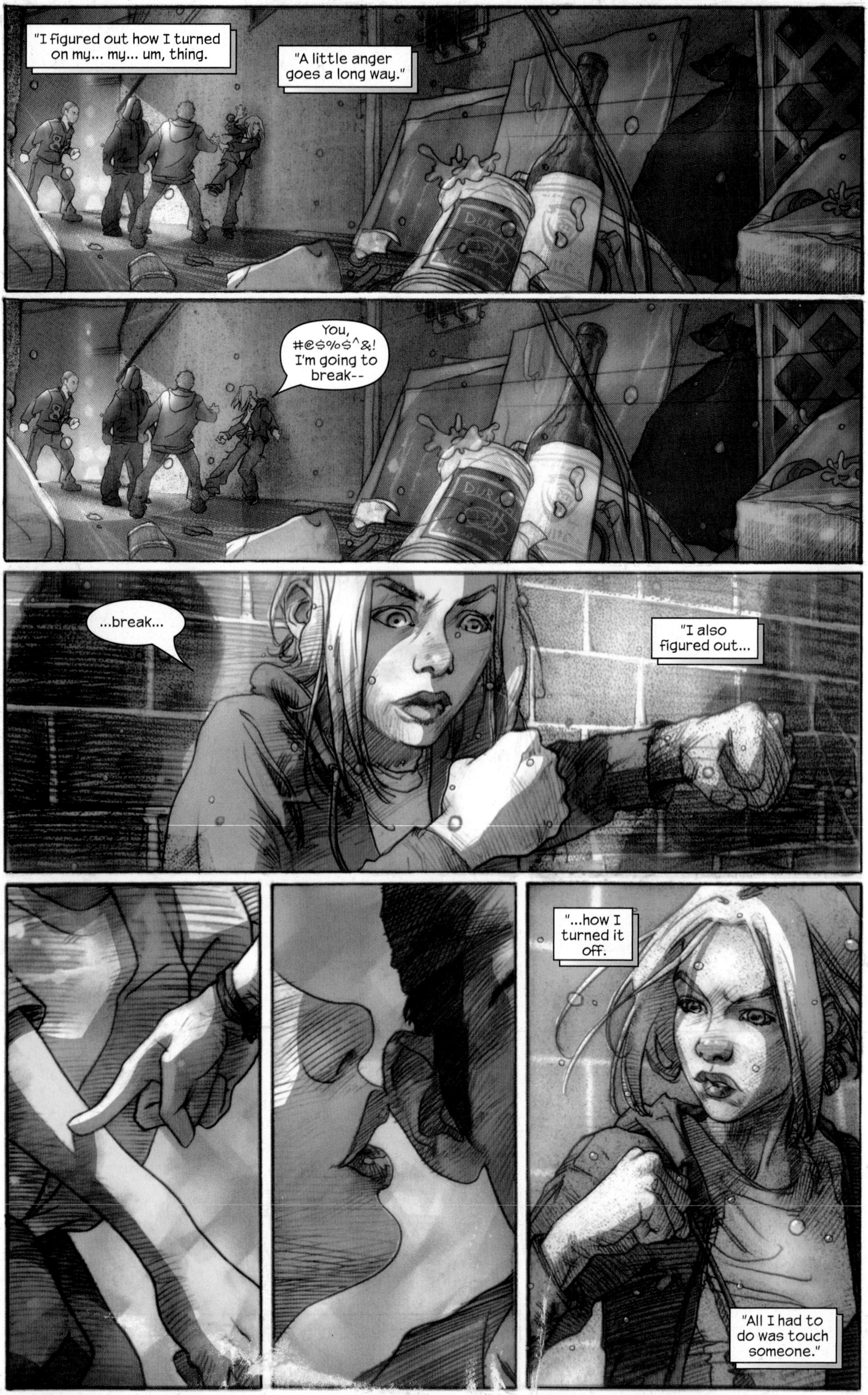
"I figured out how I turned on my... my... um, thing.
"A little anger goes a long way."
You, #@$%$^&! I'm going to break--
...break...
"I also figured out...
"...how I turned it off.
"All I had to do was touch someone."

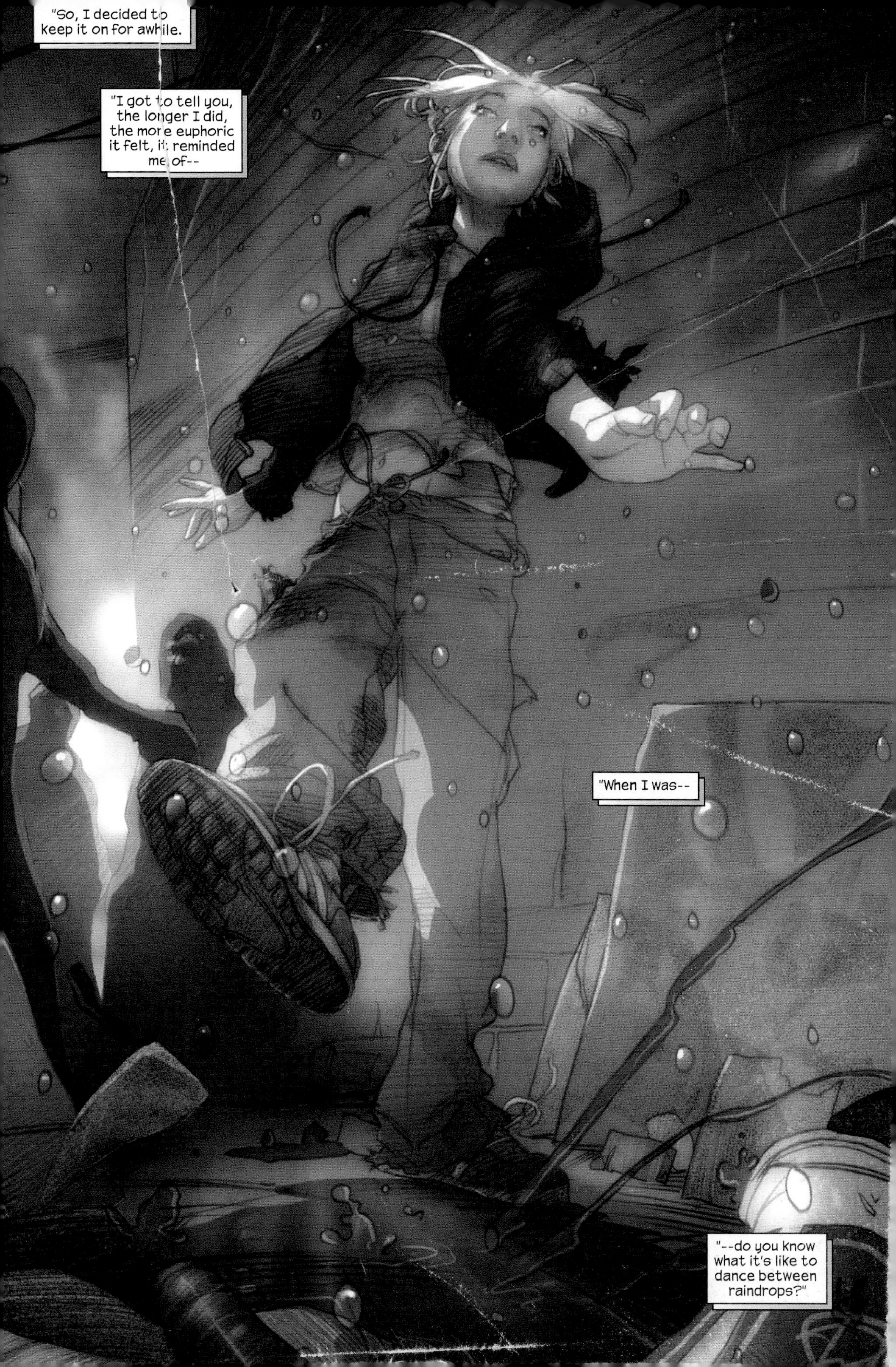
"So, I decided to keep it on for awhile.
"I got to tell you, the longer I did, the more euphoric it felt, it reminded me of--
"When I was--
"--do you know what it's like to dance between raindrops?"

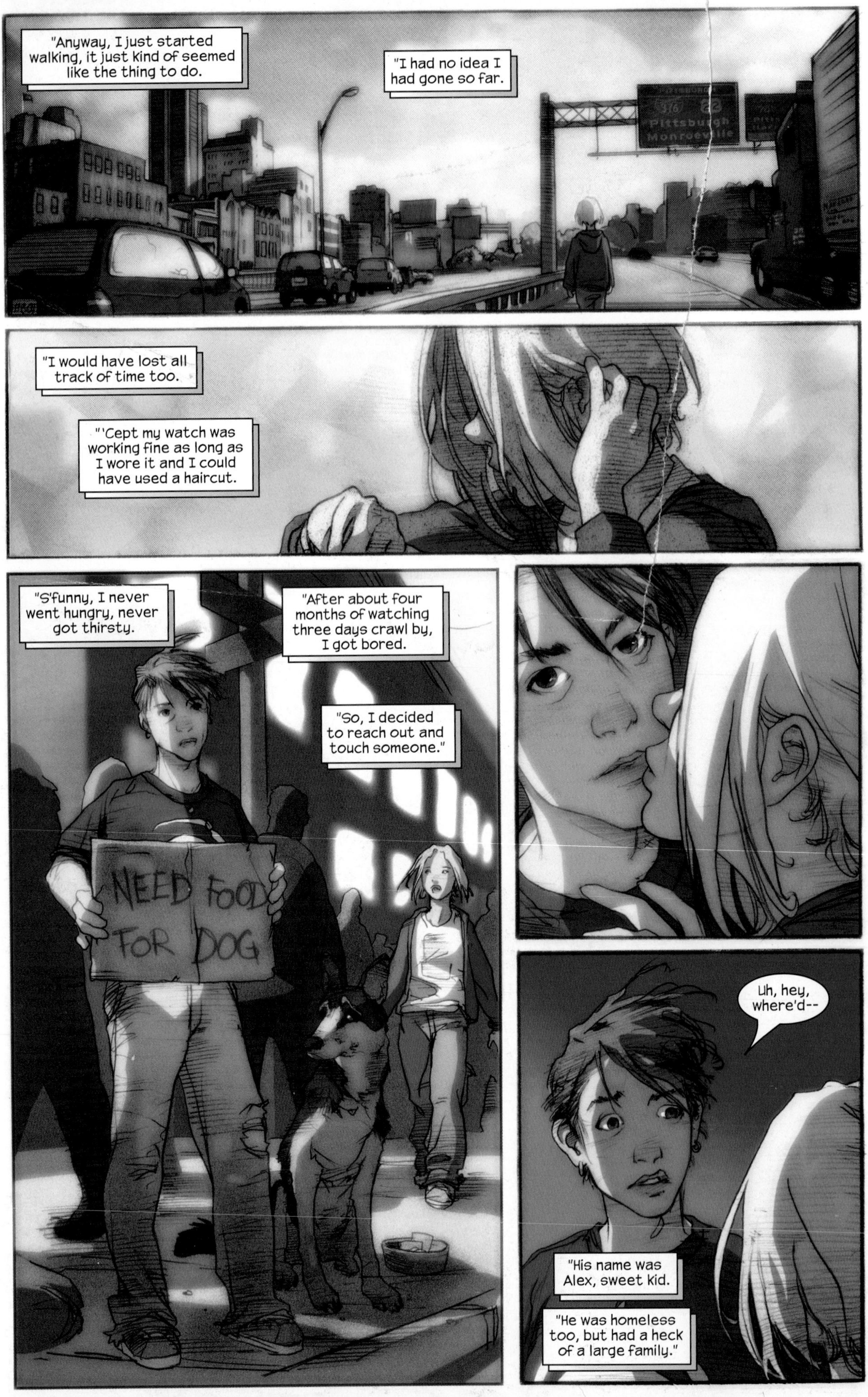
"Anyway, I just started walking, it just kind of seemed like the thing to do.
"I had no idea I had gone so far.
Pittsburgh
Monroeville
"I would have lost all track of time too.
"'Cept my watch was working fine as long as I wore it and I could have used a haircut.
"S'funny, I never went hungry, never got thirsty.
"After about four months of watching three days crawl by, I got bored.
"So, I decided to reach out and touch someone."
NEED FOOD FOR DOG
Uh, hey, where'd--
"His name was Alex, sweet kid.
"He was homeless too, but had a heck of a large family."

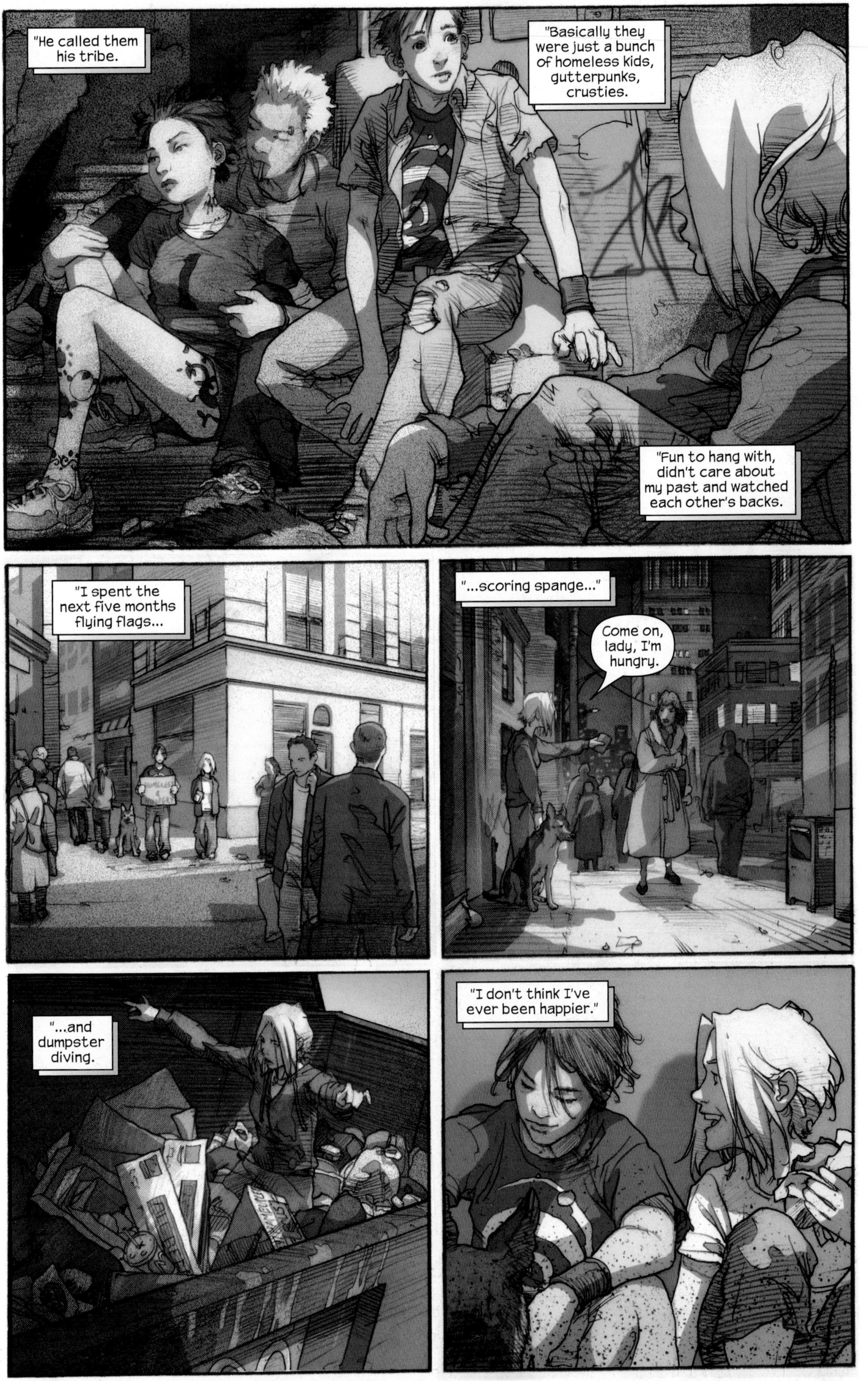
"He called them his tribe.
"Basically they were just a bunch of homeless kids, gutterpunks, crusties.
"Fun to hang with, didn't care about my past and watched each other's backs.
"I spent the next five months flying flags...
"...scoring spange..."
Come on, lady, I'm hungry.
"...and dumpster diving.
"I don't think I've ever been happier."

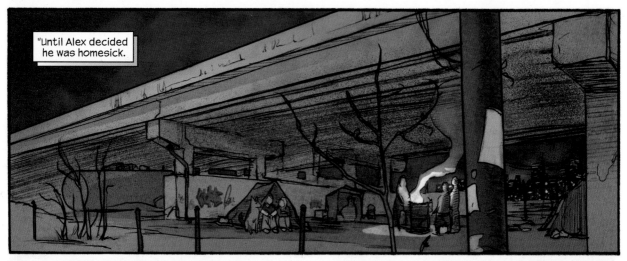

"Until Alex decided he was homesick.

"It got me thinking...

PHONE

Hel--

CLK!

"...about my family."

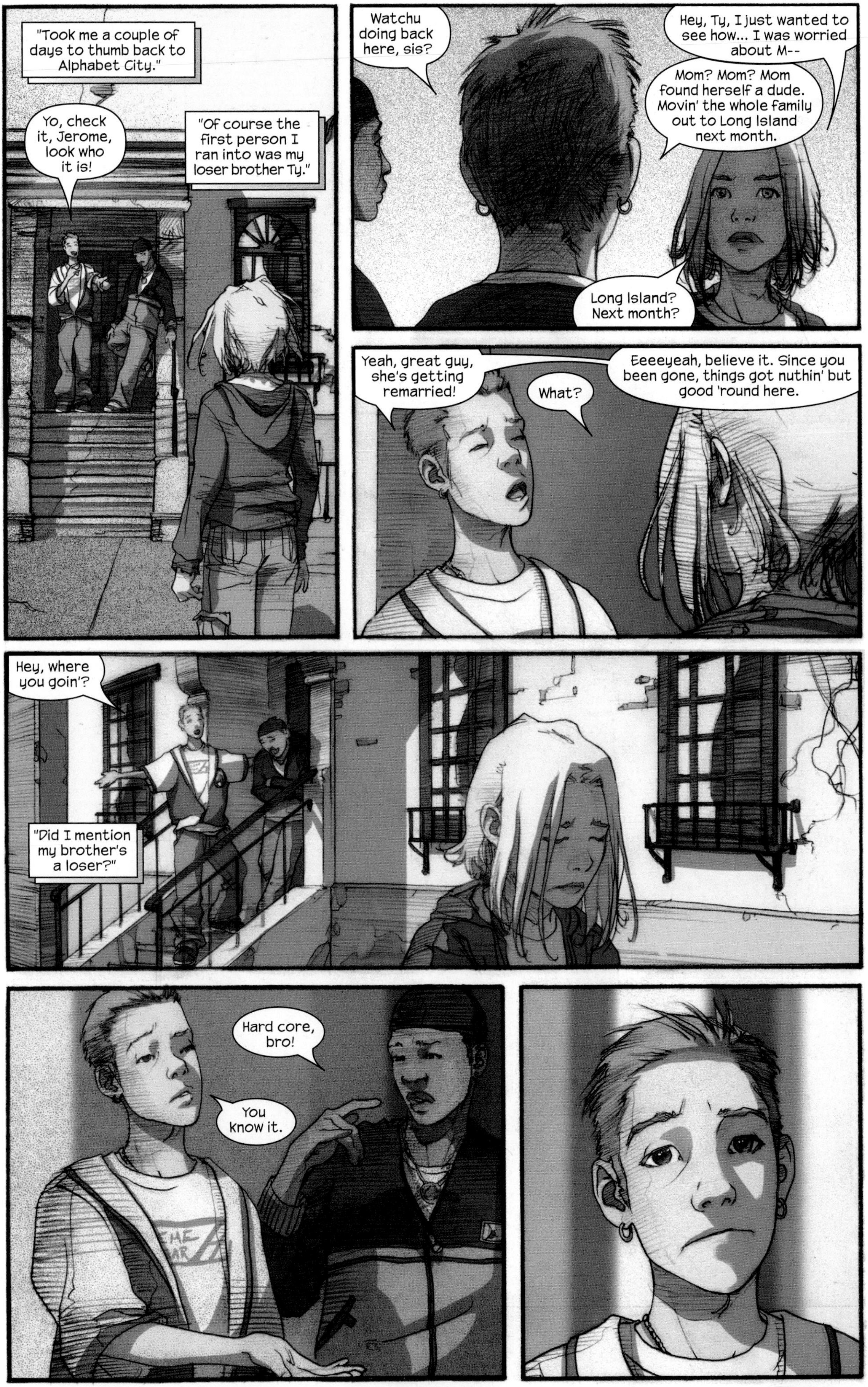
"Took me a couple of days to thumb back to Alphabet City."
Yo, check it, Jerome, look who it is!
"Of course the first person I ran into was my loser brother Ty."
Watchu doing back here, sis?
Hey, Ty, I just wanted to see how... I was worried about M--
Mom? Mom? Mom found herself a dude. Movin' the whole family out to Long Island next month.
Long Island? Next month?
Yeah, great guy, she's getting remarried!
What?
Eeeeyeah, believe it. Since you been gone, things got nuthin' but good 'round here.
Hey, where you goin'?
"Did I mention my brother's a loser?"
Hard core, bro!
You know it.

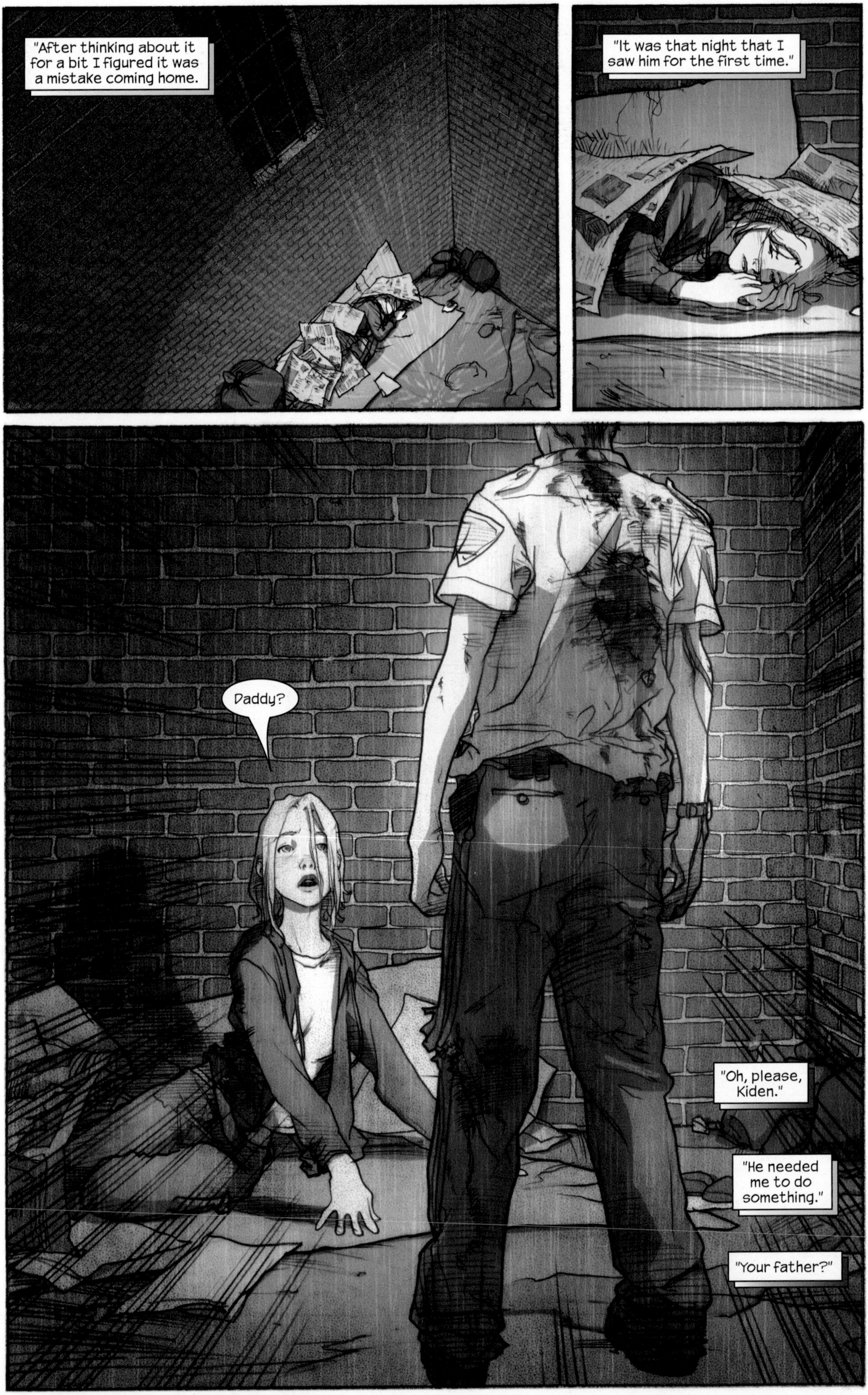
"After thinking about it for a bit I figured it was a mistake coming home.
"It was that night that I saw him for the first time."
Daddy?
"Oh, please, Kiden."
"He needed me to do something."
"Your father?"

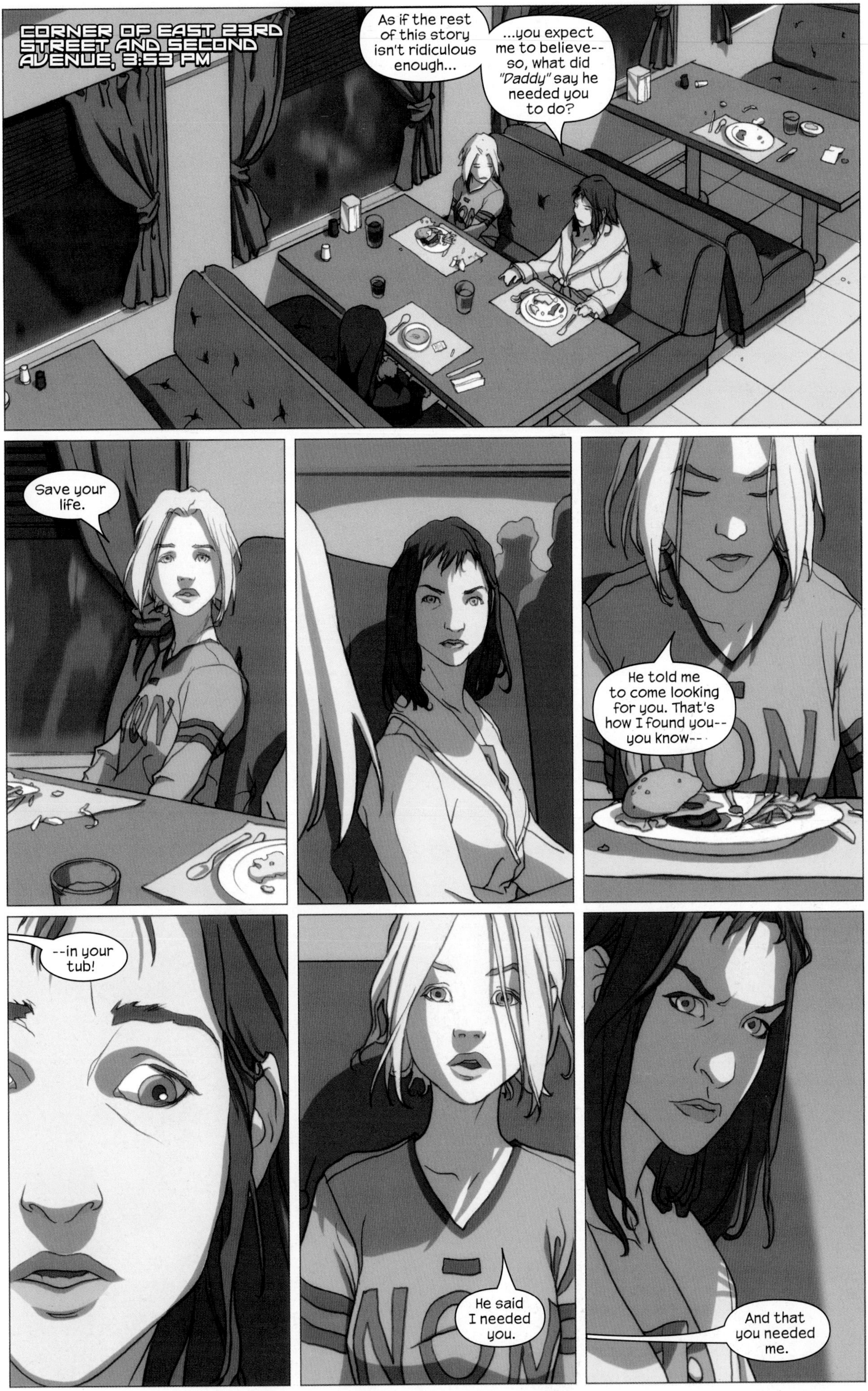
CORNER OF EAST 23RD STREET AND SECOND AVENUE, 3:53 PM
As if the rest of this story isn't ridiculous enough...
...you expect me to believe-- so, what did "Daddy" say he needed you to do?
Save your life.
He told me to come looking for you. That's how I found you-- you know--
--in your tub!
He said I needed you.
And that you needed me.

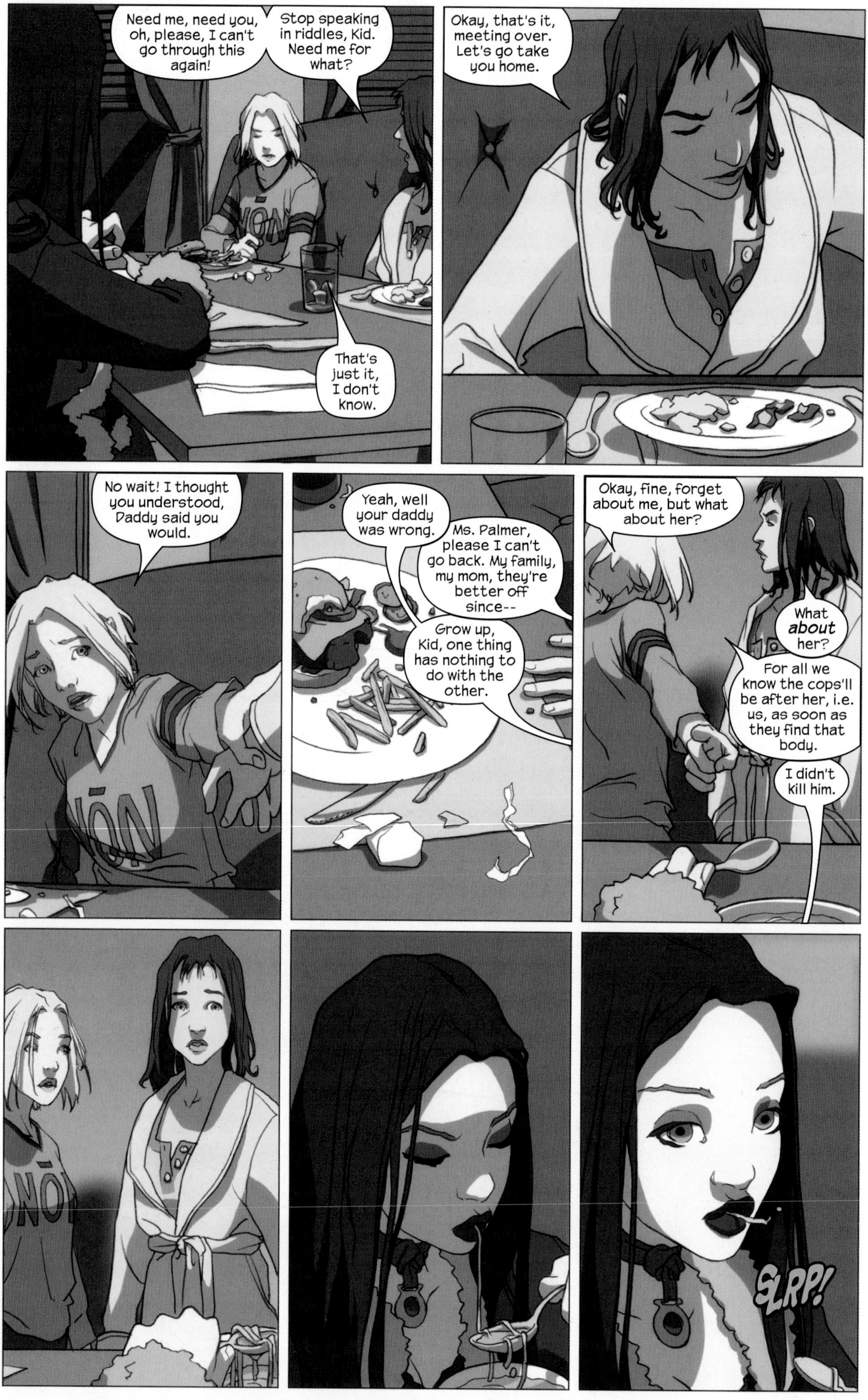
Need me, need you, oh, please, I can't go through this again!
Stop speaking in riddles, Kid. Need me for what?
That's just it, I don't know.
Okay, that's it, meeting over. Let's go take you home.
No wait! I thought you understood, Daddy said you would.
Yeah, well your daddy was wrong.
Ms. Palmer, please I can't go back. My family, my mom, they're better off since--
Grow up, Kid, one thing has nothing to do with the other.
Okay, fine, forget about me, but what about her?
What *about* her?
For all we know the cops'll be after her, i.e. us, as soon as they find that body.
I didn't kill him.
SLRP!

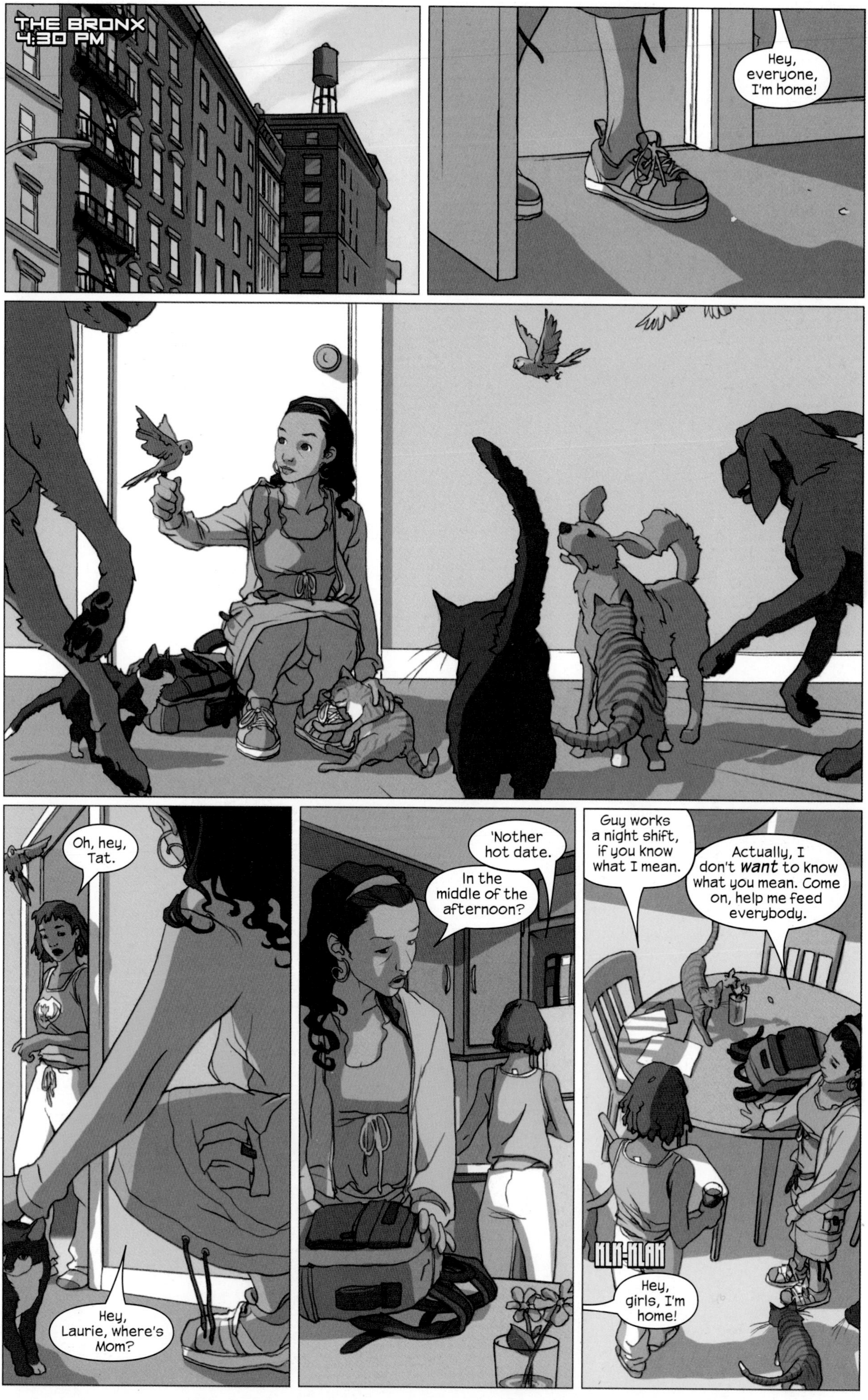
THE BRONX
4:30 PM
Hey, everyone, I'm home!
Oh, hey, Tat.
Hey, Laurie, where's Mom?
'Nother hot date.
In the middle of the afternoon?
Guy works a night shift, if you know what I mean.
Actually, I don't *want* to know what you mean. Come on, help me feed everybody.
KLK-KLAK
Hey, girls, I'm home!

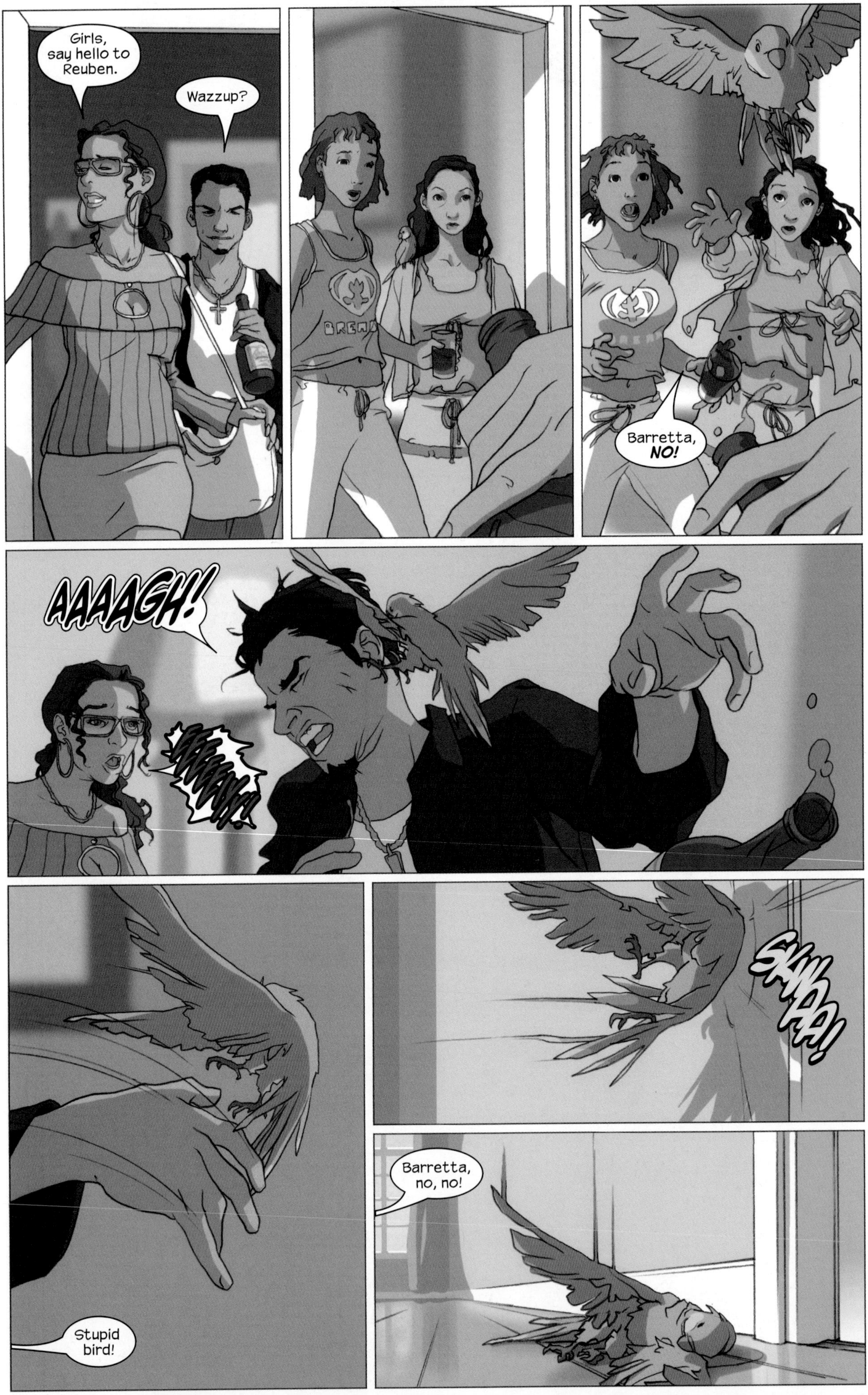
Girls, say hello to Reuben.
Wazzup?
Barretta, NO!
AAAAGH!
SKWAA!
Stupid bird!
Barretta, no, no!

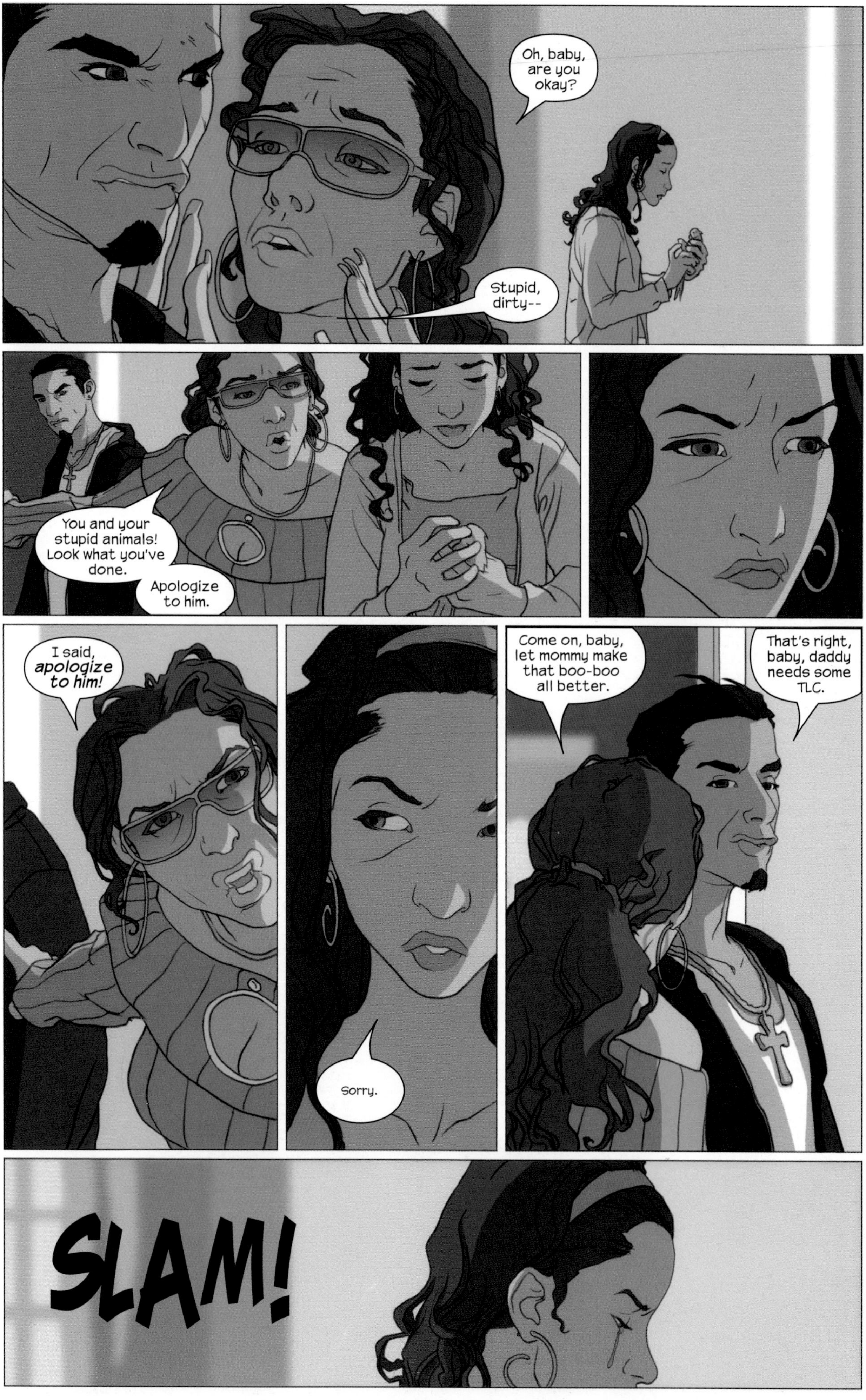
Oh, baby, are you okay?
Stupid, dirty--
You and your stupid animals! Look what you've done.
Apologize to him.
I said, *apologize to him!*
Sorry.
Come on, baby, let mommy make that boo-boo all better.
That's right, baby, daddy needs some TLC.
SLAM!

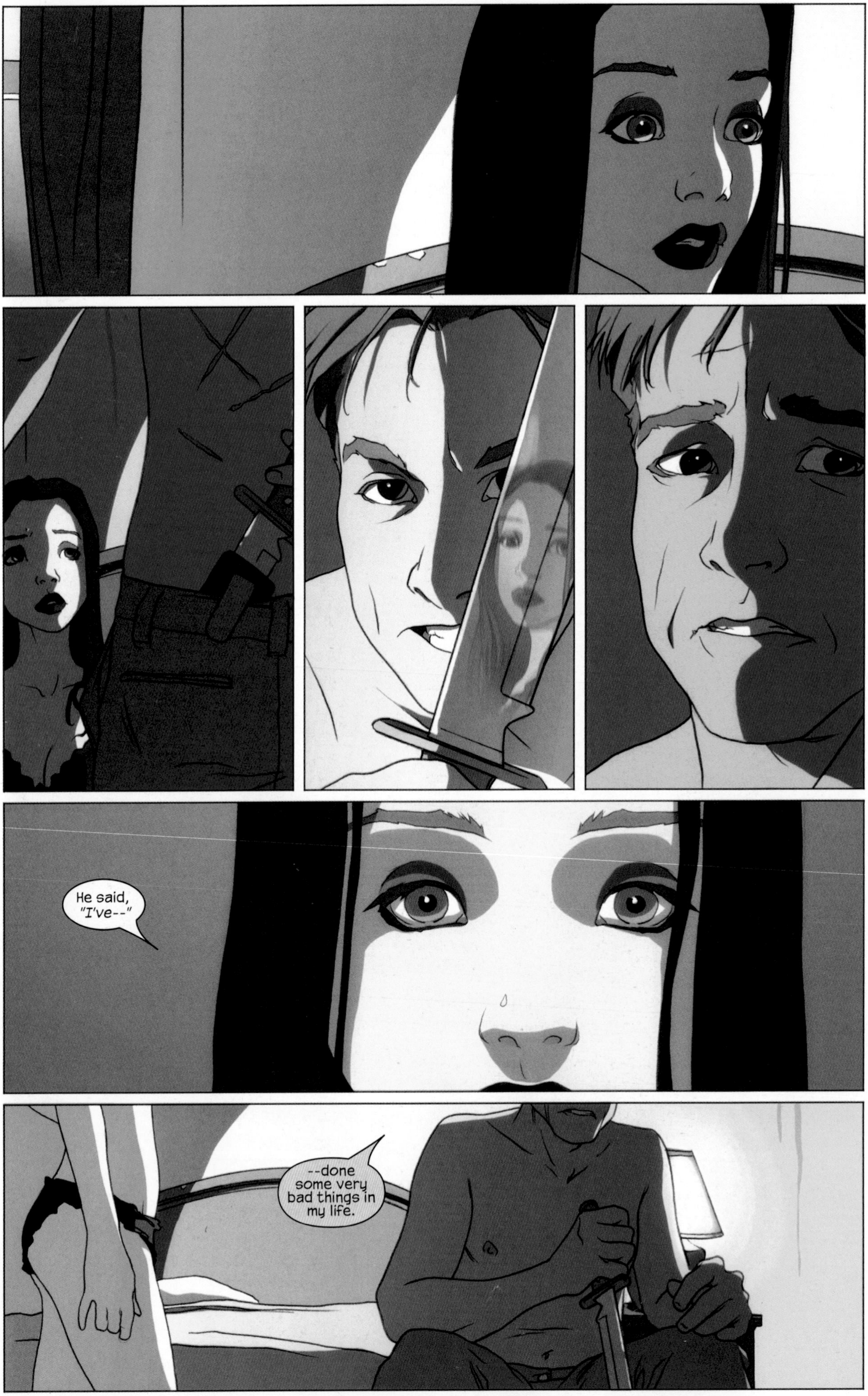
He said, "I've--"
--done some very bad things in my life.

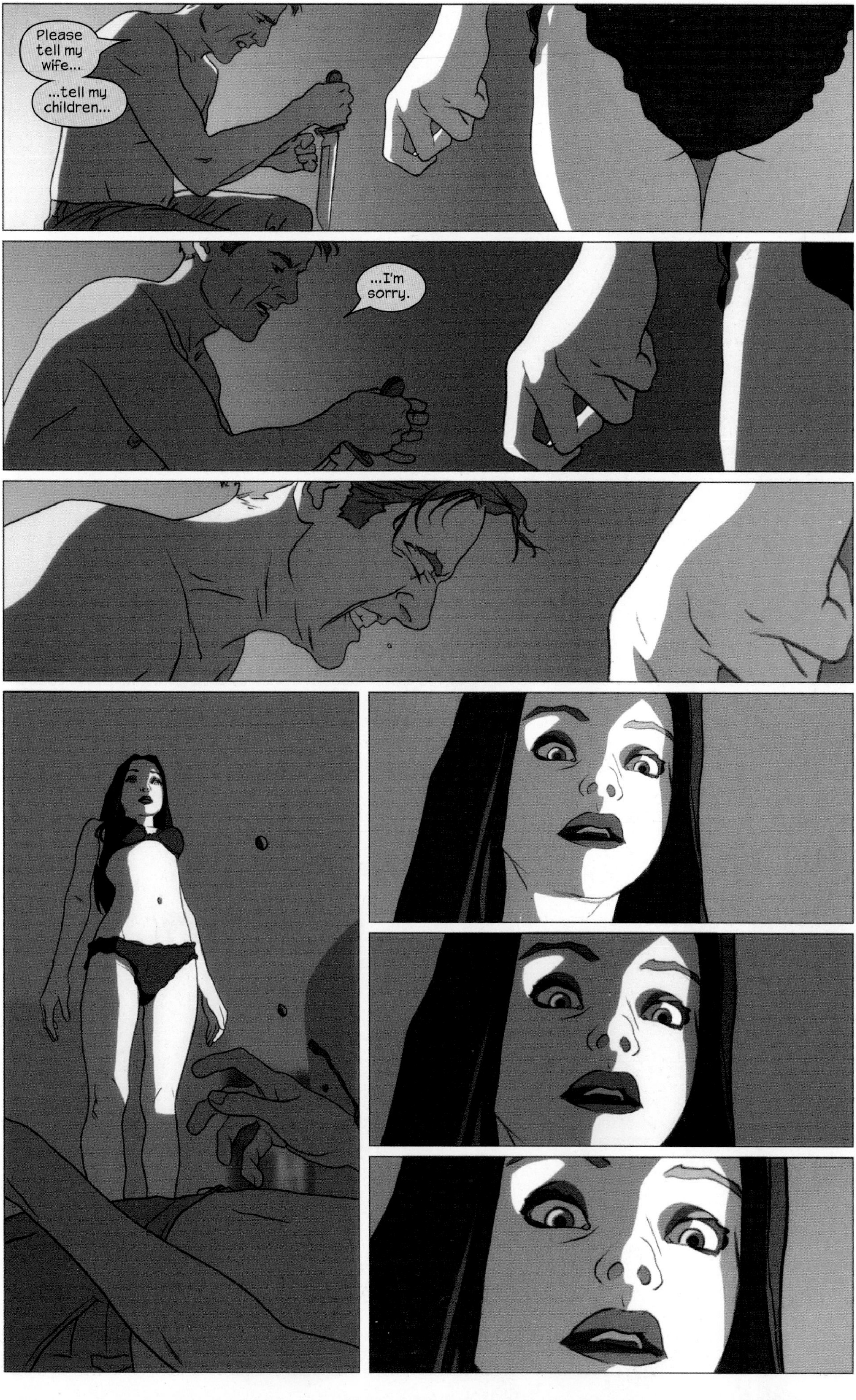

Please tell my wife...
...tell my children...
...I'm sorry.

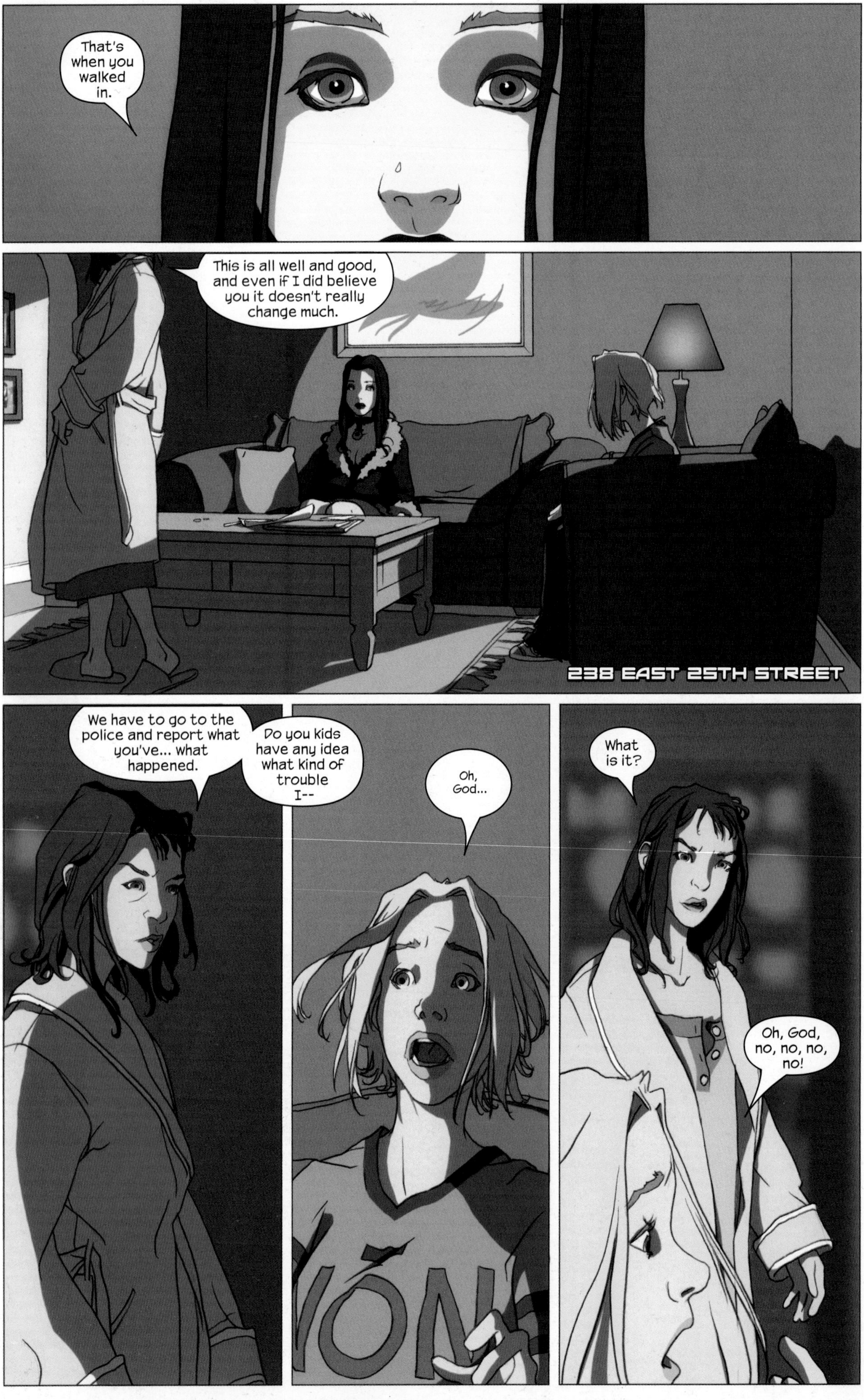
That's when you walked in.
This is all well and good, and even if I did believe you it doesn't really change much.
238 EAST 25TH STREET
We have to go to the police and report what you've... what happened.
Do you kids have any idea what kind of trouble I--
Oh, God...
What is it?
Oh, God, no, no, no, no!

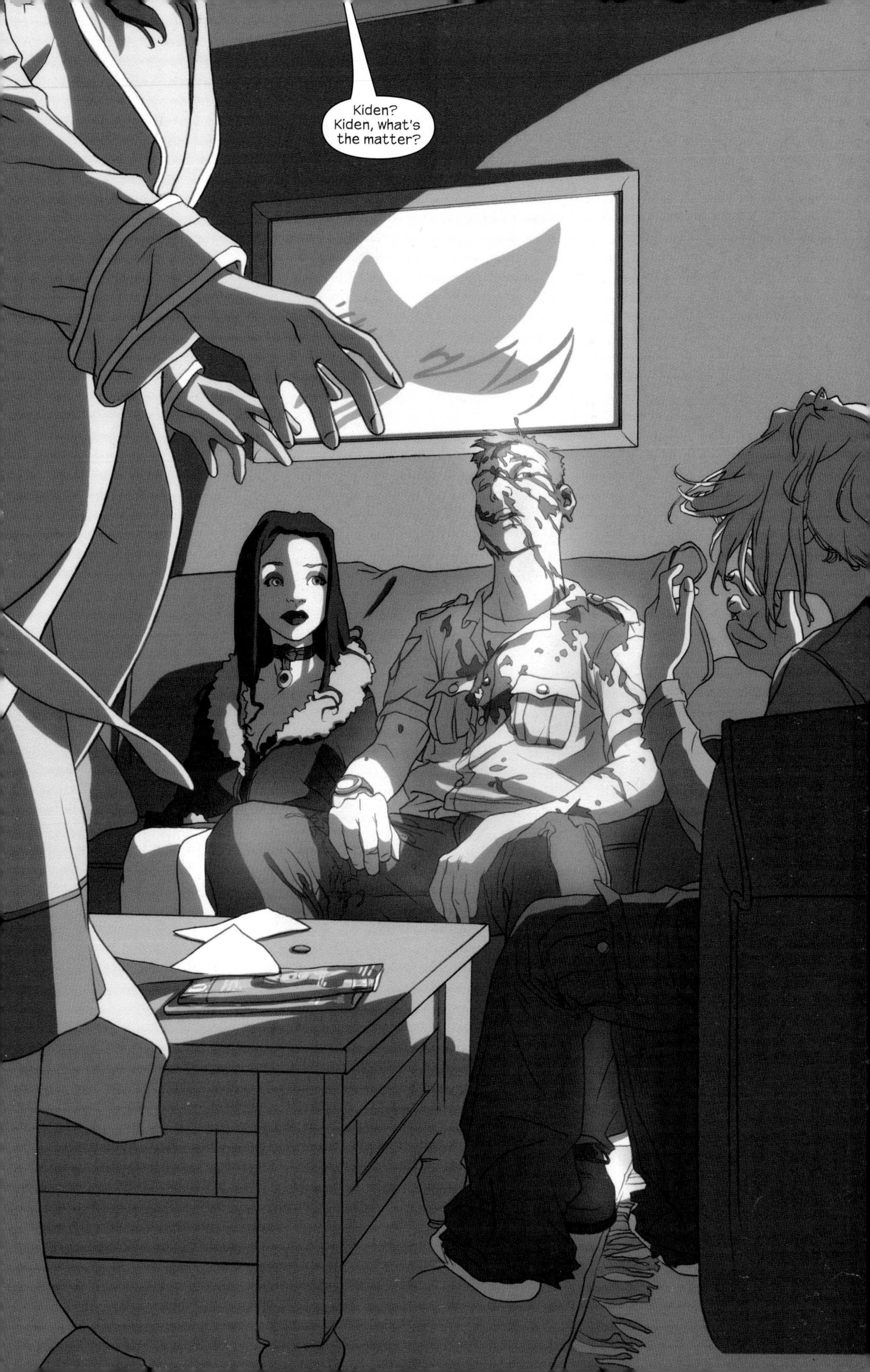
Kiden? Kiden, what's the matter?

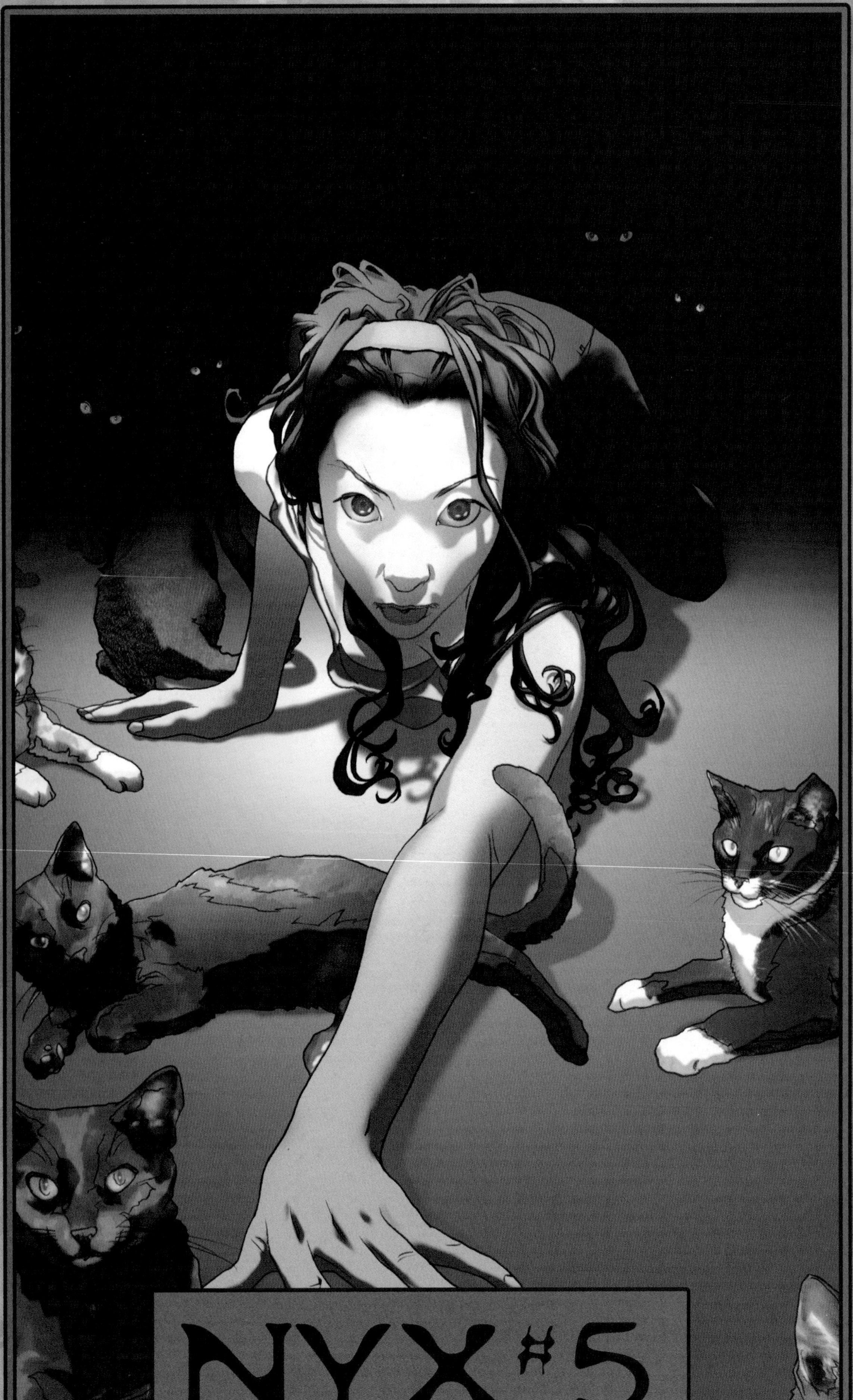
NYX #5

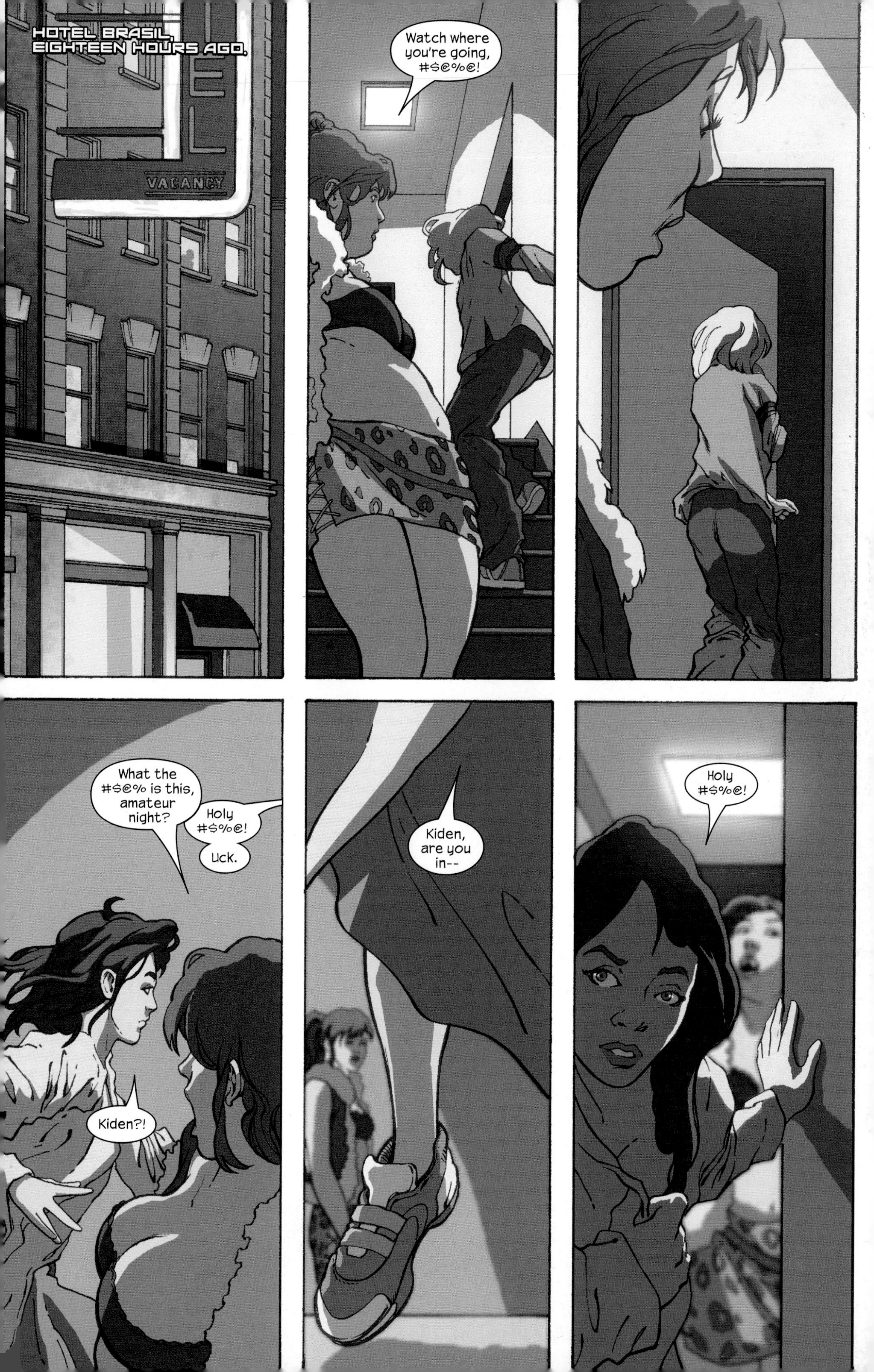
HOTEL BRASIL, EIGHTEEN HOURS AGO.
VACANCY
Watch where you're going, #$@%@!
What the #$@% is this, amateur night?
Holy #$%@!
Uck.
Kiden?!
Kiden, are you in--
Holy #$%@!

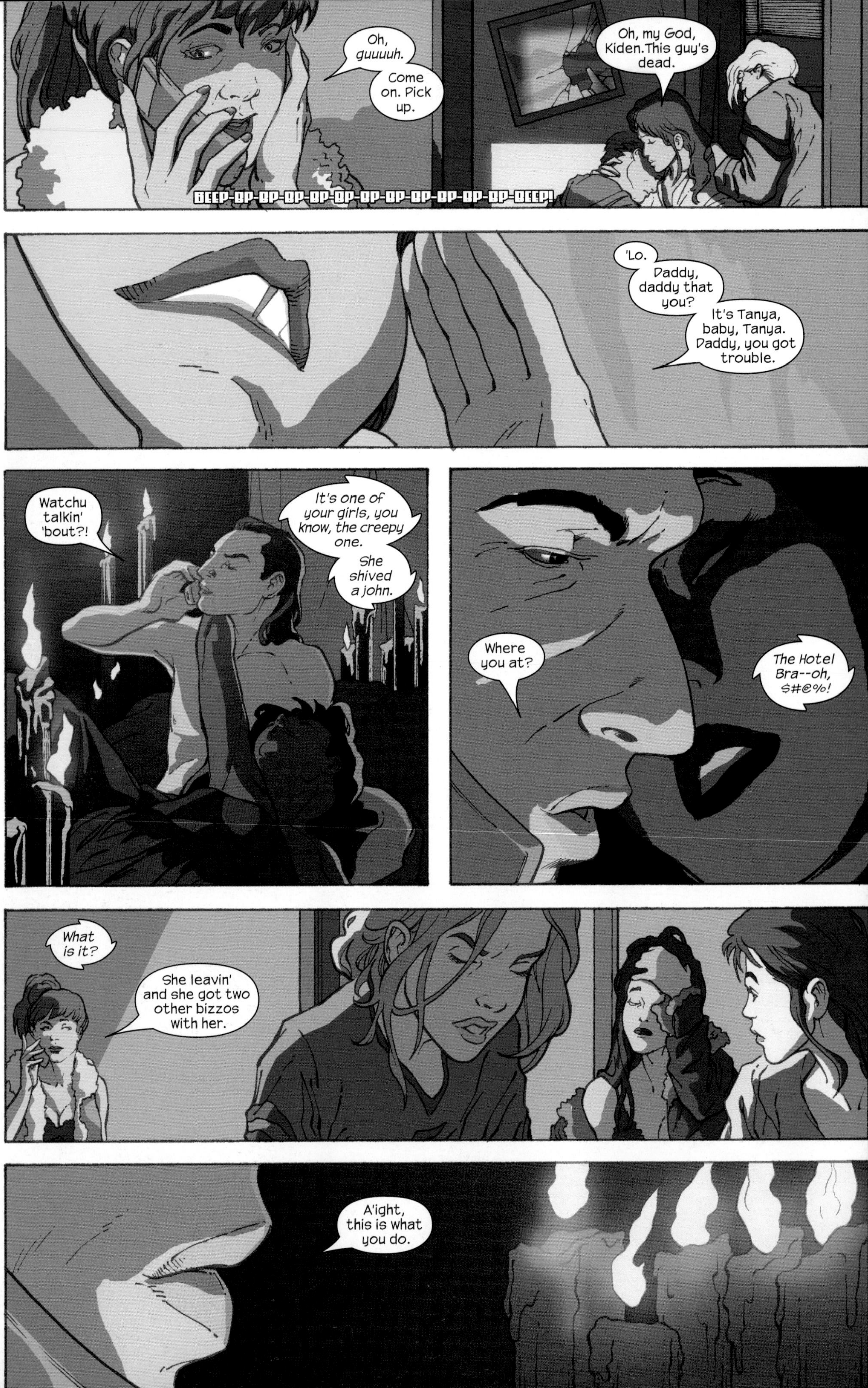
Oh, guuuuh.
Come on. Pick up.
BEEP-BP-BP-BP-BP-BP-BP-BP-BP-BP-BP-BP-BEEP!
Oh, my God, Kiden. This guy's dead.
'Lo.
Daddy, daddy that you?
It's Tanya, baby, Tanya. Daddy, you got trouble.
Watchu talkin' 'bout?!
It's one of your girls, you know, the creepy one.
She shived a john.
Where you at?
The Hotel Bra--oh, $#@%!
What is it?
She leavin' and she got two other bizzos with her.
A'ight, this is what you do.

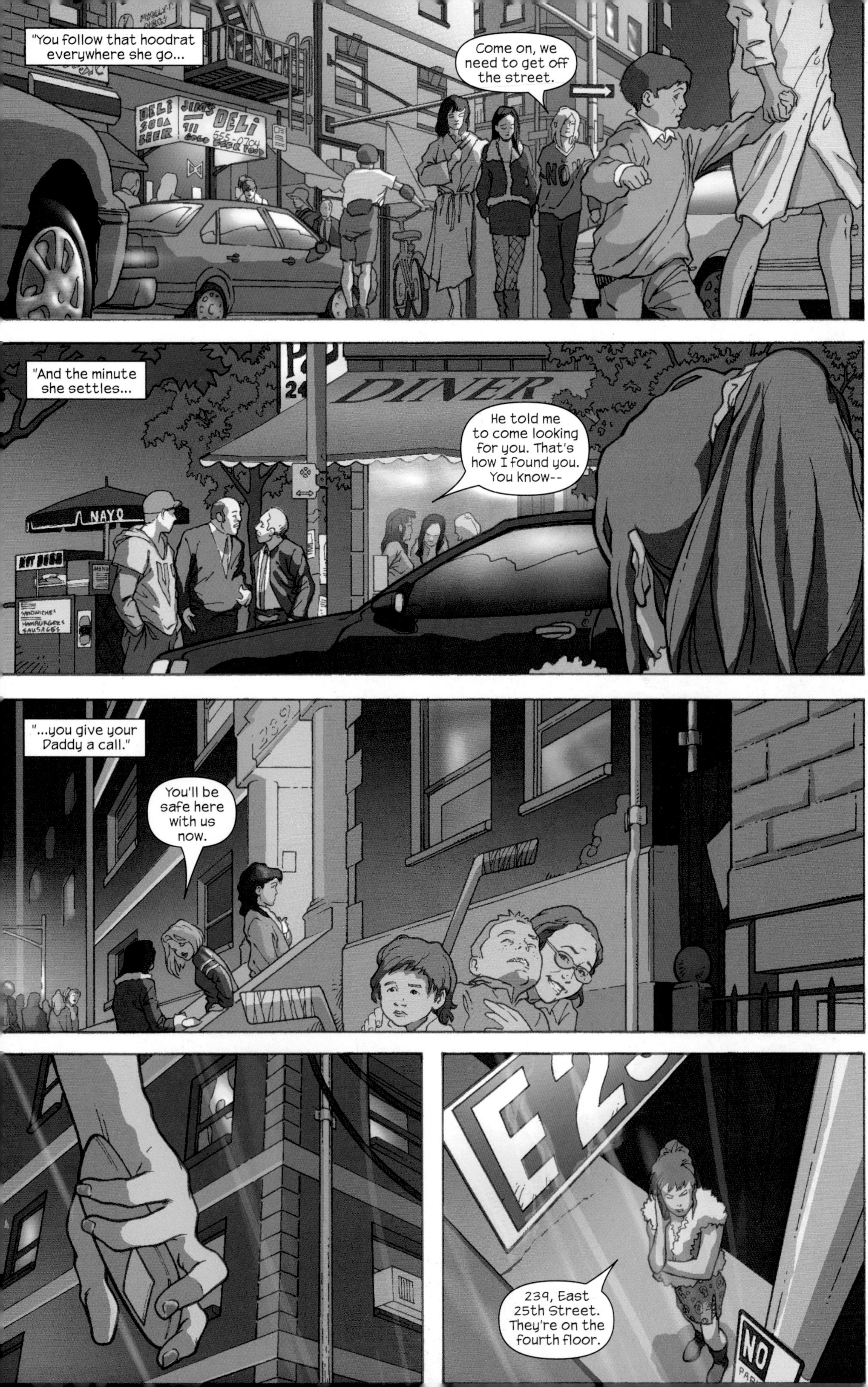
"You follow that hoodrat everywhere she go...
Come on, we need to get off the street.
"And the minute she settles...
DINER
NAYO
He told me to come looking for you. That's how I found you. You know--
"...you give your Daddy a call."
You'll be safe here with us now.
239, East 25th Street. They're on the fourth floor.

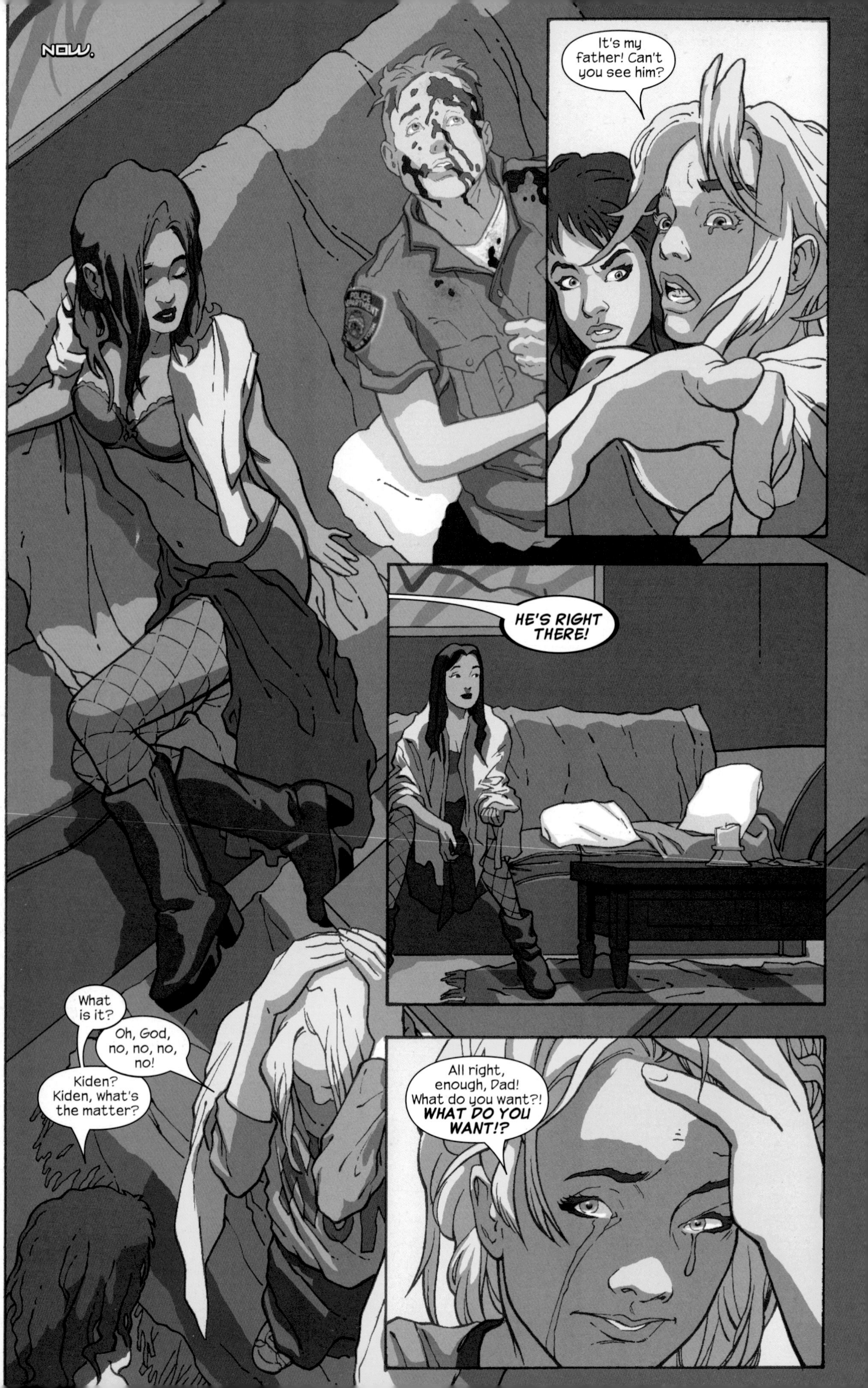
NOW.
It's my father! Can't you see him?
HE'S RIGHT THERE!
What is it?
Oh, God, no, no, no, no!
Kiden? Kiden, what's the matter?
All right, enough, Dad! What do you want?! WHAT DO YOU WANT!?

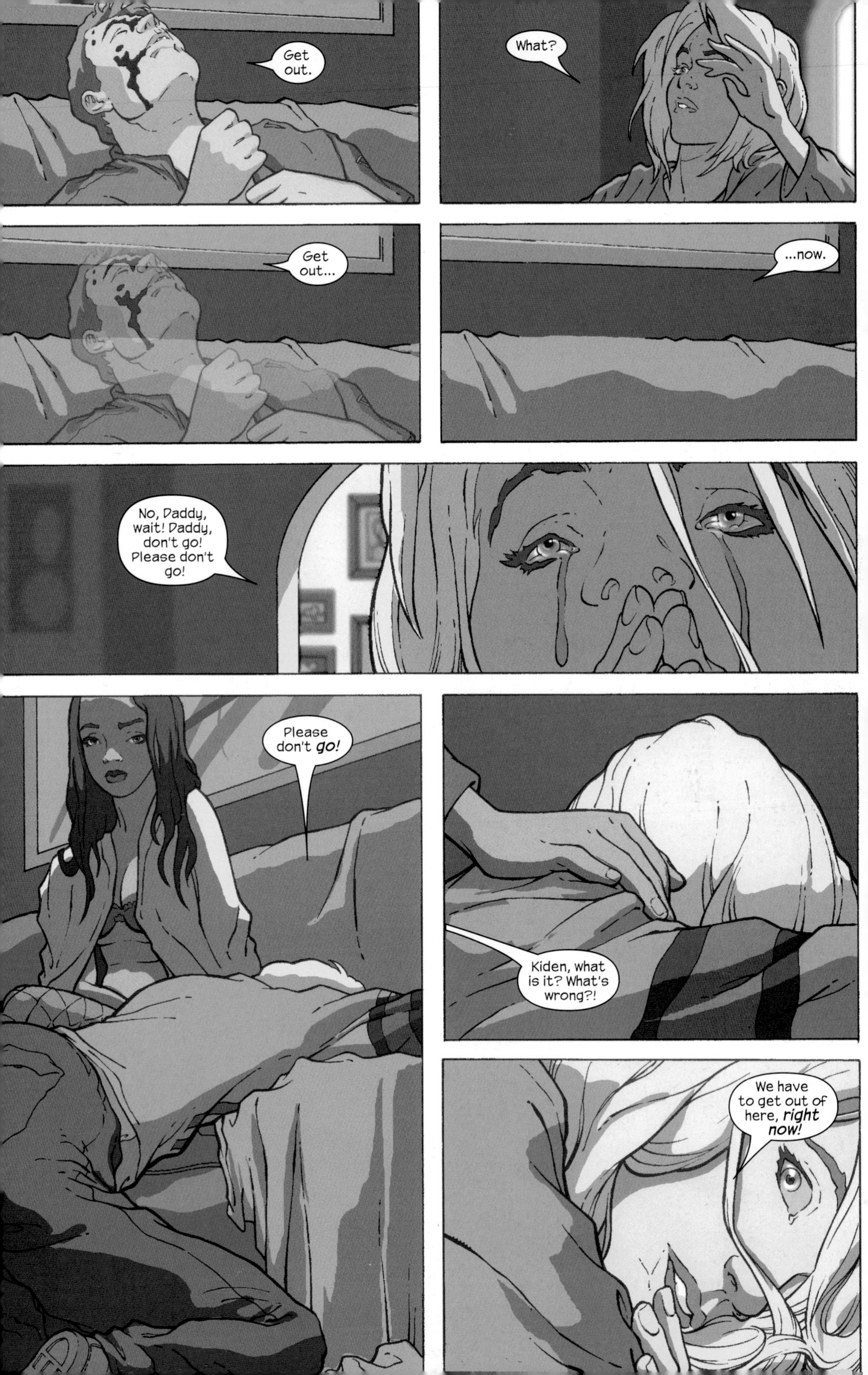
Get out.
What?
Get out...
...now.
No, Daddy, wait! Daddy, don't go! Please don't go!
Please don't go!
Kiden, what is it? What's wrong?!
We have to get out of here, right now!

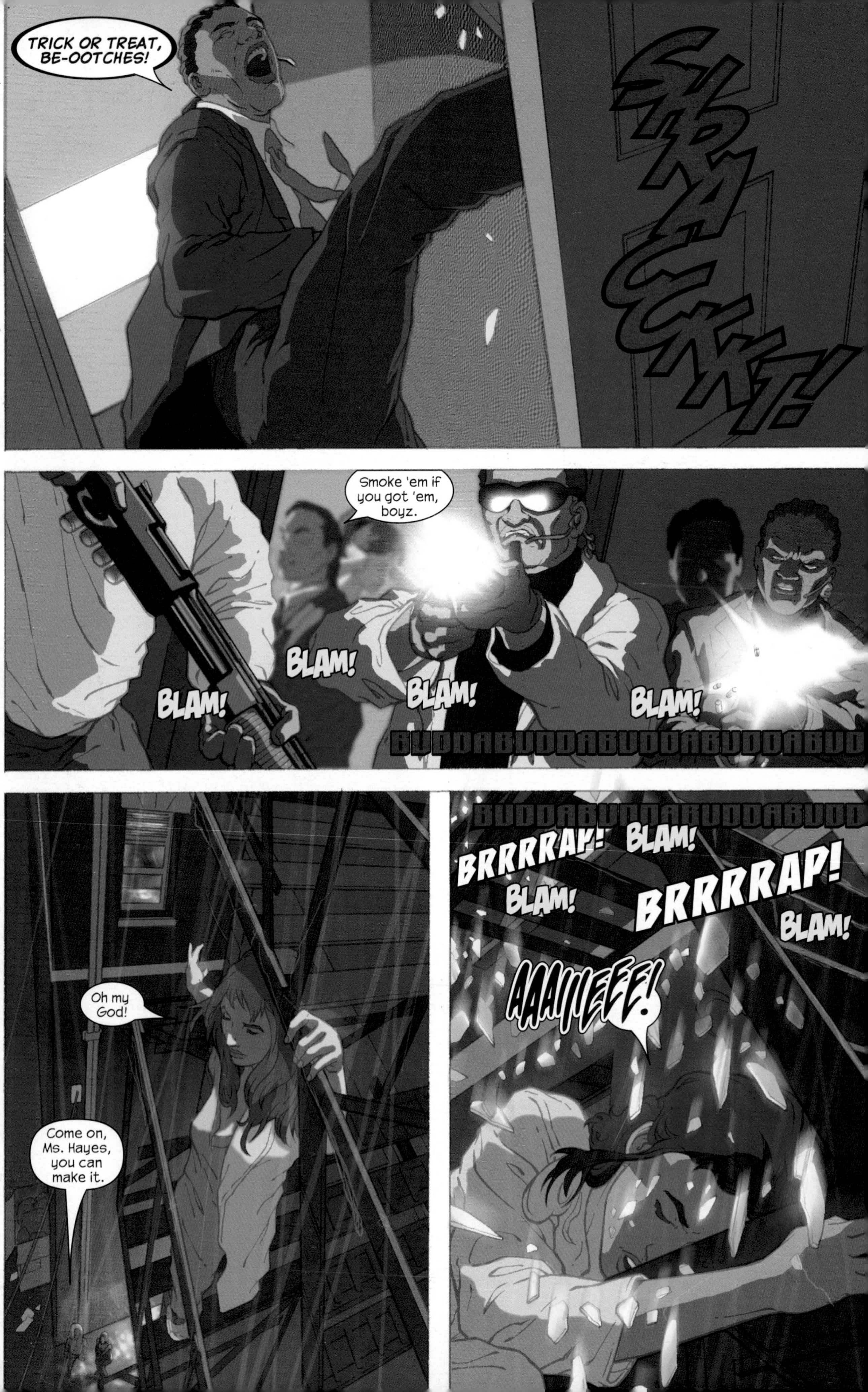
TRICK OR TREAT, BE-OOTCHES!
SKRACKKT!
Smoke 'em if you got 'em, boyz.
BLAM!
BLAM!
BLAM!
BLAM!
BUDDABUDDABUDDABUDDABUD
Oh my God!
Come on, Ms. Hayes, you can make it.
BUDDABUNNABUDDABUDD
BRRRRAP! BLAM!
BLAM!
BRRRRAP!
BLAM!
AAAIIIEEE!

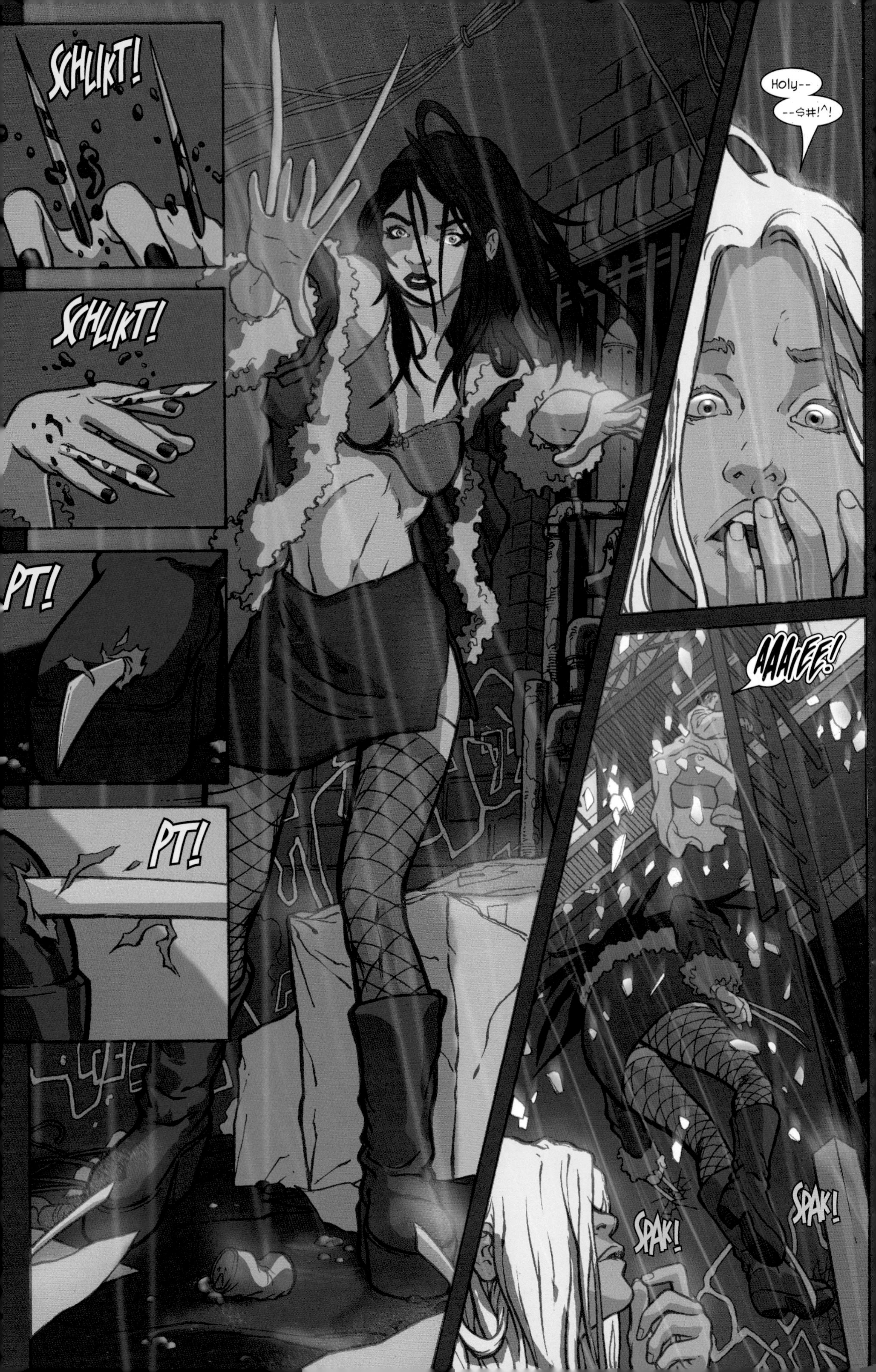
SCHLIKT!
SCHLIKT!
PT!
PT!
Holy--
--$#!^!
AAAIEE!
SPAK!
SPAK!

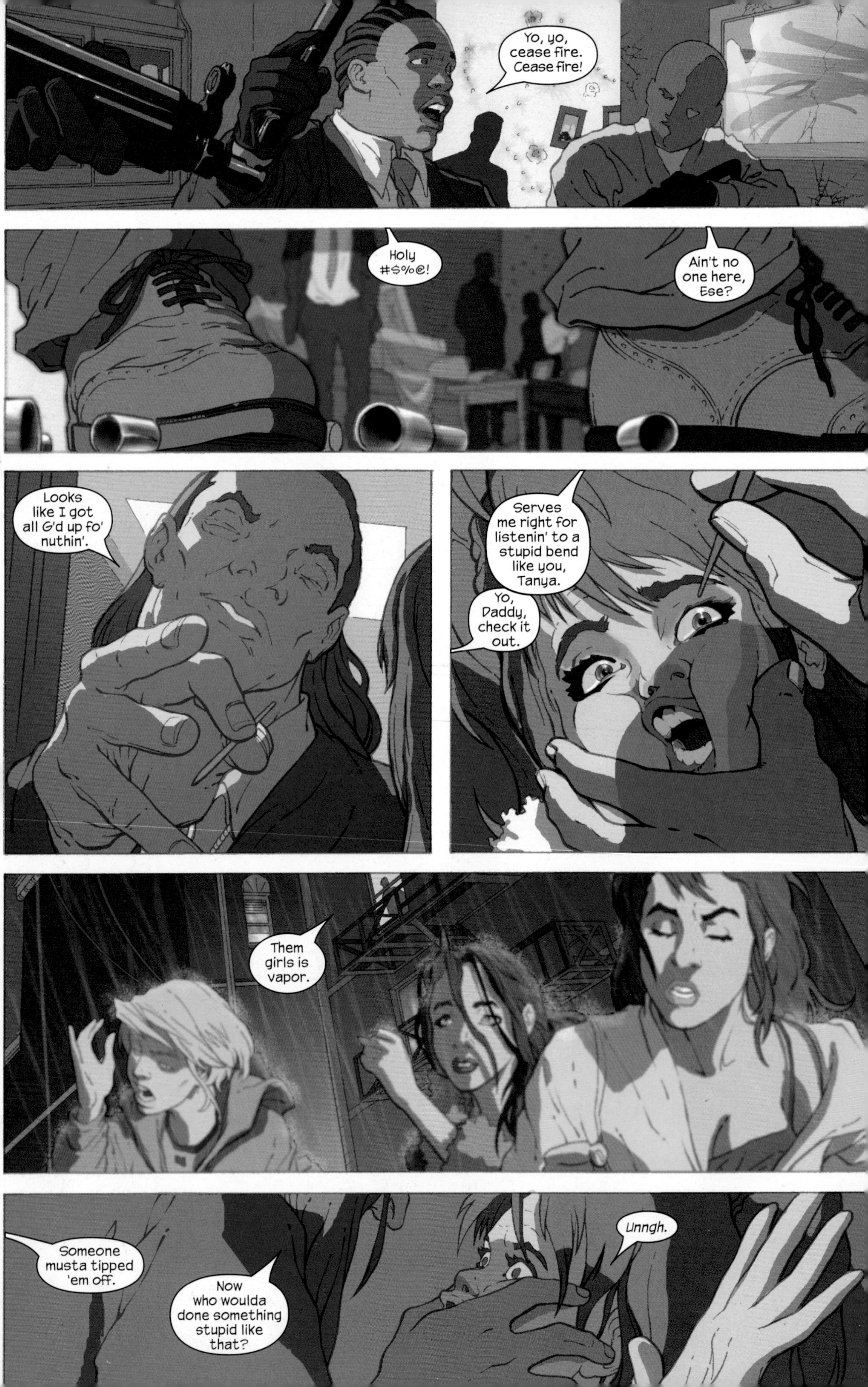
Yo, yo, cease fire. Cease fire!
Holy #$%@!
Ain't no one here, Ese?
Looks like I got all G'd up fo' nuthin'.
Serves me right for listenin' to a stupid bend like you, Tanya.
Yo, Daddy, check it out.
Them girls is vapor.
Someone musta tipped 'em off.
Now who woulda done something stupid like that?
Unngh.

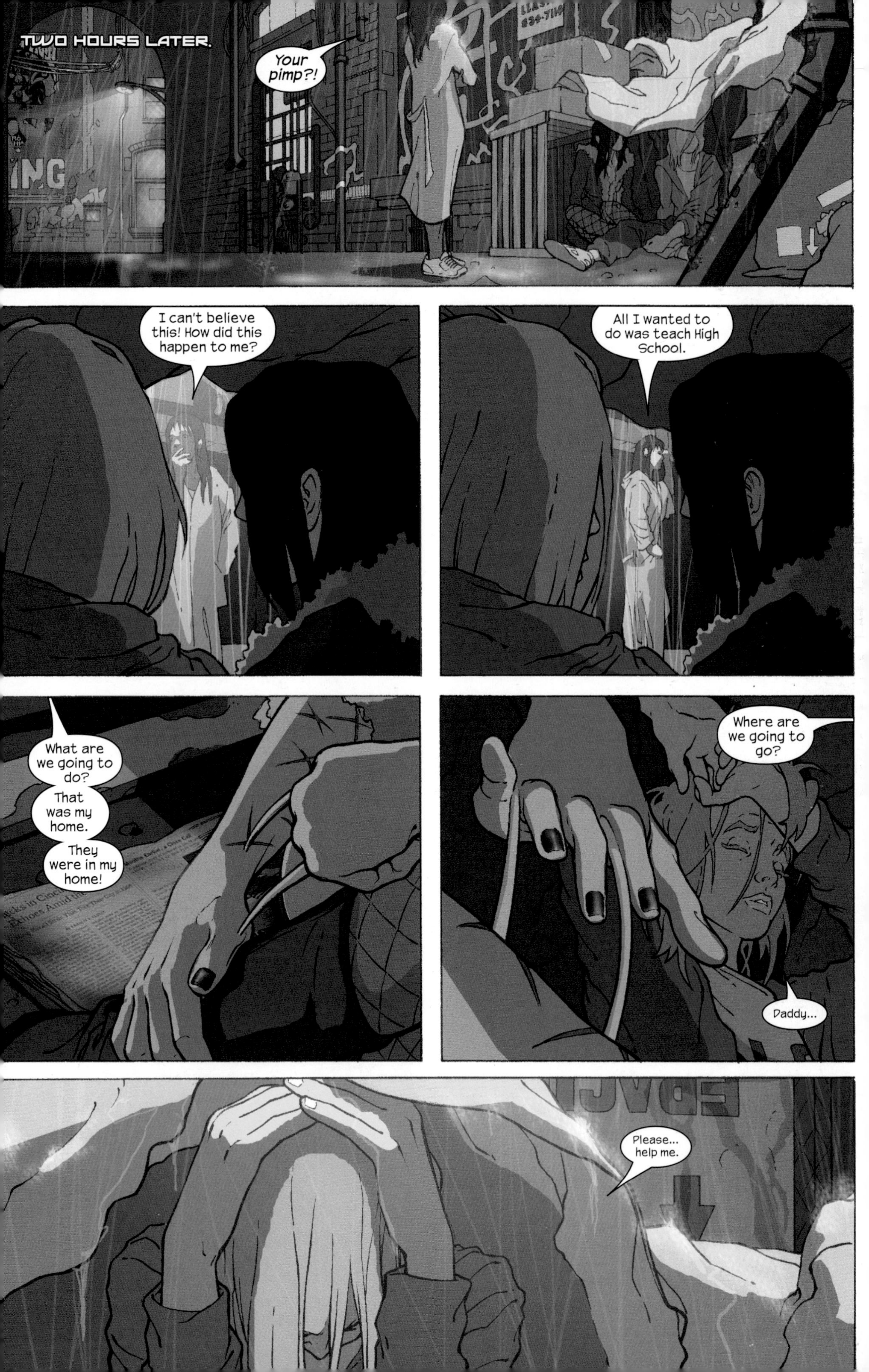
TWO HOURS LATER.
Your pimp?!
I can't believe this! How did this happen to me?
All I wanted to do was teach High School.
What are we going to do?
That was my home.
They were in my home!
Where are we going to go?
Daddy...
Please... help me.

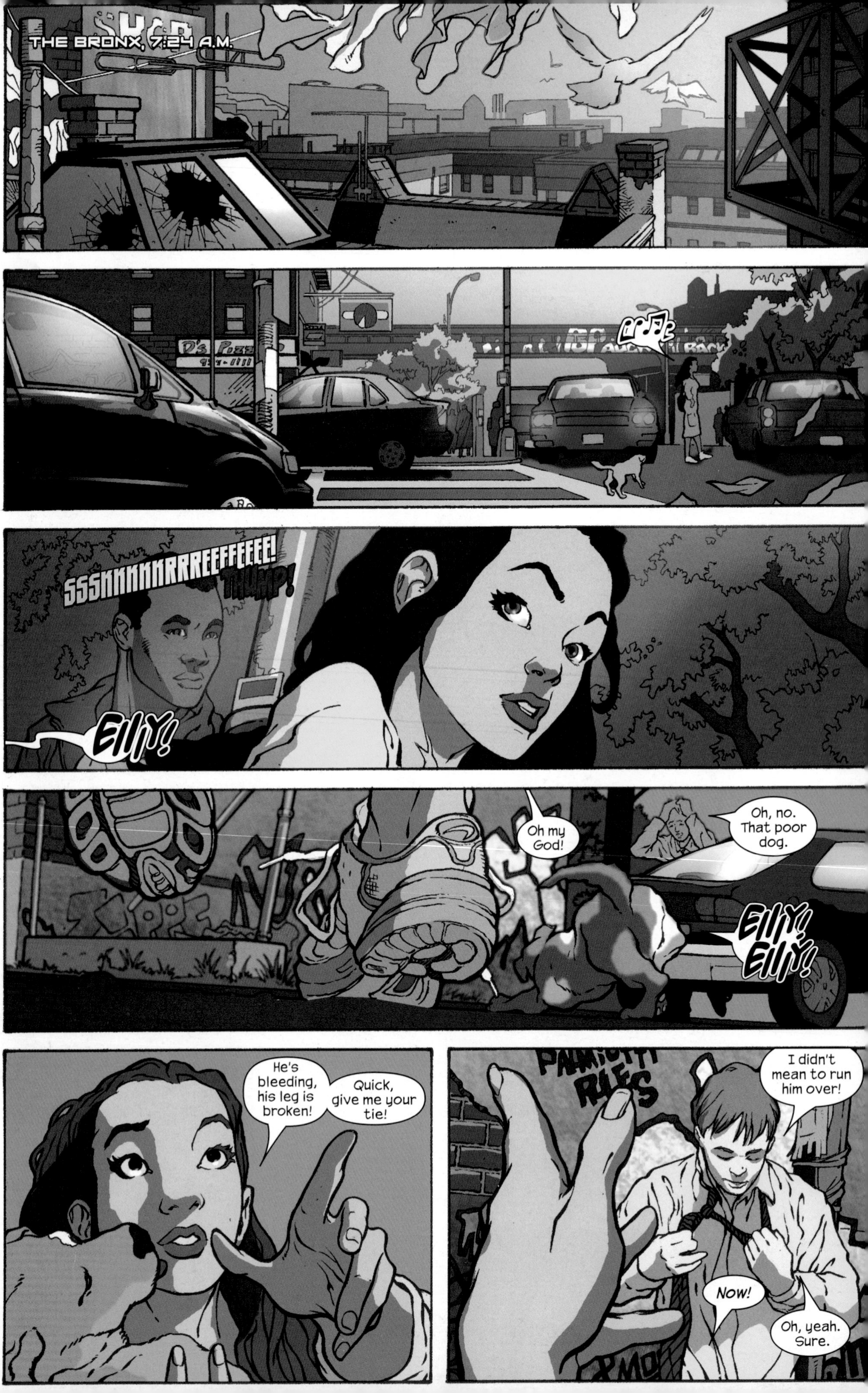
THE BRONX, 7:24 A.M.
SSSHKKKKKRRREEEEEEEE!
THUMP!
ELLY!
Oh my God!
Oh, no. That poor dog.
ELLY! ELLY!
He's bleeding, his leg is broken!
Quick, give me your tie!
I didn't mean to run him over!
NOW!
Oh, yeah. Sure.

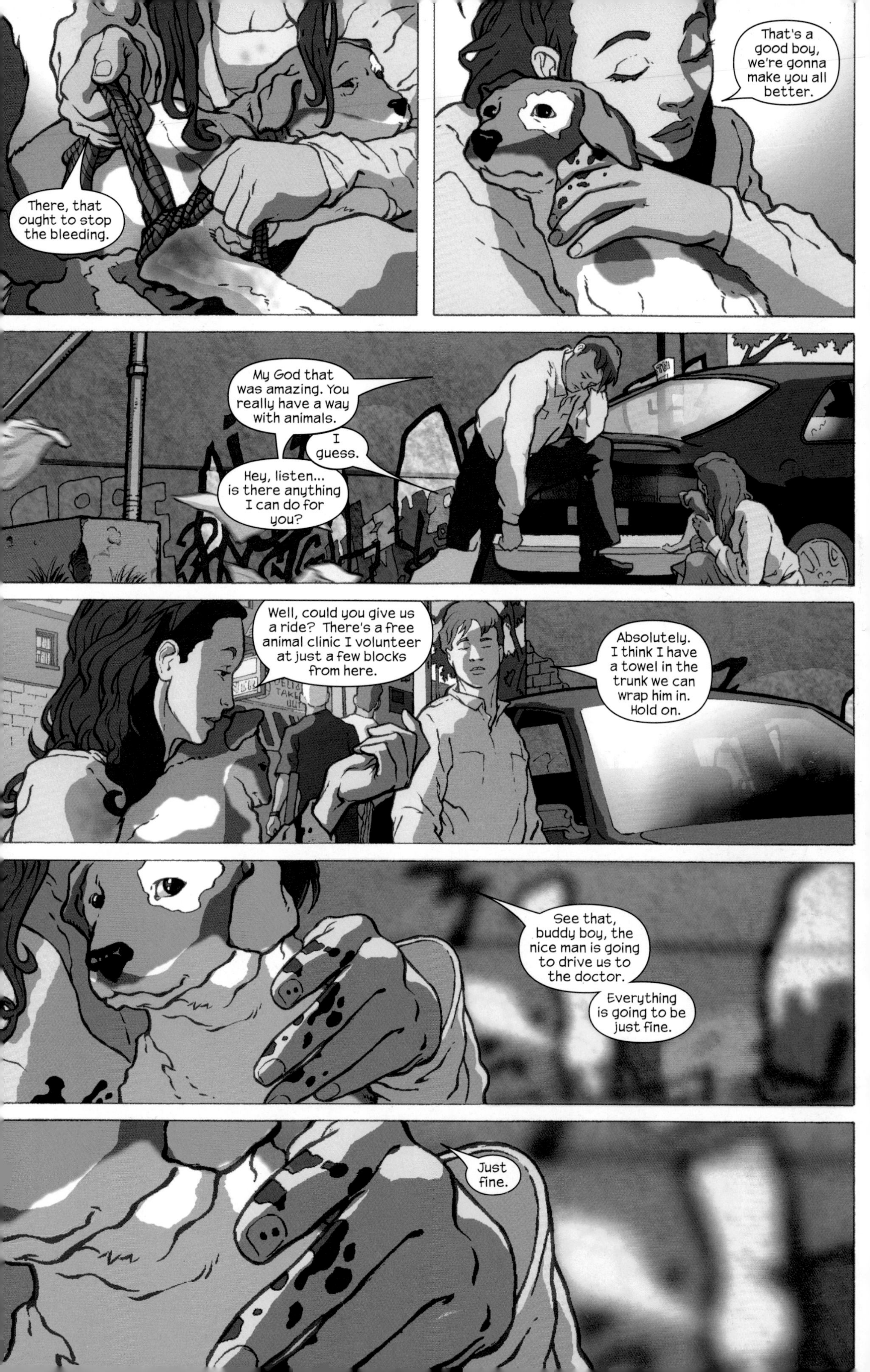

There, that ought to stop the bleeding.
That's a good boy, we're gonna make you all better.
My God that was amazing. You really have a way with animals.
I guess.
Hey, listen... is there anything I can do for you?
Well, could you give us a ride? There's a free animal clinic I volunteer at just a few blocks from here.
Absolutely. I think I have a towel in the trunk we can wrap him in. Hold on.
See that, buddy boy, the nice man is going to drive us to the doctor.
Everything is going to be just fine.
Just fine.

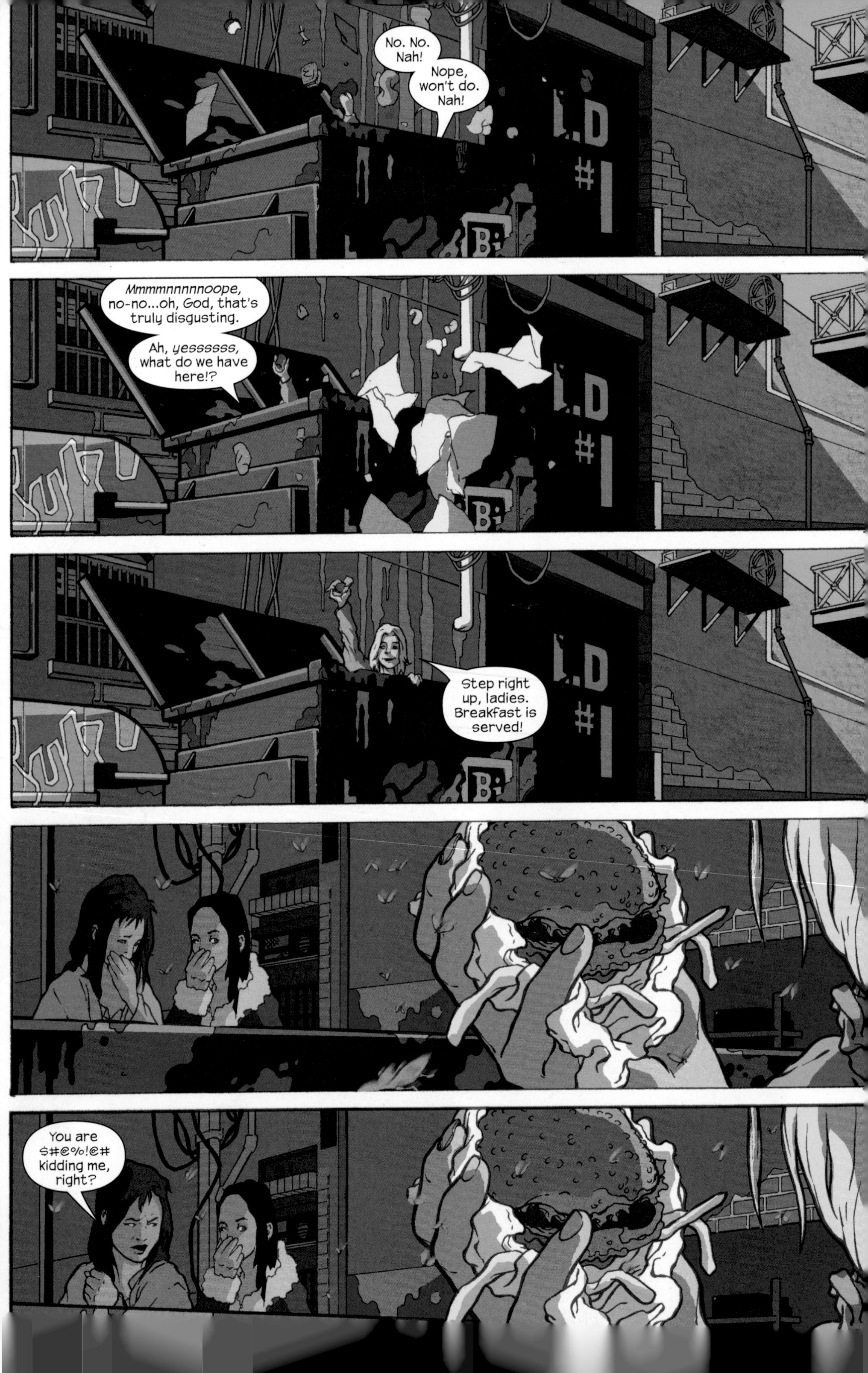
No. No. Nah!
Nope, won't do. Nah!
Mmmmnnnnnoope, no-no...oh, God, that's truly disgusting.
Ah, *yessssss,* what do we have here!?
Step right up, ladies. Breakfast is served!
You are $#@%!@# kidding me, right?

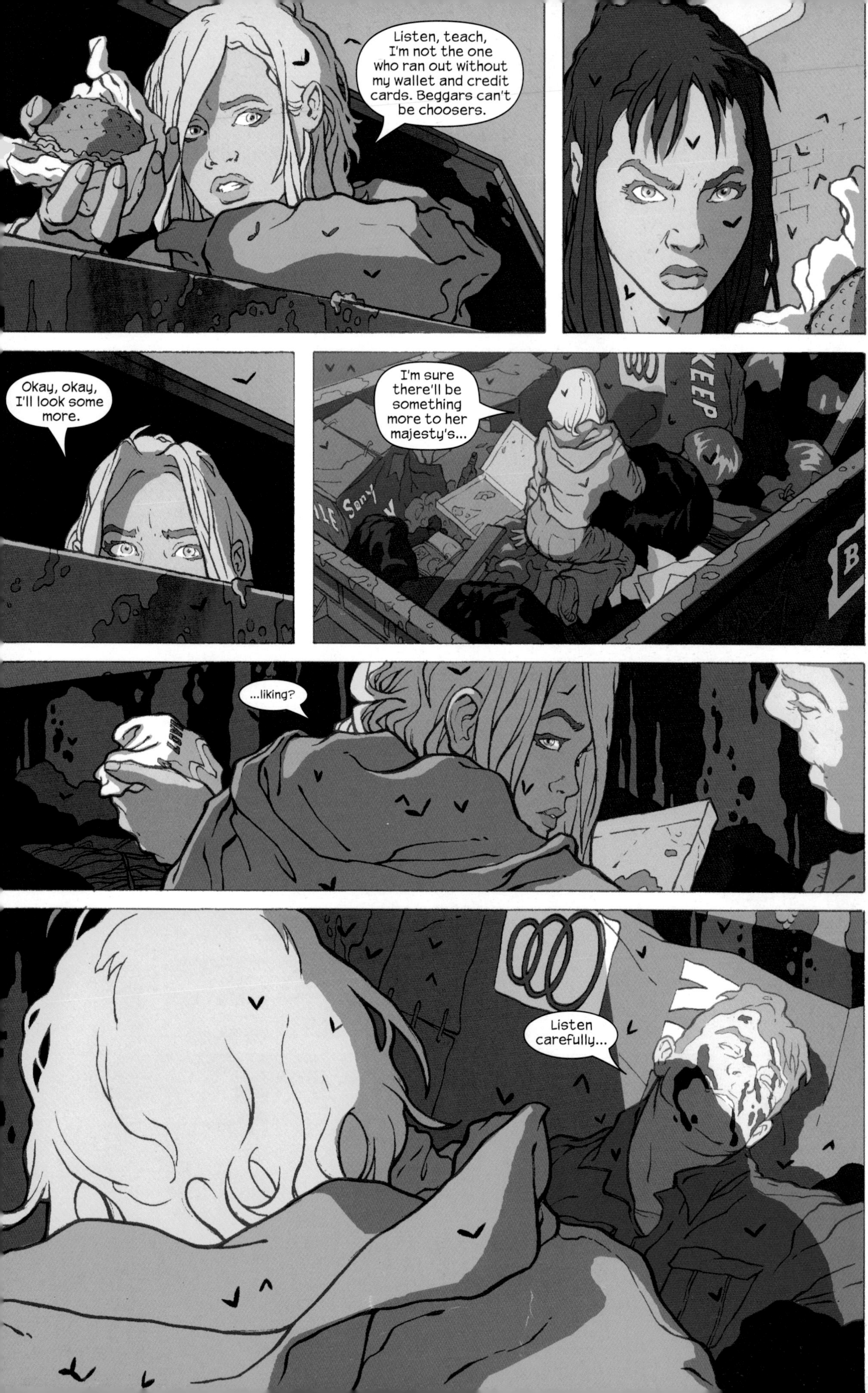

Listen, teach, I'm not the one who ran out without my wallet and credit cards. Beggars can't be choosers.
Okay, okay, I'll look some more.
I'm sure there'll be something more to her majesty's...
...liking?
Listen carefully...

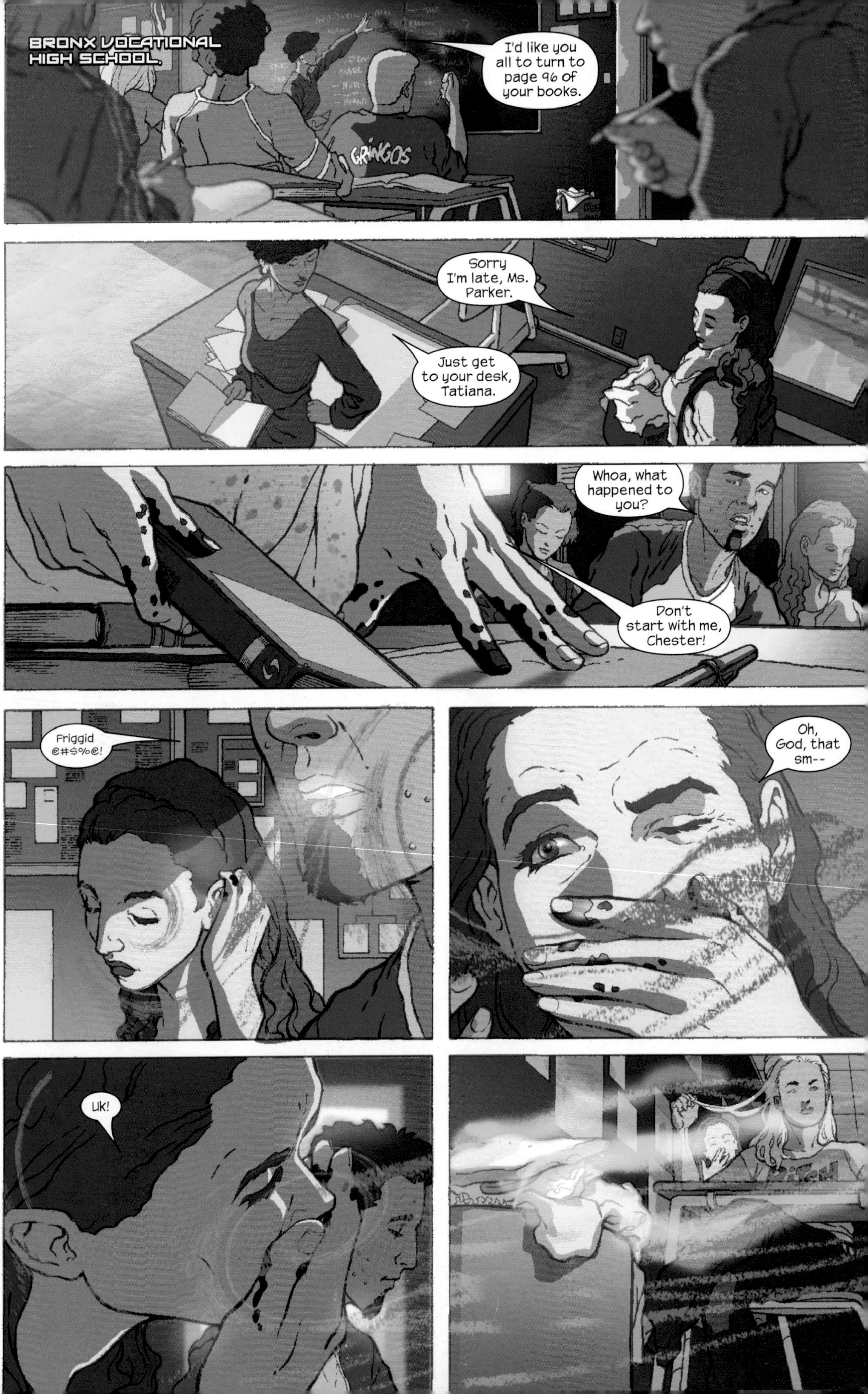
BRONX VOCATIONAL HIGH SCHOOL.
I'd like you all to turn to page 96 of your books.
GRINGOS
Sorry I'm late, Ms. Parker.
Just get to your desk, Tatiana.
Whoa, what happened to you?
Don't start with me, Chester!
Friggid @#$%@!
Oh, God, that sm--
UK!

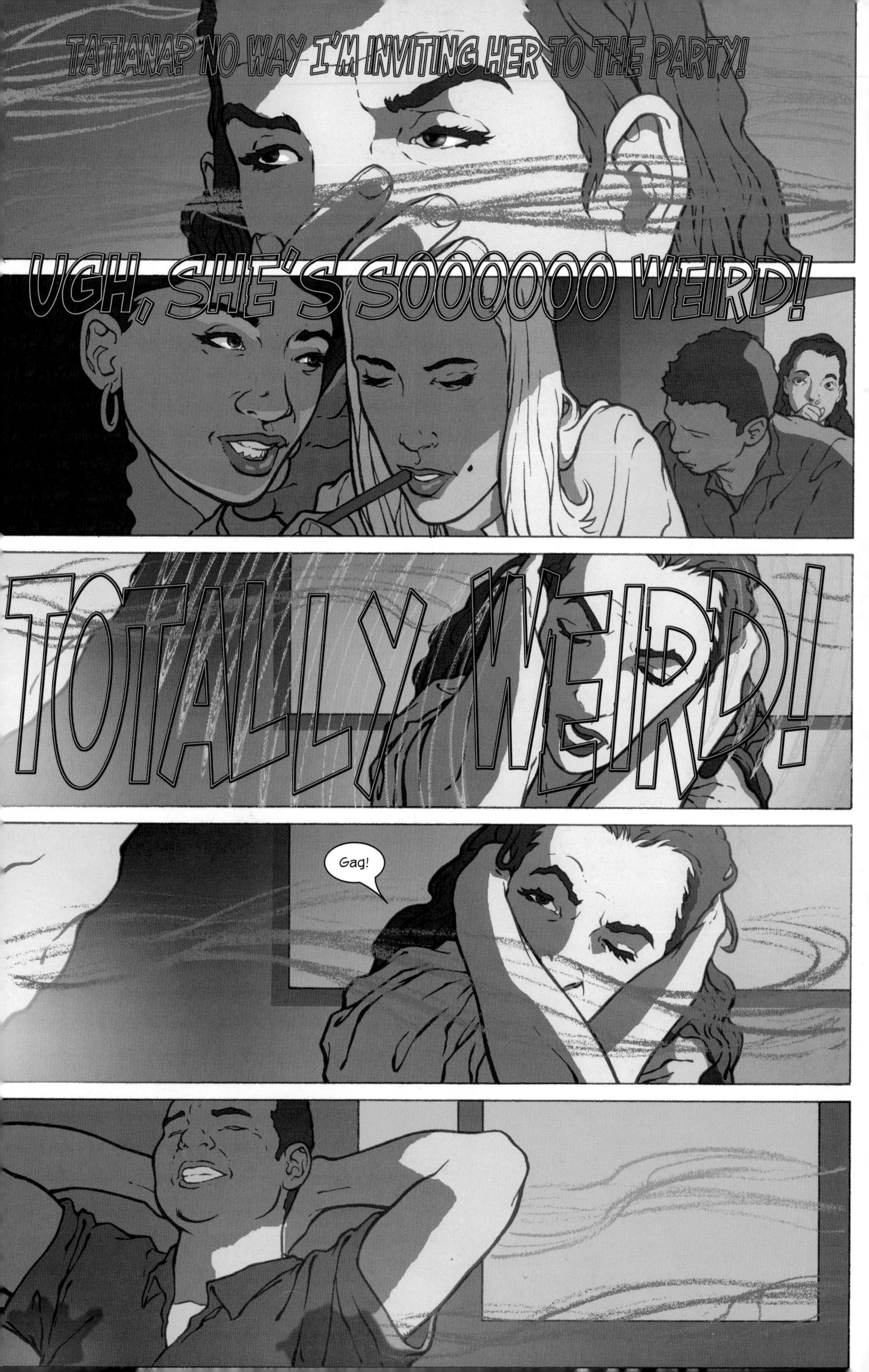
TATIANA? NO WAY I'M INVITING HER TO THE PARTY!
UGH, SHE'S SOOOOOO WEIRD!
TOTALLY WEIRD!
Gag!

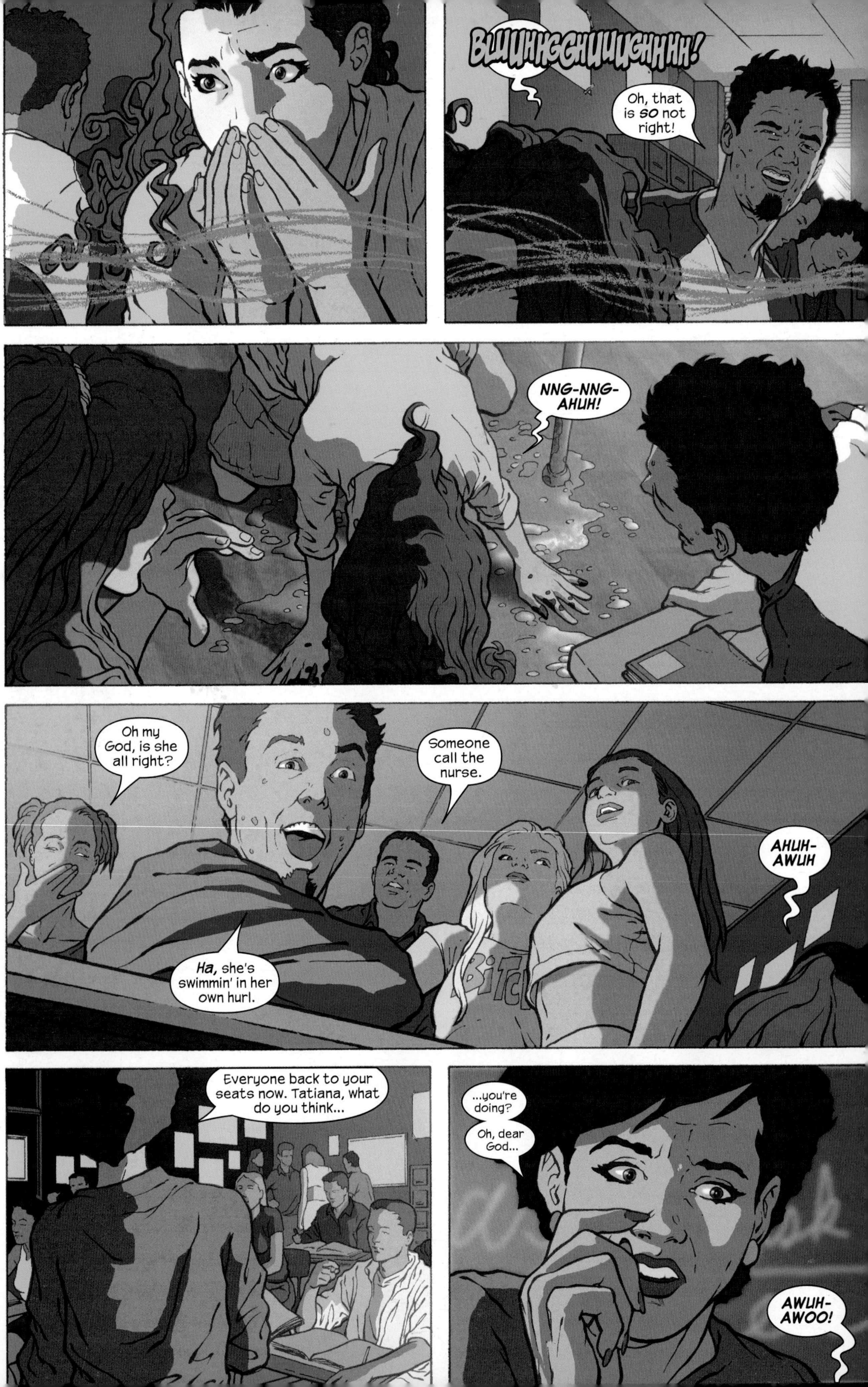
BWUUHHGGHUUUUGHHHH!
Oh, that is SO not right!
NNG-NNG-AHUH!
Oh my God, is she all right?
Someone call the nurse.
AHUH-AWUH
Ha, she's swimmin' in her own hurl.
Everyone back to your seats now. Tatiana, what do you think...
...you're doing?
Oh, dear God...
AWUH-AWOO!

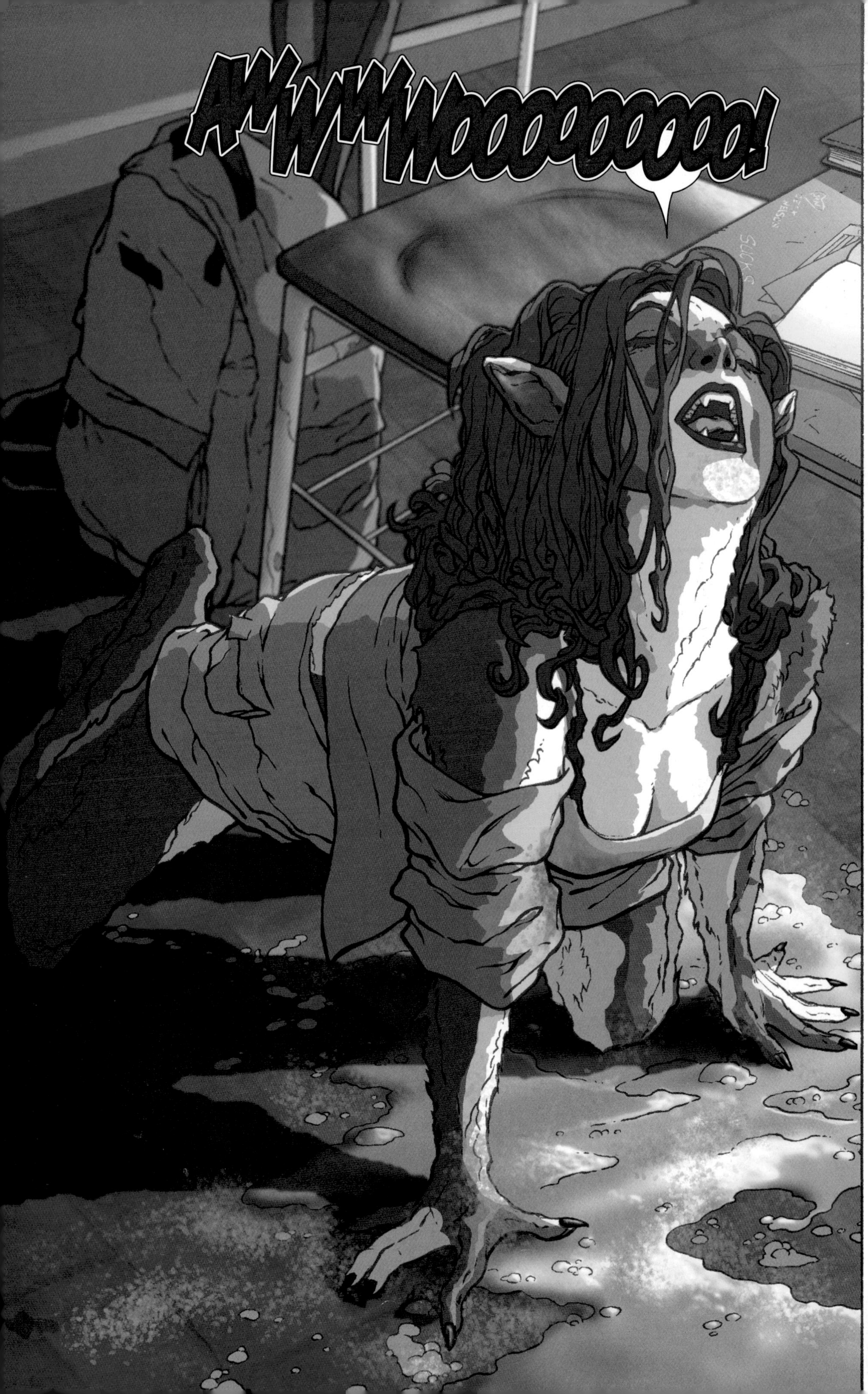
AWWWWOOOOOOOOO!
SUCKS

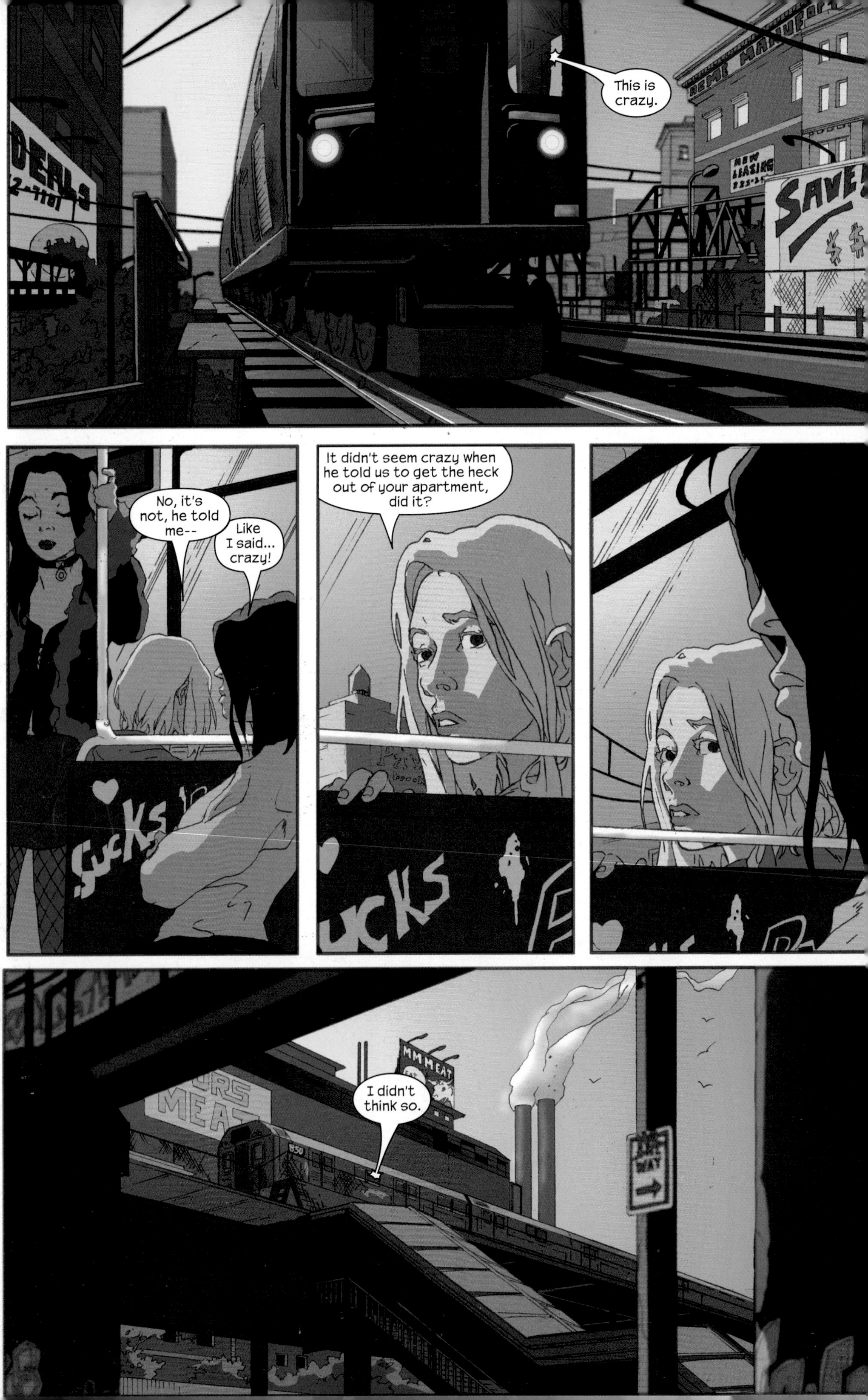
This is crazy.
No, it's not, he told me--
Like I said... crazy!
It didn't seem crazy when he told us to get the heck out of your apartment, did it?
I didn't think so.

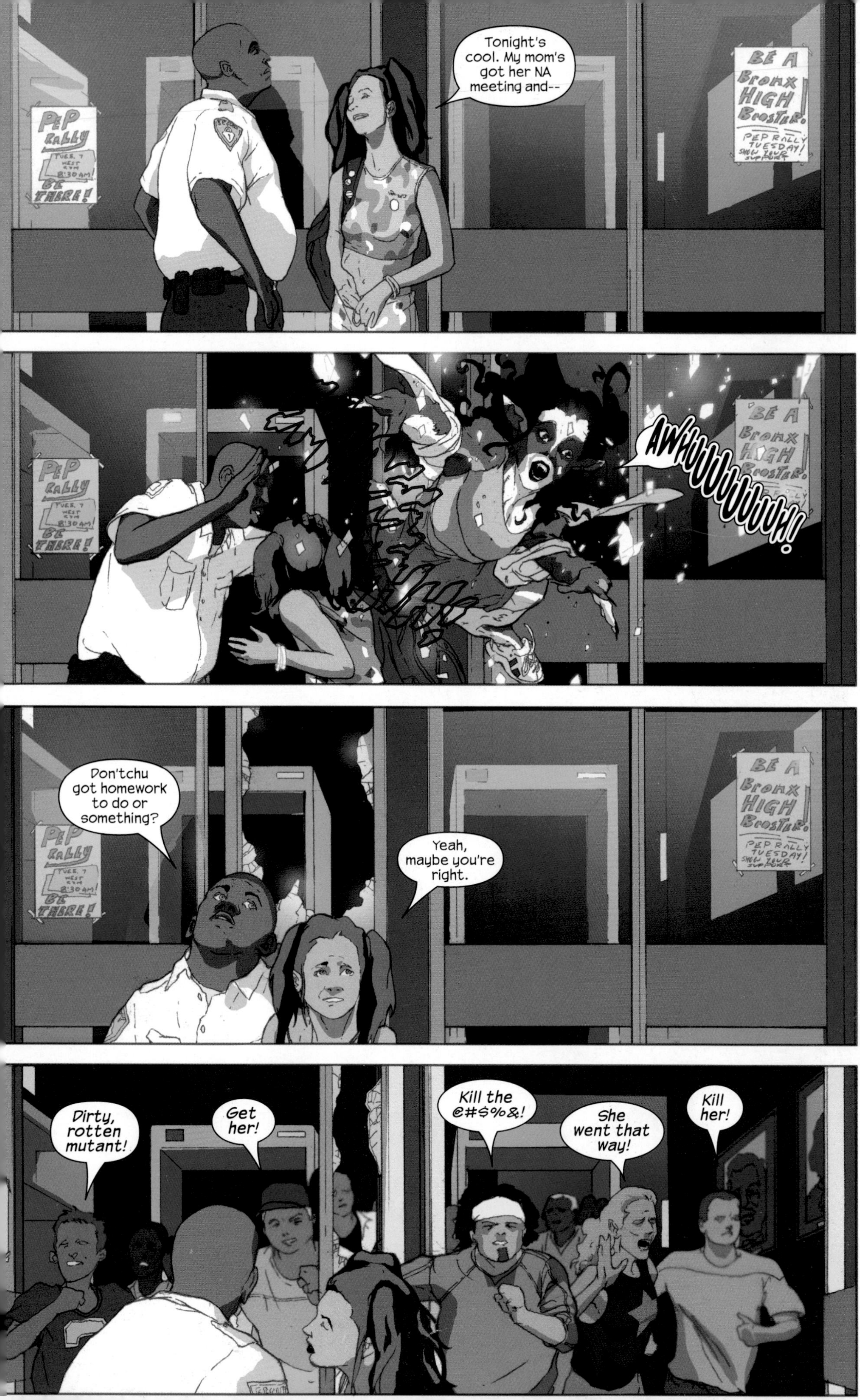
PEP RALLY
TUES. 7 WEST GYM 8:30 AM!
BE THERE!
BE A Bronx HIGH Booster!
PEP RALLY TUESDAY!
Tonight's cool. My mom's got her NA meeting and--
AWHUUUUUUUUUH!
Don'tchu got homework to do or something?
Yeah, maybe you're right.
Dirty, rotten mutant!
Get her!
Kill the @#$%&!
She went that way!
Kill her!

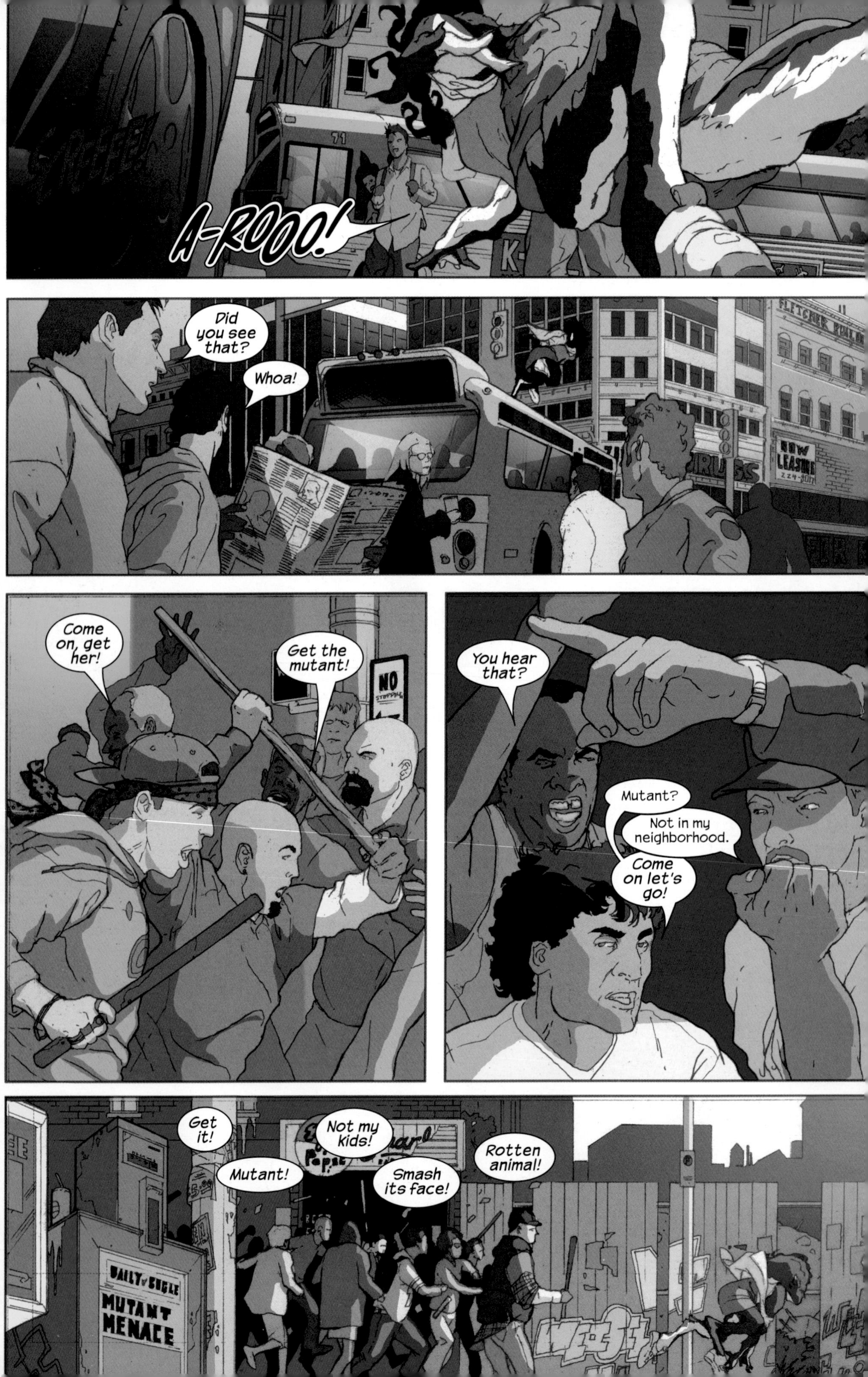
A-ROOO!
Did you see that?
Whoa!
FLETCHER BUILDING
NOW LEASING
Come on, get her!
Get the mutant!
NO
You hear that?
Mutant?
Not in my neighborhood.
Come on let's go!
Get it!
Not my kids!
Mutant!
Smash its face!
Rotten animal!
DAILY BUGLE
MUTANT MENACE

This is it, Gunhill Road. We're here.

Now what?

I--I don't know.

You're kidding me, right?

No, just give me a second and something will hit me.

AHHH!

What was that?

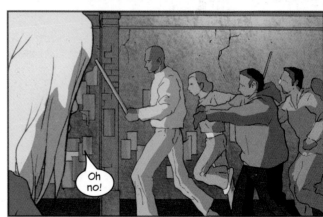

Oh no!

Kiden, get up!

Kiden, where are you going?

Come on, this is what he wanted us to see!

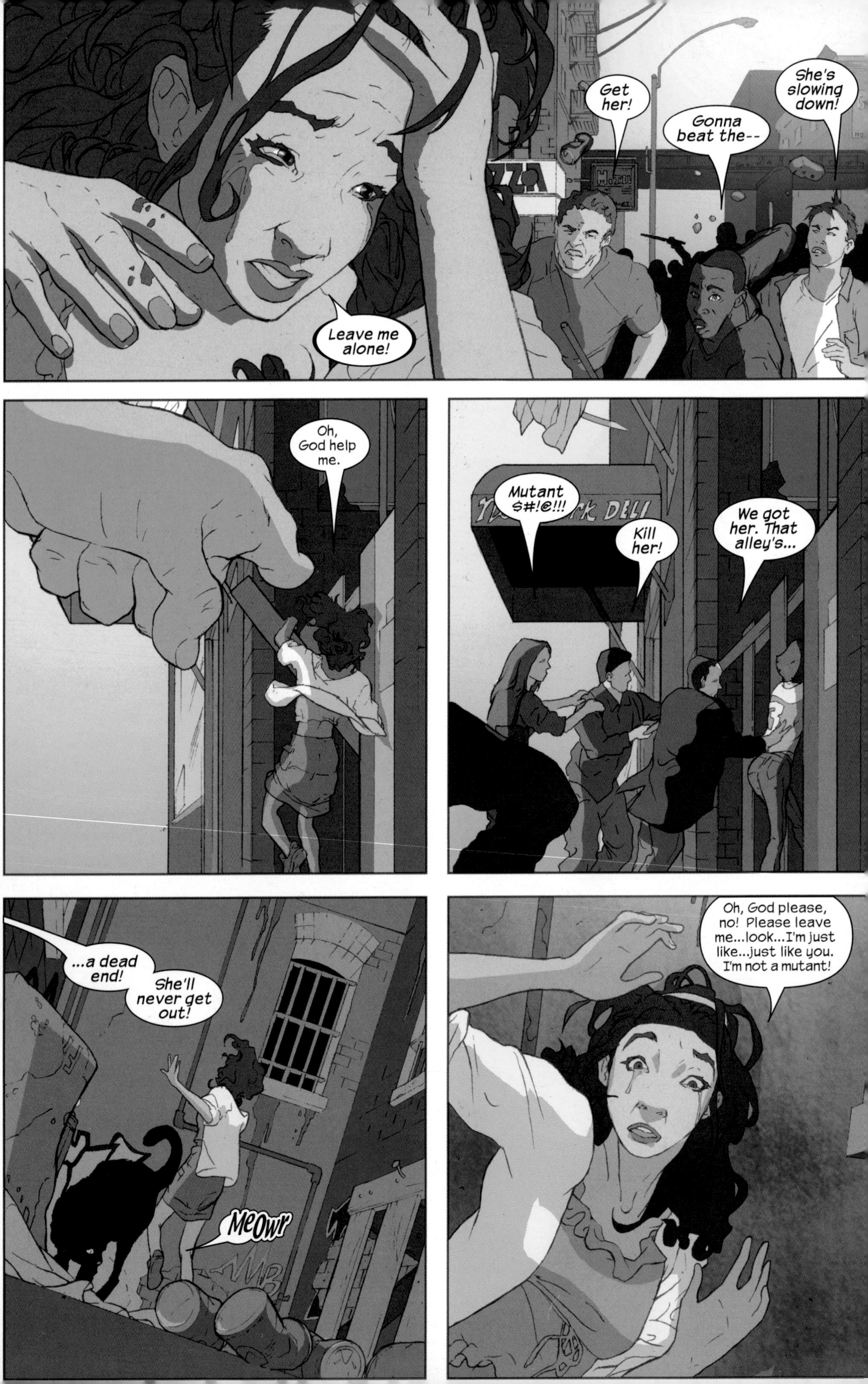
Get her!
Gonna beat the--
She's slowing down!
Leave me alone!
Oh, God help me.
Mutant $#!@!!!
Kill her!
We got her. That alley's...
...a dead end!
She'll never get out!
MEOWR
Oh, God please, no! Please leave me...look...I'm just like...just like you. I'm not a mutant!

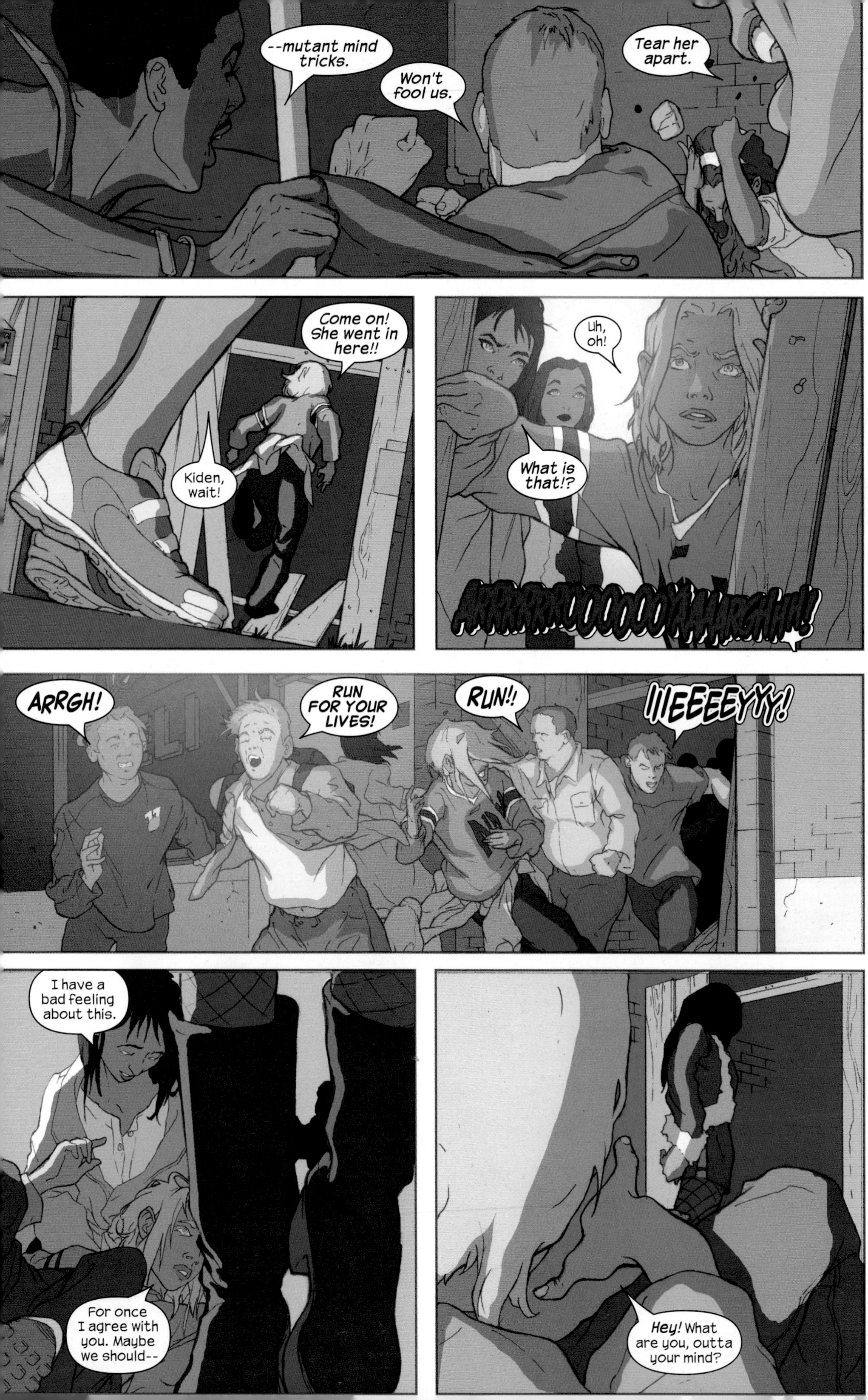
--mutant mind tricks.
Won't fool us.
Tear her apart.
Come on! She went in here!!
Kiden, wait!
Uh, oh!
What is that!?
ARRRRRRROOOOOOOYAAAARGHHH!
ARRGH!
RUN FOR YOUR LIVES!
RUN!!
IIIEEEEYYY!
I have a bad feeling about this.
For once I agree with you. Maybe we should--
Hey! What are you, outta your mind?

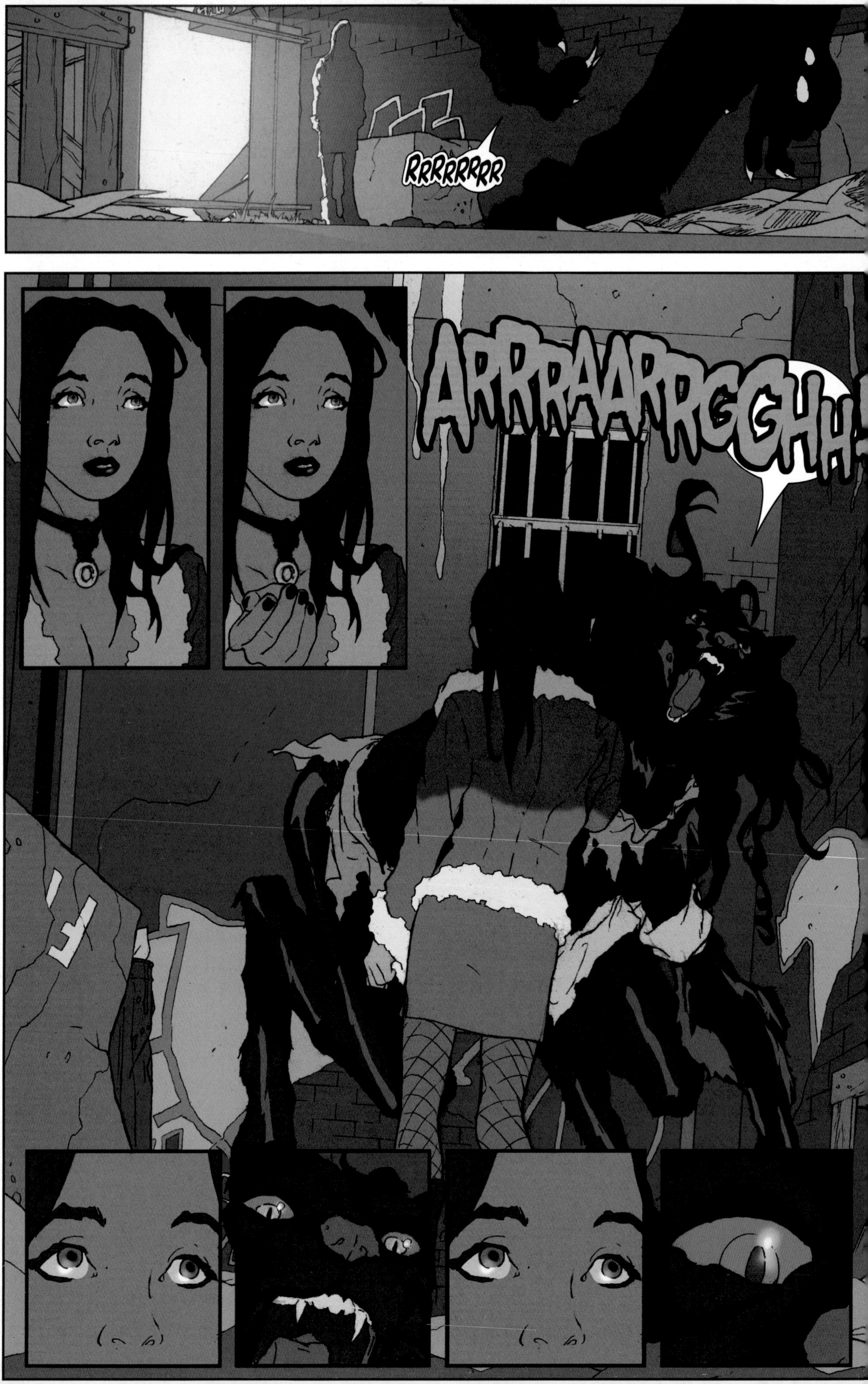
RRRRRRRR
ARRRAARRGGHH!

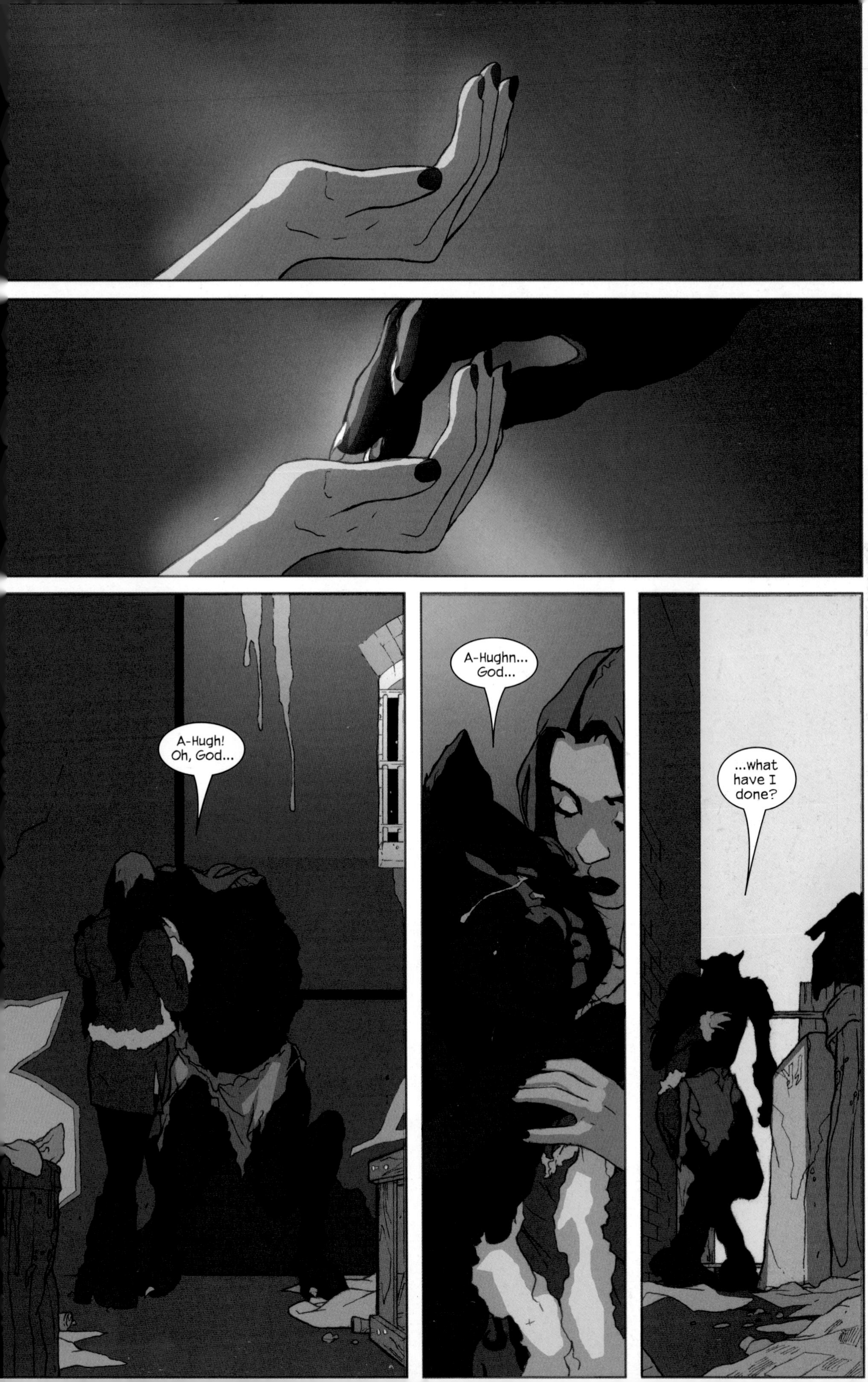
A-Hugh!
Oh, God...
A-Hughn...
God...
...what
have I
done?

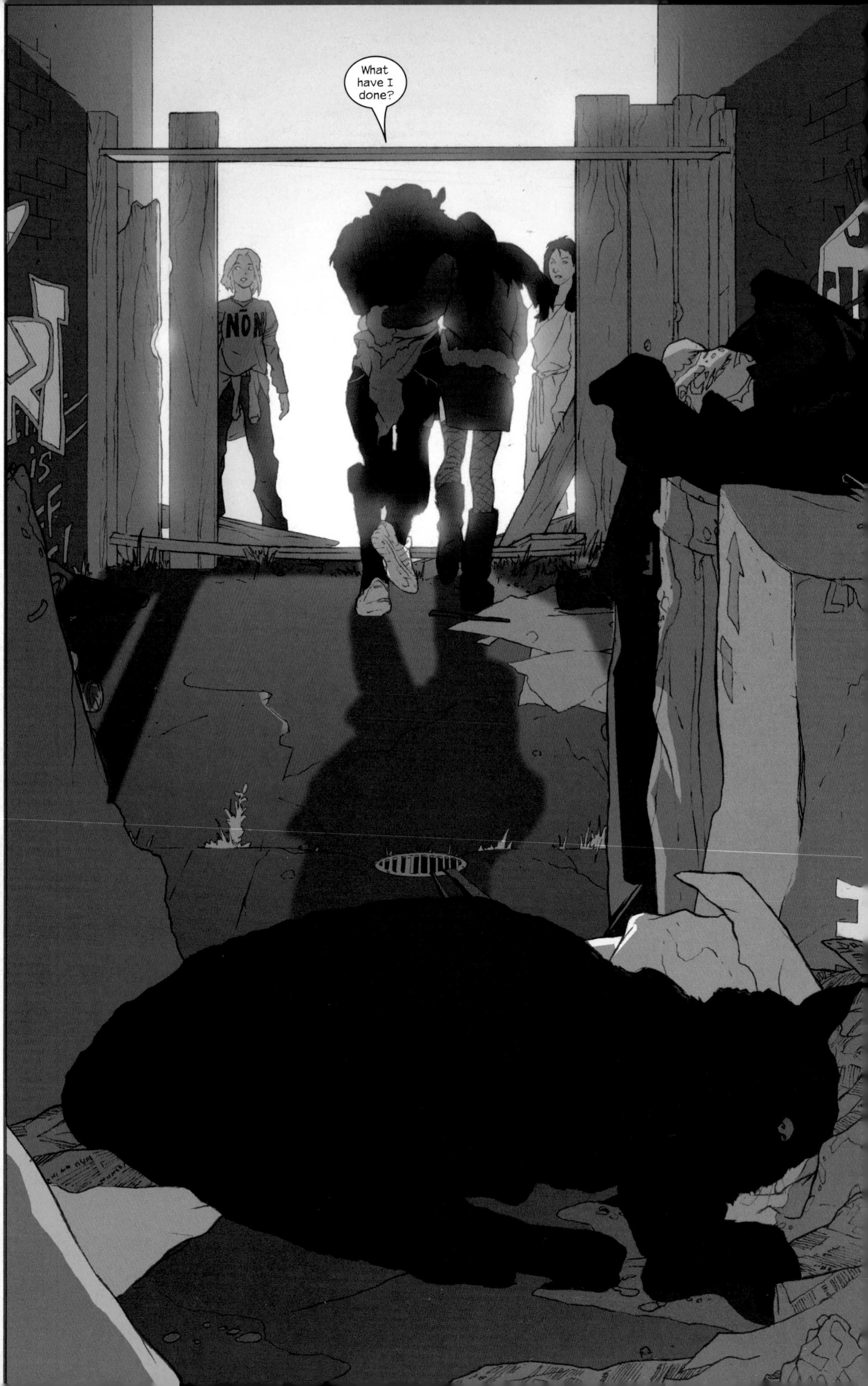
What have I done?
NŌN

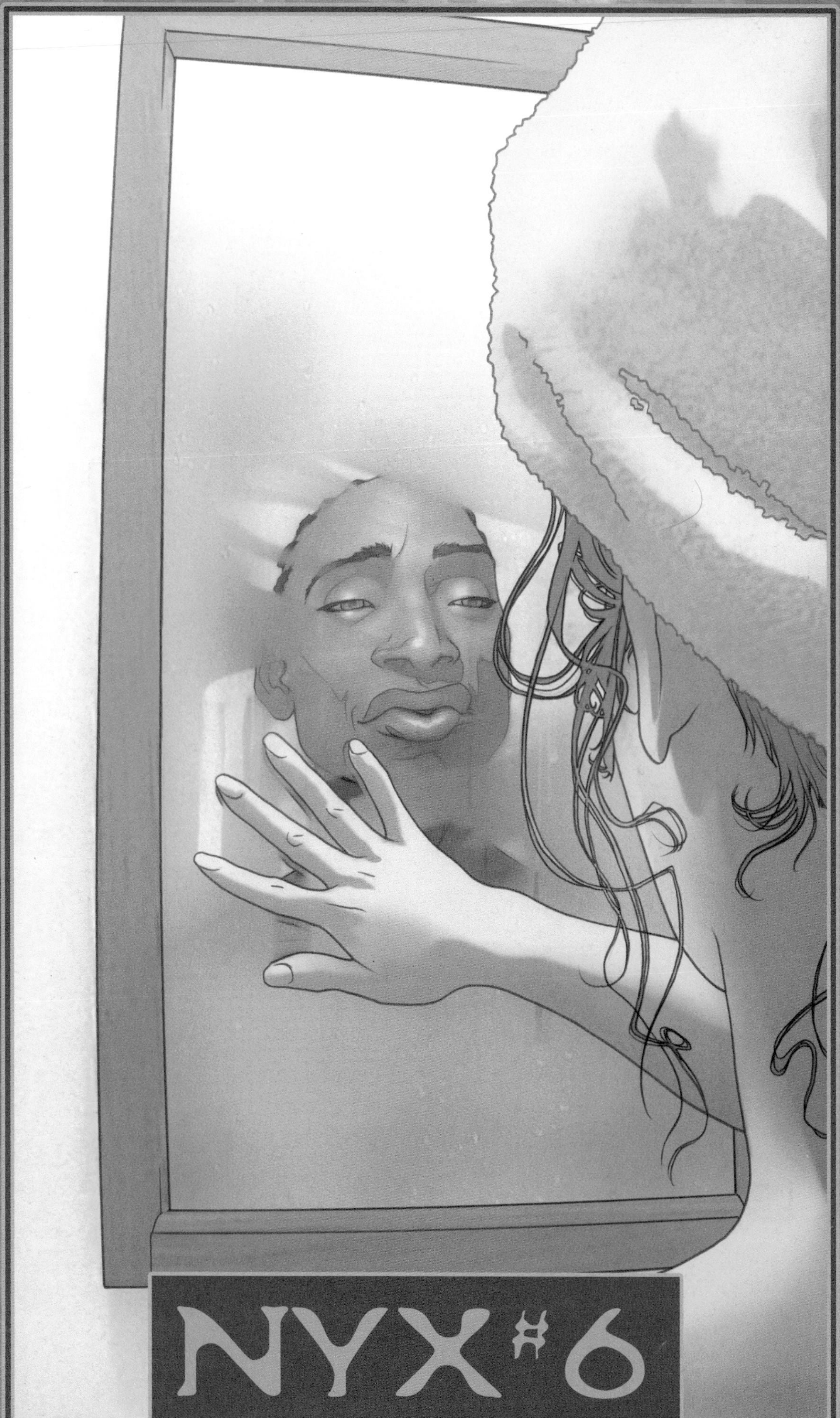
NYX #6

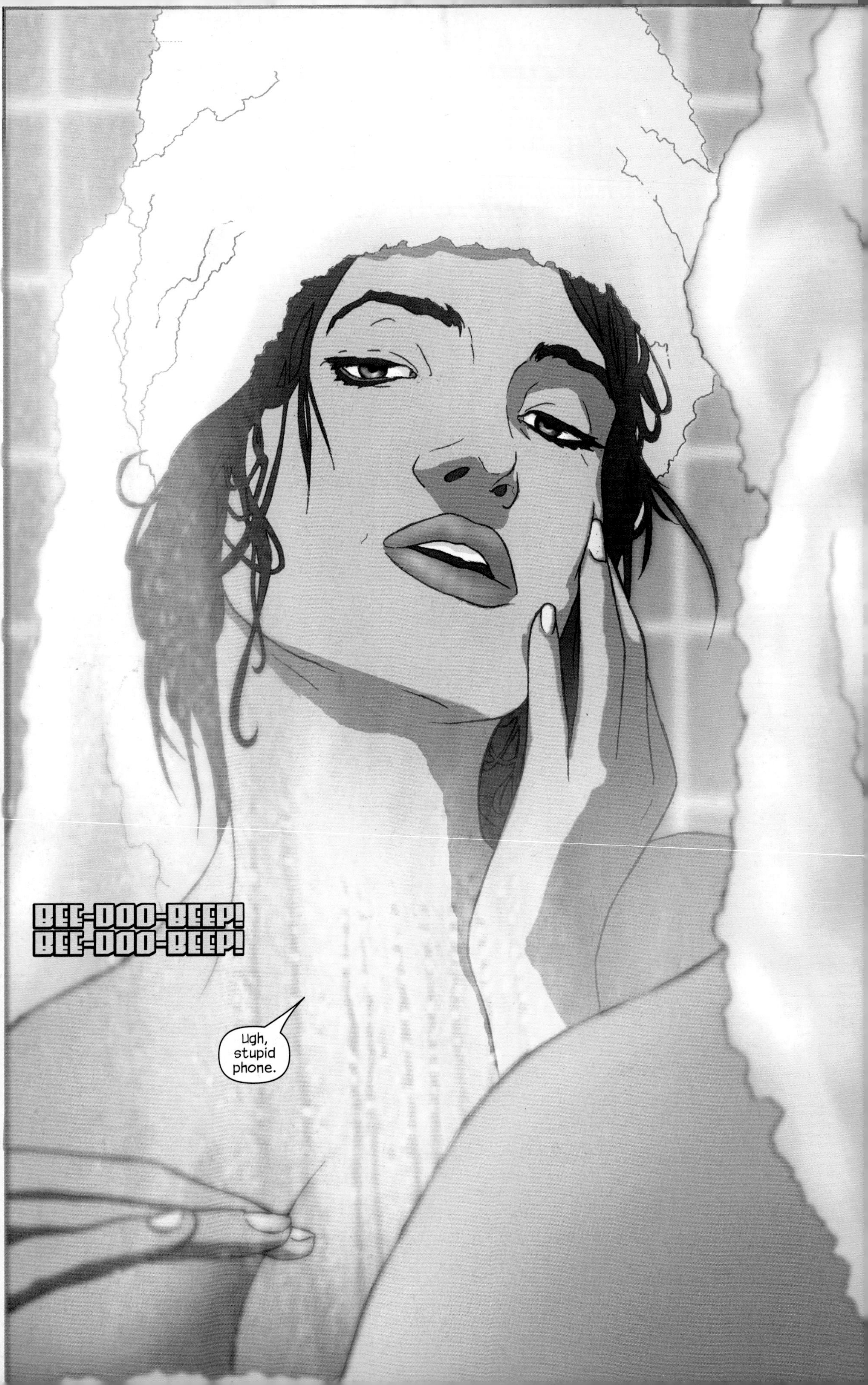
BEE-DOO-BEEP!
BEE-DOO-BEEP!
Ugh, stupid phone.

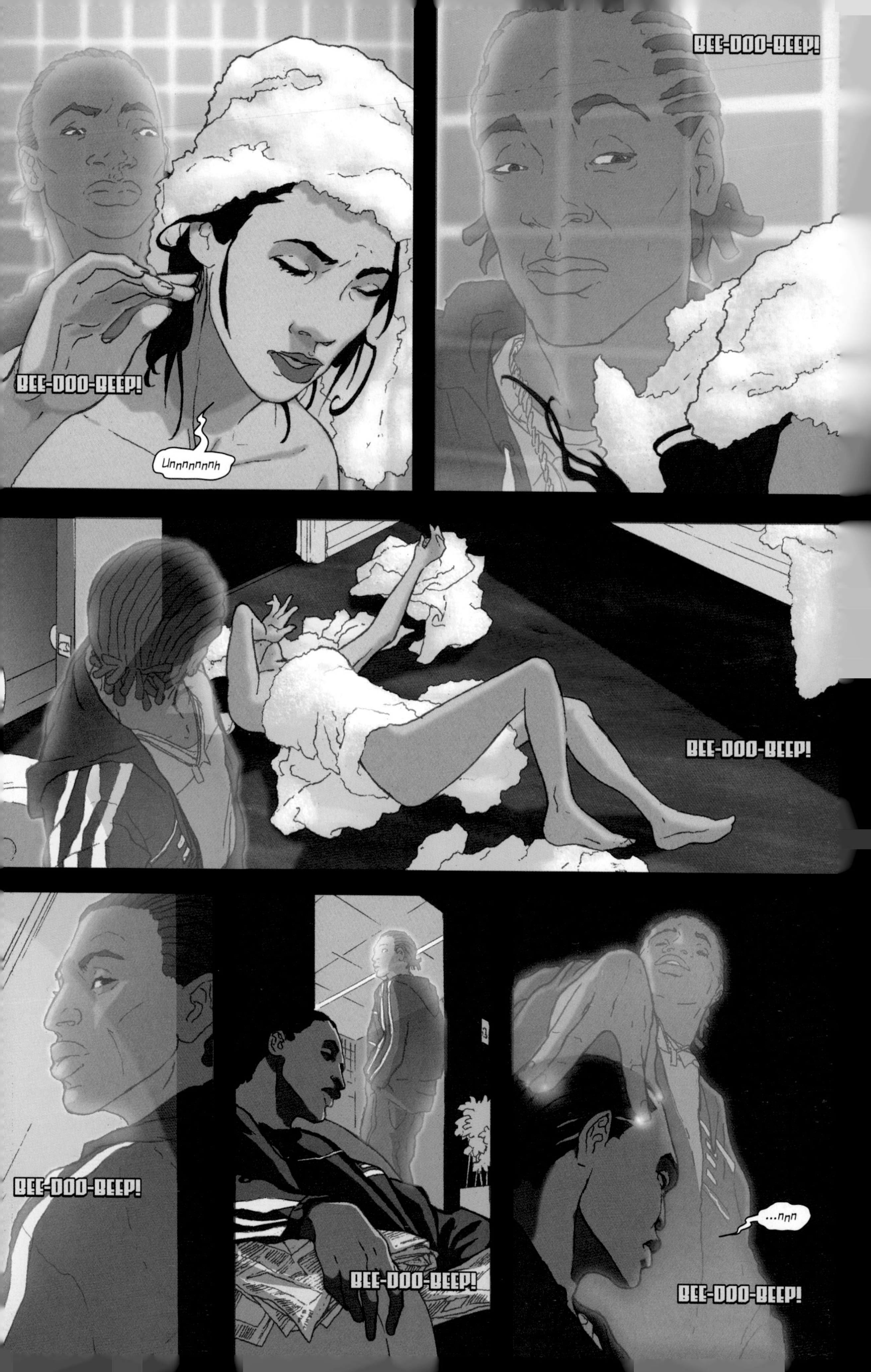
BEE-DOO-BEEP!
Unnnnnnnh
BEE-DOO-BEEP!
BEE-DOO-BEEP!
BEE-DOO-BEEP!
BEE-DOO-BEEP!
...nnn
BEE-DOO-BEEP!

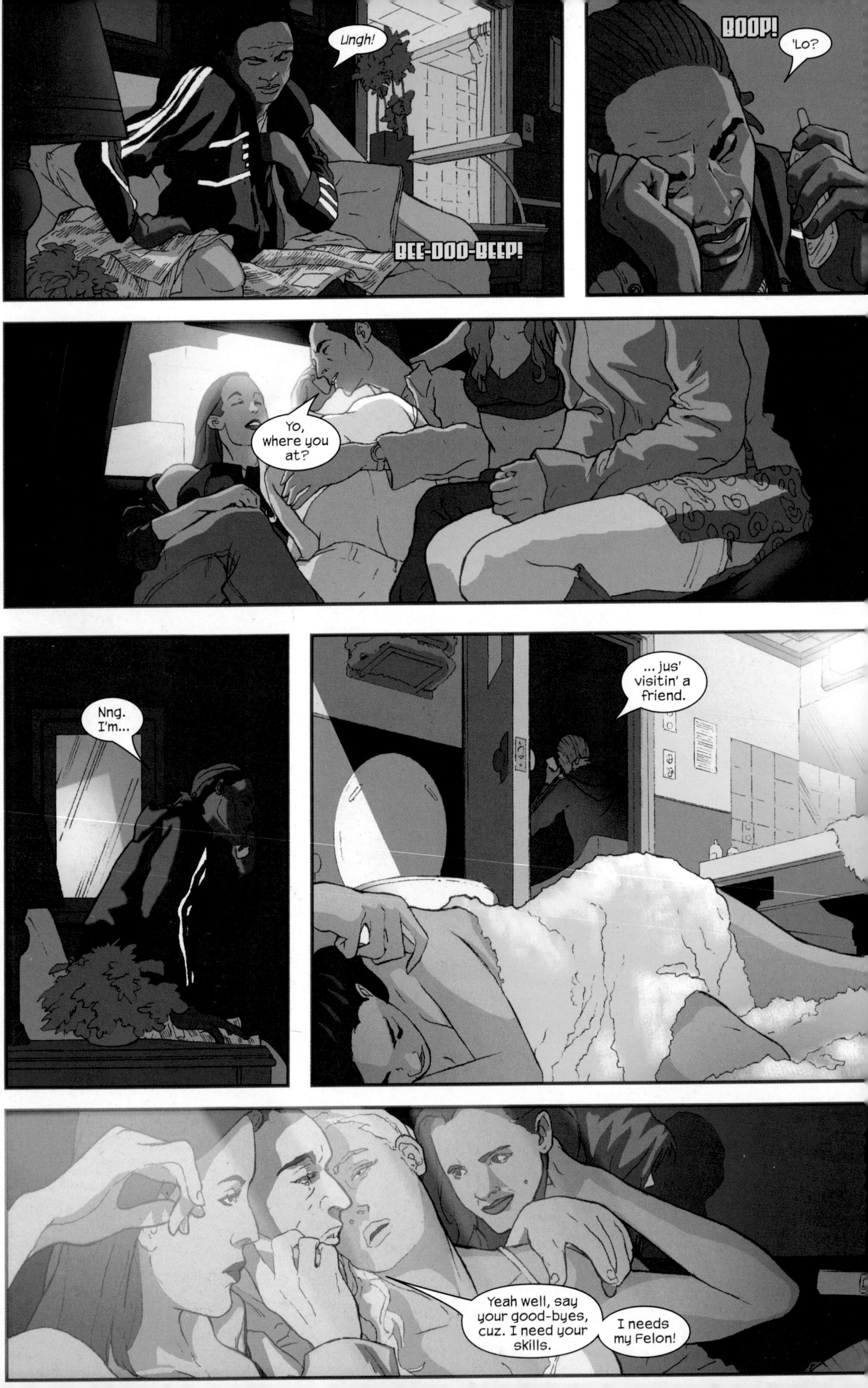
Ungh!
BEE-DOO-BEEP!
BOOP!
'Lo?
Yo, where you at?
Nng. I'm...
... jus' visitin' a friend.
Yeah well, say your good-byes, cuz. I need your skills.
I needs my Felon!

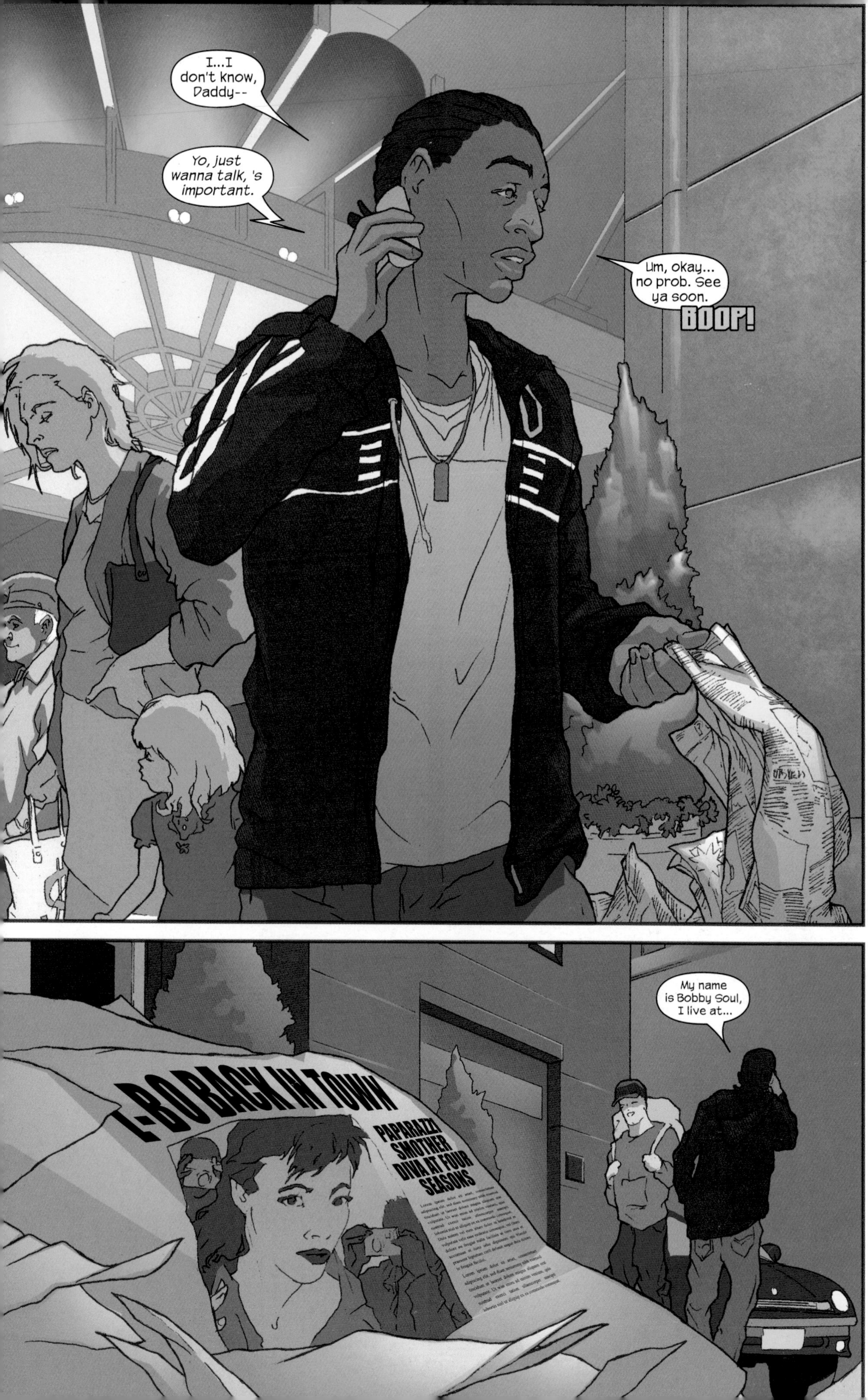
I...I don't know, Daddy--
Yo, just wanna talk, 's important.
Um, okay... no prob. See ya soon.
BOOP!
My name is Bobby Soul, I live at...
I-BO BACK IN TOWN
PAPARAZZI SMOTHER DIVA AT FOUR SEASONS

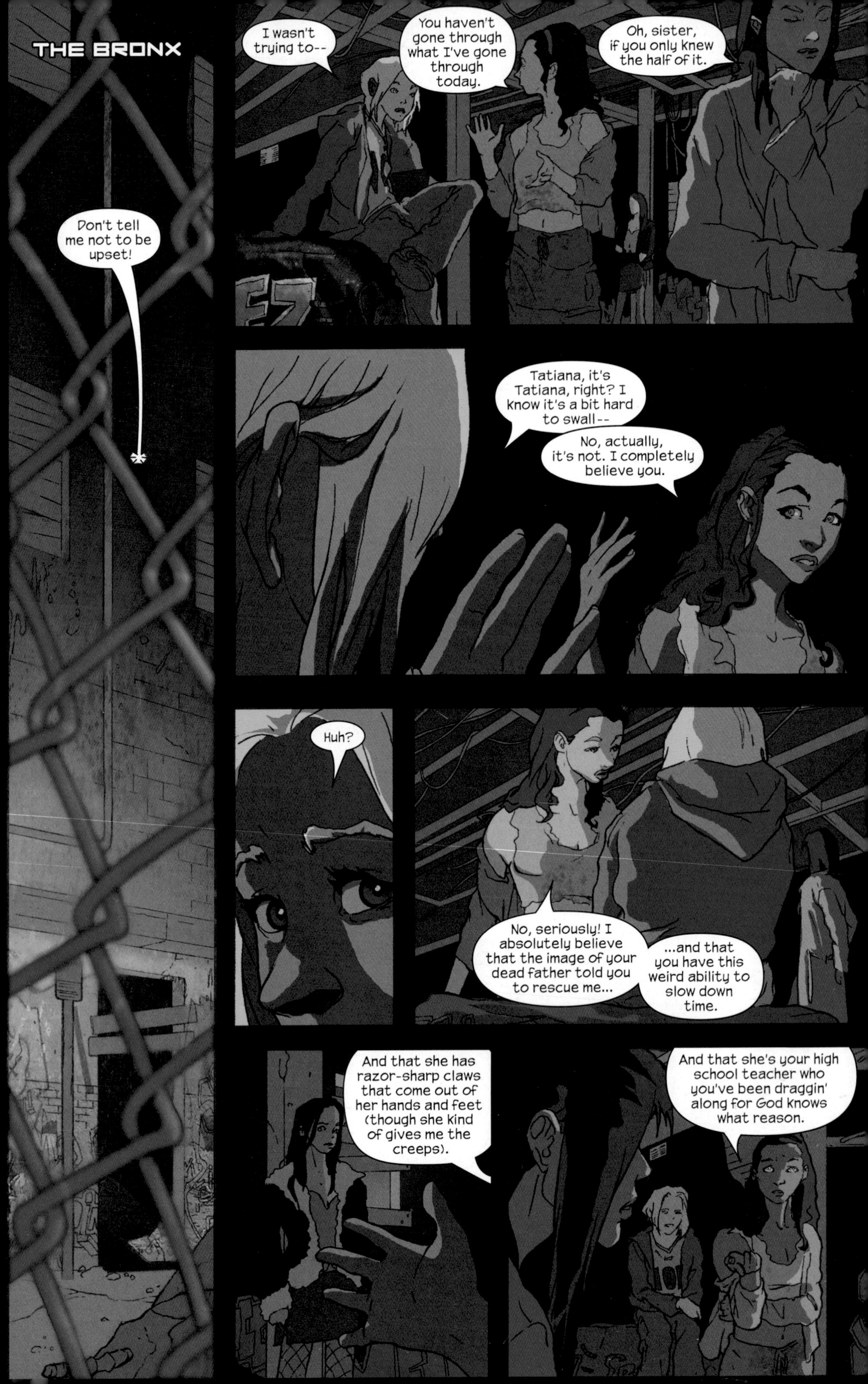
THE BRONX
Don't tell me not to be upset!
I wasn't trying to--
You haven't gone through what I've gone through today.
Oh, sister, if you only knew the half of it.
Tatiana, it's Tatiana, right? I know it's a bit hard to swall--
No, actually, it's not. I completely believe you.
Huh?
No, seriously! I absolutely believe that the image of your dead father told you to rescue me...
...and that you have this weird ability to slow down time.
And that she has razor-sharp claws that come out of her hands and feet (though she kind of gives me the creeps).
And that she's your high school teacher who you've been draggin' along for God knows what reason.

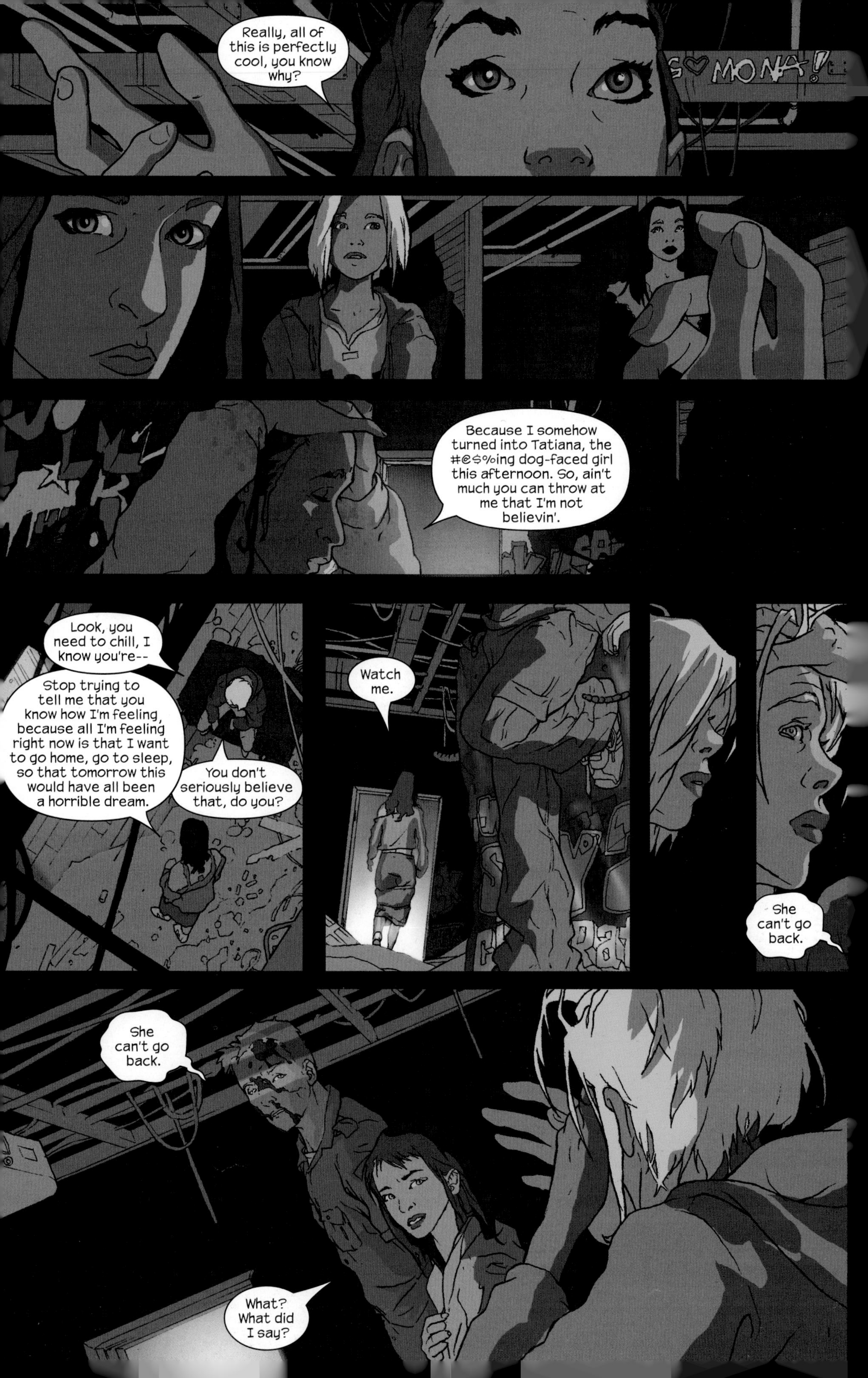

Really, all of this is perfectly cool, you know why?
♡ MONA!
Because I somehow turned into Tatiana, the #@$%ing dog-faced girl this afternoon. So, ain't much you can throw at me that I'm not believin'.
Look, you need to chill, I know you're--
Stop trying to tell me that you know how I'm feeling, because all I'm feeling right now is that I want to go home, go to sleep, so that tomorrow this would have all been a horrible dream.
You don't seriously believe that, do you?
Watch me.
She can't go back.
She can't go back.
What? What did I say?

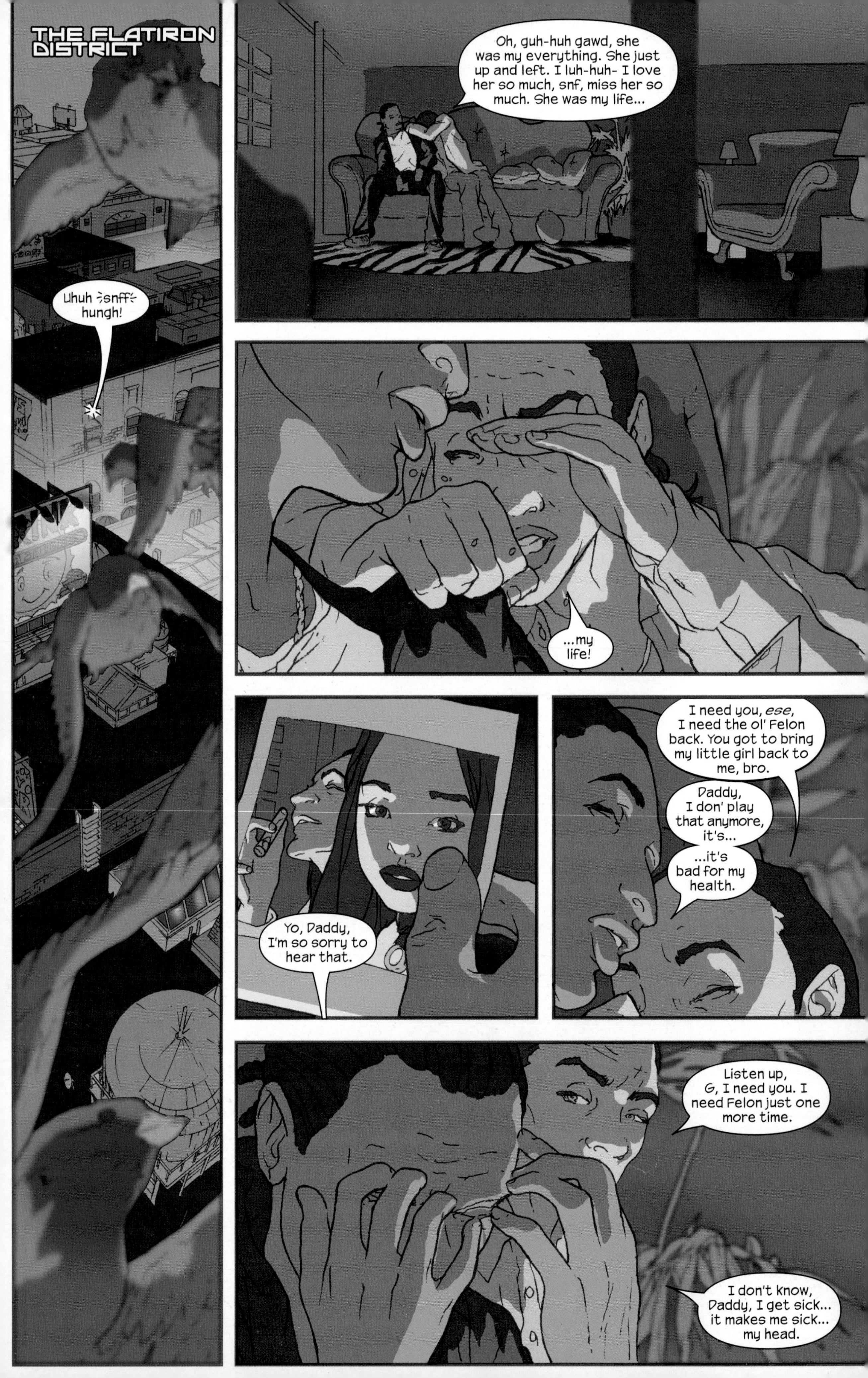
THE FLATIRON DISTRICT
Uhuh ≈snff≈ hungh!
Oh, guh-huh gawd, she was my everything. She just up and left. I luh-huh- I love her so much, snf, miss her so much. She was my life...
...my life!
Yo, Daddy, I'm so sorry to hear that.
I need you, *ese*, I need the ol' Felon back. You got to bring my little girl back to me, bro.
Daddy, I don' play that anymore, it's...
...it's bad for my health.
Listen up, G, I need you. I need Felon just one more time.
I don't know, Daddy, I get sick... it makes me sick... my head.

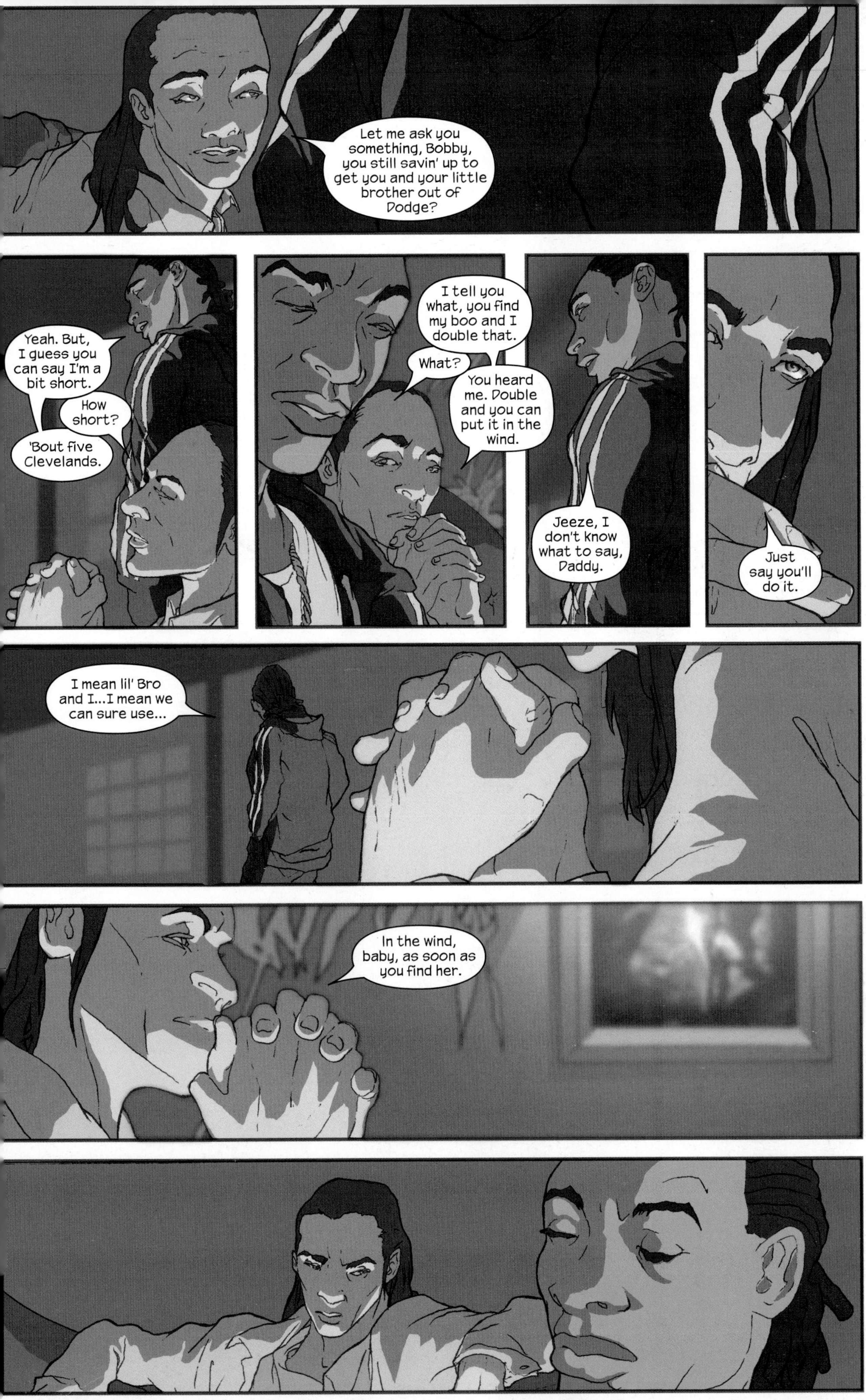
Let me ask you something, Bobby, you still savin' up to get you and your little brother out of Dodge?
Yeah. But, I guess you can say I'm a bit short.
How short?
'Bout five Clevelands.
I tell you what, you find my boo and I double that.
What?
You heard me. Double and you can put it in the wind.
Jeeze, I don't know what to say, Daddy.
Just say you'll do it.
I mean lil' Bro and I...I mean we can sure use...
In the wind, baby, as soon as you find her.

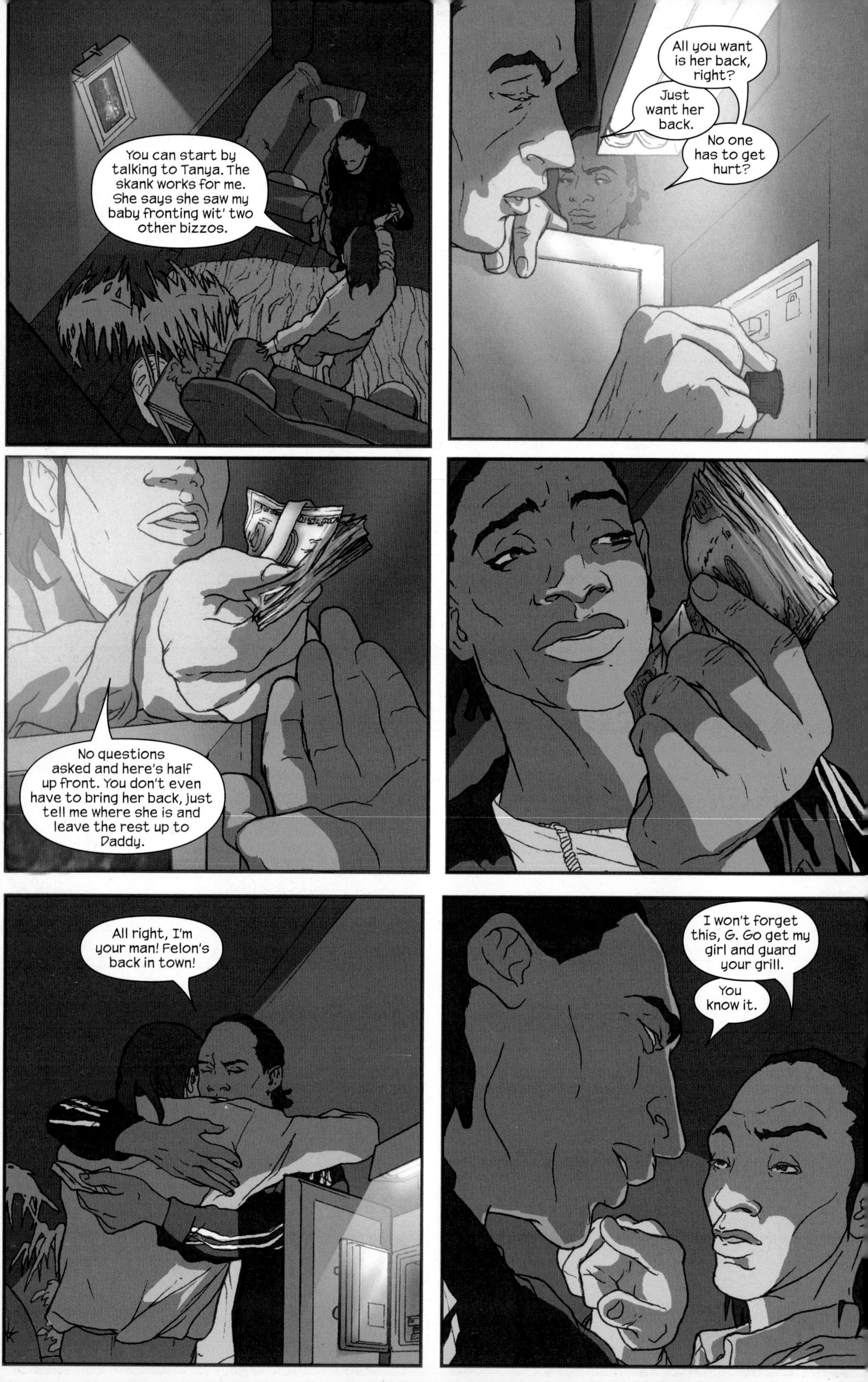
You can start by talking to Tanya. The skank works for me. She says she saw my baby fronting wit' two other bizzos.
All you want is her back, right?
Just want her back.
No one has to get hurt?
No questions asked and here's half up front. You don't even have to bring her back, just tell me where she is and leave the rest up to Daddy.
All right, I'm your man! Felon's back in town!
I won't forget this, G. Go get my girl and guard your grill.
You know it.

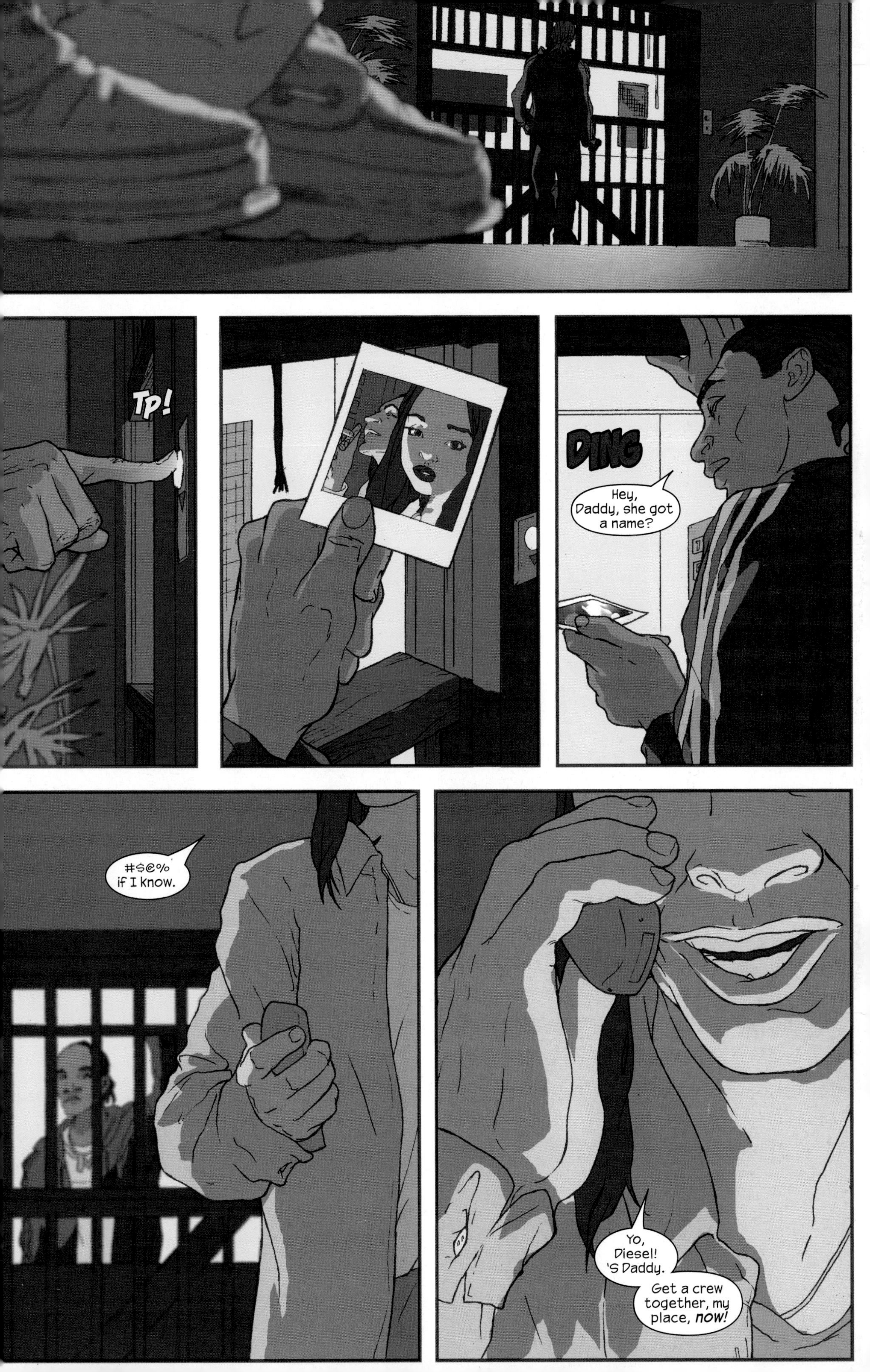
TP!
DING
Hey, Daddy, she got a name?
#$@% if I know.
YO, Diesel! 'S Daddy.
Get a crew together, my place, NOW!

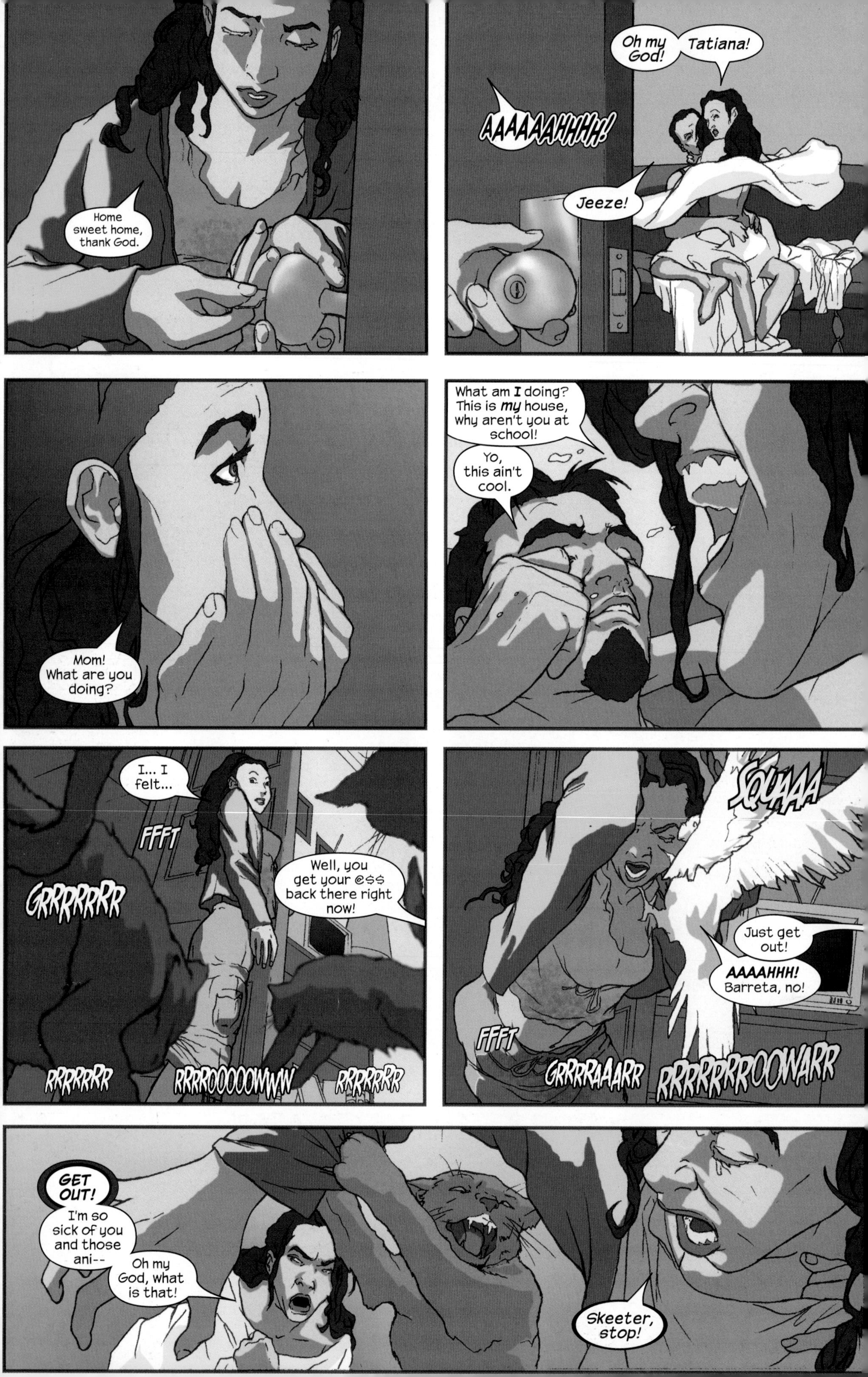
Home sweet home, thank God.
AAAAAAHHHH!
Oh my God!
Tatiana!
Jeeze!
Mom! What are you doing?
What am I doing? This is my house, why aren't you at school!
Yo, this ain't cool.
I... I felt...
FFFT
GRRRRRRR
Well, you get your @$$ back there right now!
RRRRRRR
RRRROOOOOWWW
RRRRRRR
SQUAAA
Just get out!
AAAAHHH! Barreta, no!
FFFT
GRRRRAAARR
RRRRRRROOWARR
GET OUT!
I'm so sick of you and those ani--
Oh my God, what is that!
Skeeter, stop!

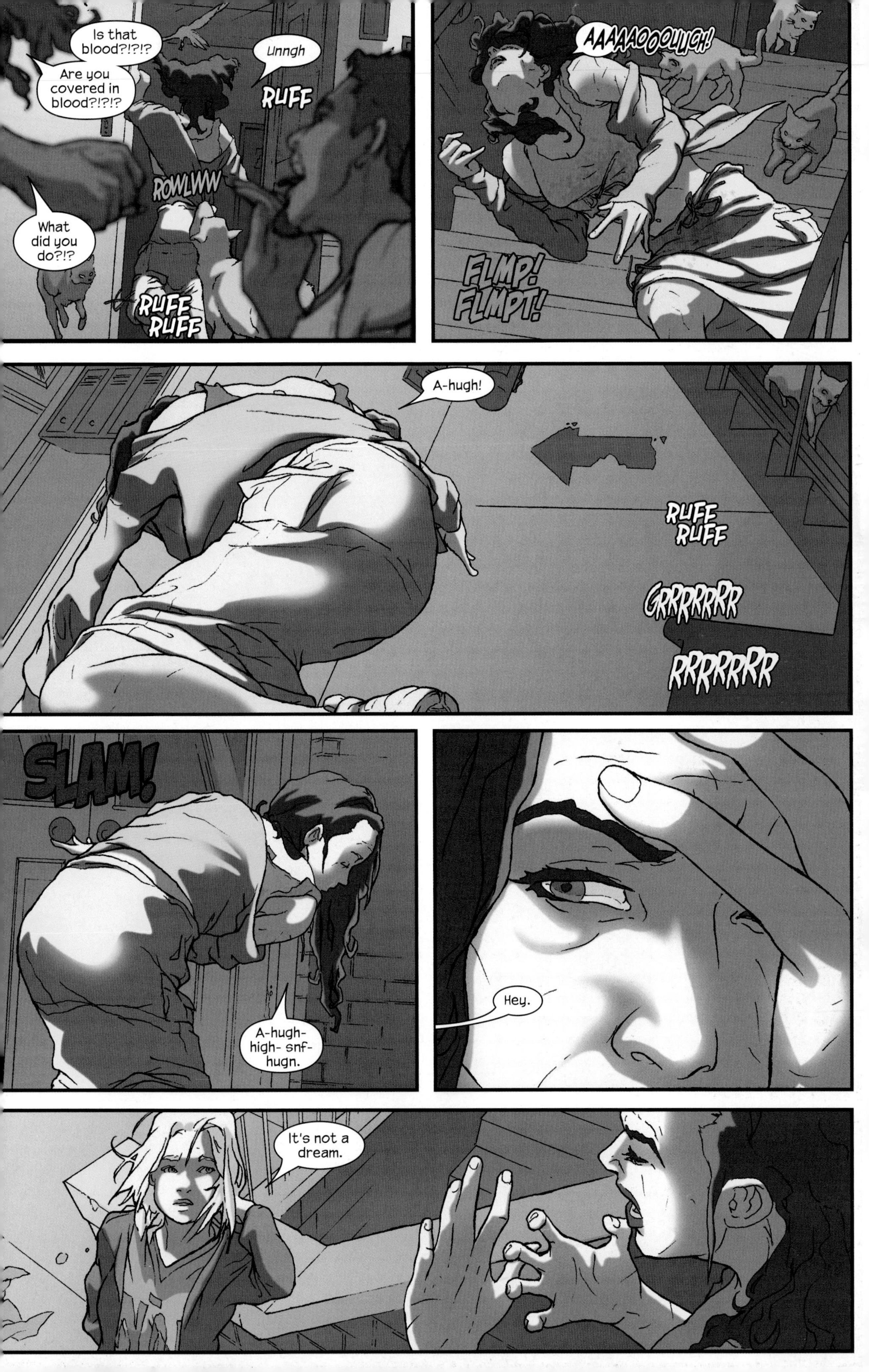
Is that blood?!?!?
Are you covered in blood?!?!?
Unngh
RUFF
ROWLWW
What did you do?!?
RUFF RUFF
AAAAAOOOUUGH!
FLMP! FLMPT!
A-hugh!
RUFF RUFF
GRRRRRRR
RRRRRRR
SLAM!
A-hugh- high- snf- hugn.
Hey.
It's not a dream.

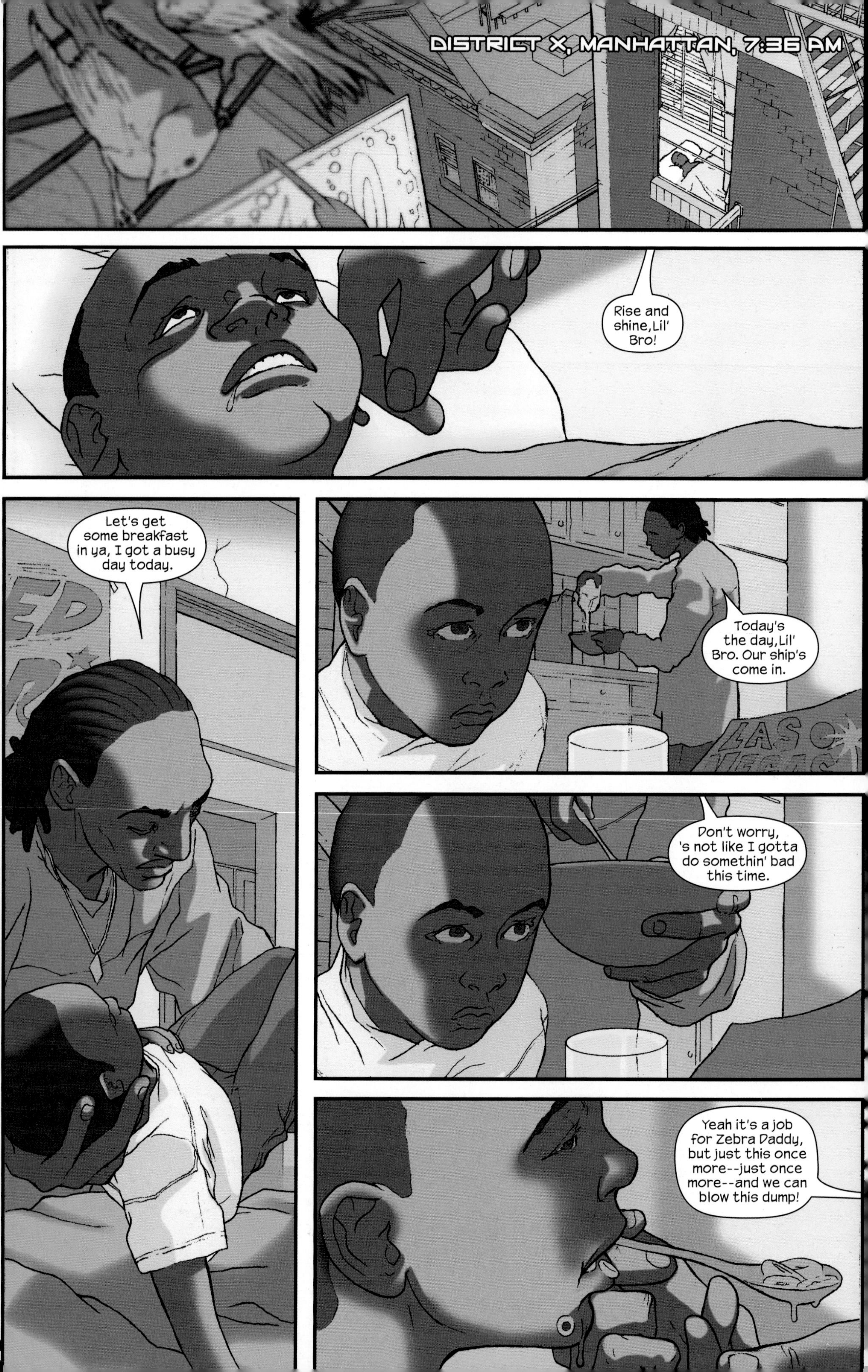
DISTRICT X, MANHATTAN, 7:36 AM
Rise and shine, Lil' Bro!
Let's get some breakfast in ya, I got a busy day today.
Today's the day, Lil' Bro. Our ship's come in.
LAS VEGAS
Don't worry, 's not like I gotta do somethin' bad this time.
Yeah it's a job for Zebra Daddy, but just this once more--just once more--and we can blow this dump!

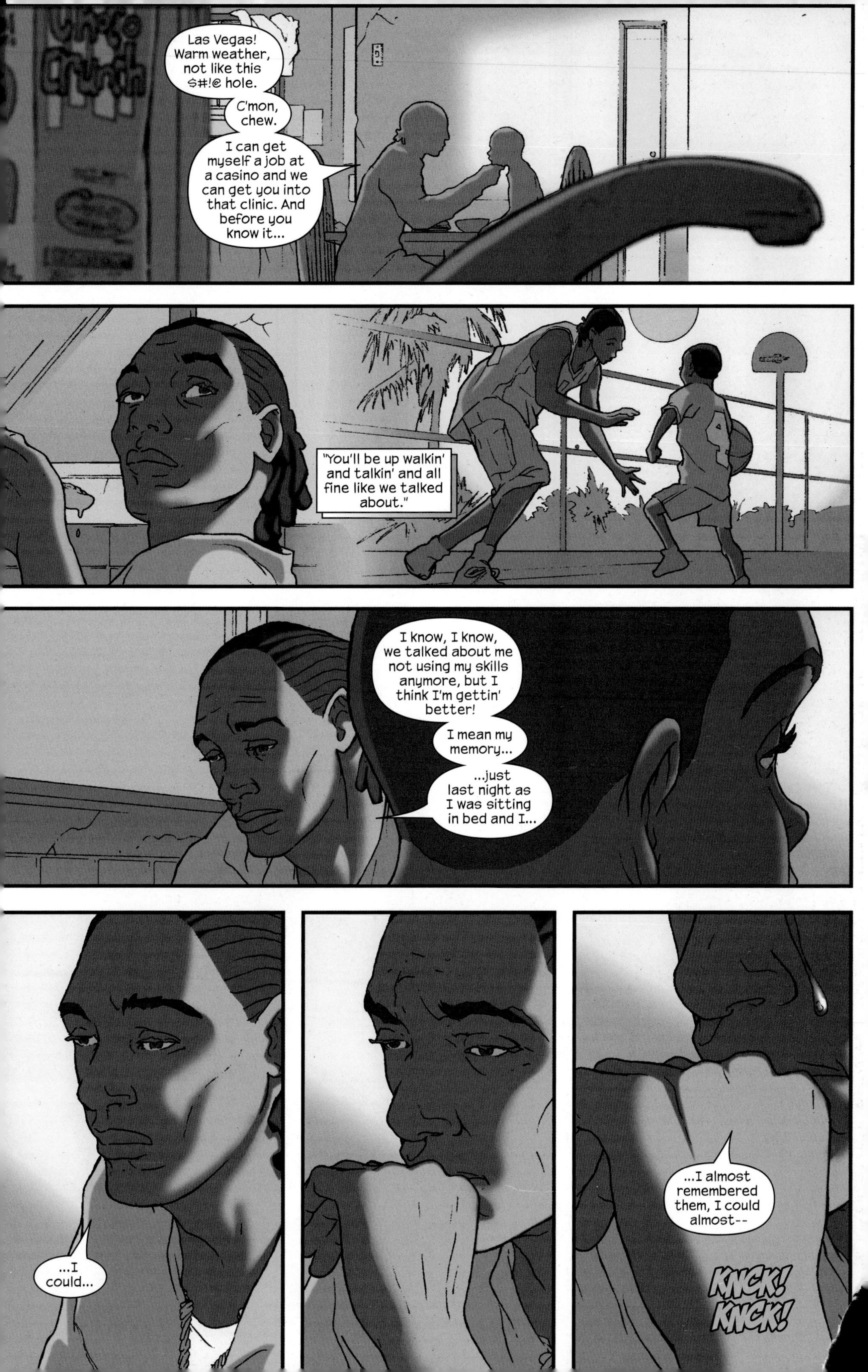
Las Vegas! Warm weather, not like this $#!@ hole.
C'mon, chew.
I can get myself a job at a casino and we can get you into that clinic. And before you know it...
"You'll be up walkin' and talkin' and all fine like we talked about."
I know, I know, we talked about me not using my skills anymore, but I think I'm gettin' better!
I mean my memory...
...just last night as I was sitting in bed and I...
...I could...
...I almost remembered them, I could almost--
KNCK! KNCK!

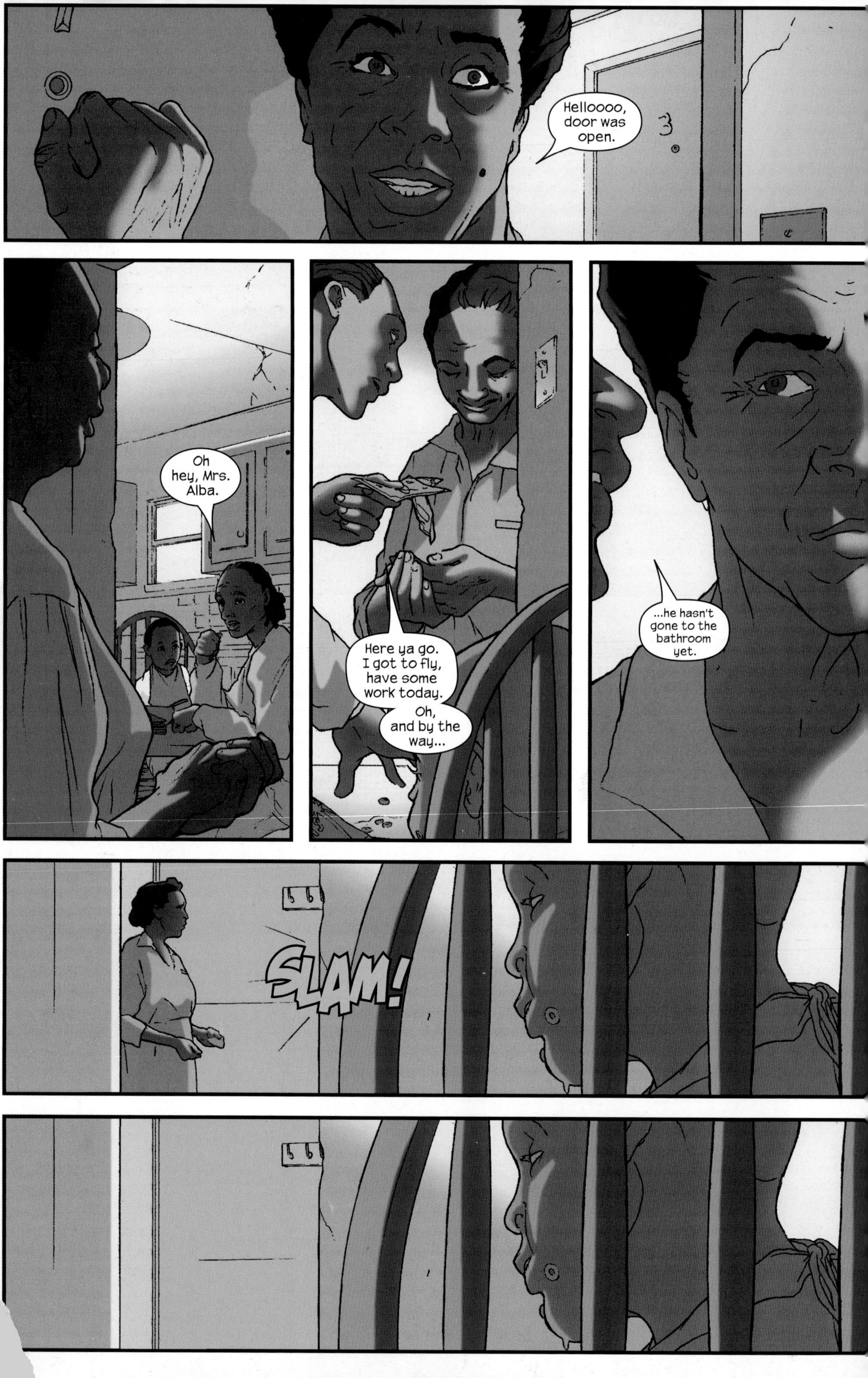
Helloooo, door was open.
Oh hey, Mrs. Alba.
Here ya go. I got to fly, have some work today.
Oh, and by the way...
...he hasn't gone to the bathroom yet.
SLAM!

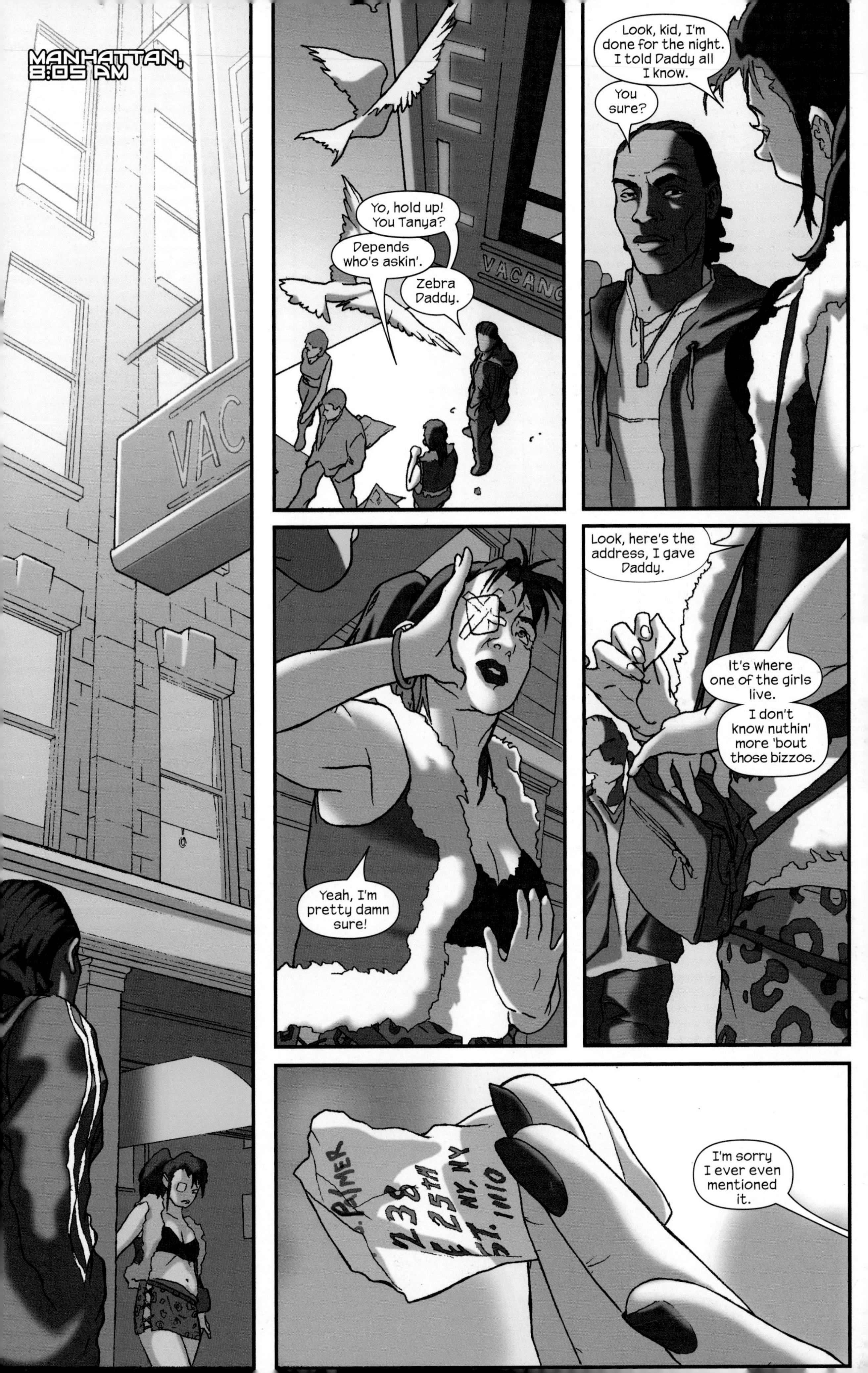
MANHATTAN, 8:05 AM
VAC
Yo, hold up! You Tanya?
Depends who's askin'.
Zebra Daddy.
VACANC
Look, kid, I'm done for the night. I told Daddy all I know.
You sure?
Yeah, I'm pretty damn sure!
Look, here's the address, I gave Daddy.
It's where one of the girls live.
I don't know nuthin' more 'bout those bizzos.
PALMER
238 E 25TH ST. NY, NY 10010
I'm sorry I ever even mentioned it.

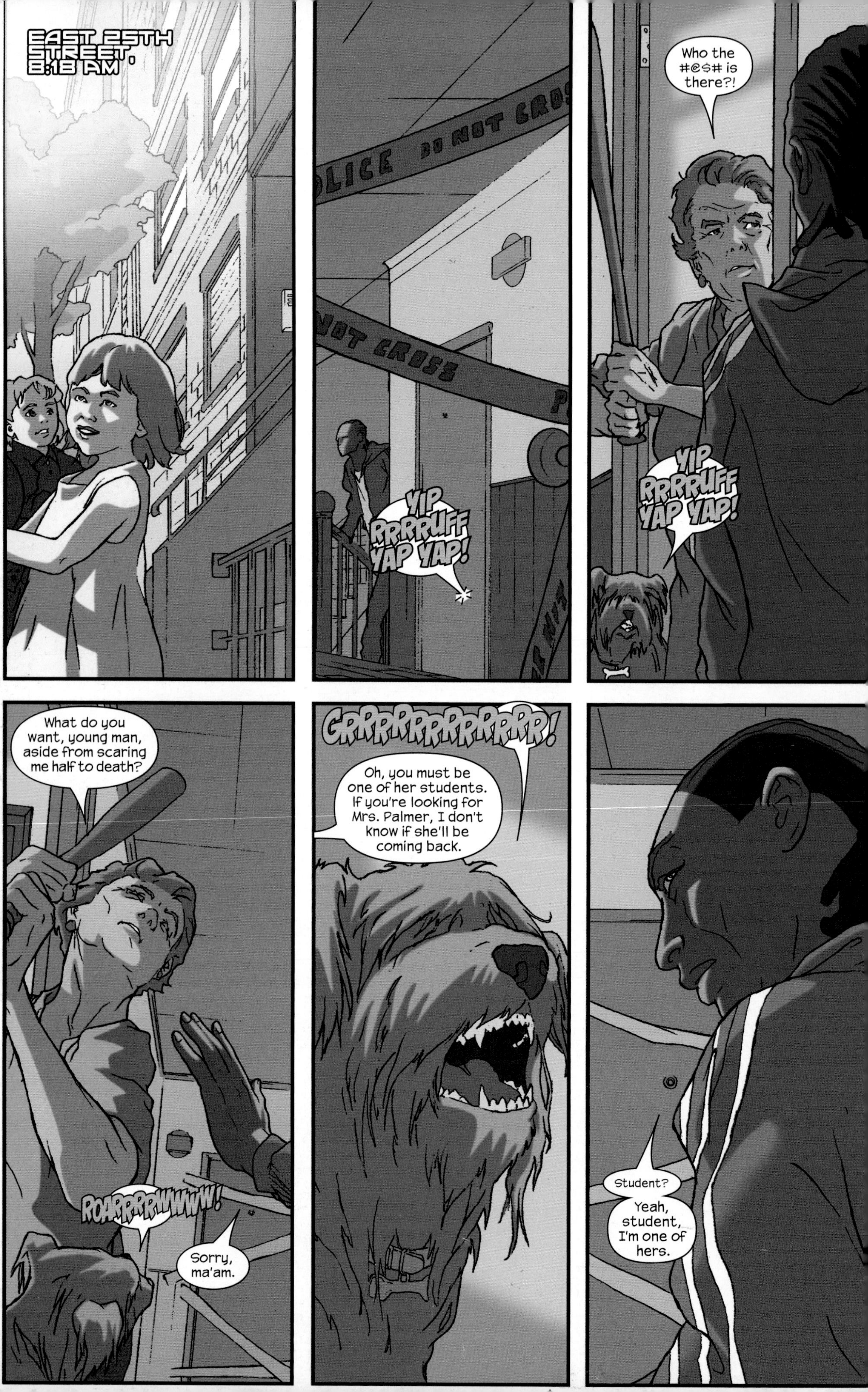
EAST 25TH STREET, 8:18 AM
YIP RRRRUFF YAP YAP!
Who the #@$# is there?!
YIP RRRRUFF YAP YAP!
What do you want, young man, aside from scaring me half to death?
ROARRRRWWWW!
Sorry, ma'am.
GRRRRRRRRRRRRR!
Oh, you must be one of her students. If you're looking for Mrs. Palmer, I don't know if she'll be coming back.
Student?
Yeah, student, I'm one of hers.

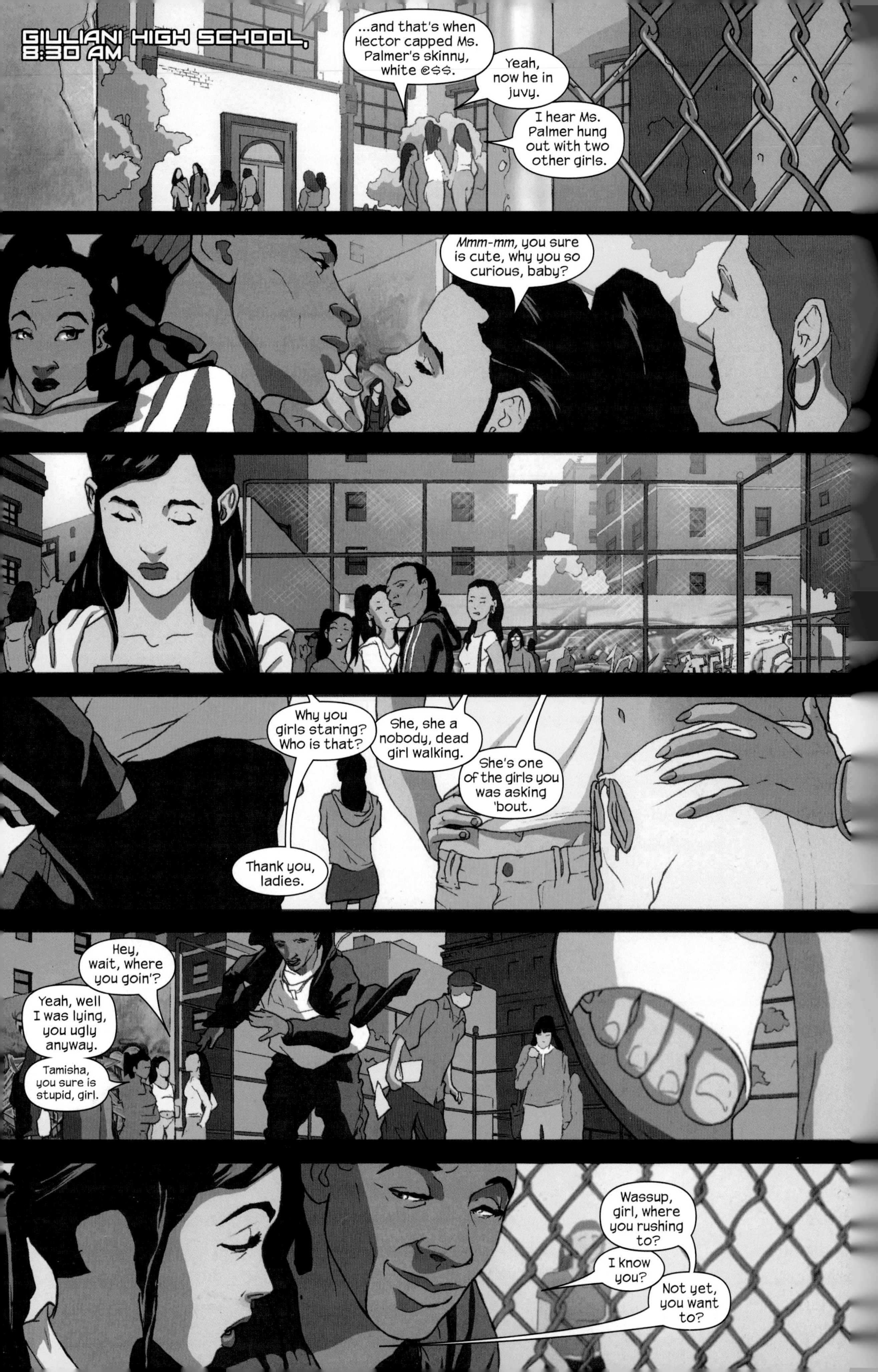
GIULIANI HIGH SCHOOL, 8:30 AM
...and that's when Hector capped Ms. Palmer's skinny, white @$$.
Yeah, now he in juvy.
I hear Ms. Palmer hung out with two other girls.
Mmm-mm, you sure is cute, why you so curious, baby?
Why you girls staring? Who is that?
She, she a nobody, dead girl walking.
She's one of the girls you was asking 'bout.
Thank you, ladies.
Hey, wait, where you goin'?
Yeah, well I was lying, you ugly anyway.
Tamisha, you sure is stupid, girl.
Wassup, girl, where you rushing to?
I know you?
Not yet, you want to?

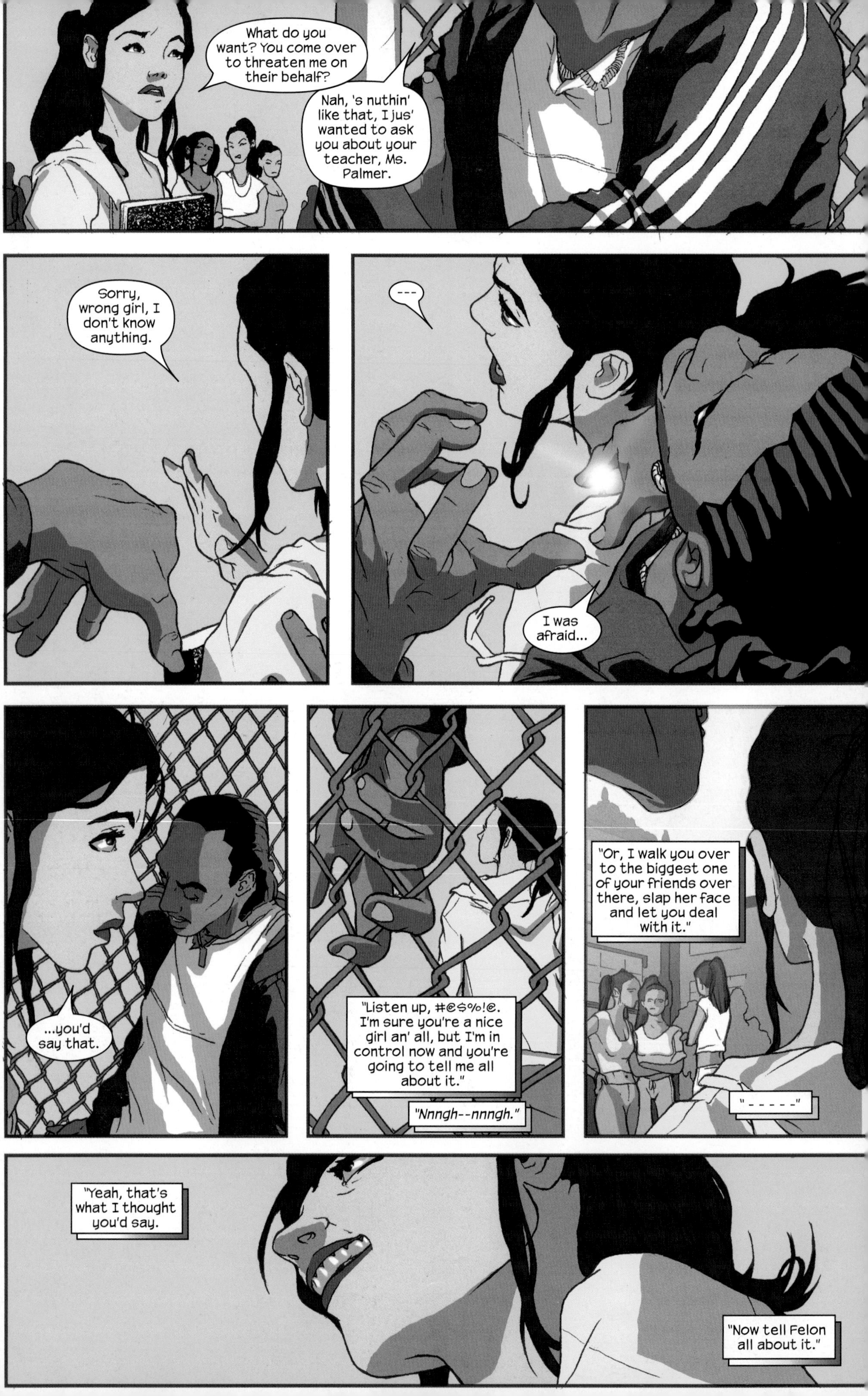
What do you want? You come over to threaten me on their behalf?
Nah, 's nuthin' like that, I jus' wanted to ask you about your teacher, Ms. Palmer.
Sorry, wrong girl, I don't know anything.

I was afraid...
...you'd say that.
"Listen up, #@$%!@. I'm sure you're a nice girl an' all, but I'm in control now and you're going to tell me all about it."
"Nnngh--nnngh."
"Or, I walk you over to the biggest one of your friends over there, slap her face and let you deal with it."
"- - - - -"
"Yeah, that's what I thought you'd say.
"Now tell Felon all about it."

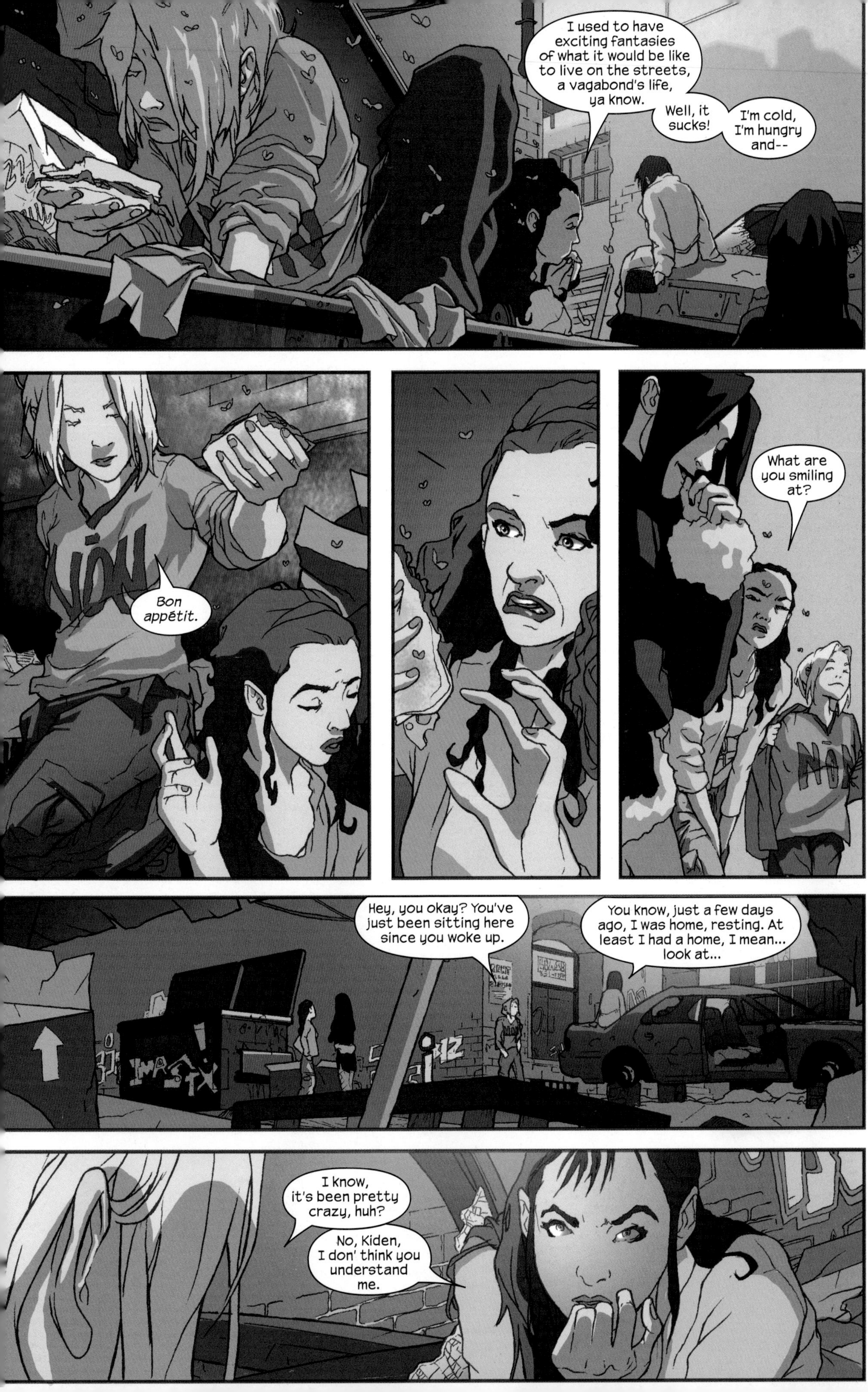
I used to have exciting fantasies of what it would be like to live on the streets, a vagabond's life, ya know.
Well, it sucks!
I'm cold, I'm hungry and--
Bon appétit.
What are you smiling at?
Hey, you okay? You've just been sitting here since you woke up.
You know, just a few days ago, I was home, resting. At least I had a home, I mean... look at...
I know, it's been pretty crazy, huh?
No, Kiden, I don' think you understand me.

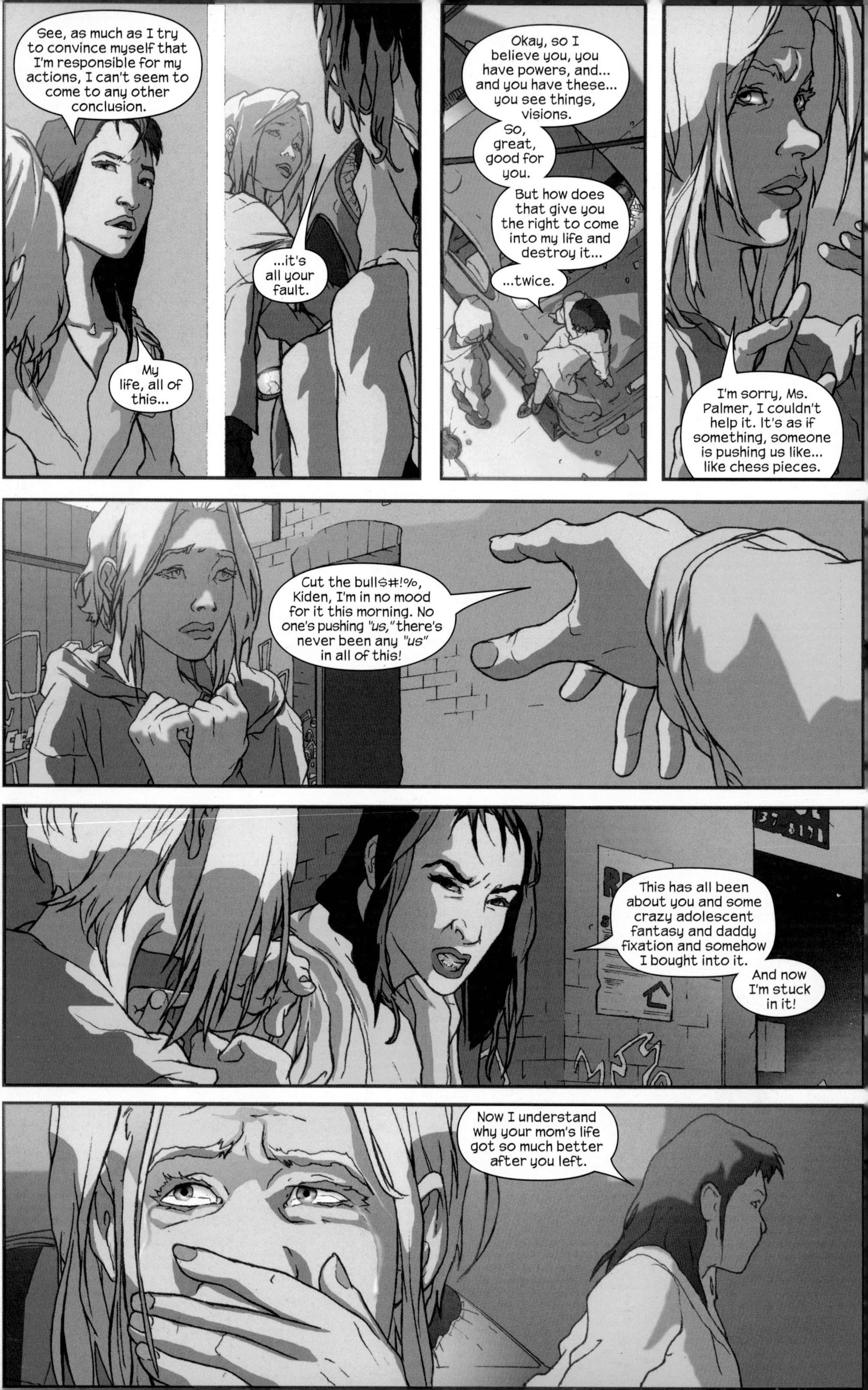
See, as much as I try to convince myself that I'm responsible for my actions, I can't seem to come to any other conclusion.
My life, all of this...
...it's all your fault.
Okay, so I believe you, you have powers, and... and you have these... you see things, visions.
So, great, good for you.
But how does that give you the right to come into my life and destroy it...
...twice.
I'm sorry, Ms. Palmer, I couldn't help it. It's as if something, someone is pushing us like... like chess pieces.
Cut the bull$#!%, Kiden, I'm in no mood for it this morning. No one's pushing *"us,"* there's never been any *"us"* in all of this!
This has all been about you and some crazy adolescent fantasy and daddy fixation and somehow I bought into it.
And now I'm stuck in it!
Now I understand why your mom's life got so much better after you left.

Whatchoo got?

Your boo's hangin' with two other girls.

Yeah, I know that.

One is named Kiden Nixon, neighborhood girl.

Alphabet City to be exact. Three brothers, single mom.

Who's the other one?

ESSEX ST

DON'T WALK

8 ESSIX

45

NIMITZ

NIXON

Soto

supt

A teacher, Cameron Palmer. You busted up her apartment yesterday. I thought you said--

That was a misunderstanding, got our signals crossed. Where they at, bro? That's all I care about.

MRS. PAL

They can be anywhere, Daddy, they beat feet, hit the streets.

Bro, I'm severely disappointed in what you're giving me here.

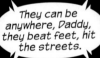

Yeah, well chill. The ways I sees it, these girls want to get out of town so they'll be coming back to teach's place to get their $#!@ together.

I suggest you get a couple of boys to camp outside her apartment and just wait.

Yeah ;sngt; you're probably right. Don't you leave ;snort; leave town until this is done.

Done? Whatchu gonna to them?

No nothin', I mean "done" like when I get my boo back.

And you can get the rest o' yo money.

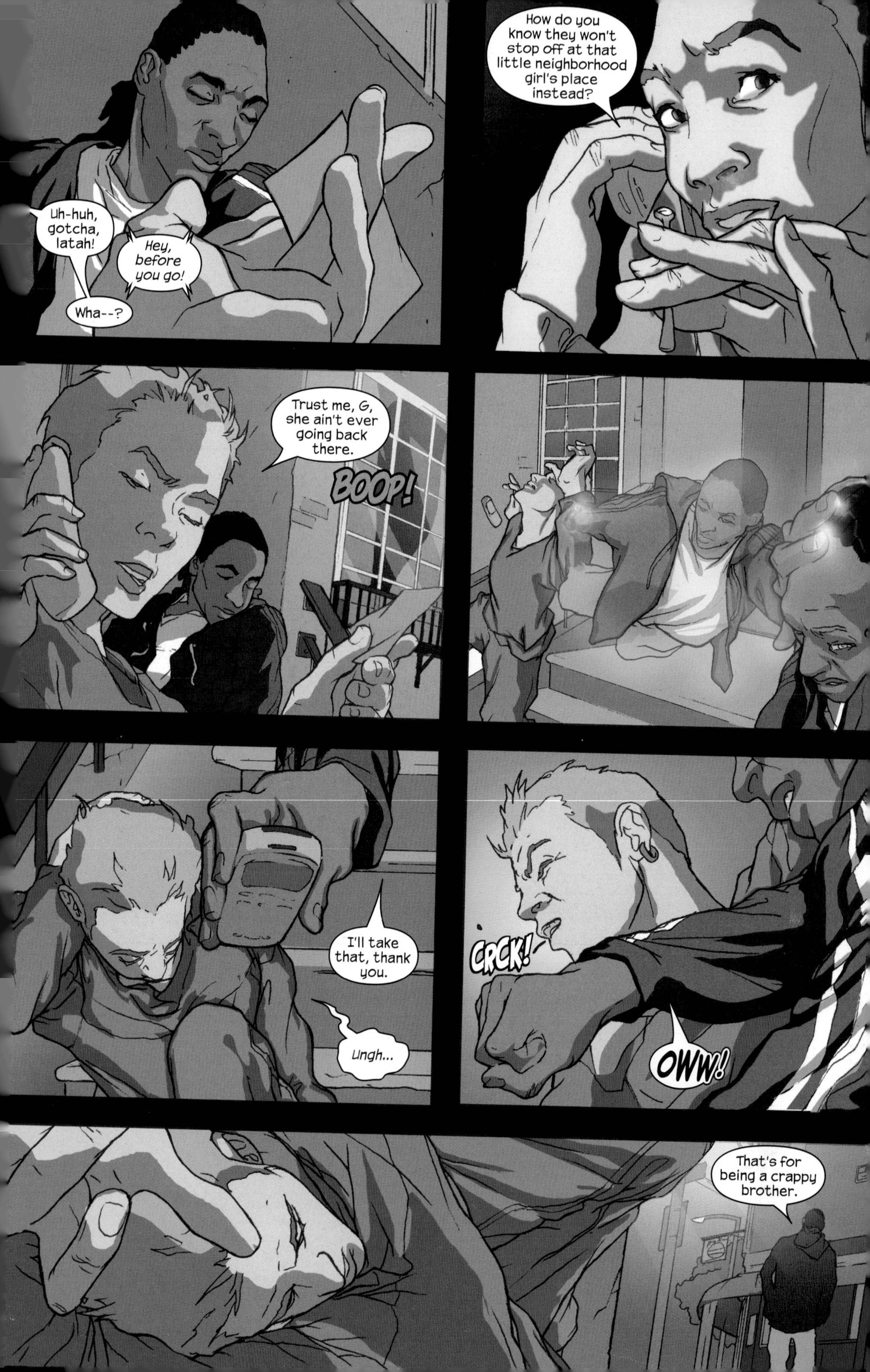
Uh-huh, gotcha, latah!
Hey, before you go!
Wha--?
How do you know they won't stop off at that little neighborhood girl's place instead?
Trust me, G, she ain't ever going back there.
BOOP!
I'll take that, thank you.
Ungh...
CRCK!
OWW!
That's for being a crappy brother.

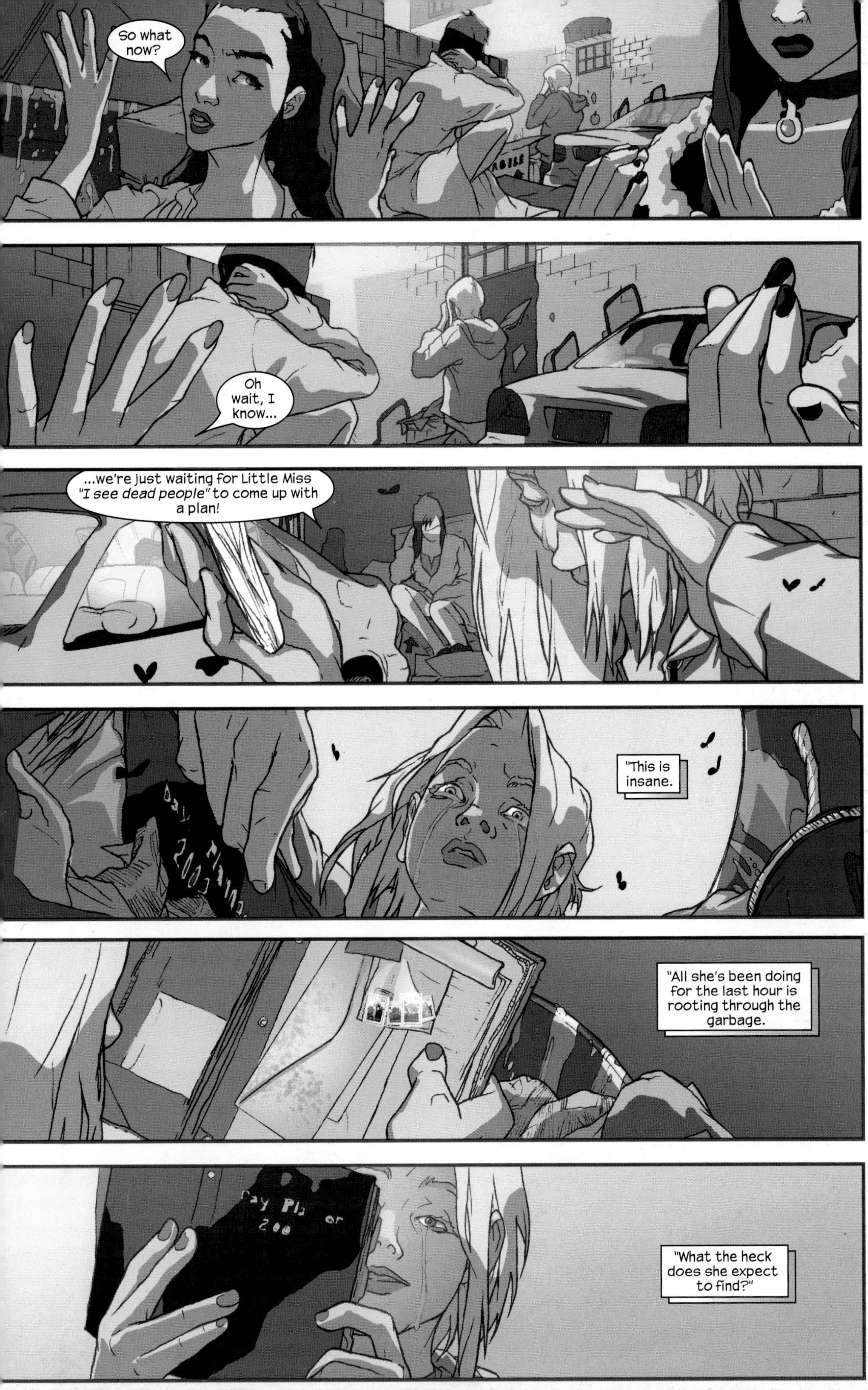

So what now?
Oh wait, I know...
...we're just waiting for Little Miss "I see dead people" to come up with a plan!
"This is insane.
"All she's been doing for the last hour is rooting through the garbage.
"What the heck does she expect to find?"

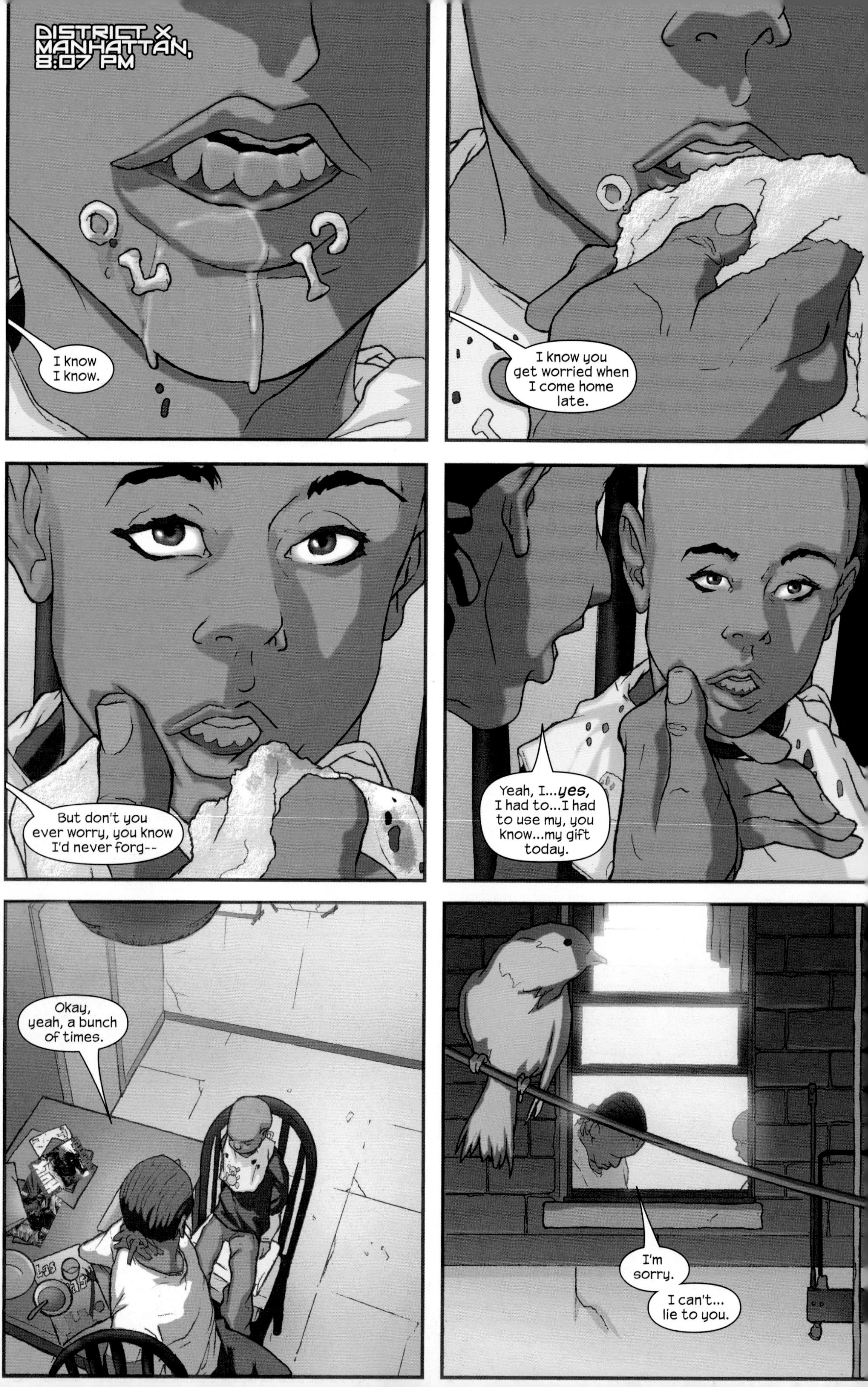
DISTRICT X, MANHATTAN, 8:07 PM
I know I know.
I know you get worried when I come home late.
But don't you ever worry, you know I'd never forg--
Yeah, I...*yes,* I had to...I had to use my, you know...my gift today.
Okay, yeah, a bunch of times.
I'm sorry.
I can't... lie to you.

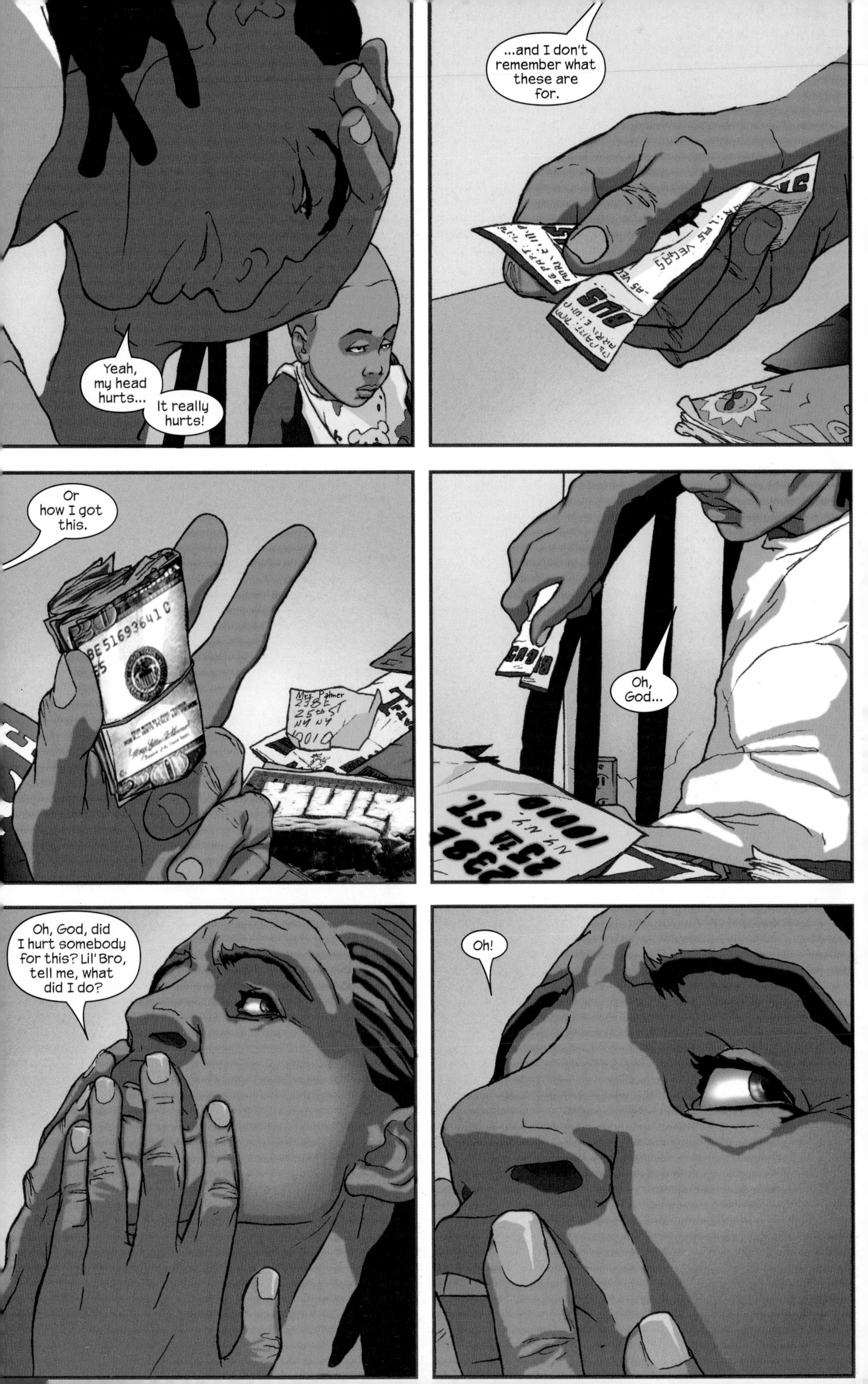
Yeah, my head hurts...
It really hurts!
...and I don't remember what these are for.
Or how I got this.
Mrs. Palmer 238 E 25th ST NY NY 10010
Oh, God...
Oh, God, did I hurt somebody for this? Lil' Bro, tell me, what did I do?
Oh!

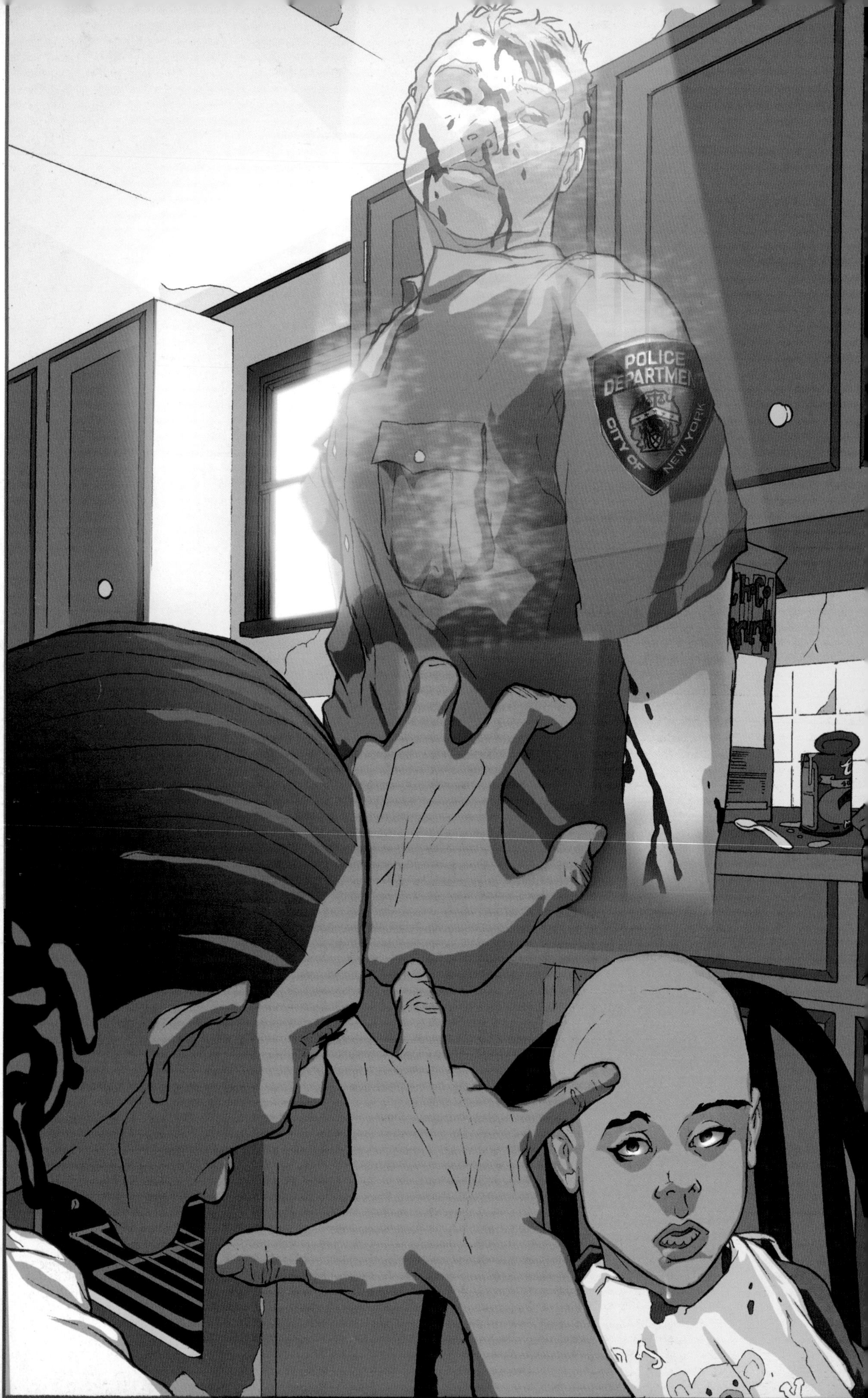
POLICE DEPARTMENT
CITY OF NEW YORK

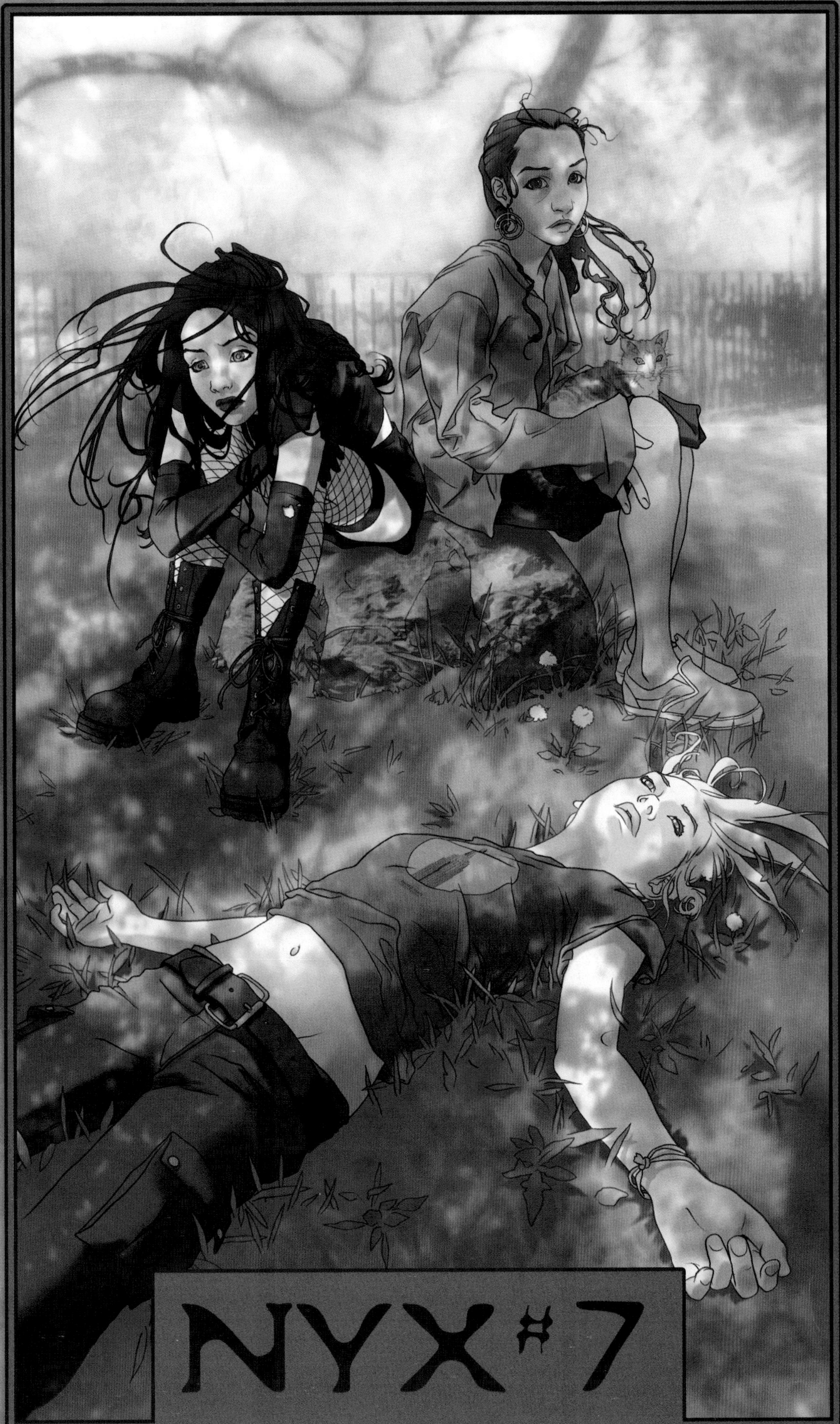
NYX #7

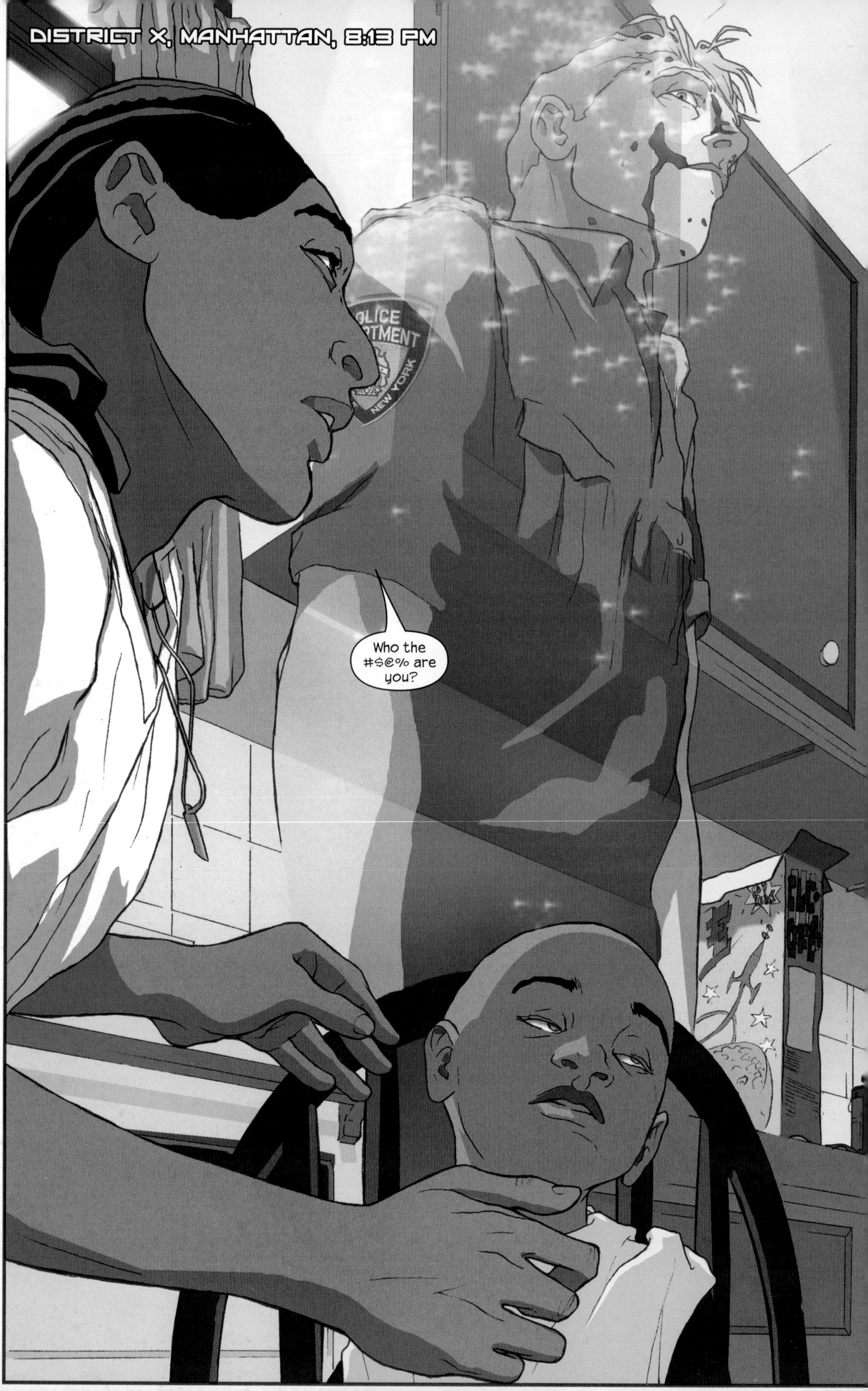
DISTRICT X, MANHATTAN, 8:13 PM
Who the #$@% are you?

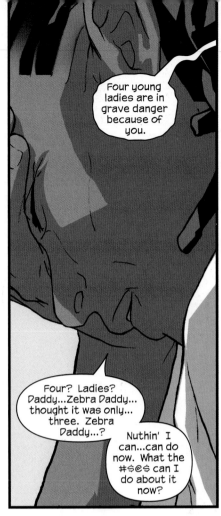

You get away right now, you get away from my little brother!

I'm not here to hurt anyone, Bobby.

How you know my name?

You've done some very bad things today, Bobby.

What are you talkin' 'bout?

Think hard, Bobby, you can remember. You know exactly what I'm talking about.

Four young ladies are in grave danger because of you.

Four? Ladies? Daddy...Zebra Daddy... thought it was only... three. Zebra Daddy...?

Nuthin' I can...can do now. What the #$@$ can I do about it now?

You know exactly what to do about it.

Huh? But Lil' Bro, I can't leave him here by himself.

Well, that's just a chance you'll have to take. Wouldn't you agree, Lil' Bro?

Mrs. Palmer
235 E 25TH ST.
NY, NY 10010

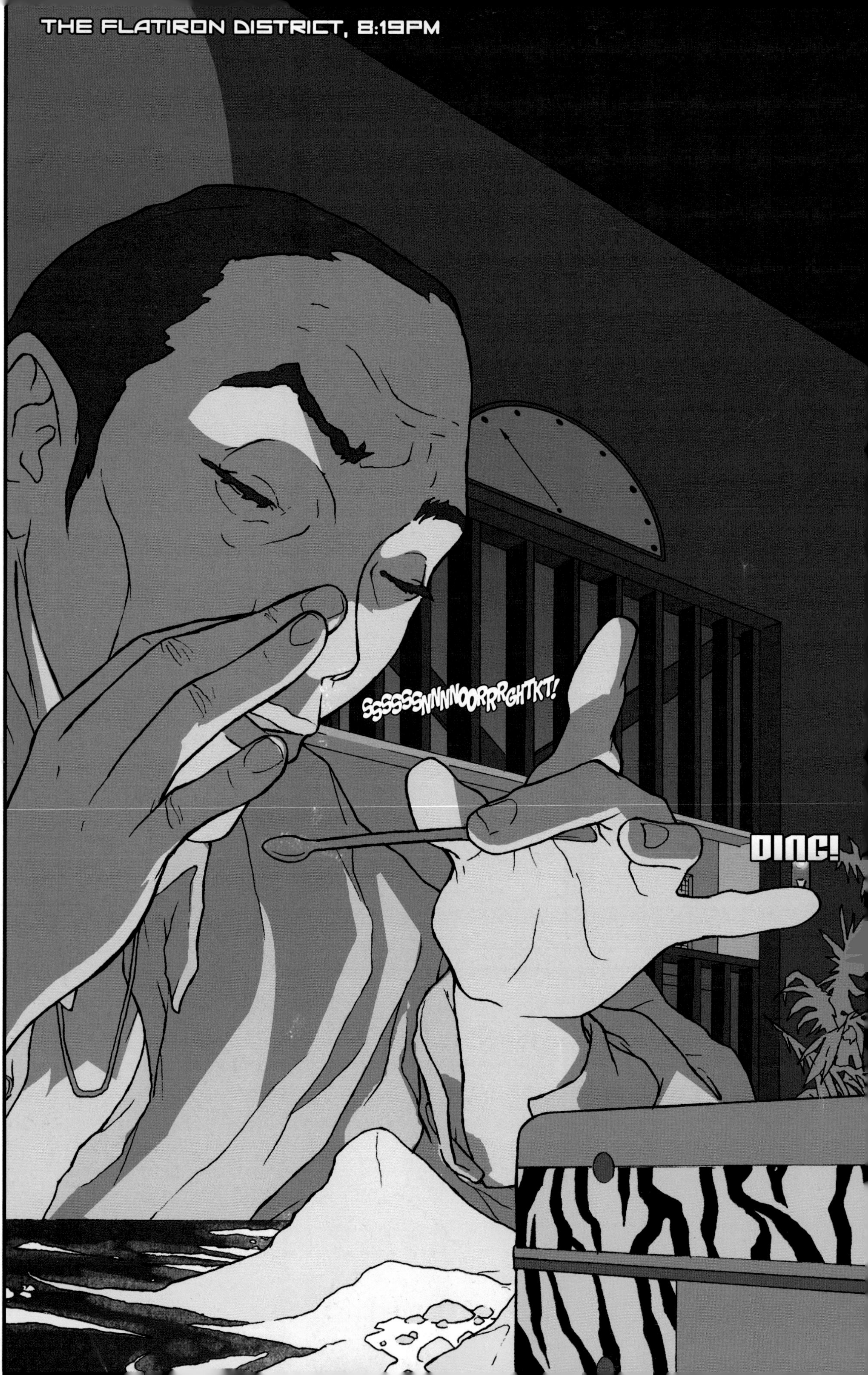
THE FLATIRON DISTRICT, 8:19PM
SSSSSSNNNNOORRRGHTKT!
DING!

Gentlemen, 's about time, I was beginnin' to think you weren't showing.

I'm sure you boys know what you're workin' for.

But you better sure as hell also know *who* you workin' for.

This isn't just 'bout money.

This ain't just 'bout pride.

This 'bout some lowly skank thought she can run out on me.

This 'bout the way we live, bruthas!

Ain't no bitch gonna $#@$ wit' dat, right!?

RIGHT!

Ain't no bitch gonna give others ideas, right!?

RIGHT!

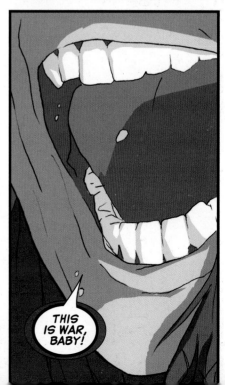

THIS IS WAR, BABY!

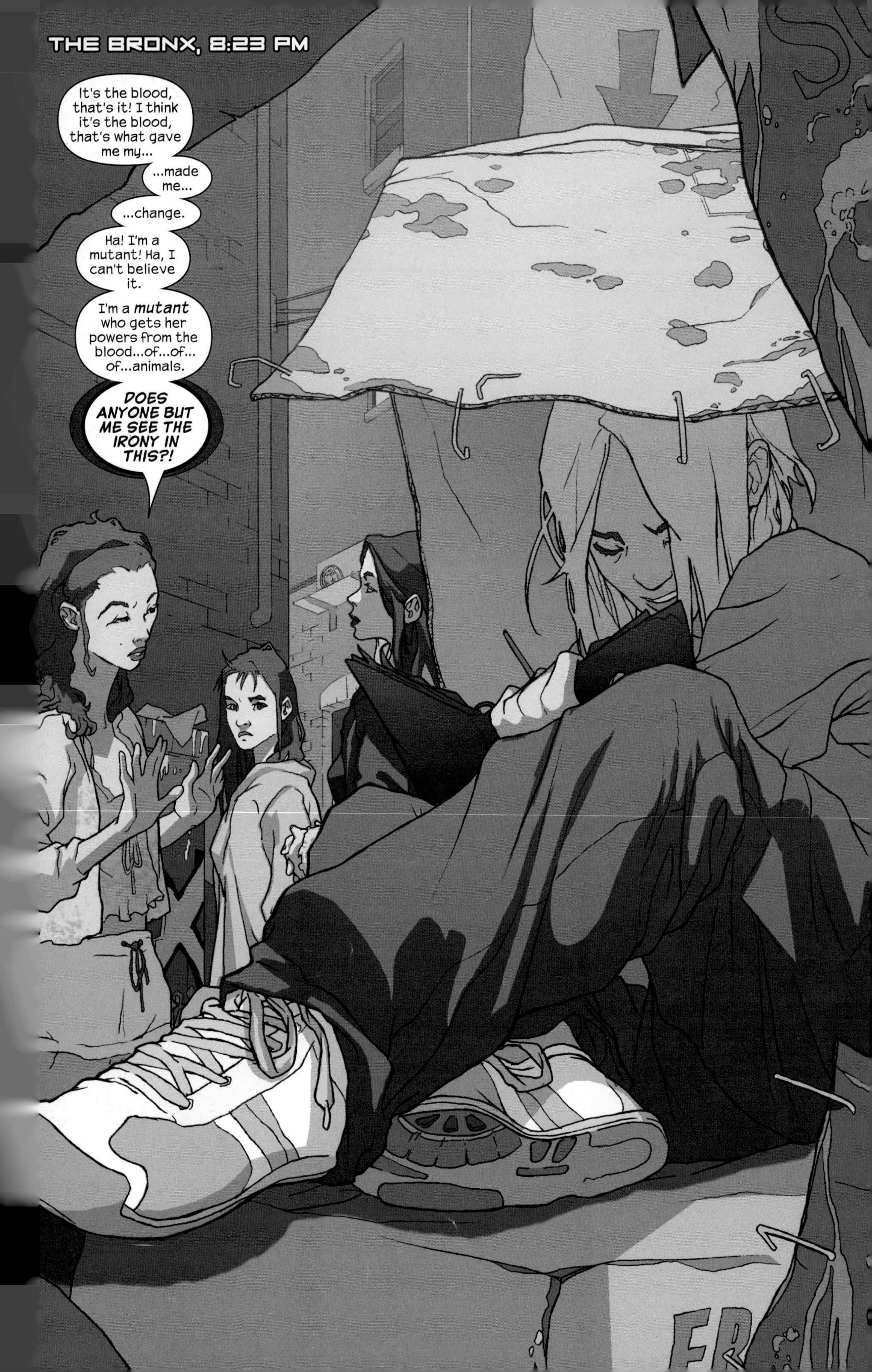
THE BRONX, 8:23 PM
It's the blood, that's it! I think it's the blood, that's what gave me my...
...made me...
...change.
Ha! I'm a mutant! Ha, I can't believe it.
I'm a *mutant* who gets her powers from the blood...of...of... of...animals.
DOES ANYONE BUT ME SEE THE IRONY IN THIS?!

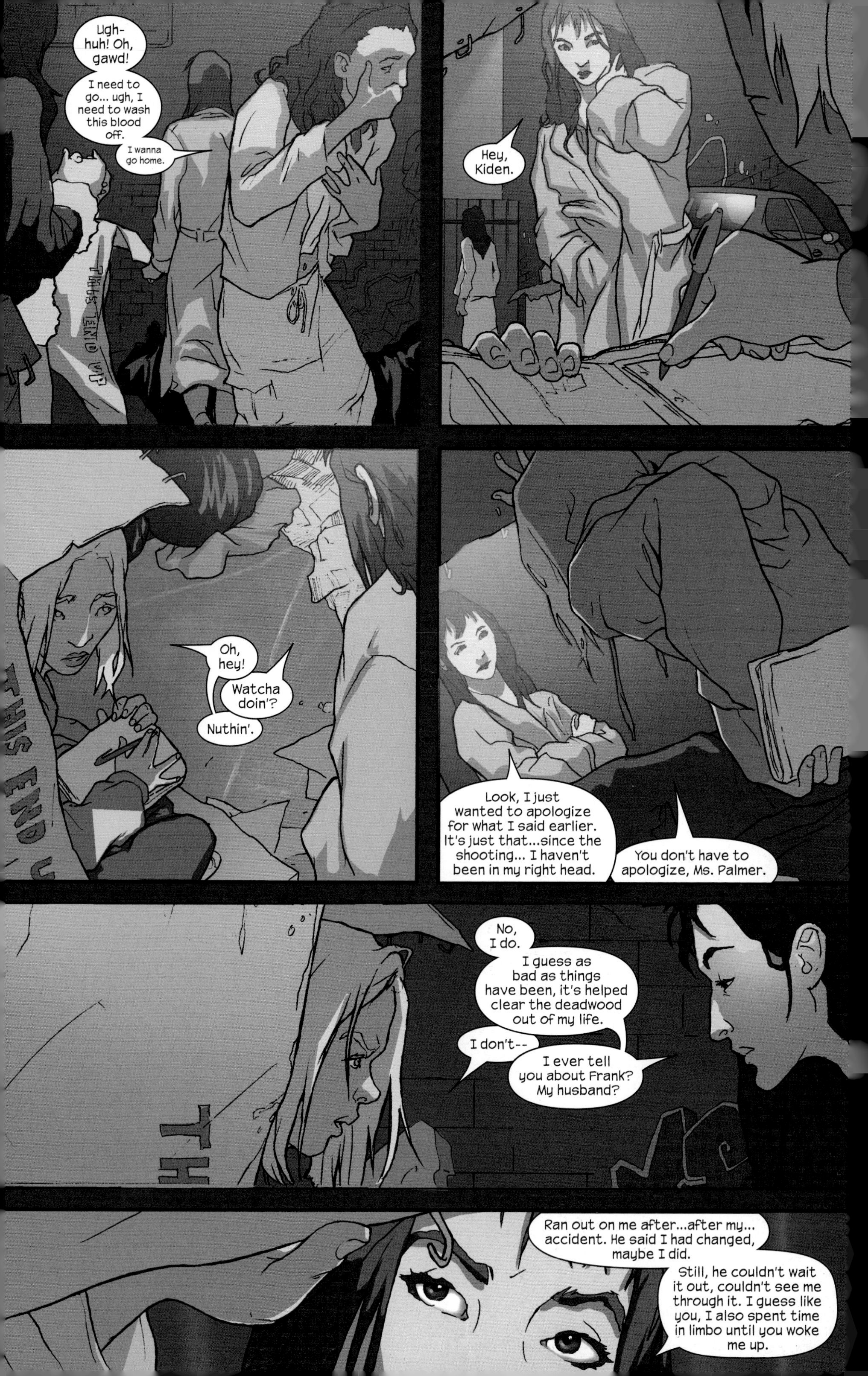
Ugh-huh! Oh, gawd!
I need to go... ugh, I need to wash this blood off.
I wanna go home.
THIS END UP
Hey, Kiden.
THIS END U
Oh, hey!
Watcha doin'?
Nuthin'.
Look, I just wanted to apologize for what I said earlier. It's just that...since the shooting... I haven't been in my right head.
You don't have to apologize, Ms. Palmer.
No, I do.
I guess as bad as things have been, it's helped clear the deadwood out of my life.
I don't--
I ever tell you about Frank? My husband?
TH
Ran out on me after...after my... accident. He said I had changed, maybe I did.
Still, he couldn't wait it out, couldn't see me through it. I guess like you, I also spent time in limbo until you woke me up.

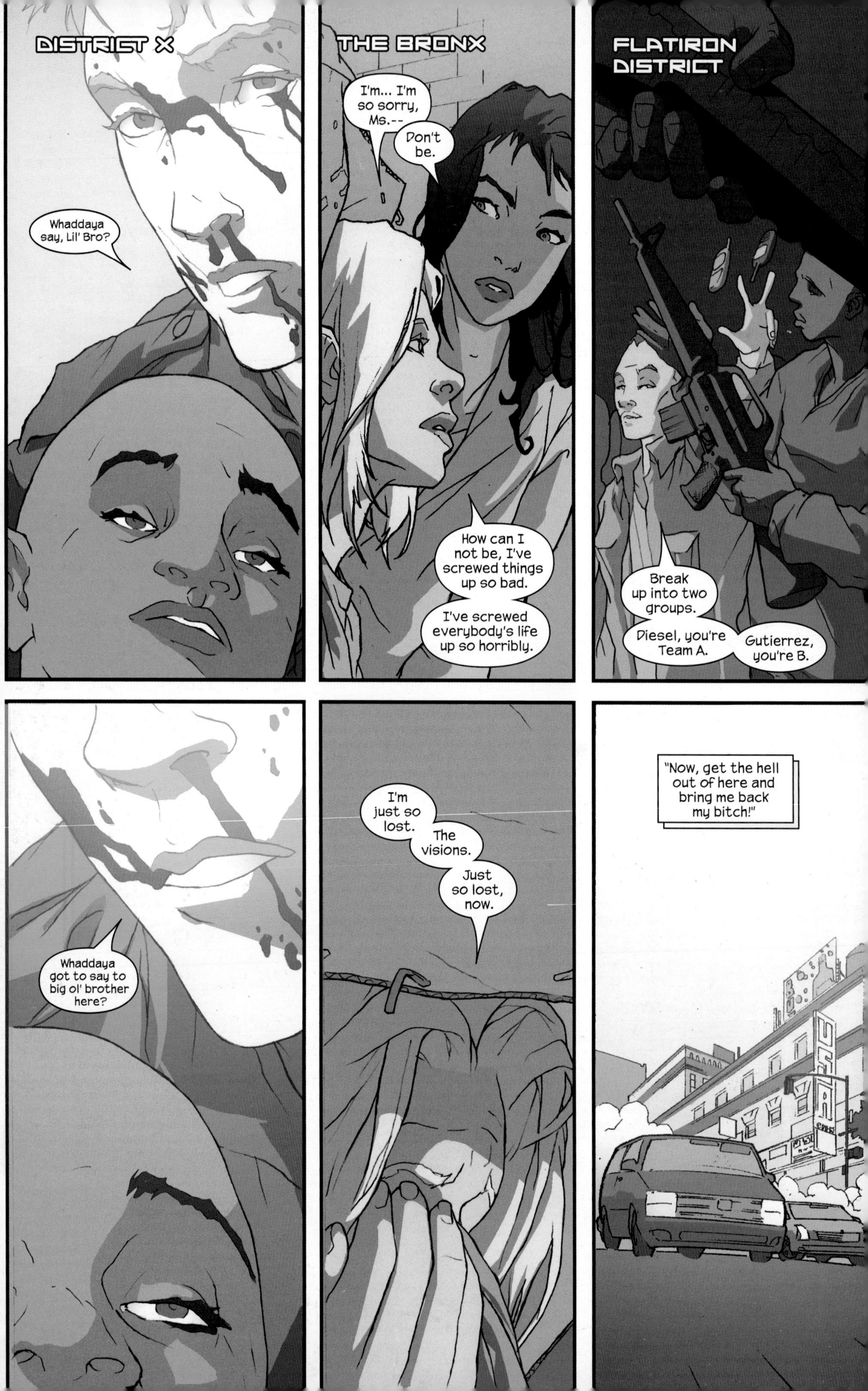
DISTRICT X
Whaddaya say, Lil' Bro?
THE BRONX
I'm... I'm so sorry, Ms.--
Don't be.
How can I not be, I've screwed things up so bad.
I've screwed everybody's life up so horribly.
FLATIRON DISTRICT
Break up into two groups.
Diesel, you're Team A.
Gutierrez, you're B.
Whaddaya got to say to big ol' brother here?
I'm just so lost.
The visions.
Just so lost, now.
"Now, get the hell out of here and bring me back my bitch!"

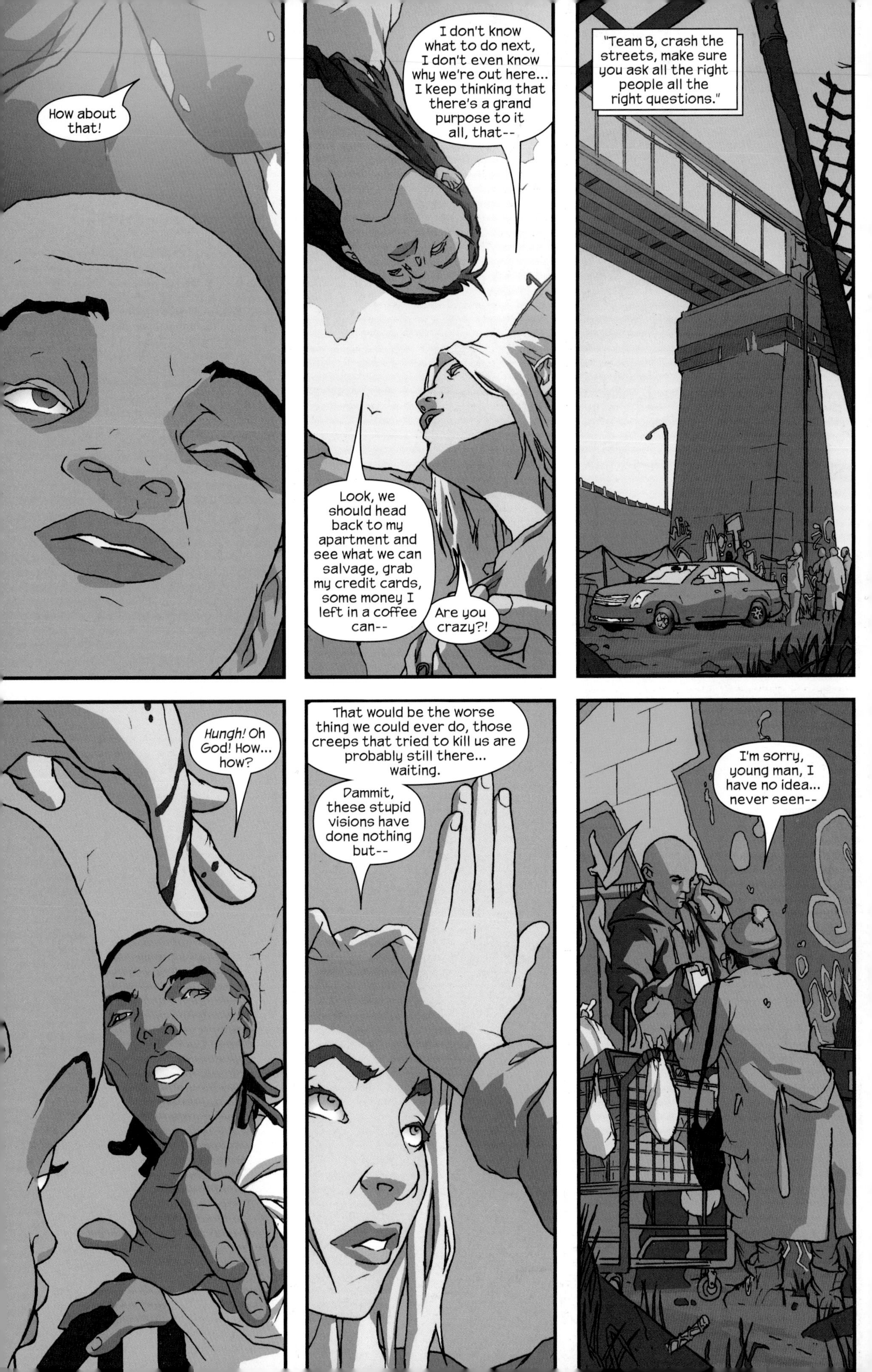
How about that!
I don't know what to do next, I don't even know why we're out here... I keep thinking that there's a grand purpose to it all, that--
Look, we should head back to my apartment and see what we can salvage, grab my credit cards, some money I left in a coffee can--
Are you crazy?!
"Team B, crash the streets, make sure you ask all the right people all the right questions."
Hungh! Oh God! How... how?
That would be the worse thing we could ever do, those creeps that tried to kill us are probably still there... waiting.
Dammit, these stupid visions have done nothing but--
I'm sorry, young man, I have no idea... never seen--

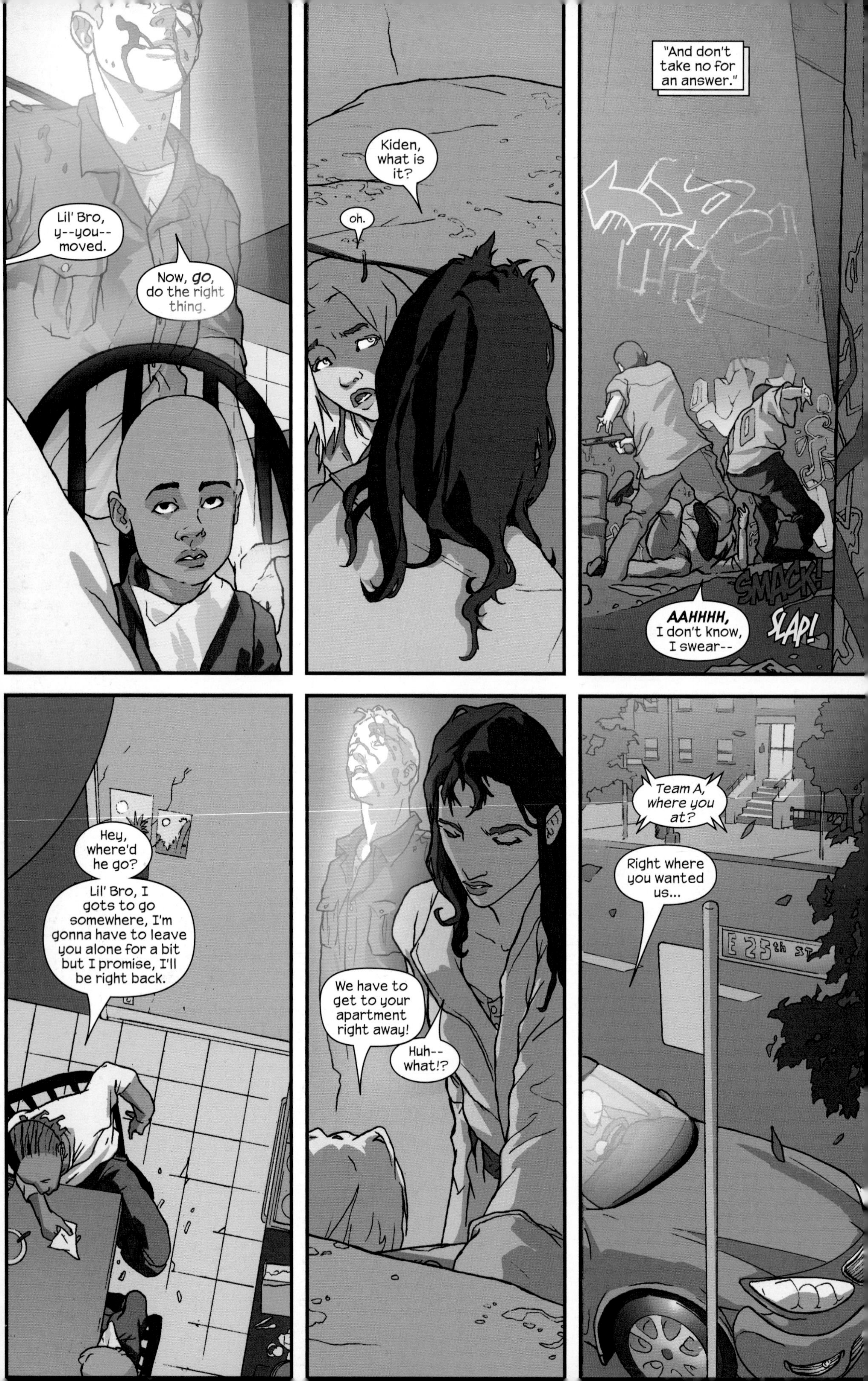
Lil' Bro, y--you-- moved.
Now, GO, do the right thing.
Kiden, what is it?
oh.
"And don't take no for an answer."
SMACK!
AAHHHH, I don't know, I swear--
SLAP!
Hey, where'd he go?
Lil' Bro, I gots to go somewhere, I'm gonna have to leave you alone for a bit but I promise, I'll be right back.
We have to get to your apartment right away!
Huh-- what!?
Team A, where you at?
Right where you wanted us...
E 25th ST

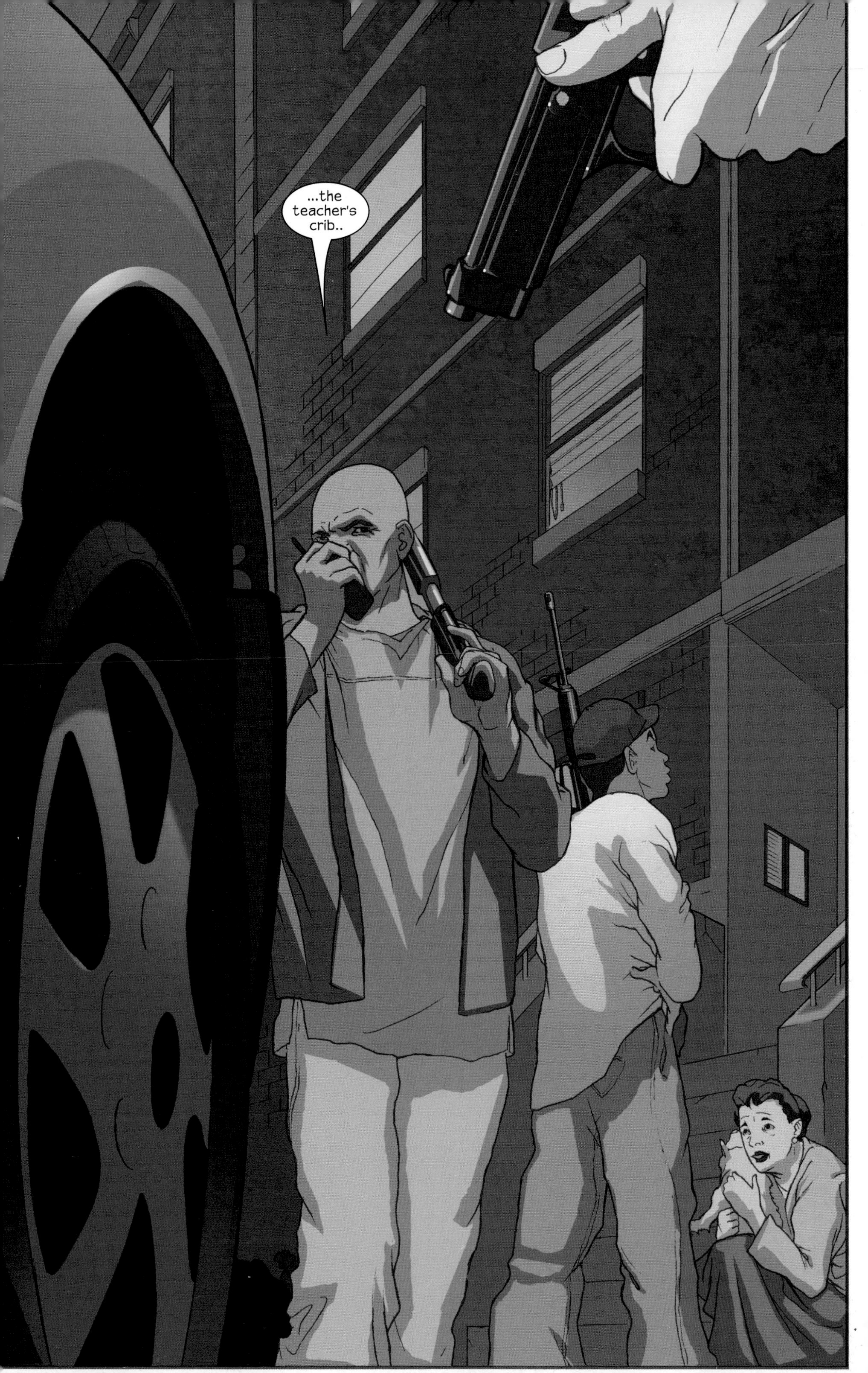
...the teacher's crib..

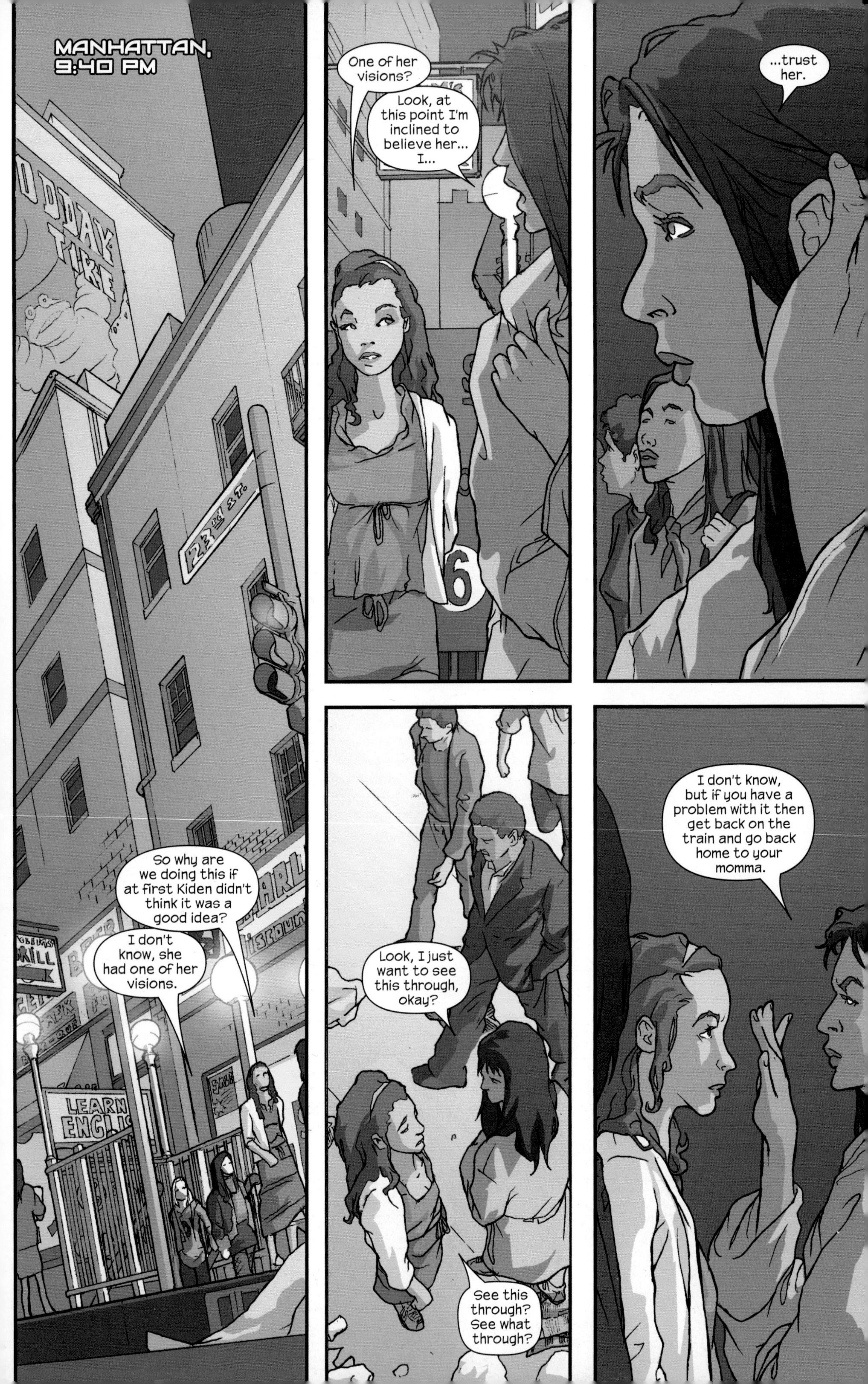
MANHATTAN, 9:40 PM
So why are we doing this if at first Kiden didn't think it was a good idea?
I don't know, she had one of her visions.
LEARN ENGLI
One of her visions?
Look, at this point I'm inclined to believe her... I...
...trust her.
Look, I just want to see this through, okay?
See this through? See what through?
I don't know, but if you have a problem with it then get back on the train and go back home to your momma.

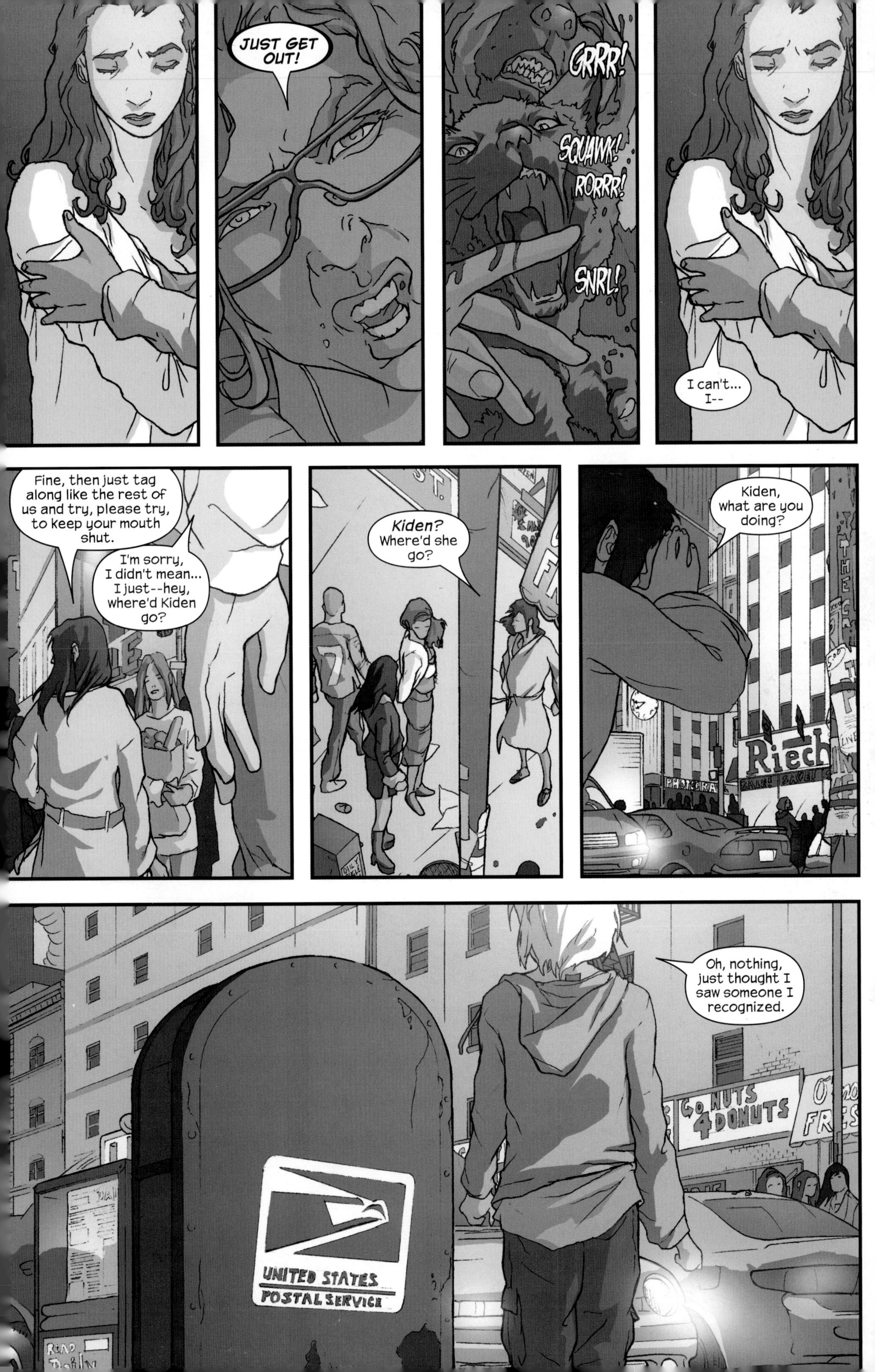
JUST GET OUT!
GRRR!
SQUAWK!
RORRR!
SNRL!
I can't... I--
Fine, then just tag along like the rest of us and try, please try, to keep your mouth shut.
I'm sorry, I didn't mean... I just--hey, where'd Kiden go?
Kiden? Where'd she go?
Kiden, what are you doing?
Riech
SALE! SAVE!
Oh, nothing, just thought I saw someone I recognized.
GO NUTS 4 DONUTS
UNITED STATES
POSTAL SERVICE

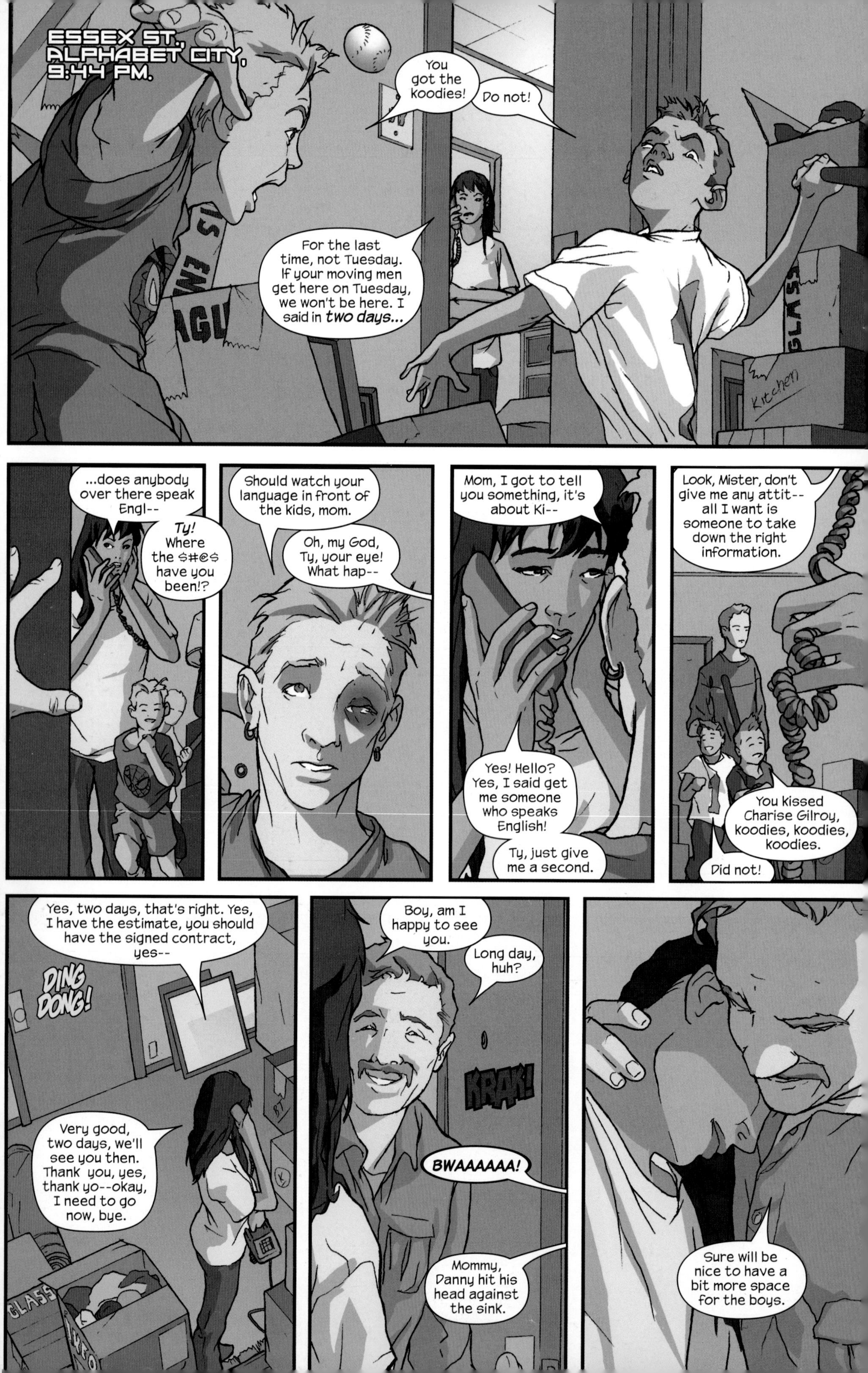
ESSEX ST., ALPHABET CITY, 9:44 PM.
You got the koodies!
Do not!
For the last time, not Tuesday. If your moving men get here on Tuesday, we won't be here. I said in *two days...*
...does anybody over there speak Engl--
Ty! Where the $#@$ have you been!?
Should watch your language in front of the kids, mom.
Oh, my God, Ty, your eye! What hap--
Mom, I got to tell you something, it's about Ki--
Yes! Hello? Yes, I said get me someone who speaks English!
Ty, just give me a second.
Look, Mister, don't give me any attit-- all I want is someone to take down the right information.
You kissed Charise Gilroy, koodies, koodies, koodies.
Did not!
Yes, two days, that's right. Yes, I have the estimate, you should have the signed contract, yes--
DING DONG!
Very good, two days, we'll see you then. Thank you, yes, thank yo--okay, I need to go now, bye.
Boy, am I happy to see you.
Long day, huh?
KRAK!
BWAAAAAA!
Mommy, Danny hit his head against the sink.
Sure will be nice to have a bit more space for the boys.

Okay, what's wrong?

You know what's wrong. It's just, my... my little girl. I can't believe we're leaving without--

Babe, I know what you're going through but even the police--

I know what they say, it just doesn't change how I feel.

Look, we won't ever stop looking for Kiden. If she's alive and out there, we'll find her or she'll find us.

I don't know, will she? Are we doing the right thing by moving?

Babe, we can't put our lives on hold because of this. This neighborhood is $#!@ and you need to think about your children that are here with you now. For god sake, Ty is dealing--

Oh my God, Ty!

Ty I'm sorry, there was something you needed to tell me?

That's for being a crappy brother.

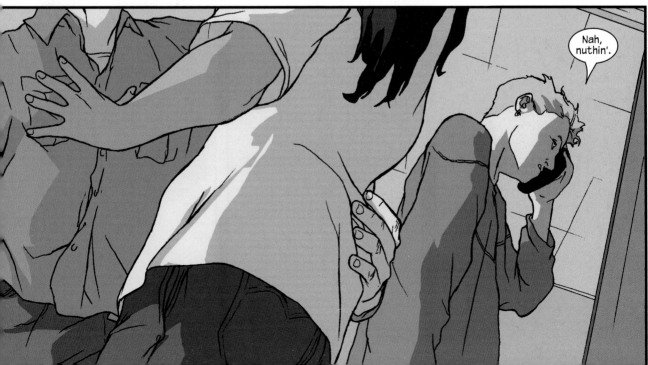

Nah, nuthin'.

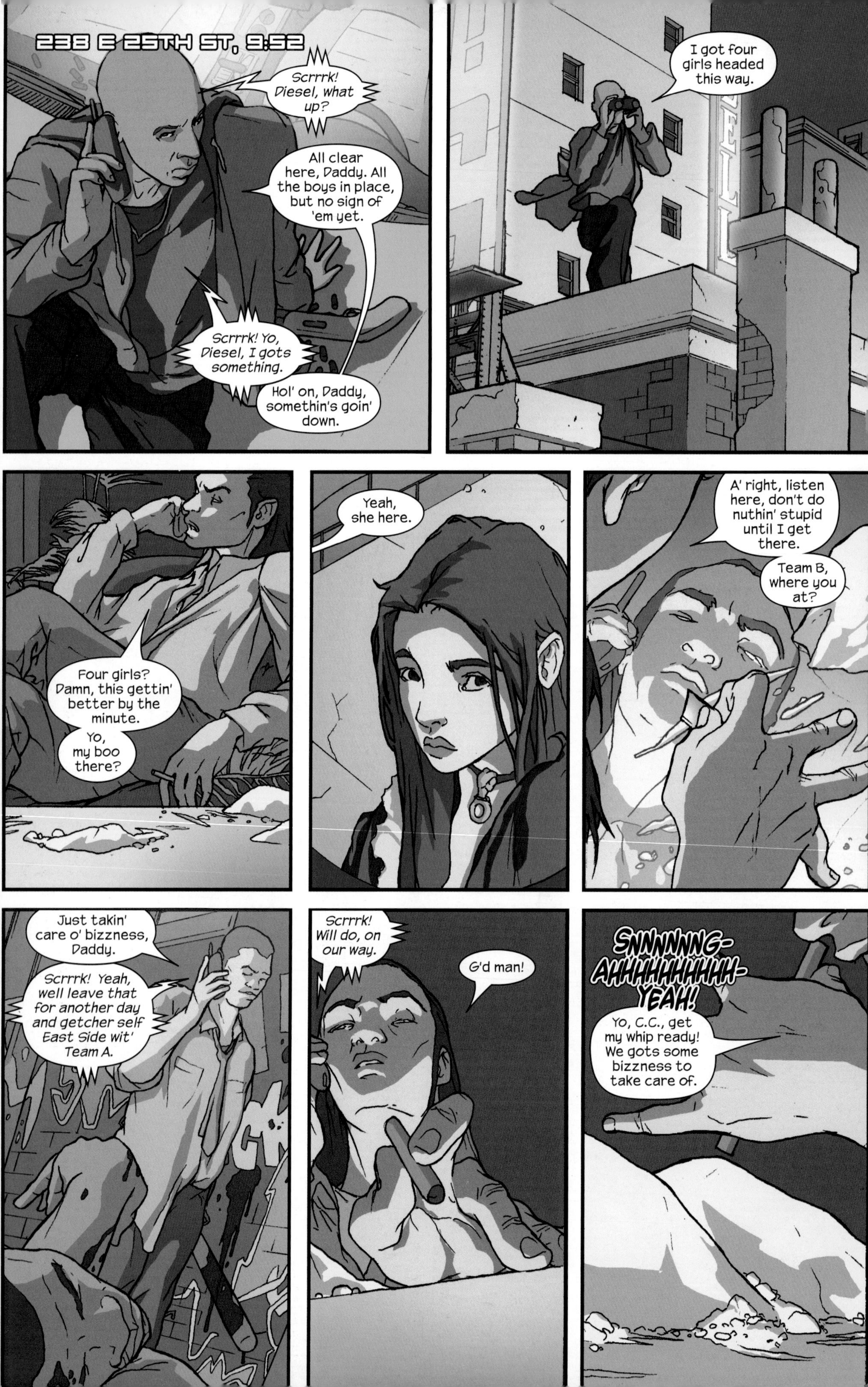
238 E 25TH ST, 9:52
Scrrrk! Diesel, what up?
All clear here, Daddy. All the boys in place, but no sign of 'em yet.
Scrrrk! Yo, Diesel, I gots something.
Hol' on, Daddy, somethin's goin' down.
I got four girls headed this way.
Four girls? Damn, this gettin' better by the minute.
Yo, my boo there?
Yeah, she here.
A' right, listen here, don't do nuthin' stupid until I get there.
Team B, where you at?
Just takin' care o' bizzness, Daddy.
Scrrrk! Yeah, well leave that for another day and getcher self East Side wit' Team A.
Scrrrk! Will do, on our way.
G'd man!
SNNNNNG-AHHHHHHHHH-YEAH!
Yo, C.C., get my whip ready! We gots some bizzness to take care of.

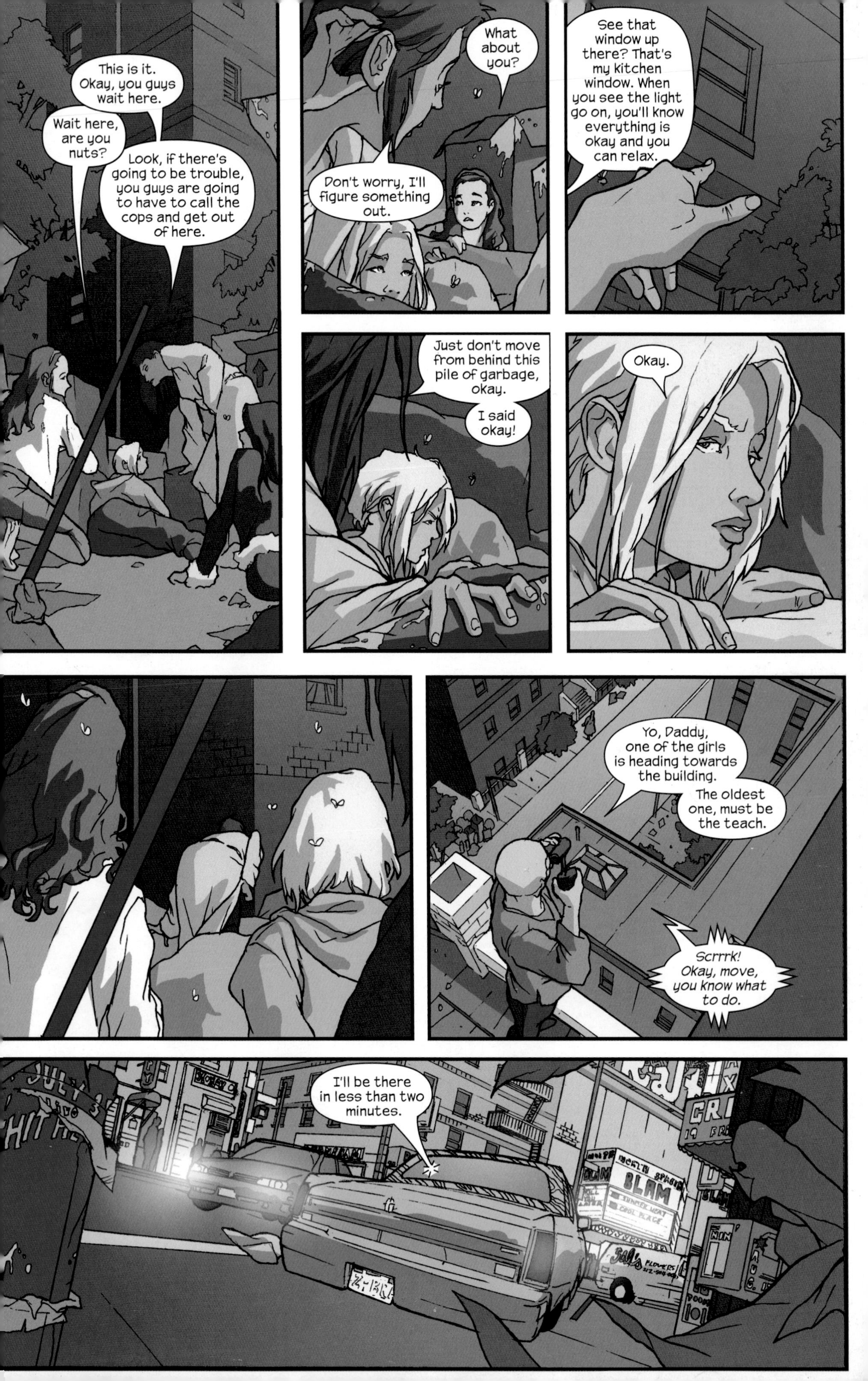
This is it. Okay, you guys wait here.
Wait here, are you nuts?
Look, if there's going to be trouble, you guys are going to have to call the cops and get out of here.
What about you?
Don't worry, I'll figure something out.
See that window up there? That's my kitchen window. When you see the light go on, you'll know everything is okay and you can relax.
Just don't move from behind this pile of garbage, okay.
I said okay!
Okay.
Yo, Daddy, one of the girls is heading towards the building.
The oldest one, must be the teach.
Scrrrk! Okay, move, you know what to do.
I'll be there in less than two minutes.
BLAM

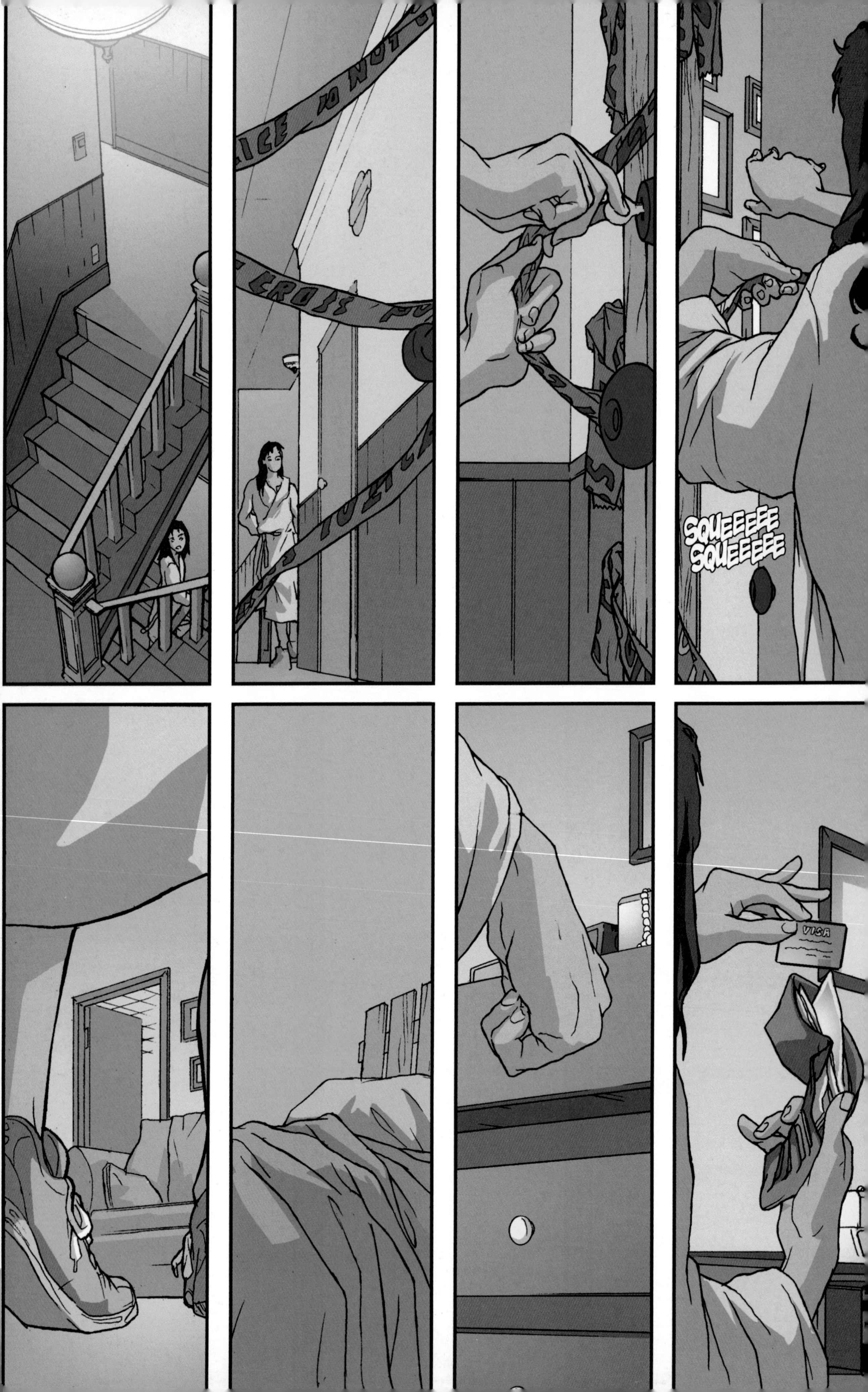
POLICE DO NOT CROSS
SQUEEEEE
SQUEEEEE
VISA

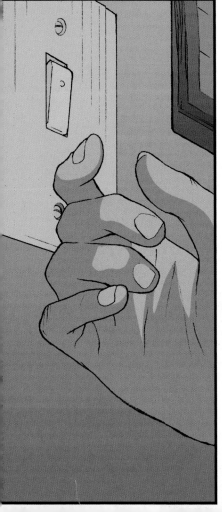

Not a word out of you, beeyatch!

UGH-KT!!!

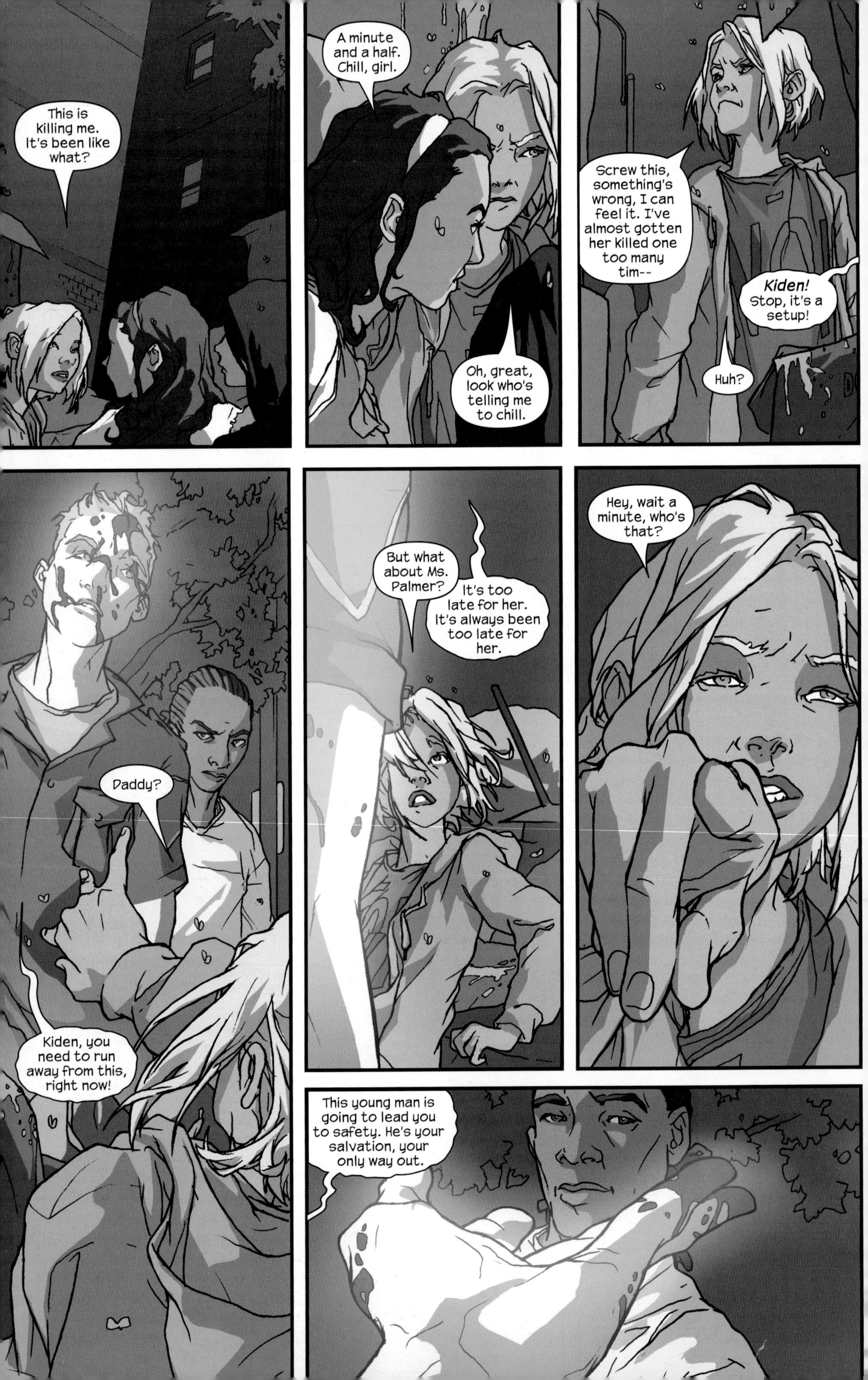
This is killing me. It's been like what?
A minute and a half. Chill, girl.
Oh, great, look who's telling me to chill.
Screw this, something's wrong, I can feel it. I've almost gotten her killed one too many tim--
Kiden! Stop, it's a setup!
Huh?
Daddy?
Kiden, you need to run away from this, right now!
But what about Ms. Palmer?
It's too late for her. It's always been too late for her.
Hey, wait a minute, who's that?
This young man is going to lead you to safety. He's your salvation, your only way out.

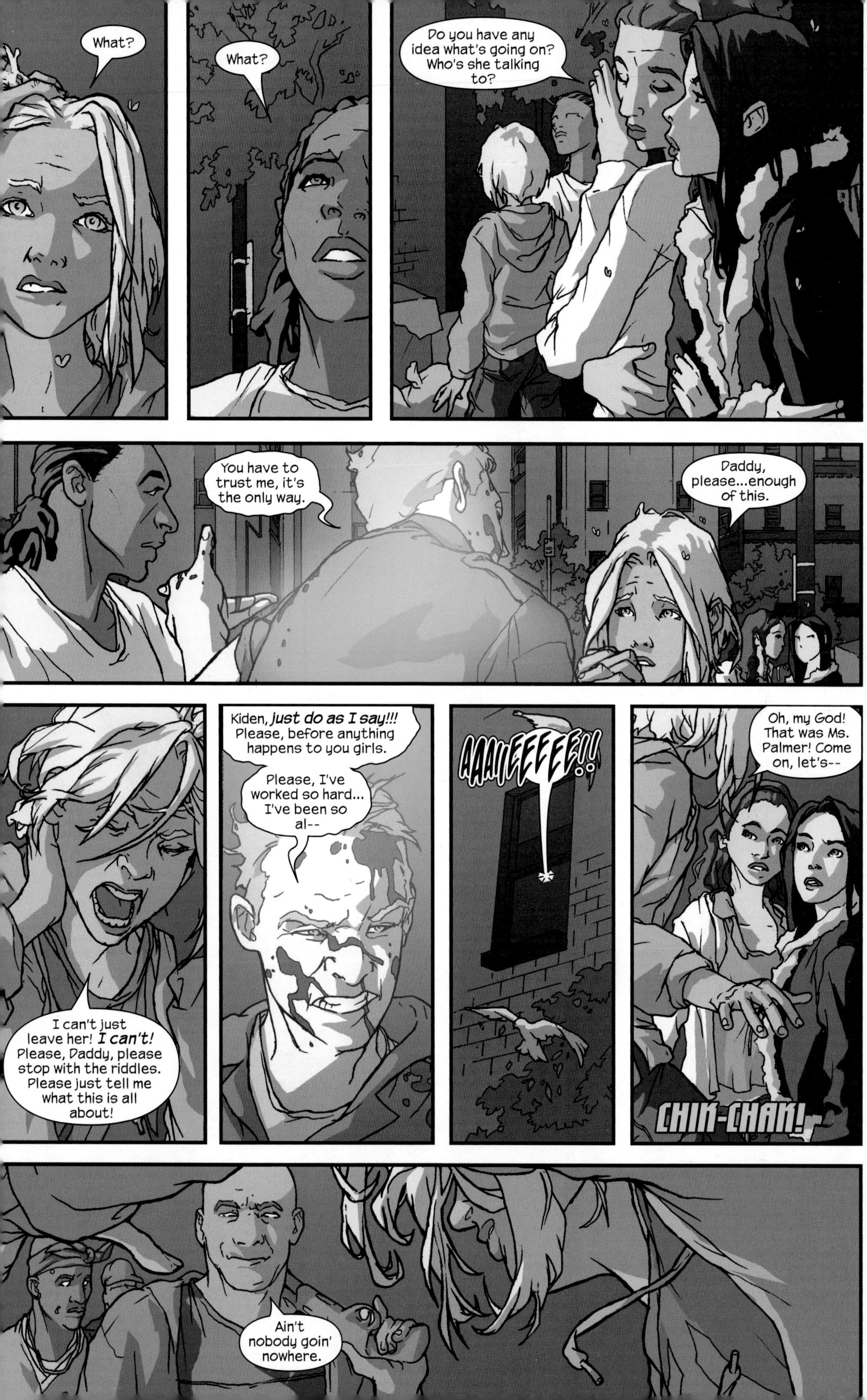
What?
What?
Do you have any idea what's going on? Who's she talking to?
You have to trust me, it's the only way.
Daddy, please...enough of this.
I can't just leave her! I can't! Please, Daddy, please stop with the riddles. Please just tell me what this is all about!
Kiden, just do as I say!!! Please, before anything happens to you girls.
Please, I've worked so hard... I've been so al--
AAAIIEEEEE!!!
Oh, my God! That was Ms. Palmer! Come on, let's--
CHIK-CHAK!
Ain't nobody goin' nowhere.

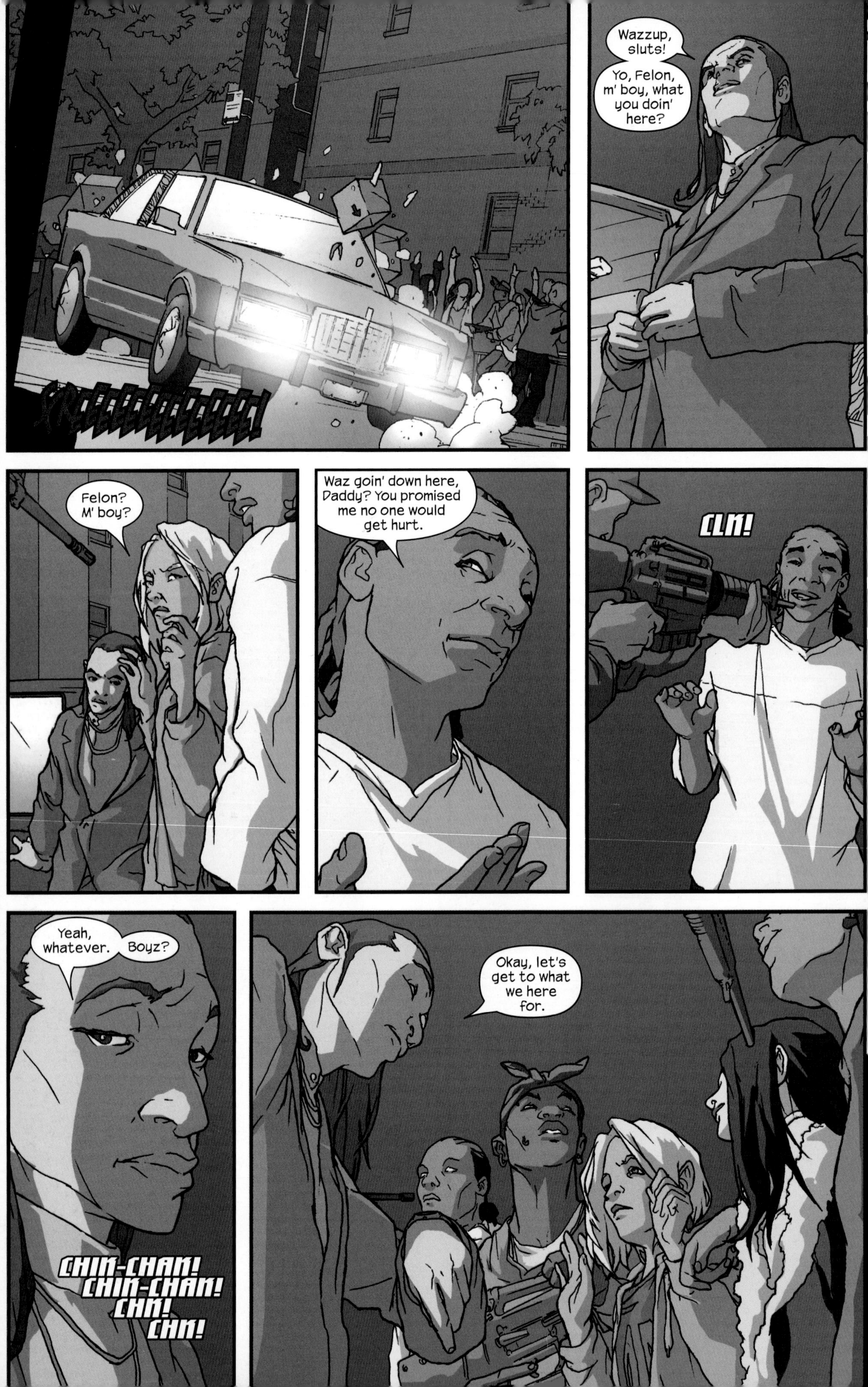
SKREEEEEEEEEEEEEEE!
Wazzup, sluts!
Yo, Felon, m' boy, what you doin' here?
Felon? M' boy?
Waz goin' down here, Daddy? You promised me no one would get hurt.
CLN!
Yeah, whatever.
Boyz?
CHIN-CHAN! CHIN-CHAN! CHN! CHN!
Okay, let's get to what we here for.

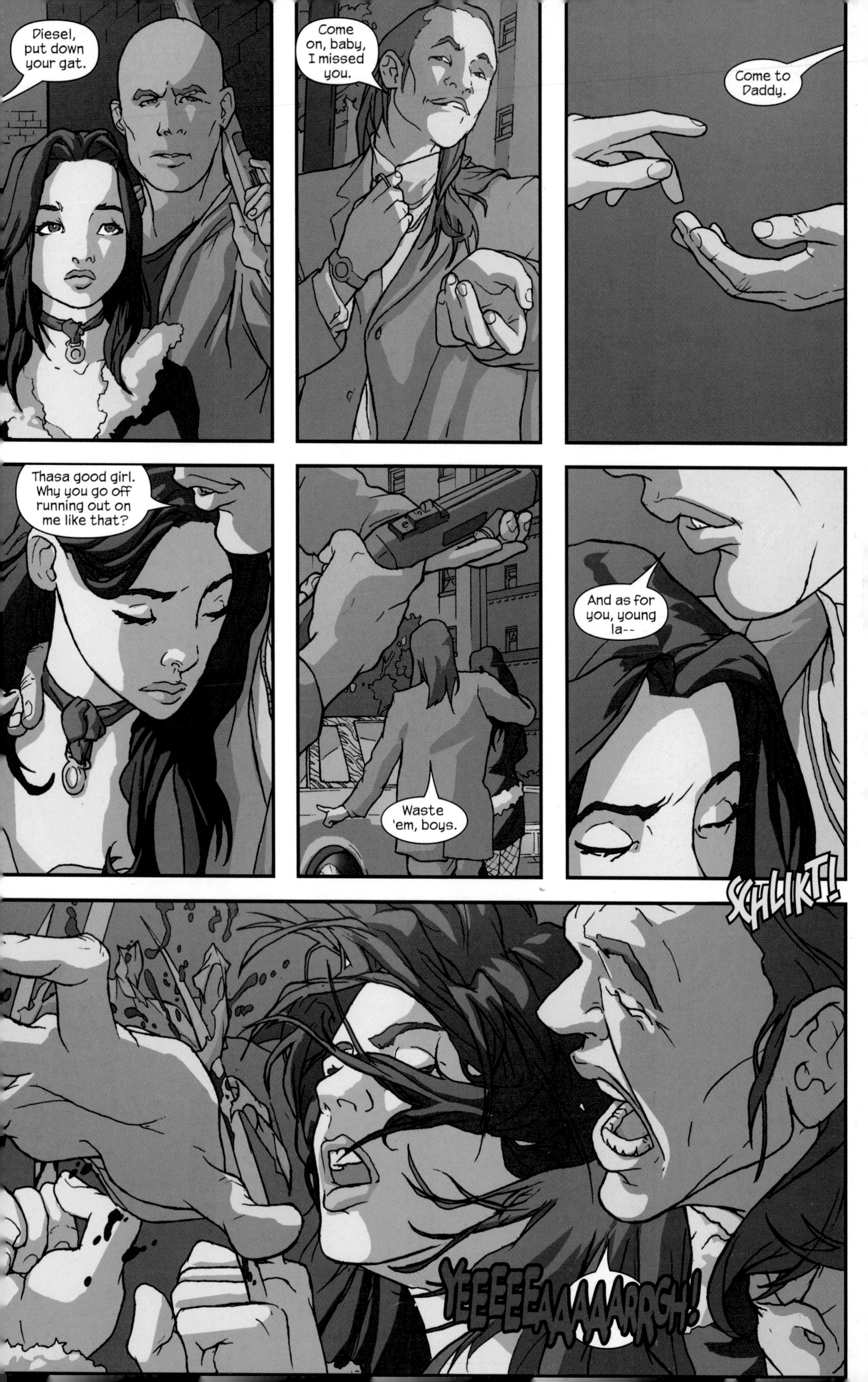
Diesel, put down your gat.
Come on, baby, I missed you.
Come to Daddy.
Thasa good girl. Why you go off running out on me like that?
Waste 'em, boys.
And as for you, young la--
SCHLIKT!
YEEEEEAAAAARRGH!

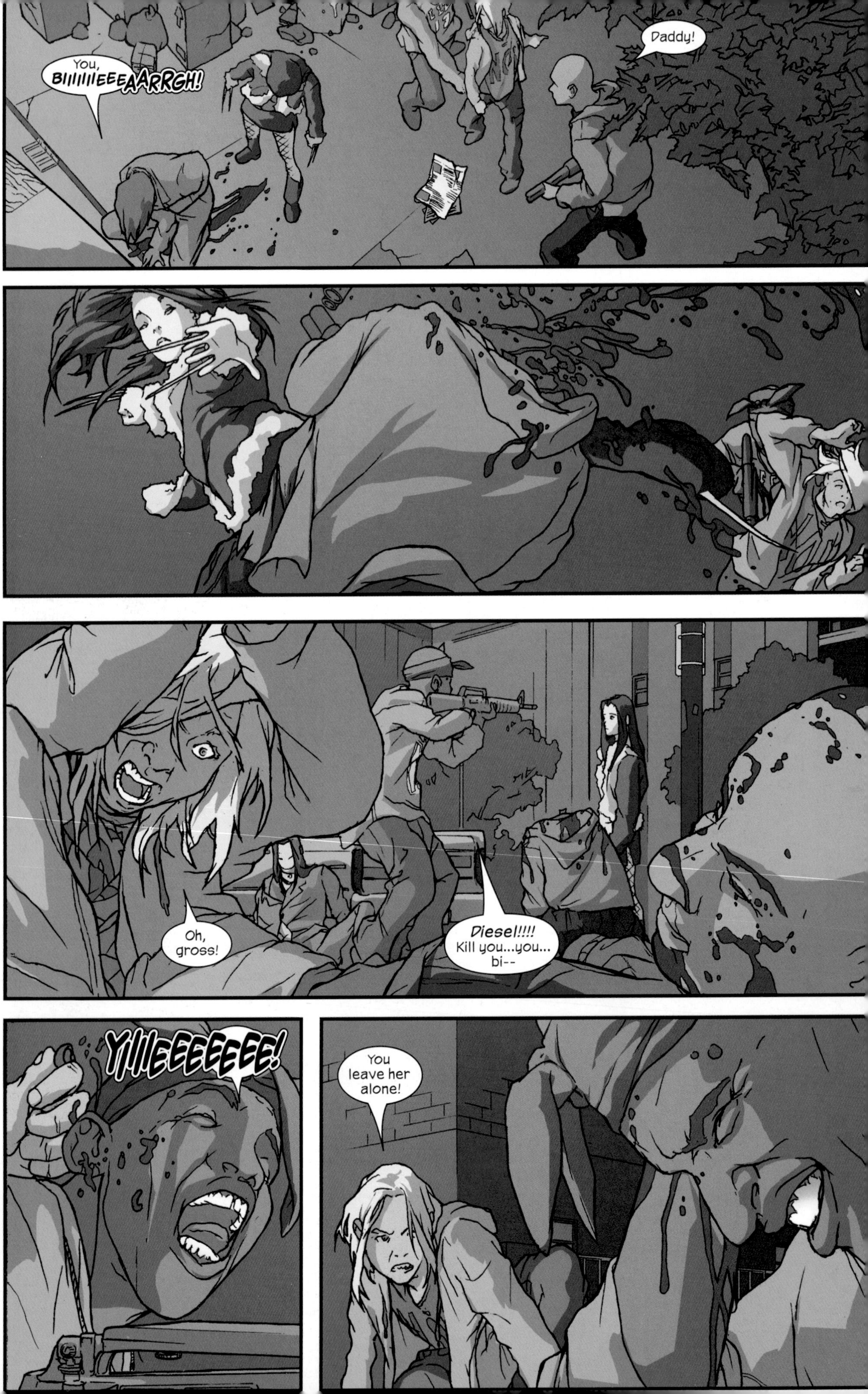
You, BIIIIIIEEEAARRGH!
Daddy!
Oh, gross!
Diesel!!!! Kill you...you... bi--
YIIIIEEEEEEEE!
You leave her alone!

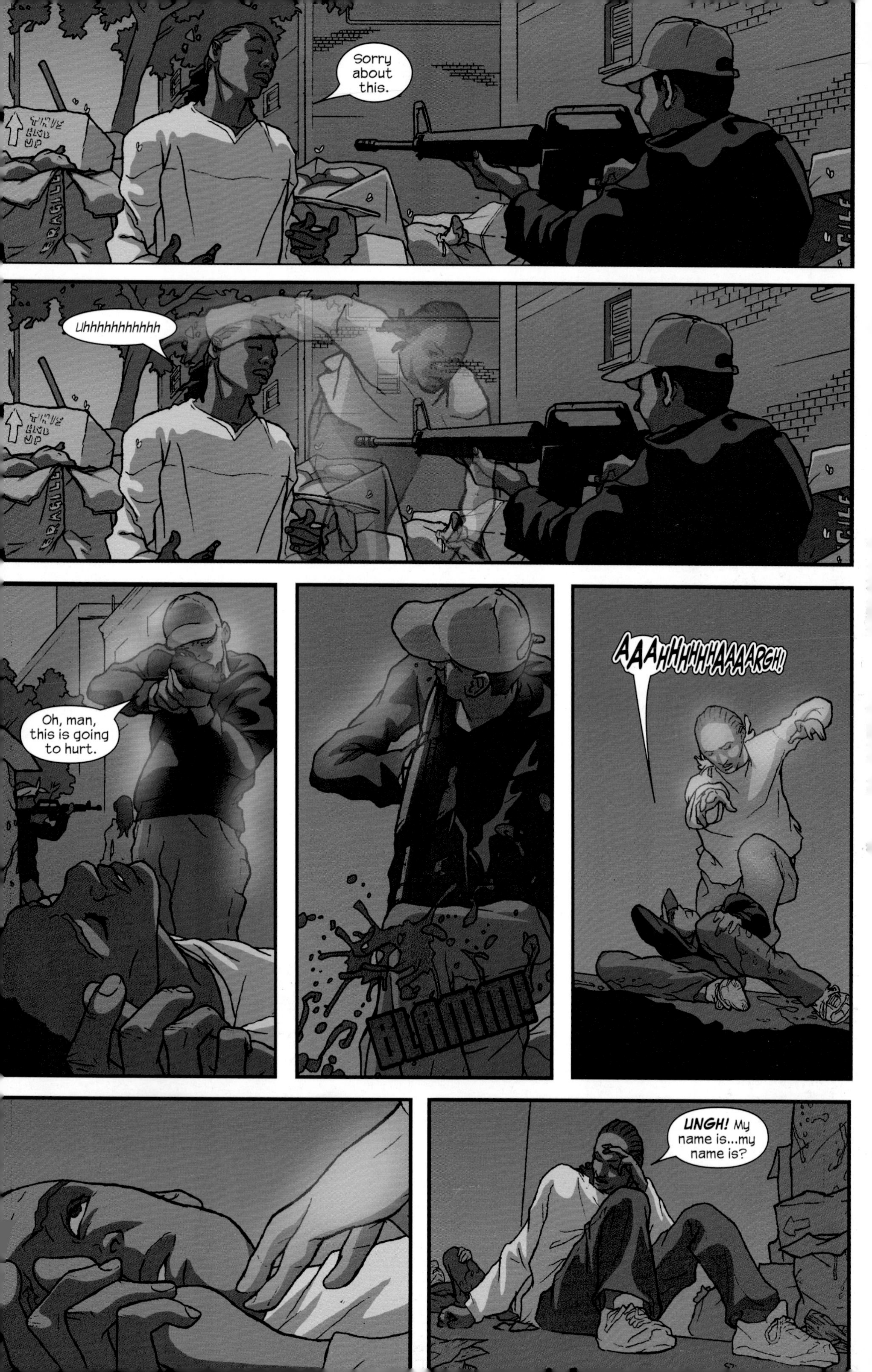
Sorry about this.
THIS END UP
FRAGILE
Uhhhhhhhhhhh
Oh, man, this is going to hurt.
BLAMM!
AAAHHHHHAAAARGH!
UNGH! My name is...my name is?

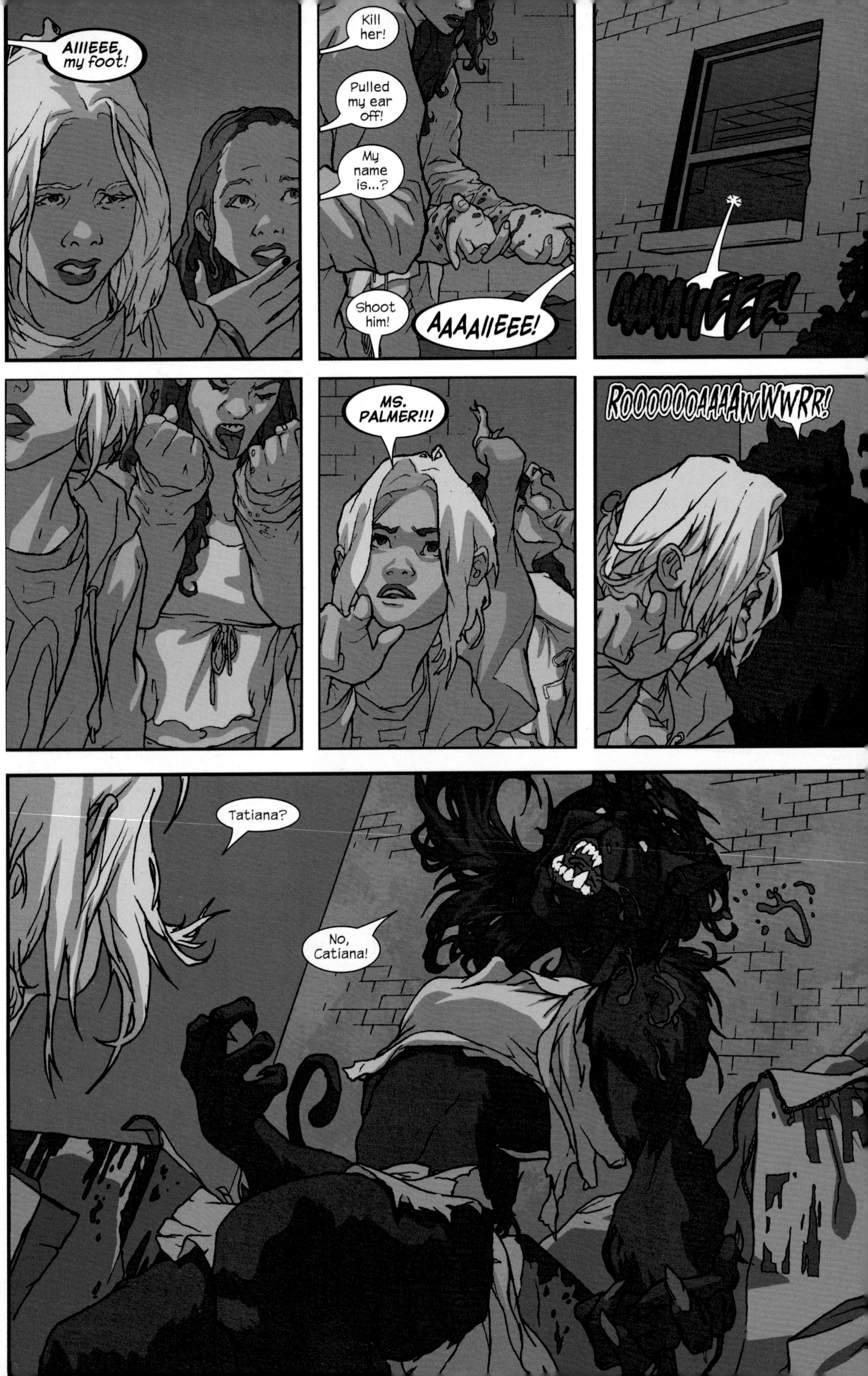
AIIIEEE, my foot!
Kill her!
Pulled my ear off!
My name is...?
Shoot him!
AAAAIIEEE!
AAAAIIEEE!
MS. PALMER!!!
ROOOOOOAAAAWWWRR!
Tatiana?
No, Catiana!

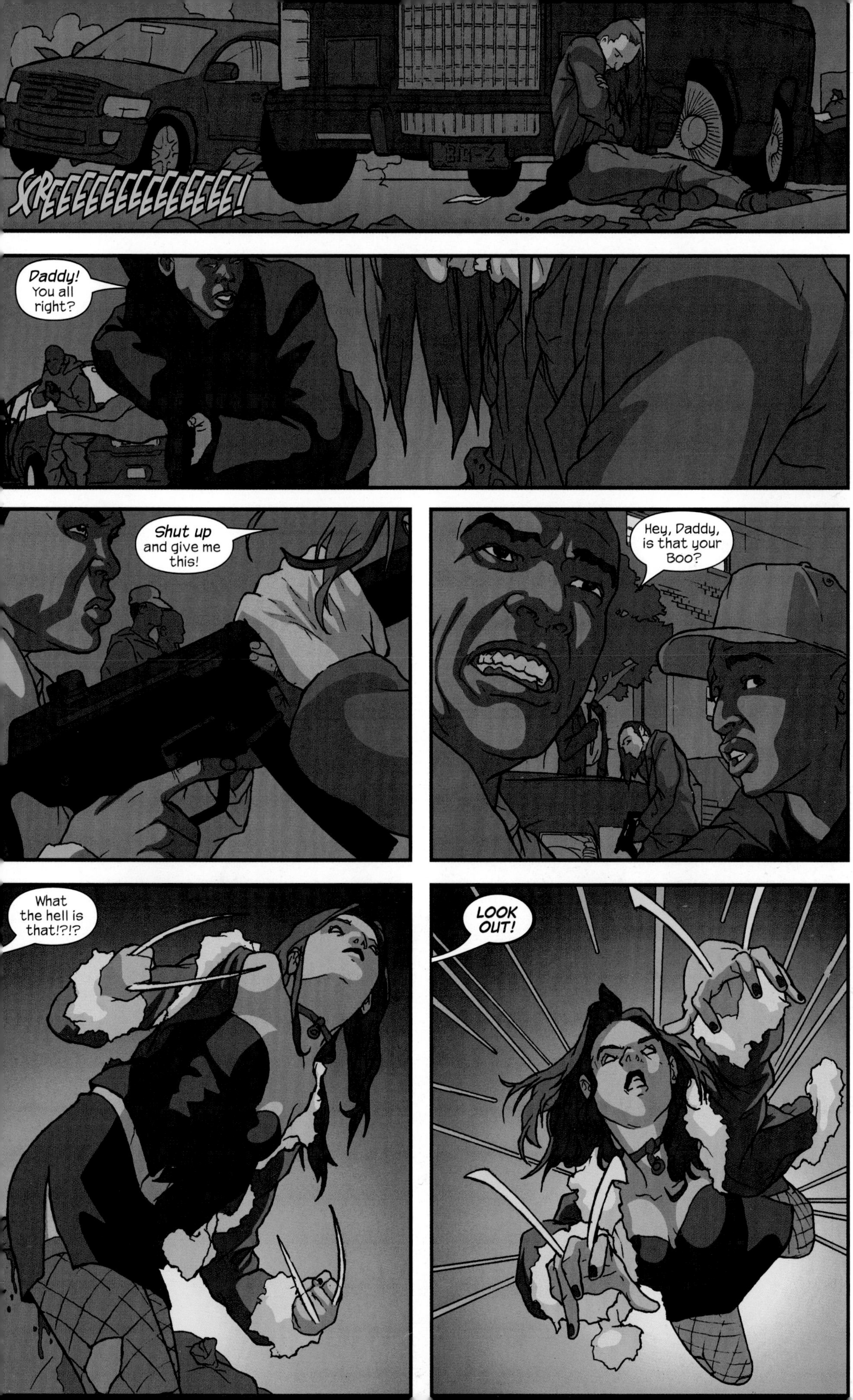

SCREEEEEEEEEEEEEEC!
Daddy! You all right?
Shut up and give me this!
Hey, Daddy, is that your Boo?
What the hell is that!?!?
LOOK OUT!

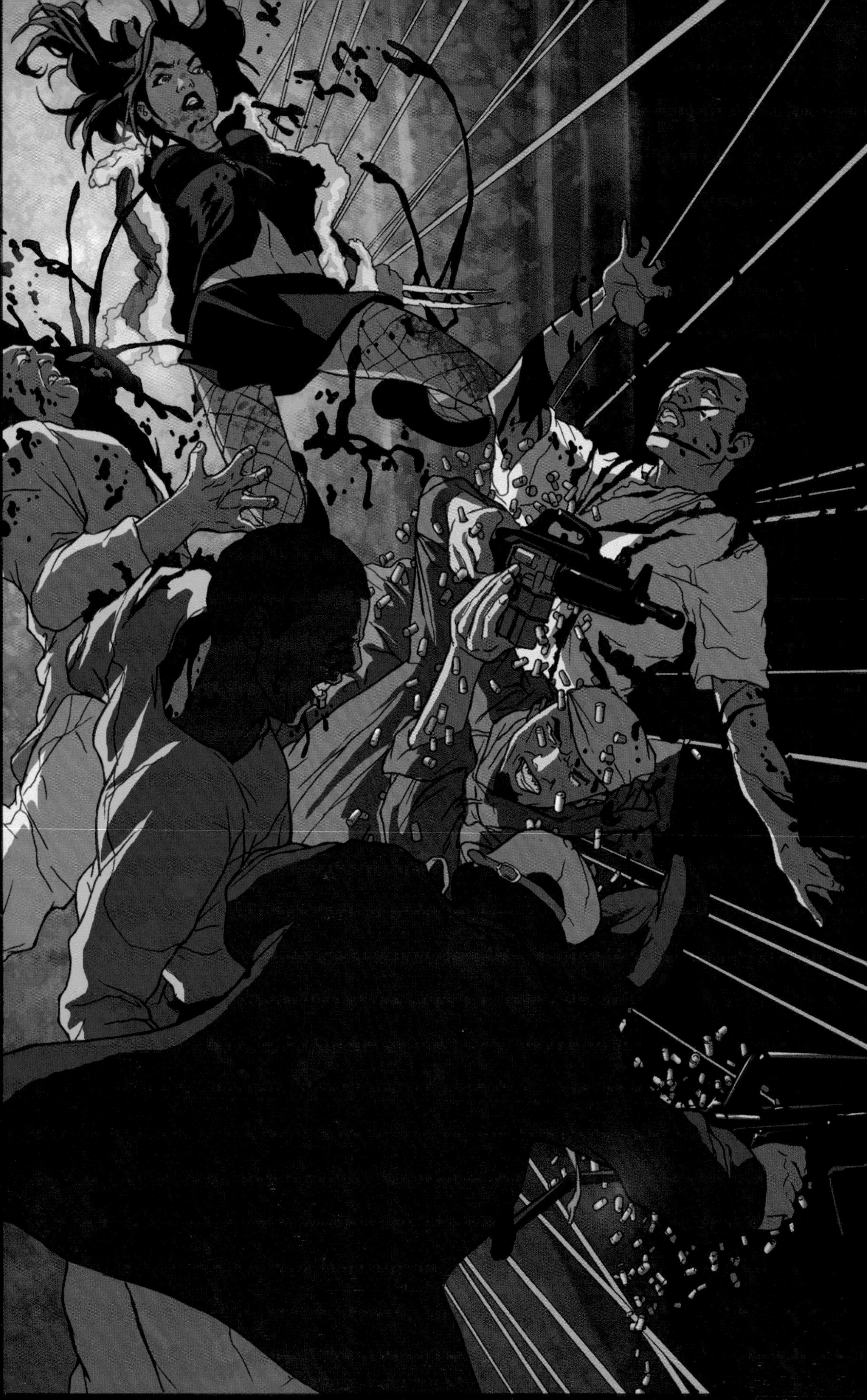

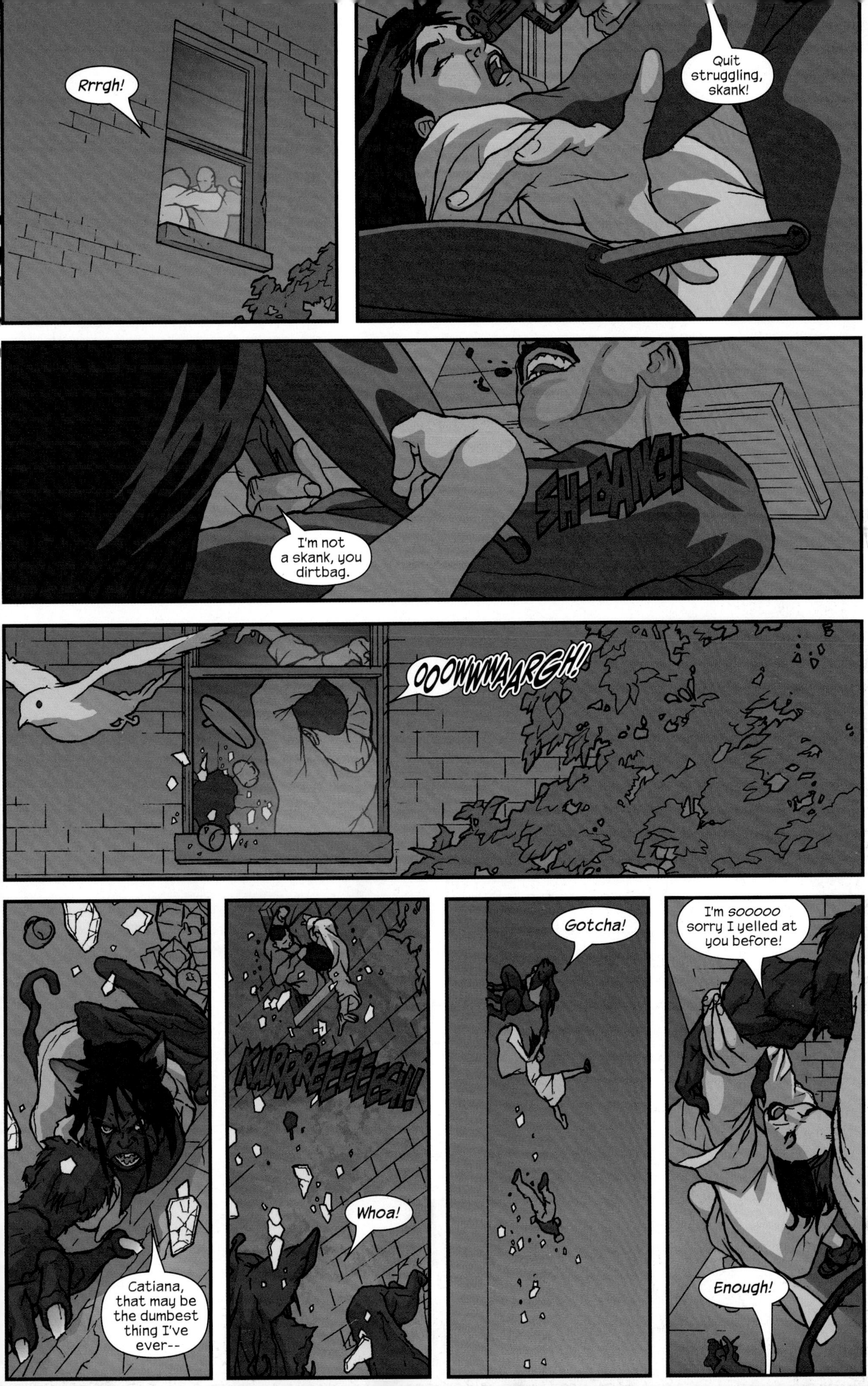

Rrrgh!
Quit struggling, skank!
I'm not a skank, you dirtbag.
SH-BANG!
OOOWWWAARGH!
Catiana, that may be the dumbest thing I've ever--
KARRREEEEECH!
Whoa!
Gotcha!
I'm sooooo sorry I yelled at you before!
Enough!

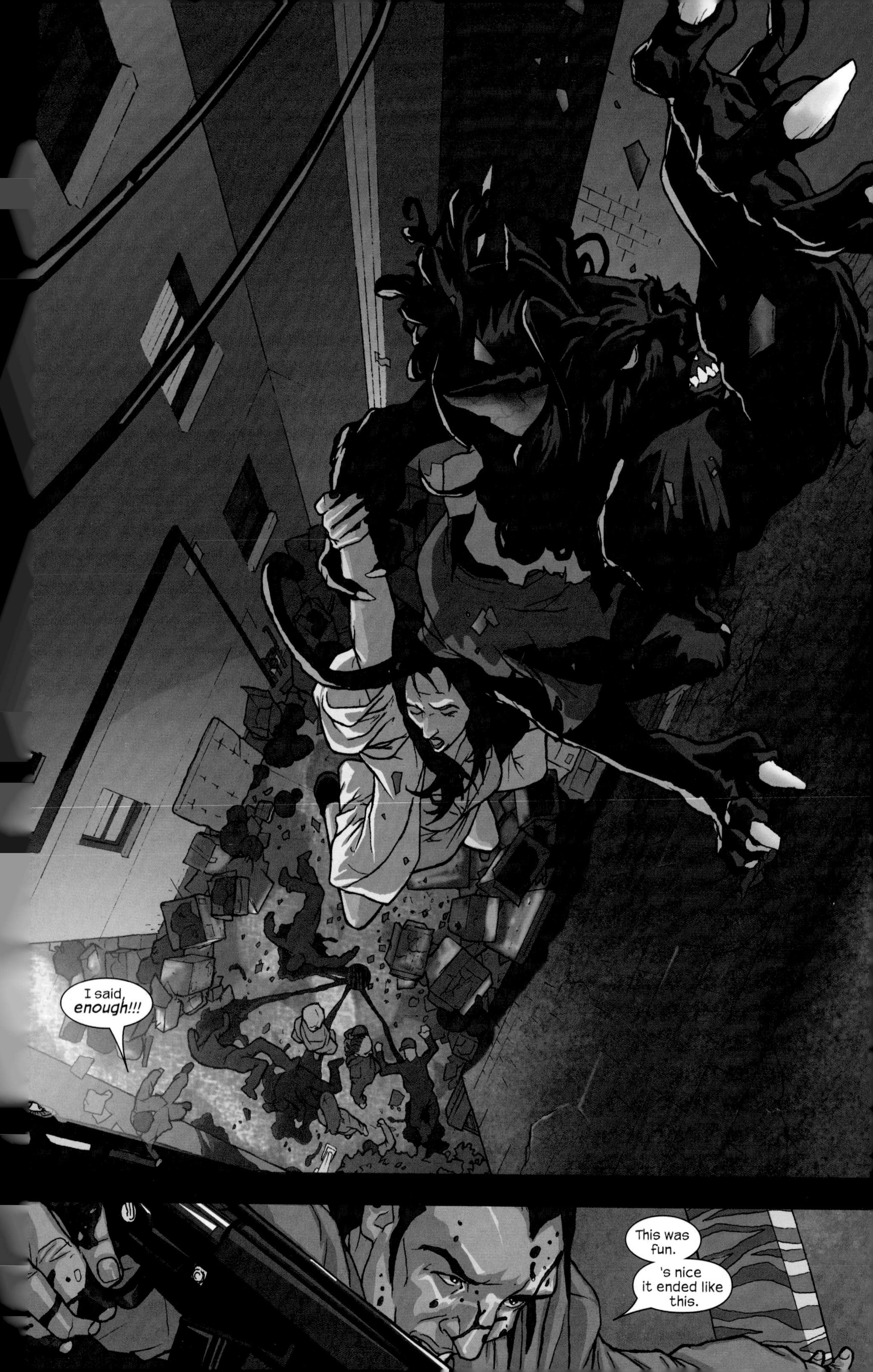

I said, enough!!!
This was fun.
's nice it ended like this.

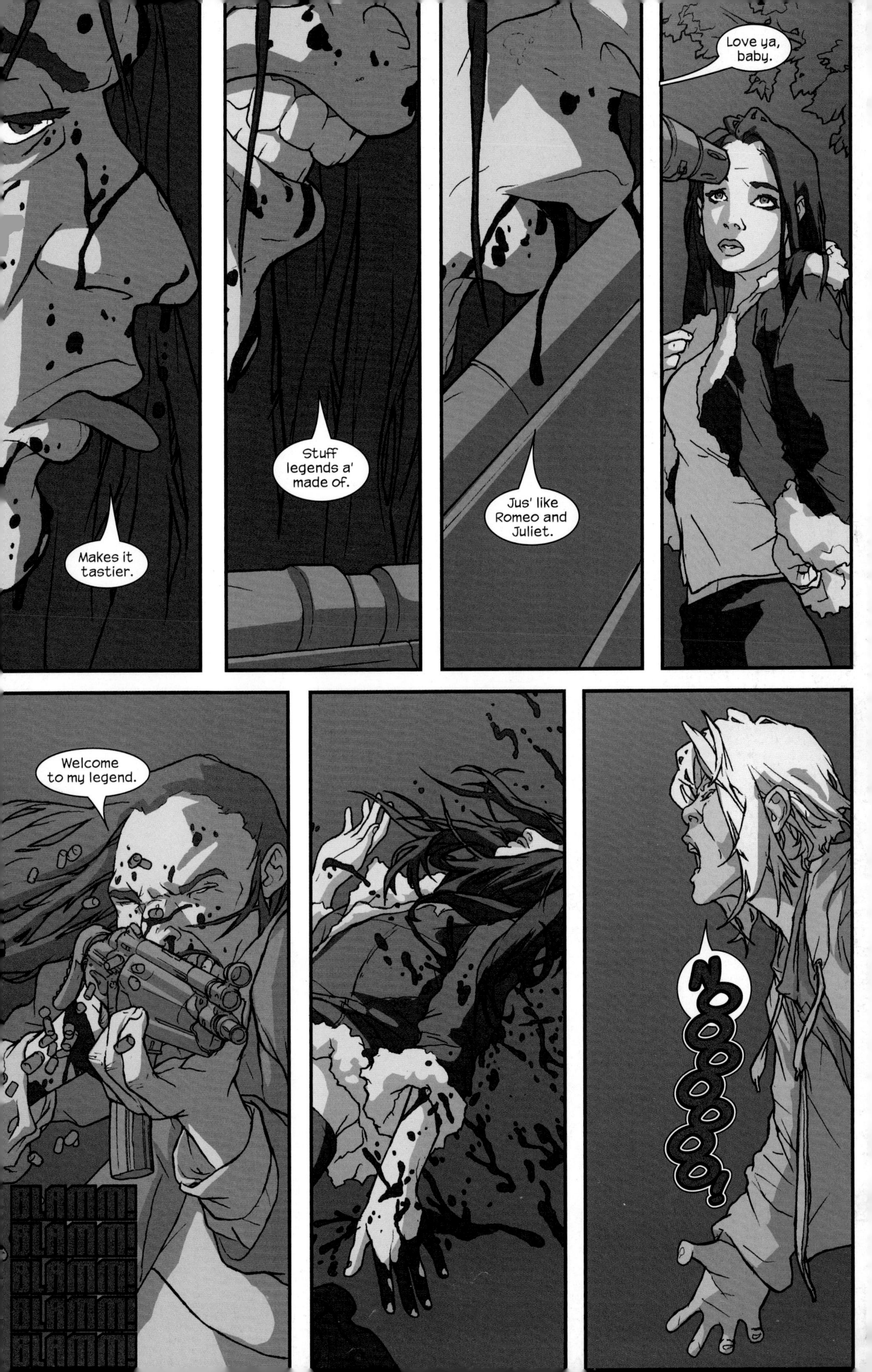

Makes it tastier.
Stuff legends a' made of.
Jus' like Romeo and Juliet.
Love ya, baby.
Welcome to my legend.
BLAMM! BLAMM! BLAMM! BLAMM! BLAMM!
NOOOOOO!

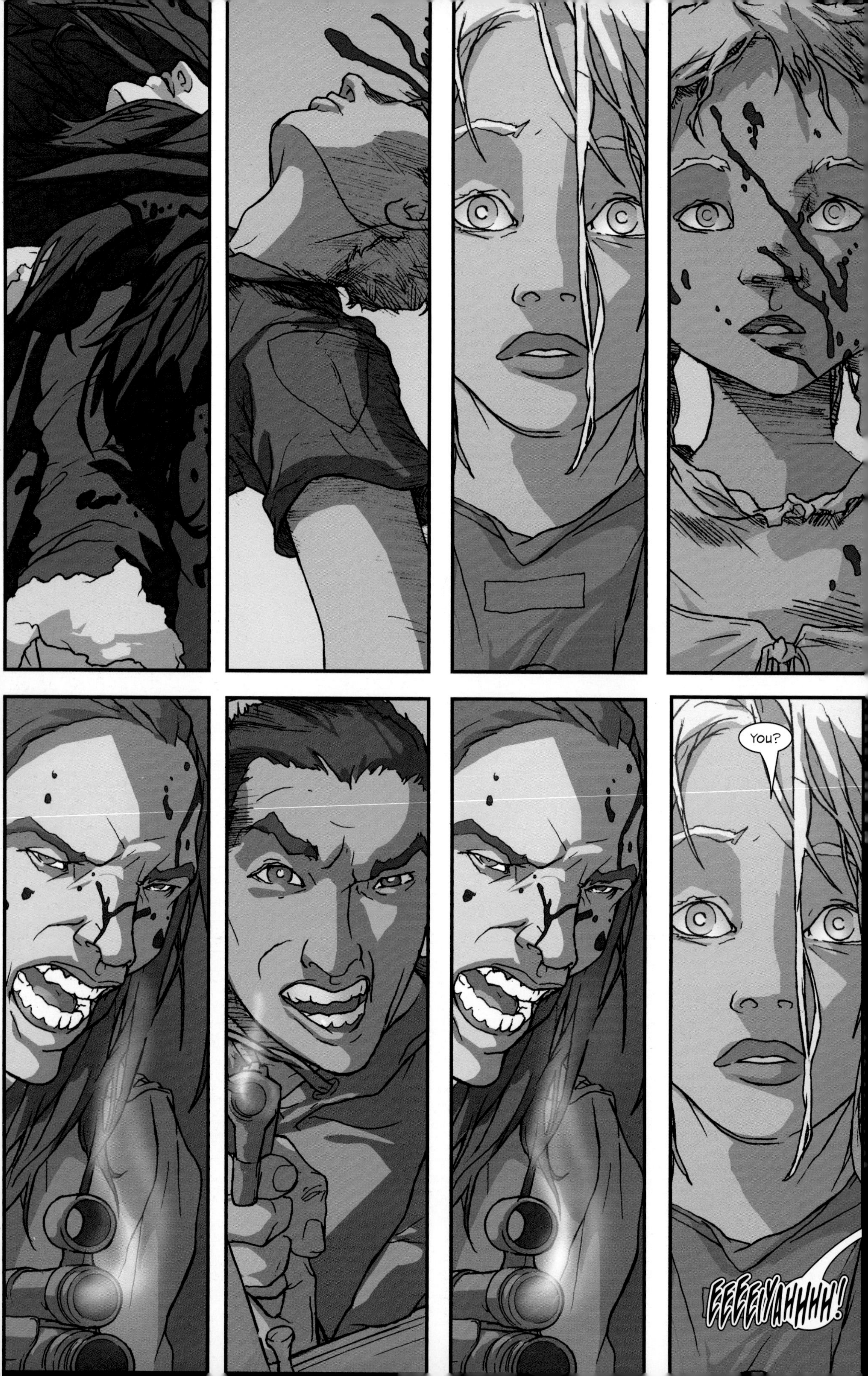
You?
EEEEIYAHHHH!

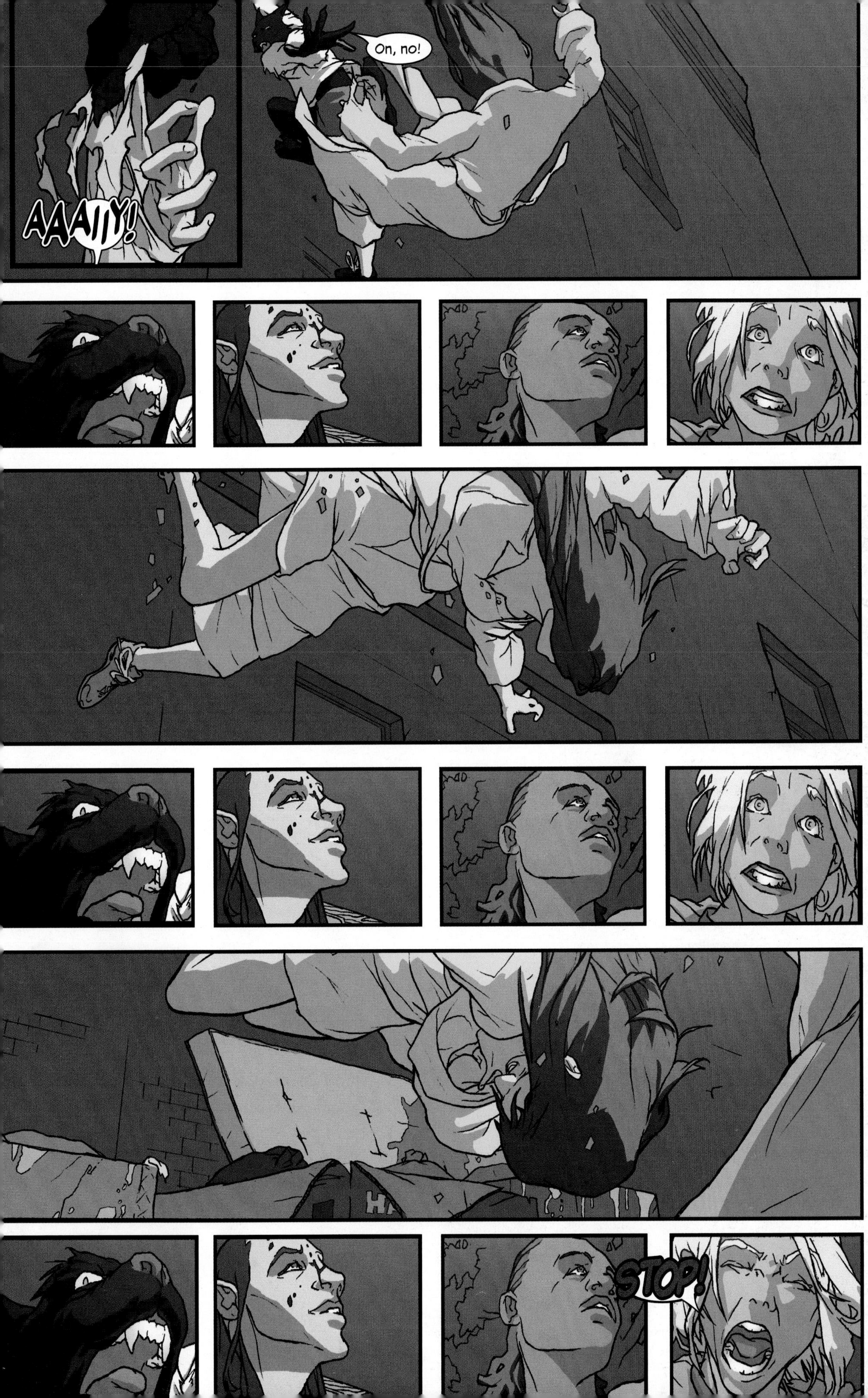
AAAIIIY!
On, no!
STOP!

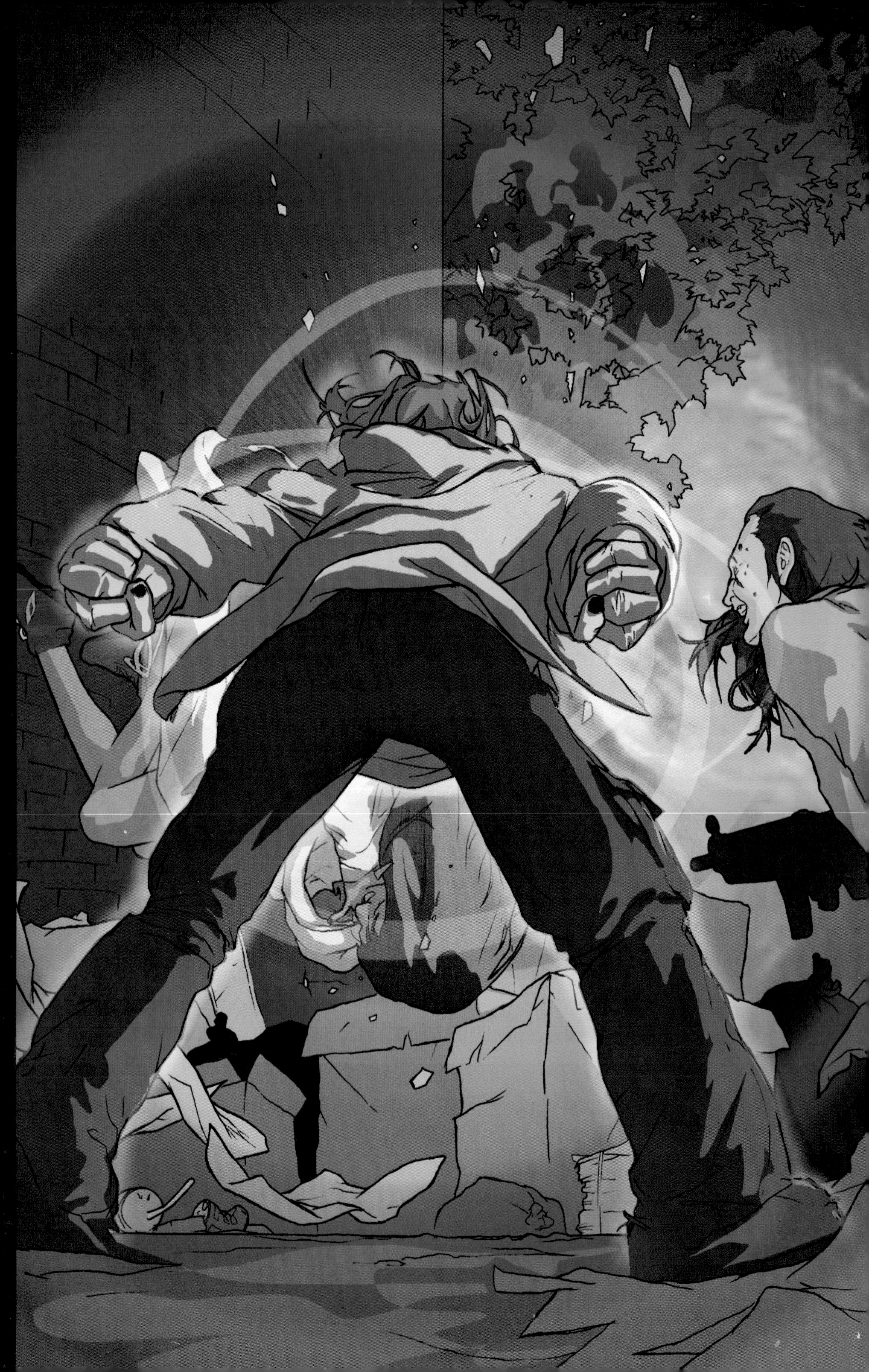

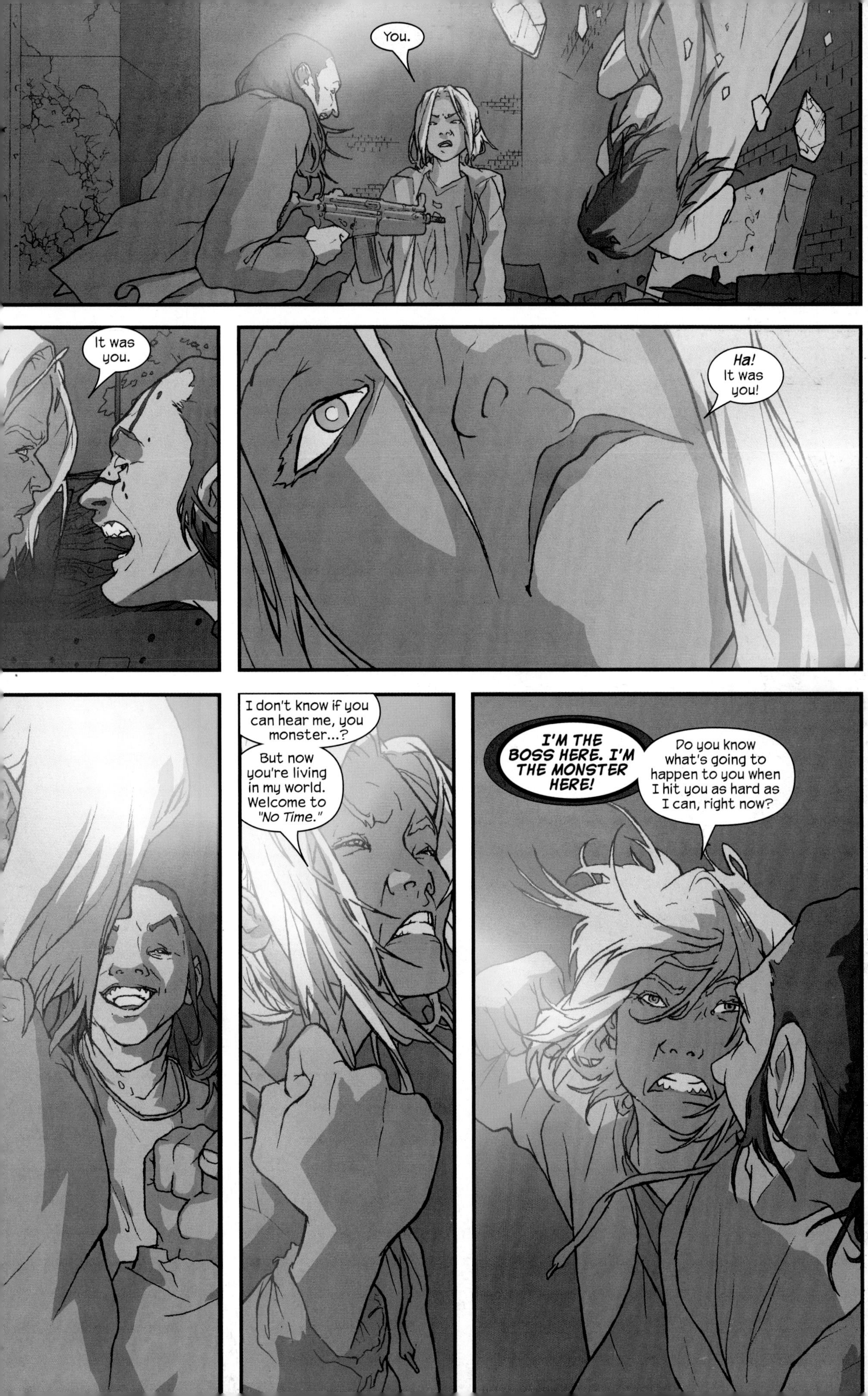
You.
It was you.
Ha! It was you!
I don't know if you can hear me, you monster...?
But now you're living in my world. Welcome to *"No Time."*
I'M THE BOSS HERE. I'M THE MONSTER HERE!
Do you know what's going to happen to you when I hit you as hard as I can, right now?

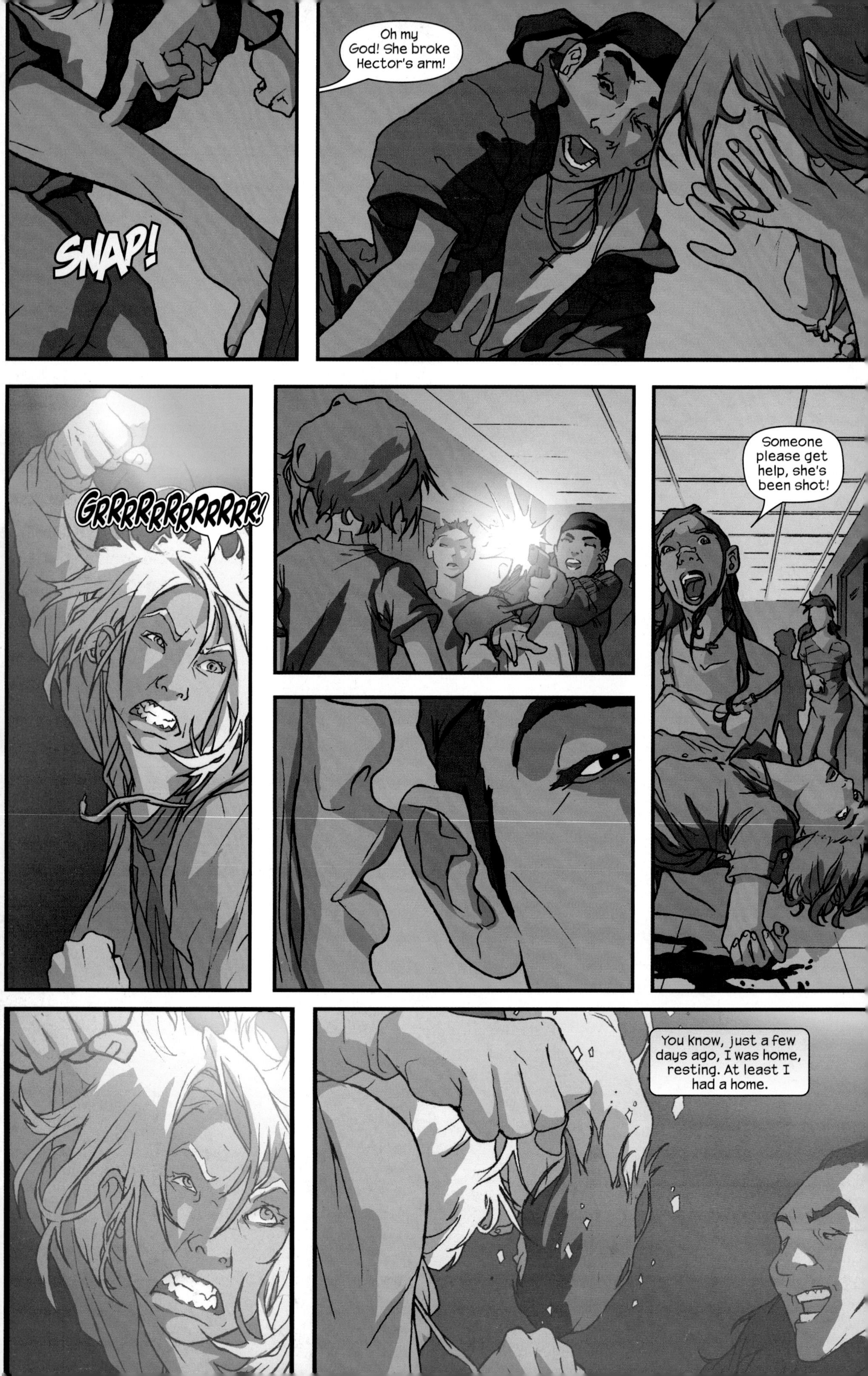

SNAP!
Oh my God! She broke Hector's arm!
GRRRRRRRRRRR!
Someone please get help, she's been shot!
You know, just a few days ago, I was home, resting. At least I had a home.

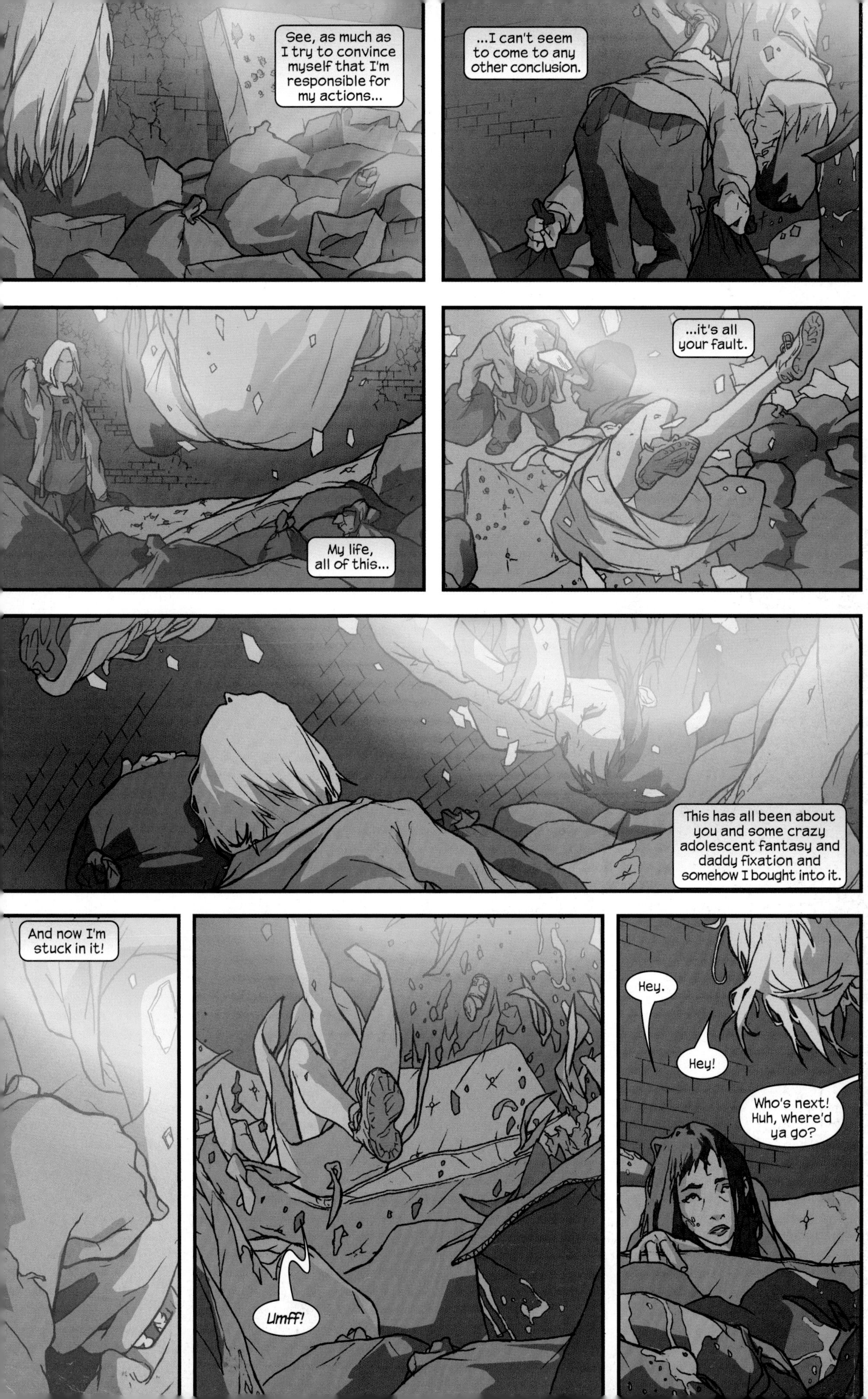
See, as much as I try to convince myself that I'm responsible for my actions...
...I can't seem to come to any other conclusion.
My life, all of this...
...it's all your fault.
This has all been about you and some crazy adolescent fantasy and daddy fixation and somehow I bought into it.
And now I'm stuck in it!
Umff!
Hey.
Hey!
Who's next! Huh, where'd ya go?

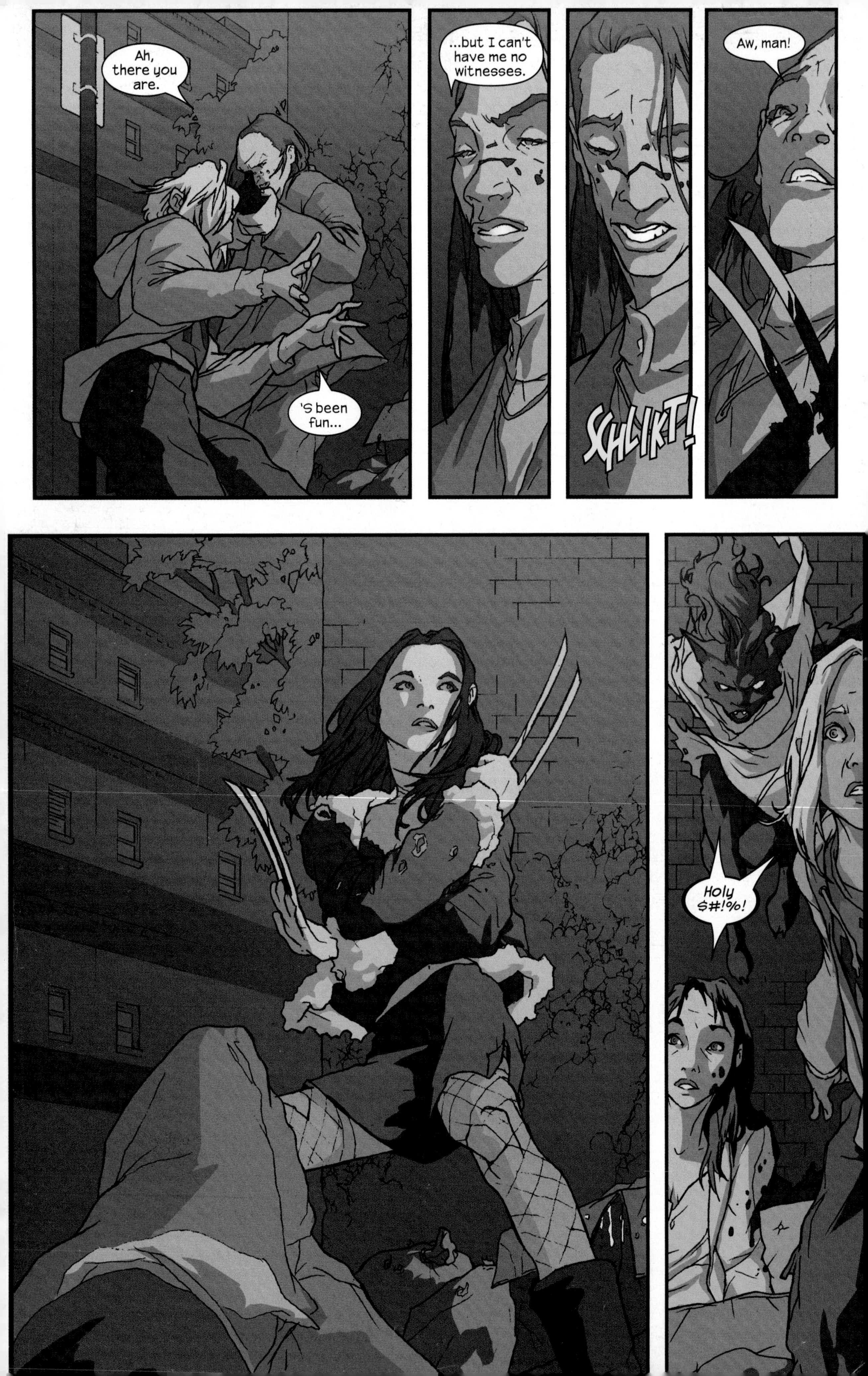
Ah, there you are.
'S been fun...
...but I can't have me no witnesses.
SCHLIKT!
Aw, man!
Holy $#!%!

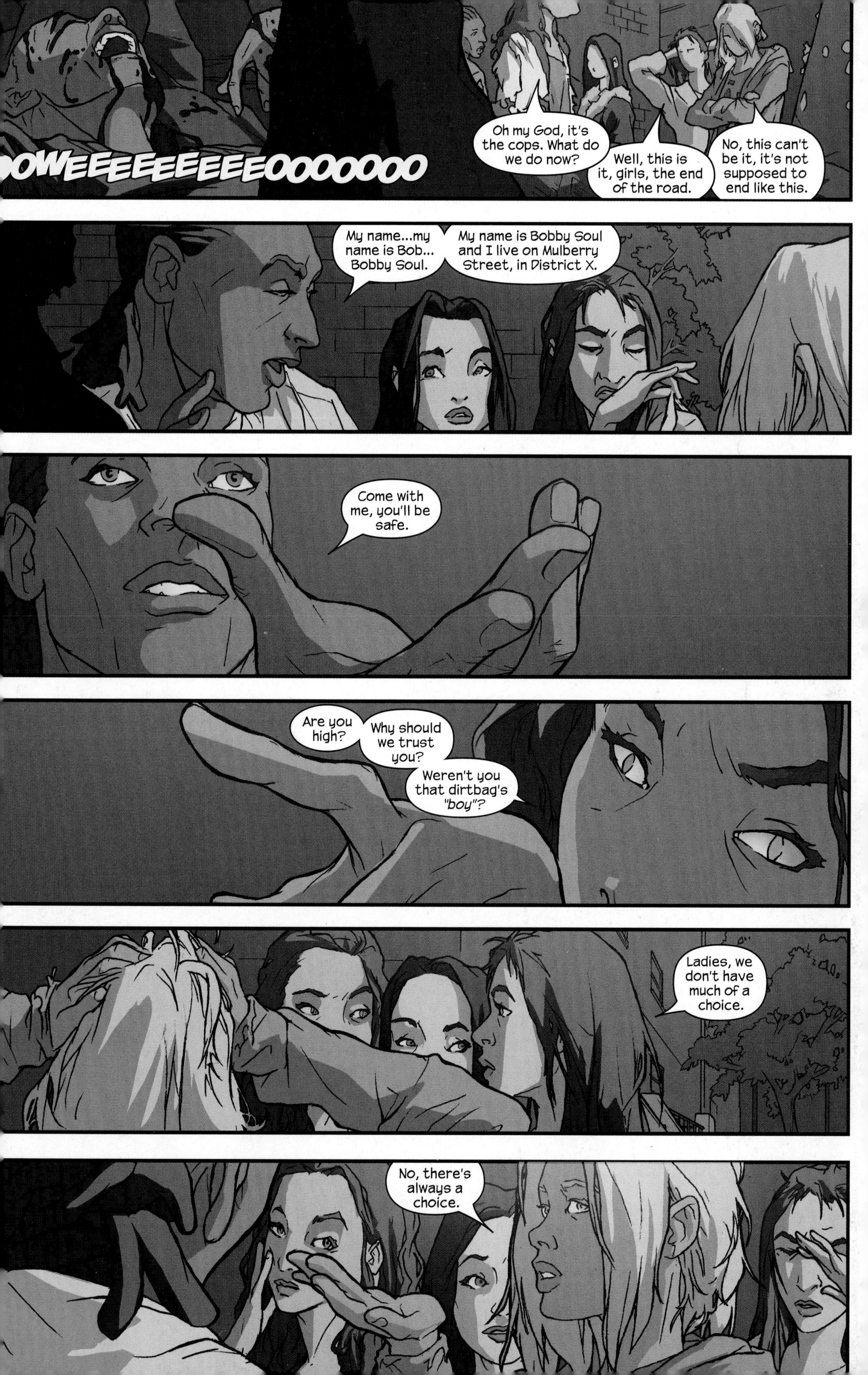

OWEEEEEEEEEOOOOOOO
Oh my God, it's the cops. What do we do now?
Well, this is it, girls, the end of the road.
No, this can't be it, it's not supposed to end like this.
My name...my name is Bob... Bobby Soul.
My name is Bobby Soul and I live on Mulberry Street, in District X.
Come with me, you'll be safe.
Are you high?
Why should we trust you?
Weren't you that dirtbag's "boy"?
Ladies, we don't have much of a choice.
No, there's always a choice.

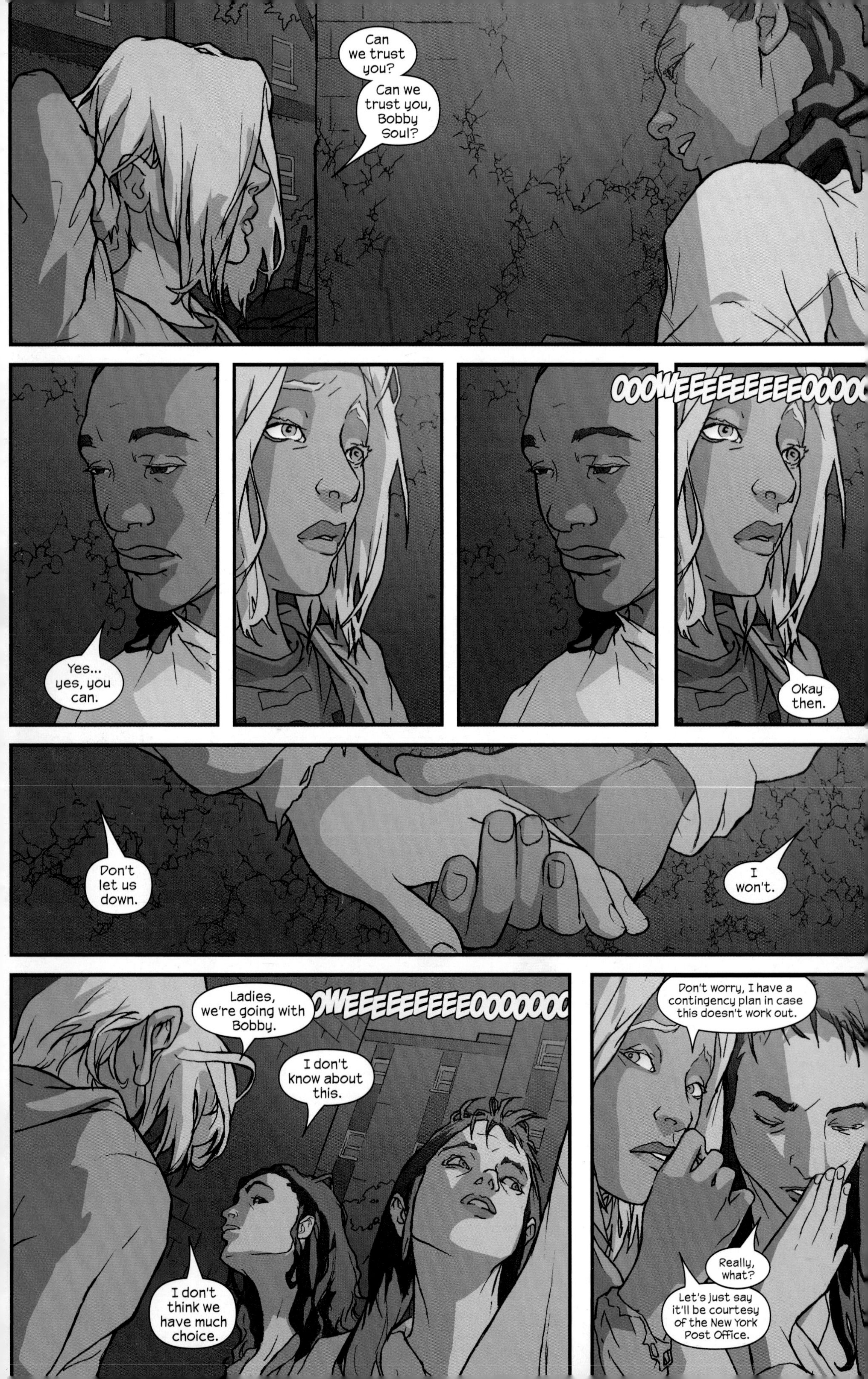

Can we trust you?
Can we trust you, Bobby Soul?
Yes... yes, you can.
OOOWEEEEEEEEEOOOOO
Okay then.
Don't let us down.
I won't.
Ladies, we're going with Bobby.
OWEEEEEEEEEOOOOOO
I don't know about this.
I don't think we have much choice.
Don't worry, I have a contingency plan in case this doesn't work out.
Really, what?
Let's just say it'll be courtesy of the New York Post Office.

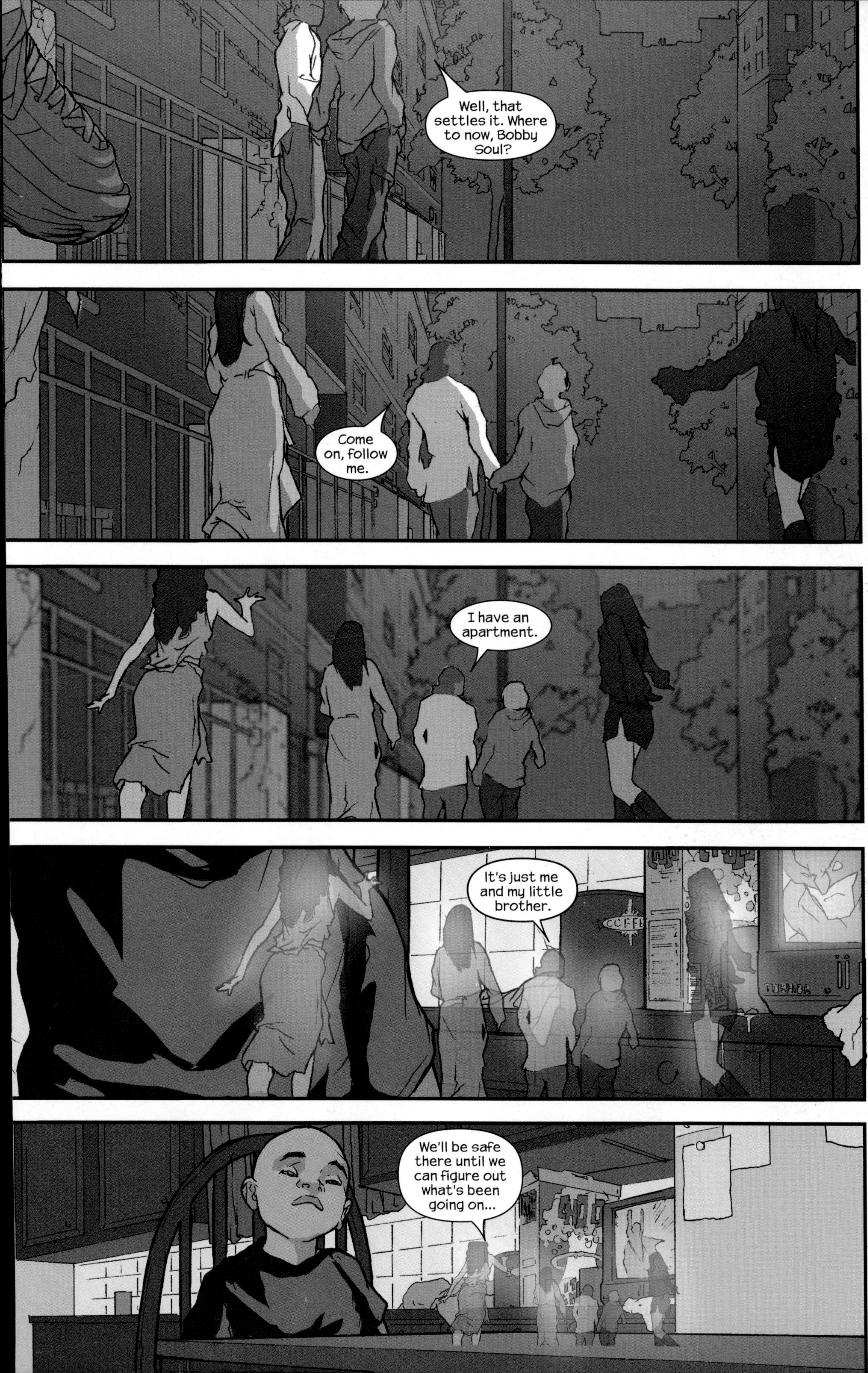
Well, that settles it. Where to now, Bobby Soul?
Come on, follow me.
I have an apartment.
It's just me and my little brother.
We'll be safe there until we can figure out what's been going on...

Well, guess it's time to get ready.

KLK!

Company's going to be over real soon.

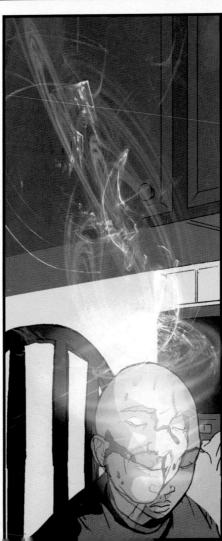

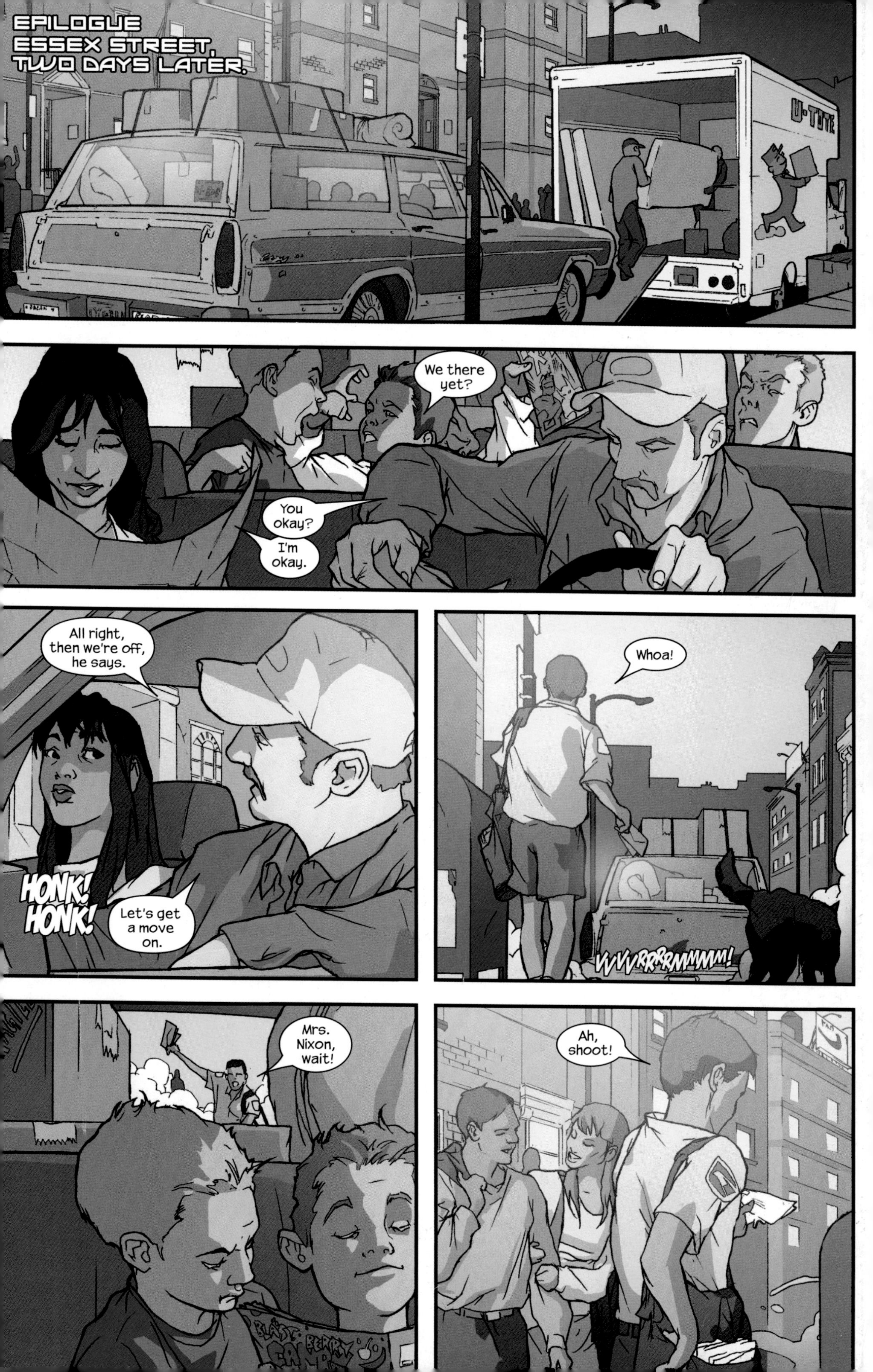
EPILOGUE
ESSEX STREET, TWO DAYS LATER.
U-TOTE
We there yet?
You okay?
I'm okay.
All right, then we're off, he says.
HONK! HONK!
Let's get a move on.
Whoa!
VVVVRRRRMMMMM!
Mrs. Nixon, wait!
Ah, shoot!

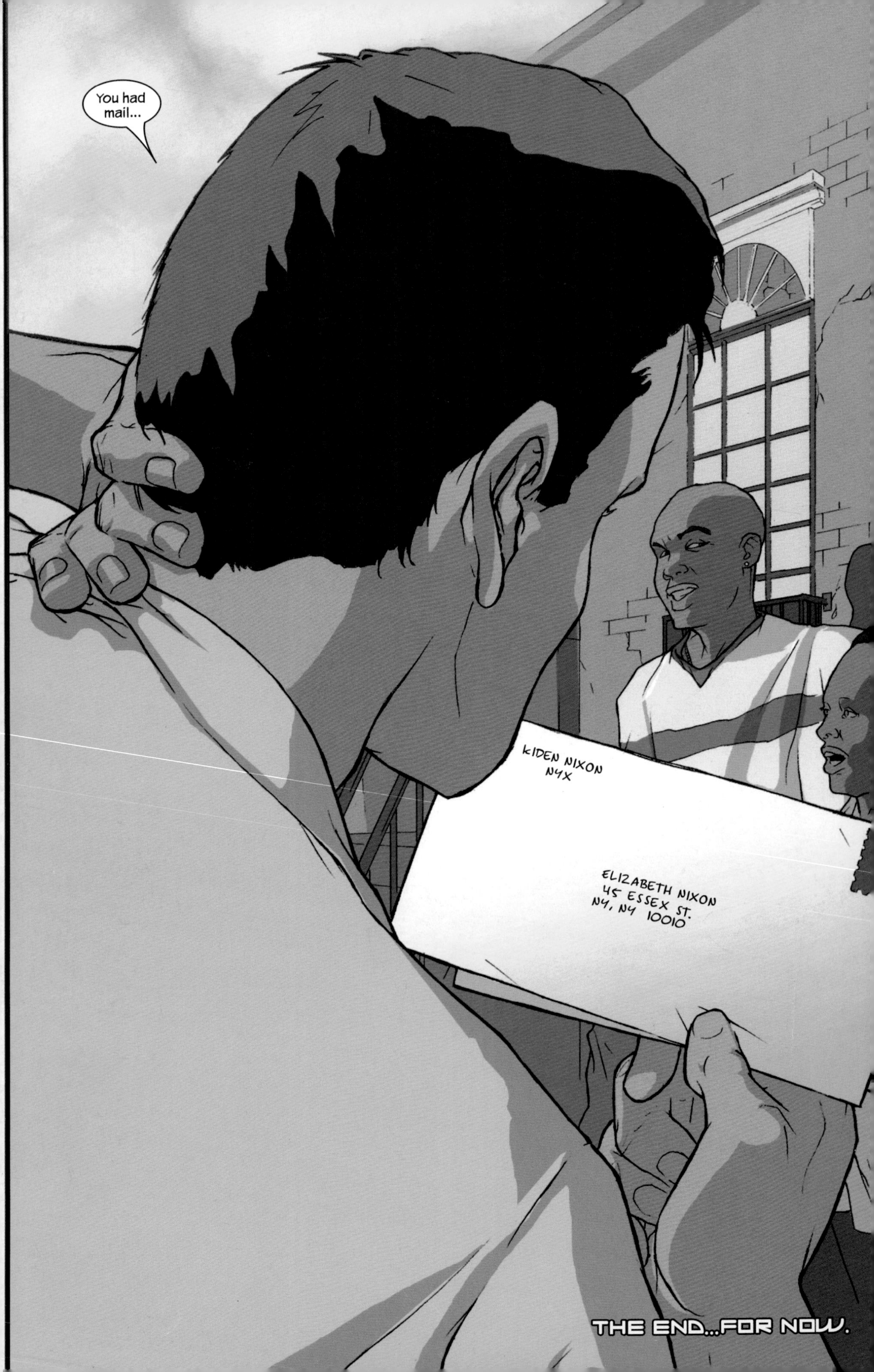
You had mail...
KIDEN NIXON
NYX
ELIZABETH NIXON
45 ESSEX ST.
NY, NY 10010
THE END...FOR NOW.

X-23 COVER SKETCHES BY BILLY TAN

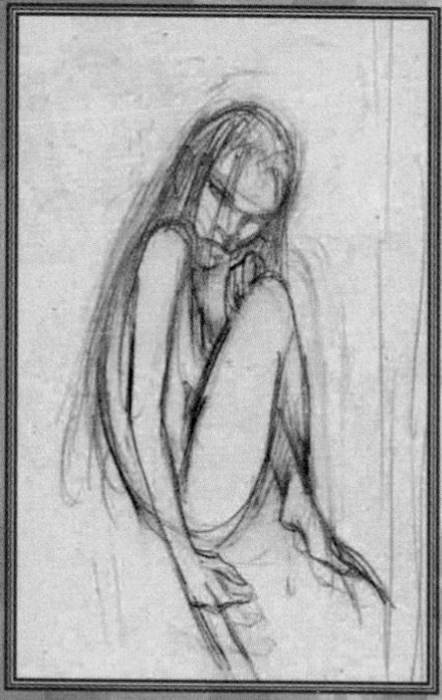
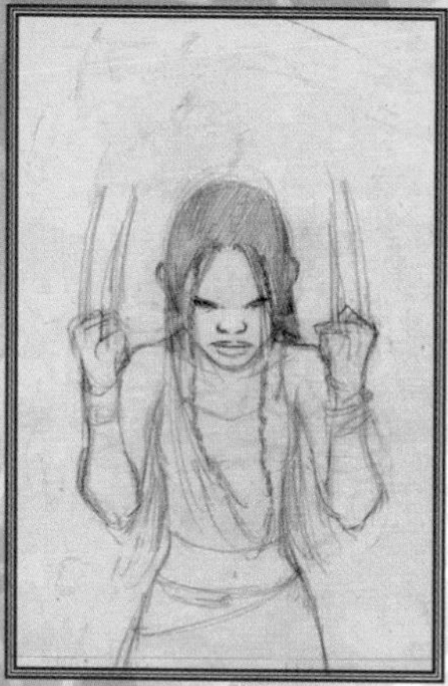
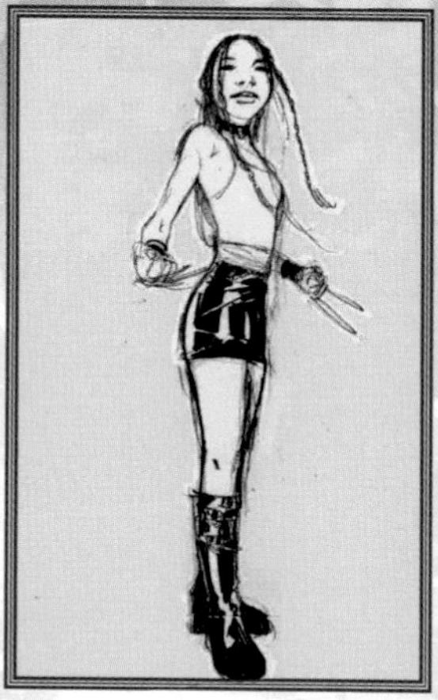
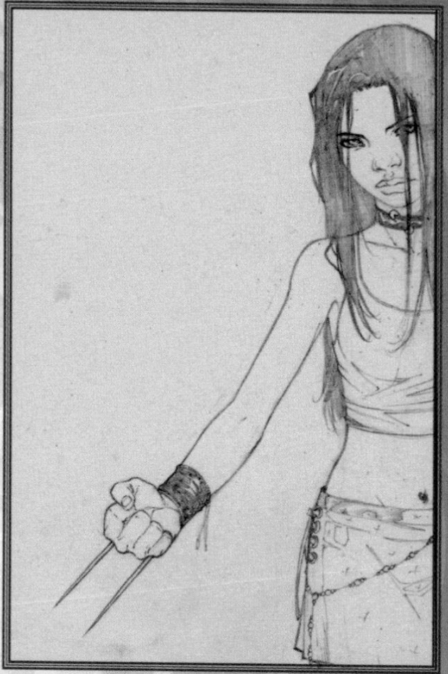
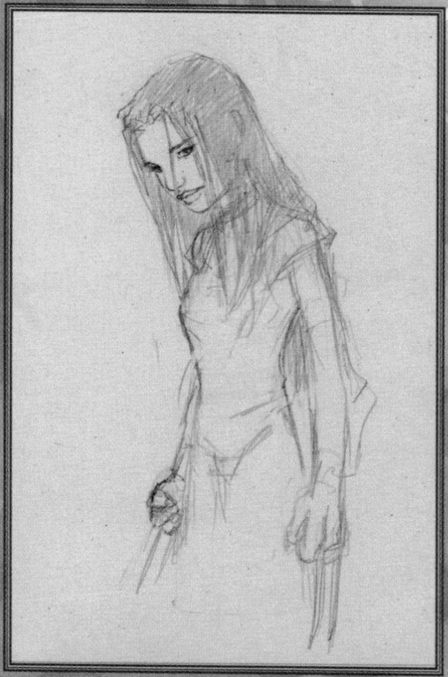
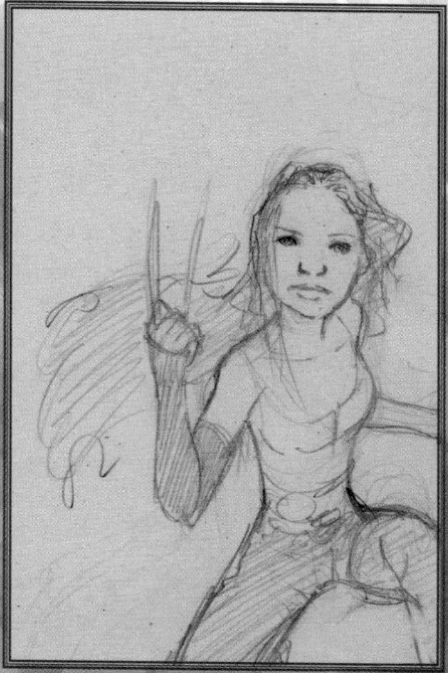
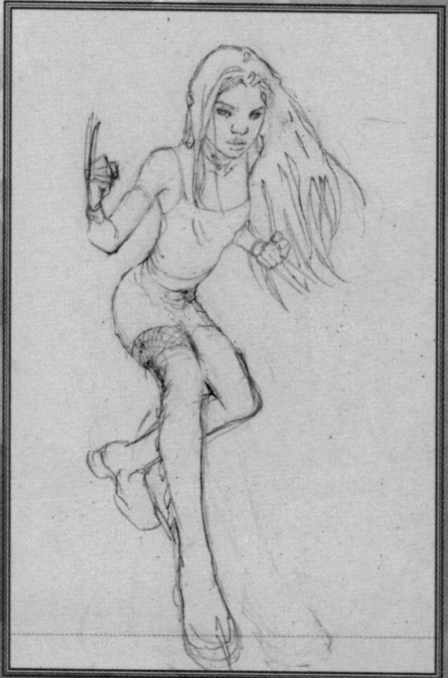
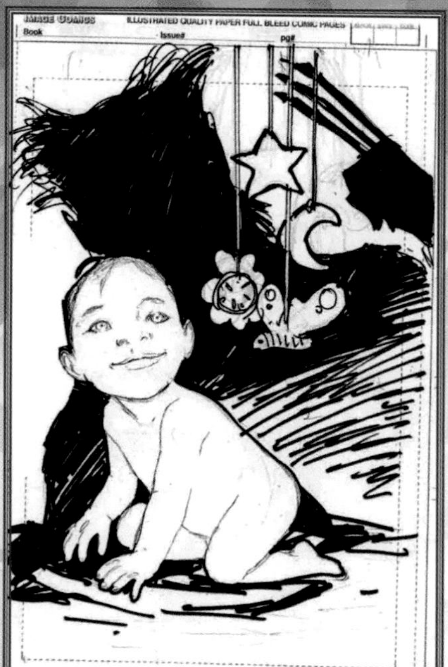
ILLUSTRATED QUALITY PAPER FULL BLEED COMIC PAGES
Book
Issue#
pg#
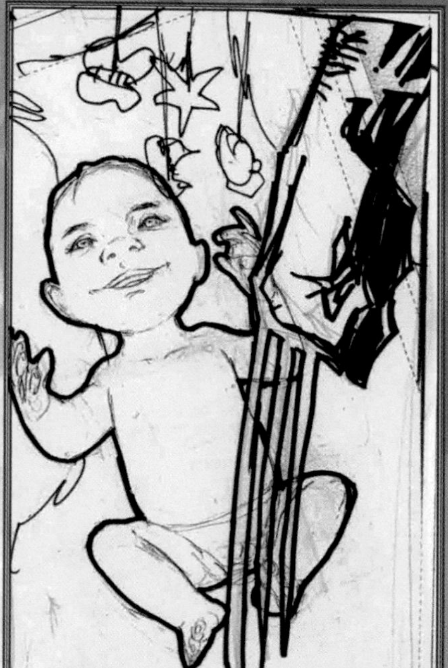

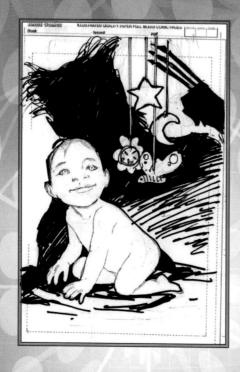

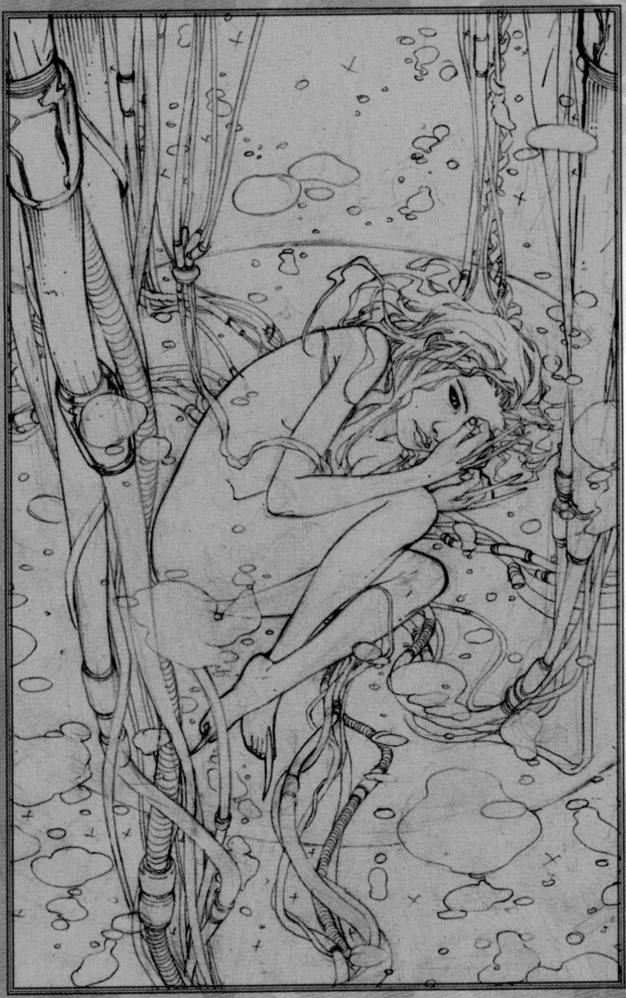

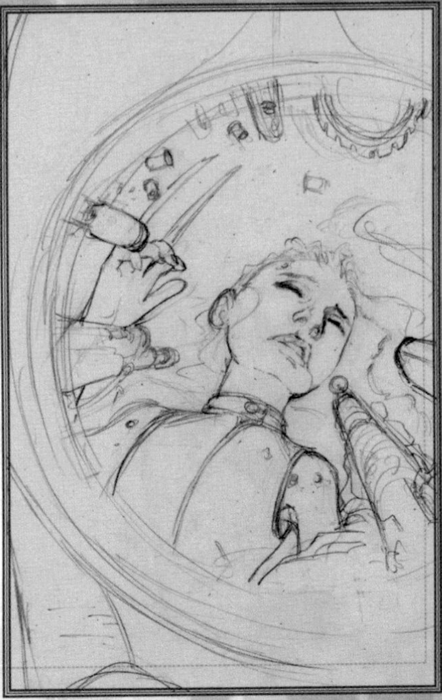

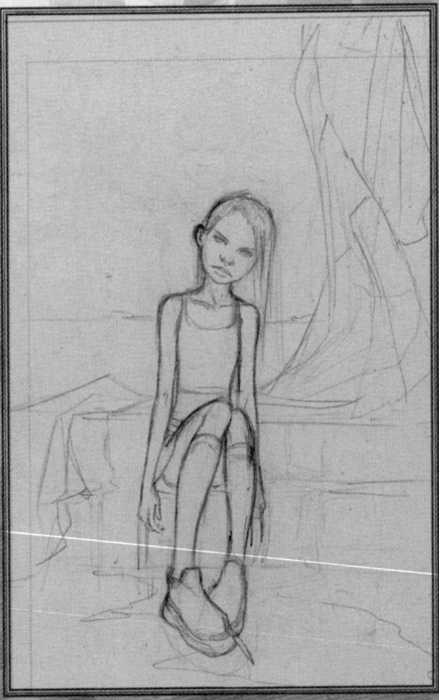

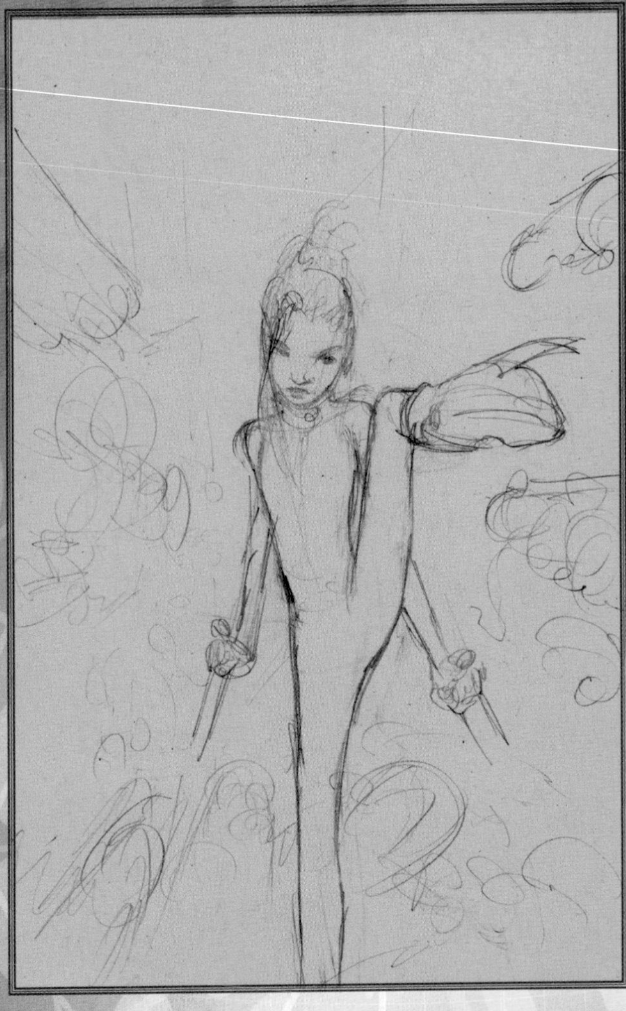

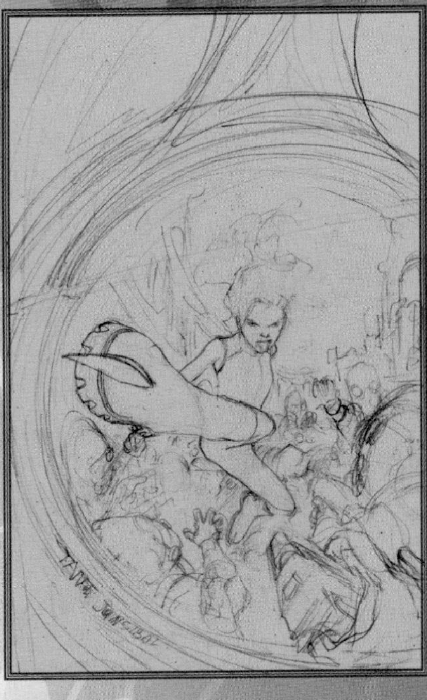

X-23 #6 Cover Pencils by Billy Tan; Inks by John Sibal; Colors by Brian Haberlin

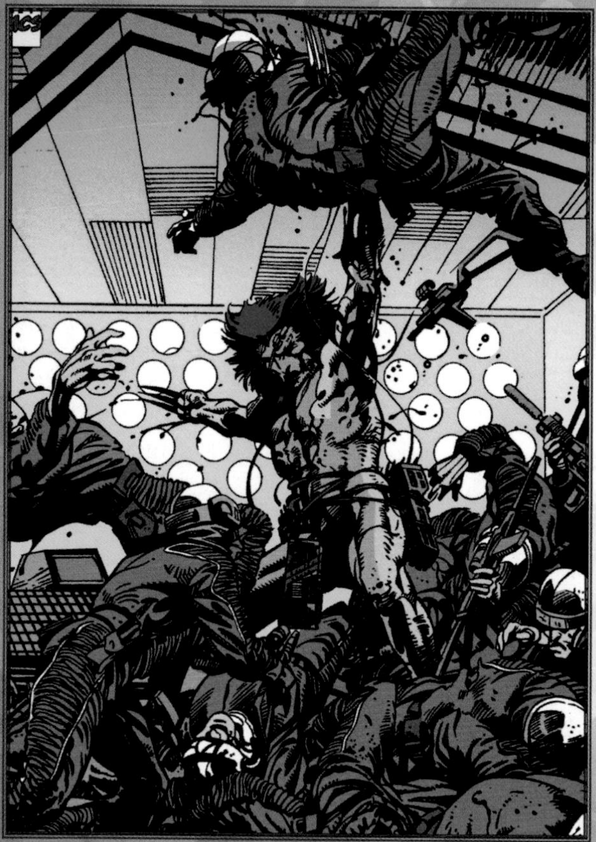

Weapon X Trade Paperback cover
by Barry Windsor-Smith

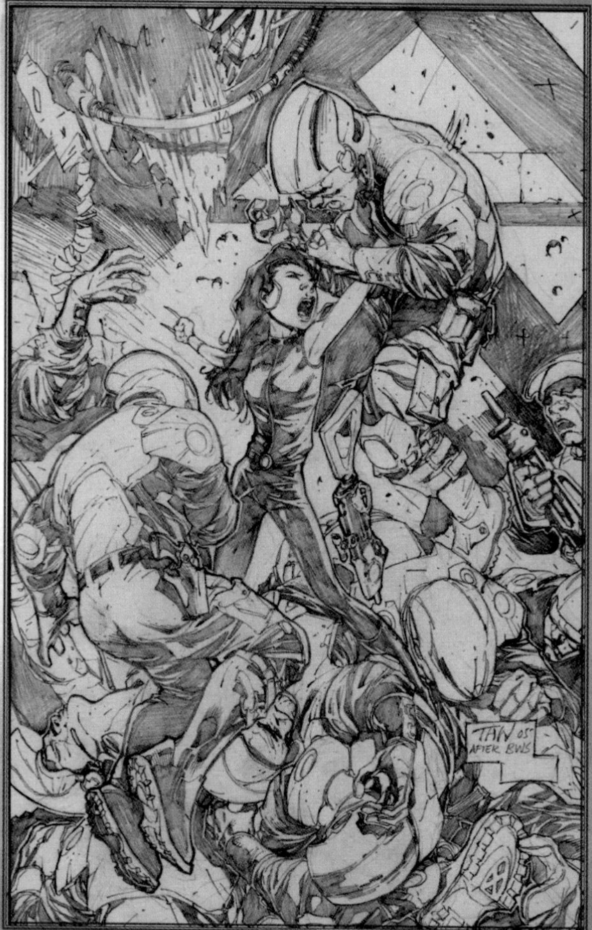
TAN 05
AFTER BWS

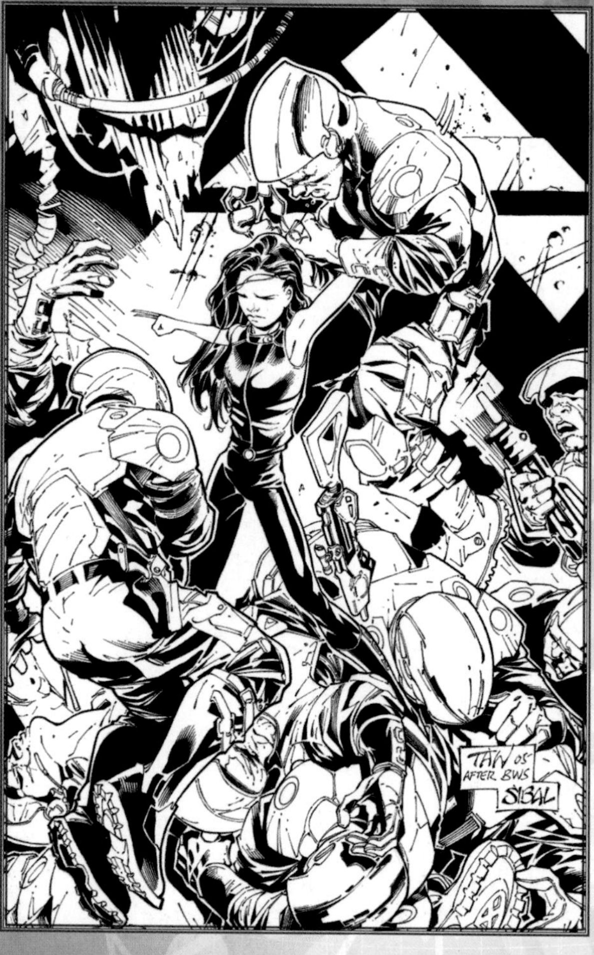
TAN 05
AFTER BWS
SIBAL

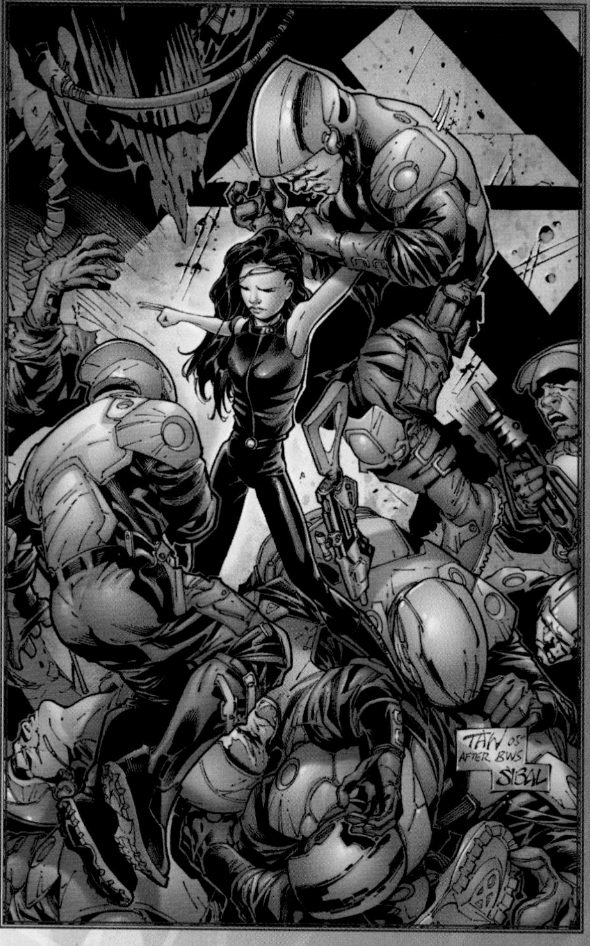
TAN 05
AFTER BWS
SIBAL

NYX SKETCHBOOK
ART BY JOSHUA MIDDLETON

ORIGINAL NYX

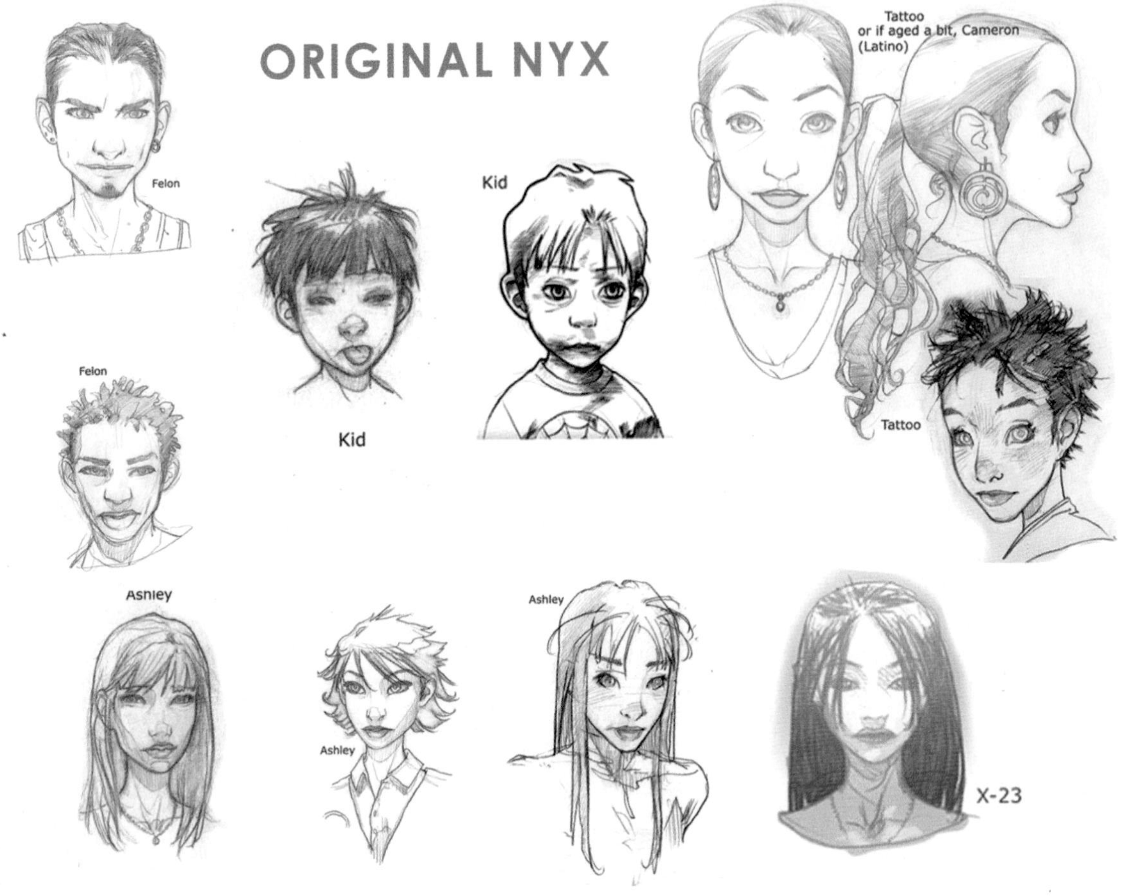
Felon
Kid
Kid
Tattoo
or if aged a bit, Cameron
(Latino)
Felon
Tattoo
Ashley
Ashley
Ashley
X-23

NEW NYX

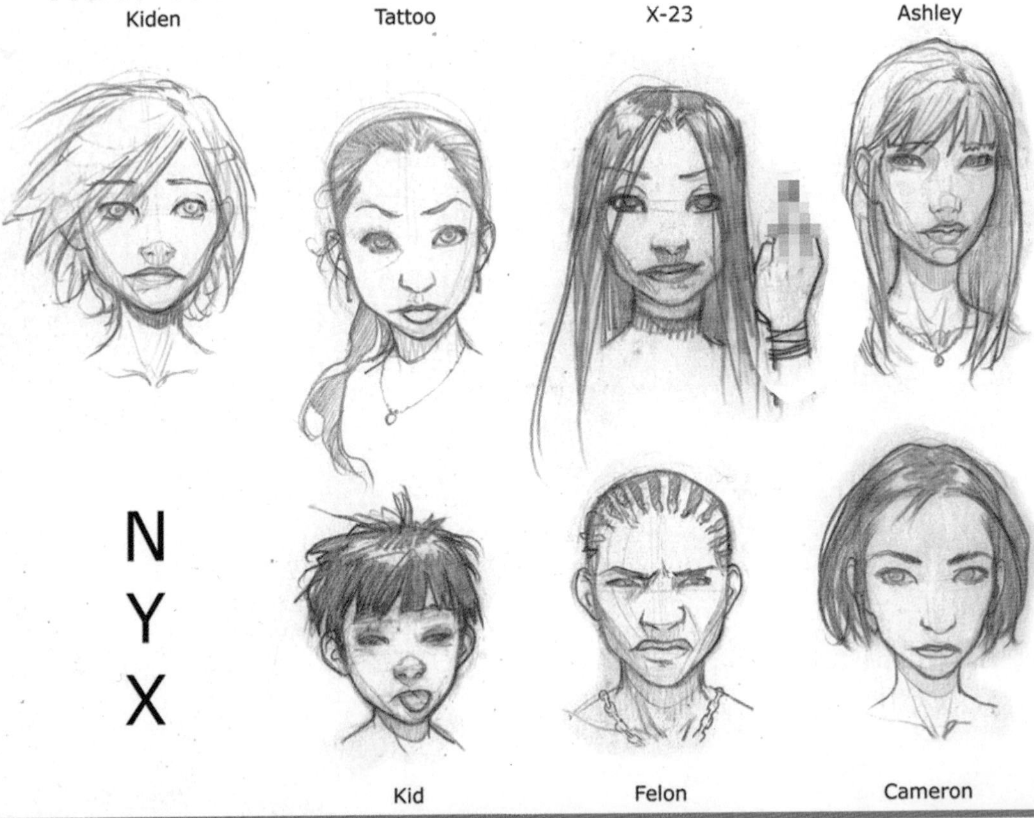
Kiden
Tattoo
X-23
Ashley
N
Y
X
Kid
Felon
Cameron

X-23

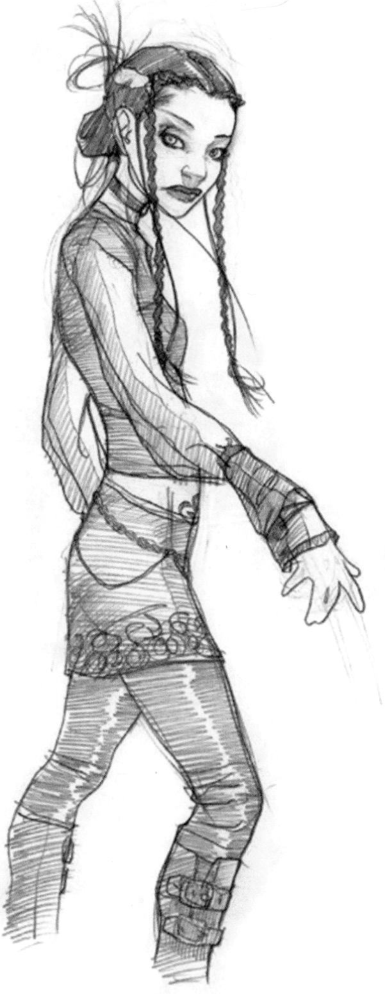

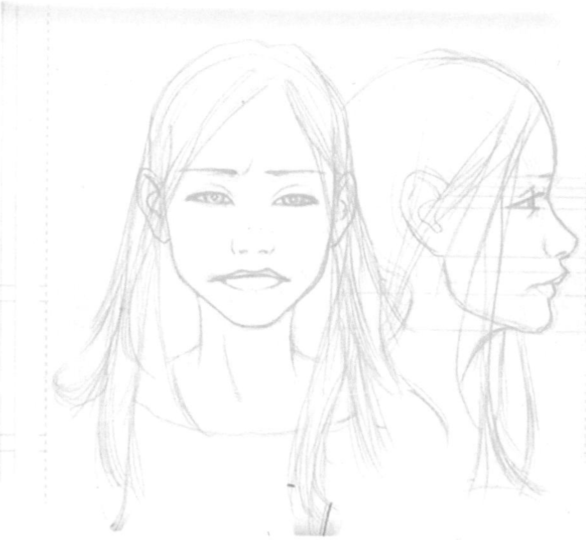

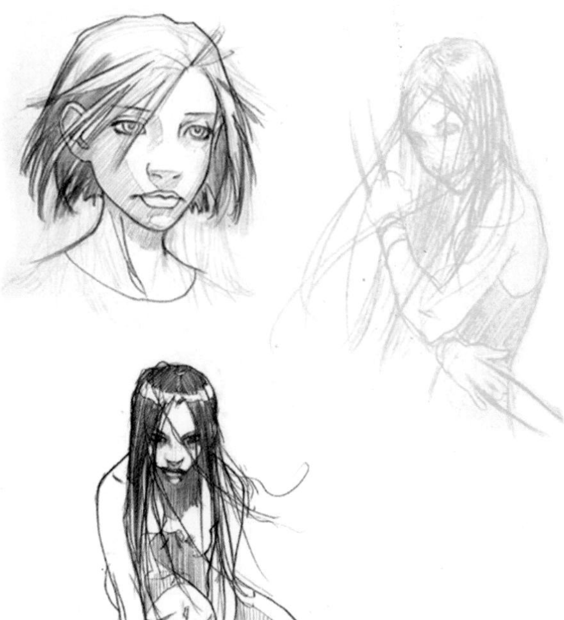

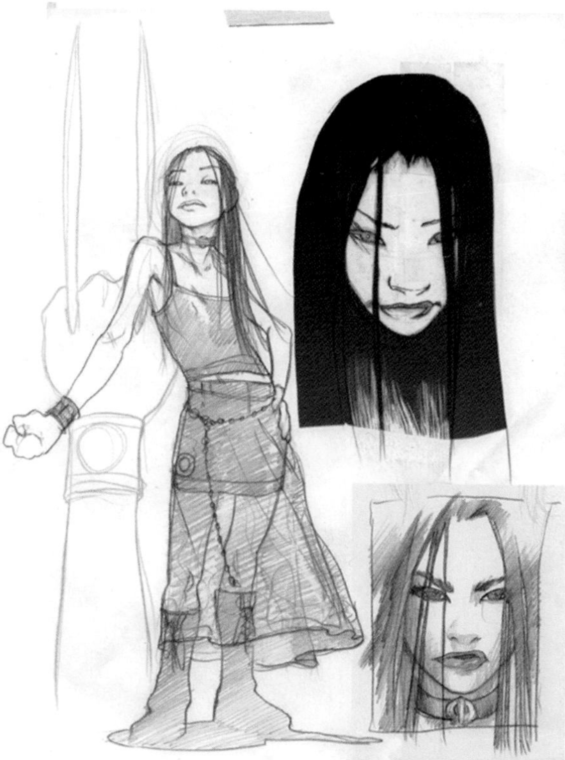

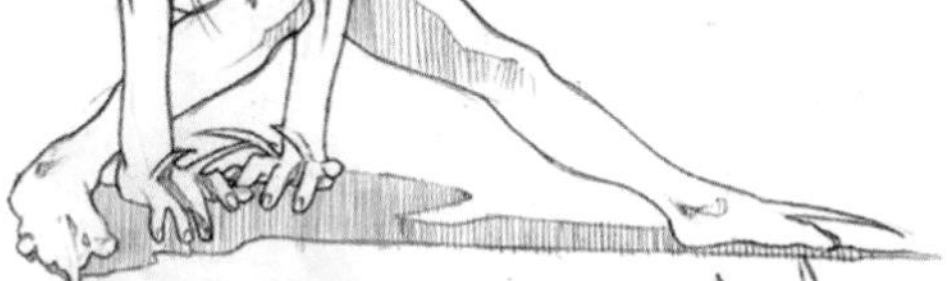

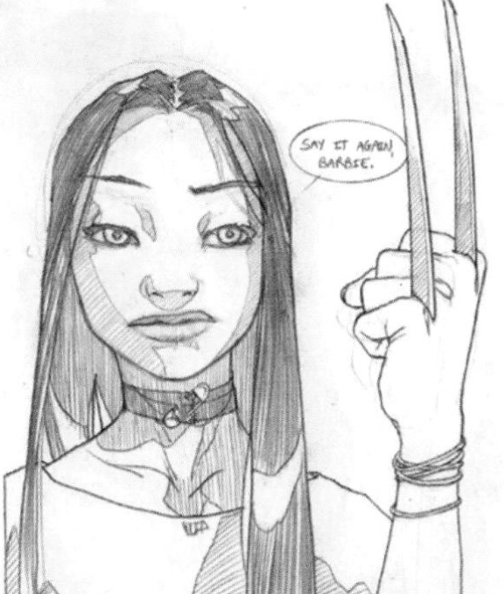
SAY IT AGAIN, BARBIE.

FELON

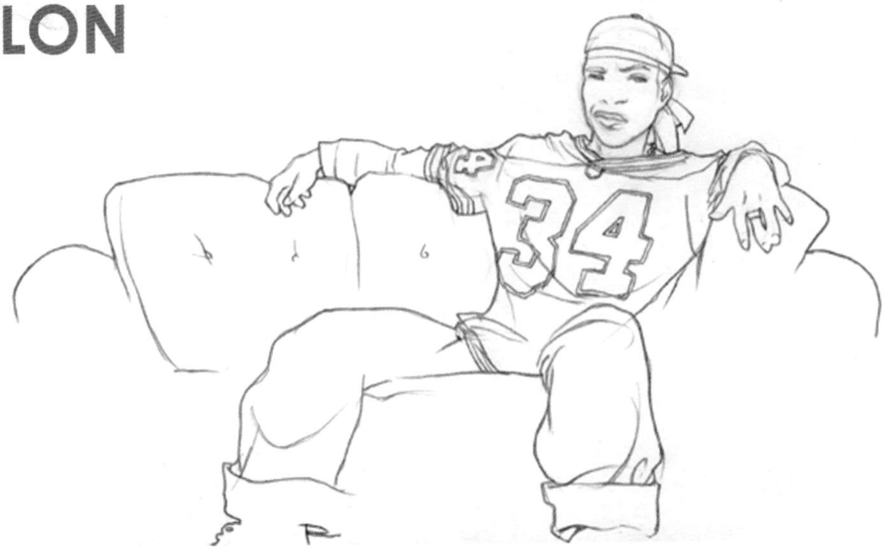

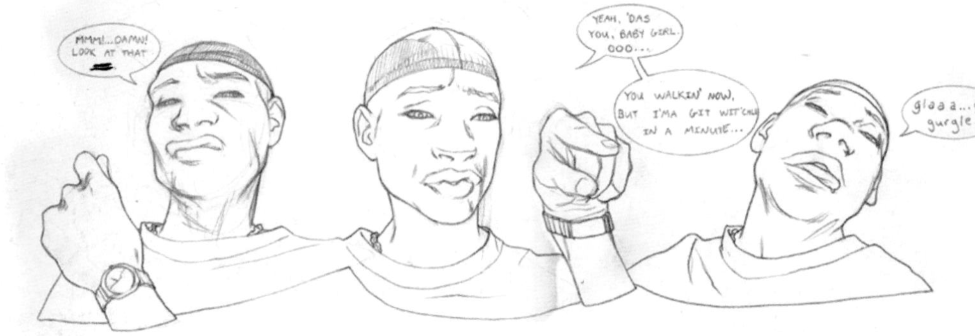
MMM!...DAMN! LOOK AT THAT [redacted]
YEAH, 'DAS YOU, BABY GIRL. OOO...
YOU WALKIN' NOW, BUT I'MA GIT WIT'CHU IN A MINUTE...
glaaa...gk... gurgle...

ZEBRA DADDY

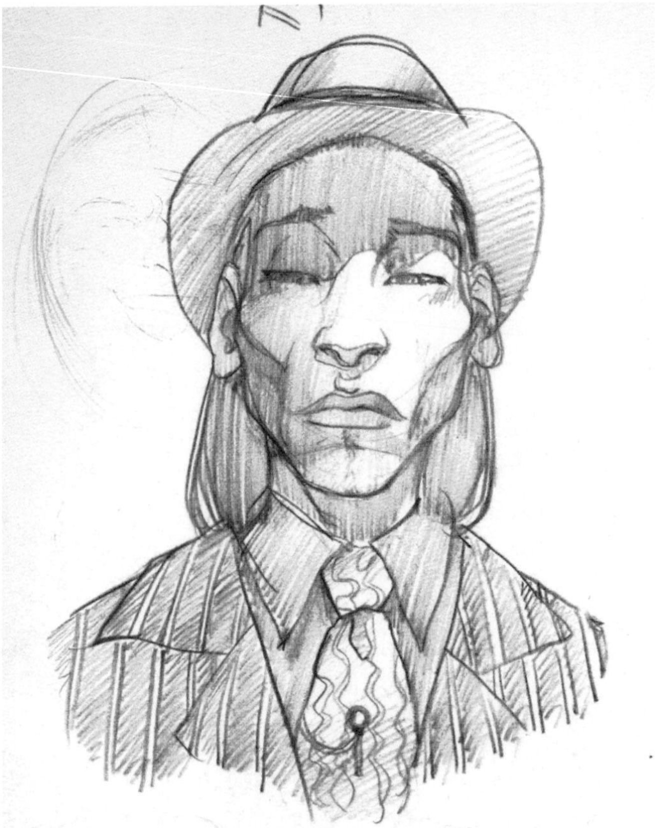

ISSUE #1 COVER PROCESS

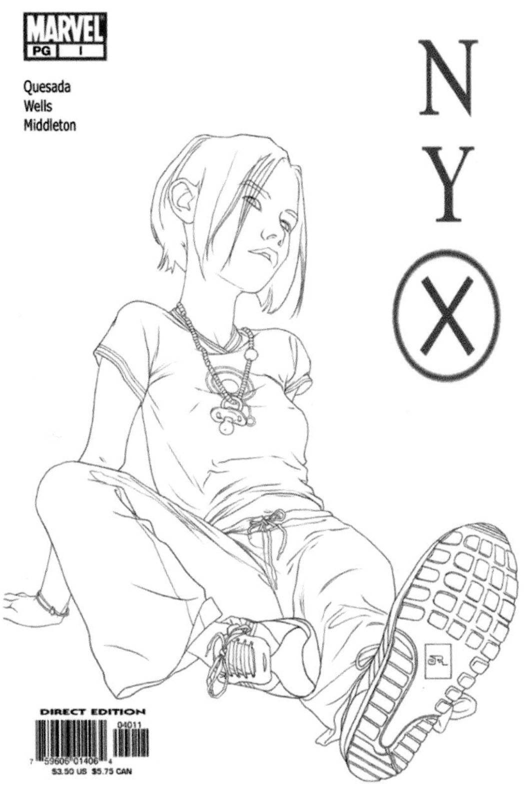
MARVEL
PG 1
Quesada
Wells
Middleton
NYX
DIRECT EDITION
$3.50 US $5.75 CAN

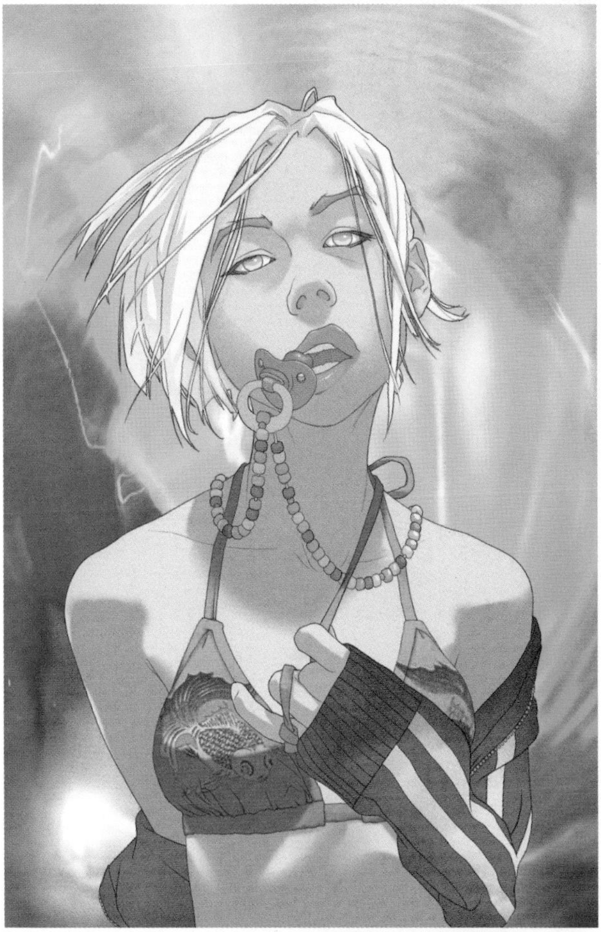

ISSUE #2 COVER PROCESS

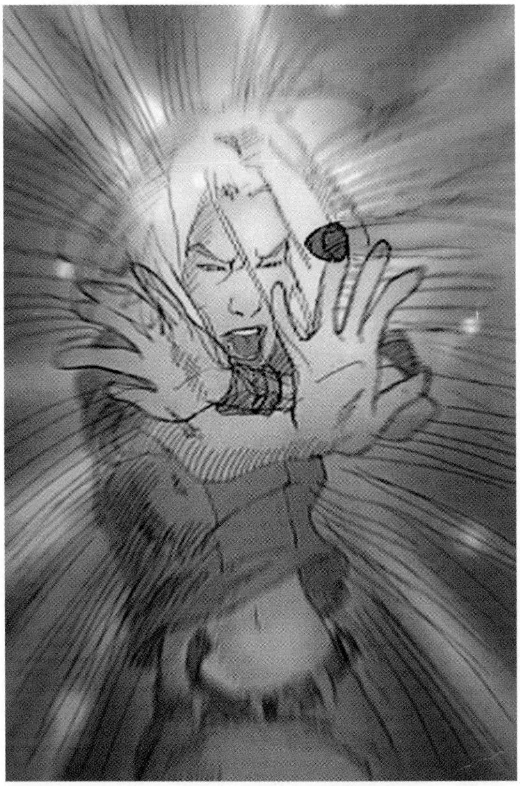

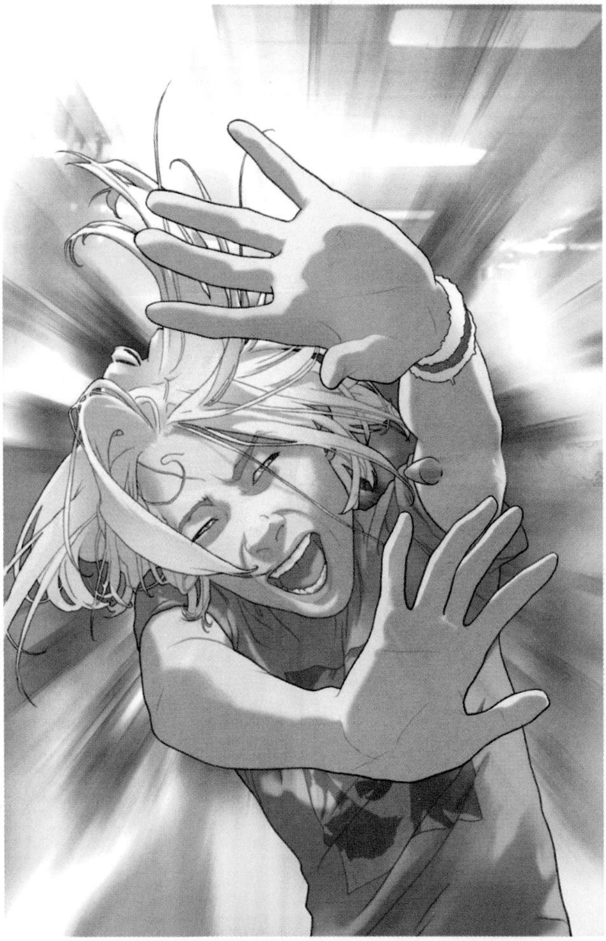

ISSUE #3 COVER PROCESS

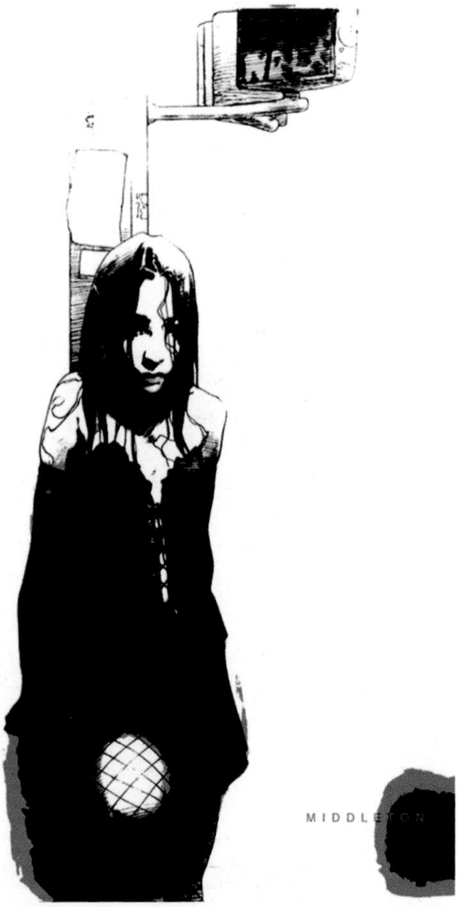
MIDDLETON

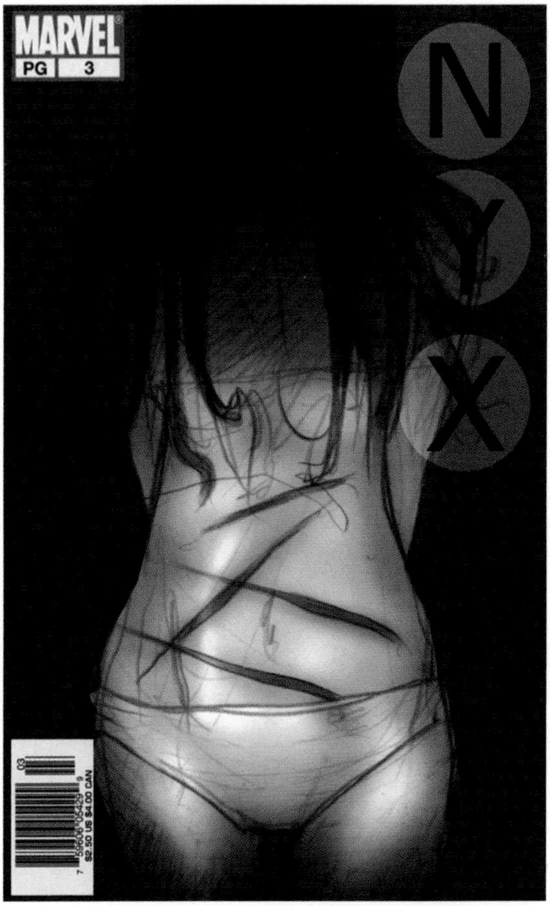
MARVEL
PG 3
N
Y
X

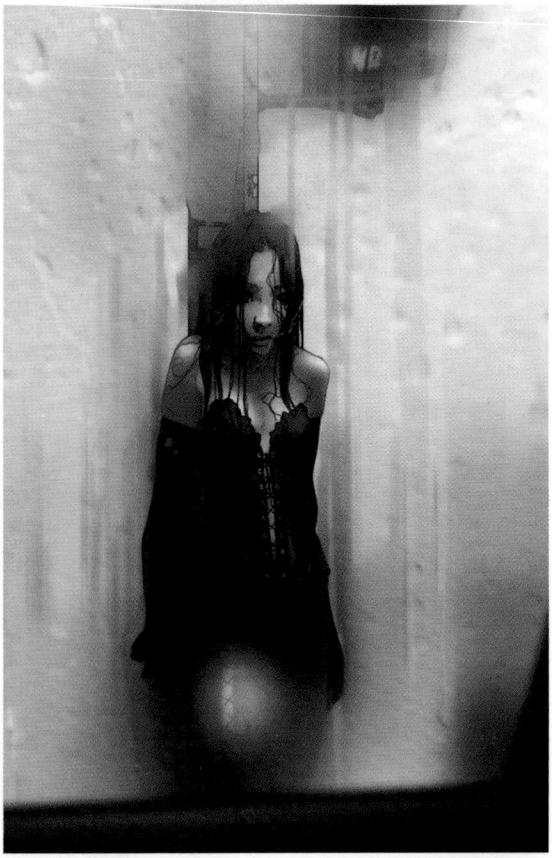

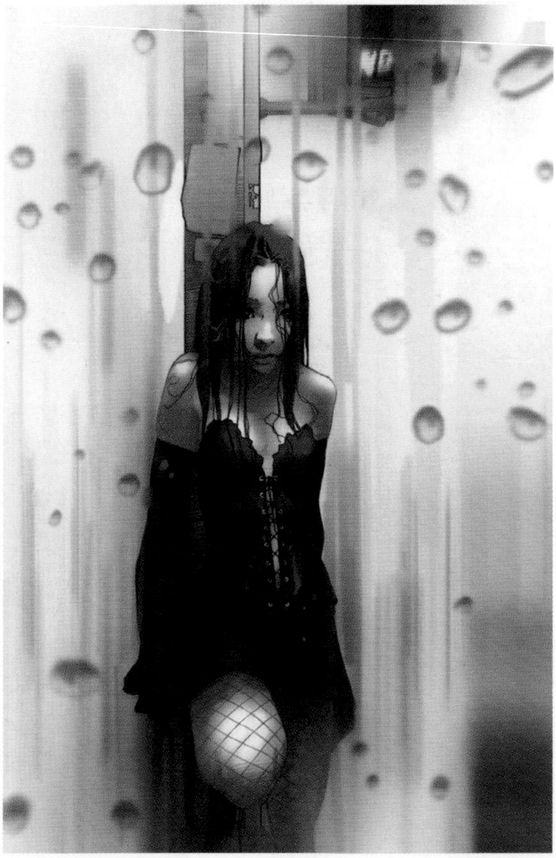

ISSUE #4 COVER PROCESS

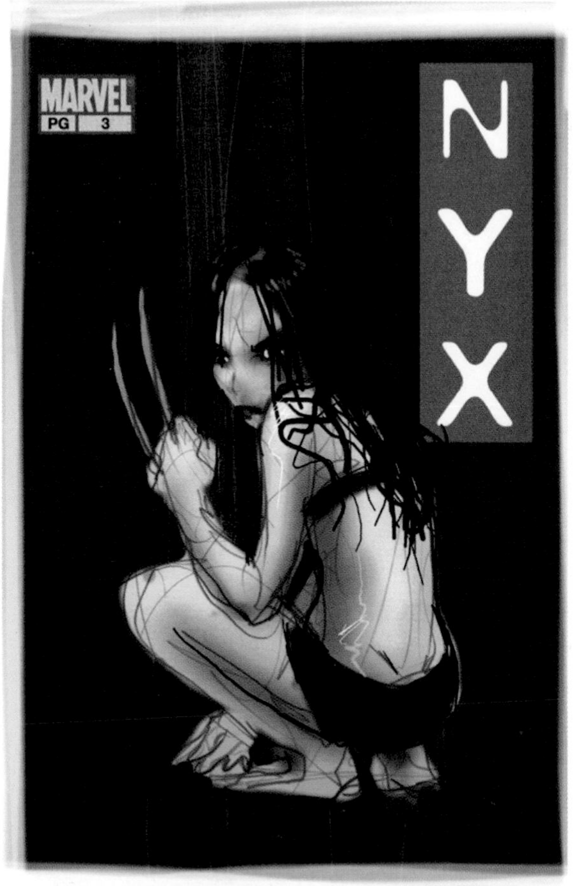
MARVEL
PG 3
NYX

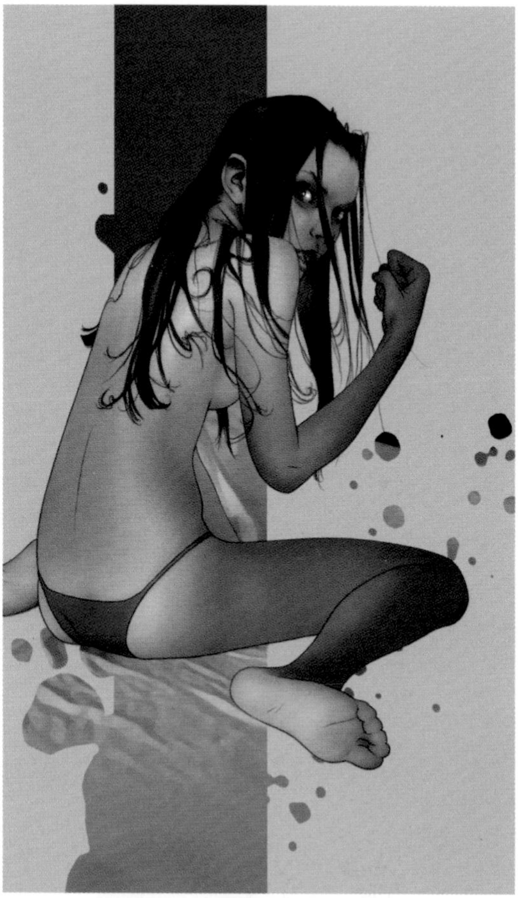

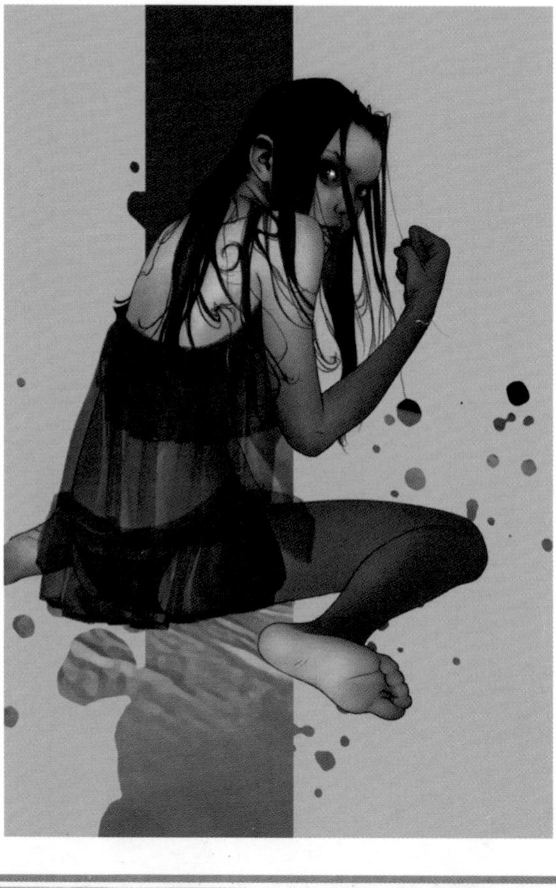

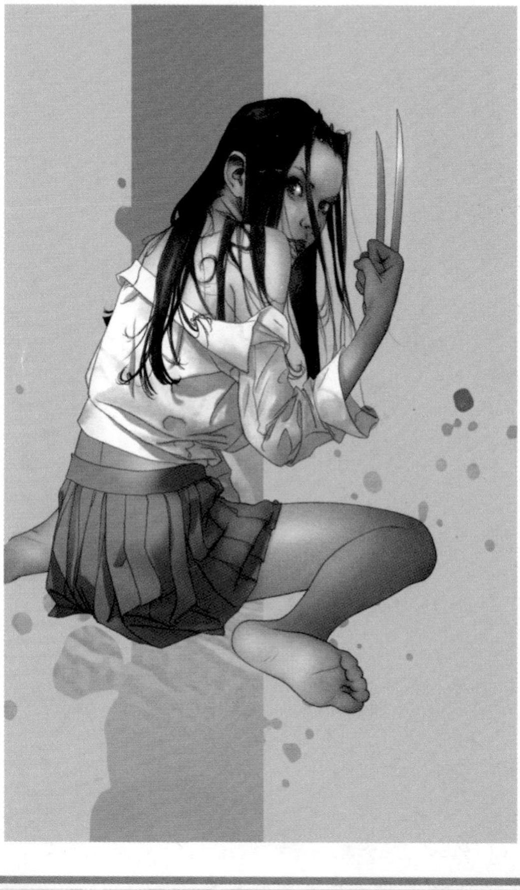

ISSUE #6 COVER PROCESS

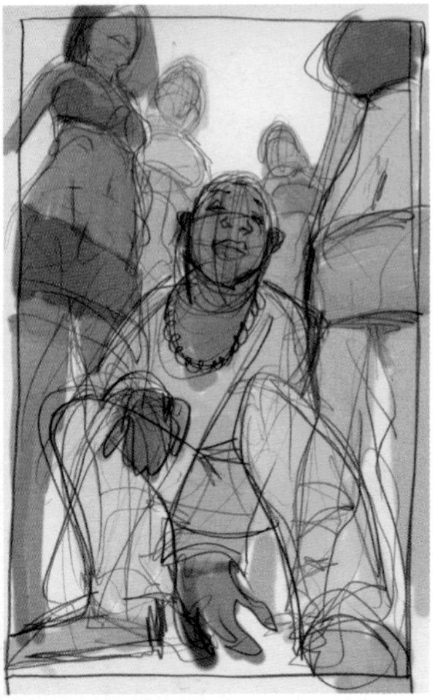
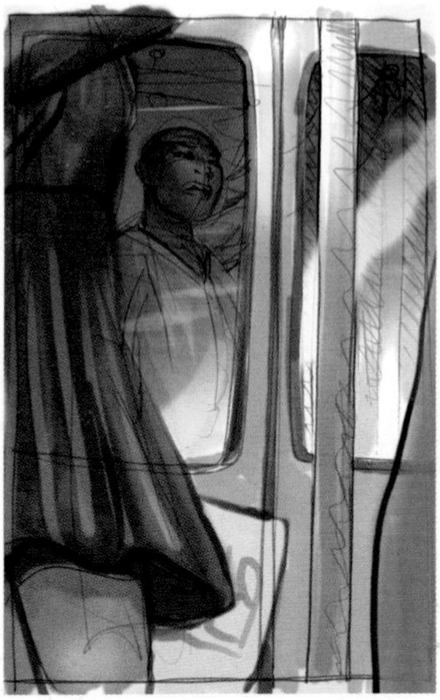
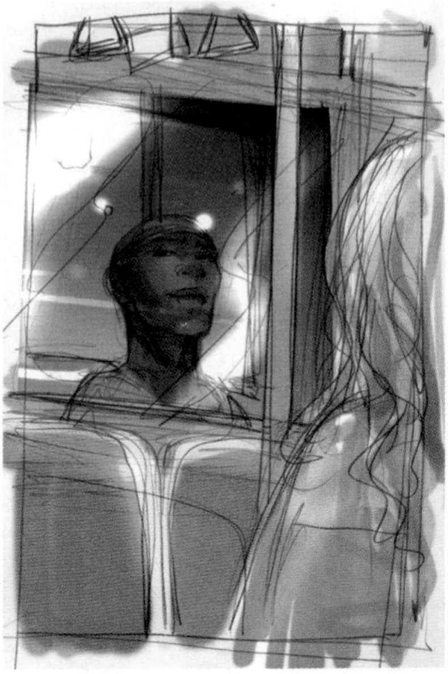
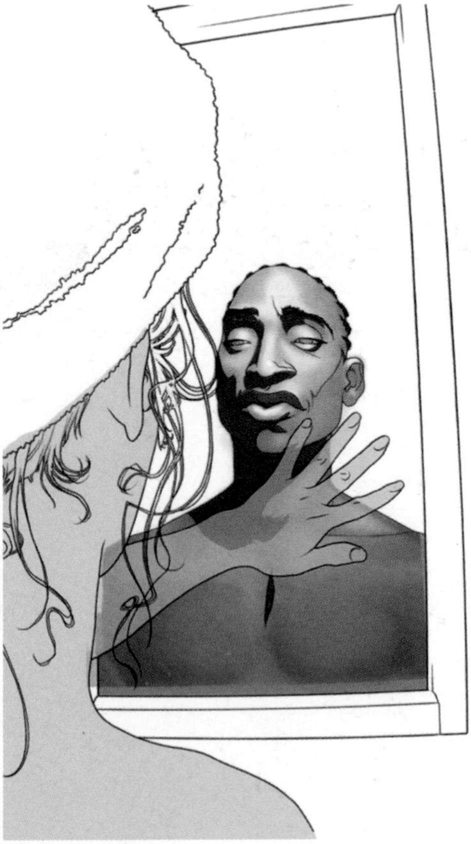
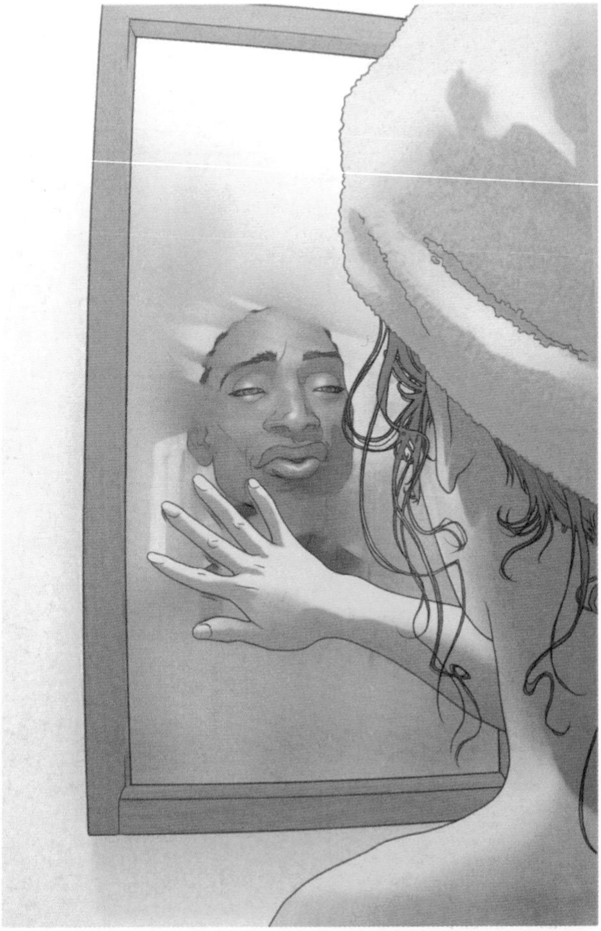

ISSUE #4 PENCILS

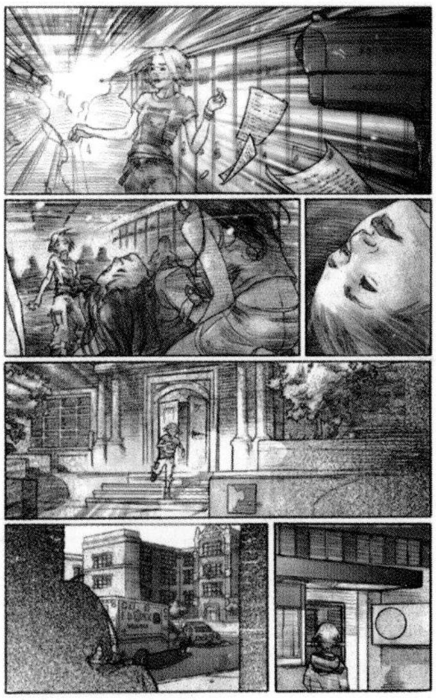

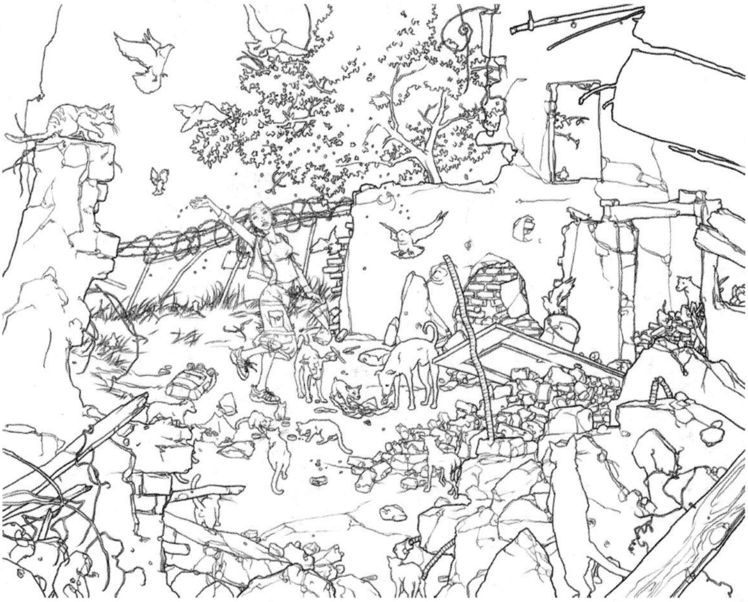

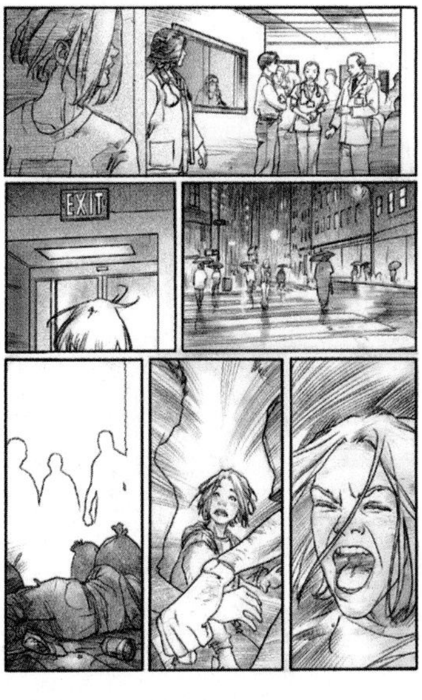
EXIT

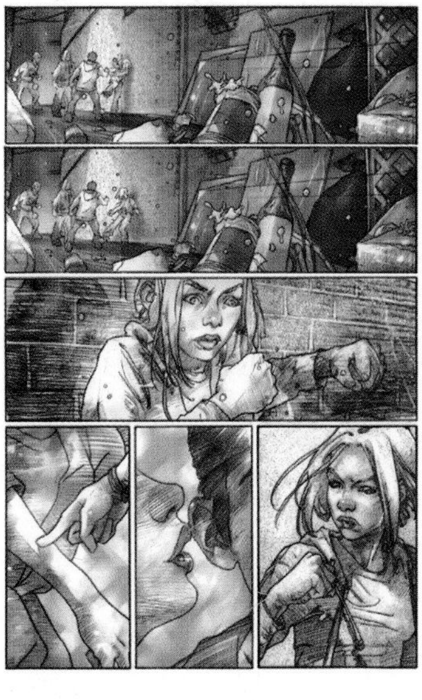

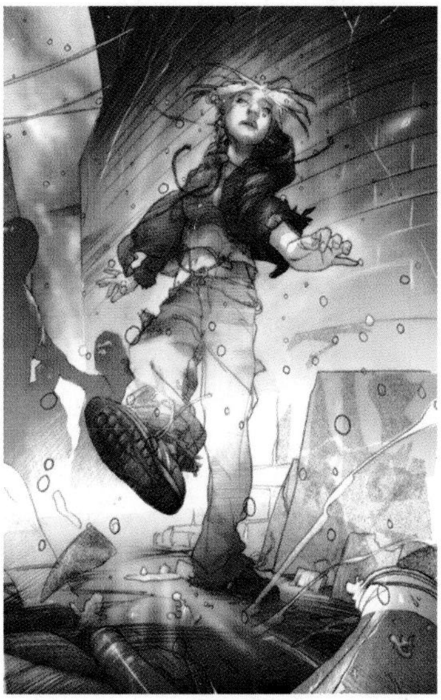

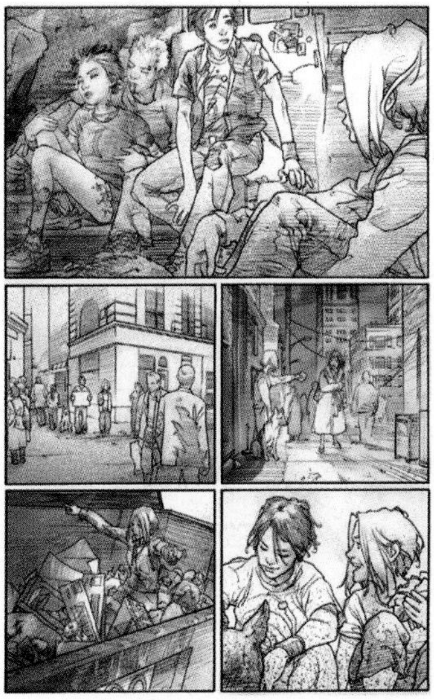

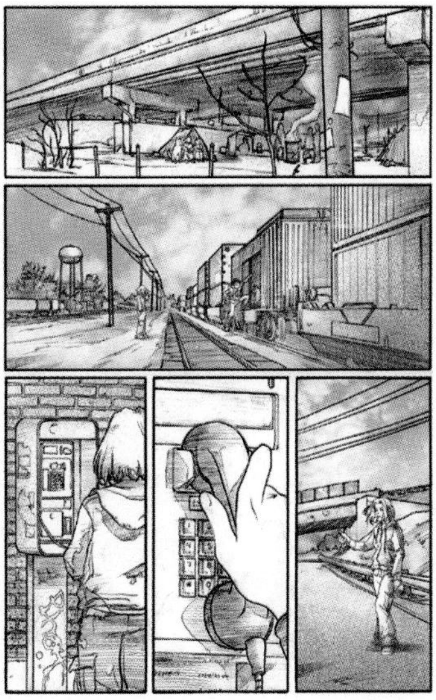

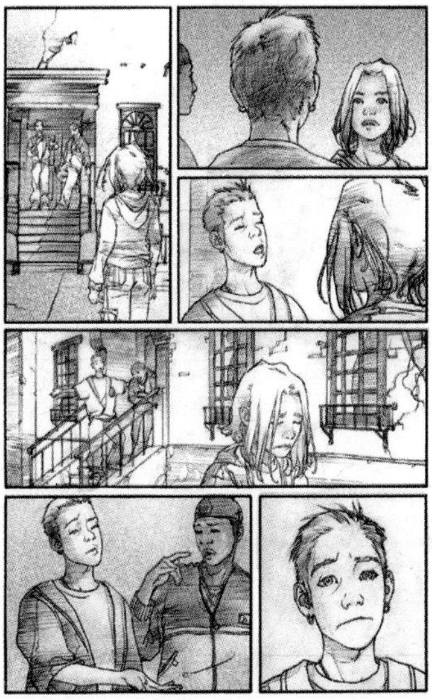

UNUSED COVER

MARVEL
PG
3
NYX

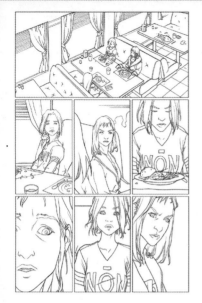

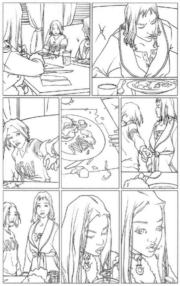

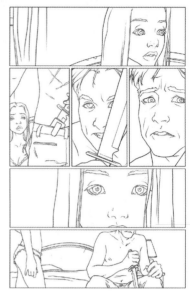

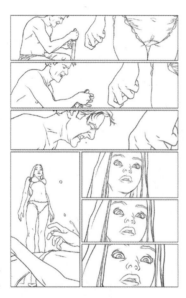

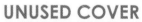

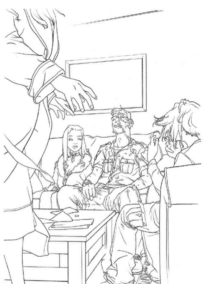

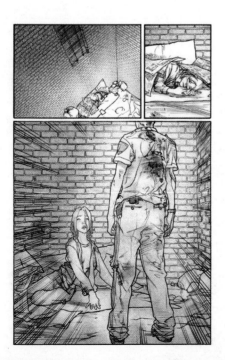

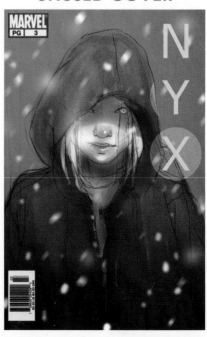